Contents

C by Discovery

Second Edition

L. S. Foster

California State University
Long Beach

Scott/Jones Inc., Publishers
P.O. Box 696
El Granada, CA 94018

C by Discovery, Second Edition
L. S. Foster

Copyright 1994, 1991 by Scott/Jones, Inc.

ISBN 1-881991-29-6

Book Production: Greg Hubit Bookworks
Book Manufacturing: Malloy Lithographing, Inc.
Illustrations: Janice Maupin
Text Design and Composition: WLF Enterprises
P.O. Box 1677
Valley Center, CA 92082

V W   5 6

ADDITIONAL TITLES OF INTEREST FROM SCOTT/JONES

The DOS-6 Coursebook
by Forest Lin

The Visual Basic Primer
by Mark Simkin

Computer Architecture and Assembly Language: The MC68000
by G.M. Prabhu and Charles Wright

The DOS Primer 2nd Ed.
by Dorothy Calvin

The 1-2-3 Coursebook: Beginning & Advanced Topics
by Forest Lin

Fortran for Scientists and Engineers, 2nd Ed.
by Gary Bronson

Assembly Language for the IBM PC Family
by William Jones

Visual Basic Coursebook
by Forest Lin

WordPerfect for Windows
by Rolayne Day

The Windows Textbook
by Stewart Venit

QuickStart in C++
by William Jones
Also available shrinkwrapped with

C by Discovery, Second Edition

QuickStart in DOS
by Forest Lin

QuickStart in WINDOWS
by Stewart Venit

QuickStart in MS Works for Windows
by Jim Payne

QuickStart in MS Office
by Jim Payne

Preface to the Second Edition

I must admit to being both astonished and gratified by the success *C by Discovery* has enjoyed since publication in 1991. Over 150 colleges and universities have adopted *C by Discovery*, and it is the instructors at those schools, as well as my own students and colleagues, who have provided the main agenda for this revision.

Changes in the Second Edition

Many of our users have requested expanded coverage of ANSI C since the transition period from early C compilers is coming to an end. Both students and instructors requested additional structure in the early programs.

Function coverage in Chapter 1 has been expanded in the spirit of presenting ANSI C function prototyping and structured programming.

ANSI C prototypes are included for all function declarations to activate the type checking of function parameters by the compiler and to prepare the students for programming in C++, which may be the next logical step in a programmer's development.

Output has been added for some of the sample programs for convenience of the student when study must take place without an available computer.

The example programs have more structure and a more standardized style throughout to provide a better model for students to follow. We decided that it was enough to mention other ways to accomplish a task, but the examples should demonstrate a preferred way.

Chapters 3 and 7 have been reworked to improve order, sequencing, and clarity. In addition, various housekeeping items have been addressed throughout the book. Any user familiar with the book will doubtless find and hopefully agree with them.

What Hasn't Changed

Short programs, each of which illustrates one or two points of the language, are presented. Each program is followed by Learning Activities that will guide the students through the thought processes necessary to make the concepts understood. Additional Learning Activities have been added, and the sequence in which the material is presented has been refined.

When a book has been as well received as *C by Discovery* has been, there is a tremendous tendency to "don't fix it if it isn't broken". Thus there is an extensive list of items in this edition that are pretty much the same as they were in the first edition. In particular, one of the changes that wasn't made deserves emphasis: the lack of inclusion of C++ and/or ideas from object-oriented programming. This decision was based on some detailed discussions with many users of the text that convinced me of two things: First, a brief coverage of C++ and object-oriented programming would not do justice to this different language and programming paradigm. Indeed, it might result in injustice to both C and C++. Instead of continuing to do one thing well, *C by Discovery* would be attempting to do two things poorly.

Second, many professors teaching out of *C by Discovery* felt that there was simply no room in their course for such discussions. There is great student and faculty interest in C++, but there is just not enough time in most C courses (or this C textbook) to provide more than lip service to that descendant of C. Faced with the decision of whether to cover one topic thoroughly, or two topics superficially, I have chosen the former.

The current sequence of topics in this text may be altered in an Alternate Edition. Please contact the publisher to give input for or to obtain information about this edition. The key differences will be the presentation of the basic data types before the presentation of control statements, some consolidation of the presentation of control statements, and an early chapter on functions.

The items that remain consistent with the earlier edition of *C by Discovery* are addressed in the Preface to the First Edition.

Preface to the First Edition

There is a saying attributed to an ancient Chinese scholar that goes something like this:

> I hear, and I forget.
> I see, and I remember.
> I do, and I understand.

Most of us learn by a combination of audio, visual and kinetic activities. Each of us has a different balance of these three elements for optimal learning. Instead of trying to teach the subject by having students only "see" and "hear," I have tried to provide a way for them to also "do and understand."

Discovering C by Doing

Programming is not a spectator sport. Much of what we try to teach about any given language becomes meaningful only when students use or "do" something with the information. In this book I have consistently tried to encourage students to roll up their sleeves and work with C, in order to appreciate not only the subtleties of the language, but also its power.

Learning Activities

As a means toward that end, "Learning Activities" are interspersed throughout this book. They provide a means of requesting a student to spend just a little more time thinking about and experimenting with a concept or an example program. An activity can be as simple as executing a program to verify the student's understanding. In many cases, an activity consists of executing a program, modifying the source, executing it again, and then undertaking the important final step of verbalizing what the experiment illustrated. The use of the text does not depend on the assignment of the Learning Activities, but I believe that learning will be much more effective when they are used.

Source Code on Disk

To help the students make more effective use of their time, the source code for the programs in the text is provided on floppy disk. This enables students to move immediately to actively learning, instead of having to spend time typing the programs. The shorter the link between "seeing" and "doing," the less diluted the "AHA" experience will be.

Selected Answers

Lastly, to "close the loop" on Learning Activities, I have provided answers to selected Activities in the back of the text. Students can determine which elements of the language are giving them a difficult time, and which have been mastered. Between the answers and the computer response to the programs, the students are able to get close to 100% feedback on these activities.

Exercises and Programming Problems

The end of each chapter contains Exercises and Programming Problems, a second type of "doing." These exercises range from questions designed to review concepts from the chapter to programming projects. In general, the exercises at the end of the chapter will take the students more time than the Learning Activities and are designed to allow the students to put the concepts learned to use.

Discovering C by Seeing

Since programming is a game of both concepts and detail, ultimate understanding of code comes from closely examining the details. Through the use of **Notes** in the example programs, the student is directed immediately to the new concepts in the code and the accompanying explanation.

Asking the students to learn to program by "seeing" annotated code is similar to asking students to learn to write essays by having them analyze works of literature. Students use analytic skills when reading someone else's program. It is a part of the educational experience and cannot be ignored, but it should be accompanied with a full educational package.

A Closer Look

I wanted this text to give more than a cursory mention to some key topics. These passages are prefaced by the term **A Closer Look,** and in many cases they exceed other C texts in depth and breadth. This discussion has been isolated in these sections for several reasons: It allows inclusion or exclusion of the material as time and interest dictate. The remainder of the text does not make reference to this material. Finally, it provides explanation of concepts for the interested student without necessitating that the point be belabored in class.

A Word of Warning

Some common programming pitfalls with the C language are presented in **A Word of Warning** sections. A mistake is made, and the student is asked to execute the program and suffer the consequences. In my observation, a student needs this experience to help avoid certain errors. Rather than have the error occur and create a moment of panic the night before a major project is due, it will occur during a non-threatening time. Even if the mistake is repeated during the coding of a major project, the experience of having seen this consequence before should help.

The Programmer's Handbook

It is impossible to give every example that a student needs in a text. At some point the student will want to know something beyond the classroom discussion and will dig into the text and reference material for the additional information necessary to solve a problem. By including the *Programmer's Handbook*, I have tried to provide a "reference within a text." In documenting the C library functions I have tried to state the type of the parameters to each function in a way that will alleviate a point of confusion.

To the Instructor

I have not found it necessary to discuss all of the sample programs in class. I have assigned them as reading material, but have chosen for discussion those that give the final picture. As specific examples, in Chapter 3, the introductory discussion on type int is recapped in the program that discusses all of the integer types. While the concepts should be mentioned, the inclusion of the earlier programs is for the students' benefit, and need not be included in class discussion. As another example, in Chapter 10, a very simple program that opens and closes a file is given. When I have included that as part of the class discussion, I invariably get some students who resist checking on the return value of fopen() even though I have stressed that it should be done. I think that students need to see this simple use as a beginning point in their learning process, but discussing it seems to leave them with the impression that it is acceptable to open files without checking for errors. By assigning it as reading, but discussing only the other versions, this problem is somewhat alleviated.

There is some flexibility in the order that the chapters can be covered. For example, Chapter 3 can come before or after Chapter 2. Also, Chapter 6 can be discussed before Chapters 4 and 5. Chapter 8 can be moved to an earlier position in the course as well.

To the Student

This book has been written for you. The programs and Learning Activities have been designed to let you learn with efficiency. It will still take some effort and dedication, but by simply executing the sample programs as you study them and following the Learning Activities, you should be able to conquer the material easily. The difference is that executing the sample programs provides the kinetic learning experience that allows you to satisfy the audio, visual, and kinetic senses necessary to learning. When the school term gets hectic, don't let up on this course. A little time spent each day with the Learning Activities should allow your mind to process the material while you are involved in other school or work activities. Don't leave it all until the end.

Acknowledgments

Good books are the result of effective collaboration between authors and reviewers. Successive editions of books can become more powerful and better teaching tools because of a "feedback loop" between the author and those professors who teach from the author's book and provide the author with classroom feedback.

One of the reasons *C by Discovery, Second Edition* is an even better book than its predecessors is because it distills classroom experiences of the earlier edition. I would like to thank each "generation" of professors who have provided my publisher with feedback. They have helped this text become a successively more effective teaching tool.

Professors Helping Develop *C by Discovery, First Edition*

Stan Wileman
University of Nebraska

Gordon Hoagland
Ricks College

Ken Collier
Northern Arizona University

Kerry Hays
San Jose City College

Stephen Allan
Utah State University

D. Hanscom
University of Utah

Charles Hall
North Carolina State University

Clifford Shaffer
Virginia Tech

Cay Horstman
San Jose State University

Mladen Vouk
North Carolina State University

Andrew Lopez
Texas A & M University

Peter Bahrs
University of Southwestern Louisiana

Thomas Cheatam
Western Kentucky University

Julius Nadas
Wilbur Wright Community College

John Crenshaw
Western Kentucky University

Duane Jordan
Texas Tech University

Stan Ferrell
Virginia Tech

Margaret Zinky
Phoenix College

Professors Helping Develop *C by Discovery, Second Edition*

The Second Edition benefits from the classroom teaching experiences of many professors. The following individuals took the time to send back annotated versions of their textbooks, summarizing their classroom experiences:

Mark Manchester
SUNY Morrisville

Anup Mathur
Virginia Tech

David Goldstein
University of Texas, Arlington

Ray Springston
University of Texas, Arlington

Brenda Sonderegger
Montana State University

Mark Weiss
University of Nebraska - Omaha

Many users of the First Edition gave particularly insightful feedback on a survey conducted by my publisher. I especially appreciated the feedback of:

Wayne Hewitt
Johnson County
Community College

William Nico
California State University
Hayward

David Sarchet
Embry Riddle
Aeronautical University

Bunny Tjadin
Montgomery College

Van Howbert
Colorado State University

Stewart Laughton
Virginia Polytechnic University

Jeff Blessing
Milwaukee School of Engineering

Reggie Kwan
Montana Tech

Sei-Jong Chung
Northern Illinois University

John Carroll
San Diego State University

Kamila Blessing
University of North Carolina
Chapel Hill

My publisher also relayed to me comments from interviews with many professors, especially concerning the extent to which object-oriented programming should be discussed in this revision. I appreciate their taking the time to speak with him and share their thoughts.

Carole Conway
Chabot College

Cliff Schaffer
Virginia Tech

Clark Nahler
Buffalo State University

William van der Beck
Los Angeles Valley College

Kay Robbins
University of Texas - San Antonio

John Carroll
San Diego State University

Bill Jones
California State University
Dominguez Hills

Vigaya Krishnamurthy
Montgomery College

Lastly, I especially appreciate those professors who were willing to discuss with me, in detail, the problems they had encountered with the First Edition of *C by*

Discovery. Often they allowed me to telephone them at home. The resulting conversations, set apart from the busy days on campus we all experience, allowed me to get a fuller understanding of their experiences teaching from this book. Their candid comments both encouraged and challenged me to improve on the First Edition.

Anne DeLaney	Willene Grady
Los Angeles Pierce College	Arapahoe Community College
Arthur Gittleman	Dale Boerker
California State University	Chabot College
Long Beach	John Lane
Martha Tilmann	California State University
College of San Mateo	Long Beach

In addition, my departmental chair, Dr. Michael K. Mahoney, and the Dean of the College of Engineering, Dr. Richard Williams, continue to provide me with support and encouragement in my writing efforts. I am fortunate to have them at California State University Long Beach. I also greatly appreciate the encouragement of my colleagues and students.

The Instructor's Resource Manual builds on the great reception to the Manual for the First Edition. I would like to thank Jan Snyder (Chaffee College) for his work on the even-number answers and Larry Weiner and Trudy Weitzen (Ohione College) for their work on the overhead transparency masters. In addition I am indebted to those professors who provided my publisher with sample course syllabuses using my text.

The text still benefits from the inclusion of the artwork first rendered by Janice Maupin, whose contribution I appreciate. My publisher, Scott/Jones, has been quite helpful in bringing to my attention the comments, complaints, and compliments of professors using the first edition. Greg Hubit has done an excellent job of coordinating the production and proofreading of the second edition. The composition for the second edition, done by WLF Enterprises, has been a tremendous improvement over that done in the first edition. Users should take comfort in expecting far fewer errors and typos.

Any mistakes that remain are, of course, my fault, and I would very much like to know about them as soon as possible. I encourage anyone finding such errors to contact me via e-mail at California State University Long Beach:

> **foster@csulb.edu**

or in care of the publisher.

Once again, I could not have completed this work without the patience, love, and understanding of my friend, spouse and partner, Dusty Foster.

L. S. Foster
California State University, Long Beach

Chapter 1

Getting Started

1.1 What to Expect from C

A programmer who considers programming in a new language should make certain observations about that language. Most programmers would consider the level of the language, the programming environment, the portability and efficiency of the programs written in that language, and ease of maintaining and modifying the programs. Each of these considerations should be evaluated in relation to the particular programming application.

Language Level

One distinction made among languages is the level. A computer language can be classified as high, intermediate, or low level. The lowest level languages, those that the computers understand directly, are the machine languages. Higher level languages more closely resemble the way human beings think and speak. Programs written in languages other than machine language must undergo some sort of translation to machine language to be executed.

Assembly languages are low-level languages because they relate directly to the underlying hardware. Operating systems, monitors, and similar programs are often written in assembly language so they can access the specifics of the hardware. Business and scientific applications are frequently programmed in higher level languages so they can be transferred (ported) from computer to computer easily.

1

In terms of language level, C is an intermediate- to high-level language, yet it allows the programmer to control the hardware. This facility is not always available in other high-level languages. Therefore C is used to write programs from business applications to operating systems.

Programming Environment

Another distinction among languages is the process of translation into machine language. The name of the translation process for an assembly language program is assembly. For higher level languages, two processes are common: interpretation and compilation.

When a program is compiled, a second program called a compiler reads each statement and translates it directly into machine language. The machine code is stored in a separate file. The program in its original form is the source code; the machine language translation of the program is the object code. After all statements in a program have been translated, program execution occurs by executing the object code. No further code processing is necessary.

When a program is interpreted, a second program called an interpreter processes the statements in the program sequentially. During execution, the interpreter translates each statement into machine language and executes it before processing the next statement. This continues until execution of the program terminates. Each time the program executes, the interpretation process is repeated.

Both methods have their advantages with different applications. Most high-level languages have developed either as a compiled language or an interpreted language, depending on the most common usage.

Traditionally, C has been a compiled language. It was developed in the early 1970s on the UNIX Operating System. The compilation of a C program in the UNIX Operating system consists of at least 5 steps: preprocessing, translating, optimizing, assembling, and link editing.

Preprocessing consists of stripping comments, expanding macros, and handling all the preprocessor directives. The preprocessor directives have a separate syntax from C. They are used for things like constant definitions, inclusion of other source code files, defining macros[1], and conditional compilation.

The translation phase of compilation on the UNIX system consists of translating the C source code to assembly language. Optimization takes the assembly language program and makes it more efficient. Assembling translates from assembly language to machine language, and link editing brings in the necessary parts of the C library and creates an executable file. All this can be done with one command, but it is also possible to stop the compilation process after any given phase and look at the resulting code.

Compilers on other operating systems may not have as many well defined steps in the compilation process, but it may still be possible to look at the code

---

1. When a macro is defined, a sequence of tokens is associated with an identifier. During the preprocess phase, the sequence of tokens replaces every occurrence of that identifier in the source code.

produced by a separate step. It is most common to look at the preprocessed source code, but the commands to do so differ from system to system.

Most implementations of C allow the source code to be divided among different files and allow each file to be compiled separately. The object code resulting from the compilation of one source module will not execute until it is linked with the remainder of the program. A program called a linker, a link editor, or a linking loader combines the object code files for each source file into an executable form. The advantages to this modular system include ease of maintenance and the possibility of more structured code. In this way, code written in C can often be combined with code written in other languages.

Portability and Efficiency of C Code

A portable program is one that executes properly without modifications on all types of computers. Few, if any, programs have this ultimate portability, but a degree of portability is a worthwhile programming goal. The source code for a portable program does not depend on any specific parts of the computer hardware. Each compiler and operating system assigns the storage for a program's use. To be portable, source code should be written in the standards for the programming language. It should not use any of the extra features supplied in a particular compiler or interpreter. The portability of source code is an advantage that any high-level language has over assembly language.

The efficiency of the object code is an advantage that assembly language has over any higher level language. Generally, object code from a well-written assembly language program is more compact and faster than that from a high-level language program with the same functionality. However, compilers have been developed that produce object code optimized in terms of speed and compactness.

Since the publication of the ANSI standards for C and the emergence of compilers meeting those standards, programmers can write source code that will port more easily to many different computers. Because C is a higher level language, its object code may not be as small or fast as that from an assembly language program. However, C object code has a reputation for being compact and fast when compared to code from programs written in other high-level languages.

Ease of Maintenance

A program's development can continue throughout its period of use. The specifics of the application may change with time, and new or previously unknown situations may uncover bugs in the original code. Either of these situations mandates that modifications be made to the original source code program. These types of changes characterize the maintenance phase of a program.

Through years of experience, programmers have developed the technique of structured programming to aid in the development of readable and easily maintained programs. This method is a desirable way of writing source code in any programming language. Three of the goals of structured programming are to write programs that are modular in nature, readable, and easily modified. Programs with these properties usually consist of many short subprograms. Each subprogram performs one task necessary to the program. Several related subprograms might be collected in a file. The subprograms in each file can be tested, debugged, and compiled separately.

Separate compilation of source code files can be a time-saving feature because a change made to one file does not require recompiling the whole program. Also, choosing the subprograms in each file carefully makes program modification easier.

Suppose a program must be modified because of a hardware change. If all the code that is dependent on the hardware in question were in one file, then modifications could be limited to that one file. In contrast, an alternate method of programming would allow the hardware-dependent code to appear anywhere in a program. A change in the hardware would then require a time-consuming and painstakingly close inspection of the program code for possible change.

C lends itself naturally to structured modular programming. A program in C can be written as a sequence of subprograms, and where appropriate, subprograms can be written as tools. Related subprograms can be kept in separately compiled files.

Object oriented programming (OOP) is one current recommendation for a sound programming technique. Among other things, it consists of identifying "objects" and the operations associated with them, and incorporating both the data and the operations in separate data types. It is possible to do object oriented programming in C, but the language was not designed to support OOP specifically. More important, the language C++ is designed to support OOP, and is based on C. Knowing C will help in learning C++.

While it is possible to write unreadable code in C, it is just as easy to write readable code. Judicious decisions about programming style result in readable, easily maintained source code.

To summarize, C is a popular programming language. It allows a programmer control over a computer that is not usually possible with other high-level programming languages. Yet, in contrast to most assembly languages, C programs can be ported to different computers with relative ease. C also lends itself naturally to structured modular programming. Subprograms are fundamental to C programs, and most implementations of C allow code to be kept in separately compiled files. Although performance varies from compiler to compiler, object code from C source programs can be expected to be compact and fast in comparison with object code from other high-level languages.

1.2 Fundamentals—Reserved Words, Identifiers, the Character Set

Reserved Words

Reserved words or keywords in C and in other programming languages are the words that are part of the language itself. They are used as control statements, data types, and other elements of the language. Although we will discuss each language element later, you might gain an overview of the features of C by inspecting the list of keywords in the Programmer's Handbook.

Identifiers or Names in C

An identifier is an allowed sequence of characters that can be used for the name of a variable, a subprogram, or another element in a program. In C, the following rules establish the allowable identifiers.

1. They can consist of letters, digits, and underscores.
2. They must start with a letter or underscore. Note that the names of functions in the C library often start with an underscore. These names were chosen in an attempt to avoid conflict with names that a programmer might choose. Therefore, it is usually better to choose identifiers that do not start with an underscore.
3. The C language is *case sensitive*; that is, it considers upper- and lowercase letters to be different. For example, `counter` and `Counter` are two different legal identifiers in C.
4. The limit on the number of significant characters allowed in an identifier can vary among compilers. Compilers following the ANSI standards for C recognize at least 31 significant characters in an identifier. Older compilers may not recognize that many characters. Additional restrictions exist for identifiers referenced in several different files since these identifier references must be resolved by a linker before program execution.
5. An identifier must not be identical to any keyword in C.

As examples,

> `count, first_char, ByteCount, TRUE,` and `char1`

are all valid identifiers; the words in the following list are not:

`1st_integer`	does not start with a letter or underscore
`void`	is identical with a keyword
`last-time`	contains the illegal character `'-'`

The Character Set

A character set for a language defines the characters that can be used in the source code, or input and output by a program. Some characters have special meaning for a language and must be available in the character set.

A character set for C should contain both upper- and lowercase alphabetic characters, the digits, and most of the punctuation, formatting, and graphic characters. The ASCII collating sequence is used most often, but other sequences such as EBCDIC could be used.

Theoretically, any C compiler will be matched to the available character set on the underlying computer so that it is possible to deviate from the above requirements. Note that C source code that uses a character set with different characteristics may not be portable. The ASCII character set is used for the examples in this text. A few of the algorithms in the examples rely on the use of ASCII characters and may not work with another character set. These algorithms will be noted when they arise.

Format of C Programs

C is a free-format language. That is, the programmer may format the source code in the way that makes it most readable. There are no requirements that code begin in a certain column, that statements must be contained on a single line, or that comments must be located in a special place.

The space, line feed, backspace, horizontal tab, vertical tab, form feed, and carriage return are called whitespace characters. Whitespace characters separate identifiers or other elements (tokens) in the source code. Otherwise, the compiler ignores them. Whitespace should be used to enhance a program's readability.

The idea of a token in a programming language is important in understanding how a compiler views a program. The compiler divides a C program into groups of characters that belong together. Each group is a token. The compiler then inspects the sequence of tokens to generate the object code. Each keyword in a language is a token; so is any identifier. Other examples of tokens include a left parenthesis, a right parenthesis, a left or right brace, and each operation symbol, like those for assignment or addition.

Learning Activities

1. Which of the following are legal identifiers? If a word is not a legal identifier, explain why not.

First	do1	Which#	struct	3meninatub
main	Number1	Why_Not	SecondChioce	Who's_on_first

1.3 Subprograms or Functions in C

A subprogram is essential in writing structured modular code. A C program is a collection of subprograms called functions. A function in C differs from those in other languages in that a value is not always associated with the function's name. Other languages may have functions as well as subroutines or procedures. In contrast, all subprograms in C are functions whether a value is associated with the function name or not.

A *function definition* in ANSI C has the following general form:[1]

```
type function_name( formal parameter declarations )
{
        variable declarations
        code
}
```

The first line is the *function heading*; it consists of the function type, the function's name, and a pair of parentheses that will enclose information about the function's parameters. The *type* refers to the function's return value. In this chapter most of the functions will have type void which means that the function does not return a value. The function's name must be an identifier in C.

The *parameters* to a function are one means by which information can be passed into and out of a function. A formal parameter declaration will contain the type and the name of the parameter. The first functions in this text will be simple. They will not need parameters; therefore the formal parameter declarations will be replaced by the keyword void to reflect that fact.

The opening and closing braces ({ and }) mark the beginning and the end of the *function block*. The block will contain local variable declarations and/or executable code. We will start with the simplest function—one with no declarations or executable code.

A function with the name does_nothing is declared below. It has the minimum components of a function, but nothing more.

```
void does_nothing( void )
{
}
```

The function's name, does_nothing, is an example of an identifier in C. The identifier followed immediately with an opening parenthesis signifies to the compiler that does_nothing is a function. (From this point on, we will follow the

---

1. For an older compiler, the first line would be replaced with the two lines:
   ```
   type function_name ( formal parameters )
   formal parameter declarations
   ```

convention of following each function name with a pair of parentheses when referring to a function in this text.) The opening and closing braces would enclose the executable code and variable declarations. In this example, there are no variable declarations or executable code between the braces. True to its name, this function does nothing.

There are seven tokens in the function `does_nothing()`. The tokens are: the keyword `void` which appears as two separate tokens, the identifier, `does_nothing`; the opening parenthesis; the closing parenthesis; the opening brace; the closing brace. Each token has a special meaning to the compiler.

The Shortest C Program

Now that we know a little about functions, we are ready to start writing C programs. Every program must contain certain elements. In particular, it must have a function with the name `main`. When a C program executes, the execution begins with the statements in the function `main()`. Example 1-1 illustrates the shortest C program that compiles without errors or warnings on an ANSI C compiler and can be executed. Note that `main()` is a function and therefore must have the same elements as the function `does_nothing()` that we saw earlier. This version of `main()` has type `void` because it does not return a value. It does not take parameters so the keyword `void` also appears between the parentheses.

Example 1-1: shortest.c

```
void main( void )
{
}
```

Because C is a free-format language, the spacing in the program is up to the programmer. The above program could be written as

```
void main( void ){}
```

just as well, but would be considerably harder to read.

Calling a Function

We will next add a line of executable code to `main()`. We will have `main()` call the function `does_nothing()` that was illustrated earlier in this section. Example 1-2 demonstrates the technique of calling a function. This is a complete program that will compile and execute on any standard implementation of C.

Recall that every C program must have a function named `main()`. This time `main()` contains an executable line of code, the call to the function named does_nothing(). When this program is executed, the function call in `main()` causes control to be passed to `does_nothing()` for execution of any code there. In this example, `does_nothing()` contains no executable statements. Therefore control passes back to the function `main()` and execution ends.

The other new program elements that are introduced in Example 1-2 are comments and function declarations.

Example 1-2: shortsub.c

```
/* This is a comment */
/*                shortsub.c
 *
 *    Synopsis    - Control is passed from the function main() to the
 *                  function sub_funct() and back.
 *
 *    Objective   - Illustrates a subfunction and function call.
 *
 */

void does_nothing( void );                                  /* Note 1 */

void main( void )
{
    does_nothing();                                         /* Notes 2 and 3 */
}

void does_nothing( void )                                   /* Note 4 */
{
}
```

As indicated in `shortsub.c`, comments in C programs start with the characters `/*` and terminate with the first occurrence of the characters `*/`. Comments are places where a programmer can make notes about the code and algorithms in the program. Comments are ignored by the compiler. Notice that a comment can begin on one line and terminate several lines later.

In this text, comments contain reference numbers for notes that explain the points and new elements of the C language illustrated by the program. Study them carefully. **Note 1**, **Note 2**, **Note 3**, and **Note 4** in the program refer to the following explanations. **Notes 2 and 3** refer to different explanations about the same line of code.

Note 1: A function declaration, also called a prototype, is a line of code that contains information about a function. When a program accesses a function other than `main()`, the other function must be declared. A function declaration consists of the function type, the function name, a pair of parentheses with the number and type of the formal parameters inside the parentheses, and a semicolon to terminate the declaration. In this example, `does_nothing()` has type `void` (it does not return a value). That `does_nothing()` does not take any parameters is indicated by the `void` between the parentheses.

In this example, the declaration of `does_nothing()` looks very similar to the function heading. Much of the same information is contained in the function declaration and the function heading. However, as we will see later, the function heading must be more specific in cases where formal parameters are involved.

Note 2: This line of code is our first example of an executable statement in C. It is terminated with a semicolon (`;`). Every statement in C must have a semicolon to terminate it.

Note 3: This statement is an example of a function call in C. A function is invoked by its name followed by a set of opening and closing parentheses. If there were actual parameters for the function call, they would appear within the parentheses. When execution reaches this line of code, the point of execution passes to `does_nothing()`.

Note 4: This line starts the definition of the function `does_nothing()`. Note the placement of `does_nothing()`. It does not need to appear before `main()` and must not appear inside `main()`. A C program is a sequence of functions. A function cannot be defined inside another function. Nesting of functions is not legal in C. Note also that the first line of the function definition, the one containing the name of the function, does not terminate with a semicolon.

Learning Activities

2. List all the separate tokens in the program shortsub.c.

3. Modify shortsub.c by adding a function named `funct()` and have both `main()` and `does_nothing()` call `funct()`.

1.4 An Introduction to Output in C

The two programs that we have seen will compile and run,[1] but they contain no productive statements. We will add executable statements to our programs gradually. The first addition is to have the program produce output. In C, input and output are not part of the language, but are supplied as functions in a collection of functions that comes with a C compiler. This library or collection of functions is known as the standard C library. The output function we will investigate first is `printf()`. Example 1-3 presents a simple usage of `printf()`. Additional uses will be discussed throughout the text. One rationale for presenting this type of program early is that once programmers know how to obtain output in a language, they can test the rest of their code.

Example 1-3: output.c

```
/*                output.c
 *
 *    Synopsis   - Displays a message on the terminal screen.
 *
 *    Objective  - Illustrate a printf() call for output in C.
 */

#include <stdio.h>                                        /* Note 1 */

void main( void )
{
      printf( "C by Discovery\n" );              /* Notes 2, 3, and 4 */
}
```

To get an overview of the program output.c, notice that it consists of the single function `main()`. There are no subprograms in this code. The function `main()` has only one statement. This one statement contains three new ideas that are described below.

Note 1: This line contains an example of a *preprocessor directive*. It begins with the symbol '#'. This #include directive causes the contents of the external file named stdio.h to be read into the source file at this location in the code. The angle brackets < and > surrounding the file name tell the compiler where to find the file. Header files consist of C source code segments. The header files that are supplied with a compiler are called

---

1. Many C compilers require the extension .c for the names of the source code files. Therefore, the names of the files for the programs in this text all end with .c.

standard header files and are generally kept in a special location in the directory structure of the computer system.

Typically, a header file might include constants, definitions of customized types, and function declarations developed for use in the source code. The file stdio.h is a standard header file supplied with each C compiler. It contains declarations of all the input and output functions in the standard C library and should be "#included" in most programs. In Section 10.8, an example program will illustrate more about the contents of this file.

Traditionally, preprocessor directives are processed in a separate phase of compilation called the preprocess phase that occurs at the beginning of compilation. On many computer systems, a separate program called the preprocessor handles the preprocessor directives. On other systems, the preprocess phase is an integral part of compilation. Other preprocessor directives are discussed in Sections 1.7, 11.7, and 11.8.

Note 2: If we read from both ends of the line toward the middle, we notice the tokens printf, (,), and ;. The semicolon terminates the statement. The parentheses suggest to the compiler (and to us) that printf() is a function. It is part of the standard C library and will print formatted output. The actual parameters to the function are inside the parentheses. The function printf() can be used in many ways which will be explored in later programs in this text.

Like all functions in C, printf() should be declared. This declaration appears in the file stdio.h; it does not need to be repeated anywhere else.

Note 3: The actual parameter to printf() is "C by Discovery\n". This is an example of a string in C. A string is a sequence of characters from the underlying character set. A programmer signifies to the compiler and the readers of the program that such a sequence is a string by enclosing the sequence in double quotes. During compilation, the compiler stores a string in the object code by storing the sequence of characters inside the pair of double quotes. It terminates that sequence with a *null character*, the first character in the ASCII collating sequence. The compiler keeps track of the location of the string in memory. When printf() outputs the string, it finds the string at the saved location. It then starts the output with the first character and stops when it reaches the terminating null. We will study strings in more depth in Chapter 5.

Notice the difference between strings and characters. In a C program, strings appear between pairs of double quotes (") while single characters appear between pairs of single quotes ('). In particular, consider the string "a" and the single character 'a'.

The single character 'a' is a member of the underlying character set; it has an integer value associated with it, namely, the value it corresponds to in the collating sequence. In ASCII, the null character corresponds to the integer 0; the horizontal tab corresponds to 9; the character '0' corresponds to 48; 'a' corresponds to 97, and so on. In C code, the character 'a' is often used interchangeably with the integer 97.

In contrast, the double quotes in `"a"` signify a string to the compiler. Strings are handled differently from single characters. Specifically, they are stored in a special place in the object code and terminated with a null character. When the compiler sees `"a"` in the source code, it stores the character `'a'` and a null character in the object code. The compiler keeps track of the location of the string in memory.

Note 4: Looking inside the string, we see the words `C by Discovery` followed by some additional symbols. The symbols `\n` end the string. The pair of characters `'\'` and `'n'` when written together as `\n` represent a newline. The backslash (`\`) is an "escape character". It "escapes" or changes the usual meaning of the character following it. Note that this is different from the escape character associated with the escape key on your keyboard.

With `\n`, the usual meaning of n as the fourteenth letter in the lowercase alphabet is no longer valid. Instead the backslash followed by an 'n' means the end of a line. On a UNIX system, this is the line feed character, the character associated with 10 in the ASCII collating sequence. On a microcomputer running the MS-DOS operating system, the `'\n'` in this context represents the carriage return-line feed combination. Note that the method of terminating a line may differ with different computer systems. The use of the `'\n'` to represent the end of a line is one way in which C source code is portable. The compiler and operating system take care of the specific details.

A Closer Look

Using the backslash to escape the usual meaning of characters and impart special meanings is a common practice in C. Other examples of this escape mechanism appear below:

`\t`	the tab character
`\b`	the backspace character
`\"`	the double quote character in a string
`\'`	the single quote character
`\\`	the backslash character
`\0`	the null character

For example, the symbols `\"` would be used to write a quoted statement within a string. The sentence of dialogue

"So what?" said she.

would be written

```
"\"So what?\" said she.\n"
```

as a string in C. Here, the usual meaning of the double quote would be to terminate the string. The backslash alters this meaning; the escaped meaning is that of a double quote. Another example is using the backslash to escape the meaning of a single quote to end the designation of a character. That is, `'\''` represents the single character `'` in C source code.

The representation of the null character by `\0` is a special case of a more general concept in C. That is, any member of the underlying character set can be represented by a backslash followed by a leading zero and its underlying integer value expressed in octal. It can also be expressed with a leading zero, an x or X, and its underlying integer value expressed in hexadecimal. For example, the character `'a'` has decimal value 97, octal value 141, or hexadecimal value 61. It can be represented to the compiler as `'a'`, 97, `'\0141'`, `'\0x61'`, or `'\0X61'`. (The x would be used when a hexadecimal value is expressed using the digits `'0'` through `'9'`, and the letters `'a'`, `'b'`, `'c'`, `'d'`, `'e'`, and `'f'`. The X would be used when the letters `'A'`, `'B'`, `'C'`, `'D'`, `'E'`, and `'F'` are used instead.) This fact is especially useful for the nonprinting characters. The BEL character can be represented by `'\007'`. (BEL is the three-character mnemonic for the character CONTROL-G that rings the bell on most terminals. This can be typed from the keyboard by holding the control key down and pressing the `'G'`.)

Learning Activities

4. *C by Discovery*   Get to know your compiler. Determine the error messages from your compiler for the following deliberate syntax errors:
   a missing closing brace
   omitting the () in a function call
   a missing " in a printf() call
   a missing ; at the end of a statement
   putting a ; after the first line in a function definition

5. Test the CONTROL-G on your terminal. Does it ring the bell? If so, try to write a C program to ring the bell.

6. Write a C program that writes three lines of text (your choice of text) to the terminal screen. Have your output double spaced (one blank line between each two lines of text).

7. What would be output by the following line of code? How would it appear on the terminal?
   ```
   printf ("\t\"whoops\b\b\b\bew\n\"\n");
   ```
   Imbed this code in a C program, compile and execute the program to verify your answer to this activity.

The Structured Approach

The following example is a structured version of output.c; it demonstrates the use of a separate function to do the output. In a structured program `main()` can be used as a *driver*. Its purpose would be to call the other functions in order or "drive the program". All of the actual tasks of the program would be done by subfunctions. To be used, each subfunction must

1. be defined,
2. be declared, and
3. be called.

Example 1-4: structur.c

```
/*                structur.c
 *
 *    Synopsis   - Displays a message on the terminal screen.
 *
 *    Objective  - Demonstrates structuring the program by using
 *                 a separate function to do the output.
 */

#include <stdio.h>

void print_title( void );                          /* Note 1 */

void main( void )                                  /* Note 2 */
{
    print_title();                                 /* Note 3 */
}
/***************************** print_title()  *****************/
/*   prints the title of the text.
 */

void print_title( void )                           /* Note 4 */
{
    printf( "C by Discovery\n" );                  /* Note 5 */
}
```

This program consists of two functions `main()`, and `print_title()`. Notice the comment line with the asterisks and the name of the subfunction. This is strictly a stylistic addition. Its purpose is to aid the reader by giving a visual separation between the two functions.

Note 1: The subfunction `print_title()` must be declared. The declaration contains the type, `void`, the function name, `print_title`, and a pair of parentheses containing the number and type of the formal parameters. In this example, `void` appears between the parentheses since the function does not take any parameters. The declaration is terminated with a semicolon. The only function that should not have a separate declaration is `main()` [1].

Note 2: The function heading for `main()` indicates that `main()` does not return any value (type `void`), and that it does not take any parameters (`void` between the parentheses).

Note 3: The executable code for `main()` consists of a call to the function `print_title()`. The function call consists of the function name, followed by the pair of open parentheses, and terminated with a semicolon. If `print_title()` had taken any parameters, the actual parameters would be inside the parentheses.

Note 4: The function heading for `print_title()` states that the type is `void` and that there are no parameters. With these simple functions, the function heading looks very much like the function declaration. We will see some differences in Section 1.7 where the use of parameters is introduced.

Note 5: The executable code for `print_title()` is inside the braces. It consists of a call to `printf()`. The actual parameters to `printf()` are the same as those in the program output.c.

When the program structur.c is executed, execution starts with the code in `main()`. The call to `print_title()` causes the point of execution to change to first line in `print_title()`. There, the call to `printf()` causes the code for `printf()` to be executed. After the execution of `printf()` completes, control returns to `print_title()`. Any additional code there would be executed. When `print_title()` completes, control returns to `main()` for the execution of any additional code there. The program terminates execution when it reaches the closing brace for the function block for `main()`.

Learning Activities

8. Add another function to structur.c. Have it output a line of asterisks. Have `main()` call your function both before and after the call to `print_title()`. Make sure to compile and run your program to test it.

---

1. As we will see in later chapters, a separate declaration is not strictly required for functions in C that return a value of type `int`. However, concerns of providing information to the readers of the program and giving the compiler the information needed to do additional type checking indicate that declarations "should" be made for all functions except `main()`.

An alternate view of having all the output done by a call to printf(). Based on *Venus Victrix (Princess Pauline Bonaparte Borghese as Venus)* by Onotonio Canova, 1808.

1.5 Input and Output with Variables

In this section, we discuss the mechanism of using variables. Variables are used to hold data while a program is executing. C requires that a variable must be declared before it can be used. The declaration establishes the name and type of the variable. When a program is compiled, the compiler reserves space in memory for each variable. The amount of space reserved depends on the type of the variable. When the program is executed, values for a variable are stored in that reserved space.

The first variables we will work with have the type `int`. The keyword `int` is the name for a built-in data type used to represent integers. The variable's name must be an identifier.

To declare a variable with type `int`, state the type, follow it with the variable name, and terminate it with a semicolon. The following line of code declares a variable of type `int` with the name `counter`:

```
int counter;
```

There are two places where a variable declaration can occur: inside of a function block and outside of a function block. If the declaration appears inside a function block, the variable name is recognized by the compiler from the point of declaration to the end of the function block; the variable would be *local to the function*.

When a variable declaration appears outside a function declaration, the variable name will be recognized by the compiler anywhere in the code from the point of declaration to the end of the file in which the source code appears. The places where a variable name will be recognized is called the *scope* of the variable. We will talk more about scope in Chapter 8.

Once a variable is declared, it can be used in many ways. A value can be given to a variable with an assignment statement. The symbol for the assignment operator is a single equal sign, =. The simplest form of an assignment statement consists of a variable name followed by an equal sign, followed by a value and terminated by a semicolon (;). The statement

```
counter = 1;
```

assigns the value 1 to the variable counter. If counter is referenced after this statement in the source code, its value will be 1.

Variables in C can be initialized or given a value in the declaration. The line of code

```
int counter = 1;
```

declares a variable named counter of type int and sets its initial value to 1. This statement would replace the following two lines of code:

```
int counter;
counter = 1;
```

The difference between a variable initialization and an assignment is that when the initialization appears in the declaration, the variable is given the initial value when it is created. In contrast, an assignment statement is executable; it can appear many times in source code and can be used to change a variable's value.

More than one variable can be declared in one declaration. Commas separate the names of the variables in the declaration. The code

```
int first, second;
```

declares two variables of type int with names first and second.

The program in Example 1-5 illustrates the techniques of declaring, initializing, and displaying the values of variables of type int. The discussion of this program follows.

Example 1-5: intvar.c

```
/*              intvar.c
 *
 *   Synopsis   - Four variables of type int are declared and
 *                initialized. Their values are displayed with
 *                calls to printf().
```

```
 *
 *    Objective   - Illustrates declaration of variables
 *                  both with and without initializers, assignment
 *                  statements and the use of printf() with
 *                  conversion specifications in its control string
 *                  to output the values of variables.
 */

#include <stdio.h>

void main( void )
{
    int first;                                            /* Note 1 */
    int second = 2;                                       /* Note 2 */
    int third,
        fourth = 4;                                       /* Note 3 */

    first = 1;                                            /* Note 4 */
    third = 3;
    printf( "first is %d, ", first );                     /* Note 5 */
                                                          /* Note 6 */
    printf( "second is %d, third is %d, and fourth is %d.\n",
                                    second, third, fourth );

}
```

 Running the Program

```
first is 1, second is 2, third is 3, and fourth is 4.
```

Again, there is a single function, main(). Nine lines of source code are between the braces that enclose the code for main(). The first four lines of code are variations of variable declarations. Two assignment statements follow, and the last two statements are variations of printf() calls. The variations are explained in the notes below.

Note 1: This line of code declares a variable named first to have type int. The type appears first, followed by the variable name and the terminating semicolon. During compilation, space will be allotted for storage of a variable of type int.

This and the other variable declarations in this program appear inside the function block for main(). These identifiers will be recognized by the compiler from the point of their declaration to the end of the function block for main(). These variables are local to main().

Note 2: In this declaration, a variable named second is declared and the initial value is set at the time of declaration. An equal sign, =, initializes the variable `second` with the following numerical value. This variable will have type `int` and will have an initial value of 2. The term *initializer* refers to the expression that follows the equal sign. This example shows the simplest form of an initializer; the initializer is 2.

Note 3: Before reading further, locate the terminating semicolon in this declaration. The declaration begins with the token `int` and continues onto the following line, where it terminates with a semicolon.

Two or more variables of the same type can be declared in the same declaration in C. This line of code declares two `int` variables named `third` and `fourth`. The names of multiple variables declared in the same declaration must be separated with commas. In this example, the variable `fourth` is given an initial value of 4 at the time of declaration. The variable `third` is not given a value at its declaration.

Note 4: The next two lines are examples of assignment statements. When these statements execute, the value 1 is placed in the storage location for the variable `first` and the value 3 is placed in the storage location for the variable `third`. A single equal sign, =, is the symbol for assignment in C.

Note 5: The `printf()` function outputs the value of the variable `first`. Here, `printf()` takes two actual parameters. The two parameters are inside the parentheses and separated by a comma. The second parameter is the variable `first`. The first parameter to `printf()` is the string

```
"first is %d, "
```

It contains instructions for the output of the value of `first`. Again, the double quotes suggest to the compiler that this is a string. The first parameter to the `printf()` function must always be a string, the *control string*.

The only unfamiliar symbols in this first parameter are the '%' and the 'd'. This combination of characters is an *embedded conversion specification*. The percent sign indicates that the next character or characters will specify that a conversion must take place before output. The 'd' suggests that a value will be converted from the internal binary representation of an `int` to decimal digits for the output. When the `printf()` function executes, it looks at its first parameter and gets the memory location of the control string. It then starts the output of the characters in that string. When `printf()` encounters the `%d`, it takes its next parameter, and converts it to a sequence of decimal digits. The decimal digits form the actual output.

Each conversion specification must be associated with an additional parameter after the control string. The value of the expression in the next parameter position is the value that is to be converted and output. Here the value of `first` is output. We will see many other conversion specifications for `printf()`. A list appears in Section F of the *Programmer's Handbook*.

Note 6: This `printf()` call is similar to the previous one, but the control string now contains three embedded conversion specifications. Also, three additional parameters follow the control string. Each conversion specification in the control string gets the value to be converted from a separate parameter. The parameters must appear in the same order as the corresponding conversion specifications. The first %d in the control string instructs printf() to convert the value in the first parameter to decimal digits; the second %d instructs printf() to convert the value in the second parameter and so on. More conversion specifications can appear in the control string, but each must be associated with an additional parameter after the control string. The function printf() takes a variable number of parameters.

Learning Activities

9.   In the printf() calls in the program intvar.c, describe the uses of each of the following characters.
   a.   " (double quotes)
   b.   \ (backslash)
   c.   , (comma)
   d.   . (period)

10.   Modify intvar.c in the following ways:
   a.   Have all the variables initialized in the declarations.
   b.   Have all the variables assigned values in the executable code.
   c.   Have all variables initialized in the declarations. Display their values with a single call to printf(). Change the values of all variables with assignment statements and use printf() to display the new values.
   d.   Add a variable named fifth, assign the value 5 to it and have that value displayed with a call to printf().

   Execute intvar.c[1] after each modification to check your changes.

11.   Modify intvar.c so that the name and value of each variable is displayed on a separate line.

12.   *C by Discovery*   Find out if it is possible to start a string on one line of source code and terminate it on another line. That is, either modify an existing program or write a short program with a string running over at least two lines. See if you get either compile or run-time errors.

---

1. The instruction "Execute intvar.c" is not technically correct. What we mean when we use an expression like that in this text is that the student should compile the source code file and execute the resulting object code file.

13. Modify intvar.c in the following ways:
    a. Initialize both `first` and `third` in the declaration instead of the assignment statements.
    b. Have all output done by a single call to `printf()`. (The statement may be too long to fit on your terminal screen. Since C is a free-format language, one statement can continue on a second line of source code. Experiment to find the positions where the statement can be legally separated into two or more lines of code.)

14. *C by Discovery*   To get to know your compiler better, determine the error messages, if any, for the following errors. If there are no compile-time error messages, try to execute the program. What happens?
    a. In a `printf()` call, what happens if the number of parameters after the control string is greater than the number of conversion specifications in the control string?
    b. In a `printf()` call, what happens if the number of additional parameters is less than the number of conversion specifications?

Input with scanf()

The function `scanf()`, from the C library, does formatted input. `Scanf()` converts input from the ASCII representation entered at the keyboard to the internal representation used by the computer. It reads a sequence of characters entered by a user and converts them to a value of the requested type. More specifically, if told to read a decimal integer, `scanf()` looks for a sequence of decimal digits and converts them to an integer value.

Like `printf()` for output, `scanf()` can be used to input many different things. In this section, we will use it to input values of type `int`.

`Scanf()` is similar to `printf()` in other ways. Both are functions in the standard C library. The first argument to both functions is a control string with embedded conversion specifications, and both functions take a variable number of parameters. There must be one additional parameter for each conversion specification in the control string.

A difference between the two functions is that `printf()` converts a stored value from its internal binary representation to an ASCII format and outputs the ASCII characters on the terminal screen. In contrast, `scanf()` reads a sequence of ASCII characters from the keyboard, converts the value to the computer's internal representation and stored the value in a memory location.

The additional arguments to scanf() tell it where to put the value it read. For example, in the statement

```
scanf( "%d", &intvar );
```

the control string is "%d". It contains a single conversion specification, %d, which suggests that the value to be input will be a sequence of decimal digits and should be interpreted as a value of type int.

The second parameter tells scanf() where to put the value typed at the keyboard. Here the input value will be stored at the memory location associated with the variable intvar. The declaration of intvar as a variable of type int must appear before its use in this line of code.

The & is the address operator. It indicates a reference to the memory address of that variable. That is, &intvar tells scanf() the location in memory where it is to store the input value.

The program input1.c in Example 1-6 illustrates the use of scanf() to input a decimal value. It also introduces the address conversion specification, %p, for use with printf() when it outputs the address of the variable intvar.

Example 1-6: input1.c

```
/*                  input1.c
 *
 *    Synopsis    - A variable of type int is declared. Its address
 *                  is output. The program then prompts for and
 *                  accepts input of an integer value. The input
 *                  value is echoed to the terminal screen.
 *
 *    Objective   - Illustrates input of an integer value with
 *                  scanf(). Shows the syntax for the address of
 *                  a variable.
 */

#include <stdio.h>

void main( void )
{
    int intvar;
    printf( "The address of intvar is %p.\n",
                                    &intvar );   /* Notes 1 and 2 */

    printf( "\nEnter an integer value: " );
    scanf( "%d", &intvar );                             /* Note 3 */
    printf( "The value you entered was %d.\n", intvar );
}
```

The example has only a single function, `main()`, with a single variable of type `int` declared. There are four other lines of code, three `printf()` calls with a call to `scanf()` between them.

Note 1: This note refers to the conversion specification in the control string to this `printf()` call. The `%p` suggests that the next parameter to `printf()` should be a memory address and that the value should be converted by `printf()` to a form appropriate for displaying an address. This form may be different on different computer systems; it is *implementation dependent*.

Note 2: The second parameter to this `printf()` call is `&intvar`. This is the address of the variable `intvar`. During compilation, memory is allocated for each variable declared. The address is the location of the memory space allocated for the variable.

Note 3: In this statement, the function `scanf()` reads the value entered by the user at the terminal. The first parameter to `scanf()` is a control string with a single conversion specification, `%d`. This suggests that the value entered should be the ASCII representation of a decimal value (a sequence of digits). The second parameter, `&intvar`, is the location in memory where `scanf()` is to store the value it reads. It needs to be an address or "pointer" value. Here it is the address of `intvar`. When `intvar` is accessed in the next line of code, its value will be the value entered from the terminal.

A Word of Caution

As will be seen in Chapters 3 and 10, `scanf()` is a multipurpose input function. Like most multipurpose input functions, it can return unexpected values if the input does not exactly match the conversion specifications. An exercise below addresses this fact.

Learning Activities

15. Execute the program input1.c to make sure that it works as you expected.

16. *C by Discovery*
   a. Experiment with erroneous inputs to input1.c. For example, type alphabetic characters instead of digits or type digits and nondigits intermixed. Try typing a few blanks or tabs before, between, and after the digits.
   b. Describe what happens in each case in part a.
   c. Try to generalize the behavior of `scanf()` for each case in part a.

17.   Add the declaration of another variable of type `int` to input1.c. Have `printf()` display the addresses of both variables on the screen. Note the relationship between the two addresses displayed.

So far we have seen the decimal conversion specification, `%d`, and the memory address conversion specification, `%p`. Besides these, both `printf()` and `scanf()` will convert an integer value to or from octal and hexadecimal.

The conversion specification for octal is `%o`. When `%o` is used with `printf()`, the corresponding parameter should be type `int`. Then `printf()` will convert the value from the internal representation to an octal representation in the octal digits `'0'`, `'1'`, `'2'`, `'3'`, `'4'`, `'5'`, `'6'`, and `'7'`. When `%o` is used with `scanf()`, the conversion goes in the opposite direction. The input is expected to be in octal digits, and `scanf()` will convert them to the internal binary format for storage in a variable of type `int`.

The hexadecimal conversion specifications are `%x` and `%X`; either one can be used with any `int` expression with both `printf()` and `scanf()`. When the conversion specification is `%x`, the characters used should be the hexadecimal digits `'0'` through `'9'`, and `'a'`, `'b'`, `'c'`, `'d'`, `'e'`, `'f'`. When the uppercase characters, `'A'`, `'B'`, `'C'`, `'D'`, `'E'`, `'F'`, are desired, the conversion specification `%X` can be used.

The program input2.c in Example 1-7 illustrates the use of these three conversion specifications in both `printf()` and `scanf()`. The discussion of that program starts here.

Example 1-7: input2.c

```
/*              input2.c
 *
 *  Synopsis    - A variable of type int is declared. The program
 *                prompts for, accepts input of, and outputs an
 *                integer value. The input and output are done
 *                three times - in decimal, hexadecimal, and
 *                octal.
 *
 *  Objective   - Illustrates input and output of an integer
 *                value with scanf() and printf() using the
 *                conversion specifications %d for decimal, %x
 *                for hexadecimal, and %o for octal.
 */
```

```
#include <stdio.h>

void main( void )
{
    int intvar;

    printf( "Enter a decimal integer value: " );
    scanf( "%d", &intvar );
                                                    /* Note 1 */
    printf( "The hexadecimal equivalent of %d is %x.\n",
                                        intvar, intvar );

    printf( "Enter a hexadecimal integer value: " );
    scanf( "%x", &intvar );                         /* Note 2 */
                                                    /* Note 3 */
    printf( "The value you entered was %o in octal.\n",
                                        intvar );

    printf( "Enter an octal integer value: " );
    scanf( "%o", &intvar );                         /* Note 4 */
    printf( "The value you entered was %d in decimal.\n",
                                        intvar );
}
```

The overview of the program reveals a single function, main(), with a single variable of type int declared. The next nine lines of code consist of three sequences of a printf() call, a scanf() call, and a printf() call.

Note 1: Note the conversion specification %x in the control string to printf(). This suggests that the value of intvar will be converted to hexadecimal when it is output. In the previous statement, scanf() read a decimal value and stored that value in the internal machine representation in the variable intvar. This value can be converted to any representation before output.

Note 2: In this call to scanf(), the value entered on the terminal is assumed to be in hexadecimal. Scanf() looks for a sequence of hexadecimal characters, '0' through '9' and 'a', 'b', 'c', 'd', 'e', 'f'. It converts the value it finds to the internal representation for type int and stores the value in intvar.

Note 3: The %o in the control string requests a conversion to octal before output. Note that the internal representation of a value of type int is in binary (base 2). Scanf() and printf() perform conversions to and from this internal representation.

Note 4: The %o indicates a conversion to octal on input by this scanf() call. Scanf() looks for a sequence of the digits '0' through '7' and, if found, converts the octal value to the internal representation and stores it in `intvar`.

Both `printf()` and `scanf()` are useful functions for conversions and formatted input and output. Remember that `scanf()` can give unexpected results if the input does not match the specifications.

Learning Activities

18. Predict the output of the program input2.c for each following input sequence:

    a. 243
        a45
        132

    b. 255
        ff
        177

19. Execute input2.c with the above input sequences to check your predictions.

1.6 Arithmetic Operations

In this section, we will investigate arithmetic operations in C. The arithmetic operations that are available for quantities of type `int` and the other integer types in C are:

    +   addition and unary plus
    –   unary minus and subtraction
    *   multiplication
    /   division
    %   remainder

The addition, (+), subtraction, (–), and multiplication, (*), operators are the usual operators that are used in mathematics. They are *binary* operators because they take two operands. For example, 2 + 3, 10 – 2, 23 * 521.

Division (/) and remainder (%) operations are also binary operations; they take two operands. However, the meanings of these operands are slightly different than that taught in mathematics.

When the division operator, /, is applied to positive integer values, / is truncating division. The fractional part is truncated. In particular, the value of 2/3 is

0, 3/2 is 1, 13/4 is 3, and so on.

If the operands of / are integers that do not have the same sign, the results may vary from compiler to compiler. Therefore, it is best, whenever possible, to code programs so that the results of integer division and the remainder operator do not depend on operands with opposite signs. This can be done with functions from the C library. How C handles the division and remainder operations and one method of avoiding the portability problem is described more fully in the next **A Closer Look** section.

If a and b are variables of type int, the expression

```
a % b
```

represents the remainder when a is divided by b. This operator is referred to as the *remainder operator*. The symbol for the operator is a percent sign. Unlike the other operators, the remainder operator is only defined for operands of type int. For example,

```
7 % 3 is 1
```

since 7 divided by 3 is 2 with remainder 1. By the same reasoning,

```
8 % 3 is 2
9 % 5 is 4
```

The modulus operator and the division operator are related by the fact that when a and b are variables of type int,

```
a = (a/b)*b + (a%b)
```

This means that the same portability problem exists with the remainder operator applied to operands with different signs as with the division operator.

C has two *unary* arithmetic operators, unary plus and unary minus. They take only one operand. The unary plus has no effect on its operand. That is, if intvar is an int variable, then +intvar has the same value as intvar; it is used in much the same way as +3 and +x might be used in algebra. The unary minus changes the sign of its operand; if intvar is positive, -intvar is negative, and vice versa.

When these operations are applied to variables of type int, the result, by default, is of type int. The effects of these operators on variables of different types is discussed in Chapter 3.

The program in Example 1-8 illustrates the arithmetic operations +, -, *, /, and % in a program with variables of type int.

Example 1-8: arith.c

```
/*              arith.c
 *
 *   Synopsis    - Calculates arithmetic operations with variables
```

```
*                       of type int and displays the resulting values
*                       in decimal.
*
*    Objective  - Demonstrates the operations +, -, *, /, and %
*                       on variables of type int.
*/

#include <stdio.h>

void main( void )
{
     int a, b, c, d;
     printf( "Enter an integer: " );
     scanf( "%d", &a );

     b = a + 4;                                              /* Note 1 */
     c = a - 3;                                              /* Note 2 */
     d = -a;                                                 /* Note 3 */
     printf( "b is %d,\nc is %d, and\nd is %d.\n\n", b, c, d );

     b = a * 3;                                              /* Note 4 */
     c = a / 3;                                              /* Note 5 */
     d = a % 3;                                              /* Note 6 */
     printf( "Now\nb is %d,\nc is %d, and\nd is %d.\n",
                                          b, c, d );
}
```

There is a single function named main(). Notice that four variables are declared of type int. Of these, only the variable a has been initialized. The declarations are followed by a sequence of assignment statements interspersed with calls to printf().

Note 1: The addition operation is illustrated here. The variable b receives the value of a + 4.

Note 2: The subtraction operation. The variable c receives the value of a - 3.

Note 3: The unary minus operation. After execution of this statement, the value of d is the negative of the value of a.

Note 4: The multiplication operation is performed here. The value of a is multiplied by 3 to get the new value of b.

Note 5: This statement demonstrates the division of two integers. Since both dividend and divisor are positive, the operation is truncating division.

Note 6: This statement illustrates the modulus operation. Again, since both divisor and dividend are positive, there is no ambiguity about the new value of d.

Learning Activities

20. a. How many lines of output will there be from arith.c?
     b. Predict the output of arith.c. Write the output in the spaces
         below. Write one character per space. Indicate end of lines with
         the symbol '\n'.

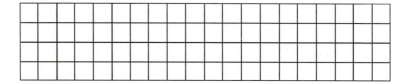

     c. Execute this program to verify your answers to parts a
         and b.

A Closer Look

We have discussed the results of a/b and a%b when both a and b are int variables that currently have positive values stored. The other cases need some explanation.

The ANSI standards for C guarantee that the absolute value of the remainder,
a%b, is less than the absolute value of the divisor, b. No other guarantees are made
about the values of a/b and a%b.

The first case we will consider is when the mathematical quotient of the two
operands is an integer. Then the result of the quotient in C is that integer. For
example, since 6 is evenly divisible by 3, we know that

> the value of (-6)/3 is -2
> the value of 6/(-3) is -2
> the value of (-6)/(-3) is 2

However, when the indicated quotient is not an integer, as in 5/(-3), (-5)/3,
or (-5)/(-3), the result may vary from compiler to compiler. The result could
be either of the two integers closest to the actual arithmetic quotient. For example,
the mathematical value of (-5)/(-3) is 1.66666, therefore, the C value will be
either 1 or 2. Similarly the value of (-5)/3 is either -1 or -2.

The result of the remainder operator involving negative integer operands
depends on the value of the corresponding quotient. For example, the values of
(-7)%(-3), (-7)%3, and 7%(-3) may vary between systems since they are
dependent on the corresponding values of (-7)/(-3), (-7)/3, and 7/(-3).

To ensure that a program is portable, its calculations should never depend on a quotient or remainder involving negative operands. This can be avoided by the use of the function abs() from the C library. This function takes a single parameter of type int and returns the absolute value of the parameter. For example, abs(-3) is 3, and abs(2) is 2. The program divrem.c in Example 1.9 shows the use of this function to make / and % portable. The other new things are the inclusion of the file stdlib.h which contains the ANSI prototype of abs() as well as prototypes of other ANSI functions, and the use of the conversion specification %% to effect the output of the character '%'.

Example 1-9: divrem.c

```
/*              divrem.c
 *
 *    Synopsis    - Prompts for and accepts input of two integer
 *                  values and displays the results of a quotient
 *                  and a remainder operation.
 *
 *    Objective   - Illustrates the abs() function and one method
 *                  of ensuring that the results of these operations
 *                  will be the same on different computer systems.
 */

/* Include Files */
#include <stdio.h>
#include <stdlib.h>                                    /* Note 1 */

void main( void )
{
    int a, b;

    printf( "Enter a positive and a negative integer. " );
    printf( "\nSeparate with a space: " );
    scanf( "%d %d", &a, &b );

                                                       /* Note 2 */
    printf( "The value of a / b is %d\n",
                            -(abs( a ) / abs( b )) );

    printf( "The value of a %% b is %d\n",             /* Note 3 */
                            -(abs( a ) % abs( b )) );
}
```

The program consists of a single function named `main()`. The program prompts for and accepts input of two integer values. The values of `a/b` and `a%b` are displayed to the screen. This value should be the same on any computer system.

Note 1: The file stdlib.h must be included since the prototype for the function `abs()` appears in that file. This function returns type `int`, and takes a single parameter of type `int`. Instead of including the header file, we could put a source code line with the function's prototype declaration,

```
int abs( int );
```

Either the header file or the prototype declaration must appear before the first call to `abs()`. Including the header file is the more popular way to make sure the function is declared.

Note 2: The following two calls to `printf()` use the function `abs()` to make sure that each of the operands to `/` and `%` are positive. Since the operands are positive, we know that `/` will produce truncating division, and `%` will give the corresponding remainder. Since the values of `a` and `b` are opposite in sign (if the user followed directions), the value of the quotient will be negative; the remainder must also be negative to make the identity `a = (a/b)*b + (a%b)` true. This may or may not match the way your compiler calculates these operations without the use of `abs()`, but this code will produce the same results on any computer system. After we have studied control statements, this algorithm can be expanded to handle the case where both operands are negative.

Note 3: Notice the characters `%%` in the control string to `printf()`. This is the method for getting `printf()` to output a single percent sign. It is handled as a conversion specification.

Learning Activities

21.   *C by Discovery*   Find out how your compiler handles integer division and the modulus operator when at least one operand is negative:

   a.   Write a short program that performs integer division and the remainder operation and outputs the results of both operations.

   b.   Test your program with different values of the operands.

   c.   Explain what happens with your compiler for a quotient `a/b` when either `a`, `b`, or both are negative integers and when the mathematical quotient of `a` divided by `b` is not an integer value.

22.   Modify divrem.c by changing the `%%` to `%`. Compile and execute the program again. Can you explain the result?

Precedence of Arithmetic Operations

The precedence of the arithmetic operations follows the rules of mathematics. The unary plus and unary minus have the highest precedence; the multiplicative operations, *, /, and %, come next; and the additive operations, + and –, have the lowest precedence. All of the arithmetic operators have precedence over the assignment operator.

High precedence

Unary Operators:	`-, +`
Multiplicative Operators:	`*, /, %`
Additive Operators:	`+, -`
Assignment Operator:	`=`

Low precedence

Within each group, the operations associate from left to right. For example, `a*b/c` is evaluated as `(a*b)/c` and `2*a + 4/b` is evaluated as `(2*a) + (4/b)`.

These precedence rules can be overruled by judicious placement of parentheses. A parenthesized expression will be evaluated first. A full precedence chart for the arithmetic operations and all other operations in C appears in the *Programmer's Handbook*.

The program in Example 1-10 illustrates precedence for some combinations of the arithmetic operations.

Example 1-10: preceden.c

```
/*                  preceden.c
 *
 *    Synopsis    - Five variables of type int are declared.
 *                  Arithmetic operations are performed and the
 *                  resulting values are displayed.
 *
 *    Objective   - To illustrate the relative precedence of
 *                  arithmetic operations and to see how the meaning
 *                  can be changed by the addition of parentheses.
 */

#include <stdio.h>

void main( void )
{
     int a=4, b=2, c=3, d, e;
```

```
d = a * -b + c;                                      /* Note 1 */
e = a * -(b + c);
printf( "d is %d, e is %d,\n", d, e );

d = a + b * c;                                       /* Note 2 */
e = (a + b) * c;
printf( "d is %d, e is %d,\n", d, e );

d = b % c + a;                                       /* Note 3 */
e = b % (c + a);
printf( "d is %d, e is %d,\n", d, e );

d = c - b / a * a;                                   /* Note 4 */
e = (c - b) / (a * a);
printf( "d is %d, e is %d,\n", d, e );

}
```

The program consists of only one function, `main()`. Variables `a`, `b`, `c`, `d`, and `e` are declared with initial values given to `a`, `b`, and `c`. The following code is broken into four sequences consisting of assignment to `d`, assignment to `e`, and a call to `printf()` to output their current values. Note that the expression assigned to `d` differs from the one assigned to `e` only in the addition of parentheses.

Note 1: The expression assigned to `d` is evaluated as

$$(a* (- b)) + c$$

by the natural precedence of the arithmetic operators.

Note 2: In this assignment, the natural precedence causes the expression `a + b * c` to be evaluated as `a + (b * c)`.

Note 3: The expression `b % c + a` is evaluated as `(b % c) + a`.

Note 4: The natural precedence of operators and order of evaluation causes the expression `c - b / a * a` to be evaluated as `c - ((b/a) * a)`.

Learning Activities

23.   Predict the output of preceden.c. Execute the program to verify your prediction and correct any mistakes in your understanding.

24.   a.   If the variables `a`, `b`, and `c` have been declared as type `int` and have the values `4`, `5`, and `2` respectively, evaluate the following expressions as they would be evaluated on your system:

   i.   `a % b - 5`
   ii.   `c - b * a`

> iii. c * c + b * a / 3
> iv. a - b - c * a % b
>
> b. To verify your answers to part a, write a short program in C that declares and initializes a, b, and c and outputs the values of the four expressions.

The program fahrcels.c in Example 1-11 accepts input of a temperature in degrees Fahrenheit and outputs the Celsius equivalent. Since this program uses variables of type int, it will not record the fractional part of the temperature. The discussion of that program is presented below.

Example 1-11: fahrcels.c

```
/*               fahrcels.c
 *
 *    Synopsis    - Converts a temperature entered in degrees
 *                  Fahrenheit to Celsius. Uses variables of type
 *                  int.
 *
 *    Objective   - To illustrate a practical use of arithmetic
 *                  operators.
 */

#include <stdio.h>

void main( void )
{
    int fahrenheit, celsius;                              /* Note 1 */

    printf( "Enter a temperature in fahrenheit: " );
    scanf( "%d", &fahrenheit );

    celsius = 5 * (fahrenheit  -  32) / 9;                /* Note 2 */

    printf( "%d in Fahrenheit is %d in Celsius.\n",
                              fahrenheit, celsius );
}
```

The function main() has two variables of type int declared. The variable fahrenheit is initialized by a call to scanf() to input its value. The Celsius temperature is calculated and output.

Note 1: The variables `fahrenheit` and `celsius` are both declared to have type `int`. In order to record the fractional part of the temperature, a different type must be used. Chapter 3 discusses other numeric types in C.

Note 2: This line of code does the conversion from Fahrenheit to Celsius. First the parenthetical expression is evaluated, then the multiplication and truncating division by the constant factors 5 and 9 are performed.

Learning Activities

25.   Compile and execute fahrcels.c. Test it with the following input values: `212`, `32`, `213`, `35`, and `40`. Check the results of the program by calculating the Celsius temperature by hand.

26.   a.   Modify the program fahrcels.c by changing the line

```
celsius = 5 * (fahrenheit - 32) / 9;
```

to

```
celsius = 5/9 * (fahrenheit - 32);
```

b.   Compile and run the modified program with the same input as for activity 25. Explain the results.

In the remainder of this section we will discuss shortcuts in the C syntax for the arithmetic operations. They are optional in use, but may allow the C compiler to perform some optimization in the object code. However, they tend to make the code harder to read. The possibility of optimization must be weighed against the style considerations when deciding whether or not to use these shortcuts in your programs. Since other programmers may use this syntax extensively, it will be necessary to recognize these shortcuts in other's code.

Compound Assignment

The first syntax shortcut is *compound assignment*. The assignment statement

```
a = a + 4;
```

can be shortened to

```
a += 4;
```

The operation `+=` is one example of *compound assignment*. When a single variable is being changed with any operation, it can be done with compound assignment. For any operation, the expression

```
a op= b        is equivalent to        a = a op (b)
```

For example,

a *= 3	is equivalent to	a = a * 3
a += 4	is equivalent to	a = a + 4

Compound assignment also can be used with division and the remainder operation. Example 1-12 illustrates this.

Example 1-12: compound.c

```
/*                  compound.c
 *
 *    Synopsis    - Uses compound assignment to change the value of
 *                  an integer variable a and displays the changed
 *                  value with printf().
 *
 *    Objective   - Illustrates compound assignment in C with
 *                  several different arithmetic operations.
 */

#include <stdio.h>

void main( void )
{
    int a = 0;

    a += 4;                                              /* Note 1 */
    printf( "a is %d.\n", a );

    a *= 3;                                              /* Note 2 */
    printf( "a is now %d.\n", a );

    a -= 4;                                              /* Note 3 */
    printf( "a is now %d.\n", a );

    a /= 2;                                              /* Note 4 */
    printf( "a is now %d.\n", a );

    a %= 5;                                              /* Note 5 */
    printf( "a is now %d.\n", a );
}
```

This program contains a single function named `main()`. An integer variable named a is declared and initialized to zero. A sequence of compound assignment statements is followed by calls to `printf()`.

Note 1: The statement `a += 4;` is equivalent to `a = a + 4;`. A new value of the variable a is established.

Note 2: Compound assignment is used with the multiplication operation. This statement is equivalent to `a = a * 3;`.

Note 3: Subtraction can be done with compound assignment also.

Note 4: This is an example of compound assignment with division. Because both operands are positive, the result is unambiguous.

Note 5: The remainder operation is applied with compound assignment. Note that the result is not ambiguous in this case either.

Compound assignment can be used whenever a single variable is being changed. It also can be used with operations other than the arithmetic operations.

Learning Activities

27. Part of the output from compound.c is given below. Complete the output by writing down the value of a in the output from each of the `printf()` calls.

    ```
    a is      _____.\n
    a is now _____.\n
    a is now _____.\n
    a is now _____.\n
    a is now _____.\n
    ```

28. What is the value of `int1` after the following code sequence has been executed?

    ```
    int int1 = 5, int2 = 7;
    int2 /= int2 - int1;
    int1 *= int1 + int2;
    ```

29. Try to find a way to compare the object or assembly code[1] generated by the statement

    ```
    a = a + 4;
    ```

    with the code generated by the equivalent statement

    ```
    a += 4;
    ```

---

1. On some systems, UNIX and Turbo C and Turbo C++ for example, it is easy to stop the compilation process and look at the assembly code. On other systems it may be impossible. If you can't look at the assembly code, try looking at the size of the object code to see if there is a difference.

Based on your comparison, give some reasons for using one form over the other. Which form do you think is preferable? Find out which one your instructor thinks is better.

The Increment and Decrement by 1 Operations

Another shortcut in source code is provided for incrementing a variable by one. The following statements increment the variable a by 1.

```
a = a + 1;
a += 1;
a++;
```

The third statement uses the increment by one operator, ++. This operator can be used immediately before or after a variable anywhere in an expression. If the ++ is placed immediately after the variable, as in a++, then the value of a is incremented after it is accessed for use in the expression. If the ++ is placed immediately before the variable, as in ++a, then the value of a is incremented before a is used in the expression.

For example, compare the two expressions a++ * 4 and ++a * 4. If the value of the variable a is 5, then the expression

```
a++  *  4
```

yields the value 20. After evaluation of that expression, the value of a becomes 6.

For the other expression, again assume the value of the variable a is 5, then the expression

```
++a  *  4
```

would have the value 24 since a would be incremented before it is multiplied by 4. Again, the value of a is 6 after evaluation of the expression.

The corresponding decrement by one operator is --. When placed immediately after a variable in an expression, as in a--, the value of the variable is decremented by one after accessing the value in the expression. The operator -- can also be placed immediately before a variable, as in --a, and the value of the variable is decremented before it is accessed in the expression.

The program incremen.c in Example 1-13 illustrates the increment and decrement by 1 operators.

Example 1-13: incremen.c

```
/*                  incremen.c
 *
 *    Synopsis     - Assigns values to b using the increment and
 *                   decrement by 1 operators with a. Displays
 *                   values of a and b.
 *
 *    Objective    - To demonstrate the increment and decrement by
 *                   1 operators.
 */

#include <stdio.h>

void main( void )
{
     int a = 3, b;

     b = a++;                                               /* Note 1 */
     printf( "b is %d, and a is %d.\n", b, a );

     b = ++a;                                               /* Note 2 */
     printf( "Now b is %d, and a is %d.\n", b, a );

     b = 5 % --a;                                           /* Note 3 */
     printf( "Now b is %d, and a is %d.\n", b, a );
                                                            /* Note 4 */
     printf( "Now b is %d, and a is %d.\n", ++b, a-- );
     printf( "Now b is %d, and a is %d.\n", b, a );
}
```

This program consists of the single function main(). Two variables of type int are declared, and the variable a is initialized to 3. The remainder of the program is a sequence of assignment statements and printf() calls.

Note 1: The current value of a is assigned to b, and a is incremented after the assignment. This leaves b with the value 3 and a with the value 4.

Note 2: In this statement, a is incremented before its value is assigned to b. This leaves both b and a with the value 5.

Note 3: Here a is decremented to 4 before the modulus operation is performed. Therefore, the value 1 is assigned to b.

Note 4: In this printf() call, the value of b is incremented before it is output while the value of a is decremented after it is output. The resulting values are output in the next call to `printf()`.

Learning Activities

30. a. Predict the output of incremen.c if each statement of the form

    ```
    printf( "b is %d, and a is %d.\n", b, a );
    ```

    or

    ```
    printf( "Now b is %d, and a is %d.\n", b, a );
    ```

    is changed to

    ```
    printf( "b is %d, and a is %d.\n", b--, a++ );
    ```

    Write the new values of a and b for each of the `printf()` calls.

    ```
    b is ____ and a is ____.\n
    Now b is ____ and a is ____.\n
    Now b is ____ and a is ____.\n
    Now b is ____ and a is ____.\n
    Now b is ____ and a is ____.\n
    ```

    b. Make the changes and execute the program to verify your answers.

31. Predict the output of the following program.

    ```
    /*                  laincr.c
     *
     *    Synopsis   -Displays values of int1, int2 and
     *                int3
     *
     *    Objective -To provide practice with automatic
     *                increment and decrement
     */

    /* Include Files */
    #include <stdio.h>

    void main( void )
    {
         int int1 = 4,
             int2 = 7,
             int3;

         int3 = ++int1 * --int2;
         printf( "%d  %d  %d\n", ++int1, int2--, --int3 );
         printf( "%d  %d  %d\n", int1, int2, int3 );
    }
    ```

1.7 Introduction to Functions and Structured Programming in C

The goals of structured programming include writing source code that is modular in nature, easily modifiable, robust (handles errors gracefully), and readable. A modular program is composed of many independent subprograms. Each subprogram or function in C should be designed to do one task, and should not be too long to be understood easily. Another programming goal is to write subprograms that are tools and can be used with little or no modification in many programs. If a subprogram is to be a useful tool, it should not depend on any variables or constants not declared in the function.

With a few new concepts we can start to write structured, modular, modifiable C code and write functions that are tools. The new C concepts are constant definitions, parameter passing, and the return statement. We will discuss those topics and present some additional information about function declarations, function definitions, and function calls in this section.

Preprocessor Constants

Defining constants add to a program's readability. They also allow a program to be more easily modified. For example, consider a situation in which a company commissions a software developer to write a payroll program. The company currently has 100 employees, and the program needs to reference a certain maximum number of employees several places in the code. The programmer, being farsighted, allows for a maximum of 150 employees, and the program works well for several years. However, the company expands beyond all expectation, and when they add their 151st employee, they experience trouble with their payroll program and call the programmer back in. If the programmer had associated the maximum number of employees with an identifier and always referenced that value by using the identifier, it would be a simple matter to change the value of the identifier and recompile the program. However, if the programmer had used the value 150 throughout the code instead of using an identifier, then he or she must painstakingly search the source code for all references to 150; determine, by context, if that value was referring to the maximum number of employees or to some other quantity; and change all of those and only those that are relevant.

In C, one way of defining constants is with the preprocessor. We discussed the preprocessor directive #include in Section 1.4. The #define directive is our second preprocessor directive. For the situation described above, the directive would be

```
#define MAXEMPLOYEES 150
```

It should appear in the source code file before other references to MAXEMPLOYEES. Older versions of C compilers may require that the character # appear in the first column of a line and that no whitespace appear between the # and the word define. These restrictions have been eased in the ANSI C standards.

During the preprocess phase of compilation, the preprocessor searches through the source code for all references to the identifier MAXEMPLOYEES and replaces each one with the expression 150. When the program is modified by replacing the value 150 with 200 or another suitable constant, it must be recompiled. The preprocessor again seeks out all occurrences of the identifier MAXEMPLOYEES and this time replaces each one with the value 200.

Function Parameters

Using parameters is one method of letting a function communicate with the rest of the program without depending directly on program variables. A function parameter is used to carry information from one function to another.

The use of parameters has its beginnings in mathematical notation. For example, in mathematical functional notation,

$$y = f(x)$$

indicates that

> 1. f is a function
> 2. its value depends on the value of x (its argument)
> 3. y takes on that particular value of f

In the mathematical context, x is called the independent variable and y is the dependent variable. In a C function definition, the terminology is somewhat different: x is called the *formal parameter* or argument to f, and y is said to store the value returned by f. However, the concept is the same. The name of the formal parameters appear throughout the code for a function.

In a C function call, the values (variables or expressions) that appear inside the parentheses are called the *actual parameters*. They must match the formal parameters in position, number and type. When a function call is made, a memory location is allocated for each formal parameter and a copy of the corresponding actual parameter is put in that memory location. All calculations involving the formal parameter use this memory location.

For example, let us try to implement the mathematical function

$$y = f(x) = x + 3$$

in ANSI C. In this chapter we will restrict the type of x to int. To implement this function, we will need to specify both a function definition and a function declaration.

The ANSI C function definition for this function would begin with the following function heading:

```
int f( int x )
```

The heading will appear before the opening brace for the function. This informs the compiler that the function f takes a single parameter that will be referred to by the name x in the body of the function and that the parameter type is int[1].

Since x has type int, x + 3 will also have type int. Therefore, the type of the function is type int. The function heading will never have a semicolon.

A value can be established for a function by means of the return statement. When execution reaches any return statement, the function stops executing and control is returned to the position immediately after the function call. When the return statement appearing in a function is followed by an expression, two additional things happen when that statement is executed. First, the expression is evaluated. Second, when the function stops executing, it returns the value of the expression to its calling environment. That value can be ignored, used and discarded, or stored in a variable with an assignment statement.

To complete the C implementation of the mathematical function $y = f(x) = x + 3$, the executable code in the function block for f() should be

```
return x+3;
```

The function declaration is similar to the function heading. For this function, the declaration would be

```
int f( int );
```

It must contain the function type, the function name, and the number and type of the formal parameters. Unlike the function heading, the declaration must be terminated with a semicolon. Another difference is that the formal parameter names need not appear in a function declaration.[2]

Function Calls

A function call in C consists of the function's name, and a pair of parentheses containing the actual parameters. A function call can appear anywhere that an expression of the corresponding type is allowed.

The following example program has the full C implementation of the mathematical function $f(x) = x + 3$. It also contains four calls to that function f().

---

1. An alternate syntax is used in older compilers to convey the same information. In this example, the alternate declaration for the function f() would be
    ```
    int f(x)
    int x;
    ```

2. Two additional facts should be noted about function declarations. First, it is syntactically acceptable to include an identifier in the formal parameter declaration in an ANSI C prototype declaration. Any identifier is accepted. It does not need to match the name of a formal parameter.

    The second fact has to do with the necessity of declaring functions. In C, type int is the default type. If a function returns type int, the declaration can be omitted. (However, some compilers will issue a warning for omitted function declarations.) However, if the declaration is omitted, then the compiler will not be able to check the type and number of parameters in function calls. Therefore, in this text we will provide the ANSI C prototype declarations of all functions other than main().

    With older compilers, a function declaration contains the name of the function, the type of the function, a pair of parentheses, and a terminating semicolon. Again, functions returning a value of type int do not need to be declared. With these older compilers, no information about the parameters is supplied with the declaration. Older compilers never check on the type and number of actual parameters in a function call.

Example 1-14: function.c

```
/*                function.c
 *
 *    Synopsis    - Makes four calls to the function f() and
 *                  displays values involving the return value of
 *                  the function.
 *
 *    Objective   - To demonstrate a function that 1) takes a
 *                  parameter, and 2) returns a value. Three
 *                  versions of function calls to f() are also
 *                  demonstrated.
 */

/* Include Files */
#include <stdio.h>

/* Function Declarations */
int f( int );        - function declaration              /* Note 1 */

void main( void )
{
     int x, y, z;

     z = 4;
     y = f( z );          - function call               /* Note 2 */
     printf( "y is %d\n", y );

     x = y + f( 3 );  - function call                    /* Note 3 */
     printf( "The value of x is %d\n", x );

     f( x );  - function call                            /* Note 4 */
     printf( "The value of f( 5 ) is %d\n", f( 5 ) );    /* Note 5 */
}

/*************************** f ()  ***************************/
/*    Takes a single parameter, and returns the parameter + 3.
 */

int f( int x )  - function definition                   /* Note 6 */
{
     return x + 3;                                       /* Note 7 */
}
```

Running the Program

```
y is 7
The value of x is 13
The value of f(5) is 8
```

This program consists of two functions, `main()` and `f()`. The purpose of `main()` is to make several calls to `f()` and demonstrate different actual parameters. The function `f()` is the C implementation of the mathematical function $f(x) = x + 3$.

Note 1: The declaration of the function `f()` indicates that this function takes a single parameter of type `int` and returns a value of type `int`. The declaration appears above `main()`. In this position, its declaration is known by all functions in the file.

In this program, the declaration of `f()` could also appear inside of `main()`. In that position, `main()` would be the only function that would know about the declaration. The significance of this will become apparent as programs get more complex.

Note 2: The line

```
y = f( z );
```

calls the function `f()` with the current value of `z` as the actual parameter, and assigns the return value to `y`. The value returned by `f()` is output by the call to `printf()` in the next statement. Notice that the name of the actual parameter does not need to match the name of the formal parameter.

Note 3: The next call to `f()` appears as an operand for an arithmetic addition operation. To evaluate the sum, C must determine the value of `f( 3 )`. This involves a call to the function `f()` with the actual parameter 3. The return value is added to `y` and assigned to `x`. In this line of code, the value returned by the function is used and discarded.

Notice that in this call, the actual parameter is a constant. The value 3 is copied into the memory location that is allocated for the formal parameter to `f()`. While the function `f()` is executing, the value in that memory location is used in place of the formal parameter. Some other languages do not allow constants as actual parameters.

Note 4: The third call to `f()` is in the line

```
f( x );
```

This time, when the `return` statement in the function `f()` is executed, the function terminates, the value of `x+3` is returned to `main()`, and execution continues on the next line of `main()`. The return value is ignored. In this case, the function call has no effect on the results of this program. This use is not considered an error, but ignoring a return value may elicit a warning message from some compilers.

This type of a function call might be used with a function that does some other tasks (like input or output) as well as returning a value. Then the other task would still be performed even if the program had no use for the returned value. For example it is very common in existing C code to ignore the return values from `printf()` and `scanf()`.

Note 5: The last call to `f()` appears as a parameter to the call to `printf()`. Evaluating the parameter causes `f()` to be called. The return value will be displayed by `printf()`.

Note 6: The function heading for `f()` has the same information as the function declaration plus the name of the formal parameter. That name will be used throughout the code for `f()`. Whenever `f()` is called, the value of the actual parameter will be substituted for the formal parameter.

Note 7: When this `return` statement is executed, control passes back to the point in the code immediately after the function call. The return value can either be assigned to a variable, used in an expression, used as a parameter to another function or ignored.

Learning Activities

32. Compile and execute function.c as it is. Then add some additional calls to the function `f()` and compile and run it again.

33. Write a function `cube()` that takes a single parameter of type `int` and returns the cube of its parameter. Use the function `f()` from funct1.c and your function `cube()` in a program that accepts input of a value x of type `int` and displays the value of the polynomial $x^3 + 3x$.

The example program convert.c of Example 1-15 gives an example of a function that communicates with the main program by means of two parameters and a `return` statement. In this program, a preprocessor-defined constant has been declared so that the program can be easily modified. The program directs the user to input a value in a given base. That value is then converted to decimal by the function `todecimal()`. The parameters inform the function of the number to be converted, `original`, and the `base` of the number. Since C does not have a facility to input numbers in bases other than decimal, hexadecimal, and octal, the input is done as if the number were decimal. The function then isolates the individual digits so that the true value of the input can be calculated.

Note that this program has many limitations. First, the program may not execute correctly on a microcomputer if the value entered is greater than 32767 because that is the largest integer value that can be handled on many computers. Second, the program will not work correctly for a number whose base is greater than 10 because the input is limited to decimal digits. Third, no error checking is done on the input values. For a base 5 number, the digits used are 0 through 4. If the user enters a digit greater than 4, the program will accept it as correct. You will learn how to correct these limitations after studying the material presented in Chapters 2 and 3. At that time the program could be rewritten using one of the loops in C.

Example 1-15: convert.c

```
/*                  convert.c
 *
 *    Synopsis    - Accepts input of a number in base 5 and displays
 *                  the decimal representation of that number.
 *
 *    Objective   - To illustrate the use of a preprocessor-defined
 *                  constant to make a program easily modifiable,
 *                  and the use of parameters and return values to
 *                  make a function independent.
 */

/* Include Files */
#include <stdio.h>

/* Preprocessor Constants */
#define BASE 5                                          /* Note 1 */

/* Function Declarations */
int todecimal( int, int );

void main( void )
{
    int original;

    printf( "Convert integers in another base to decimal\n" );
    printf( "-------------------------------------------\n" );
    printf( "Current base is %d.\n", BASE );            /* Note 2 */

    printf( "\n\nEnter an integer in base %d: ", BASE );
    scanf( "%d", &original );
                                                        /* Note 3 */
    printf( "Thank you, the converted value is %d.\n",
                                    todecimal(original, BASE) );
```

```
}

/***************************** todecimal()   ******************/
/*    Converts an integer from another base to decimal.
 *    The other base is the second parameter to the function,
 *    the number to be converted is the first.
 */

int todecimal( int number, int base )                         /* Note 4 */
{
      int digit1, digit2, digit3, digit4, digit5, converted;

      /*   isolate the digits in number    */
      digit1 = number % 10;                                   /* Note 5 */
      number /= 10;
      digit2 = number % 10;
      number /= 10;
      digit3 = number % 10;
      number /= 10;
      digit4 = number % 10;
      number /= 10;
      digit5 = number % 10;

      converted = digit1 + digit2 * base                      /* Note 6 */
                  + digit3 * base * base
                  + digit4 * base * base * base
                  + digit5 * base * base * base * base;
      return ( converted );                                   /* Note 7 */
}
```

The program consists of the functions main() and todecimal(). Note that main() consists of calls to printf() and scanf(). The declarations of those functions are in the header file stdio.h. The last printf() call contains a call to the function todecimal() as a parameter.

Note 1: The identifier BASE is defined to be the constant value 5. As it is, this program converts base 5 numbers to decimal. If a program is needed to convert base 7 numbers to decimal, this constant definition should be changed to 7 and the program recompiled. No other change is needed.

Note 2: The preprocessor finds all occurrences of the identifier BASE like the one on this line and replaces them with the value 5.

Note 3: The call to todecimal() appears as the second argument to this printf() call. In todecimal(), the first actual parameter, original, is the number to be converted and the second actual parameter is the constant BASE, indicating to the function that the first number is to be treated as base 5.

Note 4: The formal parameters to `todecimal()` are `number` and `base`. Both are of type `int`. The compiler will not consider `BASE` and `base` as the same value because of the upper/lowercase difference. It is only because `BASE` is passed as the second parameter that it takes the place of `base` here. In general, the names of the actual parameters are unrelated to the names of the formal parameters.

Note also that `todecimal()` is an independent subfunction. It does not depend directly on any values declared in `main()`. It could be moved to another program and would perform identically. If the constant `BASE` were used directly in `todecimal()` instead of being passed in as a parameter, this would not be true. An identifier, `BASE`, would have to be defined in the other programs using `todecimal()`, and the flexibility in the use of the function and the establishment of the base for the conversion would be lost.

Note 5: When the number was input by `scanf()`, it was input as decimal because there is no immediate facility for input in base 5. To interpret the number correctly, it is necessary to isolate each digit. This is done by taking the remainder when the number is successively divided by 10. For example, if the input is 124, `number % 10` evaluates to 4 and the first digit is isolated. After dividing number by 10, the expression `number % 10` evaluates to `12 % 10` or 2, and so on.

Note 6: To reconstruct the input as a base 5 number, each successive digit is multiplied by an additional factor of 5 to get the true value.

Note 7: This value is returned by `todecimal()`. The main program outputs it as a decimal value.

Learning Activities

34. Compile and test convert.c as it is. Test it with base 5 values for which you know or can easily calculate the decimal equivalent.

35. Find out if it is possible with your computer system to stop the compilation after the preprocess phase has been completed. If so, find out how to do it and inspect this file after preprocessing. You should see the substitutions of the value 5 for the identifier `BASE` throughout the code as well as certain changes caused by the included file, stdio.h. What other changes do you notice?

36. If you are not yet certain how the algorithm for isolating the digits works, put some `printf()` calls after each statement of the form
    ```
    number /= 10;
    ```
    that displays the value of the number and the digit that was just calculated. Hand calculate the values for the input value `124`.

37. Modify the program so that it will calculate the decimal equivalent for a number entered in base 7 and test it again.

38.   Will changing %d to %x in the scanf() call allow the BASE to be larger than 10? Test it by making that change, changing BASE to 12, compiling and executing it several times. Enter some base 12 numbers, using the letter a for 10 and the letter b for 11. Does the program work correctly? If it doesn't, correct it.

Language Elements Introduced in This Chapter: A Review

✓ Comments
```
/*  This is a comment.   */
```

✓ Control Statements
return   Used to impart value to a function and to return control from a function to the calling environment.

✓ Conversion Specifications
%d	conversion to or from decimal
%x	conversion to or from hexadecimal
%o	conversion to or from octal

✓ Escape Characters
'\'   escapes the usual meaning of the next character

Examples:

\t	the tab character
\c	a carriage return
\b	the backspace character
\"	the double quote character in a string
\'	the single quote character
\\	the backslash character
\0	the null character
\n	the newline character

✓ Function Definitions
Functions must have a heading and a function block. The heading contains the function type, a name (identifier), a pair of parentheses, and the formal parameters (if any). The function block would contain the declaration of the local variables and the executable code.

✓ Function Calls
Consist of the function name, a pair of parentheses, and a semicolon. Any actual parameters appear between the parentheses.

✓ **Function Declarations**

Consist of the function type, the function name, and a pair of parentheses containing the number and type of each parameter.

Example: `int f( int x )`   (ANSI Prototype)

✓ **Identifiers**

Consist of letters, underscores, and numbers. They must not start with a number and must not conflict with any keyword.

✓ **Library Functions**

- `printf("control string", parameters);`
    Does formatted output. Takes one additional parameter for each conversion specification in the control string.
- `scanf ("control string", parameters);`
    Does formatted input. Takes one additional parameter for each conversion specification in the control string.

✓ **Operators**

`=`	assignment
`+`	addition
`-`	unary minus and subtraction
`*`	multiplication
`/`	division
`%`	remainder
`+=, -=, *=,`	compound assignment
`/=, %=`	
`++`	increment by 1
`--`	decrement by 1

✓ **Preprocessor Directives**

`#include`	includes a source file or header file at that point in the code
`#define`	used to define constants for easy readability and maintainability

✓ **Types**

`int`	used to represent an integer value
`void`	indicates that a function will not return a value or that a function does not take parameters.

✓ **Variable Declarations**

Consist of the type name followed by a comma-separated list of variables and a terminating semicolon.

Things to Remember

1. Unlike most upper-level languages, C allows a programmer a measure of control over the hardware.

2. The underlying character set must have most of the characters in the ASCII collating sequence. ASCII will be used in this text.

3. C distinguishes between uppercase and lowercase alphabetics.

4. C is a free-format language.

5. All subprograms in C are called functions.

6. Every C program must have a function named `main()`.

7. If a variable is declared inside a function block, the scope of the variable is from the declaration to the end of the function block.

8. If a variable is declared outside a function block, its scope is from the point of declaration to the end of the source code file.

9. The `printf()` function will do output in C. It takes a variable number of arguments. The first argument is a control string that contains conversion specifications. One additional argument should appear for every conversion specification in the control string.

10. When operating with integers, the division operator, `/`, is related to the remainder operator by the equation

    ```
    a = (a/b)*b + (a%b)
    ```

    When the signs of a and b differ and b does not divide a evenly, the only guarantee is that the absolute value of a%b is less than the absolute value of b.

11. The precedence of the multiplicative operators, `*`, `/`, and `%`, is greater than the precedence of the additive operators, `+` and `-`. The precedence of the arithmetic operators is greater than that of assignment (including compound assignment). For operators of equal precedence, the expressions are evaluated from left to right.

12. When the increment by 1 (`++`) and decrement by 1 (`--`) operators appear in an expression, the placement of the operator determines the order of evaluation. If the operator appears to the left of a variable, the operator is evaluated before the expression, but if the operator appears to the right of a variable, the expression is evaluated first.

13. The goals of structured programming include writing source code that is modular in nature, easily modifiable, robust (handles errors gracefully), and readable.

14. Each subprogram or function should be designed to do one task and should not be too long to be understood easily. When possible, tools should be written that can be used with little or no modification in many programs. Tools should not depend on any variables or constants not declared in the function.

15. Actual parameter names are unrelated to formal parameter names.

Exercises and Programming Problems

1. Which of the following are legal identifiers in C?

to_dec	1more	forget-it	hex2dec
floater	horrendous	rub-a-dub-dub	Let_it_be_me
two+four	UPPER	l_o_n_g	_3angle

2. If x, y, and z are variables of type int with values 4, 7, and 9 respectively, what is output by the following sequence of printf() calls?

    ```
    printf( "%d, %d, %d\n", x + 2%x, ++z % x, y++ /x );
    printf ("%d, %d, %d\n", x+y+z++,  3*y/2, 3/2*y);
    printf( "%d, %d, %d\n", ++y + ++z, x  -  4, 2 * x % 3 );
    ```

3. Write a C program to output a triangle of asterisks with five rows. Your output should look like the figure below.

    ```
            *
          *  *
        *  *  *
      *  *  *  *
    *  *  *  *  *
    ```

4. Write a C program to output your initials in block letters. For example, the output from my program might be

    ```
    LLL            SSSSSSSSSSS    FFFFFFFFFFFF
    LLL            SSS      SSS    FFF
    LLL            SSS             FFF
    LLL            SSSSSSSSSSS    FFFFFFFFF
    LLL                      SSS    FFF
    LLL            SSS       SSS    FFF
    LLLLLLLLLLLL   SSSSSSSSSSS    FFF
    ```

5. Write a program to input two integer values and output their sum and their difference. A sample run of the program follows. The user input is represented in **boldface** in the sample run.

    ```
    Enter an integer: 45
    Enter another integer: 83
    45 + 83 = 128
    45 - 83 = -38
    ```

6. Write a program that accepts input of a number of seconds and outputs the equivalent number of hours, minutes, and seconds. A sample run follows with the user input indicated by **boldface**.

```
Enter the number of seconds: 3920
1 hour, 5 minutes, 20 seconds.
```

7. Write a program that will input an integer and output the minimum number of quarters, dimes, nickels and pennies needed to make up the input amount. Two sample runs follow with user input in **boldface**.

```
Enter the amount for which change must be created: 67
2 quarter(s), 1 dime(s), 1 nickel(s) and 2 penny(ies)
Enter the amount for which change must be created: 45
1 quarter(s), 2 dime(s), 0 nickel(s) and 0 penny(ies)
```

8. Write a program that adds two fractions. Your output need not be in lowest terms. A sample run follows with user input in **boldface**.

```
First Fraction:
Enter the numerator: 2
Enter the denominator: 3
Second Fraction:
Enter the numerator: 3
Enter the denominator: 8
2/3 + 3/8 = 25/24
```

9. a. Write a function that calculates and returns the area of a rectangle. Your function should take two parameters, the length and the width of the rectangle. For this problem, assume that both dimensions are integers.

   b. Write a program that prompts for and accepts input of the length and width in integers and outputs the area and the perimeter of a rectangle. Have your program call the function you wrote in part a). Below is a sample run. The user input is indicated with **boldface**.

```
Rectangle Geometry
------------------
Enter the length: 5
Enter the width: 4
A rectangle with length 5 and width 4
has area 20 and perimeter 18.
```

10. Write a program that will input a decimal value and output the equivalent value in octal and hexadecimal. Sample run with user input in boldface.

```
Enter a decimal integer: 35
35 decimal is 43 octal and 23 hexadecimal.
```

11. A grocery store is selling oranges for 9 cents apiece or one dollar per dozen.

    a) Write a function that takes a single parameter - the number of oranges - and returns the total price for those oranges.

    b) Write a program that prompts for a number of oranges, accepts input of an integer value, and outputs the total price for the oranges. Make sure your program calls the function you wrote in part a).

12. Rewrite fahrcels.c with the following structure: write a separate function to calculate the temperature in Celsius, and return that value. Have `main()` prompts for and accept input of a temperature in Fahrenheit, call your function and display the value returned by your function.

Chapter 2

Gaining Control

2.1 Expressions and Statements

In Chapter 2 we will study expressions and control statements. Expressions are sequences of tokens that can be evaluated to a numerical quantity. They range from a single number or identifier to a more complicated sequence of tokens. Expressions can contain any of the operators in C. In this section, the discussion involves expressions with either arithmetic operators or the assignment operator.

A statement is a sequence of tokens terminated with a semicolon that can be recognized by the compiler. A statement differs from an expression in that statements do not have values. The purpose of some statements like assignment statements is to change the values of variables. The purpose of other statements might be to select which set of statements to execute in a given circumstance or to cause a sequence of statements to be executed more than once. This latter type of statement is referred to as a *control statement*.

Expressions in C can be classified as *lvalues* or *rvalues*. The term *lvalue* refers to an expression that has a location in memory. For example, the name of a variable is an lvalue. Modifiable lvalues are expressions whose values can be either changed or evaluated. Modifiable lvalues can be used on the left-hand side of an assignment statement.

In contrast, an *rvalue* can be evaluated but cannot be changed. For example, the single character token '5' is an rvalue. If a variable named x has been previously declared, the expression 2*x + 5 is also an rvalue. An rvalue cannot be used on the left-hand side of an assignment statement. It may only be used on the right-hand side.

There are several types of expressions in C. We consider arithmetic expressions first. Assume x and y have been declared as variables of type int. The following table gives legal C expressions and their corresponding classification as rvalues or lvalues.

Expression	Lvalue	Rvalue
x	yes	yes
x + 3	no	yes
y	yes	yes
2*y - 7	no	yes
* (-2/y + 7 % x)	no	yes

Note that an expression can be both an lvalue and a rvalue. For example, any variable is both an lvalue and an rvalue.

The use of the assignment operator, =, creates a quantity known as an assignment expression. The assignment operator is a binary operator. It has a lower precedence than any of the arithmetic operators. An assignment expression has the form

```
expr1 = expr2
```

where expr1 must be an lvalue and expr2 is an rvalue. When this assignment expression is evaluated, expr2 is fully evaluated before the assignment is made and the assignment expression itself takes on that value.

An assignment such as

```
x = 5
```

is considered to be an expression and can appear anywhere that any other expression can appear in a C program. The lvalue on the left-hand side of an assignment expression indicates where to store the value obtained from the evaluation of the expression on the right-hand side. The numerical value of

```
x = 5
```

is 5. The assignment expression

```
x = 2 * 5 - 3
```

has the value 7 because that is the numerical value of the expression on the right-hand side of the assignment operator.

C programmers can use statements like

```
x = y = 2;
```

because this is equivalent to the parenthesized statement

```
x = (y = 2);
```

Here the first assignment assigns 2 to y and the value of that assignment expression, 2, is assigned to x. The assignment operator associates from right to left.

The program express.c in Example 2-1 illustrates expressions and the value of assignment statements. We will see more uses for expressions when we study control statements later in this chapter.

Example 2-1: express.c

```
/*              express.c
 *
 *    Synopsis    - Assigns and outputs values of the variables
 *                  x and y.
 *
 *    Objective   - Demonstrates expression statements and the
 *                  values of assignment statements.
 */

/* Include Files */
#include <stdio.h>

void main( void )
{
    int x = 1, y, z;

    printf( "Value of x, %d\n", x );                    /* Note 1 */
    printf( "Value of 2*x + 5, %d\n", 2*x + 5 );        /* Note 1 */

                                                        /* Note 2 */
    printf( "Value of assignment to x, %d\n", x = 5 );

                                                        /* Note 3 */
    printf( "Value of assignment to y, %d\n", y = 2*x++ + 1 );
    printf( "x is %d and y is %d\n", x, y );

    z = y = 4*x + 5;                                    /* Note 4 */
    printf( "y is %d and z is %d.\n", y, z );
}
```

The overview of the program reveals three declared variables of type int, a sequence of printf() calls, and some miscellaneous expression statements.

Note 1: These two familiar types of `printf()` calls illustrate that the parameters after a control string are expressions and those expressions are evaluated when the program executes.

Note 2: Since an assignment is an expression, it can appear anywhere that any other expression can appear. The assignment is made and the value of the assignment expression is displayed by the call to `printf()`.

Note 3: The value of this assignment expression is the value of the quantity being assigned to y. After the assignment, the value of x is incremented by 1. This incrementation has no effect on the value of the assignment statement or the value assigned to y.

Note 4: In this statement, the expression `4*x + 5` is evaluated first. The value is assigned to y and becomes the value of the assignment expression on the right. That value is then assigned to z. This one statement is equivalent to the statements

```
y = 4*x + 5;
z = y;
```

or the single parenthesized statement

```
z = (y = 4*x + 5);
```

In summary, the important points are that expressions are evaluated when a program executes and that an assignment is an expression that can appear in a C program wherever any other expression can appear. We will see how this fact allows C source code to be written in a compact manner.

Learning Activities

1. Before running express.c,
   a. Identify the expressions in each of the `printf()` calls.
   b. Predict the output of the program.
   c. Make a list of the expressions in the program above. Which are lvalues? Which are rvalues?
2. Compile and execute express.c to check your answer to part b in question 1. If your answer to part b was wrong, make sure you know why. Correct your concepts.

2.2 Blocks and Compound Statements

A compound statement is a sequence of statements that can be used anyplace in the syntax that a simple statement can be used. It is a common construct in most programming languages. In C, the construct that implements a compound statement is called a block. The syntax of the C language allows more than just a sequence of statements in a block; variable declarations can be included with the executable statements. Assuming that both x and y have been declared as variables of type int, both of the following are examples of blocks in C.

1.
```
        {

            x = 4;
            y = x + 3;

        }
```

2.
```
        {

            int i;

            i = 5;
            x = (i++) +3;
            y = i - 4;


        }
```

Every function must have a function block. For example, in Example 2-1, the only block is the function block associated with main(). It consists of the braces and all the declarations and statements in between. A C program can contain a block that is not a function block; it can be used everywhere any statement can be used.

A block must begin with an opening brace and terminate with a closing brace. The contents of the block may consist of declarations, statements, both or neither. All declarations in a block must appear before the statements. A block can be placed anywhere in a program that a simple statement can be placed.

When a variable is declared inside of a block, it is called a *local variable* since the compiler will only recognize its name from its point of declaration to the end of the block. This type of variable is local in the sense that the surrounding function does not know about variables declared inside an inner block. However, the statements in an inner block can access any variables that the surrounding function can access.

The program block.c in Example 2-2 illustrates variables local to functions and blocks. In general, it is a better idea not to give the same name to different variables; it is done in this example just to emphasize the point that the variable inside the block and the variable outside the block are different even when they have the same name.

Example 2-2: block.c

```
/*              block.c
 *
 *    Synopsis   - The values of two variables named i are
 *                 displayed. They are declared in two
 *                 different blocks.
 *
 *    Objective  - To illustrate block structuring of C source
 *                 code.
 */

/* Include Files */
#include <stdio.h>

void main( void )
{
    int i = 3;

    {                                                   /* Note 1 */
      int i = 5;                                        /* Note 2 */
                                                        /* Note 3 */
      printf( "In the inner block, i is %d.\n", i );
    }
                                                        /* Note 4 */
    printf( "In the outer block, i is %d.\n", i );
}
```

Running the Program

```
In the inner block, i is 5.
In the outer block, i is 3.
```

An overview of the program reveals a single function named main(). Inside main(), a variable named i of type int is declared. An inner block follows. It is delimited by the open and close braces. Inside the inner block, another variable named i is declared and initialized. Calls to printf() appear both inside and after the end of the block.

Note 1: The brace, {, signifies the beginning of an interior block in the function main(). Each block can have its own set of internal declarations and statements. A block is also known as a compound statement. Compound statements must be surrounded by braces. A compound statement can appear anywhere a statement can appear.

Note 2: This is an internal declaration. The values for this variable are unknown outside the block. Each variable declared inside a block is allocated memory that is only active while that block is executing. When there are conflicting variable names, the name in the executing block dominates.

Note 3: The printf() call displays the value of the variable i that was declared inside the block. When a single identifier like i is used to access two different variables, the variable that was declared in the nearest block to the executing statement is chosen.

Note 4: The value of the variable i that was defined in main() is displayed here. This call to printf() has no knowledge of any of the variables or statements inside the block because the memory for variables in the block was allocated temporarily and is no longer active. The value output is 3.

Learning Activity

3.   In the program block.c,

a.   Suppose that the line int i = 5; is deleted. Predict what would happen if you attempt to execute the modified program on your computer system. Choose your prediction from the choices below.

   i.   The program won't compile.

   ii.   The program compiles but has a runtime error.

   iii.   The program compiles and executes but the output is
```
In the inner block, i is 3.
In the outer block, i is 3.
```

   iv.   The program compiles and executes but the output is
```
In the inner block, i is 5.
In the outer block, i is 5.
```

   v.   The program compiles and executes with no changes from the original program.

b.   Start again from the original program. Suppose that the line int i = 3; is deleted. Predict what would happen if you attempt to execute the modified program on your computer system. Choose your prediction from the choices in part a.

c. In the original program, suppose that the line int i = 5; is changed to read i = 5;. Now predict what would happen if you attempt to compile and execute the program. Choose your prediction from the choices in part a.

In Example 2-2, the variable i that was declared in the inner block was hidden from the rest of the function main(). Another illustration of the effects of variable hiding appears in the program block2.c in Example 2-3. This program will not compile because the surrounding program does not know about the declaration inside the block.

Example 2-3: block2.c

```
/*                block2.c
 *
 *   Synopsis    - This program will not compile.
 *
 *   Objective   - To illustrate the fact that variables declared
 *                 inside a block are unknown by the rest of the
 *                 program.
 */

/* Include Files */
#include <stdio.h>

void main( void )
{
    {
        int i;                                          /* Note 1 */
        scanf( "%d", &i );
    }

    printf( "i is %d.\n", i );                          /* Note 2 */
}
```

The function main() in this program consists of a declaration and two executable statements; one of the statements is a compound statement or a block. The variable declaration is contained within the inner block.

Note 1: The variable i is declared of type int. This variable is local to the block delimited by the inner pair of braces.

Note 2: This line causes a compile-time error because it references the variable i. Since i was declared within a block and this statement is outside that block, the variable i is unknown in this part of the program.

A Word about Style

A C program or function will be more readable when all variables used within a single function are given different names. The compiler can keep variables declared inside and outside a block straight, but human beings may have problems.

As another general stylistic rule, a program is more readable if all the declarations for a function appear in one place. Therefore, this facility of allowing auxiliary declarations in a block should be used with discretion.

2.3 The if and if-else Statements

The first statement we will study is the conditional statement. A conditional statement allows a program to test a condition and then choose which code to execute next. The choice depends on the outcome of that test. The if statement is the conditional statement in C. Its syntax is

```
if (expression)
        statement
```

The expression must be in parentheses; the statement can be any allowable C statement or a block. Don't forget that all statements end with a semicolon.

The expression is referred to as the *control expression*. Any expression can be used in that position; its value will be interpreted as either true or false. During execution, the expression is evaluated. If the value is nonzero, the expression is interpreted as true and is executed. If the value of the expression is zero, the expression is interpreted as false and the statement is not executed.

The program if1.c in Example 2-4 gives a simple example of an if statement. In this program, the conditional expression for the if statement is

```
sum < 20
```

meaning sum is less than 20. If the value of sum is indeed less than 20, the value of the expression is 1 which is interpreted as true; otherwise, the value is 0 which is interpreted as false. The expression sum < 20 is called a relational expression. Other relational expressions involve equality, and the other inequalities. These will be discussed in Section 2.4.

Example 2-4: if1.c

```
/*                if1.c
 *
 *    Synopsis   - A decimal integer is input, added to CONST,
 *                 and the sum is displayed. If the sum is less
 *                 than 20, a message is issued.
 *
 *    Objective  - Illustrates the simplest form of the if
 *                 statement.
 */
/* Include Files */
#include <stdio.h>

/* Constant Definitions */
#define CONST 5

/* Function prototype declarations */
int add_const( int );

void main( void )
{
    int sum, intvar;

    printf( "Enter a decimal integer: " );
    scanf( "%d", &intvar );

    sum = add_const( intvar );
    printf( "%d + %d is %d.\n", intvar, CONST, sum );

    if ( sum < 20 )                              /* Notes 1 and 2 */
      printf( "The number is small.\n" );
}

/***************************** add_const()  *******************/
/*    returns the sum of its argument and CONST.
 */
int add_const( int intvar )
{
    return( intvar + CONST );
}
```

An overview of this program reveals two familiar preprocessor statements and two functions, main() and add_const(). The function add_const() returns the value of CONST plus its argument. The conditional statement appears towards the end of main().

Note 1: The conditional if statement starts on this line and terminates on the next. The parentheses enclosing the control expression are a mandatory part of the syntax.

Note 2: The control expression in this example is a relational expression. As would be expected, it is true when the value of sum is less than 20 and false otherwise. That is, the expression has value 1 when sum is less than 20 and 0 otherwise.

Learning Activities

4.   In the program if1.c,
  a. Circle the entire conditional statement.
  b. What is the control expression?
  c. For each of the input values below, state whether the control expression is true or false and give the output for the program. The first one is done for you.

	Input value	Control expression	Program output
Example:	10	true	10 + 5 is 15. The number is small.
	5	_____	_____
			_____
	15	_____	_____
			_____
	20	_____	_____
			_____

5.   Execute the program if1.c to check your answers to question 4.

A Word about Style

General stylistic guidelines suggest placing the statement to be conditionally executed in an indented position on a separate line. This placement is an important part of program readability.

The if-else Statement

The program if1.c displays its message only if the value of sum is less than 20. If you want the program to output a different message (or take some different actions) for any value of the variable sum, use the if-else statement. Its syntax is

```
if (expression)
        statement1
else
        statement2
```

If expression evaluates to true (nonzero), statement1 is executed. If expression evaluates to false (zero), statement2 is executed.

The program in Example 2-5 is a modification of if1.c that prints a message for any value of sum. It uses an if-else statement.

Example 2-5: if2.c

```
/*              if2.c
 *
 *   Synopsis   - A decimal integer is read as input, added to
 *                CONST, and the sum is displayed. If the sum
 *                is less than 20, one message is displayed.
 *                If not, another message is displayed.
 *
 *   Objective  - Illustrates a simple form of the if-else
 *                statement.
 */

/* Include Files */
#include <stdio.h>

/* Constant Definitions */
#define CONST 5
```

```
/* Function Prototype Declarations */
int add_const( int );

void main( void )
{
     int sum, intvar;

     printf( "Enter a decimal integer: " );
     scanf( "%d", &intvar );
     sum = add_const( intvar );
     printf( "%d + %d is %d.\n", intvar, CONST, sum );

     if ( sum < 20 )
          printf( "The number is small.\n" );
     else                                          /* Note 1 */
          printf( "Oops, too big.\n" );
}

/***************************** add_const()   *****************/
/*   returns the sum of its argument and CONST.
 */
int add_const( int intvar )
{
     return( intvar + CONST );
}
```

This program is similar to that in Example 2-4 above. The only difference is the change from an `if` statement to an `if-else` statement at the end of the function `main()`.

Note 1: This `else` is paired with the preceding `if`. When `sum` is greater than or equal to 20 the `printf()` call on the next line is executed. Stylistically, the token `else` should be on a separate line from the previous statement and should be indented as least as far as the `if`.

Learning Activities

6. In the program if2.c, for each of the given input values, state whether the control expression is true or false and give the output for the program. The first one is done for you..

	Input value	Control expression	Program output
Example:	10	true	10 + 5 is 15. The number is small.
	5	_____	_____ _____
	15	_____	_____ _____
	-20	_____	_____ _____

7.   Execute the program if2.c to check your answers to question 6.

The program if3.c in Example 2-6 illustrates the use of a numerical expression in an if-else statement. A function named odd() is defined. It takes a parameter of type int and returns the remainder when the parameter is divided by 2. That is, it returns the value 1 when the parameter is odd and 0 when the parameter is even. This value is tested in the main program with an if statement; 1 is interpreted as true since it is nonzero. The value 0 is interpreted as false.

Example 2-6: if3.c

```
/*                  if3.c
 *
 *    Synopsis    - The program prompts for and accepts input of a
 *                  decimal integer.  It then tests to see if that
 *                  integer is even or odd.  The results of the
 *                  test are displayed.
 *
 *    Objective   - Illustrates an if-else statement and the use
 *                  of a function call in a control expression.
 */

/* Include Files */
#include <stdio.h>

/* Function Declarations */
int odd( int );
```

```
void main( void )
{
      int intvar;

      printf( "Enter a decimal integer: " );
      scanf( "%d", &intvar );

      if ( odd( intvar ) )                              /* Note 1 */
            printf( "%d is odd.\n", intvar );
      else                                              /* Note 2 */
            printf( "%d is even.\n", intvar );
}

/***************************** odd()    ***********************/
/*    Returns 1 if argument is odd, 0 otherwise.
 */
int odd( int intvar )
{
      return( intvar % 2 );                             /* Note 3 */
}
```

This program consists of two functions, the mandatory function named main() and a function named odd(). Scanning the code, we see that main() has one local variable, a call to printf() for output, a call to scanf() for input, and an if-else statement. The function odd() consists of a single return statement.

Note 1: The expression in this if-else statement is a function call. C expects the function name to have a value when it returns from the call. The value is tested; a nonzero value causes the first printf() call to be executed.

Note 2: If the value returned from odd() is zero, the second printf() call is executed.

Note 3: The value returned is the remainder when the parameter is divided by 2. That is, if the parameter is 1, 3, 5, 7, . . . , the remainder is 1 and the expression odd(intvar) evaluates to 1; it would test true in the control expression for the conditional. However, if the parameter is 0, 2, 4, 6, 8, . . . , the remainder is zero, odd(intvar) is zero, and the control expression would test false. Similar results would be obtained with negative input.

Learning Activities

8. In the program if3.c predict the output for each of the following input values.

Input	Output
35	_____
-22	_____
0	_____

9. Execute the program if3.c to test your answers to question 8.

Compound if-else Statement

The statement after the else part of an if-else statement can be another if-else statement. This construct is called a *nested* or *compound* if-else statement. The syntax for this type of statement is:

```
if (expression)
        statement
else if (expression)
        statement
else if (expression)
        statement
...
else
        statement
```

The effect is to create a multiway decision statement. Exactly one of the subsidiary statements will be executed. If one of the expressions in the list tests true, the accompanying statement will be executed. If none of the statements tests true, then the statement associated with the final else will be executed.[1]

The program if.c in Example 2-7 illustrates a nested `if-else` statement. It plays a guessing game with the user.

Example 2-7: if.c

```
/*                  if.c
 *
 *    Synopsis   - Plays a one-time guessing game with the user.
 *                 The user enters a number, which is compared
 *                 with TARGET. The computer issues a diagnostic
 *                 message and then the correct result.
 *
 *    Objective  - Illustrates the if-else statement.
 */

/* Include Files */
#include <stdio.h>

/* Constant Definitions */
#define TARGET 17

/* Function Declarations */
void test( int );

void main( void )
{
    int a_guess;

    printf( "I'm thinking of an integer.\n" );
    printf( "Try to guess it now. " );

    scanf( "%d", &a_guess );

    test( a_guess );

    printf( "The number was %d.\n", TARGET );
}


/***************************** test()  *********************/
/*    compares the value of its parameter to TARGET and outputs
 *    the result.
 */
```

---

1. The final else is optional and if omitted, it is possible that none of the statements would be executed.

```
void test( int guess )
{
     if ( guess < TARGET )                        /* Note 1 */
           printf( "Too low.\n" );
     else if ( guess > TARGET )                   /* Note 2 */
           printf( "Too high.\n" );
     else                                         /* Note 3 */
           printf( "You guessed it!\n" );
}
```

An overview of this program reveals two functions, main() and test(). One variable of type int is declared in main(). Calls to printf() for output are followed by a call to scanf() for input. The functions test() is called and then printf() displays the answer to the guessing game. The compound if-else statement appears in the function test().

Note 1: The first expression in the compound if-else statement is the relational expression (guess < TARGET). If it is true, the following printf() call is executed and the if-else statement is terminated. In this case, the next statement to be executed is the call to printf() at the end of main(). If the expression (guess < TARGET) is not true, execution continues with the if after the first else.

Note 2: If guess < TARGET tests false, the next expression to be tested is the expression (guess > TARGET) that appears on this line. If it is true, the printf() call on the next line is executed. This terminates the execution of the compound if-else statement and the functions test(). Control passes to the call to printf() at the end of main(). If the expression (guess > TARGET) is not true, control stays with the compound if-else statement.

Note the indentation for the compound if-else statement. This style is one of the accepted ways of formatting this statement. Other methods of formatting are also acceptable; they usually involve more indentation. The important point is that this is a compound if-else statement and only one of the statements will be executed. The indentation for a compound if-else statement should be consistent.

Note 3: If neither of the above expressions tests true, then guess is equal to TARGET. In this case the statement following this else will be executed before the final printf() call.

Learning Activities

10. What must the input have been if the third line of output from the program if.c is

```
                         "You guessed it!"
             11.    What is the maximum number of output lines from if.c? What is
                    the minimum number of lines? Give a reason for your answer.
```

In the case of a statement with the syntax

```
if ( expression1 )
        if ( expression2 )
                if_statement;
        else
                else_statement;
```

the pairing of the `else` is with the closest `if` without a corresponding `else`. In the
above case, nothing is executed when `expression1` tests false. If `expression1`
and `expression2` test true, `if_statement` is executed; if `expression1` is true
and `expression2` is false, `else_statement` is executed. If a programmer
wishes to have the `else` paired with the first `if`, braces must be added to create a
block for the inner `if` as shown below:

```
if ( expression1 ) {
        if ( expression2 )
                ifstatement;
}
else
        else_statement;
```

In this case, when `expression1` is false, `else_statement` is executed; if both
`expression1` and `expression2` are true, `if_statement` is executed; if
`expression1` is true and `expression2` is false, nothing is executed. The program in Example 2-8 has this type of structure. The program illustrates a simple
error check on input. Code like this might be included as part of a larger program
in which execution would continue once the input was validated.

Example 2-8: errorchk.c

```
/*                    errorchk.c
 *
 *    Synopsis    - Prompts for and accepts input of an integer.
 *                  The integer is tested to see that it meets the
 *                  stated criteria.  If it doesn't, an error
 *                  message is issued.  If all criteria are met,
```

```
 *                       execution terminates silently.
 *
 *   Objective   - Illustrates the necessary grouping of if and
 *                   associated else statements.
 */

/* Include Files */
#include <stdio.h>

/* Function Declarations */
int odd( int );

void main( void )
{
    int inputint;

    printf( "Enter a positive even " );
    printf( "number that is less than 20.\n" );
    scanf( "%d", &inputint );

    if ( inputint < 20 ) {                              /* Note 1 */
        if ( odd( inputint ) )
                printf( "Sorry that number wasn't even.\n" );
        else if ( inputint <= 0 )
                printf( "That number wasn't positive.\n" );
    }                                                   /* Note 2 */
    else
        printf( "That number was too big.\n" );
}

/*************************** odd()   ***********************/
/*   returns a 1 if intvar is odd and a 0 if not.
 */

int odd( int intvar )                                   /* Note 3 */
{
    return( intvar % 2 );
}
```

This program consists of two functions, main() and odd(). The function main() consists of a printf() call followed by a scanf() call. The remainder of this function is a combination if-else statement. The function odd() consists of a single return statement.

Note 1: The if-else structure begins on this line. The brace is necessary to create a separate block for the inner `if-else` statement so that there is no possibility of pairing the second `else` with the third `if`. Note: As an alternative, the code could be restructured to avoid this problem entirely.

Note 2: The brace ends the block so that the `else` on the next line is paired with the first `if` in the program.

Note 3: The function `odd()` is identical to the function `odd()` in previous examples. This is an example of a tool that can be moved from program to program without change.

Learning Activity

12. Consider the program errorchk.c with the following changes. Remove the braces from the lines containing the comments `/* **Note 1** */` and `/* **Note 2** */`. Which of the following statements would be true?

    a. It would no longer compile.

    b. If the input was 4, the output would be
       `"That number wasn't positive."`

    c. If the input was -1, the output would be
       `"That number wasn't positive."`

    d. If the input was 8, the output would be
       `"That number was too big."`

2.4 Relational Operators and Expressions

We saw some of the relational expressions in use in the last section. The relational operators are:

`<=`	is less than or equal to
`>=`	is greater than or equal to
`==`	is equal to
`!=`	is not equal to
`>`	is greater than
`<`	is less than

For example, the expression

    x == 3

could be tested to determine whether x is equal to 3. If x is 3, the value of the expression (x == 3) is 1, which is nonzero and interpreted as true. If x is not 3, the value of $(x == 3)$ is zero (false). The expression

    3 == 2 + 1

would always test true while the expression

    3 != 2 + 1   (or 3 is not equal to 2 + 1)

would always test false.

The actual value assigned to an expression formed with a relational operator is 1 if the relation is true and 0 if it is false. The fact that the relational expressions actually have values is illustrated in the program relation.c in Example 2-9.

Example 2-9: relation.c

```
/*                relation.c
 *
 *   Synopsis    - Displays values of relational expressions.
 *
 *   Objective   - To illustrate that relational expressions are
 *                 given the values of 1 for true and 0 for false.
 */

/* Include Files */
#include <stdio.h>

void main( void )
{
    int x = 3;
                                                       /* Note 1 */
    printf( "The value of (x == 3) is %d.\n", x == 3 );
    printf( "The value of (x != 3) is %d.\n", x != 3 );

    printf( "The value of (3*x - 4 <= 3) is %d.\n",
                                        3*x - 4 <=3 );
    printf( "The value of (x >= 3) is %d.\n", x >= 3 );

                                                       /* Note 2 */
    printf( "The value of (2*x %% 3 > 3) is %d.\n",
                                        2*x % 3 > 3 );

    printf( "The value of (25 / (2*x) < 3) is %d.\n",
                                        25 /(2*x) < 3 );
}
```

This program has a single function, `main()`. One variable named x of type int is declared. The remainder of the program consists of displaying the decimal values of expressions involving x in conjunction with relational expressions.

Note 1: In each of the `printf()` calls, the expression with the relational operator is evaluated and its decimal value is output. The following points are important to understand:

1. Each expression has a value of either 1 (true) or 0 (false).
2. The expressions can involve arithmetic operators as well as the relational operators.
3. The precedence of all the arithmetic operators is higher than that of any of the relational operators, thus eliminating the need for additional parentheses.

Note 2: The `%%` in the control string to `printf()` is the conversion specification for the output of a single `%`.

Learning Activities

13.   Predict the output of relation.c. Run the program to verify your predictions. Make sure you resolve any differences between your predictions and the actual output.

14.   Consider the final `printf()` call in relation.c. What would be the output if the parentheses were removed from both occurrences of `2*x` in that statement?

A Word of Warning

One common mistake made by new C programmers, especially those who have previously programmed in Pascal, is illustrated in the program mistake1.c of Example 2-10.

Example 2-10: mistake1.c

```
/*              mistake1.c
 *
 *   Synopsis    - Accepts input of a value of type int and issues
 *                 messages about its value.
 *
 *
```

```
*    Objective  - To further illustrate that an assignment is
*                 an expression.
*/
/* Include Files */
#include <stdio.h>

void main( void )
{
    int intvar;

    printf( "Enter a decimal value : " );
    scanf( "%d", &intvar );

    if ( intvar = 3 )                                    /* Note 1 */
    printf( "It's THREE!!\n" );

    printf( "The value of intvar is %d.\n", intvar );
}
```

This program has a single variable, intvar, of type int. The printf() and scanf() calls establish a value for intvar. Then a conditional statement with an expression involving intvar is executed. Finally, the value of intvar is output by the last call to printf().

Note 1: Notice that this program outputs the line

```
It's THREE!!
```

for any input value of intvar. The mistake lies in the fact that the single equal sign, =, does assignment and an assignment expression takes on the value of the quantity being assigned. In this case the value assigned to intvar is 3, which is nonzero and therefore tests true. The printf() call will always execute and the value of intvar will always be 3 after that statement. The programmer may have meant

```
if (intvar == 3)
        printf ("It's THREE!!\n");
```

instead. This is an easy mistake to make and a hard bug to find, but some compilers offer help by issuing a warning for this use.

Learning Activities

15. Execute the program mistake1.c with several different input values to make sure that you understand what is happening.

16. Predict the output from the following program. How many lines will be output?

```
/*                exrcse2.c
 *
 *    Synopsis  -Tests relational expressions, and
 *               produces appropriate messages.
 *
 *    Objective -Provides practice with relational
 *               expressions.
 */
/* Include Files */
#include <stdio.h>

void main( void )
{
     int x = 2;

     if ( x = 3 )
         printf( "it's three!\n" );
     else if ( x = 4 )
         printf( "it's four!\n" );

     printf( "x has value %d.\n", x );
}
```

Operator Precedence

As can be seen from the precedence chart in the Programmer's Handbook, the relational operators have lower precedence than any of the arithmetic operators, but higher precedence than assignment operators. For example, in the expression

```
4 <= z + 3
```

the subexpression z + 3 would be evaluated first. The resulting value would then be compared with 4. However, the expression

```
4 <= x = z+3
```

is illegal in C. Because assignment has a lower precedence than either <= or +, the compiler interprets this expression as an attempt to assign the value z+3 to the expression 4 <= x. This is not allowed because 4 <= x does not have a storage location in memory (it is not an lvalue). This error is a compile-time error. That is, it is caught by the compiler.

Note that an assignment can be done within a relational expression with the use of added parentheses. In the expression

```
4 <= (x = z +3)
```

the assignment of z + 3 to the variable x is done before the <= operator is considered.

The comparison would be made between the value 4 and the value of x after the assignment.

Another aspect to be aware of when using relational expressions is that an expression like

        3 < x < 7

is evaluated as

        ((3 < x) < 7)

For example, if the current value of x is 0, the expression 3 < x is 0 (false). The expression 3 < x < 7 becomes 0 < 7. Because 0 is less than 7, the expression (3 < x < 7) is true when x is 0. By similar arguments, 3 < x < 7 is also true when x has the values -1, 3, 4, 7, 10, or any value. Expressions like this one should be avoided in C code.

Learning Activities

17. Predict the output of the following program:

```
/*                  exrcse1.c
 *
 *    Synopsis  - Prints out values for several
 *                expressions involving combinations
 *                of relational operators.
 *
 *    Objective - To give practice with precedence
 *                of the relational expressions.
 */

/* Include Files */
#include <stdio.h>

void main( void )
{
      int x = 4, y = 2;

      printf( "3<x<y has value %d.\n", 3<x<y );
      printf( "x<3<y has value %d.\n", x<3<y );
      printf( "3<x<1 has value %d.\n", 3<x<1 );
      printf( "3<x<2 has value %d.\n", 3<x<2 );
      printf( "3<(x=y) has value %d.\n", 3<(x=y) );
      printf( "y=x<4 has value %d.\n", y=x<4 );
}
```

18. a. How would you test to see if the value of a variable x lies between the values 3 and 7?

b. Write a short C program that prompts for and accepts input of a value of type `int` and reports whether that value is between 3 and 7. Make sure to test your program thoroughly.

2.5 The while Loop

In programming, executing a code segment more than once is called *iteration*. It is an important technique. For example, in Example 2-7 where the computer played a guessing game with the user, the game would have been more interesting if the user had been able to continue playing until the number was guessed.

A `while` loop is an iterative construct that can be used to allow this continued interchange between user and computer. The syntax of C's `while` loop is as follows:

```
while (expression)
        statement
```

The parentheses around the expression are mandatory. The statement can be a block (compound statement), a conditional statement, another `while` loop, or any of the other legal C statements that we will discuss.

When the `while` loop begins execution, the expression inside the parentheses is evaluated for the first time. If the value of `expression` is nonzero, `statement` is executed and `expression` is evaluated again. The statement is executed each time `expression` tests true (nonzero). The first time `expression` evaluates to false (zero), the loop terminates.

The program while.c in Example 2-11 is an extension of the guessing game introduced in Example 2-7. In this version the user continues to play until guessing the correct number.

Example 2-11: while.c

```
/*                  while.c
 *
 *   Synopsis    - Plays a guessing game with the user.  The user
 *                 is asked to enter choices until guessing the
 *                 computer's number.
 *
 *   Objective   - Illustrates the while statement and compound
 *                 statements in  C.
```

```
 */

/* Include Files */
#include <stdio.h>

/* Constant Definitions */
#define TARGET 17
#define LOW 0
#define HIGH 100
#define TRUE 1                                          /* Note 1 */
#define FALSE 0                                         /* Note 1 */

/* Function Declarations */
int process( int );

void main( void )
{
    int a_guess, correct;

    correct = FALSE;
    printf( "I'm thinking of a number between %d and %d.\n",
                                          LOW, HIGH );

    while ( correct == FALSE ) {                        /* Notes 2 and 3 */
        printf( "Try to guess it now. " );
        scanf( "%d", &a_guess );
        correct = process( a_guess );
    }                                                  /* Note 4 */
}

/***************************** process()  *********************/
/*   Tests its parameter to see if it is equal to TARGET.
 *   Issues a diagnostic message and returns 1 for equality
 *   and 0 for inequality
 */
int process( int guess )
{
    if ( guess < TARGET )
        printf( "Too low!\n" );
    else if ( guess > TARGET )
        printf( "Too high!\n" );
    else {
        printf( "You guessed it!\n" );
        return TRUE;
    }
    return FALSE;
}
```

The overview of this program reveals two functions, `main()` and `process()`. In `main()`, two variables of type `int` are declared. An assignment statement initializes the variable `correct` and a call to `printf()` starts the game. A `while` loop controls the code in `main()`. The statement associated with the `while` loop consists of a block with a call to `printf()`, a call to `scanf()`, and a call to the function `process()`. The return value from `process()` is assigned to the variable `correct`. The code for `process()` consists of a compound `if-else` statement. This last component is similar to the function `process()` in the program if.c in Example 2-7.

Note 1: These preprocessor statements define values for the identifiers `TRUE` and `FALSE`. With these definitions, it is possible to simulate Boolean variables. An `int` variable named `correct` is declared and initialized to `FALSE`. It is used as a flag. When the user's guess is wrong, the value `FALSE` is returned by `process()` and assigned to `correct`. When the number is guessed, the value `TRUE` is assigned to `correct`.

Note 2: The relational expression (`correct == FALSE`) serves as the test expression in the `while` loop. The expression is evaluated and if it is nonzero (true) the loop is entered. The expression must appear in parentheses.

Note 3: The statement for this `while` loop is a block. Notice the placement of the opening brace for this block. This placement is preferred by many C programmers who have learned to look at the right end of a line of code for an indication of what is coming next. Another acceptable placement for the opening brace is on a line by itself directly under the `'w'` in `while`.

Note 4: Notice the placement of the closing brace for each block. In this programming style, the closing brace is positioned in the same column as the first letter in `while`. Because the opening and closing braces for a compound statement are single characters rather than complete words, be careful where you place them. They need to be easily visible in the code.

Learning Activities

19. In while.c, what is the statement associated with the final `else` in the compound `if-else` statement?

20. Consider the following input for while.c:

         3 10 15 50 25 20 17

   a. How many times is the following statement executed?

```
printf ("Try to guess it now. ");
```

   b. How many times is the following expression evaluated?

```
(correct == FALSE)
```

Using getchar() and putchar() in a while Loop

Suppose we want to write a program that takes input from the keyboard and copies that input back to the terminal screen.[1]

A program with this property is called a filter. Two utilities, getchar() and putchar(), are provided to input and output single characters from the terminal. The utility getchar() reads a character from the keyboard and returns the corresponding integer value as type int. The utility putchar() takes an argument of type int and outputs the corresponding ASCII character on the terminal screen. The utilities getchar() and putchar() usually involve less overhead than calls to scanf() and printf() to input or output single characters.

The program in Example 2-12 reads input from standard input and echoes that input to standard output.[2] To use this program, a user must be able to signal the end of the input from the keyboard. On a UNIX system, the end of the input file can be signaled by typing CONTROL-D as the first character on a new input line. On an MS-DOS system, the end of the input file is signaled by typing CONTROL-Z. If your system has another operating system, you will need to find out how to signal the end of input from the keyboard before executing this program.

When getchar() senses the end of input, it returns a special value to the program. This value is denoted EOF and is usually -1. In the file stdio.h, a preprocessor statement is used to make the association between the value -1 and the identifier EOF, which is a mnemonic for end-of-file. A program should always reference EOF since the preprocessor definition could be changed in future systems.

The program inout1.c in Example 2-12 copies its input to its output. To terminate the program, the symbol for end of input for your system must be signaled from the keyboard.

Example 2-12:   inout1.c

```
/*                inout1.c
 *
 *    Synopsis    - Takes input from the keyboard and echoes that
 *                  input back to the terminal.
 *
 *    Objective   - Illustrates another use of the while loop and
 *                  leads into the discussion of inout2.c.
 */
```

---

1. In the terminology of C manuals, input from the keyboard is usually referred to as standard input, and output to the terminal is usually referred to as standard output. When input and output redirection is available in the underlying operating system, the terms standard input and standard output can also refer to input and output that has been redirected.
2. In contrast to this program, most filters modify the input data before it is output.

```
/* Include Files */
#include <stdio.h>

void main( void )
{
    int iochar;                                /* Note 1 */

    iochar = getchar();                        /* Note 2 */
    while ( iochar != EOF ) {                  /* Note 3 */
        putchar( iochar );                     /* Note 4 */
        iochar = getchar();                    /* Note 5 */
    }
}
```

The executable statements for this program consist of an assignment statement followed by a while loop. The statement for the while loop is compound and contains a call to putchar() and an assignment statement. The only variable is of type int.

Note 1: The variable iochar (which stands for input/output character) is declared to be of type int. It is used to receive the input characters returned by getchar(). The type int is necessary because getchar() returns a value of type int.

Note 2: Input is done with a call to getchar(). The returned value is assigned to the variable iochar.

Note 3: The value of iochar is compared with EOF. When end of input is signaled from the keyboard, getchar() returns the value EOF (defined as -1 in stdio.h) to the executing program. When the value of iochar is not EOF, the loop is entered and the compound statement is executed. When iochar is equal to EOF, the while loop terminates.

Note 4: The utility putchar() is used to output the character stored in iochar.

Note 5: Another character is read from the keyboard. This character is compared with EOF at the top of the while loop.

A Word of Warning

It is a common error to use a type char with a call to getchar(). Because getchar() must return the integer value -1, it was designed to return a value of type int. Therefore, programmers should use a variable of type int in assignment statements using getchar(). Failure to use the int type could produce programs that work on some systems and not others.

Learning Activities

21 Find out how to signal the end of input from the command line on your system.

22. Inspect the file stdio.h on your system. Find the line where EOF is defined.

23. *C by Discovery*   Execute the program inout1.c. Is the result what you expected? Describe the keyboard interaction with the program. What character must you enter in order to get the input to echo back?[1]

Note that in the previous program, the input is done in two places, before entering the `while` loop and again at the bottom of the loop. Using the concept that, in C, an assignment is an expression and therefore has a value, we can combine the two input statements into one that occurs exactly at the top of the `while` loop. The expression

```
iochar = getchar()
```

permits a character to be entered from the terminal and assigns the integer value of that character to the variable `iochar`. The value of the assignment expression is the value assigned to `iochar`. This value can be immediately compared with EOF with an expression like

```
(iochar = getchar()) != EOF
```

The assignment is made and the value of `iochar` is compared to EOF. The resulting expression is a relational expression that has the value 1 when `iochar` is not the same as EOF and the value 0 when it is the same. This is the expression that drives the `while` loop in the program inout2.c in Example 2-13. Like inout1.c, the program echoes its input to its output, but does input in only one place, in the expression at the top of the `while` loop. A `while` loop similar to the one in inout2.c is commonly used in programs that need to read through all their input one character at a time.

---

1. This activity deals with the buffered input that is encountered on UNIX, PC, and other systems. The program output may not appear until after the user presses the Return key.

Example 2-13: inout2.c

```
/*                    inout2.c
 *
 *      Synopsis    - Takes input from the keyboard and echoes that
 *                    input back to the terminal.
 *
 *      Objective   - Illustrates the use of an assignment statement
 *                    as part of the test expression in a while loop.
 */

/* Include Files */
#include <stdio.h>

void main( void )
{
        int iochar;                                     /* Note 1 */

        while ( ( iochar = getchar() ) != EOF )         /* Note 2 */
                putchar( iochar );                      /* Note 3 */
}
```

In this program, the variable `iochar` is again declared as type `int`. However, now the executable code consists of a single `while` loop whose associated statement is a single call to `putchar()`.

Note 1: Again, `iochar` must be of type `int` because it is used to store the `int` value returned by `getchar()`.

Note 2: The relational expression compares the value `EOF` with the value of the assignment expression

            iochar = getchar()

A character is input from the command line by `getchar()` and is stored in `iochar` by the assignment operator, `=`. The value given to the assignment expression is the value input by `getchar()`. If the end of input is sensed, this value will be `EOF` and the loop will terminate. Otherwise, the call to `putchar()` will be executed and another value will be input at the top of the loop.

Note 3: The call to `putchar()` causes the character stored in `iochar` to be displayed on the terminal. This statement is not executed when the end-of-file is sensed.

C accepts this type of concise and cryptic source code. There are different opinions about the desirability of programming in this style. Most people would find inout2.c harder to read than inout1.c the first time they see it. However, much of the existing C source code is written in this idiomatic style, so C programmers learn to expect and understand code like this. Some compilers may be able to better optimize this code and produce shorter and more efficient object code.

Learning Activities

24.   Which of the example programs in Chapter 1 and Chapter 2 are filters?

25.   Assuming that the input to the program inout2.c consists of the following four characters,

```
ABC<EOF signal>
```

trace execution of the program by evaluating each expression for the given input value. The trace for the input of the 'A' is shown.

	Input values			
Expressions	A	B	C	EOF signal
getchar()	65	___	___	___
iochar = getchar()	65	___	___	___
iochar	65	___	___	___
iochar != EOF	1	___	___	___
((iochar = getchar())!=EOF)	1	___	___	___

26.   Assume that iochar has been declared as a variable of type int. What are the input values, if any, that will terminate the following while loops? If you think any of the examples will produce errors, state the reason for the error and what form the error would take (compile-time or run-time for example).

```
while ( ( iochar = getchar() ) != '9' )      _____
        putchar( iochar );
while ( ( iochar = getchar() ) != 9 )        _____
        putchar( iochar );
while ( ( iochar = getchar() ) != 64 )       _____
        putchar( iochar );
while ( ( iochar = getchar() ) != '64')      _____
        putchar( iochar );
```

2.6 Logical Operators and Expressions

When a test must be made on two or more conditions in an `if-else` statement or in a loop, expressions can be combined by using the logical operators in C. They are listed below:

!	logical-not
&&	logical-and
¦¦	logical-or

The logical-and, `&&`, is a binary operator; it is used to combine two expressions into one. The syntax for using `&&` to combine two expressions is as follows:

```
expression1 && expression2
```

where `expression1` and `expression2` can be any legal C expressions. The expression involving `&&` is true (nonzero) when both `expression1` and `expression2` are nonzero. C only evaluates as much of the expression as necessary to determine the truth value.

A truth table can be used to represent the values of an expression formed with a logical-and.

expression1	expression2	(expression1 && expression2)
true	true	true
true	false	false
false	—	false

To evaluate an expression involving the logical-and, `expression1` is evaluated first. If it has a nonzero (true) value, then `expression2` is evaluated. If both expressions have nonzero values, then `(expression1 && expression2)` is given a value of `1` (true); otherwise, the value of `(expression1 && expression2)` is `0` (false). However, if `expression1` has a value of `0` (false), then the logical-and expression, `(expression1 && expression2)`, is given a value of `0` (false); `expression2` is not evaluated.

Note that the truth table contains only three possible combinations for the truth values of `expression1` and `expression2`. The cases

expression1	expression2
false	true
false	false

have been combined into the single case

    expression1   **expression2**
     false   —

This was done to emphasize the fact that the C compiler only checks the second expression when it is necessary to determine the value of the logical-and expression. The logical-and expression is false when `expression1` is false; the value of `expression2` is not checked. Some interesting consequences of this fact are presented in Example 2-14 and the exercises.

The logical-or, `||`, is also used to combine two expressions. Its syntax is:

```
expression1 || expression2
```

where `expression1` and `expression2` must be legal C expressions. No other requirement is imposed on them. A logical-or expression is true if either `expression1` or `expression2` or both are nonzero. Again, C only evaluates as much as necessary to determine the truth value.

The truth table values of `expression1`, `expression2` and `expression1 || expression2` follow:

expression1	**expression2**	**(expression1 || expression2)**
true	—	true
false	true	true
false	false	false

To evaluate a logical-or expression, `expression1` is evaluated first. If it has a nonzero value, `(expression1 || expression2)` is given a value of 1 (true). In this case, `expression2` is not evaluated. If `expression1` has a 0 value, `expression2` is evaluated. If it is nonzero, the logical-or expression is given a value of 1 (true); if `expression2` is 0, the logical-or expression is given a value of 0 (false).

The table contains only three of the four possible combinations of the truth values of `expression1` and `expression2`. C only evaluates the second expression when its value is necessary to determine the value of the logical-or statement.

A third logical operation is the logical-not, `!`. It takes a single operand. Its use in an expression has the syntax

```
!expression1
```

When this expression is evaluated, the value of `expression1` is computed. If expression1 has a nonzero (true) value, the value of `!expression1` is 0 (false). If `expression1` evaluates to 0 (false), `!expression1` evaluates to 1 (true). The following truth table illustrates this:

expression1	**!expression1**
true	false
false	true

The program logic1.c in Example 2-14 outputs the values of some logical expressions and illustrates their syntax. It does not provide an example of the use of the logical operations. That will be done later.

Example 2-14: logic1.c

```
/*                 logic1.c
 *
 *    Synopsis    - Displays a table of values of some logical
 *                  expressions. Gives examples of the effect of
 *                  evaluating the logical expressions on embedded
 *                  variable operations.
 *
 *    Objective   - To illustrate syntax and evaluation of logical
 *                  expressions.
 */

/* Include Files */
#include <stdio.h>
void main( void )
{
    int  i = 3,
         j = 0;

    printf( "Examples of the logical expressions\n" );
    printf( "-----------------------------------\n" );

                                                        /* Note 1 */
    printf( "    i && j        %d\n", i && j );
                                                        /* Note 2 */
    printf( "    i || j        %d\n", i || j );

                                                        /* Note 3 */
    printf( "    !i            %d\n", !i );
    printf( "    !j            %d\n", !j );
                                                        /* Note 4 */
```

```
    printf( "(i > 0) && (j < 7)    %d\n", (i > 0) && (j < 7) );
    printf( "(i < 0) || (j < 7)    %d\n", (i < 0) || (j < 7) );
    printf( "!(i > 5) || (j > 0)   %d\n", !(i > 5) || (j > 0) );

    printf( "\nExamples of the effects on the variables\n" );
    printf( "---------------------------------------\n" );
    printf( "Initially,    \ti = %d,\tj = %d\n", i, j );

    printf( "i || ++j      %d,", i || ++j );                      /* Note 5 */
    printf( "\ti = %d,\tj = %d\n", i, j );
    printf( "i && j++      %d,", i && j++ );                      /* Note 6 */
    printf( "\ti = %d,\tj = %d\n", i, j );
}
```

This program contains two variables of type int that are initialized when they are declared. The remainder of the program consists of printf() calls. Most of the printf() calls consist of the output of the values of some examples of logical expressions involving the variables.

Note 1: The value of the simple logical-and expression i && j is output in decimal. The possible values for this expression are 0 and 1. In this specific case the value 0 would be displayed because the expression is false since the value of j is 0 (false).

Note 2: The value of the expression i || j is output in decimal. Because the value of i is 3 (not 0), this expression is given the value 1. C will not even look at the value of j.

Note 3: This time the value of !i is output. Because i is nonzero, !i is 0.

Note 4: In the next three printf() calls, the expressions whose values are displayed involve both logical operators and relational operators. Parentheses are inserted to indicate which operations are evaluated first. The unary operator, !, has higher precedence than the binary operators. You are asked to predict the output of the rest of the program in the Learning Activities.

Note 5: In the next two printf() calls, the value of a logical-or expression is displayed along with the subsequent values of the variables i and j. Notice that in the second operand of the logical-or, i || ++j, the increment operator is applied to j. Remember that with the logical-or, if the first operand is nonzero, the second operand is not evaluated. Therefore, the increment operator has no effect since the expression ++j is not evaluated. Programmers need to be aware of this consequence of the method of evaluating logical operations.

Note 6: A similar situation exists in the next two lines of code except that the logical operator is &&. Now the second operand will only be evaluated when the first operator is nonzero. Therefore, it is only in this case that the variable j is incremented.

Learning Activities

27. a. Predict the output of the program logic1.c by filling in the blanks below:

```
Examples of the logical expressions
i && j                          ____
i || j                          ____
!i                              ____
!j                              ____
(i > 0) && (j < 7)              ____
(i < 0) || (j < 7)              ____
!(i > 5) || (j > 0)             ____

Examples of the effects on the variables
Initially,       i = ___,    j = ___
i || ++j ___,    i = ___,    j = ___
i && j++ ___,    i = ___,    j = ___
```

   b. Execute the program to verify your predictions. Make sure you resolve any differences between your prediction and the actual output.

28. a. Predict the output of logic1.c for the following values of i and j:

i	j
0	7
8	2
0	0

   b. Modify the program logic1.c to interactively ask for and accept input values for i and j. Execute the program with the three input values from part a to verify your predictions.

   c. Execute your modified program with different input values until you see the pattern and are clear about the concepts.

Precedence of the Logical Operators

Among the logical operators, the logical-not has higher precedence than the logical-and, which has higher precedence than the logical-or. The two binary operators are both left associative. That is, an expression like

```
i || j || k
```

is evaluated as indicated by the following insertion of parentheses:

```
( (i || j) || k)
```

The expression i || j is evaluated first. Then its result is combined in the second logical-or operator with k.

An Example

The program tabs.c in Example 2-15 gives an example of how to combine the concepts that we have studied to write a simple but useful program in a structured way.

The problem addressed by this program is to copy a program's input to its output but to replace every tab character and every CTRL-A with five spaces. There is no new element of the language C in this program, but we will discuss the reasons for many of the statements as well as many design decisions that were made. This is another example of a filter.

Example 2-15: tabs.c

```
/*                  tabs.c
 *
 *    Synopsis   - A filter that processes its input by replacing
 *                 every tab character and ^A character with
 *                 TABSTOP spaces.
 *
 *    Objective  - Illustrates the use of a logical operator in a
 *                 structured program that contains a useful tool.
 */

/* Include Files */
#include <stdio.h>

/* Constant Definitions */
#define TAB       '\t'
#define ALTTAB    1                          /*  CTRL-A in ASCII */
#define TABSTOP   5
#define SPACE     ' '                    /* the ASCII space character */

/* Function Declarations */
void processtabs( int tabstop, int character );

void main( void )
{
```

```
     int iochar;

     /*  The following while loop processes each input
      *  character.  If the character is one of the two
      *  designated tab characters, the function processstabs()
      *  is called. Otherwise, the character is output with
      *  putchar().
      */

     while ( ( iochar = getchar() ) != EOF )
          if ( ( iochar == TAB ) || ( iochar == ALTTAB ) )
               processtabs( TABSTOP, SPACE );
          else
               putchar( iochar );
}


/***************************** processtabs()   ***************/
/*   will output tabstop characters every time it is called.
 */

void processtabs( int tabstop, int character )
{
     int colcount = 0;

     while ( colcount++ < tabstop )
          putchar( character );
}
```

The program consists of two functions, main() and processtabs(). Since there are no new C constructs in this program, the usual notes have not been included. However, several points about the use of the C language are illustrated with this program:

1. The function main() consists of a familiar while loop that works through all the input. The input is done only at the top of the while loop. The input value is assigned to iochar and is tested against EOF. The while loop executes until the end of input is sensed.

2. Inside the while loop, each character is compared to both TAB and ALTTAB. If the input value is one of the tab characters, the function processtabs() is called to display the desired number of spaces. Otherwise, the input character is echoed back to the terminal by putchar().

3. The function processtabs() is a tool. It has one purpose: to produce some output. It is passed parameters indicating which characters and how many of them to output and then does its job and nothing more. It doesn't

access any variables outside its own code, and has no restrictions on identifier names that must be used. It also doesn't check the input characters or guess in any other way at the programmer's intent in calling its code. It is important for its use as a tool that this function does not do any input or make any decisions itself about which or how many characters to output. The function code is complete in itself. It could be used in any program as it is.

4. Notice the constant definitions. The definitions of `TAB` and `ALTTAB` allow easy modification of the program to output the spaces for other characters instead of just the tab character and `CTRL-A`. The definitions of `TABSTOP` and `SPACE` also allow ease of modification. A modification of `TABSTOP` changes the number of spaces that are output every time the function `processtabs()` is called. A modification to `SPACE` changes the character that is output.

2.7 The for Loop

The second iterative loop in C is the `for` loop. Its syntax is as follows:

```
for (initialization; test; processing)
        statement
```

where `for` is the keyword and `initialization`, `test`, and `processing` are expressions. Any or all of the three expressions may be omitted, but the opening and closing parentheses and the semicolons must be included.

The `initialization` expression is evaluated once as the loop is entered. It is generally used to initialize variables for the loop. The `test` expression is evaluated as a condition for continuing the loop. If the value of `test` is nonzero, `statement` is executed; if the value is zero, the execution of the `for` loop is terminated. The `test` expression is evaluated every time execution control reaches the top of the loop. The expression `processing` does *bottom-of-the-loop* processing. This expression is evaluated after `statement` is executed each time through the loop.

The execution of the `for` loop can be diagrammed as follows:

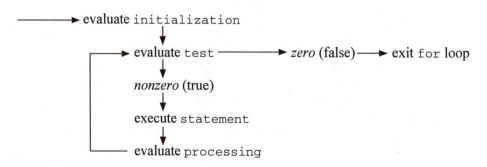

Note that a code segment equivalent to the above `for` loop can be written with the `while` loop as follows:

```
initialization;
    while (test) {
            statement;
            processing;
    }
```

Here, the statements `initialization;` and `processing;` are the expression statements that are formed by placing a semicolon after an expression. Executing these statements is the same as evaluating the expression.

Simple examples of the for loop appear in the program for.c in Example 2-16. The three variations of the for loop in the program illustrate some of the different ways the expressions can be used.[1] The comma operator is also introduced.

Example 2-16: for.c

```
/*                  for.c
 *
 *   Synopsis   - Three for loops. The first for loop counts by
 *                1; the second for loop counts by 2; the third
 *                for loop calculates a factorial.
 *
 *   Objective  - To illustrate the syntax and the flexibility
 *                of the for loop.
 */

/* Include Files */
#include <stdio.h>

/* Constant Definitions */
#define LAST 7

void main( void )
{
    int count,
        factorial;

    printf( "Counting.\n" );
    for ( count = 1; count < LAST; count++ )          /* Note 1 */
        printf( "%d\n", count );
```

---

1. One of the `for` loops calculates a "factorial". The factorial of an integer, n is denoted $n!$ and is defined as the product, $n \cdot (n-1) \cdot (n-2) \cdot (n-3) \cdot \ldots \cdot 3 \cdot 2 \cdot 1$. For example, $7! = 7 \cdot 6 \cdot 5 \cdot 4 \cdot 3 \cdot 2 \cdot 1 = 5040$. Factorials are used in several areas of mathematics.

```
        printf( "\nCounting by two.\n" );
        for ( count = 0; count < 2*LAST;
              printf( "%d\n", count += 2 ) )
            ;                                              /* Notes 2 and 3 */

        printf( "\nCalculating factorials.\n" );
        for ( factorial = 1, count = 1; count <= 7;
                                     factorial *= count++ )
            ;                                              /* Note 4 */
        printf( "%d! is %d.\n", LAST, factorial );
}
```

 Running the Program

```
Counting.
1
2
3
4
5
6

Counting by two.
2
4
6
8
10
12
14

Calculating factorials.
7! is 5040.
```

This program consists of the single function named `main()`. Two variables of type `int` are declared. The program consists of some `printf()` calls and three variations of a `for` loop.

Note 1: This is the simplest example of a `for` loop. The initialization expression consists of the assignment expression, `count = 1`. The assignment is made at the beginning of the loop execution.

The test expression is `count < LAST`. It is evaluated to determine whether the loop will execute or not. If the value is nonzero (true), the loop will execute. If it is zero, the loop terminates.

The bottom of the loop processing consists of the expression `count++`. It is evaluated (`count` is incremented) after the loop statement is executed. The `printf()` call serves as the statement in this `for` loop.

Note 2: In the second `for` loop, the initialization expression is a simple assignment. The test expression,

```
count < 2*LAST
```

is somewhat more complicated than in the first loop. Any expression can be placed in this position. This expression tests false and the loop terminates when `count` is greater than or equal to `2*LAST`.

The bottom of the loop processing can be any expression that has a value. In this example, the fact that the `printf()` library function returns a value makes this a legitimate expression. The evaluation of this expression causes the `printf()` function to be executed. Note that count is incremented by 2 when this statement is evaluated so that the loop counts by 2.

Note 3: The semicolon on this line is the *null statement*. The syntax of the `for` loop requires that a statement be included, but in this case, since the bottom of the loop processing includes a call to `printf()`, no additional code is needed. The semicolon serves as the statement required by the syntax for this loop.

Note 4: Look at the initialization expression in this `for` loop. It consists of everything from the opening parenthesis to the first semicolon. That is, the initialization expression consists of

```
factorial = 1, count = 1
```

This expression is an example of a *comma expression*; the comma is the comma operator in C. It signifies sequential execution of the expressions before and after the comma. The expression on the left is evaluated first; the actual value of the expression is discarded, but the assignment is done. Then the expression on the right is evaluated. The value of a comma expression is the value of the expression on the right.

In this loop, the bottom of the loop processing is the compound assignment statement that multiplies the variable `factorial` by the value of `count`. Then `count` is incremented by one. Again, the semicolon or the null statement is the statement required in the `for` loop. The function `printf()` is called once, after the `for` loop terminates.

Notice how flexible the `for` loop is. A loop control variable may increase or decrease by any value. The variable can change by addition, subtraction, multiplication, division or taking the remainder. However, it is not necessary to use a loop control variable. For example, the loop

```
for (;;)
    printf ("still going.\n");
```

is an infinite loop. The initialization, test, and processing expressions are all optional in the `for` loop and can be omitted, as in this example. No initialization is done, no test is made for continuing, and no processing is done at the bottom of the loop. The loop just keeps on executing.

A Word about Style

The comma has syntactic uses other than that of the comma operator. It is used in declarations, initializations, and passing parameters to functions. Programmers should be careful not to use the comma operator where it might be mistaken for one of these other uses of the comma.

Learning Activities

29. The second `for` loop in for.c displays the values 2 through 14.
    a. What values would the loop
    ```
    for (count = 0; count < 2*LAST; count += 2)
            printf("%d ", count);
    ```
    display?
    b. Rewrite the loop in part a) so that it outputs the values 2 through 14 without including the call to `printf()` in the bottom of the loop processing.

30. Write a `for` loop that outputs the following values in two ways:
    ```
    1, 2, 4, 8, 16, 32, 64, 128, 256, 512
    ```
    a.   Use a `printf()` call as the statement in the `for` loop.
    b.   Use a null statement as the statement in the `for` loop.

31. Write two different `for` loops that output the following values:
    ```
    8, 7, 6, 5, 4, 3, 2, 1
    ```

32. Write a `for` loop that outputs the first 10 positive integers in the following format:

1	2	3	4	5
6	7	8	9	10

    Use two variables, one for the value to be output and one as a column counter. Initialize both variables in the initialization expression by using the comma operator.

2.8 Making C Readable—Programming Style

By now we have discussed enough of the language to address the issue of programming style. C uses many combinations of symbols like ++ and -- for automatic increment and decrement and `&&`, `||`, and `!` for the logical operators. Because of this and other properties of the language, it is very easy to write unreadable code in C. It is only slightly more difficult to make it readable. It is important to give thought to programming style. Some points, like one command statement per line of source code and the use of mnemonics for identifiers, are standard guidelines for programming in any upper-level language.

C is a free-format language. The programmer is free to decide on the placement of the code elements as well as the names of the program elements. A clear programming style can be developed. Consistency is very important.

Some of the points in C programming style are discussed below.

Choice of Identifiers

A programmer chooses names for the variables and functions used in a program. Generally, those variables have meaning and should be named accordingly. Similarly, functions have a purpose and their names should convey that purpose. The identifiers chosen for the variable names and the function names should be mnemonic - they should portray the significance of that variable or function to the reader. For example, consider the following two statements:

```
z = x * y;
service_charge = number_of_checks * CHARGE_PER_CHECK;
```

In the first example, you can easily see that the result of multiplication operation is assigned to the variable `z`, but nothing else of meaning is apparent. However, in the second statement, the variable names indicate the intent of the statement as well as the nature of the program it might appear in. By convention, the fact that the identifier `CHARGE_PER_CHECK` is in uppercase indicates that it is a preprocessor-defined constant.

Indentation

The use of indentation is very important to a C program's readability. Typically, the amount of indentation depicts the level of nesting. For example, if the statement portion of a `while` loop consists of a compound statement, each statement in the compound statement should be indented the same amount. Also, the statements in the compound statement should be indented more than the `while` statement itself. Programs in C are more readable when the indentations are larger than two or three spaces. Traditionally, a full tab stop of indentation is used for each new level of nesting.

Consider the following code segments and notice the difference that the indentation makes. To read the code, assume that `rownum`, `colnum`, and `matrix-elt` are declared variables of type `int`, that NUMROWS and NUMCOLUMNS are preprocessor-defined constants, and that `calculate()` is a function that calculates and returns an element of a product matrix given the position. In this situation, the code segment outputs a matrix in a rectangular format. In the first code segment, the code lines are not indented at all.

```
for (rownum = 1; rownum <= NUMROWS; rownum++) {
for (colnum = 1; colnum <= NUMCOLUMNS; colnum++) {
matrixelt = calculate (rownum, colnum);
printf ("\t%d", matrixelt);
}
printf ("\n");
colnum = 1;
}
```

The next code segment differs only in its indentation. However, it should be easier to recognize the structure of the nested `for` loop.

```
for (rownum = 1; rownum <= NUMROWS; rownum++) {
    for (colnum = 1; colnum <= NUMCOLUMNS; colnum++) {
        matrixelt = calculate (rownum, colnum);
        printf ("\t%d", matrixelt);
    }
    printf ("\n");
    colnum = 1;
}
```

Placement of Braces

Several methods are acceptable for the placement of the braces that surround a block in C. The important point is consistency. A reader should be able to see the beginning and ending of a block of code by looking in the same place each time.

In this text, the following method is used:

1. The opening brace for a function block is placed in the first column; the function's closing brace appears in that column also.

2. The opening brace for a block associated with an `if`, a `while`, a `do-while` (see Chapter 6), or a `for` statement is placed on the right end of the line containing the statement's keyword. As an example, consider the nested `for` loop in the code segment above. In this way, the end of a line becomes a point of tension for the reader. The closing brace appears in the same column as the first character in the control word. That is, it appears in the same column as the `i` from the `if`, the `w` from the `while`, the `d` from the `do-while`, or the `f` from the `for` loop.

3. An independent compound statement or block has its opening brace in the column that best indicates its nesting level. The closing brace appears in the same column.

Another acceptable style is to place both opening and closing braces on separate lines in the column that conveys the nesting level of the compound statement. Two copies of a `while` loop appear below. The first loop has its braces placed in the style suggested by points 1, 2, and 3 above. Assume `count`, `number`, and `sum` have type `int`.

```c
while ( count++ < 5 ) {
        printf( "Enter a number : " );
        scanf( "%d", &number );
        sum += number;
}
```

The second loop has an alternate acceptable placement of the braces.

```c
while ( count++ < 5 )
{
        printf ("Enter a number : ");
        scanf("%d", &number);
        sum += number;
}
```

Because programming style is largely a matter of personal taste, it is not important to adopt either method. However, it is necessary to choose some method of indentation and placement of braces that indicates nesting level and to use it consistently.

"In this text...the closing braces will appear in the same column as the first character..."
Based on a limestone relief of a funeral procession, 19th Dynasty (artist unknown)

Block Structuring

Programs written in a top-down structured style are easier to read and maintain than those not written in that style. This means writing short blocks of code because it is much easier to read and understand 10 lines of code than 100. Each block should be designed to perform a single task. In C the block is usually packaged as a function. Once each block of code makes sense, the whole program follows more easily. Writing short code blocks that perform different tasks becomes more important as the length and complexity of the program increases.

Use of Parentheses

C has specific precedence rules so that the compiler will automatically know the meaning of any legal expression in a source code program. The use of parentheses aids the reader. For example, consider the following two lines of code. The first is a legal C expression. The compiler will have no problem interpreting the code, but a reader might have trouble interpreting it correctly.[1]

```
i = i + 5 % j != 3*i - 4/j % 2;
```

The second expression differs from the first only in the addition of parentheses so that a reader will not have to dig for a precedence chart.

```
i = ( ( i + (5 % j) ) != ( ( 3*i ) - ( ( 4/j ) % 2 ) ) );
```

Comments

It is hard to overstate the importance of comments in a computer program. It is so much easier to see what a program does if you can get a general idea of its function before wrestling with the details in the source code. There are many styles of commenting a program, from placing comments on every line to writing paragraphs of comments for every function and major code block. Again, the method you choose largely depends on personal taste. However, it is important to spell out the significance of every variable and function in comments and to explain the algorithms.

Comments can be helpful to a programmer during the programming process. One way might be to add comments to the line containing the ending brace for a block that indicates which block terminates at that position. For example,

```
while ( ex1 ) {
    if ( ex2 ) {
        . . .
    }       /* end of if (ex2) block */
    else {
        . . .
    }       /* end of else block */
}           /* end of while block */
```

---

1. Try to interpret this assignment statement both with and without the parentheses. What possible values could be assigned to i?

It is also important to make the comments as clear as possible. Comment lines that merely restate the code without giving more insight are useless.

Paragraphing

C source code can be made more readable by creating cohesive paragraphs of code surrounded by blank lines and comments. That is, a `while` loop with an embedded compound statement could be separated from the surrounding code by putting blank lines both before and after the loop. Consider the difference in the following two examples.

The actual code in both code segments is identical. The purpose is to calculate a non-negative integral power of an integer. The code prompts for and accepts input of an integer value for the base and a non-negative integer value for the power. Then a `for` loop is used for the actual calculation. In the first copy of the code, no paragraphing was done.

```
int base, power, count, result;
printf ("To calculate the power of a number, ");
printf ("enter an integer for the base: ");
scanf ("%d", &base);
printf ("Enter a non-negative integer power: ");
scanf ("%d", &power);
for (count = 0, result = 1; count < power; count++)
result *= base;
printf ("The result is %d\n", result);
```

In the second copy, the code was paragraphed into five separate sections by including blank lines between (1) the declarations, (2) the prompt for and input of the base, (3) the prompt for and input of the power, (4) the calculation of the result, and (5) the output of the result.

```
int base, power, count, result;

printf ("To calculate the power of a number, ");
printf ("enter an integer for the base: ");
scanf ("%d", &base);

printf ("Enter a non-negative integer power: ");
scanf ("%d", &power);

for (count = 0, result = 1; count < power; count++)
        result *= base;

printf ("The result is %d\n", result);
```

Whitespace

The judicious placement of blanks, tabs, and newlines enhances the readability of C source code. Complicated expressions can be clarified for the reader and the groupings of symbols emphasized. Consider the following two versions of a familiar C source code expression. This is the control part of a `while` loop that reads terminal input until the end of input is sensed. In the first example, no whitespace is included.

```
while((iochar=getchar())!=EOF)
```

The second example is easier to read because most of the tokens are separated by whitespace.

```
while ( ( iochar = getchar() ) != EOF )
```

However, both examples compile and execute properly.

Each element of programming style makes a small but significant difference in the readability of C source code.[1]

Language Elements Introduced in This Chapter: A Review

✓ **Blocks and Compound Statements**
- Can contain both declarations and executable code.
- Treated as a single statement.
- Delimited by a pair of braces.
- Variables declared in a block are unknown outside the block.

✓ **Control Statements**

```
if ( expression )
    statement


if ( expression )
    statement1
else
    statement2


while ( expression )
    statement


for ( initialization; test; processing )
    statement
```

---

1. Often a C compiler comes with a program that formats C source code in a specific style. The most notable example is cb, the c beautifier program that is part of the UNIX System V operating system. If such a program exists on your system, it is worth learning to use now. It makes writing programs in an acceptable style much easier, and can sometimes be used to find some elusive syntax errors.

✓ **Preprocessor Defined I/O Utilities**

getchar()   Reads a single character from standard input and returns the int value.

putchar()   Takes an int between 0 and 127 as a parameter and outputs the corresponding character on standard output.

EOF   Stands for end-of-file, usually has value -1, returned by getchar() when end of input is sensed.

✓ **Operators**

Relational operators

<=   is less than or equal to
>=   is greater than or equal to
==   is equal to
!=   is not equal to
>   is greater than
<   is less than

Logical operators

&&   logical-and
|| logical-or
!   logical-not

✓ **Comma operator**

,   causes sequential evaluation of expressions it separates

✓ **Operator Precedence**

HIGHEST PRECEDENCE

```
( )
++      --    unary +   unary -   & (address)
*       /      %
+       -
<    <=     >      >=
==          !=
&&
||
=      +=      -=     *=     etc.
,  (comma operator)
```

LOWEST PRECEDENCE

Things to Remember

1. lvalues refer to expressions that have a location in memory.

2. rvalues can be evaluated, but cannot be changed.

3. An assignment is an expression. It has the value of the quantity being assigned.

4. An expression with a nonzero value is evaluated as true; an expression with value zero is evaluated as false.

5. Each else is paired with the nearest if.

6. Remember to use == to test equality. Don't use =.

7. The relational operators have lower precedence than any of the arithmetic operators, but higher precedence than assignment operators.

8. A filter is a program that reads from standard input and writes to standard output.

9. The utilities getchar(), putchar(), and EOF are declared in stdio.h.

10. Remember to use type int to store the return value from getchar(), because getchar() returns an int value.

11. The expression ((iochar = getchar()) != EOF) is often used to drive a while loop that is to work through all the input in a program.

12. The value of an expression involving one of the logical operators is either 1 (true) or 0 (false).

13. The precedence of the logical operators from high to low is !, &&, and ||.

14. Get in the habit of using good programming style. C needs more whitespace than other programming languages.

Exercises and Programming Problems

1. Assume that the variables x, y, and z have been declared as follows:

   ```
   int x = 5, y = -1, z = 3;
   ```

   a. Categorize each expression below as either an lvalue or an rvalue.

   ```
   x + y        _____
   2*x + 3      _____
   z + 1        _____
   x++          _____
   y            _____
   x = y + 5    _____
   x <= z       _____
   ```

   b. Evaluate each of the following C expressions. (Evaluate each expression separately. Do not assume they are in a program.)

   ```
   2*x + 5      _____
   x = y % z    _____
   x >= 2       _____
   x = 3219     _____
   x == 3219    _____
   ```

```
y / z * 2        _____
! (x - 3)        _____
z || y           _____
! (y + 1)        _____
```

2. What is the output for the following program? Write each character of output in boxes like those below. Write one character per box.

```
/*              epp2.c*/

/* Include Files */
#include <stdio.h>

void main( void )
{
    int i, j;

    i = 2;
    j = 1;

    while ( (i > -5) || (j-- > 0) ) {
            if ( (j % 2) && (i-- % 3) )
                    printf ("%d", j);
            else
                    printf ("%d\n", i);
    }
}
```

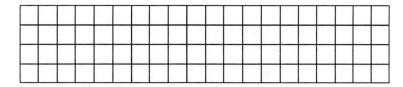

3. Will the following program compile as it appears or are there syntax errors?

```
/*              epp3.c*/
# include <stdio.h>

void main( void )
{
    int count, done

    done = 0;
    for count = 0, count < 5, count++) {
            if count % 2
            printf ("count is odd.\n, count)
}
```

    a. If there are syntax errors, fix them; preserve the original intent of the program. Make your changes on the copy of the program above.

    b. After the corrections have been made, give the output of the program.

    _____

    _____

4. Rewrite the following program with better style. Incorporate as many of the style points mentioned in Section 2.8 as possible.

```
/*                        epp4.c                        */
#include <stdio.h>
void main( void )
         {
int y,x = 0;
printf( "Enter your integers now.\n" );
printf( "Enter one integer per line, press return.\n" );
printf( ">>> " );
while( (scanf( "%d",&y ) ) != EOF ){
x=x+y; printf( ">>> " ); }printf("The sum is %d.\n", x ); }
```

(Hint: If your system has a C beautifier program, start by running this source code through that program.)

5. How many times is each indicated statement executed when the following code segment is executed? Fill in the number of times in the blank immediately to the left of the statement.

```
            int i, j;

            for ( i = 1; i <= 4; i++ )
                    for ( j = i; j >= 1; j-- )
____                    printf ( "%d ", j );
____                    i = 0;
                        j = 3*i;
            while ( i != j+4 )
____                    i = i + 1;

            i = 4;
            if (i <= 10)
____                    i++;
```

6. a. If it is possible with your system, compile the program inout2.c of Example 2-13 but stop the compilation after the preprocess phase.

    b. Compare the original source code and the preprocessed code. In the latter, circle the changes that were made by the preprocessor.

    c. Get a hard copy of stdio.h from your system and compare its contents to the changes you have circled.

  d. Try to explain how the preprocessor expands utilities like `getchar()`.

7. Write a function named `positive` that takes a single argument of type `int` and returns a value that will test true if the argument is positive and false otherwise. Test your function with the program below.

```
/*                        epp7.c                        */

/* Include Files */
#include <stdio.h>

/* Function Declarations */
int positive( int );

void main( void )
{
int inputint;

     printf( "Enter an integer and " );
     printf( "press return after the prompt.\n" );
     printf( "Signal EOF when you are done.\n" );
     printf( ">>> " );

     while ( scanf( "%d", &inputint ) != EOF ) {
          if ( positive( inputint ) )
                    printf( "That one was positive.\n" );
          else
                    printf( "That one wasn't.\n" );
          printf( ">>> " );
     }
}
```

8. The purpose of the following program is to count the whitespace, the digits, the uppercase alphabetics and the lowercase alphabetics in the input. There are bugs in the program. Fix it.

```
/*                        epp8.c                        */

/* Include Files */
#include <stdio.h>

void main( void )
{
     int    iochar,
            numdigits = 0,
            numlower = 0,
```

```
                  numupper = 0,
                  numwhites = 0;

        while ( ( iochar = getchar() ) != EOF ) {
                if ( ( iochar = ' ' ) || ( iochar = '\t' )
                                       || ( iochar = '\n' ) ) ) {
                        numwhites++;
                        putchar( iochar );
        }
                else if ( ( '0' <= iochar )
                            && ( iochar <= '9' ) ) {
                        numdigits++;
                        putchar( iochar );
        }
                else if ( ( 'a' <=  iochar )
                            && ( iochar <= 'z' ) ) {
                        numlower++;
                        putchar( iochar - 32 );
        }
                else if ( ( 'A' <=  iochar )
                            && ( iochar <= 'Z' ) ) {
                        numupper++;
                        putchar( iochar );
        }
                else putchar( iochar );
    }

        printf( "%d white characters, %d digits, ",
                                numwhites, numdigits );
        printf( "%d lowercase have been converted to",
                                numlower );
        printf( "uppercase and %d uppercase.\n", numupper );
    }
```

a. Execute the program in its present form using input for which it is easy to predict the output.

b. Analyze the program from the output obtained through the testing and tentatively make some changes.

c. Retest it after each change until you are sure that the bugs are gone.

d. Rewrite epp8.c in a more structured way. It should have more than one function.

9. The purpose of the following program is to check input. It is only supposed to accept a value between 0 and 20 and continually ask for input until the correct quantity is entered. However, there is a bug in it.

```
/*                      epp9.c                    */

/* Include Files */
#include <stdio.h>

/* Constant Definitions */
#define TRUE   1
#define FALSE  0

void main( void )
{
    int correct, inputint;

    inputint = -1;
    correct = FALSE;
    while ( !correct ) {
            if ( 0 < inputint < 20 ) {
                    printf( "Thank you.\n" );
                    correct = TRUE;
            }
            else  {
                    printf( "Enter an integer " );
                    printf( "between 0 and 20: " );
                    scanf( "%d", &inputint );

            }
    }
}
```

a. Fix the bug so that the program behaves as stated above.

b. After the program is working, modify it to give diagnostic help to the person who runs the program.

10. Write a function that will take a variable of type int and output it with a dollar sign preceding the number and a decimal place before the last two digits. For example, the value 8530 should be output as $85.30. Name your function printmoney() and have it take the variable of type int as a parameter. Test it with the program below. Your output should be:

```
$.12
$10.00
$253.04
$.00
$1.45
```

```
/*                      epp10.c                    /

/* Include Files */
```

```
#include <stdio.h>

/* Function Declarations */
void printmoney( int );

void main( void )
{
    printmoney( 12 );
    printf( "\n" );
    printmoney( 1000 );
    printf( "\n" );
    printmoney( 25304 );
    printf( "\n" );
    printmoney( 0 );
    printf( "\n" );
    printmoney( 145 );
    printf( "\n" );
}
```

11. Write a C program that plays a number guessing game with the user. A sample run for the game would be as follows: User input is in **boldface**.

```
Welcome to the game of Guess It!
I will choose a number between 1 and 100.
You will try to guess that number. If you guess wrong,
I will tell you if you guessed too high or too low.
You have 6 tries to get the number.

OK, I am thinking of a number. Try to guess it.

Your guess? 50
Too high!
Your guess? 12
Too low!
Your guess? 112
Illegal guess. Your guess must be between 1 and 100.
Try again. Your guess? 23
**** CORRECT****

Want to play again? y
OK, I am thinking of a number. Try to guess it.
Your guess? 23
**** CORRECT ****

Want to play again? n
Goodbye, it was fun. Play again soon.
```

12. Write a C program that will accept input of two positive decimal integer val-

ues and output the prime factorizations of the input values. A sample run is below. User input is in **boldface**.

```
So you want two numbers factored.
Give them to me one by one and I will do the factoring.

Number?  12
The prime factorization of 12 is 2*2*3.

Number?  1050
The prime factorization of 1050 is 2*3*5*5*7.

You're welcome. The bill is in the mail.
```

13. Indicate the output of each `printf()` call below in the spaces to the right.

```
/*                          epp13.c                    */

/* Include Files */
#include <stdio.h>

void main( void )
{
    int i, count = 0;

    for ( i = 8; i >= 0; i-- ) {
        if ( !( i%4 ) || ( i--%3 ) ) {
            i--;
            count++;
        }
    }

    printf( "%d\n", count );              _____

    printf( "%d\n", count && ++i );       _____

    printf( "%d\n", !count );             _____

    printf( "%d\n", i > 0 );              _____

    printf( "%d\n", 0 < count < 3 );      _____
}
```

14. a. The following program does not compile. Remove all syntax errors so that it compiles and runs properly. Preserve the original intent of the program.

```
/*                      epp14.c                    */

/* Include Files (/
#include <stdio.h>

void main( void )
{
        int i;

        i = 1;
        printf ("counting\n;
        while (i < 100) {
                int j = 1;
                printf ("%4d", i);
                if !(i++ % 16)   {
                        printf ("\n");
                        j++
                else printf (" ");
                }
                printf( "\nThe number of lines printed was
                                        %d.\n", j );

}
```

b. Predict the output of the program after the syntax errors have been removed. Write the output characters in the boxes below, one character per box.

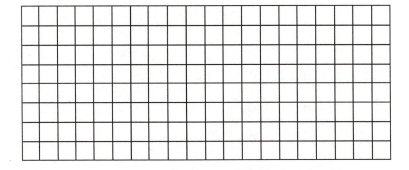

Chapter 3

Basic Data Types

3.1 Introduction to Scalar Types in C

Now that expressions, some operators, and the elementary control statements have been discussed, we will study variables and some of the basic data types in C. Variables are used to hold data while a program is executing. In C, each variable must be declared before it is used. When a variable is declared, a type is assigned to it. During the compilation/link process, memory is reserved for each variable. The amount of memory that is reserved depends on the stated type.

Types in C can be divided into scalar types, aggregate types, function types, union types and the void type. In this chapter we will discuss most of the scalar types, those that can contain only a single data value at any time. In contrast, aggregate types can store multiple data items and include arrays and structures. Union types are associated with unions in C. Aggregate and union types will be discussed in Chapters 4, 7, and 9. Function types and the void types were introduced in Chapter 1. We will discuss functions returning other types in this chapter.

Computer Memory

To understand how numbers are represented in a computer, it is necessary to understand a little bit about a computer's memory.

Every modern computer has memory. When a program is executed, the memory is used for two things. The object code is loaded into memory, and the program data (values of variables, etc.) are kept in memory.

We can talk about a bit, a byte, or a word of memory. Each bit holds 0 or 1. A byte is a sequence of several bits. For example, 8 bits = 1 byte is a popular size. Similarly, a word is a collection of one or more bytes. Two of the more common word sizes are 2 bytes and 4 bytes. Byte size and word size may vary with the computer; the sizes depend on the underlying hardware.

"The byte size . . . may vary with the computer; the size depends on the underlying hardware." From the painting *Jaguar Devouring a Crocodile* by Antoine-Louis Barye, c. 1850-1855

When a byte or word contains a number, some of the bits might be 1 and others would be 0. The resulting configuration is called a bit pattern.

For example, assume that a byte consists of 8 bits and that a word consists of two bytes. Then,

1	0	1	1	0	1	1	0

is an example of one of the possible bit patterns in a byte, and

1	0	1	1	1	1	1	0	0	0	1	1	0	0	1	0

is an example of one bit pattern in a word of memory. These bit patterns can be interpreted in different ways by the compiler. This is why it is possible to have different scalar types.

The scalar types can be classified as arithmetic types, enumerated types, and pointer types. In this chapter we will discuss the arithmetic types. Pointers will be introduced in Chapter 4 and enumerated types in Chapter 7.

The arithmetic types can be further classified as integer types and floating point types. We'll discuss the integer types first.

3.2 Integers and Different Integer Bases

In mathematics, the term *integers* refers to all the whole numbers, 0, 1, 2, 3, 4, 5, 6, . . . together with their negatives, -1, -2, -3, -4, -5, ... There is an infinite number of integers. On a computer, it is not possible to represent every integer. Instead, a range of integers is represented. The range is usually

-m, -m+1, -m+2, . . . , -2, -1, 0, 1, 2, 3, . . . m-2, m-1

where m is a power of 2. The actual value of m depends on the hardware characteristics and the particular implementation of the language.

It is important to realize that the internal representation of an integer is the 0s and 1s of a specific bit pattern. An integer is stored in a binary representation. For example, assuming that a byte consists of 8 bits and that a word consists of 2 bytes,

| 0 | 0 | 0 | 0 | 0 | 0 | 0 | 0 | 0 | 0 | 0 | 0 | 0 | 0 | 0 | 1 | represents the integer 1

| 0 | 0 | 0 | 0 | 0 | 0 | 0 | 0 | 0 | 0 | 0 | 0 | 0 | 1 | 0 | 1 | is the same as decimal 5

| 0 | 0 | 0 | 0 | 0 | 0 | 0 | 0 | 0 | 0 | 0 | 0 | 1 | 1 | 1 | 1 | is the same as 15

The representation of an integer in terms of a specific base keeps track of the multiple of each of the powers of the base that makes up the number. The multiples of each power are written in a specific location. For example, the decimal (base 10) number 125 is represented as

$$1 \cdot 10^2 + 2 \cdot 10^1 + 5 \cdot 10^0$$

The rightmost position holds the multiples of 10^0, the next position to the left holds the multiples of 10^1, and the leftmost position holds the multiples of 10^2.

If the base is 10, as in a decimal representation, the digits needed to keep track of the multiples are 0 through 9. For a base 8 (octal) number, the digits needed are 0 through 7. For a base 2 (binary) number, the digits are 0 and 1. For a base 16 (hexadecimal) number, the digits are 0, 1, . . . , 9, a, b, c, d, e, and f. The a represents the decimal 10; the b represents 11; c is 12; d is 13; e is 14; and f is 15.

The value of the hexadecimal number 1b2f is

$$1 \cdot 16^3 + b \cdot 16^2 + 2 \cdot 16^1 + f \cdot 16^0$$

Replacing the b by 11 and the f by 15, we see that the number 1b2f in hexadecimal is the same as the number 6959 in decimal. The value of the binary number 10111 is

$$1 \cdot 2^4 + 0 \cdot 2^3 + 1 \cdot 2^2 + 1 \cdot 2^1 + 1 \cdot 2^0$$

which equals 23 in decimal.

One method of conversion from decimal to binary is to divide the decimal number by 2 and keep the remainder as the first bit (rightmost bit) of the binary number. Then the quotient is divided by 2 again and the remainder becomes the second bit of the binary representation. This process continues until the quotient is zero. For example, the process of converting the number 11 to binary is shown in Figure 3-1.

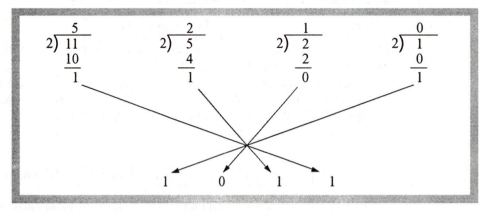

Figure 3-1

The conversion of a binary number to decimal proceeds by multiplying the leftmost bit by 2, and adding in the next bit to the right. Then the result is multiplied by 2 and added to the next bit to the right. This process continues until the rightmost bit has been added to the result. For example, the process of converting the bit pattern 10110 to decimal is shown in Figure 3-2.

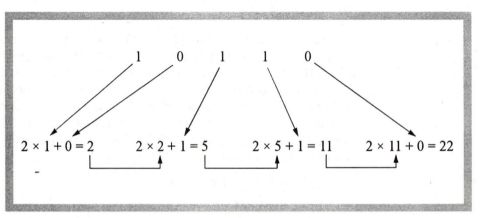

Figure 3-2

Conversions between binary and hexadecimal are easier since four binary digits translate directly to one hexadecimal digit. The table below shows the translation.

Decimal	Hexadecimal	Binary
0	0	0000
1	1	0001
2	2	0010
3	3	0011
4	4	0100
5	5	0101
6	6	0110
7	7	0111
8	8	1000
9	9	1001
10	a	1010
11	b	1011
12	c	1100
13	d	1101
14	e	1110
15	f	1111

All that is necessary to convert a hexadecimal number to binary is to convert each hexadecimal digit to binary. For example, to convert the hexadecimal number 1f3a to binary,

1	f	3	a
0001	1111	0011	1010

and the binary representation is 0001111100111010.

Learning Activities

1.   a. Convert each of the following decimal integers to binary:

   278   1295   31   832

   b. Convert each of your binary answers from part a to hexadecimal.

2.   a. Convert each of the following hexadecimal numbers to binary:

   1000   ffff   1ab   2e

   b. Convert each of your binary answers from part a to decimal.

3. Find a method of converting directly from hexadecimal to decimal and back again. Test the method with the numbers in problems 1 and 2.

4.   In an octal representation, each octal digit translates directly to three binary digits.

   a.   Construct a chart like the one above that shows the binary representation for the octal digits 0 through 7.

   b.   Use that chart to convert the following octal integers to binary:

   1735   361   14315

   c.   Use the chart to convert the following binary integers to octal:

   11010110   100011001   11010

3.3 The Integer Types

Type int Revisited

One of the integer types in C is the type int. This scalar type was first discussed in Chapter 1 where variable declarations were introduced. Output of and arithmetic operations on expressions of type int were also discussed there. The type int is a type that C provides to store integer values.

Most implementations of C let a variable of type int occupy a word in the specific computer. This allows type int to be handled very efficiently. Throughout the language, where a default type is provided, it is generally the int type. The disadvantage of associating the size of a variable of type int with the size of a word on the underlying hardware is that the size of a word varies with different hardware and creates portability problems. A word might consist of 16 bits on one computer and 32 bits on another. The largest value that could be represented with a variable of type int would vary also. For example, if an int is stored in 16 bits, the largest integer that can be represented is 32767 (2^{15} - 1). If an int is stored in 32 bits, the largest integer that can be represented is 2147483647 (2^{31} - 1).

Types short int and long int

We mentioned that the int type is handled more efficiently than the other types in C. However, the way in which it is handled usually depends on the size of a word in the hardware on which it is implemented. This is not always the most efficient use of memory, and may not always produce the desired results when a program is ported to other computers. Therefore, other integer types have been provided. These types include short int and long int, also referred to as short and long. They behave like type int with the arithmetic operators. The major difference is in the number of bytes used to store each value.

The keywords short and long loosely refer to the amount of memory needed to store the values. That is, theoretically, a variable of type short int would be used to store values that are relatively small and would take fewer bytes of memory. A variable of type `long int` would be used for larger values, those taking more bytes of memory. In reality, the specifications for the relative sizes of `short int`, `int`, and `long int` are not precise. Currently, the most common ranges for the types `short` and `long` are given below:

Type	Range
`short`	-32768 to 32767
`long`	-2147483648 to 2147483647

The range for type `int` is usually identical to either type `short` or type `long`, depending on the word size of the underlying hardware. However, as hardware technology advances, these values will change.

The ANSI standards for C include minimal ranges that must be represented by each of the integral types and methods by which the ranges on each individual computer system are specified. These concepts are discussed with Example 3-5 in Section 3.7.[1]

Input and Output of short and long Values

Like values of type `int`, values of variables of type `short int` and `long int` can be output in decimal, hexadecimal, or octal. The `printf()` and `scanf()` functions need to know if the quantity to be output or input is an `int`, a `long int` or a `short int`, and in what base to display the value.

The conversion specifications for type `long int` are as follows:

`%ld`	a `long int` value in decimal
`%lo`	a `long int` value in octal
`%lx` or `%lX`	a `long int` value in hexadecimal

An `'l'` (lowercase `'L'`) is used with the conversion specification to indicate a `long int`. Similarly, an `'h'` in a conversion specification indicates a value of type `short int` to `printf()` and `scanf()`. The conversion specifications for type `short int` are as follows:

`%hd`	a `short int` in decimal
`%ho`	a `short int` in octal
`%hx` or `%hX`	a `short int` in hexadecimal

The program ints.c in Example 3-1 illustrates the declaration of and assignment to variables of type `short int` and `long int`, displays the values in decimal, octal and hexadecimal, and gives some information about what happens when a value "overflows" the storage space allotted to it.

The output from this program is also given. This program was executed on a computer with a 16 bit word. Both type `int` and type `short` occupy 16 bits on the computer. The maximum value that can be represented in those types is 32767.

---

1. Prior to the creation of the ANSI standard for C, all that a programmer was guaranteed was that type `short` occupied no more bytes than type `int`, and type `long` occupied no fewer bytes than type `int`. It was possible for all three types to occupy the same amount of storage.

The value 32767 is assigned to all three variables. When both shortvar and intvar are incremented by 1, the mathematical value becomes 32768 which is larger than the maximum value that can be stored in those types; overflow occurs. The output of this program indicates how the overflow is handled.

Note that overflow should not occur on the variable of type long since 32768 is within the range that can be handled with that type. If more than two bytes are used to store type int, then overflow will not occur with intvar either. It is also possible (but not as likely) that type short is stored in more than two bytes so that overflow might not occur at all. You will need to execute this program on your computer system to see what happens.

Example 3-1: ints.c

```
/*              ints.c
 *
 *    Synopsis    - Declares variables with types, int, long, and
 *                  short. Displays values in decimal, octal, and
 *                  hexadecimal.
 *
 *    Objective   - Demonstrates the conversion specifications for
 *                  types short and long and potentially
 *                  demonstrates overflow.
 */

/* Include Files */
#include <stdio.h>

void main( void )
{
        short     shortvar;                          /* Note 1 */
        long int  longvar;                           /* Note 2 */
        int       intvar;

        shortvar = 32767;                            /* Note 3 */
        intvar   = 32767;
        longvar  = 32767;

                                                     /* Note 4 */
        printf( "shortvar is %hd in decimal, ", shortvar );
        printf( "%ho in octal, and %hx in hexadecimal.\n",
                                    shortvar, shortvar );

        shortvar += 1;                               /* Note 5 */
```

```
printf( "After adding 1, shortvar is %hd in decimal.\n",
                               shortvar );

printf ( "\nintvar is %d in decimal, ", intvar );
printf( "%o in octal, and %x in hexadecimal.\n",
                               intvar, intvar );

intvar++;                                              /* Note 6 */
printf( "After adding 1, intvar is %d in decimal.\n",
                               intvar );

                                                       /* Note 7 */
printf( "\nlongvar is %ld in decimal, ", longvar );
printf( "%lo in octal, and %lx in hexadecimal.\n",
                               longvar, longvar );

longvar++;                                             /* Note 8 */
printf( "After adding 1, longvar is %ld in decimal.\n",
                               longvar );
}
```

Running the Program

```
shortvar is 32767 in decimal, 77777 in octal, and 7fff in hexadecimal.
After adding 1, shortvar is -32768 in decimal.

intvar is 32767 in decimal, 77777 in octal, and 7fff in hexadecimal.
After adding 1, intvar is -32768 in decimal.

longvar is 32767 in decimal, 77777 in octal, and 7fff in hexadecimal.
After adding 1, longvar is 32768 in decimal.
```

The executable code in main() consists of assignment statements and calls to printf(). Essentially the same information is displayed for variables of type short int, int, and long int.

Note 1: A variable named shortvar is declared. Its type is short or short int. The declaration could also have been

    short int shortvar;

The keyword int is optional.

Note 2: The variable longvar is of type long or long int. The keyword int is optional here also.

Note 3: All three variables are initialized to 32767. This integer is the largest integer that can be represented with a type associated with 16 bits of memory.

Note 4: The value of `shortvar` is displayed in decimal, octal, and hexadecimal. The conversion specifications `%hd`, `%ho`, and `%hx` are used.

Note 5: One is added to `shortvar` and the result is displayed in decimal. This value (`32768`) will very probably be beyond the range your computer system handles properly for a `short int`. This causes an error commonly referred to as overflow. Make sure you execute this program to see how this error is handled on your system.

Note 6: One is also added to `intvar` and the result is displayed in decimal. The value `32767` may or may not be beyond your computer system's range for type `int`. Therefore, the output cannot be predicted unless the number of bytes used to store a value of type `int` is known. If `32768` is within your system's range for type `int` then the displayed value will be `32768`; if it isn't in range, then the value displayed for `intvar` will be the same as the final value for `shortvar`.

Note 7: The value of `longvar` is displayed in decimal with the conversion specification `%ld`. The conversion specification `%lo` causes the value to be displayed in octal, and `%lx` causes the value to be displayed in hexadecimal.

Note 8: Finally, one is added to `longvar` and the result is displayed in decimal. The value `32768` is within the range for a `long int` on any ANSI C compiler. There should be no problem with this output.

Learning Activities

5. Execute the program ints.c to see the results on your computer system. In particular, notice the final values displayed for `shortvar`, `intvar`, and `longvar` after one is added to each variable.

    a. The mathematical value should be `32768`. Which, if any of the displayed values matches the mathematical value?

    b. What is the final value displayed for `intvar`? Is it positive or negative? On your system does the storage for type `int` have the same number bytes as type `short int` or more bytes?

6. Modify ints.c by replacing the value `32767` by `2147483647` or $2^{31} - 1$. (`2147483647` is the largest signed integer value that can be stored in 4 bytes.) Execute the program again. Be sure that you understand the output. Explain your results.

3.4 The sizeof() Operator

C provides an operator named `sizeof` that gives the number of bytes associated with a specified type or a variable. The syntax of the `sizeof` operator is similar to that of a function. Its operand can be placed in parentheses. Therefore, in this text, we will refer to this operator as `sizeof()`, using the same notation as for C library functions.

The `sizeof()` operator takes either a variable, an expression or a type name as an argument and returns the number of bytes in that argument. The operator `sizeof()` does only what is necessary to determine the number of bytes in the expression. The value of a `sizeof()` operation can be determined at compile time. It never depends on runtime values of variables or expressions, only on the types involved.

For example, in

```
sizeof( int )
```

the operand is `int` and the number of bytes needed to store an `int` will be returned. In the example

```
sizeof( intvar + 3 )
```

the operand is the expression `intvar + 3`. Since `intvar + 3` has type `int`, the number of bytes needed to store an `int` will be returned here also.

Our first use for `sizeof()` is to determine how many bytes variables of type `int`, `short`, and `long` occupy. The program sizeof1.c in Example 3-2 illustrates this. Other uses for `sizeof()` will be discussed later.

Example 3-2: sizeof1.c

```
/*              sizeof1.c
 *
 *    Synopsis    - Displays the number of bytes occupied by types
 *                  int, short, and long by using sizeof().
 *
 *    Objective   - Demonstrates the use of the sizeof()
 *                  operator with different integer types.
 *                  Determines the range of the different types of
 *                  integer variables.
 */

/* Include Files */
#include <stdio.h>

void main( void )
{
```

```
    short shortvar;
    long  longvar;
                                                        /* Note 1 */
    printf( "An int has %d bytes.\n", sizeof( int ) );
                                                        /* Note 2 */
    printf( "A long int has %d bytes.\n", sizeof longvar );
    printf( "A short int has %d bytes.\n", sizeof shortvar );
                                                        /* Note 3 */
    printf( "It takes %d bytes to store shortvar + 2\n",
                                    sizeof( shortvar + 2 ) );
}
```

This program is simple in structure. A variable of type `short int` and a variable of type `long int` are declared. The executable code consists of calls to the `printf()` library function.

Note 1: In the following call to `printf()`, the operator `sizeof()` is applied to the type `int`. When `sizeof()` is applied to any C type, the value returned is the number of bytes of memory allotted for any variable of that type.

Note 2: The operator `sizeof()` is used with a variable name as an argument in the next two `printf()` calls. The `sizeof()` a `long int` and a `short int` will be displayed. Parentheses are not necessary in the syntax for `sizeof()` in this case, but they can be inserted without error.

Note 3: The `sizeof()` operator can be used with expressions as well as types and variables. The number of bytes used to store `shortvar + 2` may be different than the number of bytes used to store `shortvar`. These two expressions are different types in C. This will be explained more fully in Section 3.10.

Learning Activities

7.   If the `sizeof()` operator is available on your system, run sizeof1.c and note the values displayed for `sizeof( int )`, `sizeof shortvar`, and `sizeof longvar`. Find out the number of bits to a byte on the computer you are using.

8.   Calculate the range of values that can be handled by types `short int`, `int`, and `long int` on your system. Use the results from question 3. (Hint: You will need to know the byte size on your computer as well as the value of the `sizeof()` operator on each of the integer types. Assume that a byte contains n bits and that the `sizeof()` operator says that m bytes are occupied by a certain type. Then 2^{mn} different integers can be represented by the type in question. Half of the integers will be non-negative and half will be negative.)

9.   *C by Discovery*

a.   Predict the output of the following program.

```
/*                   la9.c                    */

/* Include Files */
#include <stdio.h>

void main( void )
{
    int j = 3;

    printf( "The sizeof( j++ ) is %d\n",
                            sizeof( j++ ) );
    printf( "The value of j is %d\n", j );
}
```

b.   Execute la9.c to check your prediction. Was the value of j incremented during the program's execution? Do more experimentation, if necessary, to understand what is happening.

c.   Explain in your own words the concept illustrated by la9.c.

A Closer Look

Of all of the data types supported by the C language the int type is the most machine dependent in terms of size and range. The sizeof() operator in C offers a very useful tool for answering questions about integer variables on a particular machine.

The actual method of storage of integers will be fairly consistent from machine to machine. Integer types are usually stored in groups of bits where the "leftmost" bit is called the *sign bit*. The sign bit tells the CPU whether to treat the number as a negative number (sign bit set to one) or a positive number (sign bit set to zero). Non-negative integers are stored as a direct binary representation of their decimal counterparts. One bit (the high order or "leftmost" bit) is typically used to indicate that a value is negative. This fact has an unusual consequence that we will develop below.

For example, assume that an int is stored in 16 bits. Then 2^{16} different values of type int can be stored. Of these, 2^{15} (0 ... 32767) will be nonnegative and 2^{15} (-32768 ... -1) will be negative.

We will establish a few values and the corresponding bit patterns.[1]

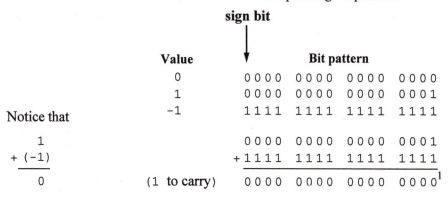

sign bit

Value	Bit pattern
0	0000 0000 0000 0000
1	0000 0000 0000 0001
-1	1111 1111 1111 1111

Notice that

```
      1          0000 0000 0000 0001
 + (-1)        + 1111 1111 1111 1111
 ─────────      ──────────────────────────
      0  (1 to carry)  0000 0000 0000 0000¹
```

The largest positive value that can be represented in 16 bits is

Value	Bit pattern
32767	0111 1111 1111 1111

When we add 1 to 32767 in the binary computer representation, we get

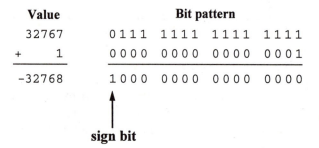

Value	Bit pattern
32767	0111 1111 1111 1111
+ 1	0000 0000 0000 0001
-32768	1000 0000 0000 0000

sign bit

which is the representation of a negative value since the sign bit is one. This is an error condition referred to as arithmetic overflow. An explanation for what happens follows:

The integer values that can be represented in sixteen bits of a computer can be put on a circle like a clock. When we add 1 to each value we progress around the circle in a clockwise direction. When we add 1 to 32767, we cross a dividing line between +32767 and -32768. Continuing to add one will eventually return the value to 0.

---

1. Note that since we are manipulating binary numbers, when one is added to one it is necessary to carry a one into the next place value. Adding one to a sixteen bit binary value consisting of all ones, results in sixteen zeros and one carry bit. Since we are only manipulating 16 bit values at this point there is no room for the 17th "carry bit"; it is not used. The resulting 16-bit value has the same bit pattern as zero.

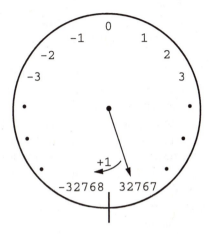

Keeping these ideas in mind we will now look at the specifications regarding the size and range of the integer types, int, short int, and long int.

The value returned by sizeof(int) is the number of bytes in the computer's word. Most microcomputers in use today have a word size of either 2 or 4 bytes (16 or 32 bits), while most time-shared computers have a word size of 4 bytes (32 bits) and some even have 8 byte (64 bit) words. The following table shows the range of numbers represented with type int on computers with different word sizes.

Computer word size	Minimum int	Maximum int
8 bits	$-2^7 = -128$	$2^7 - 1 = 127$
16 bits	$-2^{15} = -32768$	$2^{15} - 1 = 32767$
32 bits	$-2^{31} = -2147483648$	$2^{31} - 1 = 2147483647$

There is a "wrap-around" effect at each end of the range of values for any of the integer types. This information is often very useful for debugging programs. Whenever positive numbers are arithmetically manipulated and the result is an unexpected negative number it may be that the maximum value of that variable has been exceeded. Similarly, if two negative numbers are added the result may be erroneously positive. The solution to these problems is to declare the variable using a data type that allows a larger maximum value.

3.5 Character Variables

In this section, we discuss a type that will hold a member of the underlying character set. It is one of the integer types in C.

The ASCII character set consists of 128 characters. Each element of this character set can be associated with an integer value between 0 and 127. Conversely, each integral value in this range can be translated to an ASCII character[1].

The range of integers from 0 to 127 (0 to $2^7 - 1$) (and more) can be represented with 8 bits (usually 1 byte) on a computer. C provides an integer type named char to represent characters or integers in this range. Values of type char are stored in one byte of memory.

The declaration of a variable of type char is similar to declaration of a variable of type int. The simplest form of a declaration starts with the data type, followed by the variable names, and terminated by a semicolon. As with integers, a variable of type char may or may not be initialized at the time of declaration. The program charvar.c in Example 3-3 has a declaration of a variable of type char.

The program also illustrates some of the other modes of output that are available with the printf() function. For example, the value of a char variable can be output as a character with the conversion specification %c. A char variable can also be output in a numeric form. The value that is output is the integer value that corresponds to the ASCII character.

For example, in the ASCII character set, the character '0' is associated with decimal 48; the character 'B' is associated with decimal 66; and the character '{' is associated with decimal 123. These values are indicated in the ASCII character set in the *Programmer's Handbook*. The integer associated with the value of a character variable can be output in decimal form by a printf() call. This is done by specifying the %d conversion specification in the control string. The value 66 would be output by the printf() call

```
printf("%d", 'B');
```

Any variable of type char or int can also be displayed in an octal representation by specifying a %o in the conversion specification, or in hexadecimal with a %x conversion specification. The statements

```
printf( "B is character '%c', decimal %d,",'B','B' );
printf( " octal %o, and hexadecimal %x.\n", 'B','B' );
```

would output the following:

```
B is character 'B', decimal 66, octal 102, and hexadecimal 42.
```

The key thing to remember is that the computer actually stores any integer (including a value of type char) in a binary representation consisting of 0s and 1s. When an integer is output, it can be converted from this binary form to a form that is more easily read by a human being. The programmer specifies the desired form with the conversion specification in the printf() control string. The program charvar.c gives examples of this.

---

1. This is also true for character sets other than ASCII. There will be a one-to-one correspondence between some subset of the integers and the elements of the character set. However, the specific subset of the integers, the number of characters, the actual characters, and the correspondence may differ. The use of an ASCII character set will be assumed in this text.

Example 3-3: charvar.c

```
/*               charvar.c
 *
 *   Synopsis    - Variables of type char and int are declared.
 *                 The sizeof() the char type is displayed.  Then
 *                 a value is assigned to each variable and
 *                 displayed with different conversion
 *                 specifications.
 *
 *   Objective   - Illustrates the relationship between type char
 *                 and type int and some of the different
 *                 conversion specifications with printf().
 */

/* Include Files */
#include <stdio.h>

void main( void )
{
    char    charvar;                                        /* Note 1 */
    int     intvar;
                                                            /* Note 2 */
    printf( "The sizeof type char is %d byte(s).\n\n",
                                        sizeof( char ) );

                                                            /* Note 3 */
    charvar = 'c';                                          /* Note 4 */

    printf( "charvar is the character %c.\n", charvar );
    printf( "It can be displayed in decimal as %d\n",charvar );
    printf( "in octal as %o or \n", charvar );
    printf( "in hexadecimal as %x.\n\n", charvar );

    intvar = 73;
    printf( "Intvar is the decimal integer, %d.\n", intvar );
    printf( "It can be written in hex, %x,\nor octal, %o, ",
                                        intvar, intvar );

                                                            /* Note 5 */
    printf( "or even treated as the character %c.\n",intvar );
}
```

Running the Program

```
The sizeof type char is 1 byte(s).

charvar is the character c.
It can be displayed in decimal as 99
in octal as 143 or
in hexadecimal as 63.

Intvar is the decimal integer, 73.
It can be written in hex, 49,
or octal, 111, or even treated as the character I.
```

An overview of charvar.c reveals a single function, main(). Two variables are declared, one of type int and one of type char. After a printf() call involving the sizeof() operator, the code sequence of an assignment statement followed by printf() calls appears twice.

Note 1: A variable of type char is declared. The name of the variable is charvar. The declaration consists of the keyword char, the variable name, and the terminating semicolon.

Note 2: The sizeof() operator is applied to type char. The parentheses are necessary when sizeof() is used with a type. The value sizeof(char) will probably be 1 because most computers use one byte to store a character.

Note 3: An assignment statement can be used to establish the value of charvar. The single quotes indicate to the compiler that the value is from the underlying character set.

Note 4: This note refers to the following three printf() calls. The first printf() call is used to print out the value of charvar. The only way in which this statement differs from the printf() calls we have seen previously is that the new conversion specification, %c, is used to indicate that the value should be output as a character. The next two printf() calls illustrate other conversions that can be used to output char values. They can be output in decimal, octal, or hexadecimal. Decimal is indicated with a %d conversion specification, as before; the conversion specification for octal is %o, and hexadecimal output is indicated with %x. The numerical value is the number associated with the character in the underlying character set.

Note 5: In this printf() call, the character associated with a 73 in the underlying character set is displayed. With the ASCII character set, an uppercase 'I' would be displayed in the indicated place in the sentence.

Learning Activities

10. What is the underlying character set for the C compiler on the computer system you are using? Get a chart for that character set so that you can answer the following questions. A chart for the ASCII character set appears in the *Programmer's Handbook* at the end of this text.

    a. What is the subset of the integers associated with the character set?

    b. How many bits would be needed to store the largest integer in the subset?

    c. How many characters are in the character set?

    d. Are the uppercase alphabetics contiguous in the character set? What integer is associated with 'A'? With 'B'? With each of the uppercase alphabetic characters?

    e. Answer the questions in part d for the lower-case alphabetic characters.

    f. Are the digits `'0'`, `'1'`, `'2'`,...`'9'` contiguous in the character set? What integers are associated with the digits?

11. a. Predict the values that will be displayed by charvar.c when the assignments to `charvar` and `intvar` are changed to assign the comma character to `charvar` and `52` to `intvar`.

    b. Check your values in part a by modifying the program and executing it.

12. Combine the declaration and initialization of `charvar` into one declaration statement with an initializer.

3.6 Unsigned Types

The types `int`, `long`, and `short` discussed previously allow both positive and negative values. However, some applications require only non-negative values. For these, C provides the types named `unsigned int`, `unsigned long int`, and `unsigned short int`.[1]

The `sizeof()` each of these types is the same as the related signed type; the possible bit patterns are also the same. It is only the interpretation of these bit patterns

---

1. The terms `signed` and `unsigned` also apply to type `char`; this is discussed in the next section.

that differs. The range of integers that can be represented with type `unsigned int` is

$$0, 1, 2, 3, \ldots, 2^m{-}1$$

where m is the total number of bits involved in the underlying type. For example, if an `int` variable is stored in 16 bits (2 bytes), then the range of values that can be represented by an `unsigned int` is

$$0, 1, 2, \ldots, 2^{16}{-}1 \quad \text{(0 to 65535)}$$

If a variable with type `long` is stored in 32 bits, then the range of values that can be represented by an `unsigned long int` is

$$0, 1, 2, \ldots, 2^{32}{-}1 \quad \text{(0 to 4294967295)}$$

The `unsigned` types in C offer a method for increasing the maximum size of an integer variable at the expense of disallowing any negative values. The range of `unsigned int` is not any larger than `int`. Rather, it is scaled up so that the minimum integer is 0 and the maximum integer is dependent upon the computer word size. The following table shows the minimum and maximum values for `unsigned int` on various computers.

Computer word size	Minimum unsigned int	Maximum unsigned int
16 bits	0	$2^{16}{-}1 = 65535$
32 bits	0	$2^{32}{-}1 = 4294967295$

The results of the arithmetic operations on the unsigned types also differ because the result is always interpreted as a value in this range. For example, if an `int` occupies 16 bits, the result of the operation `4 - 5` when stored in an `unsigned int` will be `65535` because the bit pattern for `-1` in a signed type (all ones) is identical to the largest value that can be represented with an unsigned type. The program unsigned.c in Example 3-4 addresses this phenomenon.

A variable of type `unsigned int` can be declared in two ways. The declarations

```
unsigned positive;
```

and

```
unsigned int positive;
```

both declare a variable named `positive` with type `unsigned int`. That is, the keyword `int` is optional. Similarly, a variable named `bigvalue` of type `unsigned long int` can be declared as either

```
unsigned long int bigvalue;
```

or

```
unsigned long bigvalue;
```

Declarations of variables of type `unsigned short int` follow the same pattern.

The conversion specification used with `printf()` and `scanf()` for an unsigned decimal is `%u`. It tells the `printf()` and `scanf()` functions to convert the value to or from unsigned decimal. The `%x` and the `%o` conversion specifications indicate *unsigned* conversion to hexadecimal and octal, respectively. The `%u` conversion specification is used in Example 3-4.

In that example, a field width specifier is used with the conversion specifications in the calls to `printf()`. For example, in the conversion specification

```
%6d
```

the 6 designates a minimum field width. The value to be output will still be converted to a sequence of decimal digits; the minimum field width of 6 ensures that the output will be right justified in at least 6 spaces. The blank character will be used to pad on the left. Consider the following example,

```
printf( "\n1234567890" );
printf( "\n%6d\n", 3 );
```

The output will appear as follows:

```
1234567890
     3
```

As can be seen from Example 3.4, the minimum field width is useful in aligning output. This is a *minimum* field width since `printf()` will use more space than designated if more space is necessary to output an expression. More examples of field width are given in Section 3.9 when the output of floating point values is discussed.

In Example 3.4, error conditions are created by assigning values to variables that are not in the range of the type of the variable. Some compilers will issue a warning message because of this; others will not. In either case, the program should execute.

Example 3-4: unsigned.c

```
/*              unsigned.c
 *
 *   Synopsis    - Variables of types unsigned int and int are
 *                 declared. The same values are assigned to each
 *                 and the values are displayed by calls to
 *                 printf().
 *
 *   Objective   - To illustrate some of the differences between
 *                 the types unsigned int and int.
```

```
 */

/* Include Files */
#include <stdio.h>

void main( void )
{
    unsigned positive;                                      /* Note 1 */
    int signedvar;

    printf( "Unsigned\t  Signed\n" );
    printf( "--------\t  ------\n" );

    positive  = 65535;                                      /* Note 2 */
    signedvar = 65535;
                                                            /* Note 3 */
    printf( "  %6u\t  %6d\n", positive, signedvar );

    positive  *= 2;                                         /* Note 4 */
    signedvar *= 2;
                                                            /* Note 3 */
    printf( "  %6u\t  %6d\n", positive, signedvar );

    positive  += 3;                                         /* Note 5 */
    signedvar += 3;
                                                            /* Note 3 */
    printf( "  %6u\t  %6d\n", positive, signedvar );

    positive  = 40000;                                      /* Note 6 */
    signedvar = 40000;
                                                            /* Note 3 */
    printf( "  %6u\t  %6d\n", positive, signedvar );

    positive  = 4 - 5;                                      /* Note 7 */
    signedvar = 4 - 5;
                                                            /* Note 3 */
    printf( "  %6u\t  %6d\n", positive, signedvar );
}
```

In this program, two variables are declared, one of type int and one of type unsigned int. The same value is assigned to each variable and the value is displayed by a call to printf(), using the %u conversion specification for the unsigned int and the %d conversion specification for the int. This is repeated so that five values for each variable are output.

Note 1: The variable `positive` of type `unsigned int` is declared. The keyword `int` is optional. That is, the declaration could also have read

    unsigned int positive;

Note 2: The value `65535` is assigned to both variables. This value is the largest value that can be represented with 16 bits and an unsigned type. Note that this program will compile on most C compilers even though the value could be out of range for the variable `signedvar`. The following `printf()` call outputs both values. The `%u` conversion specification is used for the `unsigned int`.

Note 3: In all the calls to `printf()`, the control string is

    " %6u\t   %6d\n"

The conversion specification `%6u` corresponds to the parameter `positive`. The `u` causes conversion of the `unsigned` type. The `6` will cause the output of this quantity to occupy at least 6 spaces. In these `printf()` calls, the output of values of `positive` should all be aligned under the heading "Unsigned". Similarly, the conversion specification `%6d` causes the output of the variable `signedvar` to align under the heading "Signed". The tab characters ('`\t`') are also useful in aligning output.

Note 4: The values of both variables are multiplied by 2. The result of the arithmetic for the unsigned type is always the remainder when the true arithmetic result is divided by 2^m. (m is the total number of bits used to store an `unsigned int`.) If 16 bits are used to store an `int` value, there would be an overflow error on both variables.

Note 5: The value 3 is added to both values. Again, the arithmetic with the unsigned type is done modulo 2^m. That is, whenever an arithmetic result exceeds 2^m-1, the counting starts at 0 again. For example, if m = 16, the following relations hold for unsigned quantities:

    65534 + 1 = 65535 but 65535 + 1 = 0
    65535 + 3 = 2 and 2 * 65535 = 65534

Note 6: If an `int` is stored in 16 bits, this value, `40000`, will be beyond the largest value that an `int` can correctly store but in the middle of the correct range for an `unsigned int`.

Note 7: These assignment statements attempt to store a negative value in both variables. The value in the `unsigned int` will be interpreted as positive. When using `unsigned int` types, be aware that certain arithmetic operations with positive integers may yield negative results. Unless this is a planned outcome, these results will be incorrectly interpreted within the program.

Learning Activities

13.   Calculate the maximum integer value that can be stored in an `unsigned int` on your computer system. This value will be $2^m - 1$ where m is the number of bits used to store an integer.

14. Modify the program unsigned.c by replacing the 65535 with the value you calculated in part 1 and replacing the 40000 with any value between $2^{m-1} - 1$ and $2^m - 1$. Note that if $m = 16$ for your computer system, you will not have to make any modifications.

15. Predict the output of unsigned.c with the modifications you made in Learning Activity 14.

16. Execute the modified version of unsigned.c. If the results are different from your prediction, find out why and correct your understanding.

17. a. Modify unsigned.c again by declaring variables of type long and unsigned long. Test the range of long and unsigned long by having appropriate values displayed.

    b. Repeat part a. with types short and unsigned short.

18. Experiment with the program unsigned.c to help understand the concept of a minimum field width.

    a. Change the field width specifier in the first printf() call to 2. Compile and execute the program again and see how the spacing of the output changes.

    b. Change the field width specifier to 5, compile and run the program again.

    c. If you are still having trouble with the concept of a minimum field width, experiment with other values for the field width specifier.

3.7 ANSI C and Integer Types

The keyword signed is new in ANSI C. It is generally used with type char since the char type can be implemented as a signed type on some computer systems and an unsigned type on others. With the addition of the keyword signed, ANSI C provides for both signed char and unsigned char types on all systems. The declaration

```
signed char charvar;
```

declares a variable of type signed char with the name charvar. This use ensures that this char variable is signed.

The keyword signed can also be used in combination with short, int, and long in a declaration, but since those types are signed by default, it is unnecessary. The types signed short, signed int, and signed long are just other names for types short, int, and long, respectively.

The ANSI standards for C specify minimal ranges that must be represented by each of the integral types. The ranges are specified below.

Integral type		**Guaranteed range (it may be wider)**
signed	char	-127 to 127
unsigned	char	0 to 255
signed	short	-32767 to 32767
unsigned	short	0 to 65535
signed	int	-32767 to 32767
unsigned	int	0 to 65535
signed	long	-2147483647 to 2147483647
unsigned	long	0 to 4294967295

However, an implementation of C may enlarge these ranges. The actual maximum and minimum values that can be represented for each of the integral types in an implementation of ANSI C is recorded in a set of preprocessor-defined constants. These constants are declared in a header file named limits.h. Some of the constants and the corresponding meanings are listed below.

CHAR_BIT	Number of bits in a	char
CHAR_MAX	Maximum value for type	char
CHAR_MIN	Minimum value for type	char
SCHAR_MAX	Maximum value for type	signed char
SCHAR_MIN	Minimum value for type	signed char
UCHAR_MAX	Maximum value for type	unsigned char
SHRT_MAX	Maximum value for type	short int
SHRT_MIN	Minimum value for type	short int
USHRT_MAX	Maximum value for type	unsigned short int
INT_MAX	Maximum value for type	int
INT_MIN	Minimum value for type	int
UINT_MAX	Maximum value for type	unsigned int
LONG_MAX	Maximum value for type	long int
LONG_MIN	Minimum value for type	long int
ULONG_MAX	Maximum value for type	unsigned long int

Note that the minimum value that can be represented in any of the unsigned types is 0; it will not vary between implementations. The program limits.c in Example 3-5 displays the values of some of the constants in that file. There are no new language elements in this program. The output of this program is given. The program was executed on a computer with 2 byte (16 bit) words. The output may be different on your computer system.

Example 3-5: limits.c

```c
/*              limits.c
 *
 *    Synopsis   - Displays values of some constants in limits.h.
 *
 *    Objective  - To illustrate limits.h and the relative ranges
 *                 of values that can be represented with the
 *                 integral types.
 */

/* Include Files */
#include <stdio.h>
#include <limits.h>

void main( void )
{
     printf( "Contents of limits.h\n\n" );
     printf( "Constant\t     Values\n" );
     printf( "--------\t     ------\n" );

     printf( "CHAR_BIT\t%11d\n", CHAR_BIT );
     printf( "CHAR_MAX\t%11d\nCHAR_MIN\t%11d\n", CHAR_MAX,
                                      CHAR_MIN );
     printf( "SCHAR_MAX\t%11d\nSCHAR_MIN\t%11d\n", SCHAR_MAX,
                                      SCHAR_MIN );

     printf( "INT_MAX \t%11d\nINT_MIN \t%11d\n", INT_MAX,
                                      INT_MIN );
     printf( "LONG_MAX\t%11ld\nLONG_MIN\t%11ld\n", LONG_MAX,
                                      LONG_MIN );
     printf( "SHRT_MAX\t%11hd\nSHRT_MIN\t%11hd\n", SHRT_MAX,
                                      SHRT_MIN );

     printf( "UCHAR_MAX\t%11u\nUINT_MAX\t%11u\n", UCHAR_MAX,
                                      UINT_MAX );
     printf( "ULONG_MAX\t%11lu\nUSHRT_MAX\t%11u\n", ULONG_MAX,
                                      USHRT_MAX );
}
```

Running the Program

```
Contents of limits.h

Constant              Values
--------              ------
CHAR_BIT                   8
CHAR_MAX                 127
CHAR_MIN                -128
SCHAR_MAX                127
SCHAR_MIN               -128
INT_MAX                32767
INT_MIN               -32768
LONG_MAX          2147483647
LONG_MIN         -2147483648
SHRT_MAX               32767
SHRT_MIN              -32768
UCHAR_MAX                255
UINT_MAX               65535
ULONG_MAX         4294967295
USHRT_MAX              65535
```

Learning Activities

19.   If your compiler conforms to the ANSI C standards, compile and execute the program limits.c. Inspect the output for any surprises. Reconcile the results with the results of the other programs in this section (especially with the output from ints.c).

20.   If your compiler conforms to the ANSI C standards, inspect a copy of the header file limits.h to see the other values that are declared in that file.

An Example

The program factors.c in Example 3-6 applies some of the concepts we have been discussing. This program will list all prime factors of an integer greater than 2. In the execution of this program that appears below, the user input is **12**. It is printed in **boldface**.

Example 3-6: factors.c

```
/*              factors.c
 *
 *    Synopsis   - Prompts for and accepts input of an integer
 *                 that is greater than 2. Displays the prime
 *                 factors of that integer
 *
 *    Objective  - An example of a useful working program.
 */


/* Include Files */
#include <stdio.h>

void main( void )
{
     unsigned number, factor;        /* number will store the
                                      * input, and factor
                                      * drives the for loop to
                                      * find the factors.
                                      */

     printf( "This program will print the prime factors\n" );
     printf( "of an integer that is greater than 2.\n\n" );

     /* Prompt for and input the integer. */
     printf( "Enter an integer that is greater than 2 : " );
     scanf( "%u", &number );

     printf( "Prime factors of %d are ", number );
     for ( factor = 2; factor <= number; factor++ )

       /* if factor divides number evenly */
       if ( ! ( number % factor ) ) {

            /* output factor */
            printf( "%d " , factor );
            /* take the factor out of number */
            number /= factor;

            /* decrement factor so that it can test
             * for a repeated factor.
             */
```

```
            factor--;
        }
    printf( "\n" );
}
```

 Running the Program

```
This program will print the prime factors
of an integer that is greater than 2.

Enter an integer that is greater than 2 : 12
Prime factors of 12 are 2 2 3
```

This program contains a single function, `main()`. Calls to `printf()` display the purpose of the program and prompt for input. After input with `scanf()`, the prime factors are extracted with a `for` loop. To find the factors of `number`, each of the integers between 2 and `number` is tested to see if it divides `number` evenly. The test (`! (number % factor)`) is interpreted as follows: 1) The remainder when `number` is divided by `factor` is calculated and 2) the logical negation of that value is taken.

Case 1: If `factor` divides `number` evenly, the expression `(number % factor)` is zero, and the expression `! (number % factor)` has the value 1 (true).

Case 2: If `factor` does not divide `number` evenly, then the test expression (`! (number % factor)`) evaluates to 0 (false).

When a `factor` is found, it is output, the `factor` is divided out of `number`, and `factor` is decremented so that the same `factor` will be tested again in the `for` loop. In this way, repeated factors are found.

Learning Activities

21. a. Test factors.c with different inputs. What happens if the input is negative?

     b. If an error occurred with the input of a negative number, try to modify the program to handle the error properly.

22. Modify factors.c so that the output has the form

         12 = 2 * 2 * 3;

23. Note that factors.c tests all integers less than the input number as

possible factors. This is inefficient since not all integers tested are prime. In particular, the only even prime is 2.

a. Modify the program so that the only even number tested is 2.

b. Think about the amount of work a program would have to do to be sure that it was only testing primes as factors. Do you think this would be an increase or decrease in efficiency over factors.c?

3.8 If There's Time or Need: Bit Operations on the Integer Types

A special set of operations, the bit operations, can be used on the integer types. They operate on the bit pattern of the stored values. The bit operations are useful when we need to test or change specific bits in an integer quantity; this type of programming commonly occurs in operating system programming. The bit operations are:

~	bitwise-negation
>>	shift right
<<	shift left
&	bitwise-and
^	bitwise-xor
¦	bitwise-or

Before looking at a program, we will discuss examples of the bit operations. For the examples, assume that the short type occupies 16 bits of storage and that the following declarations have been made:

```
short shortvar1,  shortvar2;
char  charvar1,   charvar2;
```

The negation operator, ~ (a tilde), is a unary operator; it operates on the bit pattern of an integer quantity by replacing all the 0 bits by 1 and all of the 1 bits by 0. The syntax for the negation operator is

```
~expression
```

where the expression must have one of the integer types. For example, suppose shortvar1 is a variable of type short and has the value 5, its bit pattern (assuming 16 bits for type short) is

0	0	0	0	0	0	0	0	0	0	0	0	0	1	0	1

The bitwise-negation of `shortvar1` is denoted `~shortvar1` and has the following bit pattern:

1	1	1	1	1	1	1	1	1	1	1	1	1	0	1	0

Its value would be `-6` in signed decimal format or `fffa` in unsigned hexadecimal format.

As another example assume that `charvar1` has the value `'F'` (decimal 70). In the ASCII character set, its bit pattern is

0	1	0	0	0	1	1	0

The bit pattern of `~charvar1` is

1	0	1	1	1	0	0	1

Its value is outside the ASCII range of 0 to 127.

The bitwise-and, `&`, is a binary operator. It combines the bit patterns of two quantities of the integer types to form a third bit pattern. Its syntax is

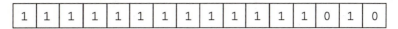

```
expression1 & expression2
```

The corresponding bits of each pattern are combined under the following rules: If both bits are 1, the corresponding bit in the result is 1; otherwise, the corresponding bit in the result is 0. The rules are summarized in the table below.

i^{th} bit in expression1	i^{th} bit in expression2	i^{th} bit in expression1 & expression2
1	1	1
1	0	0
0	1	0
0	0	0

For example, assume that `shortvar1` has value `23` and `shortvar2` has value `456`. Their bit patterns are

shortvar1
0	0	0	0	0	0	0	0	0	0	0	1	0	1	1	1

shortvar2
0	0	0	0	0	0	0	1	1	1	0	0	1	0	0	0

The bit pattern of the expression `shortvar1 & shortvar2` is

shortvar1 & shortvar2 | 0 | 0 | 0 | 0 | 0 | 0 | 0 | 0 | 0 | 0 | 0 | 0 | 0 | 0 | 0 | 0 |

and its value is 0.

Suppose `charvar1` is `'a'` and `charvar2` is `'5'`. The associated bit patterns for the ASCII character set are

charvar1 | 0 | 1 | 1 | 0 | 0 | 0 | 0 | 1 |

charvar2 | 0 | 0 | 1 | 1 | 0 | 1 | 0 | 1 |

The bit pattern for `charvar1 & charvar2` is

charvar1 & charvar2 | 0 | 0 | 1 | 0 | 0 | 0 | 0 | 1 |

This is the bit pattern for the character `'!'` in the ASCII character set.

The bitwise-or, `|`, is also a binary operation. It operates on two bit patterns to form a third. The syntax for the bitwise-or is

```
expression1 | expression2
```

A bit in the resultant pattern is a 1 if either of the corresponding bits in the operands is a 1; if both of the corresponding bits in the operand are 0, the bit in the result is 0. This rule is reflected in the table below.

i^{th} bit in expression1	i^{th} bit in expression2	i^{th} bit in expression1 | expression2
1	1	1
1	0	1
0	1	1
0	0	0

Consider the bitwise-or applied to the variables `shortvar1` and `shortvar2` with values 23 and 456 respectively. The bit patterns for `shortvar1`, `shortvar2` and `shortvar1 | shortvar2` are shown below.

shortvar1	0	0	0	0	0	0	0	0	0	0	0	1	0	1	1	1

shortvar2	0	0	0	0	0	0	0	1	1	1	0	0	1	0	0	0

shortvar1 ¦ shortvar2	0	0	0	0	0	0	0	1	1	1	0	1	1	1	1	1

The decimal value of shortvar1 ¦ shortvar2 is 479.

The next bit operation is the bitwise-xor, ^, a carat. An xor expression combines two other expressions and has the syntax

```
expression1 ^ expression2
```

It assigns 1 to the resultant bit if the corresponding bits in the two operands are different and 0 if they are the same. The rule is condensed in the table below.

i^{th} bit in expression1	i^{th} bit in expression2	i^{th} bit in expression1 ^ expression2
1	1	0
1	0	1
0	1	1
0	0	0

For example, consider the bitwise-xor applied to charvar1 and charvar2 with the values 'a' and '5' respectively. The bit patterns for charvar1, charvar2, and charvar1 ^ charvar2 are presented below.

charvar1	0	1	1	0	0	0	0	1

charvar2	0	0	1	1	0	1	0	1

charvar1 ^ charvar2	0	1	0	1	0	1	0	0

The bit pattern in charvar1 ^ charvar2 represents the character 'T'.

The effect of all the binary bitwise operations on any bit x is summarized in the table below.

Operation on the bit x	Result
0 | x	x
1 | x	1
0 & x	0
1 & x	x
0 ^ x	x
1 ^ x	~x (the negation of x)

The right and left shifts are also binary operations, but they work differently. The syntax for the right shift is

```
expression1 >> expression2
```

and the syntax for the left shift is

```
expression1 << expression2
```

where both `expression1` and `expression2` must have an integer type. The expression on the right, `expression2`, represents the number of bits that `expression1` is to be shifted; it must be non-negative. For example, assume that `shortvar1` has the value 1. The bit pattern is

shortvar1 | 0 | 0 | 0 | 0 | 0 | 0 | 0 | 0 | 0 | 0 | 0 | 0 | 0 | 0 | 0 | 1 |

The bit patterns and values of several shifts of `shortvar1` are presented below.

Shift	Bit pattern	Value
shortvar1 << 1	0 0 0 0 0 0 0 0 0 0 0 0 0 0 1 0	2
shortvar1 << 2	0 0 0 0 0 0 0 0 0 0 0 0 0 1 0 0	4
shortvar1 << 3	0 0 0 0 0 0 0 0 0 0 0 0 1 0 0 0	8
shortvar1 << 5	0 0 0 0 0 0 0 0 0 0 1 0 0 0 0 0	32
shortvar1 << 7	0 0 0 0 0 0 0 0 1 0 0 0 0 0 0 0	128

Inspecting the patterns and values above, we can see that each time `shortvar1` is shifted left by one bit the resultant value is multiplied by 2. This pattern does not hold when ones are shifted off the left edge of the bit pattern or if a one is shifted into the leftmost bit in a signed quantity. Similarly, each right shift of `shortvar1` divides its value by 2 (truncating integer division) until the value becomes zero.

As another example, suppose that `shortvar2` has the value `10,549`, which has the corresponding bit pattern

shortvar2	0	0	1	0	1	0	0	1	0	0	1	1	0	1	0	1

The following shifts have the illustrated results.

Shift	Bit pattern	Value
shortvar2 >> 1	0 0 0 1 0 1 0 0 1 0 0 1 1 0 1 0	5274
shortvar2 >> 3	0 0 0 0 0 1 0 1 0 0 1 0 0 1 1 0	1318
shortvar2 << 1	0 1 0 1 0 0 1 0 0 1 1 0 1 0 1 0	21098
shortvar2 << 3	0 1 0 0 1 0 0 1 1 0 1 0 1 0 0 0	18856

Note that in a right shift, any 1s at the right end of the bit pattern are shifted off the end and discarded. The bits at the left end of the word are filled in with 0s. Similarly, in a left shift, the bits at the left end of the word are shifted out and discarded. The bits at the right end of the word become 0s. The shifting is done to the bit patterns; the interpretation of those bit patterns depends on the type of the expression. For example, if a 1 is shifted into the leftmost bit, a previously positive expression could become negative. The interpretation of right shifts of negative expressions could vary with each implementation. The meaning is not specified by the language.

The program in Example 3-7 illustrates the bit operations. It also illustrates hexadecimal initialization of variables of type `unsigned int`. To indicate an integer in hexadecimal within C source code, it is only necessary to begin the integer with the characters `0x` or `0X` (a zero followed by an `'x'` or `'X'`). The `0x` signifies to the compiler and reader that the following value is hexadecimal and will be written using the hexadecimal digits `0, 1, 2, . . . , 9, a, b, c, d, e, f`. The hexadecimal digits `0, 1, 2, . . . , 9, A, B, C, D, E, F` are used after a leading `0X`. An octal representation of an integer can be indicated by starting the number with a leading `0`. For example, the following are different representations of equivalent values that could be used in a C source code program.

Decimal	Hexadecimal	Octal
23	0x17	027

In the following program, the variables of type `unsigned int` are initialized using a hexadecimal representation. Then the results of several combinations of the bit operations are displayed.

Example 3-7: bitop.c

```
/*              bitop.c
 *
 *   Synopsis   - Displays the results of bit operations on
```

```
*                   variables of type unsigned int.
*
*    Objective  - Illustrates operations on bits.
*/

/* Include Files */
#include <stdio.h>

void main( void )
{
    unsigned int w1, w2, w3;                              /* Note 1 */

    w1 = 0x523;                                           /* Note 2 */
    w2 = 0x746;
    w3 = 0x13a;

    printf( "w1 & w2 = %x\n", w1&w2 );                    /* Note 3 */
    printf( "w1 ¦ w2 = %x\n", w1¦w2 );                    /* Note 4 */
    printf( "w1 ^ w2 = %x\n", w1^w2 );                    /* Note 5 */
    printf( "~w1 = %x\n", ~w1 );                          /* Note 6 */

                                                          /* Note 7 */
    printf( "w1 ¦ ( ~w1 & w3 ) = %x\n", w1 ¦ ( ~w2 & w3 ) );
    printf( "~( ~w1 ¦ ~w3 ) = %x\n", ~( ~w1 ¦ ~w3 ) );

    w1 ^= w2;                                             /* Note 8 */
    printf( "w1 is %x, w2 is %x\n", w1, w2 );

    /*  Shifting bits in a word */
    w1 = 0x1;
    w2 = 0x422;
    w1 = w1 << 3;                                         /* Note 9 */
    w2 <<= 1;                                             /* Note 10 */
    printf( "w1 = %x\t w2 = %x\n", w1, w2 );
    printf( "w2 >> 2 is %x.\n", w2 >> 2  );               /* Note 11 */
}
```

 Running the Program

```
w1 & w2 = 502
w1 ¦ w2 = 767
w1 ^ w2 = 265
~w1 = fadc
w1 ¦ ( ~w1 & w3 ) = 53b
```

```
~( ~w1 ¦ ~w3 ) = 122
w1 is 265, w2 is 746
w1 = 8 w2 = 844
w2 >> 2 is 211.
```

A single function named `main()` contains variable declarations and initializations. The executable code consists of assignment statements and calls to `printf()`.

Note 1: The variables have been declared as type `unsigned int` to ensure that each of the operations is defined. This also will avoid values flipping between positive and negative when the high bit is changed by a bit operation.

Note 2: These three statements initialize the variables. The values are written as hexadecimal constants, signified by the `0x` before the value. Constant values can be written as octal constants by including a leading `0` (zero). For example, `523` is a decimal constant in C, `0523` is an octal constant, and `0x523` is a hexadecimal constant. In this program, hexadecimal is used since each hexadecimal digit translates to four bits. The effect of the bit operations will be easy to calculate.

Note 3: The value of the bitwise-and (`&`) of `w1` and `w2` is displayed in hexadecimal by this call to `printf()`.

Note 4: This statement displays the hexadecimal representation of the bitwise-or (`¦`) of the same two values.

Note 5: The bitwise-xor (`^`) with `w1` and `w2` is illustrated here.

Note 6: The bitwise-negation takes a single operand. The value of the bitwise-negation of `w1` is displayed in hexadecimal.

Note 7: The next two statements illustrate some combinations of the bit operations. In these statements, the parentheses help specify the order of evaluation. The Precedence Chart in the *Programmer's Handbook* states the precedence of the bitwise operators relative to the other C operators.

Note 8: The bitwise operators `&`, `^`, and `¦` can be used in compound assignment statements also. The given statement is equivalent to

```
w1 = w1 ^ w2
```

Note 9: The value of `w1` is shifted left by three bits. Notice that a left shift of one bit multiplies an unsigned value by 2 unless overflow occurs. Shifting by two bits multiplies this value by 4, and shifting by three bits multiplies the value by 8.

Note 10: The shift operators can also be used with compound assignment. This statement shifts the bits in `w2` one position to the left.

Note 11: The `>>` operator is the right shift. Here the result of shifting `w2` to the right two bits is displayed. Note that each shift to the right by one bit effects truncating division by two on an unsigned value until the value reaches zero. The value of `w2 / 4` is displayed by this statement.

> ## *Learning Activities*
>
> 24.   a. In bitop.c, rewrite the statement associated with **Note 9** as a compound assignment.
>
>   b. Write a statement using the bit operations that would multiply w3 by 64.
>
> 25.   Write a short program that tests the validity of all the examples presented in this section before bitop.c.

Precedence of Bitwise Operators

The precedence of the bitwise operators is as follows: The bitwise-negation has the highest precedence. The shifts are next in precedence level, followed by the bitwise-and, the bitwise-xor, and finally the bitwise-or. They associate from left to right. The precedence of these operators in comparison with the other C operators is illustrated in the *Programmer's Handbook*. However, if the expression is at all complicated, it is best to use parentheses to avoid reader confusion.

Using Masks

One common use of the bitwise operations is in working with masks. For example, the binary representation of the integer 8 in 16 bits is

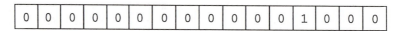

That is, the fourth bit is 1 and all the rest are 0. The value 8 can be used to test the fourth bit of an integer variable. For example,

```
shortvar1 & 8
```

will be 0 (false) if the fourth bit of shortvar1 is 0 and nonzero (true) if the fourth bit is 1. This type of expression can be used as the expression to be tested in a conditional statement or a loop.

The value 8 can also be used to set the fourth bit in any expression. The expression

```
shortvar1 | 8
```

is guaranteed to have a 1 in the fourth bit. The fourth bit of shortvar1 can be set using that expression in conjunction with an assignment statement as in

```
shortvar1 = shortvar1 | 8;
```

or more simply with the compound assignment statement

```
shortvar1 |= 8;
```

As an example of the practical use of the bitwise operations, consider a word processing package that uses the ASCII character set and stores each character in a single byte. There are 128 ASCII characters, ranging from 0 to 127, and these can be represented in the low order 7 bits of a byte. The eighth (high order) bit of each byte can be used to keep track of the program's formatting options. This is done by using the bit patterns with a 1 in the eighth bit to depict the different options for formatting. For example, the value 128, with bit pattern

1	0	0	0	0	0	0	0

might be used to toggle underlining. The value 129 with bit pattern

1	0	0	0	0	0	0	1

might be used to toggle bold print. The value 141 might be used to indicate a carriage return inserted by the word processing program rather than by the author; this value differs from the usual carriage return in the ASCII character set only by the eighth bit being set. The value 138 might play the same role for the linefeed character. If another program, like one to list the file at the terminal, needs to access the information in this file, the other program will not understand the word processor's special use of the eighth bit. Some of these special bytes need to be removed and some of them need to have the eighth bit reset to 0.

The program listit.c in Example 3-8 is a filter that will delete any byte in its input with the eighth bit set to 1, with the exception of the values 138 (the word processor's version of the line feed character) and 141 (its version of a carriage return). For these exceptional values, the program will simply set the eighth bit to 0. The program is written as a filter; for lengthy input, it can be executed with input redirection from an input file. If input redirection is not available on your computer system, you will probably test the program with short segments of input.

Example 3-8: listit.c

```
/*                      listit.c
 *
 *   Synopsis    - Masks out the high bit on characters
 *                 WP_LINEFEED and WP_CARRETURN and deletes other
 *                 characters with the high bit set while copying
 *                 input to output.
```

```
 *
 *    Objective  - Illustrates use of masks with bit operations.
 */

/*   Include Files */
#include <stdio.h>

/* Constant Declarations */
#define HIGHBIT         128                              /* Note 1 */
#define NOHIGHBIT       127
#define WP_LINEFEED     138
#define WP_CARRETURN    141
void main( void )
{
    int iochar;

    while ( ( iochar = getchar() ) != EOF ) {
        if ( HIGHBIT & iochar ) {                        /* Note 2 */
            if ( ( iochar == WP_LINEFEED ) ||
                 ( iochar == WP_CARRETURN ) )
                                                         /* Note 3 */
                putchar( iochar & NOHIGHBIT );
        }                                                /* Note 4 */
        else
            putchar( iochar );
    }
}
```

Several preprocessor constants are defined. The function main() consists of a single while loop that will read terminal input character by character until end-of-file is sensed. The body of the while loop contains a single if-else statement. The statement associated with the if is another if statement.

Note 1: The preprocessor constant HIGHBIT has the following bit pattern:

1	0	0	0	0	0	0	0

That is, the first bit is 1 and all other bits are 0. This will be used to test a byte to see if the high bit is 1. The preprocessor constant NOHIGHBIT has a 0 in the high bit and all the other bits are 1. That is, it has the bit pattern

0	1	1	1	1	1	1	1

NOHIGHBIT will be used with & to set the high bit to 0. The next two preprocessor constants define the exceptional values discussed above.

Note 2: The expression (HIGHBIT & iochar) will have a nonzero value when iochar has its high bit set and 0 otherwise. This is an example of masking. The lower bits have been masked out.

Note 3: The high bit will be 0 in the expression NOHIGHBIT & iochar since the high bit in NOHIGHBIT is 0. However, the lower seven bits will be identical to those in iochar. In this expression, the high bit of iochar was masked out; the low bits were unchanged.

Note 4: This brace delimits the end of a block that was opened on the line marked by /* **Note 2** */. There is a single if statement inside this block. Note that the braces are necessary in this case to insure correct execution of the program. Without them, the following else would be paired with the closest if.

Learning Activities

26. What would be the output (if any) when each of the bytes whose bit patterns appear below is input to listit.c?

Bit pattern								**Output**

| 1 | 0 | 0 | 0 | 1 | 0 | 1 | 0 | _____

| 0 | 1 | 1 | 0 | 1 | 0 | 0 | 0 | _____

| 1 | 1 | 1 | 1 | 0 | 1 | 0 | 0 | _____

| 1 | 0 | 0 | 0 | 1 | 1 | 0 | 1 | _____

27. If the braces on the lines marked by /* **Note 2** */ and /* **Note 4** */ in listit.c were omitted, give the output of the modified program for the same four bytes.

28. If your system can do input and output redirection, create a file with the four bytes above (you might have to write a program to create the file) and run both versions of the program to check your answers.

29. Suppose that MASK is a preprocessor constant defined by

        #define MASK   0x7c

and that iochar is of type int.

a. What is the bit pattern for MASK?

b. Using the value from part a, write the value of the bits that are determined in the expressions below. Put a question mark for each bit that depends on the value of iochar. The first two bits in the first expression have been done for you.

Expression	Bits
MASK ¦ iochar ? 1	__ __ __ __ __ __
MASK & iochar	__ __ __ __ __ __ __ __

3.9 Floating Point Types

Values like 2.5, 3.14159, 2.467e+002, 4.0, and 2.718 are known as floating point values in C. These values may have a nonzero fractional part. The representations, 2.5, 3.14159, 4.0, and 2.718 are expressed in decimal notation. The representation 2.467e+002 is an exponential representation that is equivalent to 246.7. The number after the 'e' indicates the number of places that the decimal point must be moved to represent the number in decimal notation. As other examples,

```
2.954200e+01   is the same as 29.542
3.04215e-0003  is the same as .00304215
```

Floating point numbers can be used as constants or stored in variables of the appropriate type. An example of a preprocessor directive to declare a floating point constant is

```
#define PI 3.14159
```

C provides the types float, double, and long double to store floating point values as variables. The difference between the types deals with the *precision* of a floating point number (the number of digits to the right of the decimal point that are stored). The type float is used for single-precision floating point numbers. The type double is for double-precision floating point numbers. The type long double is for extra precision; this type has been added to the C language by the ANSI standards. The method of storing floating point numbers and the actual number of decimal places stored depends on the underlying hardware. Therefore, it could be different with different computers.

Not all of the real numbers can be represented with the floating point types. Each floating point type represents certain real numbers within a certain range. The actual range and the numbers that can be represented may vary with the implementation, but the ANSI standards guarantee that the numbers that can be represented with type float form a subset of those that can be represented with type double, and those that can be represented with type double form a subset of those that can be represented with type long double.

By default a floating point constant (like 123.4567) that appears in a C program will be interpreted by the compiler as type double. To specify a constant of type float, an f or F must be appended to the constant as in 123.4567f. To specify a constant of type long double, an L or l should be appended. For example, `123.4567L` would have type `long double`.

The ANSI C compilers supply a header file named float.h that contains implementation-dependent information about the range of each type of floating point variable. The information is similar to the information in the header file limits.h for the integer types.

A declaration of a variable of type `float` minimally consists of the keyword, `float`, followed by the variable name and terminated with a semicolon. For example,

```
float floatvar;
```

declares a variable of type `float` named `floatvar`. Similarly, the code segment

```
double doublevar;
long double ldvar;
```

declares two variables, one of type `double` named `doublevar` and one of type `long double` named `ldvar`.

Floating point variables can be initialized when they are declared in the same way as variables of the integer types. For example,

```
float floatvar = 2.765;
```

declares a variable named `floatvar` of type `float` with the initial value `2.765`.

Some of the operations that can be used with expressions of type `float`, `double`, or `long double` are the arithmetic operators (+, −, *, and /), the relational operators (==, !=, <, <=, >, and >=), and the logical operators (!, &&, and ||). The result of any of the arithmetic operators when applied to values of type `double` is another value of type `double`. However, when a relational or a logical operator is applied to a value of type `float` or `double`, the result will be of type `int`. Examples appear below. Assume that each of the numeric quantities has type `double`.

Expression	Value	Type
`2.5 + 5.7`	`8.2`	`double`
`2.5 <= 3.62`	1 (true)	`int`
`2.5 == 3.62`	0 (false)	`int`
`2.5 / 3.62`	0.6906	`double`
`2.5 && 3.62`	1 (true)	`int`
`2.5 ¦ 3.62`	not defined	Syntax error
`!2.5`	0 (false)	`int`
`!0`	1 (true)	`int`

These results are consistent with the interpretation of `0` as false and of `1` or any nonzero quantity as true. The expression `2.5 && 3.2` is true because both operands are interpreted as true. Also, `!2.5` is false because `2.5` is nonzero (true). The bit operations cannot be used with the floating point types.

Input and Output of Floating Point Values

The functions `printf()` and `scanf()` have conversion specifications for `float`, `double`, and `long double` values. The conversion specifications for `scanf()` are `%e`, `%f`, and `%g` for `float` values, `%le`, `%lf`, and `%lg` for `double` values, and `%Le`, `%Lf`, and `%Lg` for `long double` values.

With the `scanf()` function, all of these conversion specifications work for values in either a decimal or exponential format. The `'l'` is a *length specifier* that indicates that the corresponding argument will have type `double`; `'L'` is a length specifier that specifies the corresponding argument will have type `long double`. For example, the statements

```
scanf( "%f", &varname );
scanf( "%e", &varname );
```

expect to read a floating point value and expect the variable `varname` to have type `float`. The statements

```
scanf( "%lf", &varname );
scanf( "%le", &varname );
```

expect a floating point value also. The `'l'` (lowercase L) indicates that `varname` is expected to be of type `double`. In the statements,

```
scanf( "%Lf", &varname );
scanf( "%Le", &varname );
```

the variable `varname` is expected to have type `long double`. The `'L'` for type `long double` is new with ANSI C.

The conversion specifications for `printf()` indicate the desired format for the output. The conversion specifications `%f`, `%e`, `%E`, `%g`, and `%G` can be used with types `float` and `double`. The conversion specifications for type `long double` are `%Lf`, `%Le`, `%LE`, `%Lg`, and `%LG`. The effect of the conversion specifications `%f`, `%e`, and `%E` with `printf()` are illustrated in the following example. The value `3456.78` can be output in the following forms:

```
3456.780000    with the statement    printf("%f\n", 3456.78);
3.456780e+003  with the statement    printf("%e\n", 3456.78);
3.456780E+003  with the statement    printf("%E\n", 3456.78);
```

The `%f` conversion specification writes the floating point number in decimal form. The `%e` conversion specification writes the number in exponential notation; the number after the `e` in the exponential notation is the power of 10 that must be multiplied by the number before the `e` in that notation. The `%E` conversion is the same as the `%e` except that an uppercase `E` is used in the output.

The `%g` and `%G` conversion specifications may write the floating point value in either decimal or exponential notation. The `%G` specification would use an upper case `'E'` whenever the `%e` specification would display in exponential notation with a lower case `'e'`. Consult the *Programmer's Handbook* for details.

The field width and the precision (the number of digits to the right of the decimal point) for the display of a floating point number can also be controlled. In the examples above, the default field width and precision was used. The minimum field width (minimum number of spaces used to display a number) can be specified by placing a decimal integer between the '%' and the conversion specification. For example:

```
printf( "123456789012345678901234567890123\n" );
printf( "The number is %15f\n", 1.2 );
```

should give the following output:

```
123456789012345678901234567890
The number is         1.200000
```

The output of the string of digits is included only to illustrate that 15 spaces are used for the output of 1.2. The 15 spaces include the digits, the decimal point, a sign (if desired), and blank padding to the left of the number.

The precision is specified by a period followed by a decimal integer that indicates the number of decimal places to be displayed. For example, the statement

```
printf("123456789012345678901234567890123\n");
printf ("The number is %15.2f\n", 1.2);
```

should give the output below:

```
123456789012345678901234567890
The number is            1.20
```

The syntax for the integer and floating point conversions is illustrated in the program floatpt.c in Example 3-9. The declaration of a variable of each built-in floating point type is also illustrated. The operator sizeof() will return the number of bytes of storage used for the floating point types. This information is displayed first in this program.

Example 3-9: floatpt.c

```
/*                  floatpt.c
 *
 *    Synopsis   - The values of variables of type float, double,
 *                 and long double are initialized and displayed
 *                 in different formats by printf().  The sizeof()
 *                 each type is also displayed.
 *
 *    Objective  - Illustrates declaration, assignment, and
 *                 some of the output options with printf()
 *                 of floating point variables.
 */
```

```c
/* Include Files */
#include <stdio.h>

void main( void )
{
    float       floatvar;                                    /* Note 1 */
    double      doublevar;
    long double ldvar;
                                                             /* Note 2 */
    printf( "The number of bytes in a float is %d.\n",
                                    sizeof( float ) );
    printf( "The number of bytes in a double is %d.\n",
                                    sizeof( double ) );
    printf( "The number of bytes in a long double is %d.\n",
                                    sizeof( long double ) );

    floatvar = 65.328f;                                      /* Note 3 */
                                                             /* Note 4 */
    printf( "floatvar has the value %7.2f.\n", floatvar );
    printf( "It can also be written in the form %10.3e.\n",
                                            floatvar );
    printf( "It can also be written in the form %10.3E.\n",
                                            floatvar );
    printf( "It can also be written in the form %10.3g.\n",
                                            floatvar );

    doublevar = 1.2465e-5;                                   /* Note 5 */
    printf( "doublevar has the value %6.3f.\n", doublevar );
    printf( "It can also be written in the form %7.5e.\n",
                                            doublevar );
    printf( "It can also be written in the form %7.5E.\n",
                                            doublevar );
    printf( "It can also be written in the form %7.5g.\n",
                                            doublevar );

    ldvar = 584.365E+17L;                                    /* Note 6 */
                                                             /* Note 7 */
    printf( "ldvar has the value %7.2Lf.\n", ldvar );
    printf( "It can also be written in the form %10.3Le.\n",
                                            ldvar );
    printf( "It can also be written in the form %10.3LE.\n",
                                            ldvar );
    printf( "It can also be written in the form %10.3Lg.\n",
                                            ldvar );
}
```

The program consists of variable declarations, assignment statements, and calls to printf().

Note 1: Variables of type float, double, and long double are declared.

Note 2: The number of bytes occupied by each of the floating point types is output using the sizeof() operator.

Note 3: Decimal notation can be used in assignment statements to variables of type float, double, and long double. The floating point constant 65.328f has type float.

Note 4: The next four calls to printf() give examples of output using four of the different conversion specifications that are available for type float.

Note 5: Exponential form can also be used for a floating point constant. In this assignment statement, the floating point constant 1.2465e-5 has type double. It could be written as 0.000012465.

Note 6: In exponential notation, the exponent can be signified with either 'e' or 'E'. This floating point constant (584.365E-17L) has type long double.

Note 7: The conversion specifications in these printf() calls include the 'L' to indicate that the value is of type long double.

Learning Activities

30. Execute the program floatpt.c to become familiar with the notation used for floating point types.

31. If you have an ANSI C compiler,
    a. Inspect the header file float.h to see its predefined constants and their meaning.
    b. Write a program to output the values of these constants using printf() and the appropriate conversion specifications.
    c. Experiment with output and calculations with values like FLT_MAX + 1 to discover how out-of-range values are handled. Do they cause compile-time errors, runtime errors, or no noticeable errors?

Two Examples

The program slope.c in Example 3-10 pulls together concepts that we have already discussed to create a useful program. In this program, the user is asked to enter the x and y coordinates of two points. The program will then calculate the slope and the y-intercept of the line through the two points and output the equation of the line.

Example 3-10: slope.c

```
/*                    slope.c
 *
 *    Synopsis    - The user enters the coordinates of two points
 *                  and the program will display the equation of
 *                  the line through those two points.
 *
 *    Objective   - To illustrate the use of floating point types
 *                  in an applied program.
 */

/* Include Files */
#include <stdio.h>

/* Function Declarations */
void print_result( float, float, float, float );

void main( void )
{
    float x1, y1, x2, y2;                        /* The points */


    /*  Input the coordinates of the points */
    printf( "Enter the first point.\n" );
    printf( "x: " );
    scanf( "%f", &x1 );
    printf( "y: " );
    scanf( "%f", &y1 );

    printf( "Enter the second point.\n" );
    printf( "x: " );
    scanf( "%f", &x2 );
    printf( "y: " );
    scanf( "%f", &y2 );

    print_result( x1, y1, x2, y2 );
}

/***************************** print_result()  ****************/
/*    Calculates the slope and y-intercept of a line and displays
```

```
 *     the equation of the line
 */
void print_result( float x1, float y1, float x2, float y2 )
{
     float slope, y_int;

     /*  Check for a vertical line */
     if ( x1 != x2 ) {
          /* the line is not vertical, calculate
           * the slope and y intercept
           */

          slope = ( y2 - y1 ) / ( x2 - x1 );
          y_int = y1 - slope * x1;

          /* Check for a horizontal line */
          if ( slope == 0 )                    /* horizontal line */
               printf( "The equation is y = %5.2f\n",y1 );
          else {
               printf( "The equation is " );
               printf( "y = %5.2fx + %5.2f\n",slope, y_int );
          }
     }
     else                                      /* vertical line */
          printf( "The equation is x = %5.2f\n", x1 );
}
```

The program consists of the functions main() and print_result(). The program uses printf() calls for prompts and for the output of results. Input is done with scanf(). In print_result(), the program checks to see if the line is vertical before calculating the slope. If this check were not done, the calculation of slope might cause an error by attempting to divide by zero.

Learning Avtivities

32.   In testing slope.c, find out what happens when an integer is input as a coordinate of a point. Does an error condition occur? Is the output correct?

33.   *C by Discovery*

a.   When executing slope.c, what happens on your system when an alphabetic character is typed as the first character of the coordinate of a point? This should create an error condition. Is it caught at compile time, at runtime, or not at all?

> b. Think of a way to avoid this potential error. Don't implement it at this time.
>
> 34. Rewrite slope.c to omit the calculation of the slope for a horizontal line (HINT: In a horizontal line, y1 equals y2).

The program circle.c illustrates the use of functions that return a floating point type instead of type int or type void. In the *Learning Activities* that follow you will see what happens when the declarations of these functions are omitted.

Example 3-11: circle.c

```
/*                  circle.c
 *
 *    Synopsis    - Accepts input of the radius of a circle and
 *                  displays the area and circumference.
 *
 *    Objective   - To illustrate the declaration and use of
 *                  functions with type other than int.
 */

/* Include Files */
#include <stdio.h>

/* Constant Definitions */
#define PI 3.1415926

/* Function Declarations */
double area( double );                                      /* Note 1 */
double circumference( double );

void main( void )
{
    double radius;

    printf( "Program to calculate area and circumference " );
    printf( "of a circle.\n" );
    printf( "------- -- --------- ---- --- ------------- " );
    printf( "-- - -------\n" );

    printf( "Please enter the radius : " );
    scanf ( "%lf", &radius );
```

```
       printf( "A circle with radius %5.2f has area %5.2f.\n",
                             radius, area( radius ) );
       printf( "The circumference of the circle is %5.2f.\n",
                             circumference( radius ) );
}

/***************************** area()   ********************/
/*    calculates the area of a circle given its radius.
 */
double area( double r )                               /* Note 2 */
{
       return( PI*r*r );
}

/***************************** circumference()  **************/
/*    calculates the circumference of a circle given its radius.
 */
double circumference( double r )                      /* Note 2 */
{
       return( 2*PI*r );
}
```

This program consists of three functions, main(), area() and circumference(). The function main() announces the intent of the program, accepts input of a value for the variable radius and displays the results of the calls to the other two functions.

Note 1: The prototype declarations of the subfunctions appear here. Since they are above all of the functions in the file, the declarations will be known to all functions in the file. Since main() is the only function that calls the subfunctions, another location for these declarations would be in the declaration section of the function block for main(). In that position, the declarations would be local to main(), and other functions would not know about them.

The functions area() and circumference() both take a parameter of type double and return a value of type double. The declaration of the parameters to these functions is part of the ANSI C prototypes. Both of these functions must be declared because they return values other than type int. Using the ANSI C prototype enables the compiler to check the type and number of parameters in function calls.

These declarations and others like them could also be collected in a header file developed especially for this program. The #include preprocessor directive would be used to include the contents of the header file in the program. We continue the discussion of communication between different parts of a program in Chapter 8.

Note 2: The type declaration precedes the function name in the definition of each of the functions, area () and circumference (). The type name can be omitted when the function returns a value of type int, but including it gives more information to anyone reading the program.

Learning Activities

35. Execute circle.c to make sure that it works correctly as given. (If you do not have an ANSI C compiler, the function declarations will need to be modified.)

36. *C by Discovery*   Modify circle.c in each of the following ways. You will be creating error conditions. After each modification try to compile and execute the program again. Notice how your system handles each of the errors. Is an error caught at compile time, at runtime, or not caught at all? If the program executes, does it give the correct results?

    a. Remove the declaration of area () that appears above the function main ().

    b. Remove the function type declaration from the definition of area ().

    c. Remove both of the declarations mentioned in parts a and b.

    d. Try to generalize from these experiences about how your compiler handles function types, function declarations, and function return values.

    e. Devise and perform experiments like those in parts a through d to test your compiler's handling of the declaration of function parameters.

3.10 Types of Expressions and Automatic Conversions

In C, every expression has an associated type. Operators and operands within the expression combine to determine the expression's type.

Expressions whose final value is the result of a logical operator or a relational operator have type int. The operators involved are !, &&, | |, ==, !=, <, <=, >, and >=. The result of any of those operations can be thought of as true or false. C assigns a value of 1 to a true statement and a value of 0 to a false statement.

Some type conversions are automatically performed in calculating the final value of expressions involving the arithmetic operators. These conversions need to be understood in order to understand C's treatment of types. The general concept is presented below. The actual conversion rules appear in the *A Closer Look* section.

First, all values of type char or short (or unsigned char and unsigned short) are changed (promoted) to type int (or unsigned) before any processing is done.[1]

Because of the initial promotion of types char, unsigned char, short, and unsigned short, the actual calculation of the value of an arithmetic expression is done with the types int, unsigned, long, unsigned long, float, double, and long double. If all the operands in an arithmetic expression have the same type, then the expression will retain that type.

In C it is possible to write expressions in which the operands are of different types. When this is done, explicit rules are applied to determine the expression's type. The general idea is that when the result of a binary operator is evaluated, both operands are converted to a single type that will accurately represent all the possible values but not waste storage space.

With only minor exceptions, the automatic conversions in C can be viewed as finding a dominating type in an expression involving a binary operator, and converting the values in that expression to that dominating type. A list of the dominating types from most to least dominating follows:

```
long double
double
float
unsigned long
long
unsigned
int
```

Exceptions:

1. For any expression involving only char, signed or unsigned char, short, or unsigned short, the dominating expression will be of type int or unsigned.
2. For expressions consisting of types long int and unsigned int, the dominating type depends on the implementation. It may be either unsigned long int or long int.

Ranges of values that can be represented by different types are implementation dependent. That is, some compilers may represent a short with 16 bits, an int with 16 bits, and a long with 32 bits while others may represent a short with 16 bits, an int with 32 bits, and a long with 32 bits. Similar size differences occur in the floating point types.

The ANSI standard for C requires that two header files be supplied with information on the ranges that can be represented with the arithmetic types.

The file limits.h contains information about the range of values that can be

---

1. The types char, unsigned char, short, and unsigned short are used for storage only, not for calculations.

represented by the integral types. Values from limits.h were output by the program limits.c from Example 3-5. The file float.h contains similar information for the floating point types.

A Closer Look

The actual rules for automatic conversions on the types in an arithmetic expression are as follows.

1. The types `char`, `short`, `unsigned char`, and `unsigned short` are converted to type `int` if all the values of the original type can be represented in type `int`. If some values cannot be represented in type `int`, the conversion is to type `unsigned int`.

2. After the initial conversions of types `char`, `short`, `unsigned char`, and `unsigned short`, expressions involving the unary operators `-`, `--`, and `++` will have a type matching the type of the operand.

For example, if `intvar` is a variable of type `int`, and `floatvar` is a variable of type `float`, then the expressions `-intvar`, `--intvar`, and `intvar++` are all of type `int`. The expressions `-floatvar`, `--floatvar`, and `floatvar++` are all of type `float`. Note also that `-charvar` is of type `int` even if `charvar` was declared to have type `char`.

In expressions involving only the binary arithmetic operators, `+`, `-`, `*`, `/`, the type of the expression depends on the operands.

3. If both the operands are of the same type, the expression will have that type.

For example, after the declaration

```
int intvar1, intvar2;
```

the expressions `intvar1 + intvar2`, `intvar1 - intvar2`, `intvar1 * intvar2` and `intvar1 / intvar2` are of type `int`. As mentioned in Chapter 1, the operator `/` produces truncated quotients when both operands are of type `int`. For example, `3 / 2` is equal to `1`.

The expressions resulting from combinations of operations like

```
(intvar1 * 2) / (intvar2 - 24)
```

where `intvar1` and `intvar2` are still of type `int` have the `int` type also.

Similarly, after the declarations

```
float floatvar1, floatvar2;
```

the expressions `floatvar1+floatvar2`, `floatvar1-floatvar2` and `(floatvar1-floatvar2) / (floatvar1+floatvar2)` are all of type `float`.

For the remaining expressions containing binary operations and more than one arithmetic type, at most one of the following conversions takes place for each binary operator in the expression. The following rules are applied in order:

4. If an expression contains an operand of type `long double`, the other operand

is converted to `long double` before calculating the expression's value. The conversion is finished.

5. Otherwise, if there exists an operand of type `double`, the other operand is converted to type `double` before calculation. This concludes the conversion in this case.

6. Similarly, if one operand is of type `float`, the other operand is converted to type `float` and the conversion terminates.
    If the conversion is not finished, the operands must all be of the integral types `long`, `unsigned long`, `int`, or `unsigned int`.

7. Of these, the type `unsigned long` dominates in that one operand of type `unsigned long` causes the other operand to be converted to that type.

8. Operands of types `long int` and `unsigned int` in the same expression are converted to type `long int` if the range of values that can be represented by type `unsigned int` is a subset of the range that can be represented by type `long`. Otherwise, both values are converted to type `unsigned long int`.

9. Otherwise, if one operand has type `long`, the other is converted to type `long`.

10. If one operand has type `unsigned`, the other operand is converted to type `unsigned`.

11. Otherwise, both operands are of type `int`.

After all automatic conversions have taken place, the arithmetic operations are applied. The type of the resulting expression matches the type of the operands after conversion.

Examples

For example, assume that the declarations

```
short    s;
unsigned u;
double   d;
```

have been made. In evaluating the expression

```
(s + u) * d
```

the following automatic conversions are made:

1. Before starting the evaluation, `s` is converted to type `int`.

2. In evaluating the result of the addition operation, `s` is converted from type `int` to type `unsigned`. The bit pattern remains the same, but assuming that an `int` occupies 16 bits of memory, the value -3 would be interpreted as 65533 (or $65536 - 3$). Note that 65535 is the largest value that can be represented with an `unsigned int`.

3. The addition is performed. It yields an expression of type `unsigned int`.

4. Since the multiplication operator combines an operand of type `unsigned`

int with an operator of type double, the unsigned int value is converted to type double before multiplying.

5. The multiplication is performed. The type of the resulting expression is double.

Learning Activities

37. If you have an ANSI C compiler and if you didn't do this in an earlier learning activity, write a program that will output some of the constants in the header file float.h. Pattern your program after limits.c. Inspect the output and reconcile this with your understanding of the internal representation of floating point variables.

38. Consider the following declarations:

```
char      c1, c2;
int       i;
long      l;
unsigned u;
unsigned short us;
unsigned long ul;
float     f;
double    d;
```

What are the types of the following expressions?

```
c1 + 3
(us + f) * i
(ul % c1) / i
us + c1
d + f + ul
u + l
3 * us
c1 + c2
```

3.11 Forced Type Conversions

After the automatic conversions, the operands of a binary operator are of the same type. By default, the resultant expression has the same type as its converted operands. However, sometimes it is necessary or preferable to compare or calculate with different types, and sometimes the default conversions do not give the desired resultant type. A *type cast* can be used in these situations.

The type of an expression can be temporarily changed with a type cast. A cast consists of a pair of parentheses enclosing a type specifier. It is a unary operator in C. For example

```
( float )
```

is the syntax for a cast to type `float`. Even if the variable `intvar` has been declared of type `int`, the expression

```
( float ) intvar;
```

will have type `float` in the expression in which it was used. The type of `intvar` is not permanently changed. Similarly, the cast

```
( unsigned ) expression
```

forces `expression` to be interpreted as an `unsigned int`. The cast

```
( short ) expression
```

forces `expression` to be treated as a `short  int`. Each of these interpretations are in effect for the current calculation only.

A cast can be constructed with any of the basic types in C. The data types we will study in later chapters are candidates for casts as well as the scalar types presented in this chapter.

Example 3-12 shows one use for a type cast. The purpose of the program cast.c is to calculate the average of three integers. The method used is to input the integers as type `int`, add them, and then divide the sum by 3. The choice of type `int` could be dictated by storage efficiency as well as potential other uses for these variables if the program were to be expanded. The problem is that if the three data values and their sum are of type `int`, when the sum is divided by 3 (another `int` value), the result will also be of type `int`; the division would be truncating integer division. One solution is to use a cast to type `float` on the variable `sum`. That would force this value to type `float`, and the division would no longer truncate the fractional part.

Example 3-12: cast.c

```
/*                 cast.c
 *
 *    Synopsis    - Accepts input of three integers and displays
 *                  their average.
 *
 *    Objective   - Illustrates one use of type casts.
 */

/* Include Files */
#include <stdio.h>

/* Function Declarations */
void intro( void );
void results( int, int, int );

void main( void )
{
    int first_num, second_num, third_num;

    intro();

    scanf( "%d", &first_num );
    scanf( "%d", &second_num );
    scanf( "%d", &third_num );

    results( first_num, second_num, third_num );
}

/***************************** intro()  ********************/
/*    Displays an introduction to the program
 */
void intro( void )
{
    printf( "This program  will calculate the " );
    printf( "average of three integers.\n" );
    printf( "Enter the integers now. " );
    printf( "Press Return after each one.\n" );
}

/***************************** results()  *****************/
/*    Calculates and displays the average of its arguments
```

```
 */
void results( int num1, int num2, int num3 )
{
    float average;                                      /* Note 1 */
    int sum;

    sum = num1 + num2 + num3;
    average = ( float ) sum / 3;                        /* Note 2 */
    printf( "The average of your data is %6.3f.\n", average );
}
```

The function `intro()` displays information and instructions on how to use this program. The three `scanf()` calls accept input of the data values. The function `results()` calculates the average and displays it.

Note 1: Notice that `average` has been declared of type `float`. This is necessary so that fractional values can be represented.

Note 2: The variable `sum` is of type `int`. The number 3 is also an `int`. Normally, the expression

> `sum/3`

would also be of type `int`. In order to force it to be of type `float`, a cast is used. The cast consists of a set of open and close parentheses enclosing a type name. The cast is a unary operator and has higher precedence than the division operator. The variable `sum` is interpreted as a `float` value; the operation performed in this statement is floating point division instead of integer division because of this cast.

Many other uses for type casts will arise later in the text. One of their main uses is in C library functions. The library functions are very serviceable, but some return types that are not identical to the types used in a program even though the information returned by the function is in a format that can be used. A type cast might be used with a library function to force the conversion of the returned value to match the existing types in a program.

There are no restrictions on the use of type casts. Any type in a C program can be cast to any other type. However, data might be lost. For example, if `doublevar` had been declared as type `double`, then the cast

> `(char) doublevar`

would minimally truncate the fractional part of `doublevar` when evaluating the expression. If the integer part of `doublevar` was outside the range representable by a `char`, additional data would be lost.

Learning Activities

39. a. Run cast.c several times with different input to make sure that you see what is happening. Input numbers whose sum is not evenly divisible by 3.

    b. Remove the cast from the sum/3 statement and execute the program again to see what the difference is.

    c. Explain what happens in your own words.

40. Obtain and read a copy of the manual entry for scanf().

41. *C by Discovery*   The program cast.c instructs the user to separate the input values with carriage returns.

    a. Is this necessary for the program to work correctly?

    b. If not, can you modify the scanf() calls so that it is necessary?

Language Elements Introduced in This Chapter: A Review

✓ Constant Expressions
- Leading 0X or 0x indicates a hexadecimal number.
- Leading 0 indicates an octal number.
- All other numerical constants are assumed to be decimal.

✓ Conversion Specifications

Type	Conversion specifications
char:	%c for character representation
	%d for the corresponding integer value
long int:	%ld for signed decimal representation
	%lx for unsigned hexadecimal representation
	%lo for unsigned octal representation
short int:	%hd for signed decimal representation
	%hx for unsigned hexadecimal representation
	%ho for unsigned octal representation
unsigned int:	%u for unsigned decimal representation
	%x for unsigned hexadecimal representation
	%o for unsigned octal representation
unsigned short int:	%hu for unsigned decimal representation
	%hx for unsigned hexadecimal representation
	%ho for unsigned octal representation
unsigned long int:	%lu for unsigned decimal representation
	%lx for unsigned hexadecimal representation
	%lo for unsigned octal representation

In all the following floating point representations, 5 is the minimum field width, and 2 is the precision.

float:

> With `printf()` and `scanf()`
>
> > `%5.2f` for decimal point representation
> > `%5.2e` for exponential representation
> > `%5.2g` for minimal space representation
> >
> > With `printf()` only
> > `%5.2E` for exponential representation
> > `%5.2G` for minimal space representation

double:

> With `scanf()` only
>
> > `%5.2lf` for decimal point representation
> > `%5.2le` for exponential representation
> > `%5.2lg` for minimal space representation
> >
> > With `printf()` only
> > `%5.2f` for decimal point representation
> > `%5.2e` for exponential representation
> > `%5.2g` for minimal space representation
> > `%5.2E` for exponential representation
> > `%5.2G` for minimal space representation

long double:

> With `printf()` and `scanf()`
>
> > `%5.2Lf` for decimal point representation
> > `%5.2Le` for exponential representation
> > `%5.2Lg` for minimal space representation
> >
> > With `printf()` only
> > `%5.2LE` for exponential representation
> > `%5.2LG` for minimal space representation

✓ Function Types
- Can be any of the scalar data types

```
double  circle( double radius )  /* ANSI  prototype */
```

✓ Operators

`sizeof()` Takes an expression or a type as an argument and returns the number of bytes allocated for that type.

Bit operators

~	negation
&	bitwise-and
¦	bitwise-or
^	bitwise-xor
>>	shift right
<<	shift left

Cast operator

(type)

✓ **Types**

Integer Types:	Hold integers
char	Holds a character from the underlying character set. Can be signed or unsigned.
short int	Minimum range: -32768 to 32767
long int	Minimum range: -2147483648 to 2147483647
Unsigned Types:	Represent non-negative integers
unsigned short	Minimum range 0 to 65535
unsigned long	Minimum range 0 to 4294967295
unsigned char	Usual range 0 to 255
unsigned int	Range usually depends on word size
signed	Allow signed and unsigned char (ANSI C only)
Floating Point Types:	for numbers with fractional parts
float	Single precision representation
double	Double precision representation
long double	Extra precision representation (ANSI C only)

Things to Remember

1. Computer memory is divided into bits, bytes, and words.
2. A range of integers can be represented from

   -m, -m+1, -m+2, . . . , -2, -1, 0, 1, 2, 3, . . . m-2, m-1

   where m is a power of 2. The power of two is dependent on the computer being used.
3. Since bit patterns can be interpreted differently, we have different types in C.
4. ANSI C has specified the minimal ranges for each type. The range was not specified before these standards appeared.
5. In ANSI C, information about the integer types is in the header file limits.h.
6. The precedence of the bitwise operators from highest to lowest is ~, >> and <<, &, ^, ¦.

7. A common use of the bit operators is to test or set certain bits with a mask.

8. In ANSI C, information about the floating point types is kept in the header file float.h.

9. Types `char`, `short`, `unsigned char`, and `unsigned short` are not used for calculation. They are used for storage only.

10. When types `char` or `short` are used in an expression or when an expression involves mixed types, C's automatic conversions occur before the expression is evaluated.

11. A cast can be used to temporarily change the type of an expression.

12. When casting from a longer type to a shorter type, data may be lost.

Exercises and Programming Problems

1. a. Write a program that will accept input of a sequence of 20 integers and display their average.

   b. Modify the original program so that the value displayed for the average is the integer closest to the actual average. For example, if the actual average is 67.8, the rounded value 68 should be output. If the average is 24.3, 24 should be output. The average 38.5 should be rounded to 39.

2. a. Write a program that will accept input of a sequence of float values and display the maximum and the minimum of those values.

   b. Repeat problem 1b for the program you wrote in 2a.

3. Write a program using bit operations that will test each input integer to see if it is divisible by 4.

4. Write a program that will update a bank balance. A sample run is below. The user's response is in **boldface**.

```
BANK ACCOUNT PROGRAM
--------------------

Enter the old balance: 1234.50
Enter the transactions now.
Enter an F for the transaction type when you are finished.

Transaction Type (D=deposit, W=withdrawal, F=finished): D
Amount: 568.34
Transaction Type (D=deposit, W=withdrawal, F=finished): W
Amount: 25.68
Transaction Type (D=deposit, W=withdrawal, F=finished): W
Amount: 167.40
Transaction Type (D=deposit, W=withdrawal, F=finished): F
```

```
Your ending balance is  $1609.76
Program Ending
```

5. Write a program that converts an integer into another base. The input integer could be in decimal, octal, or hexadecimal. The output could be converted into either of the bases. A sample run is below. The user's response is again in **boldface**.

```
INTEGER CONVERSION PROGRAM
--------------------------

Base of input (d=decimal, h=hexadecimal, o=octal): d
Number: 178
Base of output (d=decimal, h=hexadecimal, o=octal): h
The integer 178 in decimal is equivalent to b2 in hexadecimal.
Another number? (Y/N) Y

Base of input (d=decimal, h=hexadecimal, o=octal):  o
Number:  423
Base of output (d=decimal, h=hexadecimal, o=octal): d
The integer 423 in octal is equivalent to 275 in decimal.
Another Number? (Y/N) N

Goodbye!
```

6. Expand the program from exercise 5 to accept input of an integer in a binary representation and to include an option to output the binary representation of the input number.

7. Write a program to output an ASCII chart like the one in the *Programmer's Handbook*. Take pains to make the output look as much like that chart as possible. Don't try to reproduce the shading or double lines.

   The characters from 0 through 1f hexadecimal are control characters. Experiment or read a manual to determine which of the control characters rings the bell on the terminal. Which is the carriage return? The line feed? The horizontal tab? The form feed?

8. Write a program that will accept an integer between 1 and 100 as input and will output its prime factors. (A prime factor of a number is a prime number that divides the number evenly. A prime number is a number that is greater than one whose only factors are itself and 1. For example, 2, 3, 5, 7, 11, 13, and 17 are prime numbers.) A sample run of the program is below. The user's input is in **boldface**.

```
Enter a number between  1 and 100:  345
TOO LARGE!  Enter a number between 1 and 100:  -15
TOO SMALL!  Enter a number between 1 and 100:  34
The prime factors of 34 are  2 and 17.
Another number?  (Y/N)  Y
```

```
Enter a number between 1 and 100:   83
The number 83 is prime.
Another number?  (Y/N)  N
Goodbye!
```

9. A bank wants to classify its customers as "Regular," "Special," or "VIP" according to their bank balance. A customer with less than $10,000 is a "Regular" customer. A customer who has between $10,000 and $50,000 is "Special." A customer with more than $50,000 is a "VIP." The home office wants a monthly report on the number of "Regular," "Special," and "VIP" customers at each branch. The office is not interested in names, addresses, or actual balance in this report. Write a program that a bank employee can run to generate a report to send to the home office. The employee will enter the current bank balance for each customer. The computer will tally the figures and create the report.

10. The Acme Real Estate Company is planning an apartment complex. The company figures that during the first year, its income will be $450 per month from each studio apartment, $550 per month from each one-bedroom apartment, and $700 per month from each two-bedroom apartment. Each studio apartment will be 200 square feet in size; each one-bedroom apartment will be 300 square feet in size, and each two-bedroom apartment will be 450 square feet in size. The building cost is $75 per square foot. To aid in planning, the company wants a program that will allow it to input the number of studios, one-bedroom, and two-bedroom apartments and will calculate the total size of the building needed to house the apartments, the total building cost, and the expected income for the first year and output those results in report form. Write this program and structure it so that Acme can enter as many sets of data as desired at one time.

A sample run is below.

```
ACME REAL ESTATE PLANNING PROGRAM
---------------------------------
How many studio apartments?  5
How many one-bedroom apartments? 12
How many two-bedroom apartments? 10
Report for 5 studio apartments
12 one-bedroom apartments
10 two-bedroom apartments
               Space            Costs            Income
    Studios:   1000             75000            27000
One-Bedrooms:  3600            270000            79200
Two-Bedrooms:  4500            337500            84000
-------------------            ------            ------
Totals Space:  9100    Cost:  682500            190200
Do you want to enter another set of data (y/n)?  n
Thank you
```

Pointers and Arrays

In this chapter, we will look at pointers and arrays. A pointer type is a scalar type; it holds one value at a time. The value that can be stored in a variable of pointer type is a memory address. An array is an aggregate type that stores multiple data values with the same type. Even though they seem to be different concepts, a special relationship exists between arrays and pointers in C. This relationship needs to be carefully examined.

4.1 Getting Started with Pointers

The concept of a pointer is an important one in many programming languages. It is doubly important in C because of the ways in which arrays, strings, and function parameters are implemented. Because this concept is so critical, we will start with the basics.

Computer Memory and Addresses

The amount of memory available for a program to use varies from computer to computer, but whatever the size, a program keeps track of the memory in use by a numbering system. A number is associated with each byte or word. That number is called the address of the byte or word. Some computers have an address assigned to each byte; these are referred to as byte-addressable computers. Other computers are word-addressable; they assign an address to each word, but not necessarily to each byte.

For illustration, let's assume the following memory configuration for a computer. A byte consists of 8 bits and each word consists of 2 bytes. Suppose that the computer has 1 megabyte or 2^{20} bytes of memory. Assume the computer is byte addressable and the addresses range from 0 through $2^{20} - 1$. We can picture the memory in the two ways shown in Figure 4-1.

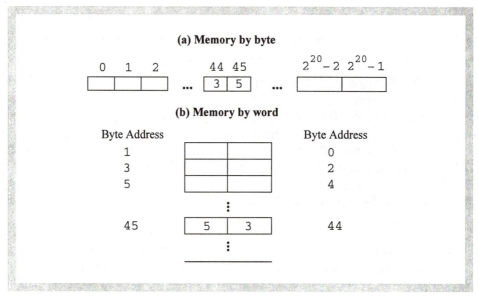

Figure 4-1

In parts a and b of the Figure, the value 3 is stored in the byte with address 44, and the value 5 is stored in the byte with address 45. The interpretation of the values is up to the program, the programmer, and the operating system. Each value stored in a byte may be interpreted separately, or two or more bytes may be interpreted together.

Now consider an error-free C program with an integer variable declared. When the program is loaded into memory, the loader will decide where the current value of the variable will be stored. An appropriate number of bytes will be reserved for values of the variable. That space is referenced by its address.

C has several mechanisms that allow a programmer to access the memory address of a variable during program execution. One mechanism that we have already seen is to specify the address of a variable with the & operator. This operator, discussed previously in relation to the function scanf(), is used to show scanf() where to put a value that it reads. C allows us to print the addresses of variables during program execution. This is illustrated in the program in Example 4-1.[1]

Example 4-1: address1.c

```
/*                  address1.c
 *
 *   Synopsis    - Prints the address of a variable.
 *
 *   Objective   - Illustrates addresses in memory and C's ability
 *                 to display them.
 */

/* Include Files */
#include <stdio.h>

void main( void )
{
    int intvar;

    printf( "The values of intvar are stored in the memory" );
    printf( " location %p.\n", &intvar );                    /* Note 1 */
}
```

This program has one variable of type int. The executable code consists of two calls to printf(). The output from this program cannot be predicted without precise knowledge of the action of the loader.

Note 1: The syntax, &intvar, refers to the address of the variable intvar. When the %p conversion specification is used, the memory address assigned by the computer for the location of the variable intvar is converted to a form suitable for displaying an address before output. The form used by the %p conversion specification can vary with computer systems. Besides the %p format, addresses of memory locations are often displayed in either hexadecimal (%x) or octal (%o).

---

1. The programs in this chapter are designed to illustrate the underlying concepts of pointers and arrays. Very few programs in this chapter illustrate using the concepts. The uses of pointers are discussed throughout the remainder of the text.

> ## *Learning Activities*
>
> 1. How many lines of output will address1.c generate?
> 2. What modifications need to be made if the address of `intvar` is to be output in octal? In hexadecimal?
> 3. To get to know your compiler, modify address1.c by adding a character variable and variables of type `float` and `double`. Have each of their addresses output by the program. Are the addresses related as you would expect? Consider the `sizeof()` each data type in answering this question.

Pointers

Another technique to determine the address of a variable is to use a pointer variable. A pointer variable stores the address of a memory location. When we say that a pointer variable *points* to another variable we mean that it stores the address of the memory location allocated for values of the other variable.

In C, pointers are considered to be separate data types. Each of the data types `char`, `int`, `float`, and `double` has a corresponding pointer data type, pointer-to-char, pointer-to-int, pointer-to-`float`, and pointer-to-double. In fact, every data type has a corresponding pointer type. Note that this allows data types such as a pointer-to-pointer-to-int and so on. The term *double indirection* applies to pointers to pointers.

In a pointer variable declaration, the pointer type consists of the underlying type plus an asterisk, `*`, placed immediately to the left of the variable name. The notation `int *` signifies the type pointer-to-int. The notation `char *` signifies the type pointer-to-char. The `*` following any type name signifies a pointer to that type. The fact that pointers are data types implies that we can declare variables of pointer types and assign and access their values in a way similar to variables of other types.

Declaring a pointer variable is the same as declaring a variable of any other type. The type is followed by the variable name. For example, the declaration

```
int *intptr;
```

declares a variable named `intptr` that has type `int *` or pointer-to-int. Similarly, the declaration

```
char *charptr;
```

declares a variable named `charptr` that has type `char *`. Pointers to the other types are declared in the same way. The program address2.c in Example 4-2 illustrates the declaration and a very simple use of a pointer variable. The program was executed on a MS-DOS system to get the output. The output from your system may be different.

Example 4-2: address2.c

```
/*                  address2.c
 *
 *    Synopsis   - Prints the address of a variable.
 *
 *    Objective  - Demonstrates pointers as addresses in memory.
 *                 Gives the syntax of declaring a pointer to an
 *                 integer and one technique for initializing a
 *                 pointer.
 */

/* Include Files */
#include <stdio.h>

void main( void )
{
    int intvar;
    int *ptr_to_intvar;                              /* Note 1 */

    printf( "The value of ptr_to_intvar is %p.\n",
                                ptr_to_intvar );     /* Note 2 */

    ptr_to_intvar = &intvar;                         /* Note 3 */

    printf( "The address of intvar is %p.\n", &intvar );
    printf( "The value of ptr_to_intvar is %p.\n",
                                ptr_to_intvar );     /* Note 4 */
}
```

Running the Program

```
The value of ptr_to_intvar is 0000.
The address of intvar is FFF4.
The value of ptr_to_intvar is FFF4.
```

Variables of type `int` and `int *` are declared. The value of the pointer variable is displayed before and after initialization. The address of the `int` variable is also displayed.

Note 1: A pointer to an integer is declared. The tokens `int *` are used to indicate the data type pointer-to-`int`. The variable name follows the asterisk.

Note 2: The value of the pointer variable is printed. Since no initialization has been done, this value could contain garbage data from some previous use of memory or could contain the value zero. In either case the value would not refer to a legitimate memory location. Referencing an improper memory location will most likely cause a runtime error. Pointer variables, like all other variables in C, must be explicitly initialized. Some compilers will give warning messages for uninitialized pointers.

Note 3: This assignment statement is used to initialize the value of the pointer variable. After the execution of this statement, the two variables `intvar` and `ptr_to_intvar` are related, as shown below. The addresses shown are fictitious.

Variable	Address	Contents
`ptr_to_intvar`	7802	8000
	•	
	•	
	•	
`intvar`	8000	????

Note 4: The value of the variable `ptr_to_intvar` is identical to the address of the variable `intvar` that was output by the previous `printf()` call.

Learning Activities

4. The syntax for declaring a pointer-to-`int` is
```
int *variable_name;
```
Experiment with address2.c and your compiler to see if either of the following forms is allowed.[1]
```
int * variable_name;
int* variable_name;
```

5. What would the expression `&ptr_to_intvar` reference?

---

1. The syntax presented in the text is the most commonly used, but many people think that one of these alternate forms is clearer. A choice for your style should be made.

6.   Write a declaration of a variable named `char_ptr` of type pointer-to-char, and another variable of type `char`. Rewrite address2.c to use the variable `char_ptr` to output the address of a character variable.

4.2 Pointer Arithmetic

To further understand a pointer to a type as a separate data type, consider the program address3.c in Example 4-3. It is a modification of address2.c.

Example 4-3: address3.c

```
/*                address3.c
 *
 *    Synopsis    - Uses pointers to print the addresses of a char
 *                  variable and an int variable and the address of
 *                  the next available memory location for each
 *                  data type.
 *
 *    Objective   - Illustrates what is meant by a pointer-to-int
 *                  being a separate data type. Demonstrates syntax
 *                  of declaring a pointer-to-char variable,
 *                  initialization of pointer variables, and
 *                  the result of adding 1 to pointer variables
 *                  of different types.
 */

/* Include Files */
#include <stdio.h>

void main( void )
{
    int intvar, *int_ptr;                               /* Note 1 */
    char charvar, *char_ptr = &charvar;                 /* Note 2 */

    int_ptr = &intvar;

    printf( "The address of charvar is %p.\n", char_ptr );
    printf( "The next character could be stored at %p.\n",
                                    char_ptr + 1 );   /* Note 3 */

    printf( "The address of intvar is %p.\n", int_ptr );
```

```
        printf( "The next integer could be stored at %p.\n",
                                    int_ptr + 1 );     /* Note 4 */
}
```

Variables of type int, int *, char, and char * are declared. Their values are initialized and output with calls to printf().

Note 1: Notice the declaration of an integer variable and a pointer-to-int on the same line. A comma is used to separate the two variable declarations.

Note 2: Here, a character variable and a variable of type pointer-to-char are declared on the same line of code. Further, char_ptr has been initialized to point to charvar. C's initialization features are available with pointer types also. Note that int_ptr could have been initialized in this way.

Note 3: Since pointer-to-char is a separate data type, the expression char_ptr + 1 references the next potential address of a character. The + 1 adds the sizeof() one char to the address in char_ptr.

Note 4: Again, since pointer-to-int is a separate data type, the expression int_ptr + 1 references the next potential address of an integer. That is, the 1 in the above expression is interpreted as 1 integer address. In this case the + 1 adds the sizeof() one int to int_ptr. It may be necessary to execute the program address3.c and think about the results to fully understand this concept.

Learning Activities

7.   Execute the program address3.c. Are the results what you expected?

8.   Use the output from address3.c to predict the output from the statements
```
        printf( "%p\n", char_ptr + 2 );
        printf( "%p\n", int_ptr + 2 );
```
if they were added to your program. Verify your predictions by modifying and executing the program.

9.   Which of the following statements will be true for all implementations of C?

The value of (int_ptr + 1) is 1 more than that of int_ptr.

The value of (int_ptr + 1) is 2 more than that of int_ptr.

The value of (int_ptr + 1) is 4 more than that of int_ptr.

The value of (int_ptr + 1) is sizeof(int) more than that of int_ptr.

10.   Predict the relationship between (&intvar + 1) and (int_ptr + 1). Check the actual relationship by making appropriate modifications to address3.c and executing it.

The previous program introduced the concept of pointer arithmetic. Certain arithmetic operations are allowed that either combine two pointers or combine a pointer and an integer.

As demonstrated in the last program, an integer value can be added to a pointer variable. An integer can also be subtracted from a pointer variable. For example, if floatptr had been declared as type float *, the expression

```
floatptr + 1
```

would also have type float *. It would evaluate to the address of the location in memory where the next float value could be located. Its value would be sizeof(float) larger than the address in floatptr. The values floatptr + 2 and floatptr - 1 are also potential addresses of values of type float. Their relationship is described by Figure 4-2.

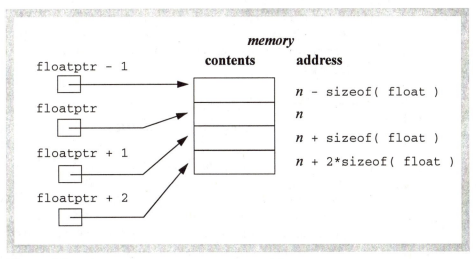

Figure 4-2

In illustrations like this figure, an arrow from a pointer variable to a rectangle representing a memory cell indicates that the address of that memory cell is stored in the pointer variable. In Figure 4-2 the memory location pointed to by floatptr has address n. Hence, the contents of floatptr is n. The contents of floatptr - 1, floatptr, floatptr + 1 and floatptr + 2 will differ by a multiple of sizeof(float).

In the expression ++floatptr, the value of floatptr would be incremented by sizeof(float). The variable floatptr would then reference the next potential location in memory where a float value could be stored. Note that this could be an illegal memory reference unless that location in memory had been allocated to store a value of type float. Similarly, after evaluation of the expression floatptr--, floatptr would contain the previous possible address of a float value. The memory reference would only be legal when that location is designated to hold values of type float.

If floatptr1 and floatptr2 have both been declared as type float * and initialized with legitimate addresses of float values, the expression

```
floatptr1 - floatptr2
```

is defined to be the integer k such that

```
floatptr2 + k == floatptr1
```

The integer k will represent the number of float values that could be stored between the two addresses. The subtraction of two pointer variables is only defined when both variables are pointers to the same type. Note that the expression

```
floatptr1 + floatptr2
```

is *not* a legitimate expression in C.

Allowable operations on pointers include the pointer arithmetic just discussed, assignment to a variable with a pointer type, and comparison of two pointers with the relational operators. It is also legal to cast a pointer type to another pointer type or to an integer type.

Learning Activities

11. Write a short C program that declares pointer variables to each of the basic types char, short, int, long, float, and double. Have your program output the values of several of the pointer arithmetic expressions like those given previously with floatptr. Predict the output of your program and then compile and execute it. (Hint: You will need to know the sizeof() each of these basic types in order to predict properly.) Reconcile any differences between your predictions and the actual output.

12. *C by Discovery*   Modify your program by adding an expression involving the sum of two pointers like floatptr1 + floatptr2. This should cause an error condition. Is it a compile-time error or a runtime error? Experiment to find out.

4.3 Dereferencing a Pointer Variable

We have used pointers to print the addresses of variables in an executing program with the main objective of illustrating the basic concepts of pointers. In practice, this technique could be useful for debugging programs, but is not often a permanent part of a program.

In this section, we learn how to determine the value pointed to by a pointer. This value can be either accessed or changed through pointer operations.

If `int_ptr` is declared as a pointer-to-`int`, we know that legal values for `int_ptr` are addresses of integers. To get to the contents of an address stored in a pointer variable, we use the *dereference* operator `*`. If the syntax

```
*int_ptr
```

is used in any expression other than a declaration, it refers to the contents of the current address in `int_ptr`. Using `*` in this way is known as dereferencing a pointer. Figure 4-3 demonstrates this relationship in two different ways.

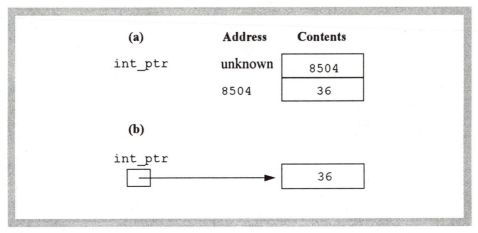

Figure 4-3

In parts a and b of the Figure, `*int_ptr` has the value 36. In general, an upper-level language gives a programmer little or no control over the memory addresses that are used by a program. That is, a programmer controls *what* is stored in memory, but not *where* it is stored. However, C does allow the programmer some control over where the program data is stored. A diagram similar to Figure 4-3b is commonly used to show the relationship between a pointer and its contents. The program pointer.c in Example 4-4 illustrates the distinction between a pointer (an address) and its contents (the contents of the address).

Example 4-4: pointer.c

```
/*                  pointer.c
 *
 *    Synopsis    - Assigns a value to a char variable twice and
 *                  prints that value and its memory address.
 *
 *    Objective   - Demonstrates how to reference the contents of a
 *                  pointer variable.
 */

/* Include Files */
#include <stdio.h>

void main( void )
{
    char c,
        *ptr_c = &c;                                        /* Note 1 */

    c = 'Q';

    printf( "The value of c is %c.\n", c );
    printf( "ptr_c points to %c.\n", *ptr_c );             /* Note 2 */
    printf( "The character %c is stored in hex %x.\n", c, ptr_c );

    *ptr_c = 'r';                                           /* Note 3 */

    printf( "The value of c is now %c.\n", c );            /* Note 4 */
    printf( "ptr_c now points to %c.\n", *ptr_c );
    printf( "The character %c is stored in hex %x.\n", c, ptr_c );
}
```

Variables of type char and char * are declared and initialized. The remainder of the code consists of assignment statements and calls to printf().

Note 1: A character variable and a variable of type pointer-to-char have been declared. Since C is a free-format language, the char declaration begun on the previous line continues until the ; on this line. The syntax *ptr_c has two different meanings. If it is preceded by a data type in a declaration (as it is here), it signifies the declaration of a pointer to that data type. However, in any other context, it is the dereference operator and signifies the contents of a pointer type variable.

Note 2: After initializing the value of the character variable, that value can be accessed either by referencing the character variable as in the previous `printf()` call, or by dereferencing the corresponding pointer variable as shown in this line of code.

Note 3: Assignments can be made to the contents of a properly initialized pointer variable. The contents of the address that is currently in the variable `ptr_c` are changed. Notice that the syntax `*ptr_c` can be used on the left side of an assignment statement as well as the right.

Note 4: The previous assignment statement changed the value of the variable `c` also. The execution of these two `printf()` calls will illustrate that fact.

The unary operators, `&` and `*`, in the syntax of pointers have equal precedence with each other and the unary arithmetic operators. Expressions combining them are evaluated left to right. The unary operators have higher precedence than the binary operators. For the full picture on precedence, see the chart in the *Programmer's Handbook.*

Learning Activities

13. Execute the program pointer.c to verify that your understanding of the output is correct.

14. Given the declaration

    ```
    char *char_ptr;
    ```

    and the following memory configuration,

Variable	Address	Contents
char_ptr	100	108
	⋮	
	108	'H'
	109	'e'
	110	'l'
	111	'l'
	112	'o'
	113	'\n'

    state the value that is referenced by each of the following expressions, if possible. Some of the values may be unknown.

    ```
    *char_ptr
    *char_ptr + 1
    *(char_ptr + 1)
    (*char_ptr) + 1
    *char_ptr + 3
    ```

```
*&char_ptr
&char_ptr
&char_ptr + 2
```

15. Write code to change the value of the variable c in pointer.c to 'A' in two different ways. One way must involve using the variable ptr_c.

16. Modify pointer.c so that it will use pointers to initialize and change the value of an integer variable.

The asterisk, *, appears in the declaration of a pointer variable. It also appears when the pointer is dereferenced to access the contents of the address stored in the pointer variable. This seems to be two different uses for the symbol *, but another way of interpreting a declaration makes the syntax more straightforward. Consider the declaration

```
int *intptr;
```

We can interpret this declaration in the following way:

1. An expression of the form *intptr is an int.

2. Therefore, intptr is a pointer-to-int since *intptr is the symbol for a dereferenced pointer.

This method of interpreting C declarations will help to demystify the declarations in later chapters.

Pointer Initialization and the NULL Pointer

When a pointer is declared, the C compiler will set aside storage for the value of the pointer (an address); however, it will not initialize the pointer. A newly declared pointer will not reference a legal memory address. It is up to the programmer to properly initialize a pointer type variable. A pointer is generally initialized with an assignment statement. As it has been shown, it is legal to assign the address of a declared variable of the proper type to a pointer type variable. It is also legal to assign the value of another pointer type to a pointer variable. That is, both of the following statements are legal.

```
int_ptr = &intvar;
int_ptr1 = int_ptr2;
```

In C, it is also possible to make assignments like

```
int_ptr = (int *)1000;
```

to assign the address 1000 to int_ptr. Note that the value 1000 will be converted to the type pointer-to-int with the cast (int *).

There are several cautions to be observed when trying a direct address assignment such as this. In a multi-user multi-tasking environment, take care to use addresses within the allotted memory space. If an ordinary user tries to read or write outside of his or her memory space, a runtime error will occur. In some implementations of C on microcomputers, these assignments are always legal, but writing into certain memory locations may erase other data needed by the operating system. Note that it is partially because C has the capability to access specific memory locations that it is an appropriate language for writing operating systems.

The identifier NULL is defined to be 0 in several of the standard header files including stdio.h. NULL has a special use with pointers. It can be assigned to all types of pointer variables.

The assignment

```
pointervar = NULL
```

is the programmer's way of indicating that pointervar does not point at a legal memory address. It is a value that a program can test in a condition. This condition can be included as part of a test for a loop or a conditional statement. Some examples appear below; they illustrate different ways of accomplishing the same thing.

1)

```
if ( pointervar != NULL )
     do_something();
if ( pointervar )
     do_something();
```

2)

```
while ( ( j < 5 ) && ( pointervar == NULL ) )
     do_something();

while ( ( j < 5 ) && ( !pointervar ) )
     do_something();
```

The program in Example 4-5 illustrates a simple use of the value NULL. More will be seen later in the text.

Example 4-5: pointer2.c

```
/*                  pointer2.c
 *
 *    Synopsis    - Accepts input of a single character entered
 *                  from the keyboard and prints the entered value
 *                  unless it was a newline.
 *
```

```
 *     Objective   - Illustrates use of NULL and relational
 *                    expressions with pointers.
 */

/* Include Files */
#include <stdio.h>                                          /* Note 1 */

void main( void )
{
     int c, *input_ptr = &c;                                /* Note 2 */

     printf( "Please enter a character from the keyboard" );
     printf( " or press return.\n" );

     if ( ( *input_ptr = getchar() ) == '\n' )              /* Note 3 */
           input_ptr = NULL;                                /* Note 4 */

     if ( input_ptr == NULL )                               /* Note 5 */
           printf( "Just a return was typed.\n" );
     else
           printf( "The character %c was entered.\n", *input_ptr );
}
```

"The program asks for input of a character and uses if and if-else statements to test the input and decide on the appropriate output." Based on *The Creation of Man* by Michelangelo, 1508.

Variables of type int and int * are defined. The program prompts for input of a character and uses if and if-else statements to test the input and decide on appropriate output.

Note 1: The value NULL is defined as 0 in stdio.h. The line #define NULL 0 could be used instead if there is no other need for the file stdio.h. When NULL is defined this way, it can be accessed as both a character and an integer because it causes a replacement in the source code before compilation and is not tied to any type.

Note 2: Again, the declaration of the pointer variable only allots space for the pointer. The declaration of the int variable c and the initialization of input_ptr as the address of c assigns a valid memory location to the pointer.

Note 3: Input is done with getchar(). This time the value returned is stored as the contents of input_ptr and then tested to see if the first character input was a return (newline).

Note 4: The value NULL is assigned to a pointer variable in the case where a return was the first key pressed.

Note 5: The value of input_ptr is tested. If the value of the pointer is NULL, the return key was pressed. In terms of programming style, this test could have been made directly on the contents of input_ptr (or c), but there are times when it is handy to be able to test the value of the pointer itself rather than the contents. The objective of this program was to illustrate that technique in a simple situation. The other relational tests that can be used either with a pointer and NULL or with two pointer variables are equality (==), inequality (!=), is greater than (>) or greater than or equal to (>=), or is less than (<) or less than or equal to (<=).

Learning Activities

17.   Why has input_ptr been declared as a pointer-to-int and why is c declared as an integer? In this program should these variables have been declared as types char * and char instead?

18.   Which of the other operators could have been used to test to see if input_ptr was NULL? Rewrite that conditional statement in two different ways.

4.4 Passing Parameters to Functions

The first use we will see for pointers is in passing parameters to functions. Examples of functions that take parameters have appeared earlier in the text. This section will explore the role of pointers in parameter passing.

Recall that the parameters in the definition of the function are called formal parameters. The parameters that appear in function calls are known as actual parameters. The names and types of the formal parameters must appear inside the parentheses that follow the name of the function in the definition.

In other languages, two basic methods of passing parameters to subprograms may be available. Parameters could be *passed by reference* or *passed by value*. A parameter that is passed by reference is also called a *variable parameter*. For variable parameters, the address of that parameter's storage location is known to the subprogram so that operations may be done directly on the parameter. The subprogram will be able to change the value of a variable parameter. If a parameter is passed by value (that is, it is a *value* parameter) to a subprogram, a copy is made of the current value of that parameter. The function will operate on the copy of the parameter. When a parameter is passed by value, the original parameter will not be changed by the subprogram.

In C, all parameters are passed by value. The actual parameters to a C function will not be changed by the function. However, it is sometimes desirable to have a subprogram effect a change on a variable from another part of the program. In these situations, pass by reference parameters can be simulated. The simulation technique is to pass the *address* of the variable as an actual parameter to a function. The address itself can not be modified by the function, but the contents of that address can be changed. The corresponding formal parameter will be declared as a pointer. The program param.c of Example 4-6 demonstrates the fact that parameters in C are passed by value and illustrates the method of simulating pass by reference parameters.

Example 4-6: param.c

```
/*                 param.c
 *
 *    Synopsis   - Displays the values of variables and parameters
 *                 before, during, and after a function call.
 *
 *    Objective  - Illustrates passing parameters by value and
 *                 by reference.
 */

/* Include Files */
```

```c
#include <stdio.h>
/* Function Declarations */
void changit( int, int * );

void main( void )
{
    int x, y, *int_ptr;

    x = 1;
    y = 3;
    int_ptr = &y;                                          /* Note 1 */

    printf( "In main before the call to changit," );
    printf( " x = %d, y = %d, *int_ptr = %d\n", x, y, *int_ptr );

    changit( x, int_ptr );                                 /* Note 2 */

                                                           /* Note 3 */
    printf( "In main after the call to changit," );
    printf( " x = %d, y = %d, *int_ptr = %d\n", x, y, *int_ptr );
}

/********************************* changit()  ****************/
/*   Assigns values to x and *int_ptr and displays the
 *   assigned values.
 */
void changit( int x, int *int_ptr )                        /* Note 4 */
{
    x += 5;
    *int_ptr += 5;                                         /* Note 5 */
                                                           /* Note 6 */
    printf( "In changit, x = %d, *int_ptr = %d.\n", x, *int_ptr );
}
```

 Running the Program

```
In main before the call to changit, x = 1, y = 3, *int_ptr = 3
In changit, x = 6, *int_ptr = 8.
In main after the call to changit, x = 1, y = 8, *int_ptr = 8
```

The function `main()` declares and initializes variables and displays their values before and after a call to the function `changit()`. The function `changit()` makes assignments to its parameters and displays their values.

Note 1: The variable `int_ptr` has been declared as type pointer-to-`int`. Here it is initialized to contain the address of the variable `y` in preparation for the call to `changit()`. The function `changit()` will be used to change the value of `y`.

Note 2: In the call to `changit()`, the actual parameters are `x` and `int_ptr`. Both of these parameters are passed by value. A copy will be made of their current values and `changit()` will work on the copies. However, by passing the address of the variable `y` as a parameter to the function, we have constructed a situation in which `y` is passed by reference to `changit()`. We have set up the situation so that `changit()` can change the value of `y`.

Note that an equivalent call to `changit()` can be made that does not necessitate the use of a pointer variable. That call would be

```
changit(x, &y);
```

The output of the program would be identical when this function call replaces the existing one.

Note 3: The values of the variables are output after the call to `changit()`. The value of `x` is unchanged by the execution of the function, but the value of `y` (which is `*int_ptr`) has been changed.

Note 4: The first formal parameter to `changit()` is `x`[1]; it corresponds to the actual parameter `x` in the function call. Any changes to the formal parameter `x` that occur during the execution of the function will be discarded when the function terminates.

The second formal parameter to `changit()` corresponds to the actual parameter `int_ptr`. It is of type `int *`. The parameter will be an address of an integer. Declaring the parameter in this way allows the function to make a change to the variable `y` in `main()`. The use of a pointer is necessary when simulating pass by reference.

Note 5: In the previous statement, a change was made to the formal parameter `x`. This change affects only the copy of `x`, not `x` itself. In this statement, a change is made to the contents of the address in `int_ptr`. This will change the corresponding variable `y` in `main()`. The function `changit()` can directly access the address of the variable in the calling function and therefore it can modify its contents.

Note 6: The values of the formal parameters are displayed by this `printf()` call. They will be different from the values of the variables `x` and `*int_ptr` in `main()`. The function `changit()` can change its formal parameters; the corresponding actual parameters in the calling function may or may not be changed.

---

1. In this example, the name of the actual parameter matches the name of the formal parameter. This does not have to be the case. The same names for actual and formal parameters were chosen in this case to show the relationship between the values.

A Closer Look

An "execution environment" for a function is created when a function is called and destroyed when it terminates. The environment includes values for the function's local variables and parameters. Each time the function is called, the current values of the actual parameters are copied to the execution environment where the function will access them. Changes to the parameters are made to these copies. The values of the actual parameters are only touched when the address of that parameter is passed to the function.

In the program param.c, when `changit()` is called, both the function `main()` and the function `changit()` are active. The diagram in Figure 4-4 indicates the two separate execution environments for these functions. The values for each variable indicate the original values and trace the changes that occur.

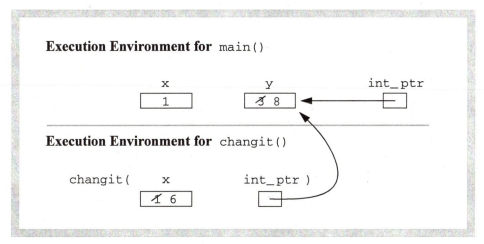

Figure 4-4

The lines through values in the boxes illustrate the changes that take place during execution of the program. Notice that the value of x in `main()` was not touched. The modification was made to the copy of x that was passed to `changit()`. Notice also that the value of int_ptr in `main()` will not be touched, but the value of `*int_ptr` (that is, y) will be changed.

Learning Activities

19.   Complete the following program so that the output is as stated. Fill in the formal parameters, the function definition, the declaration of `switchxz()` in or above `main()`, and the actual parameters.

OUTPUT:

```
1:  y is 4, x is 5, and z is 7.
2:  y is 4, x is 7, and z is 5.
```

PROGRAM:

```c
/*              la19.c                                    */

/* Include Files */
#include <stdio.h>

/* Function Declarations */
/* fill in declaration of switchxz() here */

void main( void )
{
     int x, y, z, *int_pointer;

     x = 5;
     y = 4;
     z = 7;

     int_pointer = &x;
     printf( "1: y is %d, x is %d, and z is %d.\n",
                                       y, x, z );
     switchxz(        ,        );             /*  fill in */
     printf( "2: y is %d, x is %d, and z is %d.\n",
                                       y, x, z );

}

void switchxz(        ,        )              /*  fill in */
{
     /*  fill in code that will result
      *  in the values for x and z being switched.
      */
}
```

HINT: The function `switchxz()` takes two parameters and must interchange the values of x and z. The actual parameters should be the address of x and the address of z. The formal parameters should be declared appropriately. In the function code for `switchxz()`, the parameters should be dereferenced to access the values of x and z. For example, if the actual parameter is &x and the formal parameter is ptr_x, the expression *ptr_x will translate to the value of x.

20. Predict the output from the following program by filling in values in the blanks below. Execute the program to verify your prediction.

PROGRAM:

```c
/*              la20.c                                    */
```

```
/* Include Files */
#include <stdio.h>

/* Function Declarations */
void p1( int*, int );

void main( void )
{
    int    int1, int2, int3;

    int1 = 3;
    int2 = 7;
    int3 = 2;

    p1( &int3, int2 );
    printf( "Back in main, int1 is %d, int2 is %d, ",
                                    int1, int2 );
    printf( "and int3 is %d.\n\n", int3 );

    p1( &int3, int3 );
    printf( "Back in main, int1 is %d, int2 is %d, ",
                                    int1, int2 );
    printf( "and int3 is %d.\n", int3 );
}

void p1( int *i, int j )
{
    *i = *i  +  3;
    j  = 4 * j;
    printf( "In p1, *i is %d, and j is %d.\n", *i, j );
}
```

OUTPUT:

```
In p1, *i is ____, and j is ____.
Back in main, int1 is ___, int2 is ____, and int3 is ___.

In p1, *i is ___, and j is ___.
Back in main, int1 is ___, int2 is ___, and int3 is ___.
```

Using Pointers and Parameters

Now that we know how to use pointers to simulate pass by reference parameters, it makes it possible to provide more structure to our programs. As a simple example, suppose we need to write a program to calculate the area of a rectangle. Three steps are involved: obtaining the values of the length and width as input, calculating the area, and displaying the results. A solution appears in Example 4-7. Each step is written as a separate function; the function main() drives the program by calling each of the functions in order. The variables length, width, and area are declared in main(). Communication between main() and the subfunctions is done with parameters and return values.

In particular, look at the function `get_input()`. Since it's major task is to accept the input of the length and the width of the rectangle, it needs to be able to change the values of the variables `length` and `width` that are declared in `main()`. The technique of simulating pass by reference is used to allow this to happen.

Example 4-7 area.c

```
/*                  area.c
 *
 *    Synopsis    - Accepts input of values for the length and
 *                  width of a rectangle, calculates and displays
 *                  the area of the rectangle.
 *
 *    Objective   - Illustrates how to structure a program so that
 *                  input is done in a separate function.
 */

/* Include Files */
#include <stdio.h>

/* Function Declarations */
void get_input( double *, double * );
double calculate( double, double );
void display( double );

void main( void )
{
    double length, width, area;                          /* Note 1 */

    get_input( &length, &width );                        /* Note 2 */

    area = calculate( length, width );

    display( area );
}

/****************************** get_input() *******************/
/*    accepts input of two values of type double.
 */
void get_input( double *len_ptr, double *wid_ptr )       /* Note 3 */
{
    printf( "Enter the length > ");
    scanf( "%lf", len_ptr );                             /* Note 4 */
```

```
    printf( "Enter the width > " );
    scanf( "%lf", wid_ptr );                              /* Note 4 */
    return;
}


/***************************** calculate()    *****************/
/*    returns the product of its arguments
 */
double calculate( double val1, double val2 )
{
    return( val1 * val2 );
}


/***************************** display()    *******************/
/*    displays the area of a rectangle
 */
void display( double a )
{
    printf( "The area is %5.2f\n", a );
}
```

The program consists of the functions `main()`, `get_input()`, `calculate()`, and `display()`. The subfunctions correspond exactly to the three identified tasks that need to be performed by the program. In `main()`, the variables are declared and the functions are called.

Note 1: The variables `length`, `width`, and `area` are used by the subfunctions. They are declared in `main()` and made available to each subfunction through the parameter passing mechanism.

Note 2: The function `get_input()` needs to initialize the values of the variables `length` and `width`. The addresses of these variables are the actual parameters to the function. This technique simulates pass by reference and allows the function `get_input()` to change the values of the variables.

Note 3: The corresponding formal parameters to `get_input()` are declared as type `double *`.

Note 4: The input of the values is done with calls to `scanf()`. The second parameter to `scanf()` in each call is the corresponding formal parameter. It is the address of the variable that will be initialized by the call to `scanf()`. Note that since `len_ptr` and `wid_ptr` are addresses, it is not necessary to use the address operator, `&`, in this case.

As an aside, we have finally discovered the reason that the parameters to `scanf()` that appear after the control string must be addresses. The function `scanf()` uses the technique of simulating pass by reference to allow it to change program values when it accepts, converts and stores input.

Learning Activities

21.   Execute the program and make sure you understand why it works.
22.   Rewrite the example program circle.c from Section 3.9 in a structured way where the function main() drives the program by simply calling the necessary subprograms.

A Mathematical Example—Calculating Exponents

The program exp.c in Example 4-8 calculates the value of e^x where x is input by a user. The calculation is done by expanding the Taylor series for e^x,

$$1 + x + \frac{x^2}{2!} + \frac{x^3}{3!} + \dots + \frac{x^n}{n!}$$

The expansion stops when the last term, $x^n/n!$, is less than some value epsilon which is between 0 and 1. The value of epsilon is also input by the user as an indication of the desired precision of the answer. The program is implemented with three functions. Values of variables declared in main() need to be changed by the other functions. The technique of passing the address of a variable as a parameter to a function is used.

Example 4-8: exp.c

```
/*                  exp.c
 *
 *   Synopsis    - Accepts input of float values for x and epsilon
 *                 and calculates e to the x using the Taylor
 *                 series. The series is expanded to the point
 *                 where term is less than epsilon.
 *
 *   Objective   - Illustrates the use of pointers and the address
 *                 operator in simulating pass by reference.
 */

/* Include Files */
#include <stdio.h>
```

```
/* Function Declarations */
void intro( void );
double e_to_the_x( double, double, int * );
void getinput( double *, double * );

void main( void )
{
     double x, epsilon, exp_val;
     int num_terms;

     intro();

     getinput( &x, &epsilon );

     exp_val = e_to_the_x( x, epsilon, &num_terms );

     printf( "e raised to the power %.5lf is %.5lf.\n",
                                         x, exp_val );
     printf( "The value was approximated with %d terms.\n",
                                         num_terms );
}

/******************************** intro()  *****************/
/*    Displays messages about the program.
 */
void intro( void )
{
     printf( "This program will calculate the value of e " );
     printf( "raised to the power x.\nYou will be asked to" );
     printf( " enter a real number x,\nand a value epsilon" );
     printf( " that gives an indication of the desired " );
     printf( " accuracy.\n" );
}

/******************************** e_to_the_x()  *************/
/*    Uses the Taylor series expansion to calculate e to the x.
 *    The series is terminated when the term is less than
 *    epsilon. The desired precision and the actual precision
 *    are passed between e_to_the_x() and the calling function
 *    in the parameter precision.
 */
double e_to_the_x( double x, double eps, int *num_terms_ptr )
{
     double term = 1, value = 0;
     int count = 1;
```

```
        while ( term >= eps ) {
                value += term;
                term *= x;
                term /= count++;
        }

        *num_terms_ptr = count - 1;
        return( value );
}


/*********************************** getinput()  ***************/
/*    inputs two values of type double.  Values are passed back
 *    in the parameters x_ptr and eps_ptr.
 */

void getinput( double *x_ptr, double *eps_ptr )
{
        printf( "\nEnter a value for x : " );
        scanf( "%lf", x_ptr );
        printf( "Enter a value for precision that is < 1: " );
        scanf( "%lf", eps_ptr );
}
```

The program consists of four functions, main(), intro(), e_to_the_x() and getinput(). The function intro() tells the user how to use the program. The function getinput() will accept input of a value for x and a value for epsilon. The function e_to_the_x() will calculate the value of e^x. It also keeps track of the number of terms used in the Taylor Series expansion and returns that number of terms in the formal parameter num_terms_ptr. The function main() calls the other functions, keeps track of the variables, and displays the results. This program is a compilation of concepts and techniques we have studied earlier. No new concepts are presented.

Learning Activities

23. Compile and execute exp.c. Test it with several different sets of input. Check the answers given with this program against the results given by a hand calculator.

24. Change the types of x, epsilon, val, and the parameters to the functions to have type float or float * instead of double or double *. Execute the program again with different inputs. Are the results different?

25. Modify the function e_to_the_x() to calculate the numerator

and denominator of each term separately. The numerator will be a power of x and the denominator will be $n!$ (n factorial). Test the program again. Do the results differ?

4.5 One-Dimensional Arrays

The concept of an array is common to most programming languages. In an array, multiple values of the same data type can be stored with one variable name.

Arrays are used to store collections of related data. When we declare variables to be arrays, we can use the name of the variable to access all the elements in the collection.

Suppose an array named `test_scores` will be used to store the scores on a test. This array might be visualized as follows:

test_scores

89	75	93	68	77	83	78	65	92	73
0	1	2	3	4	5	6	7	8	9

In this example, the variable name is `test_scores`. It is a collection of ten data objects, $89, 75, 93, 68, \ldots, 73$. Each data object is said to occupy one *cell* of the array. The numbers, $0, 1, \ldots, 9$, that appear below the array cells are the *indices* into the array. The variable name and an index inside a pair of brackets are used to access the contents of the cells of the array. For example,

```
test_scores[2]
```

refers to the value 93 that is stored in the cell with the index 2.

To use arrays in a C program, we will need to know how to declare arrays[1], how the individual cells are addressed, and how to initialize arrays.

An array declaration contains the following information: the type of elements that will be stored in the array, the name of the array, and the fact that this variable is an array. When the memory must be allocated (that is, when the declaration is also a definition), the number of cells in the array must also be stated. For example, if all the test scores to be stored in the array `test_scores` are integers, the declaration (and definition) of this variable would be

```
int test_scores[10];
```

The type of the array elements is `int`, the variable name is `test_scores`, and

---

1. The distinction between a definition and a declaration of a variable becomes more important when we discuss arrays. A variable definition causes storage to be allocated for the variable while a variable declaration gives the characteristics of the variable. Every variable definition is a declaration, but there are times when a variable needs to be declared but memory does not need to be allocated. That is, some variable declarations are not definitions. The distinctions will become clearer later in this chapter.

there will be ten cells in the array. The indices of the cells will be 0, 1, 2, 3, . . . , 9. In C, integers are the only choice for array indices; the first cell will always have index 0 and the last cell will always have index one less than the total number of cells.

When this array is defined, a contiguous[1] block of memory is allocated that is large enough to hold ten elements of type int. The elements will be stored in order of the indices.

The program scores.c in Example 4-9 illustrates defining an array and initializing an array with user input. It might appear as a function in a teacher's grading program.

Example 4-9: scores.c

```
/*                  scores.c
 *
 *    Synopsis    - Accepts input of 10 integers from the keyboard
 *                  into an array of ints.
 *
 *    Objective   - Illustrates basic array definition and
 *                  access of array elements.  Includes an example
 *                  of specifying a minimum field width in a
 *                  printf() call.
 */

/* Include Files */
#include <stdio.h>

void main( void )
{
    int test_scores[10];                                /* Note 1 */
    int i;

    printf( "Please enter the ten test scores now.\n" );
    for ( i = 0; i < 10; i++ ) {                        /* Note 2 */
        printf( "#%2d > ", i+1 );                       /* Note 3 */
        scanf( "%d", &test_scores[i] );                 /* Note 4 */
    }
    printf( "Thank you.\n" );
}
```

There is a single function, main(). Two variables are defined. The function

---

1. When we talk about a contiguous block of memory for an array, we mean that all the array cells are placed in adjacent memory locations. No holes or unused bytes are present within the memory block for the array.

body consists of a `for` loop surrounded by two `printf()` calls. The body of the `for` loop contains calls to `printf()` and `scanf()`.

Note 1: The variable `test_scores` is defined as an array of 10 elements of type `int`. The indices will be the integers 0 through 9.

Note 2: In the `for` loop, the variable `i` will act as an index into the array. It will consecutively take on the values 0 through 9. The loop terminates when `i` is incremented to `10`.

Note 3: The `printf()` call outputs a prompt for each of the test scores. For the user's convenience, the test scores are numbered 1 through `10` instead of the index values of 0 through 9.

Notice the 2 preceding the `d` in the conversion specification. This specifies a minimum field width of 2 spaces for the output of the decimal value. The decimal will be aligned on the right. The effect is cosmetic. The single-digit numbers, 1 through 9, will be output in the same column as the 0 in the two-digit number `10` in the output.

Note 4: The expression `test_scores[i]` will reference the cell of the array `test_scores` with the index `i`. As `i` proceeds from 0 through 9 in the `for` loop, all cells of the array will be accessed. The `&` or address operator can be used with an array reference to inform `scanf()` where to store the input value. In the next section, a more efficient way of indicating this will be discussed.

Learning Activities

26. Modify scores.c by writing and calling two C functions: one to calculate the average of the test scores and one to display that value.

27. To make sure that you understand the concept of the minimum field width in a conversion specification, delete or comment out the `scanf()` call in the `for` loop and:

   a. Change the `for` loop so that the loop control variable starts at `300` and terminates at `309`. Change it again so that it starts at `991` and terminates at `1000`. Execute the program each time and notice the spacing of that output. (Hint: the array reference in the call to `printf()` in the loop will need to be changed also.)

   b. Modify the program to output the index `i` with a minimum field width of `10`. Execute the program again and notice the output spacing.

   c. Give a general description of the effect of the minimum field width on the spacing of decimal output. Be as complete as possible.

The sizeof() an Array

The operations allowed on an array element are those allowed on any expression with the same underlying type. There is only one operator that can act on the array as a whole: the `sizeof()` operator. This operator indicates the total amount of memory used by the array. For purposes of the following example, assume that an `int` occupies two bytes. Consider the following definition:

```
int example[4];
```

The value of the expression

```
sizeof( example )
```

would be 8 since four `int`s occupy $4 \times 2 = 8$ bytes.

4.6 Initialization of Arrays

When arrays are initialized at the time of declaration, the initial values are placed in a comma-separated list enclosed in braces. In this chapter the initial values are constant. We will look at some examples of array initialization before considering an example program.[1]

```
char name[6] = { 'S', 'a', 'l', 'l', 'y', '\0' };
```

In this example, a variable named `name` is declared. It is an array of six elements of type `char`. The indices of the array range from 0 to 5. The values of the cells of the array at the start of the program execution are given below:[2]

S	a	l	l	y	\0
0	1	2	3	4	5

Establishing the values in the array `names` can also be done with six assignment statements at the beginning of the program:

```
name[0] = 'S'; name[1] = 'a';    name[2] = 'l';
name[3] = 'l'; name[4] = 'y';    name[5] = '\0';
```

As a second example of initializing an array at the time of declaration, consider the following:

```
int numbers[8] = { 4, 0, 5, 6 };
```

A variable named `numbers` is declared to be an array of type `int`. There will be

---

1. Older (non-ANSI) compilers may not allow the initialization of all arrays at the time of declaration. For more information about this and non-constant initial values, see Chapter 8.
2. In C it is typical to terminate an array of characters with a null character so that it can be treated as a string. Further discussion about arrays and strings will be presented in Chapter 5.

eight cells in the array; the indices will run from 0 through 7. In this example, the first four cells of the array have been initialized. The contents of the array appears below:

4	0	5	6	0	0	0	0
0	1	2	3	4	5	6	7

Note that the number of initial values was less than the number of cells in the array. In this case the compiler assumes that the values are for the first cells of the array. When some cells in an array have been initialized, any cell that is not explicitly given an initial value is initialized to 0 by the compiler.

The third example of declaring and initializing elements of an array follows:

```
float dollars[] = { 1.37, 45.68, 3.45 };
```

In this example, a variable named `dollars` is declared to be an array of type `float`. Note that the number of cells in the array was not placed inside the braces. In this case, the number of cells will be equal to the number of initial values. The array `dollars` will have the following configuration at the start of program execution:

1.37	45.68	3.45
0	1	2

Because three initial values were given, the array will have three cells. Each cell will contain one of the initial values.

The program in Example 4-10 illustrates the `sizeof()` operator and the declaration and initialization of arrays in several ways.

Example 4-10: array1.c

```
/*              array1.c
 *
 *   Synopsis    - Three arrays are declared and initialized.  For
 *                 each array, the value in the storage cell with
 *                 index 3 is displayed.
 *
 *   Objective   - Illustrates declaration, initialization, and
 *                 accessing of elements in arrays.
 */

/* Include Files */
```

```
#include <stdio.h>

/* Constant Definitions */
#define NUMCHARS   10
#define NUMFLOATS   8

void main( void )
{
    char chararray[NUMCHARS];                        /* Note 1 */
    int intarray[] = {                               /* Note 2 */
            2, 1, 3, 5, 4, 8, 3, 7 };
    float floatarray[NUMFLOATS] = {                  /* Note 3 */
            1.2, 3.4, -2.3, 1.4, 4.5 };
    int index;


                                                     /* Note 4 */
    for ( index = 0; index < NUMCHARS; index++ )
        chararray[index] = 127 - index;


                                                     /* Note 5 */
    printf( "chararray occupies %d bytes.\n",
                        sizeof( chararray ) );
    printf( "intarray occupies %d bytes.\n",
                        sizeof( intarray ) );
    printf( "floatarray occupies %d bytes.\n",
                        sizeof( floatarray ) );


                                                     /* Note 6 */
    printf( "The element in chararray with index 3 is '%c'.\n",
                                        chararray[3] );
    printf( "The element in intarray with index 3 is %d.\n",
                                        intarray[3] );
    printf( "The element in floatarray with index 3 is %5.2f.\n",
                                        floatarray[3] );
}
```

 Running the Program

```
chararray occupies 10 bytes.
intarray occupies 16 bytes.
floatarray occupies 32 bytes.
The element in chararray with index 3 is '|'.
The element in intarray with index 3 is 5.
The element in floatarray with index 3 is  1.40.
```

This program consists of the function `main()`. Three arrays are declared. Two are initialized at the time of declaration and one is initialized with a `for` loop. Three calls to `printf()` display the `sizeof()` each array. Then three calls to `printf()` display an element of each array.

Note 1: An array of characters named `chararray` is declared. The number of storage cells is 10; the cells will be indexed from 0 through 9. During compilation, space will be allotted for 10 characters. No initialization is done on `chararray` at time of declaration.

Note 2: This time an array of integers is declared. Its name is `intarray`. Since the number of storage cells is not given inside the brackets, the number of cells will be equal to the number of initial values in the list. In this case the number is 8. The indices will start at 0 and terminate with 7.

The array `intarray` is initialized by the numbers in the braces following the declaration. The first cell will contain 2, the second will contain 1, and so on.

Note 3: The identifier `floatarray` will refer to an array of elements of type `float`. The first value (with index 0) will be 1.2; the value with index 1 will be 3.4, etc. Note that the number of cells in the array has been declared to be 8, but that there are only five values between the braces for the array initialization. The five values will be put in the cells with indices 0 through 4. The remaining cells will be initialized with the value 0.

Note 4: This `for` loop initializes the cells in `chararray`. In a structured program, the initialization should be done in a separate function, but, done properly, that involves passing an array to a function as a parameter which will not be discussed until Section 4.8.

Note 5: The `sizeof()` operator can be used with arrays. For example, the value of the expression `sizeof(intarray)` will be

((number of cells in the array) times (`sizeof(int)`))

The value is the total number of bytes used by the array. To demonstrate this, the `sizeof()` each array is output.

Note 6: In the following three `printf()` calls, individual storage cells are accessed by stating the name of the array followed by square brackets that contain the index of the storage cell desired.

A Word of Warning

There are only two times in C when an array can be declared without putting the number of cells inside the square brackets. To understand them fully, the difference between a declaration and a definition becomes important. In a definition, the number of cells must be either explicitly or implicitly stated so that the compiler will know how much memory to allocate.

The first time the number of cells in an array can be omitted from the square brackets in a declaration is when the array is being initialized with its declaration.

This is the case with the array intarray in the program array1.c. The number of initial values will indicate the number of cells to be allocated.

The second time the number of cells in an array does not need to be in the square brackets in a declaration is when the array is being declared, but no memory is being allocated. That is, in a declaration that is not a definition, it may be possible to omit the number of cells in the array. One example is when an array is passed as an argument to a function. We will discuss this in Section 4.8. In all other cases, it is extremely important to indicate the number of cells in the array between the square brackets.

Learning Activities

28. a. Try to compile the program array1.c. Your compiler may not allow the initialization of the arrays intarray and floatarray. If it doesn't, add the word static in front of the type in both of those array declarations. The reasons for this will be discussed in Chapter 8.

  b. Predict the output of array1.c on your computer system and then execute it. Make sure the results are what you expect. (Note: your results may NOT match those given in the text.) Did you predict the correct values for the results of the sizeof() operator? Reconcile any differences between your predictions and the actual output.

29. Modify the program array1.c to display the contents of the cell with index 6 in floatarray. This cell was not initialized at the time of declaration. What value was in the cell?

30. Modify the program array1.c again to display intarray[9]. Note that intarray[] was declared with 8 initializers. Therefore, the indices should start at 0 and go through 7. Accessing intarray[9] is an error. How does your compiler and system handle this error?

31. In three different ways, declare and initialize an array to hold the even integers between 0 and 20 inclusive.

32. Write a declaration of an array of 24 characters. Initialize this array at declaration time with null characters in the first three spaces.

33. Consider the declaration

        int intarray[] = {9, 5, 2, 3, 8, 7, 4};

  a. How would the cell that contains the 7 be referenced?

  b. What is the array index associated with the cell containing the 9?

  c. Write the necessary declarations and statements to assign the sum of the contents of the third and the fifth cells in the array to a variable named sum.

d. How would the declaration above differ from the one below?

```
int intarray[7] = {9, 5, 2, 3, 8, 7, 4};
```

Which declaration is better in a stylistic sense? When might the first declaration be used instead of the second?

e. Predict what might happen during execution of the statement

```
intarray[7] = 24;
```

Put the declaration from part d. and the assignment statement in a program and test it to see if you were right. Try to generalize your findings.

Another Word of Warning

The program bounds.c in Example 4-11 has a bug in it. The programmer was not careful about the range of the indices into the array. In general, C compilers do not check the indices of an array during program execution to see that they are within the correct bounds. This is because the omission of subscript range checking makes a program execute faster. Therefore, it is up to the programmer to insure that an index into an array is within the legal range.

Example 4-11: bounds.c

```
/*                  bounds.c
 *
 *    Synopsis    - The program is supposed to increment each
 *                  element of an array and display the value of
 *                  an unrelated variable.  It has a bug in it.
 *
 *    Objective   - To illustrate a typical error and the fact that
 *                  the compiler does not check on array bounds.
 */

/* Include Files */
#include <stdio.h>
void main( void )
{
     int array[10];
     int nextvar = 5;
     int i;
```

```
        printf( "nextvar is %d.\n", nextvar );              /* Note 1 */
        for ( i = 0; i <= 10; i++ )                          /* Note 2 */
                array[i]=i;
        printf( "nextvar is now %d.\n", nextvar );           /* Note 3 */
}
```

This program consists of a single function, `main()`. Inside `main()`, the value of the variable `nextvar` is displayed both before and after a `for` loop initializes the contents of an array of type `int`.

Note 1: The value of `nextvar` is output.

Note 2: The variable `array` was declared to be an array of integers with 10 cells. Therefore, the legal indices go from 0 to 9 inclusive. In this `for` loop, the loop control variable `i` proceeds from 0 to 10, and each time a value is assigned to `array[i]`. The location accessed by `array[10]` is outside the array. Most compilers will not catch this error, either at compile time or at runtime.

Note 3: The value of `nextvar` is output again. In many implementations of C, the memory location of `nextvar` will be adjacent to that of the array. When a value is assigned to the illegal expression `array[10]`, the value would actually be stored in the location `nextvar`.

Learning Activities

34. Investigate the behavior of bounds.c on your system. Execute it to see if the value of `nextvar` was changed by the program. Add statements to display the addresses of the variables `array`, `nextvar`, and `i`. Is `nextvar` adjacent to the array? If your system does not change the value of `nextvar`, research the method utilized for memory allocation from the documentation supplied with the compiler.

35. Experiment to see if it is possible to change the value of `i` by accessing an array element where the index is outside of the declared index range. How far away is the memory location of `i` from that of `array`? Will your compiler allow you to go that far outside the bounds of the array?

36. Modify the program array1.c of the previous section to accept the input of an array index as an integer, check to ensure it is within the proper range, and then display the array elements from `chararray`, `intarray`, and `floatarray` with that index.

4.7 An Array as a Pointer

In C, a very specific relationship exists between an array and a pointer. It is necessary to understand this relationship thoroughly.

In Section 4.1 we introduced the concept of a pointer. In review, a pointer variable holds an address of a memory location. The variable is said to point to that memory location.

A pointer variable declaration consists of a type followed by an asterisk followed by an expression list, terminated with a semicolon. In simple cases, each expression in the list is a variable name. For example,

```
int *intpointer;
```

declares a variable named `intpointer` with type pointer-to-int (`int *`). The only memory locations that `intpointer` can legally point to are those designated to hold a quantity of type `int`. Once the pointer variable `intpointer` has been declared and initialized, the contents of the memory address stored in `intpointer` are accessed by referring to `*intpointer` in the program.

Allowable operations with pointers include assignment (`=`), comparisons (`==`, `!=`, `<=`, `<`, `>`, `>=`), and certain arithmetic operations with the integers as discussed in Section 4.2.

To illustrate the connection between an array and a pointer, consider the following declaration:

```
int intarray[10];
```

When the compiler processes this array declaration, it sets aside a region in memory large enough to store 10 quantities of type `int`. It also associates the address of the first cell in the array with the name `intarray` in the symbol table for the program. Therefore, anywhere in a C program that the identifier `intarray` is used alone (without any accompanying brackets), the name evaluates to the address of the first cell in the array. The quantity `intarray + 1` is the address of the second cell in the array, and so on. The expressions `*intarray` and `intarray[0]` both refer to the contents of the first cell in the array. The expressions `*(intarray + 1)` and `intarray[1]` both refer to the contents of the second cell in the array, and so on. Thus, the name of an array can be used in a manner very similar to that of a pointer.

Arrays are similar to pointers, but there are differences in the two concepts. The name of an array evaluates to the address in memory of the first element in the array. It can be used on the right hand side of an assignment statement, but not on the left. It can be evaluated, but it cannot be changed. The location of the array is fixed in memory and cannot be moved during program execution. In contrast, a pointer variable can be both evaluated and changed. It can be used on both the right and left hand side of an assignment statement.

Since the concepts of an array and a pointer are so closely linked, C allows the assignment of values between the two types. After the following declarations,

```
int intarray[10], *intpointer;
```

the identifier `intarray` refers to the address of the first element of the region set aside to hold 10 values of type `int`. The identifier `intpointer` remains uninitialized, but is designated to store the address of an `int`. The assignment

```
intpointer = intarray;
```

assigns the address of the first cell in `intarray` to `intpointer`; that is, it makes `intpointer` *point* to the first cell in the array.[1]

Review of Pointer Arithmetic

Recall that in Section 4.2, we demonstrated that for a pointer variable named `ptr`, the meaning of `ptr + 1` is dependent on the type of quantity that `ptr` points to. Consider the following declarations:

```
char   *  charptr;
int    *  intptr;
double *  dblptr;
```

If `intptr` has been initialized to point to an integer, then `intptr + 1` is the address of the next integer. In a byte-addressable computer, it is `sizeof(int)` bigger than `intptr`. Similarly, `dblptr + 1` will be the address of the next memory location for a value of type `double`. It is `sizeof(double)` bigger than `dblptr` in numerical value. The value of `charptr + 1` is usually 1 more than the value of `charptr` because `sizeof(char)` is 1. The next program in Example 4-12 illustrates these concepts. The values of `demoarray` and `demoptr` are addresses and will very probably be different when the program is executed on your computer system.

Example 4-12: arrayptr.c

```
/*                  arrayptr.c
 *
 *    Synopsis    - Prints information about the address, the
 *                  sizeof(), and the contents of an array, using
 *                  both array and pointer notation.
 *
 *    Objective   - To illustrate the relationship between pointers
 *                  and arrays and to demonstrate some of the
 *                  different methods to access array elements.
 */


/* Include Files */
```

---

1. This assignment could have been made as an initialization at the time of the declaration of `intpointer`, providing that `intarray` was the first of the variables declared.

```c
#include <stdio.h>

void main( void )
{
                                                        /* Note 1 */
    char    demoarray[5] = {'D', 'E', 'M', 'O', '!'};
    char    *demoptr = demoarray;
    int     i;

                                                        /* Note 2 */
    printf( "demoarray is %x.\n", demoarray );
    printf( "sizeof( demoarray ) is %d.\n",
                            sizeof( demoarray ) );
    printf( "sizeof( demoarray[0] ) is %d.\n",
                            sizeof( demoarray[0] ) );

                                                        /* Note 3 */
    printf( "\ndemoptr is %x.\n", demoptr );
    printf( "sizeof(demoptr) is %d.\n", sizeof( demoptr ) );
    printf( "sizeof( *demoptr ) is %d.\n",
                            sizeof( *demoptr ) );

    printf( "\ni\tdemoarray[i]\t*(demoarray+i)\t*demoptr\n" );
    printf( "-\t------------\t--------------\t--------\n" );

    for ( i = 0; i < 5; i++, demoptr++ )                /* Note 4 */
                                                        /* Note 5 */
        printf( "%d\t    %c    \t    %c    \t    %c\n",
                i, demoarray[i], *( demoarray + i ), *demoptr );
}
```

Running the Program

```
demoarray is fff0.
sizeof( demoarray ) is 5.
sizeof( demoarray[0] ) is 1.

demoptr is fff0.
sizeof(demoptr) is 2.
sizeof( *demoptr ) is 1.
```

```
i     demoarray[i]  *(demoarray+i)  *demoptr
-     ------------  --------------   --------
0          D              D             D
1          E              E             E
2          M              M             M
3          O              O             O
4          !              !             !
```

The body of the single function `main()` consists of calls to `printf()` followed by a `for` loop. The body of the `for` loop is another call to `printf()`.

Note 1: The variables for this program are an initialized array of 5 elements of type `char` and a `char *` variable that is initialized to point to the array. The variable `i` will be used to control the `for` loop.

Note 2: The first three `printf()` calls give the address of the array, the `sizeof()` the array, and the `sizeof()` the first element in the array. The `sizeof()` the array is the total number of bytes in the whole array.

Note 3: The next three `printf()` calls give the address that is currently in the variable `demoptr`, the `sizeof( demoptr )` and the `sizeof()` the quantity pointed to by `demoptr`. Note that the address in `demoptr` should be identical to the address of `demoarray`. However, `sizeof( demoptr )` should give the number of bytes necessary to hold an address on the computer system. This illustrates one of the differences between pointers and arrays.

Note 4: The `for` loop will print out a table of the three named quantities. Notice the use of the comma operator; both `i` and `demoptr` will be incremented during the bottom of the loop processing.

Note 5: Each of the expressions to be output by `printf()` references exactly the same quantity. The output from this loop should demonstrate the equivalences of the three different expressions. Notice that a pointer variable can be and was used to traverse the array.

Learning Activities

37.   Modify arrayptr.c by attempting to assign a value to `demoarray` after the `for` loop (or try to use the increment by 1 operator, `++`, on `demoarray`). This is an error because the array cannot be moved in memory during execution (`demoarray` is a constant value). How does your system handle this error? Is it caught at compile time, at runtime, or not caught at all?

Toward Efficiency

The last example showed that `*(demoarray + i)`, `demoarray[i]`, and `*demoptr` refer to the same quantity. Most programmers are more comfortable with the notation `demoarray[i]` because this syntax is similar to that used to access array elements in many other languages. However, in C, the expression `*demoptr` is the most efficient of the three expressions to access an element in an array of `int`s, since both of the other expressions must undergo evaluation to find the address of the array element, and this evaluation involves extra calculation. Therefore, it is very common to use a pointer to access array elements in an attempt to optimize the program's performance.

4.8 Arrays as Parameters to Functions

Arrays can be passed as parameters to functions; however, in contrast to other variable types, it is not possible to pass a copy of an array as a parameter.[1] Instead, the address of the array serves as the parameter and the function can access the array elements through the address.

There are two ways of declaring an array as a parameter to a function. The first makes use of the relationship between pointers and arrays. As an example,

```
doit( int *intarray )
{
    /* function code */
}
```

would declare `intarray` as the parameter to `doit()`. The notation indicates that the address of the first element of the array is what the function sees.

In the second syntax the comparable part of the code would be

```
doit( int intarray[] )[2]
```

Note that the function will have no knowledge of the number of elements in the array from the declaration. It will only know the base address and the element type of the array. This makes programming tools using arrays much easier and more flexible.

Inside the code for the function body, either of the two notations (the subscripting notation with brackets, `[]`, or the pointer arithmetic notation with the indirection operator, `*`) can be used to access the array elements. Stylistically, it is

---

1. An exception to this statement occurs when an array is a component of another data structure and a copy of the other structure is passed as a parameter. In this case, a copy of the array is passed also. See Chapter 7.
2. The corresponding declarations for older compilers would be

```
        doit( intarray )
        int *intarray;
```
and
```
        doit( intarray )
        int intarray[];
```

better to be consistent with the notation chosen, at least throughout the code for any function.

The program in Example 4-13 gives an example of input and output of arrays. A function is invoked for both the input and the output of an array. The array is passed as a parameter to both functions.

Example 4-13: arraypar.c

```
/*                  arraypar.c
 *
 *    Synopsis    - Accepts input of int values (an inventory) from
 *                  standard input into an array and displays them
 *                  on standard output.
 *
 *    Objective   - To illustrate passing an array as a parameter
 *                  to a function.
 */

/* Include Files */
#include <stdio.h>

/* Constant Definitions */
#define MAX  20

/* Function Declarations */
void print_inventory( int[], int );                     /* Note 1 */
int input_inventory( int *, int );                      /* Note 2 */

void main( void )
{
    int inventory[MAX];                                 /* Note 3 */
    int num_items;

    printf( "Please enter the number of items in stock." );
    printf( "  Enter -1 when you are done.\n" );

                                                        /* Note 4 */
    num_items = input_inventory( inventory, MAX );
                                                        /* Note 5 */
    print_inventory( inventory, num_items );
}

/***************************** input_inventory()  *************/
/*    Accepts input of MAX or less values of type int and stores
```

```
 *    them in an array.  Returns the number of items entered.
 *    Checks for overflowing the end of the array.
 */
int input_inventory( int *inventory, int maxnum )          /* Note 6 */
{
     int index = 0;

     scanf( "%d", ( inventory + index ) );
     while ( index < maxnum-1 && *(inventory + index) != -1 ) {
          index++;
          scanf( "%d", ( inventory + index ) );          /* Note 7 */
     }
     if ( index == maxnum - 1 ) {
          printf( "No room for more items.\n" );
          return ( index+1 );
     }
     else return ( index );
}
/****************************** print_inventory()  ************/
/*    Displays the values in an array of ints.  The parameter
 *    numitems indicates the number of meaningful items in the
 *    array.
 */
void print_inventory( int inventory[], int numitems )      /* Note 8 */
{
     int index;

     for ( index = 0; index < numitems; index++ ) {
          printf( "Item number %d:\t\t", index+1 );
          printf( "Number on hand  %5d\n", inventory[index] );
     }
}
```

The program is made up of the functions `main()`, `input_inventory()`, and `print_inventory()`. The function `main()` is a driver; it outputs a message with `printf()`, calls `input_inventory()` to do some input, and calls `print_inventory()` to do some output. Both `input_inventory()` and `print_inventory()` are controlled by loops that traverse the array.

Note 1: The ANSI prototype declaration of `print_inventory()` contains the name of the function, the return type, and the number and type of the parameters. The syntax `int[]` indicates that the first parameter to the function is an array of `int`s. The second parameter is of type `int`, and will contain the number of meaningful entries in the array.

Note 2: The ANSI C prototype declaration of the function `input_inventory()` appears on this line. The syntax `int  *` declares the first parameter to be a pointer-to-int (that is, an address of an int). When the function is called, this parameter will be the address of the first cell in the inventory array.

Note 3: The array inventory is declared to store twenty int values.

Note 4: The function input_inventory() takes two actual parameters: the address of the array inventory, and the total number of cells in the array. The value returned is the total number of items that were entered by the user and stored in the array inventory.

Note 5: The function print_inventory() also takes two actual parameters: the address of the array, and the number of cells that have data stored in them.

Note 6: When an array is passed as a parameter, its name and type must appear between the parentheses after the function name in the function declaration. Since the address of the array is passed to the function, the pointer notation can be used to declare the parameter. The pointer notation is used throughout the function body.

Note 7: A call to scanf() accepts input of a decimal integer. Recall that scanf() requires the address of the memory location where the input value is to be stored. The name inventory is the address of the base of the array. The expression

```
inventory + index
```

is the address of the cell with the proper offset. For each iteration of the while loop, values are read into successive cells of the array. There are two tests for terminating the while loop. If twenty values are entered, the loop will terminate, and the array will be full. If the inventory contains fewer than twenty items, the user is directed to enter -1 from the terminal as a sentinel value. Note that -1 is an appropriate sentinel since it could not be the inventory of any item.

Note 8: This parameter declaration demonstrates that the array notation can be used as well as the pointer notation. The array notation is used throughout this function. Stylistically, consistent notation should be used throughout a function.

Learning Activities

38. a. Rewrite input_inventory() using array notation throughout that function. Compile and execute the code with both functions written in array notation. If there is a facility for timing the execution of a program on your computer system, time the execution of the modified program and record the results.

    b. Rewrite the function print_inventory() using pointer notation instead of array notation. Using the original version of input_inventory() (in pointer notation also), compile and execute the modified program. If possible, time the execution of this version of the program and record the results.

c. Compare the two versions of the program arraypar.c. Is there a difference in the size of the object code? Was there a difference in the execution time of the program? Draw any conclusions you can about the efficiency of each version.

39.   Many beginning C programmers are tempted to put the number of elements in the array into the parameter declarations when an array is passed as an argument to a function. Starting with the version of arraypar.c that you modified in 38a above, change both parameter declarations of the array `inventory` to include the number of cells. Make both declarations read

```
int inventory[20];
```

Attempt to compile and run the program. What did you discover? If it runs correctly, compare the size of the executable versions of the code. Compare the contents of the two executable files. What conclusions, if any, can you draw? (On most systems, the `20` will be ignored and the two versions will be identical. Does this happen on your system?)

40.   If you do not have an ANSI C compiler, change both function definitions to conform to your compiler's requirements.

41.   Write a function that will sum the elements in an array of `ints`. Have your function take the array address and the number of elements as parameters and return the sum of the elements. Modify arraypar.c to have `print_inventory()` call this function and output the total of the inventory items after the output of the array contents.

42.   If you chose to write your function in array notation, rewrite it in pointer notation. Otherwise, rewrite it in array notation.

Language Elements Introduced in This Chapter: A Review

✓ **Arrays**
  • Indices always go from 0 to one less than size of array.
  • Accessing elements:
```
chararray[index]
*( chararray + index )
```
  • Initializing:
```
char chararray[10] = { '1', '2', '3' };
/* only the first three cells are initialized */
```

```
char constarray[] = { '1', '2', '3' };
/* the array will have only three cells    */
```

✓ Constant Definitions
- NULL is defined as 0 in stdio.h and many other header files.

✓ Operators
- The address operator
  - &   gives the address of a variable.
- The dereferencing operator
  - *   used with an address, gives the contents of that address.
- The sizeof() operator
  - used with an array returns the number of bytes in that array.

✓ Parameters to Functions
- To simulate pass by reference: pass the address of a variable to the function, e.g.,

  ```
  funct( int x, int *y )
  /* funct() will be able to change whatever
   * value y points to */
  ```

- To pass an array as a parameter to a function, pass in the address only, e.g.,

  function declaration:
  ```
  funct( int *array )
  funct( int array[] )
  ```

  function call:
  ```
  int array[50];
      ...
  funct( array );
  ```

✓ Types
- Pointer types
- One-dimensional arrays

✓ Variable Declarations
- Pointers:
  ```
  char * charptr;
  int  * intptr;
  ```
- Arrays:
  ```
  char  chararray[12];
  float floatvals[20];
  ```

Things to Remember

1. A pointer holds a memory address.
2. Each pointer type, `char *`, `int *`, and so on, is a distinct type. The pointer arithmetic is defined differently for different pointer types.
3. Like all other variables, pointers must be initialized to point to something meaningful before either reading or writing their contents.
4. Setting a pointer to `NULL` indicates that it doesn't point anywhere.
5. The declaration `int *ptr;` indicates that `*ptr` is an `int` and that `ptr` is the address of an `int`.
6. Parameters to a function are passed by value. A function cannot change the value of a variable in the calling environment that is passed in as a parameter.
7. Remember to explicitly allocate space for an array either by placing the number of cells inside the brackets when declaring or by initializing all cells of the array.
8. Be careful: C will allow you to overrun the bounds of your array.
9. The name of an array without any brackets gives the address of the first cell of the array.
10. Pointers can be used to traverse arrays efficiently.
11. If the efficiency of a program is a major concern, array element access can be done more efficiently with pointer notation.
12. When an array is passed as a parameter to a function, only the address is passed in.

Exercises and Programming Problems

1. Consider the program you wrote for exercise 1 of Chapter 3. Make the following modifications to the program. For every variable in your program, add a declaration of a pointer variable of each type and initialize the pointer to point to the original variable. Modify the executable code in the program so that all data is accessed via pointer variables instead of the original variables.

2. a. Write a program that contains declarations of one variable of each of the basic types (`int`, `char`, `long`, `short`, `unsigned`, `float`, `double`) as well as declarations of one variable of each of the pointer types (pointer-to-`int`, pointer-to-`char`, pointer-to-`long`, etc.). Initialize each of the pointer variables to point to the corresponding variable of the base type. Initialize each of the nonpointer variables also. Have your program use the pointer notation to display the address of each of the nonpointer variables. Use the dereferencing `*` to output the value of each nonpointer variable. Use the address operator, `&`, to output the address of each of the pointer variables. Compile and execute your program.

    b. Use the values displayed from the execution of your program to draw a diagram of memory (a memory map) during your program's execution. Use the diagrams in Figure 4-2 as a model.

    c. Modify your program by changing the order of the variable declarations. Then execute it again and see if the memory map changes.

3. Write a program to accept input of elements to be stored in an array of type `float` and to output those values in reverse order.

4. The following program is designed to input values for an array of three `ints` and then display the contents of the array. It does not work correctly. For example, try to enter the value 1 for each cell in the array. Because the problem has to do with memory management, the addresses of the variables are output before the array initialization begins. Find the bug in the program.

```
/*               prob3.c
 *
 * Synopsis    - Designed to input values into an array
 *               of three ints and then display the
 *               contents of that array. Has a bug in it.
 *
 * Objective   - To provide practice debugging a program
 *               with a common mistake.
 */
/* Include Files */
#include <stdio.h>

void main( void )
{
    int intarray[3], count;

    printf( "intarray  %x,   &count  %x.\n",
                                intarray, &count );
    for ( count = 0; count <= 3; count++ ) {
            printf( "Cell #%d : ", count );
            scanf( "%d", intarray+count );
    }

    printf( "The contents of the array are: " );
    for ( count = 0; count <= 3; count++ )
            printf( "%d\n", intarray[count] );
}
```

5.   a. Write a function named `addarray()` that returns the sum of the elements of an array of `int` values. Your function should take two parameters, the array, and the number of elements in the array. Make your function work with the program below.

```
/*              arraysum.c
 *
 *  Synopsis    - Displays the value returned by the
 *                function addarray() with two different
 *                sets of parameters.
 *
 *  Objective   - To provide a test program for the
 *                function addarray() written for an
 *                exercise. The answers should be 55 and 0.
 */

/* Include Files */
#include <stdio.h>

/* Function Declarations */
int addarray( int *, int );

void main( void )
{
    int     array1[10] = { 1, 2, 3, 4, 5, 6, 7, 8, 9, 10 },
            array2[4]  = { 0, 0, 0, 0 };

    printf( "The sum of the elements in array1 is %d.\n",
                                    addarray( array1, 10 ) );
    printf( "The sum of the elements in array2 is %d.\n",
                                    addarray( array2, 4 ) );
}
```

b. If you used array subscript notation in your function `addarray()`, change it to pointer notation. If you used pointer notation initially, rewrite the function with array subscript notation. Test the new version of your function with the program in part a.

6. Write a menu-driven mini-statistics package. A user should be able to enter up to 200 items of `float` data. The program should calculate the number of items in the data, the mean, the standard deviation, the variance, the median and the mode of the data. A sample run follows. The symbol `<EOF>` in the sample run below should be replaced with `CTRL-Z` or `CTRL-D` or the end-of-file symbol on your system.

```
Mini-Stat Package
-----------------
This program will perform the following:
1)   Enter data.
2)   Display the data and the following statistics:
     the number of data items, the high and low values
```

in the data, the mean, median, mode, variance and
standard deviation.

3) Quit the program.

Your choice? **1**

Enter one data item after each prompt. Press return
after each one. Signal with <EOF> when you are done
with data input.
Item #1 : **25**
Item #2 : **36**
Item #3 : **27.5**
Item #4 : **28**
Item #5 : **32**
Item #6 : **33.25**
Item #7 : **<EOF>**

This program will perform the following:
1) Enter data.
2) Display the data and the following statistics:
    the number of data items, the high and low values
    in the data, the mean, median, mode, variance and
    standard deviation.
3) Quit the program.

Your choice? **2**
Data Items:
25   36   27.5   28   32   33.25
Number of data items : 6
Largest data item   : 36
Smallest data item   : 25
Mean   : 30.292
Median   : 30
Mode   : no mode
Variance   : 14.21
Standard Deviation   : 3.77
This program will perform the following:
1) Enter data.
2) Display the data and the following statistics:
    the number of data items, the high and low values
    in the data, the mean, median, mode, variance and
    standard deviation.
3) Quit the program.

Your choice? **1**

```
Do you want to add new data to the existing sample? (Y/N)  Y
Signal with <EOF> when you are done.
Item #7  :  29.7
Item #8  :  28.2
Item #9  :  35.3
Item #10 :  28
Item #11 :  <EOF>

This program will perform the following:
1)  Enter data.
2)  Display the data and the following statistics:
    the number of data items, the high and low values
    in the data, the mean, median, mode, variance and
    standard deviation.
3)  Quit the program.
-----------------------------------------------------------
Your choice? 2

Data Items:
25      36      27.5      28      32      33.25      29.7      28.2
35.3    28
Number of data items : 10
Largest data item    : 36
Smallest data item   : 25
Mean                 : 30.295
Median               : 28.95
Mode                 : 28
Variance             : 12.03
Standard Deviation   : 3.469

This program will perform the following:
1)  Enter data.
2)  Display the data and the following statistics:
    the number of data items, the high and low values
    in the data, the mean, median, mode, variance and
    standard deviation.
3)  Quit the program.
-----------------------------------------------------------
Your choice? 3

Thank you and goodbye!
```

7. Assume that an address and a variable of type int both occupy four bytes of memory. Predict the output of the following program.

The answers for the first few are given.

```
/*                ptrex.c
 *
 *  Synopsis   - Illustrates different ways of addressing
 *               pointers and arrays.  Outputs the values
 *               of expressions relevant to the arrays.
 *
 *  Objective  - To provide practice with pointer and
 *               array expressions.
 */

/* Include Files */
#include <stdio.h>

void main( void )
{
    static int intarray[5] = {
                     32, -123, 4, 2, -24      };
    static char chararray[5] = {
                     'e', 'f', 'g', 'h', 'i' };

    int  *int_ptr  = intarray;
    char *char_ptr = chararray,
         ch = 'a';

                                         /* ANSWERS */

    printf( "%d\n", int_ptr );       /* _8204_____ */

    printf( "%d\n", char_ptr );      /* _8224_____ */

    printf( "%d\n", &int_ptr );      /* _16756484_____ */

    printf( "%d\n", *int_ptr );      /* _____ */

    printf( "%d\n", intarray[4] );   /* _____ */

    printf( "%d\n", chararray[4] );  /* _____ */

    printf( "%d\n", intarray + 1 );  /* _____ */

    printf( "%d\n", chararray + 1 ); /* _____ */

    printf( "%d\n", int_ptr + 1 );   /* _____ */

    printf( "%d\n", char_ptr + 1 );  /* _____ */
```

```
        printf( "%d\n", *int_ptr + 1 );      /* _____ */

        printf( "%d\n", *char_ptr + 1 );     /* _____ */

        printf( "%d\n", *(int_ptr + 1) );  /* _____ */

        printf( "%d\n", *(char_ptr + 1) ); /* _____ */

        printf( "%d\n", &intarray[0] );      /* _____ */

        printf( "%d\n", ++*int_ptr );        /* _____ */

        printf( "%d\n", *int_ptr++ );        /* _____ */

        printf( "%d\n", ++(*int_ptr) );      /* _____ */

        printf( "%d\n", ++*intarray );       /* _____ */

        printf( "%d\n", *&ch );              /* _____ */

        printf( "%d\n", 3**int_ptr );        /* _____ */
}
```

8. Find and correct the bugs in the following program.

```
/*                   bug.c
 *
 *   Synopsis    - Supposed to accept input values of 10
 *                 integer values for the array, add 5 to
 *                 each value, and display the values in the
 *                 array, but it doesn't work.
 *
 *   Objective   - To provide practice in finding a common
 *                 mistake.
 */

/* Include Files */
#include <stdio.h>

/* Function Declarations */
void init_array( int[], int );
void add_five( int[], int );
void print_array( int[], int );

void main( void )
{
    int intarray[10];
```

```
        init_array( intarray, 10 );
        add_five( intarray, 10 );
        print_array( intarray, 10 );
}

void init_array( int array[], int numelts )
{
    int i;

    printf( "Please enter values for the array:\n" );
    for ( i = 0; i < numelts; i++ ) {
        printf( "%d: ", i );
        scanf( "%d", array+i );
    }
}

void add_five( int array[], int numelts )
{
    int i = -1;

    printf( "\nAdding five to each element of the array.\n" );
    while ( i++ < numelts - 1 );
        array[i] += 5;
}

void print_array( int array[], int numelts )
{
    int i;

    printf( "\nThe values in the array are:\n" );
    for ( i = 0; i < numelts; i++ )
        printf( "%d\t", *( array+i ) );
    printf( "\n" );
}
```

9. The following program contains a function named `bubble_sort()` and a function named `swap()`. Together they are supposed to implement the bubble sort algorithm to sort the elements in an array of integers. The function `main()` contains a call to `bubble_sort()` and a `for` loop to print the values in the array. The program has a bug in it.

```
/*              bubble.c
 *
 *  Synopsis    - Attempts to implement a bubble sort of an
 *                array of integers. It has a small bug in
 *                it.  Fix the bug.
 *
 *
 *
```

```
*     Objective -  Gives practice in debugging.
*/

/* Include Files */
#include <stdio.h>

/* Function Declarations */
void bubble_sort( int[], int );
void swap (int, int );

void main( void )
{
    int index, data[10] = {
                  10, 3, 4, 8, 2, 5, 9, 7, 1, 6 };

    bubble_sort( data, 10 );

    for ( index=0; index < 10; index++ )
          printf( "%d ", data[index] );
    printf( "\n" );
}

void bubble_sort( int data[], int num_elts )
{
    int i, j;

    for ( i = 0; i < num_elts; i++ )
          for ( j = num_elts-1; j > i; j-- )
                if ( data[j] < data[j-1] )
                      swap( data[j], data[j-1] );
}

void swap( int a, int b )
{
    int temp;

    temp = a;
    a = b;
    b = temp;
}
```

a. Fix the bug in the program. The array should be sorted when it is output.

b. Rewrite the program so that a user may enter up to 100 values and the program will sort them.

10. Look up another sorting algorithm (quicksort, heap sort, insertion sort or

merge_sort, for example). Implement that sort in C and test it. You may want to replace the call to `bubble_sort()` in your program from exercise 9b with a call to your new sorting function to implement a program to test your code.

11. The function `sin(x)` has the following infinite series expansion:

$$x - \frac{x^3}{3!} + \frac{x^5}{5!} - \frac{x^7}{7!} + \ldots + \frac{x^{2n+1}}{(2n+1)!} + \ldots$$

a. Write a program similar to exp.c in Example 4-8 that will calculate the `sin(x)` when the user enters x in radians. Make sure your functions are declared correctly and that you pass the parameters to the functions. Have the calculated value of `sin(x)` output in `main()`.

b. After the program in part a is working, modify it so that the user can enter the angle in degrees instead of radians.

12. a. Write a C function that will input values into an array of type `int`. Have the array and the number of elements in the array passed as parameters to your function. Use a local pointer variable to traverse the array.

b. Write a C function that will output the contents of an array of type `int`. Have the array and the number of elements in the array passed as parameters. Use a local pointer variable to traverse the array.

## Chapter 5

Strings

5.1 Introduction to Strings

In computer science, a string is a sequence of characters from the underlying character set. There are different methods for handling strings in different languages. A string in C is a sequence of characters terminated by a null character, '\0'.

String constants were first discussed in Chapter 1. A string constant is used as the first parameter in a call to `printf()`. Recall the statement from the program output.c of Example 1-3:

```
printf ("Testing 1, 2, 3\n");
```

The expression `"Testing 1, 2, 3\n"` is a string constant. A string constant appears in a C program inside a set of double quotes (").

When the compiler sees a sequence of characters enclosed in double quotes, it stores the sequence in a special place in the object code and appends a terminating '\0' to the end of the character sequence. For example,

T	e	s	t	i	n	g		1	,		2	,		3	\n	\0

It then associates the string constant with the address of the memory location of the first character in the string.

If the statement

```
printf ("Testing 1, 2, 3\n");
```

appeared in a program, the characters in the string would be stored in the executable code with a terminating null character (`'\0'`) appended. The memory address of the location where the `'T'` is stored would be the parameter to `printf()`. When that statement is executed, `printf()` will look at the address and start its output with the character found at that address. It stops output when it reaches the terminating null character.

The concept of a string is very closely related to that of a character array and to that of a pointer to a character. A string is very much like an array of characters in that the characters in the string are stored in contiguous memory locations. One difference is that a string must have a null character as the string terminator while a character array does not require the `'\0'`.

Because it is handled as the address of its first character, a string is like a pointer-to-`char`. In fact, since the compiler handles the string `"Testing 1, 2, 3\n"` as the address of the `'T'`, the string could be assigned to a `char *` variable. For example,

```
char *stringptr;
...
    stringptr = "Testing 1, 2, 3\n";
```

Then the call to `printf()` could be rewritten as

```
    printf( stringptr );
```

C allows the use of the array indexing syntax to access the individual elements of a string. For example, after the above sequence of code, the notation `stringptr[0]` would be the `'T'`, `stringptr[6]` would be the `'g'`, and `stringptr[7]` would be the first blank character.

Pointer arithmetic and dereferencing could also be used to access the individual characters in the string. For example, `*stringptr` would be the `'T'`, and `*(stringptr + 6)` would be the `'g'`.

With `printf()`, the conversion specification `%s` signals the output of a string. When `printf()` sees `%s` in its control string, it expects the corresponding parameter to be the address of the first character in a string. It again starts output with the byte found at that address and proceeds displaying subsequent bytes until it encounters a null character. For example, the string `"Testing 1, 2, 3\n"` could be output with the following call to `printf()`:

```
    printf( "%s", stringptr );
```

Note that the `%s` conversion specification can be used with `scanf()` too. When `%s` appears in the control string for `scanf()`, the corresponding parameter should be the address of an array with enough space to handle the input. The string that `scanf()` will put in the array will be the first sequence of characters that does not contain a whitespace character. The input will terminate and leave the first whitespace character in the input buffer. For example, if the input is

H	e	l	l	o		t	h	e	r	e	\n

scanf() will place

H	e	l	l	o	\0

in the array. The

	t	h	e	r	e	\n

will remain in the input stream.

The program string1.c in Example 5-1 illustrates the basic concept of a string and some of the acceptable notation for accessing elements of a string. Both the array and the pointer syntax are illustrated.

Example 5-1: string1.c

```
/*              string1.c
 *
 *   Synopsis    - Displays a string, address of a string and
 *                 some characters from the string.
 *
 *   Objective   - To illustrate how C compilers handle strings.
 */

/* Include Files */
#include <stdio.h>

void main( void )
{
     char *stringptr;                                      /* Note 1 */

     stringptr = "Testing, 1, 2, 3\n";                     /* Note 2 */

     printf( stringptr );                                  /* Note 3 */
     printf( "%s", stringptr );                            /* Note 4 */
     printf( "%p\n", stringptr );                          /* Note 5 */

                                                           /* Note 6 */
     printf( "First Character: %c\n", stringptr[0] );
                                                           /* Note 7 */
     printf( "Second Character: %c\n", *( stringptr + 1 ) );
}
```

This program consists of the single function `main()`. The executable code consists of assignment statements and calls to `printf()`.

Note 1: A variable of type `char *` is declared. It will be used to hold the address of the first character in a string.

Note 2: A string is assigned to the variable with type `char *`. The compiler stored the string in a special place in the executable code and in this statement, the address of the first character, `'T'`, is assigned to `stringptr`.

Note 3: The variable `stringptr` can be used as the first parameter to `printf()`. This emphasizes the fact that `printf()` looks for the address of the first character of its control string.

Note 4: This call to `printf()` illustrates the `%s` conversion specification. It indicates that a string is to be displayed. The corresponding parameter to `printf()` should be the address of the first character in the string.

Note 5: The address of the first character in the string is displayed. The `%p` conversion specification is used in the control string to `printf()`. This emphasizes the fact that `stringptr` really contains the address of a character which is a numerical quantity. That quantity could be output in decimal or octal as well as hexadecimal.

Note that `printf()` can access the same argument in two different contexts, as a string and as a numerical address. When it expects a string, it assumes that the value it finds is the address of the first character to be output. When it expects a numerical value, it does the conversion to the desired output format and displays the resulting value. The meaning comes from the context.

Note 6: The first character in the string is displayed. Even though `stringptr` was declared to be type `char *`, the syntax for array indexing can be used to access a character. This is allowed since the concept of an array of type `char` is so closely related to a pointer-to-`char`.

Note 7: The second character in the string is displayed. This time, the dereferencing operator, `*`, is used. The expression `stringptr + 1` is the address of the second character; `*(stringptr + 1)` is the character. Pointer arithmetic is used to designate the address of that memory cell.

Learning Activities

1. Compile and execute string1.c. Make sure you understand everything in this program.

2. The output of the second character in the string could be done by incrementing the value of `stringptr` instead of using pointer arithmetic. Modify string1.c to use this technique. You will need to

> increment the value of stringptr by one and then dereference it to access the stored character. What happens in the final call to `printf()`?

Arrays and String Manipulation

When a program needs to manipulate a string, the string is usually stored in an array that has sufficient space for all of the array manipulation. C provides a method of storing a string in an array at the time the array is declared. For example, the declaration

```
char string_array[ 80 ] = "Testing 1, 2, 3\n";
```

declares an array of 80 chars, and stores the string Testing 1, 2, 3\n in it. A terminating null character is also stored to delimit the end of the string.

Once the string is stored in the array, the manipulation of the string could be done with assignment of values to the cells of the array. The program manip.c in Example 5-2 illustrates how this is done. This program was executed on a computer with two byte words and a segmented addressing scheme. The address displayed could be different on your computer system.

Example 5-2:   manip.c

```
/*                  manip.c
 *
 *   Synopsis    - Displays a string and its address. Changes the
 *                 string and displays it again.
 *
 *   Objective   - To illustrate how an array can be used to store
 *                 and manipulate a string.
 */

/* Include Files */
#include <stdio.h>

void main( void )
{
                                                    /* Note 1 */
    char work_string[ 512 ] = "One two, buckle my shoe\n";

                                                    /* Note 2 */
    printf( work_string );
```

```
        printf( "%s", work_string );
        printf( "%p\n", work_string );

        *( work_string + 7 ) = '\n';                      /* Note 3 */
        work_string[ 8 ] = '\0';                          /* Note 4 */

        printf( work_string );
}
```

 Running the Program

```
One two, buckle my shoe
One two, buckle my shoe
FDF6
One two
```

The single function `main()` consists of the declaration and initialization of an array, a series of calls to `printf()`, and assignment statements.

Note 1: An array of type `char` named `work_string` is declared and initialized to hold the string `"One two, buckle my shoe\n"`. We will manipulate this string in the program and the string will be stored in an array for manipulation.

The number of cells in this array is much larger than is actually needed by the program. This was done to make the point that the array must have sufficient memory for all possible string manipulations that a program will do. If characters are added to the end of the string, and there is not enough cells in the array then other valuable data may be overwritten. The final choice for the number of elements in an array used for string manipulations will depend on the actual manipulations and possibly the maximum number of characters that the operating system allows in a line of text.

Note the syntax of the initialization of this array of type `char`. This syntax is only legal with the declaration of the array. This initialization causes the characters in `"One two, buckle my shoe\n"` to be placed in the array.

Note 2: The next three calls to `printf()` mimic the first three calls to `printf()` in the program string1.c. This points out the ways in which an array of characters containing a string is similar to a pointer to a character that is initialized to point to a string.

Note 3: The next two assignment statements change some of the characters in the string `work_string`. Access of the individual characters in the string can be done in two ways: using pointer arithmetic and array notation.

The first assignment statement, done with pointer arithmetic, places a newline, '\n', immediately after the word "two". The comma is over-written.

Note 4: The second assignment statement uses array subscripting and places a '\0' after the newline to terminate the string at this point. The following call to printf() displays the modified string. Output stops at the first null character.

Note that both array subscripting and pointer arithmetic can be utilized to access memory locations within the string stored in an array. Recall that the name of an array evaluates to the address of the first element in the array.

Learning Activities

3. Replace the line
    ```
    char work_string[ 512 ] = "One two, buckle my shoe\n";
    ```
    with the two lines
    ```
    char work_string[ 512 ];
    work_string = "One two, buckle my shoe\n";
    ```
    and attempt to compile and execute the program again. What happens? Explain the meaning of the assignment statement and why it doesn't work. This illustrates one of the differences between a pointer variable and an array variable.

4. Write a program like string1.c and have it display the poem
    ```
    One two, buckle my shoe.
    Three four, shut the door.
    ```
    on separate lines as shown, then manipulate those strings so that the program displays
    ```
    One two three four!
    ```
    on one line.

5.2 Variable Strings

As seen in Example 5-1, a string can be assigned to a char * variable. Some compilers will allow any of the characters in the string to be changed by accessing the characters using the pointer variable. The access of individual characters can be done either with array subscripting notation or with pointer arithmetic. However, an error occurs if an attempt is made to append new characters to the end of the string. This error may (or may not) cause a program to crash or corrupt the program's data.

The problem arises because of the amount of memory allocated for the string. A programmer is only guaranteed that there is a byte allocated for each character in the string plus one for the terminating '\0'.

As seen in Example 5-2, if a program needs to process strings of unknown or changing length, enough space must be allocated for a string of maximum length. This can be done with an array of characters. If the programmer wants to treat an array of characters as a string, it is necessary to write a terminating null into the array after the last meaningful character.

The program strngio1.c in Example 5-3 illustrates the creation of a string from an array of characters. It accepts input of characters for the string from the keyboard and displays the resulting string with printf(). The function inputstring() in this program is a useful tool. It reads the characters from the system input buffer, stopping at the '\n', and stores them in a buffer that is internal to the program. It replaces the '\n' with '\0' so the input can be treated as a string. The only parameter to inputstring() is the address of the first character in the input buffer.

Example 5-3: strngio1.c

```
/*                  strngio1.c
 *
 *     Synopsis    - Accepts a line of text as input from the
 *                   keyboard and echoes it to the terminal screen.
 *
 *     Objective   - To illustrate the use of an array to create a
 *                   string and point out the connection among
 *                   pointers, arrays, and strings.
 */

/* Include Files */
#include <stdio.h>

/* Function Declarations */
void inputstring( char * );                             /* Note 1 */

void main( void )
{
     char inputarray[512];                              /* Note 2 */
     char *inputptr = inputarray;

     printf( "Enter a line of text.\n> " );
     inputstring( inputptr );                           /* Note 3 */
     printf( inputarray );
}
```

```
/********************************* inputstring()  ***********/

/*   Accepts input of a line of text from the keyboard and stores
 *   it in the array pointed to by its argument.
 */

void inputstring( char *inputptr )
{
                                                         /* Note 4 */
     while ( ( *inputptr++ = getchar() ) != '\n' )
     ;

     *( --inputptr ) = '\0';                             /* Note 5 */
}
```

Two functions, `main()` and `inputstring()`, make up this program. In `main()`, the executable code consists of two calls to `printf()` and a call to the function `inputstring()`. The function `inputstring()` consists of a while loop to do the input and an assignment statement.

Note 1: The declaration of the parameter to the function `inputstring()` is made in the prototype syntax of ANSI C. (It must be changed on systems without an ANSI C compiler.)

Note 2: Space is allocated by declaring an array of `512` characters. This will serve as the internal buffer to hold the line of text entered from the keyboard. It is unlikely that a line entered from the keyboard will exceed this length. To be more precise, the maximum length of an input line should be researched in the operating system documentation. In the next declaration, a pointer to `char` variable is defined and initialized to point to the array.

Note 3: A call to the function `inputstring()` is made. The argument to this function is the address of the first character of the buffer where the input text is to be stored.

Note 4: In this `while` loop, the call to `getchar()` reads a single character and assigns it to the address pointed to by the parameter `inputptr`. Then `inputptr` is incremented to point to the next position in the array and the value is compared to a newline character. All of this is done in the expression of the `while` loop. The loop has an empty body.

Note 5: After the input of the line is done, a null character, `'\0'`, is placed in the position of the original newline character. The newline character had already been put in the buffer and `inputptr` incremented to point to the next position. Therefore, `inputptr` must be decremented before the assignment is made.

Learning Activities

To answer the following questions, it may be necessary to test the concept by modifying the program strngio1.c, compiling it, and executing it.

5. Could `inputptr` have been used as an argument to the second call to `printf()` in `main()`? Why or why not?

6. Could `inputarray` have been used as the actual parameter to `inputstring()`? Why or why not?

7. Are both variables in `main()` necessary? Why or why not? If not, which could be eliminated and why?

"The input and output of strings is often done in sea (C)." Based on *The Herring Net* by Winslow Homer, 1885.

5.3 Input and Output of Strings

The input and output of strings is done often in C programs. Consequently, standard library functions have been written to do string I/O. The library function `gets()` reads a string from standard input, and the library function `puts()` writes a string to standard output. Other library functions that can be used for string input and output will be discussed in Chapter 10.

The library function `gets()` acts very much like the function `inputstring()` from our last example. It takes a single parameter, which is the address of an array where the input is to be stored. The array must be declared in the program. It reads each character in the input stream and stores them in successive locations in the array until it finds a newline character in the input. The newline character is discarded and `'\0'` is placed in the buffer to terminate the string.

One difference between `gets()` and `inputstring()` is that `gets()` returns a value of type `char *`. If the input was successful, `gets()` will return the address of the buffer where it put the input string. If an error occurs or the end-of-file was encountered in the input, a NULL pointer is returned. In either of these latter cases, there is no guarantee about the contents of the array.

The function `puts()` displays a string on standard output; it returns a value of type `int`. It also takes the address of an array declared in the program as a parameter. It expects to find a string stored there. It will output each successive byte at that location until the first `'\0'` is encountered. The `'\0'` is not output; instead a newline is output in its place. If an error occurred during output, `puts()` signals the error by returning the value EOF. No special significance is attached to values other than EOF that are returned by `puts()`.

Notice that it is possible to output a string with `printf()`. The statements

```
printf( string );
```

and

```
printf( "%s\n", string );
```

will both display the contents of the `char *` variable `string`. In the latter case a final newline character is output so that the `printf()` call has the same effect as the call

```
puts( string );
```

In terms of use, `puts()` is a single-purpose function; it outputs a string. In contrast, `printf()` is a multipurpose function; it can be used to output integers (in decimal, octal or hexadecimal), characters, and strings. Furthermore, it can be used to produce formatted output and will pad with blanks, justify within a field, and so on. It is a much bigger piece of code and carries a great deal more overhead.

The program in Example 5-4 has the same functionality as strngiol.c. It accepts a line of text from standard input and echoes it to standard output. However, the function inputstring() from strngiol.c is replaced with the library function gets() and output is done with the library function puts(). Some error handling is included as well.

Example 5-4: strngio2.c

```
/*              strngio2.c
 *
 *   Synopsis    - Prompts for and accepts a line of text as input
 *                 from standard input with the standard library
 *                 function gets(). Echoes the line to standard
 *                 output with puts().
 *
 *   Objective   - To illustrate gets() and puts().
 */

/* Include Files */
#include <stdio.h>                                    /* Note 1 */

void main( void )
{
    char inputarray[512];                             /* Note 2 */
    char *inputptr;

    printf( "Enter a line of text.\n> " );
    inputptr = gets( inputarray );                    /* Note 3 */
    if ( inputptr != NULL )                           /* Note 4 */
        puts( inputptr );                             /* Note 5 */
    else
        puts( "error in input\n" );                   /* Note 6 */
}
```

The single function main() prompts for input and calls gets() to do the input. Then puts() is called to do the output. The value returned by gets() determines the output.

Note 1: The function gets() must be declared as type char * since it does not return the default type, int. On most systems this declaration is in the file stdio.h.

Note 2: A buffer of 512 bytes is declared to hold the input. The size of the buffer could be adjusted according to system requirements and knowledge about the nature of the input to the program.[1]

Note 3: This call to gets() accepts the input of a line of text from standard input. The actual parameter to gets() is the address of the array where the input is to be stored. The return value from gets() is assigned to the variable, inputptr.

Note 4: The return value of gets() is checked. Upon encountering either the end-of-file or an error, gets() will return a NULL pointer, a pointer whose value is NULL. Otherwise, gets() returns the address of the first character of the input buffer.

Note 5: The function puts() is called to output the string. The parameter is the address of the buffer where the string is stored.

Note 6: In this puts() call, the parameter consists of the string enclosed in double quotes. During compilation, the string is stored with a terminating '\0', and the address of the first character in the string becomes the effective parameter. When the output is done, puts() appends a new-line character to the string.

Learning Activities

8.   Execute strngio2.c with several sets of input to make sure it works as you expect.
   a.   What is output if the return key is pressed immediately after the prompt?
   b.   What is output if end-of-file is signaled immediately after the prompt?
   c.   Distinguish between the contents of inputarray and inputptr in the two cases mentioned in a and b. What are the different values returned by gets() and why?

9.   In your own words, explain the difference between a NULL pointer, a null string, and a null character.

10.   Can either inputptr or inputarray be eliminated from strngio2.c? Why or why not? Explain fully.

11.   Modify strngio2.c by replacing the calls to puts() with calls to printf() and compile and execute the modified program. Compare the sizes of the executable code and, if possible, the execution times for the two versions of the program. What are your conclusions?

---

1.   The size of a buffer is open to debate. Many programmers will go with an array of 80 cells since few users will type more than that. Others would go with the system limit on input lines. The main point is that the buffer must be sufficiently large to hold the line of input and the terminating null character because the library function gets() does not check on the bounds of the array. If the input contains more characters than the array has cells, gets() will place the extra characters in the next memory location and overrun the bounds of the array.

12. *C by Discovery*   In section 5.1, the behavior of `scanf()` in accepting input of a string was discussed. This Learning Activity asks you to explore the action of `scanf()` and the `%s` conversion specification.

a. Write a short program that accepts input of a string using `scanf()` and the `%s` conversion specification. Have the string output with `puts()`.

b. Test the program with several different inputs until you understand what `scanf()` does with the `%s` conversion specification.

c. Modify your program to read the character after the input string also. Test the program again with input like

```
"Hello there",
"Hello                    there",
and
"Hello\tthere".
```

Does the program behave as you expected?

d. Explain `scanf()`'s behavior in your own words.

A Word of Warning

Allocation of memory for the characters in a string must be done during the compilation process. It is important to be aware of which declarations allocate what memory. Consider the following declarations:

```
char inputarray[512];
```

and

```
char *inputptr;
```

The declaration of `inputarray` causes 512 bytes of memory to be set aside for use during the program. The declaration of `inputptr` causes only enough memory for the address of a `char` to be allocated. This is normally only two or four bytes.

A common error could arise from misunderstanding the documentation for some of the C library functions. For example, most versions of the documentation for `gets()` indicate that the parameter must be of type `char *`, an address of a character buffer (that is, an array). What the documentation may not make clear is that the buffer space must be allocated by the program. The function `gets()` uses whatever address is passed to it. It does not provide the buffer.

The program in Example 5-5 illustrates this error. It attempts to perform the input and output of a string. However, an error occurs because of the lack of memory allocated. This is a very common mistake by beginning C programmers. The misunderstanding is further compounded by the fact that the program may appear to run correctly on some computer systems. For example, on a microcomputer system, the user is allowed to write into any memory address. If a pointer happens to be pointing to an unused portion of memory, execution may proceed without noticeable error. The program is more likely to cause an error on a multi-user system where restrictions on memory use are more stringent. In any case, writing to unallocated space is an error whether the program crashes or not. Some of the newer compilers now give warning messages about this type of error.

Example 5-5: strwarn.c

```
/*                 strwarn.c
 *
 *    Synopsis    - Attempts to accept input of a line of text with
 *                  the library function gets().  There is an error
 *                  in the program because space for the input line
 *                  was not allocated.
 *
 *    Objective   - To point out a common error made by beginning C
 *                  programmers.
 */

/* Include Files */
#include <stdio.h>

void main( void )
{
    char *prompt = "Enter a line of text.\n> ";
    char *inputptr, *inputptr1;                         /* Note 1 */

    printf( prompt );
    inputptr1 = gets( inputptr );                       /* Note 2 */
    if ( inputptr1 != NULL )
        puts( inputptr1 );
    else
        puts( "Error in input\n" );
}
```

The structure of this program is very much like that of strngio2.c. The function main() displays a prompt for a line of text, calls gets() to do the input, and then calls puts() to do some output. The string output by puts() depends on the value returned by gets(). The major difference between strngio2.c and strwarn.c is the declaration of the variables.

Note 1: Two variables of type char * are declared. They are uninitialized. They may have garbage values left over from a previous use of that memory. The amount of memory allocated for each of these variables is only the amount necessary to hold the address of a character. No buffer space is allocated.

Note 2: The parameter to gets() is inputptr, one of the uninitialized pointers. The function gets() will attempt to store the input line at the memory location specified by inputptr. The error arises since inputptr does not point to a valid memory location. No buffer has been allocated.

Learning Activities

13. Execute strwarn.c on your system. Do you get a warning message when you compile it? Does it execute properly, or does it crash?

14. Modify strwarn.c so that it outputs the address of inputptr before the call to gets(). Find out as much as you can about that address. Is it part of the program address space? Is it part of the operating system address space?

An Example

The programs we have seen so far in this chapter process only one line of input. The program counter.c in Example 5-6, however, reads through multiple lines of input until end-of-file is signaled. The library function gets() is designed to return a NULL pointer when it sees end-of-file. The while loop is driven by comparing the value returned by gets() with NULL. When a NULL pointer is found, the while loop terminates. A while loop using gets() to read until end-of-file has the following form:

```
while (( inptr = gets( inarray )) != NULL )
        processing();
```

The program counter.c in Example 5-6, reads lines of text from standard input and counts the number of extra blanks in the text. The text needs one blank to separate words; if there are two blanks between words, one of the blanks is "extra". Only the extra blanks are counted. The program has another interesting feature: the function countem() has the job of counting the blanks and advancing a pointer into an array to the next nonblank character. Because the pointer to the current position of the array is declared local to main(), countem() needs to be passed an address of the pointer as a parameter to deal with the pass by value feature of C. Carefully inspect the declaration of the parameter, the function call, and the reference to the parameter inside the function to see the method.

Example 5-6: counter.c

```
/*              counter.c
 *
 *    Synopsis    - Reads standard input and keeps a count of the
 *.                 number of extra blanks in the input.
 *
 *    Objective   - To illustrate a loop to read through many
 *                  lines of input and a method of having a
 *                  function change a pointer parameter.
 */

/* Include Files */
#include <stdio.h>

/* Function Declarations */
int countem( char ** );                                     /* Note 1 */
void process_line( char *, int * );

void main( void )
{
     char inarray[512], *inptr;                             /* Note 2 */
     int  white_count = 0;

     printf( "Enter text. Signal end of file when done.\n" );
     printf( "> " );

                                                            /* Note 3 */
     while ( ( inptr = gets( inarray ) ) != NULL ) {
                                                            /* Note 4 */
            process_line( inptr , &white_count );
            printf( "> " );
     }
     printf( "There were %d unnecessary spaces.\n", white_count );
}

/***************************** process_line()  ***************/
/*    Processes a line of text by looking for blanks, calling
 *    countem() to count the blanks, and updating the running
 *    total of the number of blanks.
```

```
        */
void process_line( char *ptr, int *num_white_ptr )
{
        int count;

        while ( *ptr != '\0' ) {
                if ( *ptr == ' ' ) {
                        count = countem( &ptr );                    /* Note 5 */
                        if ( count >= 2 )
                                                                    /* Note 6 */
                                *num_white_ptr += count - 1;
                }
                else
                        ptr++;
        }
}


/***************************** countem()   ********************/
/*    Returns the number of blanks it finds and advances the
 *    pointer to the first nonblank character.
 */

int countem( char **ptr )                                           /* Note 7 */
{
        int counter = 0;

        while ( **ptr == ' ' ) {                                    /* Note 8 */
                counter++;
                ( *ptr )++;                                         /* Note 9 */
        }
        return( counter );
}
```

The program consists of the functions main(), process_line() and countem(). The code in main() consists of printf() calls and a while loop. Each pass through the while loop handles one line of input. The function process_line() looks at the input, one character at a time, and counts any blanks. The function countem() is called only when a blank character is found in the input array. It counts the number of blanks at that location and advances the pointer to the next nonblank character in the array.

Note 1: The function declarations indicate how these functions communicate with each other and main(). The function process_line() takes two pointers as parameters. The first is a pointer to the beginning of the array where the input resides. The second is a pointer to the int variable that will store the running total of the number of blank characters encountered. The function `process_line()` updates the value of the actual parameter; therefore, it must know the address of the actual parameter for the change to be known in `main()`.

The formal parameter to `countem()` is the address of a `char` `*`. In C, that type is denoted `char` `**`. The function `countem()` needs to change the value of a pointer variable and therefore receives the address of the pointer as a parameter.

Note 2: The array `inarray` will hold the input. The pointer `inptr` will serve as a pointer to the current position in the array.

Note 3: Input is done with the library function `gets()`. When it reads a line of input, it will return a pointer to the first character of `inarray`. That return value serves to initialize the value of `inptr`. If `inptr` is NULL, `gets()` encountered either an error or the end of the input, and the `while` loop will terminate. If `inptr` is not NULL, the function `process_line()` is entered with the actual parameter `inptr` pointing to the first character of `inarray`.

Note 4: The actual parameters to `process_line()` are the pointer to the beginning of the array storing the input, and the address of the variable `white_count`. The value of `white_count` will be changed by the function and the updated value must be known by `main()` for the final `printf()` call. Note that the value of the first parameter is also changed by `process_line()`, but `main()` does not need the value of this parameter.

Note 5: The actual parameter to `countem()` is the address of `inptr`. Because `countem()` needs to advance (that is, change) `inptr`, the *address* of `inptr` must be passed as the parameter.

Note 6: To access the `int` variable `white_count` that was declared in `main()`, the parameter `num_white_ptr` needs to be dereferenced. This compound assignment statement updates the value of `white_count`.

Note 7: The formal parameter `ptr` has type `char` `**` (that is, the address of the address of a `char`). The function `countem()` will look at successive characters in the buffer until it finds a nonblank. It needs to advance the pointer to the part of the buffer that has not been processed. Therefore, it needs to change a pointer variable in `main()`. For this change to be effective after the function `countem()` terminates, the address of the pointer must be passed as the parameter.[1]

Note 8: The character in the array is accessed by dereferencing the parameter `ptr` twice. The first dereference accesses the value of `inptr` in `main()`. The second dereference accesses the contents of the address in `inptr`.

Note 9: The pointer, originally declared in `main()`, is accessed by dereferencing `ptr`. Because `ptr` contains the address of the pointer variable, `*ptr` is the value of the pointer.

---

1. This is a simplistic introduction to the important concept of a `char` `**` variable. The concept will be discussed in more detail in Chapter 9.

Learning Activities

15. a. Compile and execute counter.c to see that it works. Test it with the following input:,

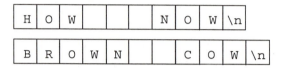

There are five blanks in the input. Two are needed to separate the words. Therefore, this program should classify the other three as extra blanks. Does it?

   b. Test it with input of your choosing. Does it work for blanks at the beginning of an input line? At the end? A line consisting of nothing but blanks? If you find any cases where this program does not work, fix it.

16. Look at the line with the statement `(*ptr)++;` Are the parentheses necessary? What is referenced if the parentheses are omitted?

17. The definition of `countem()` starts with the line

```
int countem( char **ptr )
```

What does the `int` do? Is it necessary? Why or why not?

5.4 The Common String Library Functions

As mentioned earlier, strings are commonly used in C programs. Because of this, many utilities have been written that have been included in the standard C library. In the last section we investigated `gets()` and `puts()`, the standard C library functions designed to do string input and output from the terminal. More string input and output functions will be discussed in Chapter 10.

Utilities for other string manipulations are included in the library also. In this section we will discuss some of the more commonly used string-handling functions.

Library functions are available to find the length of the string, make a copy of a string, compare two strings, and concatenate one string to the end of another.

strlen()

The library function for calculating the length of a string is `strlen()`. It takes an address of a string as a parameter and returns an integer type.[1]

The parameter to `strlen()` should point to the first character of the null-terminated string for which the length is to be calculated. Typical calls to `strlen()` would be

```
length = strlen( "How now brown cow" );
```

or

```
length = strlen( stringptr );
```

In both examples `length` would have been declared with the appropriate integer type. In the second example, `stringptr` should point to the string whose length is to be calculated. The quantity returned by `strlen()` is the number of characters in the string before the first null character; it does not count the terminating null character in determining the length. For example, the value returned by `strlen( "How now brown cow" )` is 17.

strcpy()

The `strcpy()` library function makes a copy of a string. It takes two parameters. The first parameter must be the address of the array where the copy will be located. The space must be allocated in the program. The second parameter has type `char *` and is the address of the first character in the string to be copied. It must be terminated with a null character. Typical calls to `strcpy()` would be

```
strcpy( copy, original );
```

or

```
strcpy( copy, "original string" );
```

In both cases, the character buffer referred to by `copy` must be the address of an array allocated by the program even though many versions of the documentation indicate that the type is `char *`. The function `strcpy()` does no memory allocation. The value returned by `strcpy()` is its first parameter, a pointer to the buffer where the copy was placed.

strcat()[2]

The function `strcat()` does string concatenation, appending one string to the

---

1. ANSI C has specified that the type returned by `strlen()` coincide with the type returned by the operator `sizeof()`. In the standard header file stddef.h, this type is declared as type `size_t`; it will be be one of the integer types, but the actual type may differ on different computer systems. In compilers that do not support the ANSI standard, the function type of `strlen()` is usually `int`.

2. In ANSI C, placing two string *constants* next to each other in the source code produces the concatenation of the two strings. For example,

```
printf("%s\n", "How now" "brown cow" );
```

displays

```
How nowbrown cow
```

end of the other. The first parameter must be the address of an array (sometimes documented as type char *) containing a null-terminated string. The second parameter must have type char *, and must point to a null-terminated string. In addition, there must be adequate unused space in the array pointed to by the first parameter to hold the string being appended there. If a char * variable named result points to the string "one two, button my shoe" at the beginning of a large buffer, the call

        strcat(result, "three four");

would yield the null-terminated string, "one two, button my shoethree four" in the location pointed to by result. (The lack of a blank character created "shoethree.") If adequate space was not available for the additional characters in the buffer result, strcat() would write over whatever was next in memory. The value returned to strcat() is its first parameter.

strcmp()

The standard library function strcmp() compares two strings by comparing the position of their characters in the underlying character set. It takes two parameters of type char *. Both must point to null-terminated strings. The return value from strcmp() is of type int and has the following meanings:

1. If the two strings are identical, the return value is zero (0).

2. If the first string is lexicographically less than the second (the first differing character comes earlier in the underlying character set), the value returned is negative.

3. If the first string is lexicographically greater than the second, the value returned is positive.

For example, with the ASCII character set,

        strcmp("now is the time", "She sells sea shells");

returns a positive value because 'S' appears in the character set before 'n'. The value returned by

        strcmp("Bingo", "Parcheesi");

would be negative. The parameters could also be arrays of characters containing null-terminated strings. For example, if phrase is a char * variable pointing to a null-terminated string and attempt_to_match is an array of type char that was initialized by input from the terminal, the call

        strcmp(phrase, attempt_to_match);

would return 0 if the strings were identical and some nonzero value if they differed.

   The functions strlen(), strcat(), strcmp(), and strcpy() are only a few of the string-handling functions in the string library. *The Programmer's Handbook* gives an abstract of many of the functions commonly included with a C compiler.

The program in Example 5-7 illustrates some of the manipulations possible with these functions.

Example 5-7:   strnglib.c

```
/*                strnglib.c
 *
 *    Synopsis    - Displays information about two strings,
 *                  the length, and their lexical comparison. Then
 *                  concatenates them into a character buffer and
 *                  displays the result.
 *
 *    Objective   - To illustrate basic use of the string library
 *                  functions, strlen(), strcat(), strcpy(), and
 *                  strcmp().
 */

/* Include Files */
#include <stdio.h>
#include <string.h>                              /* Note 1 */

void main( void )
{
    char workstring[512];                        /* Note 2 */
    char *string1 = "I know an old lady";
    char *string2 = "who swallowed a fly";

    puts( string1 );
    puts( string2 );
    if ( strcmp( string1, string2 ) > 0 )        /* Note 3 */
            printf( "string1 is > string2.\n" );
    else
            printf( "string1 is <= string2.\n" );

                                                 /* Note 4 */
    printf( "The length of string1 is %d.\n", strlen( string1 ) );
    printf( "The length of string2 is %d.\n", strlen( string2 ) );

    strcpy( workstring, string1 );               /* Note 5 */
    if ( !strcmp( string1, workstring ) )        /* Note 6 */
            printf( "Copy completed successfully!\n" );
```

```
        else
                printf( "Error found in copy.\n" );

        strcat( workstring, " " );                              /* Note 7 */
        strcat( workstring, string2 );
        printf( "The work string now contains:\n\t\"%s\"\n",
                                                workstring );
        printf( "The length of the work string is now %d.\n",
                                                strlen( workstring ) );
}
```

 Running the Program

```
I know an old lady
who swallowed a fly
string1 is <= string2.
The length of string1 is 18.
The length of string2 is 19.
Copy completed successfully!
The work string now contains:
    "I know an old lady who swallowed a fly"
The length of the work string is now 38.
```

There is one function named `main()` with three variables defined, two initialized `char *` variables, and an array of type `char`. Most of the statements perform output.

Note 1: The standard header file string.h has been included. This file contains the declarations of the functions in the string library. For example, the functions `strcpy()` and `strcat()` return a `char *` value instead of the default `int` type and therefore must be declared as such. The declarations are in string.h. An alternate, but not as popular technique would be to place the prototypes

```
        char *strcat( char *, char * );
        char *strcpy( char *, char * );
        int strlen( char * );
        int strcmp( char *, char *);
```

in the source code and not include the file string.h. Note that the type of all the parameters can be documented as `char *` even though some of them must be arrays (as discussed earlier).

Note 2: Buffer space is allocated for some string manipulation.

Note 3: The function `strcmp()` will compare the two strings, `string1` and `string2`. The comparison is made character by character until either the end of a string is reached or a character in one of the strings appears earlier in the ASCII collating sequence than the corresponding character in the other string. The value returned by `strcmp()` is tested. If it is positive, the first `printf()` call is executed. Otherwise the second `printf()` call is executed.

Note 4: In each of the next two calls to `printf()`, the second parameter is the value returned by a call to `strlen()`. That value will be output in decimal.

Note 5: This call to `strcpy()` copies the string pointed to by `string1` into the buffer. All of the characters, including the terminating `'\0'`, will be copied into `workstring`. From this point on, `workstring` can be treated as a string. In this call to `strcpy()`, the return value is ignored.

Note 6: The value returned by `strcmp()` is used to determine if `workstring` and `string1` point to identical strings. Note that `strcmp()` returns 0 if the two strings are identical; therefore, the negation of the value will test true when the strings are the same. A more readable version of this `if` statement might be

```
if ( strcmp( string1, workstring ) == 0 )
```

Note 7: The next two calls to `strcat()` illustrate the concatenation of strings to the string in `workstring`. In the first call, a string with a single blank, `" "`, is concatenated to the end of `workstring` to separate the words. It is important that `workstring` contains sufficient space for the results of these operations because `strcat()` does not check for space. The value returned by `strcat()` is ignored in both cases.

Learning Activities

18. a. Go over the description of the string library functions used in strnglib.c to make sure that you know what each does.

   b. Predict the output of strnglib.c and then execute it to verify your prediction.

19. a. Rewrite the program strnglib.c so that it will compare `string1` and `string2` and display the result with either <, =, or > (depending on which is correct).

   b. Rewrite the program so that a user can enter `string1` and `string2`. Test it to make sure everything works as it should.

A Word of Warning

The requirement that memory be allocated in the first parameters to both `strcat()`

and `strcpy()` is an important one. The library functions assume that the memory exists, and the programmer really wants the function to do the concatenation or the copy. Example 5-8 shows what can happen when the memory needed has not been allocated.

Example 5-8: strngerr.c

```
/*                  strngerr.c
 *
 *    Synopsis    - Initializes two strings and displays the
 *                  strings and their locations. Displays the
 *                  strings again after concatenating the
 *                  second string to the end of the first one.
 *
 *    Objective   - To demonstrate a common error in memory
 *                  allocation when using the string library
 *                  functions.
 */

/* Include Files */
#include <stdio.h>
#include <string.h>

void main( void )
{
        char *string1 = "I know an old lady who swallowed a ";
        char *string2 =
          "spider that wiggled and jiggled and tickled inside her";

        puts( string1 );
        puts( string2 );
                                                        /* Note 1 */
        printf( "\nstring1 begins at %p, and ends at %p.\n",
                string1, string1 + strlen( string1 ) );
        printf( "string2 begins at %p, and ends at %p.\n\n",
                string2, string2 + strlen( string2 ) );
                                                        /* Note 2 */
        strcat( string1, " horse.  She's dead of course." );
        puts( string1 );
        puts( string2 );
}
```

There is a single function `main()`. Two `char *` variables are defined and initialized. The executable code consists of calls to functions for output, and a single call to `strcat()`.

Note 1: The address of the beginning and the end of both `string1` and `string2` are displayed with the next two `printf()` calls. In most systems, these strings will be located close to one another.

Note 2: The following call to `strcat()` will concatenate the second parameter onto the end of `string1`. No extra memory has been allocated for this concatenation. Therefore, `strcat()` will be writing over whatever is next to it in memory.

Learning Activities

20.   Execute strngerr.c. Were any compile errors or warnings issued? Did the program crash? If not, did the content of `string2` change during program execution?

21.   If this program compiled cleanly and did not crash on your system, execute strngerr.c again and record the addresses of the beginning and end of `string1` and `string2` that are displayed by the first two calls to `printf()`.

a.   Four addresses were displayed. What are the characters stored in those addresses? Do `string1` and `string2` originally point to adjacent locations? How many bytes lie between them?

b.   Diagram the part of memory where the strings are kept so that you can associate an address for each character in both `string1` and `string2`.

c.   Hand execute the call to `strcat()` by replacing the characters in the proper place in your memory diagram.

d.   Does your diagram coincide with the strings that are displayed by the program?

e.   If `string2` was not changed during execution of strngerr.c, would it be possible to change it by concatenating a longer string to `string1`? If it appears to be possible, try it.

5.5 Examples with strlen() and strchr()

The program chlincnt.c in Example 5-9 reads standard input and counts the number of characters and lines in its input. It is similar to utilities provided by many operating systems. The function `gets()` is used to accept input of a line at a time and `strlen()` counts the number of characters in the line.

Example 5-9:   chlincnt.c

```
/*                 chlincnt.c
 *
 *    Synopsis    - Counts the number of characters and lines
 *                  in standard input.
 *
 *    Objective   - Illustrates a use for strlen() in conjunction
 *                  with gets().
 */

/* Include Files */
#include <stdio.h>
#include <string.h>

void main( void )
{
    char inarray[512];                              /* Note 1 */
    char *inptr;
    int line_count = 0,                             /* Note 2 */
        char_count = 0;

    printf( "Enter your text now." );
    printf( "Signal end-of-file when done.\n" );
    printf( "> " );
                                                    /* Note 3 */
    while ( ( inptr = gets( inarray ) ) != NULL ) {
            line_count++;                           /* Note 4 */
            char_count += strlen( inptr ) + 1;      /* Note 5 */
            printf( "> " );
    }
    printf( "%d lines, %d characters\n", line_count, char_count );
}
```

The program is simple in structure. The single function main() consists of a while loop using gets() to read through all of the terminal input.

Note 1: The array inarray will hold each line of input.

Note 2: The variables line_count and char_count will keep a running total of the number of lines and characters, respectively. They are both initialized to zero.

Note 3: The while loop is designed to read through multiple lines of input. Each time, the value returned by gets() is tested. When gets() sees the end of the input file, it returns a NULL pointer and the loop terminates.

Note 4: Since gets() attempts to read a line of input each time it is called, line_count is incremented each time the read is successful (that is, each time gets() doesn't return a NULL pointer).

Note 5: The line of input is placed in inarray and the newline is replaced with a null character so that inarray contains a string. A call to strlen() returns the number of non-null characters in the string. Because the newline was input and discarded by gets(), the calculation of the character count must be adjusted by adding 1 for the newline. Note: If your system translates a carriage return pressed on the keyboard to a carriage return/line feed combination for a newline, you may need to add 2 instead of 1 to compensate.

Learning Activities

22. a. Test chlincnt.c with some simple input for which you know the correct answer. For example, test it with an immediate signal of end-of-file; test it with one line of input with four characters before the return; test it with an immediate carriage return for one line. Test it by typing some meaningless control characters. Does it count the control characters? Test it by pressing the tab key during your input. How many characters are counted for the tab key?

  b. Find out if your system has a utility that counts characters and lines in its input. If it does and will read from the terminal, compare the output from this program with the output from that utility. Is it the same? Do you need to adjust the character count for the end of a line?

  c. If your system will allow input redirection, redirect the input to come from a file. Does the program still behave correctly?

  d. Does chlincnt.c correctly count the end-of-line character(s)? If not, correct it.

23. Is inptr necessary in chlincnt.c? If not, modify the program to eliminate this variable.

24. Is this program a filter? Why or why not?

Many functions besides the ones just discussed have been written for the string library. The ones that are included with an ANSI C compiler are described in the *Programmer's Handbook*.

As an example of another string library function, consider the function strchr(). It is a part of the standard C library and is included with any ANSI C compiler. It takes two parameters. The first is of type char * and must point to a null-terminated string. The second parameter is of type char. The function strchr() searches the first parameter string for an occurrence of the character in the second parameter and returns a pointer to the first occurrence of that character in that string. If the character is not found in the string, strchr() returns a NULL pointer.

Example 5-10 uses strchr() to break an array of characters into "words". For this program, a word is considered to be a sequence of nonblank characters delimited with blanks. The array of characters is initialized by reading a line of text from standard input. Each word is displayed on standard output on a separate line.

Example 5-10: strchrex.c

```
/*                  strchrex.c
 *
 *    Synopsis    - Accepts a line of text as input from standard
 *                  input and displays each of the space-delimited
 *                  words in the input on a separate line on
 *                  standard output.
 *
 *    Objective   - To illustrate the string library function
 *                  strchr().
 */

/* Include Files */
#include <stdio.h>
#include <string.h>

void main( void )
{
    char instring[512];
    char *currentpos, *lastpos;                     /* Note 1 */

    printf( "Enter a line of text.\n> " );
    gets( instring );                               /* Note 2 */
    lastpos = instring;

                                                    /* Note 3 */
    while ( ( currentpos = strchr( lastpos, ' ' ) ) != NULL ) {
        *currentpos++ = '\0';                       /* Note 4 */
        puts( lastpos );
```

```
        lastpos = currentpos;                          /* Note 5 */
    }
    puts( lastpos );
}
```

The program consists of the single function `main()`. One array of type `char` and two `char *` variables are defined. After the input is done, a `while` loop is used to process the array that holds the input line. Each iteration of the `while` loop outputs one "word".

Note 1: The pointer `lastpos` will always point to the beginning of the word to be output; `currentpos` will point to the end of the word.

Note 2: The buffer `instring` is initialized by a call to `gets()`.

Note 3: The call to `strchr()` begins its search for a blank character at the memory location pointed to by `lastpos`. It returns a pointer to the first blank character. If no blank is found before the terminating null character, `strchr()` returns a `NULL` pointer. In this program, the return of a `NULL` pointer by `strchr()` signifies that the whole input line has been processed.

Note 4: The blank character found by `strchr()` is replaced by `'\0'`. This creates a null-terminated string that consists of a single word. The pointer `lastpos` points to the beginning of the word. Note that `currentpos` is incremented after the assignment so that, theoretically, it points to the beginning of the next word.

Note 5: In preparation for another iteration of the `while` loop, `lastpos` is updated to point to the beginning of the next word.

Learning Activities

25.   Test strchrex.c with several different input lines to see that it works as you expect it to.

26.   Test strchrex.c with a line that does not contain any blank characters. Is the behavior what you would expect?

27.   Test strchrex.c with input that contains two or more adjacent blanks. Describe what happens. Is this the behavior that a user would expect? If necessary, modify the program so that there are no blank lines in the output.

28.   a.   Write a function that will accept a null terminated string as a parameter and return a pointer to the first non-blank character in that string. The function should return a `NULL` pointer if it finds the end of the string before it finds a character that is not a blank.

> b. Rewrite strchrex.c using the function you wrote in part a. to advance the pointer each time a blank is found.

These last two sections are not a comprehensive treatment of the string library functions. They are meant to provide examples. A partial list of the string-manipulating functions in the standard C library appears in the *Programmer's Handbook*. That and the documentation with your compiler are strongly recommended as reading material.

5.6 Two Versions of strcat()

The string-handling functions in the standard C library are nothing more than ordinary C functions that have been written as tools to perform specific tasks. These functions are compiled and the object code is put into a library where it can be linked with a C program. The linker will search specified libraries to find the necessary code.

We will explore how one of the string-handling functions might have been written. You will be asked to write your own version of other string-handling functions in the exercises.

Two versions of the `strcat()` library function are presented in Examples 5-11 and 5-12. One is written with array notation and the other with the more efficient pointer notation.

Example 5-11: strcat1.c

```
/*              strcat1.c
 *
 *   Synopsis   - Concatenates its second argument onto its
 *                first argument.  It uses array notation.
 *
 *   Objective  - To illustrate one version of the string library
 *                function strcat().
 */

char *strcat( char old[], char new[] )
{
    int oldindex = 0,
        newindex = 0;

    while ( old[oldindex++] != '\0' )        /* Note 1 */
        ;
```

/* **Note 1** */

```
        oldindex--;                                             /* Note 2 */
        while ( ( old[oldindex++] = new[newindex++] ) != '\0' )
            ;
        return( old );
}
```

This code is a single function, not a program. It will not run without a function main().

Note 1: This while loop with null statement body finds the end of the first string, old. It compares each character with the null character and increments oldindex after the comparison.

Note 2: The index is decremented since it referenced one cell beyond the '\0'. The while loop assigns successive characters to the end of old and compares each character to '\0'. The first character of new overwrites the '\0'. The terminating '\0' from new is copied to old to terminate the concatenated string.

The next version of strcat() does exactly the same thing using the pointer syntax to access the characters in the strings.

Example 5-12:   strcat2.c

```
/*                  strcat2.c
 *
 *   Synopsis    - Concatenates its second argument onto its
 *                 first argument.  It uses pointer notation.
 *
 *   Objective   - To illustrate one version of the string library
 *                 function strcat().
 */

char *strcat( char *oldpart, char *newpart )
{
        char *current = oldpart;

        while ( *current++ != '\0' )                            /* Note 1 */
            ;

        current--;                                              /* Note 2 */
        while ( *current++ = *newpart++ )
            ;
        return( oldpart );
}
```

Again, this file would need to be linked with a function `main()` that contains a call to `strcat()` in order to be executed.

Note 1: The `while` loop looks for the end of the first string. Each character is compared to `'\0'`.

Note 2: The second `while` loop copies the second string to the end of the first string. The sequence of events is as follows. The character pointed to by `newpart` is copied to the space pointed to by `current`. The value of the assignment is tested. If it tests true (nonzero) both `current` and `newpart` are incremented. It tests false and the loop terminates when the `'\0'` is copied.

Learning Activities

29.   Include the code for `strcat()` from strcat1.c in the program strnglib.c. Compile and execute it with each version to make sure that the behavior is the same.

30.   Do the same for the code for `strcat()` from strcat2.c.

Language Elements Introduced in This Chapter: A Review

✓ **Conversion Specifications**

`%s`   a string is to be output with `printf()`
`%s`   a whitespace-delimited string is to be input with `scanf()`

✓ **Library Functions**

`gets()`   inputs a line of text from standard input
`puts()`   outputs a string to standard output
`strlen()`   calculates the length of a string
`strcpy()`   makes a copy of a string into an array of `char`
`strcat()`   concatenates one string to the end of another
`strcmp()`   compares two strings lexicographically
`strchr()`   searches for a character in a string

✓ **Types**

`char **`   an address of an address of a `char`

Things to Remember

1. A string in C is a sequence of characters terminated by a null character, `'\0'`.
2. The compiler handles a string as an address of the first character.
3. A string may be used as an initializer for either an array of `char` or a pointer to `char`.
4. `gets()` will return the address of the array where the input is stored or a `NULL` pointer in case of error or end-of-file.
5. Memory must be allocated in the program for `gets()` to use to store the input.
6. A `while` loop to process many lines of terminal input with `gets()` would be written as

    ```
    while ( gets( inarray ) != NULL )
            processing();
    ```
7. If a function is to change the value of a pointer in its calling environment, a pointer to the pointer should be passed in as a parameter. If the pointer is a pointer to `char`, the parameter type should be declared as `char **`.
8. Memory must be allocated for the first parameter of `strcat()` and `strcpy()`.
9. Individual characters within a string can be accessed with either array-indexing syntax or pointer arithmetic syntax. The pointer syntax is more efficient.
10. The standard header file string.h contains declarations of the functions in the string library.

Exercises and Programming Problems

1. a. Write a program that reads standard input and counts all "words" in its input. For this program, a word will be delimited by blank spaces, tab characters, or newlines. Test your program thoroughly.

    b. Package the word-counting part of your program as a function and write a new program that counts words (defined as in part a), characters, and lines in its input. You may want to borrow some of the code from chlincnt.c.

2. Write a program that will read standard input and echo each line to standard output with a line number and a tab preceding it. When you run this program and enter lines from the terminal, lines of input will be interspersed with lines of output. If your system has output redirection and you redirect output to a file, the file will look like the input with the lines numbered. An example of a run with terminal input and output is below. The user's input is in **boldface**.

    ```
    Enter your text:
    This is line 1
    ```

```
1          This is line 1
This is line 2
2          This is line 2
This is the last line of input
3            This is the last line of input
```

3. Write your own version of puts(). Do not use printf(). Test your program by including it in one of the programs in the text that uses puts(), recompiling and executing it. If a version of puts() appears in the source file, the library version will not be linked into the object code.

4. Write a program that will read standard input and, where possible, replace each sequence of blank spaces with one or more tab characters and then echo the modified input to standard output. You may assume that tab stops occur at columns 1, 9, 17, 25, and so on.

   The output from this program should appear identical to the input even though the characters might not be the same. In the sample run below, the user's input is in **boldface**. Blank characters have been denoted with ⌴, and tabs have been denoted with ⌷tab⌷.

   ```
   12345678901234567890
   12345678901234567890
   Name⌴⌴⌴⌴Numb.⌴⌴⌴⌴⌴Id
   Name[ tab ]Numb.[ tab ]⌴⌴Id
   Bolt⌴⌴⌴⌴23⌴⌴⌴⌴⌴⌴⌴⌴⌴⌴a1
   Bolt[ tab ]23[   tab   ]⌴⌴a1
   ```

   The first line of input was included in the example to establish the column count. It was echoed unchanged by the program. The second and third lines of input had repeated spaces between the words. The program echoed these lines with some of the spaces replaced by tabs. On a terminal, the output should look identical to the input. (Hint: Before designing your program, decide how your program should handle backspace characters.)

   This program would be used on a system that allowed input and output redirection. It would produce text that looked identical to the input text but contained fewer characters and therefore took up less memory or disk space. Running the program at a terminal without redirection would alternate lines of input and output as shown.

5. Write a program that does the opposite of the program in exercise 4. Have it replace each tab in its input with an appropriate number of blank characters so that the output appears unchanged but in reality will contain no tab characters.

6. Write your own version of a function that meets the specifications for strchr() in the standard C library. Compile it with strchrex.c from Example 5-9 to test it. It should work the same as the original program.

7. a. Look up the specifications for the library function `strstr()` in the
        Programmer's Handbook. Predict the output of the following program.

```
/*                  strtst.c
 *
 *   Synopsis    - Calls strstr() twice to find substrings
 *                 in "how now brown cow".  One should be
 *                 found, the other is nonexistent.
 *
 *   Objective   - To provide a test program for personal
 *                 version of strstr().
 */

/* Include Files */
#include <stdio.h>
#include <string.h>

void main( void )
{
    char string[] = "How now brown cow";
    char *substring;

    substring = strstr( string, "own" );
    if ( substring == NULL )
            printf( "Not found.\n" );
    else
            printf( "%s\n", substring );

    substring = strstr( string, "red" );
    if ( substring == NULL )
            printf( "Not found.\n" );
    else
            printf( "%s\n", substring );
}
```

    b. Write your own version of `strstr()`. Test your function with the pro-
        gram in part a.

8. a. Write a function in C that takes an array of `char` and a `char **` expres-
        sion as parameters. The array of type `char` would contain a string that
        possibly starts with a sequence of decimal digits. Have the function con-
        vert the sequence of decimal digits it finds to type `int` and return the con-
        verted value. Have the function set the contents of its second parameter (a
        `char *` value) to point to the first character in the array that was not con-
        verted. For example, if the function was called `convert()` and the call to
        `convert()` was

```
        intval = convert( array, &charptr );
```

where `array` contained the string

| 2 | 7 | 4 | A | D | A | M | S | \0 |

then after the call, `intval` would contain the value `274`, and `charptr` would point to the `'A'` in the string.

b. Test your function with the program below.

```
/*                  testconv.c
 *
 *  Synopsis    - Inputs lines with gets() and passes the
 *                string to conv().  Outputs the value
 *                returned by conv() and the remainder of
 *                the string.
 *
 *  Objective   - To provide a test program for the
 *                user-written function to convert a string
 *                of digits to type int.
 */

/* Include Files */
#include <stdio.h>
#include <string.h>

/* Function Declarations */
int conv( char [], char ** );

void main( void )
{
    int intval;
    char array[80], *remainder;

    while ( gets( array ) != NULL ) {
            intval = conv( array, &remainder );
            printf( " %d, %s\n", intval, remainder );
    }
}
```

9. a. Write your own version of `strcpy()` using array notation.

   b. Write another version of `strcpy()` using pointer notation.

10. a. Test the program below with many different input strings. Try to figure out how the value returned by `strcmp()` is calculated.

```
/*                  strcmps.c
 *
 *  Synopsis    - Outputs the values returned by library
```

```
*                       function strcmp().
*
*  Objective   - To investigate the return value from
*                strcmp().
*/

/* Include Files */
#include <stdio.h>
#include <string.h>

void main( void )
{
    char string1[80];
    char string2[80];
    int result;

    printf( "Enter the first string: " );
    gets( string1 );
    printf( "Enter the second string: " );
    gets( string2 );

    if ( ( result = strcmp( string1, string2 ) ) > 0 )
            printf( "string1 > string2\n" );
    else if ( result < 0 )
            printf( "string1 < string2\n" );
    else
            printf( "string1 = string2\n" );

    printf( "result is %d\n", result );
}
```

b. Write your own version of strcmp() that returns the same value as the
    library version does. Test it with the program above.

## Chapter 6

Keeping Control

6.1 Introduction

In Chapter 2, we discussed expressions and some of the C control statements. In this chapter, we present the remaining C control statements. These include the do-while loop and a multiway decision statement, the switch statement. Statements similar to these exist in many other languages.

C also contains statements that alter the flow of control. These can give the language more flexibility and make a program more readable and easier to write. However, as with any statement that alters the established flow of control of a program in any language, these statements should be used with care so that the program remains structured.

The last topic of this chapter is recursion. When using recursion, a programmer must be aware of what is happening to the control of the program. Two examples are discussed in this chapter.

6.2 The do-while Statement

The do-while statement is another looping structure available in C. The do-while loop has the following syntax:

```
do
        statement
while ( expression )
```

The words do and while are the keywords. The expression can be any legal C expression, but it must appear in parentheses. The statement can be any legitimate statement in C. For example, it can be an assignment statement, any of the control statements, a function call, or a block.

The execution of the do-while loop starts with the execution of statement; the evaluation of expression follows. If expression is not 0, statement is executed and expression is evaluated again. This process is repeated until expression evaluates to zero.

Note that the test for loop continuation appears *after* the statement in this loop construction. One consequence is that the statement in a do-while loop will always be executed at least once. In contrast, in a while loop the test expression for loop continuation is located *before* the statement, and if the test expression is false, the statement in a while loop will not be executed at all. Both loops are included in the C language to provide flexibility for the programmer.

The program do.c of Example 6-1 illustrates the use of the do-while loop. It also reminds us of the fact that parameters passed to C functions are passed by value.

Example 6-1: do.c

```
/*                      do.c
 *
 *      Synopsis    - A user is asked to enter an integer. The digits
 *                    in the number are displayed in reverse order
 *                    and then in the original order.
 *
 *      Objective   - Demonstrates the do-while statement and pass by
 *                    value for parameters.
 */
```

```
/* Include Files */
#include <stdio.h>

/* Constant Declarations */
#define RADIX 10

/* Function Declarations */
void reverse( int );

void main( void )
{
     int number;

     printf( "Enter a decimal number: " );
     scanf( "%d", &number );

     printf( "\nDigits reversed: " );
     reverse( number );
     printf( "Original number : %d\n", number );        /* Note 1 */
}

/****************************** reverse()   ******************/
/*    Displays the digits of the parameter in reverse order
 */
void reverse( int number )
{
     do {                                                /* Note 2 */
          printf( "%d", number % RADIX );
          number /= RADIX;
     }
     while ( number != 0 );                              /* Note 2 */

     printf( "\n" );
}
```

An overview of this program reveals two functions: the mandatory function main() and a function named reverse(). A preprocessor constant RADIX is defined as 10. The function main() consists of a variable declaration, calls to printf(), a scanf() call that accepts input of an integer, and a call to the function reverse() and a final printf() call. The function reverse() consists of a do-while statement followed by a call to printf().

Note 1: This printf() call provides another illustration that parameters in C are passed by value. The function actually works on a copy of the actual parameter and does not touch the variable in main(). The parameter number was changed in the function reverse(), but when accessed again in `main()`, `number` still has its original value.

Note 2: In this example of the `do-while` loop, the expression to be evaluated is the relational expression

```
( number != 0 )
```

It must be in parentheses. The statement for this `do-while` loop is the compound statement consisting of a `printf()` call followed by a compound assignment statement. It is delimited by braces.

The `do-while` loop is always executed at least once. The expression is evaluated at the bottom of the loop. A nonzero (true) value causes the loop to be repeated while a zero (false) value causes the loop to terminate.

Learning Activities

1. Predict the output of the function `reverse()` for each of the following input values.
   a. 4235
   b. 19843
   c. 2200000000
   d. -234

2. a. Run do.c and test it with the four input values in activity 1.
   b. Did the program handle the minus sign in the input as you predicted? What would be a reasonable way for this program to handle negative integers as input? Modify the program so that it handles negative input in the way you think is most appropriate.
   c. Was the output for the input 2200000000 what you predicted? If it wasn't, try to explain what happened.

6.3 The switch Statement

The `switch` statement provides C programmers with a multiway decision statement. Depending on the results of a test on an expression, any number of alternative statements could be executed.

The usual syntax of the `switch` statement is illustrated below:

```
switch (expression1)  {
    case c1:
        statement
    case c2:
        statement

        .

        .

        .

    default:
        statement
}
```

The keywords in the above construct are the words switch, case, and default. The expression expression1, which follows the keyword switch, is a control expression. Any legal C expression with one of the integer types may be used here. The syntax demands that it be in parentheses.

The switch statement must be followed by a statement. In normal use, as shown above, the statement is a compound statement composed of two types of statements. The first type is of the form

```
case const_expr: statement
```

This is called a case labeled statement. The colon is a mandatory part of the syntax. The const_expr in each case labeled statement must be a constant expression and must have one of the integer types. There can be multiple case labeled statements, but each const_expr must have a distinct value.

The second type of statement that may appear in the compound statement is another type of labeled statement. It carries a default label and has the form

```
default: statement
```

The inclusion of the default labeled statement in a compound statement associated with a switch statement is optional. When included, it is usually the last statement in the compound statement.

When a switch statement is executed, the control expression, expression1, is evaluated and tested to see if the value matches one of the values c1, c2, and so on. When a match is found, control is passed to the case labeled statement with the matching value and *all statements that appear from that point to the end of the* switch *statement could be executed*. This includes the statements associated with all of the following case labels as well as the statements associated with the default.[1] If a default labeled statement is included, it is executed when no match between the control expression and the constant expressions c1, c2, and so on is found. If no default labeled statement is present and no match is found, no action is taken.

The program switch.c in Example 6-2 illustrates the syntax and execution flow of the switch statement.

Example 6-2: switch.c

```
/*              switch.c
 *
 *   Synopsis   - Displays a triangle of numbers.
 *
 *   Objective  - To illustrate the syntax and flow of control
 *                of the switch statement.
 */


/* Include Files */
#include <stdio.h>

void main( void )
{
    int test_value;

    printf( "Enter an integer between 0 and 9: " );
    scanf( "%d", &test_value );
    switch ( test_value ) {                            /* Note 1 */
      case 9:   printf( "9 9 9 9 9 9 9 9 9 9\n" );
                                                       /* Note 2 */
      case 8:   printf( " 8 8 8 8 8 8 8 8\n" );
      case 7:   printf( "  7 7 7 7 7 7 7\n" );
      case 6:   printf( "   6 6 6 6 6 6\n" );
      case 5:   printf( "    5 5 5 5 5\n" );
      case 4:   printf( "     4 4 4 4\n" );
      case 3:   printf( "      3 3 3\n" );
      case 2:   printf( "       2 2\n" );
      case 1:   printf( "        1\n" );
      case 0:   printf( "00000000000000000\n" );
                                                       /* Note 3 */
      default : printf( "-----------------\n" );
    }
}
```

1. In Section 6-4 we will see how to change this default behavior. This involves using the switch statement in conjunction with the break statement. The resulting construct is more complete, useful, and flexible.

The program consists of the single function `main()`. It contains a call to `printf()`, a call to `scanf()` to do input, and a `switch` statement. The `switch` statement has `printf()` calls associated with all the cases.

Note 1: In this example, the program "switches" on the value of `test_value`. Its value is compared to the constant expressions listed in the `case` labeled statements below. The result of this comparison determines which statements are to be executed next.

Note 2: Notice that the values in the `case` labels are all constants. If the value of `test_value` matches one of these values, execution starts with the corresponding statement. The statements preceding the one with the matching value are not executed. *The statements after the one with the matching value are also executed.*

Note 3: If no match is found with the values after the case labels, the statement associated with the default label is the only one executed.

Learning Activities

3.   Run the program switch1.c with each of the following input values: 9, 2, 4, 3, 0, 10, a. Are the results what you expected each time? If not, read the material again and reconcile the execution results with the discussion of the behavior of the `switch` statement.

4.   *C by Discovery*   What happens when a variable is used as one of the values associated with a `case` label? Modify the program by declaring a variable of type `int`, initializing the variable to 2, and replacing the value 2 in the appropriate `case` labeled statement with your new variable. Then try to compile and execute the program again to test this concept.

6.4 Altering the Flow of Control

In this section we discuss the `continue` and `break` statements. Both statements are used in conjunction with the `while` loop, the `for` loop, and the `do-while` loop. They both alter the flow of control set up by those loops. The `break` statement is also used in conjunction with the `switch` statement. Since these statements alter the flow of a program, they should be used with discretion. An acceptable use would be to handle errors; they should not be used to avoid structuring a program.

The continue Statement

A continue statement is used inside a loop. When it is encountered during program execution, it causes control to pass to the point after the last statement in the loop body instead of executing the next statement as it would normally. The syntax of the continue statement is very simple; it consists of the keyword continue followed by a semicolon, as in

```
continue;
```

The action of the continue statement within a while loop can be diagrammed as follows:

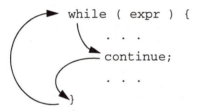

```
while ( expr ) {
    . . .
    continue;
    . . .
}
```

In the above diagram, any statements in the block that are below the continue statement would never be executed. After the continue statement executes, expr (in the while loop) would be evaluated and execution would continue from that point. The use of the continue statement is usually somewhat different than illustrated in the diagram. The continue would very probably be a part of a conditional statement. This use is illustrated in the example program.

With a do-while loop, execution would be as shown below:

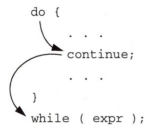

```
do {
    . . .
    continue;
    . . .
}
while ( expr );
```

After execution of the continue statement, expr would be evaluated and execution would continue from that point. The statements below the continue statement and above the evaluation of expr would be skipped. Again, the continue statement would be more likely to appear inside a conditional statement so that it would only be executed when certain conditions are met.

When a `continue` statement appears within a `for` loop, execution again passes to the point after the last statement in the body of the `for` loop.

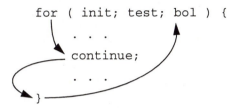

```
for ( init; test; bol ) {
        . . .
    continue;
        . . .
}
```

Then expression `bol` would be evaluated, `test` would be evaluated, and execution would proceed from that point.

The program in Example 6-3 illustrates the use of the `continue` statement. The program will read a line of input from the keyboard and output it to the monitor. Every tab character in the input will be replaced by a backslash and a lowercase `'t'`. For example, the input

        NAME<Tab>AGE

would be echoed as

        NAME\tAGE.

Code similar to this could be used in writing an editor program where it might be desirable to display the difference between a tab and a sequence of spaces. The code that does the work has been packaged as a function in order to be used as a tool in several different programs.

Example 6-3: continue.c

```
/*              continue.c
 *
 *   Synopsis   - Echoes its input to its output with each tab
 *                character replaced with '\t'.
 *
 *   Objective  - To illustrate the continue statement.
 */

/* Include Files */
#include <stdio.h>

/* Function Declarations */
```

```
void showtabsinline( void );

void main( void )
{
    printf( "Enter a line with tab characters in it.\n\n" );
    showtabsinline();
}


/***************************** showtabsinline()  ************/
/*   Reads and echoes a line of text from standard input. Every
 *   tab character in the input is replaced by the two characters
 *   '\' and 't'.
 */
void showtabsinline( void )
{
    int iochar;

    while ( ( iochar = getchar() ) != '\n' ) {
        if ( iochar == '\t' ) {
            putchar( '\\' );
            putchar( 't' );
            continue;                              /* Note 1 */
        }
        putchar( iochar );                         /* Note 2 */
    }
    putchar( '\n' );
}
```

This program consists of two functions. The function main() is very simple. It consists of a printf() call that asks for input and a call to the function showtabsinline(). It serves only to test the secondary function. When software tools are being developed, they can be tested with a driver program such as main(). The function can be tested with many different inputs, and then can be used with a high degree of confidence. The function showtabsinline() uses a while loop to read until a newline is read. Each character is processed separately.

Note 1: This continue statement is used in conjunction with a while loop. It appears inside an if statement and is only executed when the input character is a tab. In this case, the backslash (\) and the 't' are output before the continue statement causes execution to return to the top of the while loop, where another character is read.

Note that this and most other programs can easily be structured so that the continue statement is not necessary. Most stylistic guidelines caution against using the continue statement to avoid proper structuring of a program.

Note 2: This putchar() statement is skipped whenever a tab character is read in the input, but is executed every time a character other than a tab is read. All other characters in the input will be echoed to the output. Only the tab characters will be replaced in the output.

Learning Activities

5.   Execute continue.c with several different inputs to see how it works.

6.   Modify continue.c so that it skips all characters in the input except tab characters, and outputs just the string "\t" for each tab character.

The break Statement

The break is another statement that alters the flow of control of a for loop, a while loop, or a do-while loop. The break statement can also be used in conjunction with the switch statement. The syntax of the break statement is very simple. It consists of the keyword break followed by a semicolon, as in

```
break;
```

When a break statement is encountered during execution of a while, for, or do-while loop, it causes execution of the loop to terminate and control to pass to the point immediately after the loop. This execution flow is diagrammed below with each of the loops.

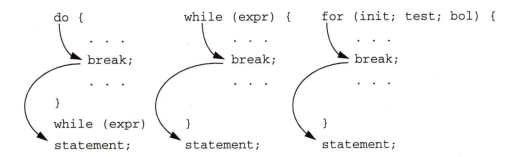

Any statements following the break in the above diagrams would never be executed. The expressions for continuing each loop would not be evaluated nor would the expression bo1 in the for loop. Again, this diagram is solely to indicate the flow of execution. Actual use would differ and is illustrated in the example below.

In the case of nested loops, a break statement would only break out of the closest loop. It does not break out of the whole nested formation.

The program break.c in Example 6-4 will read a line of input from the keyboard and echo that line to the terminal until the character '#' is read in the input. The input after the '#' is ignored. For example, the character '#' might signal the beginning of a comment or it might signal the beginning of a different type of information that would be handled by another part of the program. This program illustrates the use of the break statement to terminate a loop early.

Example 6-4: break.c

```
/*                break.c
 *
 *    Synopsis    - Accepts input of a line of text and displays
 *                  the part of a line before the SENTINEL
 *                  character.
 *
 *    Objective   - To illustrate the break statement.
 */

/* Include Files */
#include <stdio.h>

/* Constant Declarations */
#define EOLN      '\n'
#define SENTINEL  '#'

/* Function Declarations */
void readtosentinel( void );

void main( void )
{

    printf( "The sentinel character is %c.\n", SENTINEL );
    printf( "Enter a line with a sentinel in it.\n\n" );

    readtosentinel();

    printf( "\n\nThat was the first part of the line.\n" );
}
```

```
/***************************** readtosentinel()  *************/
/*   Reads a line of text from standard input. Stops when either
 *   a SENTINEL character or an EOLN is read.
 */
void readtosentinel( void )
{
     int iochar;

     while ( ( iochar = getchar() ) != EOLN ) {
       if ( iochar == SENTINEL ) {
           break;                                       /* Note 1 */
       }
       putchar( iochar );
     }
}
```

This program has two functions. The function `main()` is a driver. Its purpose is to ask for input and to call the function `readtosentinel()`. The function `readtosentinel()` reads through a line of input and outputs the characters it read until the SENTINEL character is encountered. A function similar to this one might be used to position the pointer in the input stream so that another function could process the information that appears after the SENTINEL character.

Note 1: The `break` statement is used in conjunction with a `while` loop. It appears inside an `if` statement and will only be executed when a SENTINEL appears in the input stream. When this happens, the `while` loop will terminate and control will be passed to the end of the function and back to `main()`.

This program could be easily restructured to avoid the use of the `break` statement. Like the `continue` statement, the `break` should be used with discretion.

Learning Activities

7.   Test the program break.c with several different input lines. Devise tests so that you can answer the following questions.

   a.   How does the program react when no SENTINEL character appears in the input? Is this acceptable behavior?

   b.   How does it react when two SENTINEL characters appear in the input stream? Is this what a user might expect? How (or where) should a user be notified of this behavior?

8. Modify break.c so that it will just read (and not output) the data on a line of input until SENTINEL is encountered. After SENTINEL is read, the program should continue to read the input line and echo the input to the terminal.

The break Statement in Conjunction with the switch Statement

The program switch.c in Section 6.3 illustrates that when a switch statement is executed and a match is found between the control expressions and the constant expressions, all of the following statements are executed by default.

In some cases, we don't want statements in all the case labeled statements to be executed when a match is found. The break statement can be used to control which statements are executed. For example, in the following code, if the runtime value of expr matches the value of expr2, statement2 is to be executed, but not statement3 or any of the following statements.

```
switch (expr) {
        case expr1:  statement1
        case expr2:

                        statement2
                        break;
        case expr3:  statement3

                 . . .
        default:     statement_default
}
next_statement;
```

When a break statement is encountered in a switch statement body, it transfers control to the statement immediately following the switch statement. In the above illustration, next_statement would be executed after the break. As another example of execution of the above "code segment", if expr matches expr1, then statement1, statement2, and next_statement will be executed in that order.

The program in Example 6-5 shows a typical use of the break and switch statements together. The program outputs a menu and inputs the menu choice. The program then echoes the menu choice. This program could be extended to process the response in an appropriate way by writing a function to process each of the menu choices.

Example 6-5: switch2.c

```
/*                    switch2.c
 *
 *    Synopsis    - Displays a menu, accepts a choice from a user,
 *                  and processes the response.
 *
 *    Objective   - Illustrates the switch and break statements
 *                  together.
 */

/* Include Files */
#include <stdio.h>

/* Function Declarations */
void processresponse( char );
int menu( void );

void main( void )
{
    char iochar = 0;

    do {
        iochar = menu();                                /* Note 1 */
        processresponse( iochar );
    }
    while ( iochar != '0' );
}

/***************************** menu()  *********************/
/*    Displays the menu choices and accepts input of the user's
 *    response. The first character of the response is returned.
 */

int menu( void )
{
    char response[40];

    printf( "The following games are available:\n" );
    printf( "--------------------------------\n\n" );
    printf( "1. Guessit\n" );
    printf( "2. Nim\n" );
    printf( "----------\n" );
```

```
        printf( "Choose a game or type 0 to exit.\nYour choice?   " );

        if ( gets( response ) == NULL )
            return( '0' );                                    /* Note 1 */
        else
            return( response[0] );                            /* Note 1 */
}


/***************************** processresponse()  ***********/
/*   Takes action depending on the value of its parameter.
 */

void processresponse( char iochar )
{
        switch ( iochar ) {                                   /* Note 2 */
                case '0':  break;                             /* Note 3 */
                case '1':  printf( "You have chosen guessit.\n" );
                           break;                             /* Note 4 */
                case '2':  printf( "You have chosen nim.\n" );
                           break;                             /* Note 4 */
                                                             /* Note 5 */
                default:   printf( "Illegal input.\n" );
                           printf( "Choose 0, 1, or 2.\n" );
        }
}
```

Three functions constitute this program. The function `main()` is a driver. It calls both of the other functions. A `do-while` loop is used to continue the program until the user decides to terminate it. The function `menu()` consists of `printf()` calls to output the menu and a call to `gets()` to do the input. The function `processresponse()` looks at its parameter and uses a `switch` statement to decide on the next action.

Note 1: The value returned by `menu()` is passed to `processresponse()` for appropriate action. After return from `processresponse()`, the value is tested. If the value is `'0'`, the program is terminated; otherwise, the menu is displayed and the choice is processed again. Looking at the function `menu()`, we see that the user can terminate the program by typing `'0'` to the menu prompt or signaling end-of-file.

Note 2: The `switch` is done on the parameter `iochar`. Its value will be compared with the values in the `case` labeled statements below to determine the next program action.

Note 3: The `break` is used to terminate execution of the statements in the `switch` statement. If `iochar` has the value `'0'` control will pass to the point immediately following the `switch` statement. In this program, control would pass to the end of the function `processresponse()`.

Note 4: For the next two case labeled statements in the switch statement body, the break is used in the same way. If iochar has either the value '1' or '2', the corresponding printf() call would be executed and control would pass to the point immediately after the switch statement.

Note 5: The printf() calls associated with the default label will be executed only in the case that iochar has a value other than '1', or '2'. The use of break causes these statements to be skipped if iochar matches one of the values in the case labels.

A Closer Look

The function processresponse() is a "stub" function. It does not complete the action desired, but instead is used during program development to test another program part. In this case, it could be used to test the handling of the input and assure that meaningful characters are passed to processresponse() each time. Using function stubs during program development is a technique that can lead to programs with fewer bugs.

Learning Activities

9. a. Execute the program switch2.c. Test it with each of its requested inputs to make sure that it behaves as expected.

   b. Test the program by responding with more than one character to the menu. For example, what happens if you type "12" in response to the prompt "Your choice?" What happens if you type "quit"?

   c. Experiment by placing comment symbols around one or more of the break statements and executing the program again. Make sure you understand the functionality of the break statement in this context.

10. Note that gets() was used to do the input even though only one character was needed and inspected by the program.

   a. Modify the program to have the input done by getchar(). Test it thoroughly. What problems exist with getchar() that are handled properly with gets()?

   b. Could the input be done with scanf()? If so, modify the program to use scanf() for the input.

   c. Once the program is expanded to play the games Nim and Guessit, what difference would the choice of library input functions make to the rest of the program?

6.5 Getting Out Gracefully

The two concepts discussed in this section are the `return` statement and the `exit()` library function. Both are used to alter the flow of control set up by other program elements.

The return Statement

The `return` statement is used to terminate execution of a function. When it is executed, it causes control to pass from the function back to the position where it was called. It could be used to provide a point of exit from a function other than at the end of the function block or to allow a function to return a value.

The `return` statement can be used in two different ways. First, the keyword `return` could be simply followed by a semicolon, as in

```
return;
```

For this use, the function type should be `void`. In the second syntax, the `return` statement is followed by an expression,

```
return expression;
```

where `expression` can be any legal C expression. As we saw in Chapter 3, the type of the function must match the type of `expression`.

When a `return` statement with the first syntax is executed in a function other than `main()`, it causes the execution of the function to terminate. Execution resumes in the calling function at the position following the function call. The following diagram indicates this.

```
main()
{
      . . .
    f1();
    printf ("returned\n");
      . . .
}
f1()
{
      . . .
    return;
      . . .
}
```

When the `return` statement is used with an expression, control is passed to the point in the calling function immediately after the function call and the value of the expression becomes the value returned by the function. We saw examples of this use in Chapters 1 and 3.

The `return` statement can be used in `main()` also. When executed there, it will cause the program to cease execution. When the `return` statement is used with an expression, the value of that expression is returned to the program's calling environment. This is one way for C programs to communicate with a command interpreter.

Suppose we want to write a function to read to a position in an input line that is delimited by '`#`'. Example 6-6 implements this function with the `return` statement. The program is similar in concept to the one in Example 6-4 that illustrated the `break` statement, but this time we assume that the processing of the line would take place after our function has positioned the input pointer correctly.

Example 6-6: return1.c

```
/*                    return1.c
 *
 *    Synopsis    - Positions input stream to either the character
 *                  after '#' or at the end of the input line.
 *
 *    Objective   - To illustrate the simplest form of the
 *                  return statement.
 */

/* Include Files */
#include <stdio.h>

/* Constant Declarations */
#define END_OF_LINE    '\n'
#define DELIMITER      '#'

/* Function Declarations */
void look_for_delimiter( void );


void main( void )
{
                                                        /* Note 1 */
    printf( "Enter a line of text with a '#'.\n> " );
    look_for_delimiter();
    printf( "Done looking!\n" );                        /* Note 1 */
}
```

```
/***************************** look_for_delimiter()  *********/
/*   Reads a line of text, character by character. Returns when
 *   a DELIMITER is found in the input.
 */
void look_for_delimiter( void )
{
    int iochar;

    while ( ( iochar = getchar() ) != END_OF_LINE ) {
        if ( iochar == DELIMITER )
                return;                                    /* Note 2 */
    }
    printf( "At end of line\n" );                          /* Note 3 */
}
```

The program contains the functions main() and look_for_delimiter(). In main(), there is a request for input, a call to look_for_delimiter(), and a printf() call after look_for_delimiter() finishes executing. Again main() is a driver function; its purpose is to prepare for execution of look_for_delimiter() and to call it. In look_for_delimiter(), each passage through the while loop compares a character to the delimiter '#'. The while loop will terminate if a newline is seen or if '#' is found in the input stream.

Note 1: These two printf() calls surround the call to the function look_for_delimiter(). The first asks the user for relevant input, and the second reports that the function has finished executing. The output serves as a trace through the execution of this program. If look_for_delimiter() were used as a tool in a larger program, statements like these would not appear in the final version. However, they could be included as an aid during the development phase of a program.

Note 2: This return statement will only be executed when '#' is found in the line of input. In that case, control will immediately return to the function main() at the statement following the call to this function. Note that this provides a second point of exit from the while loop.

Note 3: This printf() call might be included during the development phase of a program to provide an additional trace through the program. It will only be executed when there is no '#' in the input stream. The message serves to let the user know that fact, and that exit from the function look_for_delimiter() took place at the end of the function block. This printf() call would probably be removed after the function had been fully tested.

Learning Activity

11.　Execute return1.c with several different input lines to make sure that it behaves as you expected.

In the second syntax, the `return` statement is followed by an expression. When this type of statement is executed, the expression is evaluated and that value becomes the return value of the function. In this case, the function result can be assigned to a variable. For example, if a function `max()`, that calculates the maximum of a set of values, terminates by executing a `return` statement with an expression, then a call to the function might be combined with an assignment statement, as in

```
maxnum = max();
```

The value returned by `max()` is assigned to `maxnum` and can be referenced later in the program.

The next example is an extension of the previous example. In Example 6-6, the function `look_for_delimiter()` was to read input until the character `'#'` was found in the input or until the end of the input line. The calling function would not know which case had occurred in the input stream. Using the `return` statement with an associated expression, the function can communicate which case it found. This modification is made in Example 6-7.

Example 6-7:　return2.c

```
/*                  return2.c
 *
 *   Synopsis   - Positions input stream to the character after
 *                '#' or after the end of the input line.
 *
 *   Objective  - To illustrate a return statement with an
 *                expression.
 */

/* Include Files */
#include <stdio.h>

/* Constant Declarations */
#define END_OF_LINE     '\n'
#define DELIMITER       '#'
```

```
/* Function Declarations */
int look_for_delimiter( void );

void main( void )
{
    int found;

    printf( "Enter a line of text with a '#'.\n> " );
    found = look_for_delimiter();                        /* Note 1 */
    if ( found )                                         /* Note 2 */
        printf( "found a %c.\n", DELIMITER );
    else
        printf( "read until end of line.\n" );
}

/***************************** look_for_delimiter()   **********/
/*   Reads a line of input and compares each character to a
 *   DELIMITER. Returns 1 when a DELIMITER is found, and 0
 *   otherwise.
 */
int look_for_delimiter( void )
{
    int iochar;

    while ( ( iochar = getchar() ) != END_OF_LINE ) {
        if ( iochar == DELIMITER )
            return 1;                                    /* Note 3 */
    }
    return 0;                                            /* Note 4 */
}
```

The structure of this program is very similar to that of the previous example program. It contains the function main() and a subfunction look_for_delimiter(). The function main() is a driver; it requests input for the subfunction to process, calls the subfunction, and reports the status at return from the subfunction. The subfunction look_for_delimiter() uses a while loop to read a line of input and processes each input character separately.

Note 1: Since the return statement is used with an associated expression, the subfunction look_for_delimiter() returns a value. The value returned is assigned to the variable found.

Note 2: The value returned by the subfunction is checked by this if statement. If the value of the variable found is nonzero, the printf() call in the body of the if is executed; if found has a zero value, the printf() call in the body of the else is executed. In the current program, the findings are simply output. In later development, the printf() calls could be replaced with calls to functions that further process the input in each case.

Note 3: This `return` statement is only executed when a `'#'` is found in the input. When that happens, execution of the subfunction will terminate and control will return to `main()`. The subfunction's return value is `1`; the next source statement executed will be the assignment of that value to the variable `found`.

Note 4: This `return` statement will only execute when the input line does not contain a `'#'`. Exit from the `while` loop resulted from a newline being read. This fact is communicated by the return value of zero. If this `return` statement is executed, control is passed back to `main()` and the next execution is that of assigning the value `0` to the variable `found`. This method of communication between functions by their return values is very commonly used.

Learning Activities

12.   Execute the program return2.c with several different lines of input to make sure that you understand how it operates.

13.   *C by Discovery*   To see how your environment handles certain situations,

a.   Modify the program return1.c by changing the line

```
look_for_delimiter();
```

to

```
found = look_for_delimiter();
```

and try to compile and execute the program again. (You will also have to declare the variable `found`.) If the program compiles, modify it again to have it display the value of `found`. Generalize from this experience to understand what happens when such an assignment is made and the function does not return a value.[1]

b.   Modify the program return2.c by changing the line

```
found = look_for_delimiter();
```

to

```
look_for_delimiter();
```

and try to compile and execute the program again. Did anything appear to be amiss with the function call? Try to explain the results of your compilation and/or test runs.

14.   Modify return2.c so that the variable `found` is not needed.

---

1. Many of the older compilers will allow compilation and execution of code with the described error condition. Many of these errors have been eliminated with the advent of ANSI C.

The exit() Library Function

The `exit()` function is available in the library on many implementations of C. This function provides a drastic means of altering the program's flow of control. When executed, `exit()` causes the program to terminate. Control is returned to the underlying operating system.

The `exit()` function takes a single parameter of type `int`. Therefore, a call to `exit()` might have the form

```
exit( 0 );
```

or

```
exit( 1 );
```

or

```
exit( 255 );
```

This value is passed to the calling environment (the operating system) and could be used to indicate the reason why the program terminated. By convention, a parameter of 0 indicates normal termination. Different nonzero values between 1 and 255 can be chosen by the programmer to indicate different reasons for program termination.

When used in `main()` the statement

```
return expression;
```

is equivalent to the statement

```
exit( expression );
```

The `exit()` library function differs from the `return` statement when it appears in a function other than `main()`. The `return` statement causes control to pass back to the calling function. The `exit()` library function causes program termination from *any* function from which it is called.

Example 6-8 illustrates a use of the `exit()` library function to indicate an error in input. The function `convert()` expects a sequence of digits in its input. It converts the sequence to a value of type `int`. The sequence of digits should be terminated by a space or a newline in the input stream. A character other than a digit or a space appearing in the input stream is considered an error condition. One method of handling this type of error might be to display an error message and terminate the program. That is the approach taken in this example. Note, however, that the error handler is a separate function so that it can be changed if desired.

The character typing library is also introduced. The header file ctype.h contains declarations of utilities that are provided to determine the type of any character. We specifically look at the utility `isdigit()` in this program. It reports whether or not its argument is a digit between `'0'` and `'9'`. Chapter 11 contains additional information about the utilities declared in ctype.h.

Example 6-8: exit.c

```
/*              exit.c
 *
 *    Synopsis    - Reads a stream of digits for its input, converts
 *                  the input to an integer value, and displays it.
 *                  Finding a nondigit in input is an error.
 *
 *    Objective   - To illustrate error handling with the exit()
 *                  library function.
 */

/* Include Files */
#include <stdio.h>
#include <ctype.h>                              /* Note 1 */
#include <stdlib.h>                             /* Note 2 */

/* Constant Declarations */
#define BLANK           ' '
#define END_OF_LINE     '\n'

/* Function Declarations */
int convert( void );
void error( void );

void main( void )
{
    printf( "Enter a positive integer > " );
                                                /* Note 3 */
    printf( "The value entered was %d.\n", convert() );
    exit( 0 );                                  /* Note 4 */
}

/******************************** convert() ***************/
/*    Reads standard input until either a BLANK, an END_OF_LINE
 *    or a nondigit is found. If only digits are found, the
 *    function returns the converted value as type int. Otherwise,
 *    the function error() is called.
 */
int convert( void )
{
    int ch,
        sum = 0;
    while ((( ch = getchar() ) != BLANK ) && (ch != END_OF_LINE )) {
```

```
        if ( !isdigit( ch ) )                         /* Note 1 */
            error();
        sum = sum * 10 + ( ch - '0' );                /* Note 5 */
    }
    return ( sum );
}


/******************************** error()  ***************/
/*   Displays an error message and terminates the program with
 *   exit value 1.
 */
void error( void )
{
    printf( "Nondigit in input. Program terminated.\n" );
    exit( 1 );                                        /* Note 6 */
}
```

Three functions make up this program. The function `main()` is a driver program and only serves to ask for input, call the function `convert()`, and report on the value returned. The function `convert()` uses a `while` loop to read until either an `END_OF_LINE` or a `BLANK` is read. The processing of the digits is done inside the `while` loop. The function `error()` does the error handling.

Note 1: The header file ctype.h is a standard part of each implementation of C. It contains many declarations of utilities that deal with character types. It is included in this example to allow a call to the utility `isdigit()` that appears in the second line referenced by **Note 1**. The utility `isdigit()` is defined in the file ctype.h. It looks at its parameter and returns a value of 1 if the parameter is one of the digits `'0'`, `'1'`, `'2'`, ..., `'9'`; it returns a value of 0 if the parameter is not a digit.

Chapter 11 and the *Programmer's Handbook* contain information on other similar utilities that can be used to determine the nature of a character. Also, Learning Activity 15 starts investigation of another utility in ctype.h

Note 2: The header file stdlib.h contains declarations of many of the standard library functions. It is needed in this program because the declaration of `exit()` is usually in this file.

Note 3: The function call to `convert()` is made in this `printf()` call. The return value is displayed by `printf()`.

Note 4: This `exit()` call will be executed when no errors were found in the input and the program terminates normally. Traditionally, the argument of 0 to `exit()` will signify normal termination of the program to the calling environment. Nonzero values are used to signify error conditions.

Note 5: Conversion from a string of characters to a value of type `int` takes place on this line. The variable `sum` was initialized to `0` and accumulation of the value is done in this variable. The final value of `sum` is returned by `convert()`.

Note that this algorithm will only work when the digits `'0'` through `'9'` are contiguous in the underlying character set. The code depends on C's automatic conversion from character to integer.

Note 6: This `exit()` call will only be executed when the function `error()` was called from `convert()`. When executed, `exit()` causes the program to terminate. The value of `1` is passed to the calling environment. By convention, `0` signifies normal termination, and a value of `1` (or any other nonzero value) would indicate an error.

"It is a convention of the exit( ) function that 0 signifies normal termination, and 1 signifies an error." Based on *Archangel Saint Michael* by Andrea della Robbia, c. 1475.

Learning Activities

15. a. Find out if the file ctype.h is available on your system. If it is, inspect it. In particular, look for the definition of `isdigit()` and see if you understand the code.

   b. Without looking further in ctype.h, write a function named `islower()` that takes a single parameter. The function `islower()` should return 1 if its parameter is between `'a'` and `'z'`, and 0 otherwise. Write a short driver program that will test your function.

   c. Look at the other utility definitions provided in ctype.h so that you have a good idea of what facilities are available there.

16. Run the program exit.c.

   a. Test it with several strings of digits to make sure that the conversion is done correctly.

   b. Test it with a single string of input digits followed by a `<Enter>` to make sure that the algorithm terminates correctly in this case.

   c. Test it with a string of digits separated from other input on the line with a blank character. Try a tab character as a separator. Modify the program, if necessary, so that it handles each of these cases correctly.

   d. Finally, test the program with some nondigit input to see that the `exit()` library function behaves as you thought it should.

6.6 If There's Time or Need: The goto Statement and Labels

The `goto` statement in C allows transfer of control from one position in a function to another statement in the same function. The destination statement must be marked with a label.

A label in C is an identifier. It must be associated with a statement by using the following syntax:

```
label : statement;
```

The statement can be any legal statement in C.

The syntax of the `goto` statement follows:

```
goto identifier;
```

where `identifier` is a label associated with a statement in the same function as the `goto`.

The program in Example 6-9 illustrates a use of the `goto` statement. The program has the same functionality as exit.c in Example 6-8, but the error handling is done with a `goto` statement instead of a function call.

Example 6-9: goto.c

```
/*                  goto.c
 *
 *    Synopsis    - Expects a stream of digits in input. The digits
 *                  are converted to an integer value and output.
 *
 *    Objective   - To illustrate error handling with the goto
 *                  statement.
 */

/* Include Files */
#include <stdio.h>
#include <ctype.h>
#include <stdlib.h>

/* Constant Declarations */
#define BLANK           ' '
#define END_OF_LINE     '\n'

/* Function Declarations */
int convert( void );

void main( void )
{
    printf( "Enter a positive integer > " );
                                                    /* Note 1 */
    printf( "The value entered was %d.\n", convert () );
    exit( 0 );
}
/******************************** convert()  **************/
/*    Reads a line from standard input until either a BLANK, an
```

```
 *     END_OF_LINE or a nondigit is seen. Returns the int value
 *     of the input string in the first two cases; displays an
 *     error message and terminates the program in the last case.
 */
int convert( void )
{
        int ch,
            sum = 0;

        while ((( ch = getchar() ) != BLANK ) && ( ch != END_OF_LINE )) {

            if ( !isdigit( ch ) )
                    goto error;                                 /* Note 2 */
            sum = sum * 10 + ( ch - '0' );
        }
        return ( sum );
                                                                /* Note 3 */
error:  printf( "Nondigit in input. Program terminated.\n" );
        exit( 1 );
}
```

The program contains the function `main()` and the function `convert()`. The function `main()` only contains code necessary to initialize for, call, and report on the return of the function `convert()`. Like exit.c in Example 6-8, the function `convert()` uses a `while` loop to read in the string of digits. Each digit is processed separately. It uses the utility `isdigit()` defined in the header file ctype.h to check on errors in input. Only the error handling is different.

Note 1: The function `main()` asks for input and displays the value returned by `convert()`. The call to `convert()` is in the second call to `printf()`.

Note 2: The `goto` statement is only executed in case `isdigit(iochar)` returns 0. Control will transfer from this position in the program to the statement at the bottom of the function with the label `error`. The intervening statements will not be executed.

Note 3: When a nondigit is read in the input stream, control will transfer to this point in the program. The `printf()` call will give the error diagnostic and the program will terminate. Note that this code is only reached by means of the `goto` statement. If there is no error in input, the previous `return` statement will transfer control back to the function `main()`.

Learning Activities

17.   Test goto.c with many different inputs to verify that it behaves as you expected.[1]

18.   Modify the program goto.c by moving the `printf()` call labeled `error` and the subsequent `exit()` statement to the end of the function `main()`. Try to compile and execute the modified program. Try to explain what happens and why.

A Word of Warning

Much has been written about the use and misuse of the goto statement. Although opinions differ on the proper use of this statement, most authorities agree that indiscriminate use of the goto statement is one deterrent to structured programming.

In addition to the effect that goto has on the structure of a program, situations arise in the source code where the effects of using goto have some unexpected deleterious consequences. A major example of this is when the goto statement is used to jump into the middle of a block, as in the following code segment:

```
iochar = getchar();
if ( isdigit( iochar ))
    goto calculate;
         .
         .                              /* other code */
         .
    {                                   /* a block */
        int i = 0;                      /* local variable */
        while ( isdigit( iochar )) {
             i = i + 1;
                                        /*labeled statement */
calculate: for ( j = 1; j < i ; j++ )
                sum = 10 * ( iochar - '0' )
            iochar = getchar();
        }                               /* end while */
    }                                   /* end block */
```

---

1. Some compilers will issue a warning message for this program since the function `convert()` does not actually return a value when an error occurs. The program could be rewritten to eliminate this warning, but much of the existing C code that uses the goto to handle errors will have this structure.

The local variable `i` in the block is not guaranteed to be initialized properly when the block is not entered from the top. If the block is entered by means of the `goto` statement above, the value of `i` could be garbage. The code would be unreliable.

6.7 If There's Time or Need: Using Recursion

Recursion occurs when a function or subprogram calls itself or calls a function which in turn calls the original function. C allows recursion.

In mathematics, a recurrence relation is a formula in which the desired expression involving a positive integer, n, is described in terms of corresponding values for integers less than n. Initial conditions or starting values (usually for $n = 0$, or $n = 1$) must also be given. The following formulas for powers of x and for factorials are simple examples of recurrence relations.

	Formula	**Initial Condition**
Power:	$x^n = x \cdot x^{n-1}$	$x^0 = 1$
Factorial:	$n! = n \cdot (n-1)!$	$0! = 1$

Using the initial condition, the formulas can be evaluated for any positive integer n. For example, 4! can be calculated using the recurrence relation in the following steps:

$$4! = 4 \cdot 3! \qquad \text{using} \quad n! = n \cdot (n-1)!$$
$$= 4 \cdot 3 \cdot 2! \qquad \text{using} \quad (n-1)! = (n-1) \cdot (n-2)!$$
$$= 4 \cdot 3 \cdot 2 \cdot 1! \qquad \qquad \cdot$$
$$= 4 \cdot 3 \cdot 2 \cdot 1 \cdot 0! \qquad \qquad \cdot$$
$$= 4 \cdot 3 \cdot 2 \cdot 1 \cdot 1 \qquad \text{using} \quad 0! = 1$$
$$= 24$$

One way of implementing a recurrence relation on a computer is to code a recursive function. As the initial condition allows the calculation of a recurrence relation to terminate, it also provides a way of terminating the sequence of recursive calls of a function. It is extremely important that every recursive function be given a termination condition that is sure to occur. Otherwise, the execution would be out of control.

A recursive function to calculate factorials is demonstrated in the program recurs.c in Example 6-10. The function `main()` serves only as a driver to call the recursive function and output the value returned by the function.

Example 6-10: recurs.c

```
/*                  recurs.c
 *
 *    Synopsis   - Inputs a positive integer, calculates its
 *                 factorial, and outputs the result.
 *
 *    Objective  - A simple example of a recursive function.
 */

/* Include Files */
#include <stdio.h>
#include <ctype.h>                                       /* Note 1 */
#include <stdlib.h>

/* Constant Declarations */
#define BLANK            ' '
#define END_OF_LINE      '\n'

/* Function Declarations */
int factorial( int );
int convert( void );
void error( void );

void main( void )
{
     int n;

     printf( "Program to Calculate Factorials.\n" );
     printf( "------- -- --------- ----------\n" );
     printf( "\nEnter a positive integer value : " );

     n = convert();                                      /* Note 2 */

     printf( "\n%d! is %d.\n", n, factorial( n ) );
}

/********************************** factorial()  ************/
/*    Uses a recursive algorithm to calculate the factorial
 *    of its argument.
 */
int factorial( int n )
{
```

```
        if ( n == 0 )                              /* Note 3 */
            return ( 1 );
        else
            return ( n * factorial( n-1 ) );       /* Note 4 */
}


/********************************** convert()  **************/
/*    Reads standard input until either a BLANK, an END_OF_LINE
 *    or a nondigit is found. If only digits are found, the
 *    function returns the converted value as type int. Otherwise,
 *    the function error() is called
 */
int convert( void )
{
    int ch,
        sum = 0;

    while ((( ch = getchar() ) != BLANK )
                    && (ch != END_OF_LINE )) {
        if ( !isdigit( ch ) )                       /* Note 1 */
            error();
        sum = sum * 10 + ( ch - '0' );              /* Note 4 */
    }
    return ( sum );
}


/********************************** error()  **************/
/*    Displays an error message and terminates the program with
 *    exit value 1.
 */
void error( void )
{
    printf( "Nondigit in input. Program terminated.\n" );
    exit( 1 );                                      /* Note 5 */
}
```

This program consists of four functions: `main()`, `factorial()`, `convert()`, and `error()`. The function `main()` requests input and calls the functions `convert()` and `factorial()` to do input conversion and factorial calculation. The functions `convert()` and `error()` were those used in Example 6-8 in Section 6.5.

Note 1: The header file ctype.h is included so that the utility `isdigit()` can be accessed.

Note 2: The function `convert()` from the program exit.c is used to input the integer. In this statement, the value returned by `convert()` is assigned to the variable n. The function `convert()` and the accompanying error handler embrace the concept of software tools. These tools can be moved to a different program without rewriting.

Note 3: The function `factorial()` is the recursive function. The first clause in the `if` statement implements the termination condition for the factorial recurrence relation. This allows exit from the function without encountering a recursive call. Every recursive function must supply a method of exit from the recursion.

Note 4: This statement contains the recursive call to the function `factorial()`. When this occurs, control passes back to the beginning of the function. The earlier call to `factorial()` does not terminate but, instead, waits for the subsequent calls to terminate and return a value. If this program were used to calculate 4!, the hand calculation above indicates that there would be five calls to the function `factorial()` active at one time. The first call would be from the function `main()` with the parameter 4. Subsequent calls would be made by the function `factorial()` itself with the parameters 3, 2, 1, and 0, in that order. The initial value would be returned by the call with parameter 0, and that would allow the preceding calls to `exit` once they received the value for which they were waiting.

Learning Activities

19. a. Run the program and test it with the values 4, 6, 2, and 3 to make sure that it runs correctly.

   b. Modify recurs.c by including some `printf()` calls that will provide an execution trace. Make each message different and have the message indicate the position from which it is output. There should be a statement at the beginning and the end of the `main()`, and one for each time the function `factorial()` is entered and exited. The `printf()` messages from the function `factorial()` should mention the value of the parameter as well as whether it is entering or exiting the function. Both of the `return` statements in `factorial()` should be immediately preceded by `printf()` calls. (You may have to restructure the `else` clause to get a true trace.) Once the trace is working properly, test the program again with the above input so that you can count how many calls to `factorial()` are active at one time.

   c. If you know how to use the debugger on your system, you may choose to trace through the execution of this program in the debugger.

20. Test the program with some larger numbers as input. There is no mechanism in the program to determine when the value returned by `factorial()` exceeds the value that can be handled by a vari-

able of type `int`. On some systems this overflow error occurs for small values of `n`.

    a. Determine the largest value for which the function returns the correct value on your system.

    b. Modify the program so that the value is correct for larger values of `n`. This can usually be done by changing the type on some variables. What type will handle the largest result on your system?

21. a. Replace the call to our function `convert()` with a call to the C library function `scanf()`. Test the program now. In particular, what happens when there are errors in input? For example, what happens when the input consists of just an `'a'`, or the sequence of characters `2a3`? Do you prefer the behavior of the program with `scanf()` or with `convert()`? Why?

    b. The function `scanf()` can return an indication of error. Read your documentation on `scanf()` or the information in the *Programmer's Handbook*, and restructure the program to use `scanf()` for input and to output an error message for input errors.

A Closer Look

Recursive functions tend to use a lot of memory. In Chapter 4, we discussed execution environments (also called activation records) of functions in conjunction with parameter passing. Here we will look at them in conjunction with recursive calls to a function.

The activation record of a function contains the local variables and parameters for a function (along with other information). The activation record is in existence only while the function is active (that is, its execution has not reached a `return` statement or the closing brace for its block). Thus, the activation record for `main()` would be in existence during the full time of program execution, but the activation records for other functions were created when the function was called and destroyed when the function terminated.

When a recursive function calls itself, the original activation record is not destroyed, because that function is still active. Another activation record for the function is created with each recursive call. The activation records are "stacked up." None are destroyed until they complete execution. Below is the collection of activation records that are active at one time for the function `factorial()` in recurs.c. In each activation record, the only variable shown is the parameter `n`. The first activation record created was the one with `n` equal `4`. Then the activation records to the right were created one at a time until finally the activation record with n equal 0 was created.

n = 4	n = 3	n = 2	n = 1	n = 0

Five calls were active at one time. The calls terminate in the order opposite to their creation. The call to factorial() with n equal 0 uses the initial condition and terminates instead of making another recursive call. That allows the call with n equal 1 to calculate its return value and terminate. This pattern continues until the value of 4! has been calculated.

This was a simple example. If the example were more complicated or if the initial call to factorial() had a larger parameter, the memory usage would be much higher. In spite of the large amount of memory it may use, recursion is a handy problem-solving tool. Some problems lend themselves naturally to recursive thinking.

Another Example of Recursion

Consider the problem of sorting an array. One approach might be to

1. Divide the array in half.
2. Sort the first half.
3. Sort the second half.
4. Merge the two halves together.

To sort the first half, this approach would be applied again: divide it in half, sort the first half, sort the second half, and merge the two halves together. This approach could be continued until half of one of the divided arrays was a single element and did not need sorting. Steps 2 and 3 would be implemented as recursive calls.

For example, consider the following array:

3	1	8	2

Sorting the array with this approach is diagrammed below. In each case the call taking the action is listed. Each of the four steps in the algorithm above are executed in each recursive call to sort a portion of the array. The indentations also indicate the levels of recursion in each step.

First Call

1. Divide the array in half.

3	1		8	2

2. Sort the first half.

Second Call

1. Divide the array in half.

3		1

2. Sort the first half.

| 3 | Done
|---|

3. Sort the second half.

| 1 | Done
|---|

4. Merge the two halves together.

1	3

3. Sort the second half.

Third Call

1. Divide the array in half..

8		2

2. Sort the first half.

| 8 | Done
|---|

3. Sort the second half.

| 2 | Done
|---|

4. Merge the two halves together.

2	8

4. Merge the two halves together.

1	2	3	8

The array has been sorted.

This approach has been documented in a well-known sorting algorithm, the merge sort algorithm. It is a recursive algorithm. An implementation in C appears in Example 6-11. Consider that code now.

Example 6-11: mergsort.alg

```
/*                  mergsort.alg
 *
 *    Synopsis    - The merge sort algorithm package.
 *                  Not a complete program.
 *
 *    Objective   - A second illustration of a recursive function.
 */


/* Include Files */
#include "mergsort.h"                                    /* Note 1 */


/********************************* merge_sort()  ***********/
/*    A recursive sorting algorithm. Upon entry, to_sort is the
 *    array with the elements to be sorted. The elements will
 *    be contiguously placed in the array. first is the index
 *    of the first element and last is the index of the last.
 */
                                                         /* Note 2 */
void merge_sort( int to_sort[], int first, int last )
{
    if ( first < last ) {                                /* Note 3 */
                                                         /* Note 4 */
        merge_sort( to_sort, first, (first+last)/2 );
                                                         /* Note 5 */
        merge_sort( to_sort, (first+last)/2 + 1, last );
                                                         /* Note 6 */
        merge( to_sort, first, (first+last)/2,
                        (first+last)/2 + 1, last );
    }
}


/********************************* merge()  ***************/
/*    A utility function for merge sort, merges two lists.
 *    Both lists are in the array lists. The first list starts
 *    at index first1 and goes through index last1.  The second
 *    list starts at index first2 and goes through index last2.
 *    The two lists are contiguous in the array.
 */
void merge( int lists[], int first1, int last1,
                         int first2, int last2 )
{
```

```
    int temp[MAX_ARRAY];
    int index, index1, index2;
    int num;

    index = 0;
    index1 = first1;
    index2 = first2;
    num = last1 - first1 + last2 - first2 + 2;

    /* while there are still elements in both lists,
     * put the smallest element in the temporary array.
     */
    while (( index1 <= last1 ) && ( index2 <= last2 )) {

          if ( lists[index1] < lists[index2] )
                  temp[index++] = lists[index1++];
          else
                  temp[index++] = lists[index2++];
    }

    /* after one list is empty, fill the temporary array
     * with the remaining elements in the other list
     */
    if ( index1 > last1 )                 /* first list is empty */
          move( lists, index2, last2, temp, index );
    else                                  /* second list is empty */
          move( lists, index1, last1, temp, index );

    /* copy the list to original array */
    move( temp, 0, num-1, lists, first1 );
}

/******************************** move() *****************/
/*   A utility function for merge sort, copies the array
 *   list1 from positions with index first1 to last1 to the
 *   array list2 starting at the position with index first2.
 */
void move( int list1[], int first1, int last1,
           int list2[], int first2 )
{
    while ( first1 <= last1 )
          list2[ first2++ ] = list1[ first1++ ];
}
```

This algorithm consists of three functions: merge_sort(), merge(), and move(). The function merge_sort() is recursive and the notes below refer to that code. Both `merge()` and `move()` are fairly straightforward. Nothing new is presented in that code.

Note 1: The header file mergsort.h has been created with the declarations necessary for using this sorting package. It contains a declaration of each of the functions as well as the definition of MAX_ARRAY. It reads as follows:

```
/*              mergsort.h
 *
 * Contains declarations necessary for use
 * of the merge_sort() package.
 */


/* Constant Declarations */
#define MAX_ARRAY  512


/* Function Declarations */
void merge_sort( int[], int, int );
void merge( int[], int, int, int, int );
void move( int[], int, int, int[], int );
```

In this `#include` directive, the double quotes (") indicate that the search for this header file should start with the current directory instead of the directory where the standard header files are kept. The angle brackets (<) indicate that the usual directories for the standard header files should be searched.

Note 2: The first parameter to `merge_sort()` is an array. No size has been specified for that array; the parameters `first` and `last` indicate the portion of the array that is to be sorted. This function can be used for any array that has no more than MAX_ARRAY elements. If it is to be used for a larger array, only the declaration of MAX_ARRAY in mergsort.h needs to be changed.

Note 3: The test (`first < last`) provides the way out of the recursion. Each time the array is divided in half, the indices `first` and `last` are changed. When the portion of the array to be sorted has only one element, `first` is equal to `last` and this call to `merge_sort()` will terminate. This allows the algorithm to proceed to the merge phase for that portion of the array. Eventually, the algorithm will terminate with a sorted array.

Note 4: The first recursive call to `merge_sort()` will sort the first half of the array. The indices of that half are from `first` to (`first+last`)`/2` inclusive.

Note 5: The second recursive call to `merge_sort()` sorts the remaining portion of the array.

Note 6: The call to `merge()` will merge the two halves back together. At each step the element in the final array will be the smaller of the next elements in each half of the array.

Learning Activities

22. Carefully go through the example with four elements to make sure that you understand how the recursion works.
23. Carefully read the code for merge() and move().
24. Hand execute the algorithm for the array to_sort[] that appears below:

    to_sort[]

5	1	4	7	2	6	3

    Keep track of the activation records for merg_sort(). Each activation record should contain a value of first, a value of last, and the array to_sort[]. You could model your hand execution after the example of sorting the array with four elements.
25. Does this algorithm require distinct elements in the array? To find out, hand execute an example with three elements where two are the same.

The program mergsort.c in Example 6-12 will test the merge sort algorithm. It allows the user to input any array of integers with up to 512 entries and will output the array in sorted order. The code for the merge sort was taken directly from the file mergsort.alg that was discussed previously. The other functions were added to allow input and output of the array.

Example 6-12: mergsort.c

```
/*                  mergsort.c
 *
 *    Synopsis    - Allows a user to input elements into an array,
 *                  sorts the array, and displays it in sorted order.
 *
 *    Objective   - To provide a program to test the merge sort
 *                  algorithm.
 */
```

```
/* Include Files */
#include "mergsort.h"                                      /* Note 1 */
#include <stdio.h>
#include <ctype.h>

/* Constant Declarations */
#define DONE    0                                          /* Note 2 */
#define MORE    1
#define ERROR  -1

/* Function Declarations */
void print_array( int[], int, int );
int fill_array( int[] );
int get_int( int * );

void main( void )
{
     int num;
     int array[MAX_ARRAY];

     num = fill_array( array );
     merge_sort( array, 0, num-1 );
     print_array( array, 0, num-1 );
}

/********************************** fill_array()  ************/
/*   Allows the user to enter integers for an array of
 *   integers.  Returns the number of elements entered
 *   into the array.
 */
int fill_array( int empty[] )
{
     int    count = -1,
            more = MORE;

     printf( "Enter your integers now. Enter 'Q' to quit\n" );
     printf( "%3d : ", ++count + 1 );

     while  ( count < MAX_ARRAY ) {
            more = get_int( empty + count );

            if ( more == ERROR ) {                         /* Note 3 */
                printf( "Error in input - Try again\n" );
                printf( "%3d : ", count+1 );
                continue;
            }
```

```
        if ( !more )                                    /* Note 4 */
            break;
        printf( "%3d : ", ++count+1 );
    }
    return ( count );
}


/********************************** print_array()  ************/
/*   Displays the elements of an array of ints from the
 *   position with index first to the position with index
 *   last, inclusive.
 */
void print_array( int array[], int first, int num )
{
    int index;

    for ( index = first; index <= num; index++ )
        printf( "%3d: %5d\n", index+1, array[index] );
}


/********************************** get_int()  ***************/
/*   Accepts input of an integer from standard input.
 *   Returns the integer in the location pointed to by intptr,
 *   and returns DONE if user signals quit, ERROR if a nondigit
 *   was seen, or MORE if neither of the above occurred.
 */
int get_int (int *intptr)
{
    int    ch;
    char   remainder[80];
    int    digit_count = 0;

    *intptr = 0;
    while ( isdigit(ch = getchar() )) {
                                                        /* Note 5 */
        *intptr = *intptr * 10 + ( ch - '0' );
        digit_count++;
    }
    switch ( ch ) {                                     /* Note 6 */
        case 'Q':
        case 'q':
                gets( remainder );                      /* Note 7 */
                return ( DONE );
        case ' ':
                gets( remainder );
```

```
            case '\n':
                        if ( digit_count )
                                return ( MORE );
                        else
                                return ( ERROR );
            default:
                        gets( remainder );
                        return ( ERROR );
    }
}


/********************************* merge_sort()  *************/
/*   A recursive sorting algorithm. Upon entry, to_sort is the
 *   array with the elements to be sorted. The elements will
 *   be contiguously placed in the array. first is the index
 *   of the first element and last is the index of the last.
 */
                                                            /* Note 2 */
void merge_sort( int to_sort[], int first, int last )
{
    if ( first < last ) {                                   /* Note 3 */
                                                            /* Note 4 */
            merge_sort( to_sort, first, (first+last)/2 );
                                                            /* Note 5 */
            merge_sort( to_sort, (first+last)/2 + 1, last );
                                                            /* Note 6 */
            merge( to_sort, first,(first+last)/2,
                                    (first+last)/2 + 1, last );
    }
}


/********************************* merge()  *****************/
/*   A utility function for merge sort, merges two lists.
 *   Both lists are in the array lists. The first list starts
 *   at index first1 and goes through index last1.  The second
 *   list starts at index first2 and goes through index last2.
 *   The two lists are contiguous in the array.
 */
void merge( int lists[], int first1, int last1,
                        int first2, int last2 )
{
    int temp[MAX_ARRAY];
    int index, index1, index2;
    int num;

    index = 0;
    index1 = first1;
```

```
        index2 = first2;
        num = last1 - first1 + last2 - first2 + 2;

        /* while there are still elements in both lists,
         * put the smallest element in the temporary array.
         */
        while (( index1 <= last1 ) && ( index2 <= last2 )) {

                if ( lists[index1] < lists[index2] )
                        temp[index++] = lists[index1++];
                else
                        temp[index++] = lists[index2++];
        }


        /* after one list is empty, fill the temporary array
         * with the remaining elements in the other list
         */
        if ( index1 > last1 )                   /* first list is empty */
                move( lists, index2, last2, temp, index );
        else                                    /* second list is empty */
                move( lists, index1, last1, temp, index );

        /* copy the list to original array */
        move( temp, 0, num-1, lists, first1 );
}


/********************************** move()   ******************/
/*    A utility function for merge sort, copies the array
 *    list1 from positions with index first1 to last1 to the
 *    array list2 starting at the position with index first2.
 */
void move( int list1[],int first1, int last1,
                        int list2[], int first2 )
{
        while ( first1 <= last1 )
                list2[ first2++ ] = list1[ first1++ ];
}
```

The program contains the functions main(), fill_array(), print_array(), and get_int() in addition to the functions necessary for the merge sort. Since the merge sort algorithm was discussed previously, the notes below concentrate on the rest of the program. The function main() is a driver. It calls fill_array() to input the array elements, merge_sort() to sort the array, and print_array() to output the array. The function fill_array() calls get_int() to input each integer; fill_array() prompts for the input, counts the number of integers input, and handles the values returned from get_int(). The function print_array()

displays the elements in the array. The function `get_int()` does the actual input of the integers; we have seen the algorithm used for conversion before in the function `convert()` in exit.c. This function is different in that it does a little bit of error handling.

Note 1: The file mergsort.h is included to provide the declarations needed for the merge sort algorithm.

Note 2: The values `MORE  (1)`, `DONE  (0)`, and `ERROR  (-1)` are the values returned by `get_int()`.

Note 3: The value `ERROR` is returned when `get_int()` finds an element other than a decimal digit in the input. When this happens, `fill_array()` gives the user another chance to input an integer without either keeping or counting the input that was in error. The `continue` statement effectively transfers control to the beginning of the `while` loop.

Note 4: If `get_int()` returned `DONE`, then `!more` will test true. Then the `break` statement will break out of the `while` loop without displaying an additional prompt or incrementing `count`.

Note 5: The algorithm for converting from the character input to an integer is the same as that from earlier programs. It depends on the contiguity of the digits in the ASCII collating sequence.

Note 6: On exit from the `while` loop, the variable `ch` contains something other than a digit. The `switch` statement allows action depending on the contents of `ch`. If `ch` contains `'q'` or `'Q'`, the user has signaled that input is done; `get_int()` passes this information on by returning `DONE`. If `ch` contains a `'  '` (blank character) or a newline, then the input is correct and the user is not done; `get_int()` passes this information on by returning `MORE`. In any other case, an error has occurred and `get_int()` returns `ERROR`.

Note 7: If `ch` contains anything other than a newline, a call to `gets()` will flush the buffer.

Recursion has advantages and disadvantages. The major advantage is that some problems are easily solved with a recursive approach. More evidence of this appears in the study of data structures where tree traversal can easily be done recursively.

On the other hand, recursion can use a lot of memory. Every time the function is called, a new activation record is created. This activation record contains space for local variables, parameters, saved register values, and return addresses. If many calls to a recursive function are active at one time, a lot of memory is used.

Another disadvantage is that the recursion is often difficult to program and control. If a recursive function does not work the first time, it can be extremely difficult to find the problem.

Learning Activities

26. Compile and execute mergsort.c several times to make sure that it works with different sets of data.

27. a. If you are still having trouble understanding the recursion, put in some `printf()` calls to output the values of `first` and `last` as `merge_sort()` is entered. If you want, the function `print_array()` can be used to output the portion of the array that is to be sorted. By running the program with this trace, you should be able to see the recursive calls with the different parameters.

    b. If you know how to work with the debugger on your system, you could execute the program with the debugger to watch the recursion. This method is preferred by many programmers.

28. a. In the line

        printf ("%3d: %5d\n", index+1, array[index]);

    what is the purpose of the 3 and the 5?

    b. Consider the `while` loop in `fill_array()`. What are the ways of exiting the `while` loop? Which do you think the programmer intended to be used more often?

29. Note that the function `get_int()` is a first attempt to write a robust input routine. There are still problems with `get_int()`. Can you think of some? For example, what if the number input is greater than the largest integer that your system can handle? How could that problem be fixed?

Language Elements Introduced in This Chapter: A Review

✓ **Control Statements**

```
do
        statement
while (expression);

switch (expression1)  {
        case   c1:
                statement
        case   c2:
                statement

                .
                .
                .

        default:
                statement
}

continue;

break;

return;

return expression;

label : statement

goto label;
```

✓ **Header Files**

```
ctype.h          for character typing
```

✓ **Library Functions**

```
exit()           causes termination of its program
```

✓ **Other Utilities**

```
isdigit()        returns 1 if its argument is a digit, 0 otherwise
```

Things to Remember

1. Every `do-while` loop will execute at least one time.
2. The values in the `case` labeled statements must be constant integral expressions.
3. When the `switch` statement finds a match in one of the `case` values, control is passed to that `case` labeled statement and execution continues from that point in the program.

4. Both the `continue` and the `break` statement work with the `for`, the `do-while`, and the `while` loop. The `break` statement is also used with the `switch` statement.

5. When a `continue` or `break` statement is used in a set of nested loops, it only applies to one loop, the innermost loop that contains the `break` or `continue`.

6. The `return` statement transfers execution control out of a function and back to the calling environment.

7. When the `return` statement is used with an expression, the expression determines both the value and the type of the function using it.

8. A `return` statement can be used to provide more than one point of termination of a function.

9. The parameter to `exit()` can be used to signal the reason for program termination. A value of 0 traditionally means normal termination. Other values can be chosen to represent various error conditions.

10. When used in `main()` the statement `return expression;` is equivalent to the statement `exit (expression);`

11. The `goto` statement is used to transfer control to some labeled statement in the same function. It cannot transfer control out of a function.

12. The `goto` statement is a deterrent to structured programming. Its use should be reserved for deeply nested code.

13. Recursion occurs when a function or subprogram calls itself or calls another function that causes the original function to be called.

14. Recursion can be used to implement recurrence relations.

15. Algorithms using recurrence tend to use more memory than iterative algorithms.

Exercises and Programming Problems

1. Rewrite the function `convert()` from Example 6-8 so that a negative integer can be input. Test your new function with the program exit.c from the same example. How does it handle the following inputs?

    a. `2378`   b. `-264`   c. `0238`   d. `5-47` (an error)

    Is the action of the program desirable? Fix any bug you might have encountered in your testing.

2. Modify the error handling in goto.c from Example 6-9 to allow the user to enter another line in case the first had a mistake in it.

3. Write a function that will read a string consisting of digits, possibly a decimal point and possibly a minus. If that string has the syntax of a floating point number in decimal representation, your function should convert that string to

a value of type `float`. Test your function with a program similar to exit.c. Make sure that it appropriately handles input like

a. `3.78`   b. `-45.893`   c. `3.4.5` (an error)   d. `-.25`

4. Modify the programs continue.c and break.c from Section 6.4 so that the `continue` and `break` statements are not used in either program.

5. Write a program that will count the number of vowels, consonants, punctuation marks, and whitespace in its input. The input will be English text. For this program, the space, tab, and newline will be considered the whitespace characters. The punctuation marks consist of a period, a semicolon, a comma, a question mark, and an exclamation point. Vowels are `'a'`, `'e'`, `'i'`, `'o'`, and `'u'`. The rest of the alphabetic characters are the consonants. The output should report the number of characters in each category. Use the `switch` statement appropriately in your program. Test it thoroughly.

6. Write a program that writes a check. The user should enter the date, the check number, the payee, the amount and a memo. For example, consider the following run of the program (user input is in **boldface**):

```
Check Writing Program
----- -------- -------

Date: 11/29/91
Check Number: 351
Payee: Fears and Slowbuck
Amount: 350.13
Memo: Payment on Account 345-678-91


    ----------------------------------------------------------

                                                   Check 351

                                        Date   11/29/91

    Pay to the
    Order of            Fears and Slowbuck              $ 350.13
    Three Hundred Fifty Dollars and thirteen cents

    Memo: Payment on Account 345-678-91 --------------------
    ----------------------------------------------------------
```

Assume that the largest check that can be written is for $9999.99. Your program should output values like 300.00, 50.14, 0.12 properly both in numbers and in words.

7. Write a program that plays a number guessing game with the user. A sample run of the game program would be as follows (user input is in **boldface**:

```
Welcome to the game of Guess It!
```

```
I will choose a number between 1 and 100.
You will try to guess that number. If you guess wrong, I
will tell you if you guessed too high or too low.

You have 6 tries to get the number.

OK, I am thinking of a number. Try to guess it.
Your guess? 50
Too high!
Your guess? 12
Too low!
Your guess? 112
Illegal guess.  Your guess must be between 1 and 100.
Try again.  Your guess? -20
Illegal guess.  Your guess must be between 1 and 100.
Try again.  Your guess? 23

***CORRECT*****

Want to play again? y

OK, I am thinking of a number.  Try to guess it.

Your guess? 85
Too high!
Your guess? 12
Too low!
Your guess? 57

***CORRECT*****

Want to play again ? n

Goodbye, it was fun.
Hope to play Guess It with you again soon.
```

Hint: Look up the library functions rand() and srand(). Use them to establish the number to be guessed so that the number will be different each time the game is played.

8. Write a C program that outputs a bank statement. The user should be allowed to enter a beginning balance and the transactions one at a time. When the transaction is a deposit, the user precedes the transaction amount with 'D'; a withdrawal amount is preceded by 'W'; a check transaction is preceded by 'C' and should include the check number. The program should output a full report of all transactions and a final balance. In the statement, the checks should be sorted by check number. A suggested program run appears below. The user's input is in **boldface**.

```
XYZ Bank Statement Program
--- ---- --------- -------

Enter beginning balance: 1427.89

Enter transactions:
(W)ithdrawal, (D)eposit, (C)heck (Q)uit: D
Amount:  2478.36
(W)ithdrawal, (D)eposit, (C)heck (Q)uit: C
Check Number: 1035
Amount:  95.23
(W)ithdrawal, (D)eposit, (C)heck (Q)uit: W
Amount:  160
(W)ithdrawal, (D)eposit, (C)heck (Q)uit: C
Check Number: 1032
Amount:  46.41
(W)ithdrawal, (D)eposit, (C)heck (Q)uit: W
Amount:  45.50
(W)ithdrawal, (D)eposit, (C)heck (Q)uit: C
Check number: 1033
Amount:  25.72
(W)ithdrawal, (D)eposit, (C)heck (Q)uit: Q

Thank You!

              B A N K    S T A T E M E N T
              - - - -    - - - - - - - - -
                        Beginning Balance:    $1427.89

1 Deposit:
      $2478.36          Total deposits:       $2478.36
2 Withdrawals:
      $160.00
      $ 45.50           Total withdrawals:    $ 205.50
3 Checks:
      1032    $ 46.41
      1033      25.72
      1035      95.23
                        Total checks:         $ 167.36
                                              --------
                        Final Balance:        $3533.39
```

Note: the checks need not be entered in numerical order.

9. a. Write a program that reads English text as its input and echoes it to the
        output except that every time the characters .P are found in the input, a
        single blank line is output. For example, the following two inputs:

```
text followed by .P followed by text
```

and

```
text followed by
.P
followed by text
```

should both give output in the form

```
text followed by

followed by text
```

with a single blank line between the two text lines.

b. Extend your program from part a. to indent the text five spaces whenever the characters .I are encountered in the input. Indentation will indicate that a new line of output should be started and indented. For example, the two inputs

```
text .I more text
```

and

```
text
.I
more text
```

should both give the output below.

```
text
     more text
```

10. Write a recursive function that implements the recurrence relation to calculate the nth power of a floating point value x. Both n and x should be parameters to the function. The return value of the function will be the value of x^n. To test your function, write a program to output the following table.

```
                          Powers
             1     2     3     4     5     6     7

      1 ┆    1     1     1     1     1     1     1
Bases 2 ┆    2     4     8    16    32    64   128
      3 ┆    3     9    27    81   243   729  2187
```

and so on to some reasonable number. Be careful of overflow errors.

11. Give the output of the following program for the given input.

```
/*                        epp11.c                        */

/* Include Files */
#include <stdio.h>

/* Function Declarations */
void stackit( void );
```

```
void main( void )
{
    stackit();
}

void stackit( void )
{
    int iochar;

    if (( iochar = getchar() ) != '\n' ) {
        stackit();
        putchar( iochar );
    }
}
```

Input: How now brown cow?

12. The binomial coefficients can be defined recursively as

$$\binom{n}{r} = \binom{n-1}{r} + \binom{n-1}{r-1}$$

with the initial conditions that

$$\binom{1}{1} = 1 \quad \text{and} \quad \binom{1}{0} = 1$$

Write a program with a recursive function that will input n and r and calculate the corresponding binomial coefficient.

13. Modify the program do.c of Example 6-1 as necessary to obtain the answers to the following questions. Try to compile and execute it for each modification.

a. What happens when reverse() is called without any parameters?

b. What happens when reverse() is called with too many parameters?

c. Explain what you think is happening.

## Chapter 7

Structuring the Data

7.1 Introduction to Structures

Aggregate types are types that are designed to hold multiple data values. An array is one aggregate type. The second aggregate type that we will study in C is a structure. In contrast to an array, which will hold many data values of the same type, a structure can concurrently hold multiple data values of different types.

For example, if a program is being designed to keep track of an inventory of automobile parts, the information about each part includes the part identification, the price, and the number of items currently in stock. An array of eight characters might be appropriate for the part identification, whereas the price would be a floating point value, and the number of items in stock would be an integer. If we use a structure, we can design a single variable to hold all three pieces of data. The declaration of the structure might be

```
struct auto_part {
        char  id[8];
        float price;
        int   cur_inv;
};
```

In the above declaration, the word `struct` is a keyword in C. It signals the declaration of a structure. A pair of matching braces surrounds the declaration of the members of the structure. The declaration of a member of a structure looks very much like a variable declaration. For example, the declaration of the member

339

named `id` appears as

```
char id[8];
```

inside the braces. The member named `id` is an array of 8 `chars`.

This structure has three members: `id`, `price`, and `cur_inv`. These members represent the identification, the price, and the number of items in inventory for an automobile part. Each member has been given a type that fits the nature of one piece of data about an auto part.

The declaration above tells the compiler what the programmer means by a `struct auto_part`. It describes the structure, but does not declare any variables. The identifier `auto_part` is an optional tag. When a tag is included, the pair of words

```
struct auto_part
```

can be used elsewhere in the program as a type to declare variables and parameters with this structure. For example, the declaration of a variable named `a_part` as a structure with these three members would be

```
struct auto_part a_part;
```

Like all C declarations, this one consists of the type, `struct auto_part`, followed by the variable name, `a_part`, and a terminating semicolon.

A variable of a structure type can be initialized at the same time that it is declared. The initializers appear inside a set of matching braces; commas separate the values for the different members. The following declaration is an extension of the declaration of `a_part` to include initial values. For example,

```
struct auto_part a_part = { "J-145D", 4.79, 12 };
```

declares a variable named `a_part` of type `struct auto_part` and initializes each member[1]. The initial contents of the `id` array is the string `"J-145D"`. The initial value of the `price` member is `4.79`, and the initial value of the `cur_inv` member is `12`. The variable `a_part` could be pictured in the following way.

```
          a_part
      id | J | - | 1 | 4 | 5 | D | \0 | \0 |
   price |        4.79          |
 cur_inv |   12   |
```

It is possible to initialize only some of the members in a structure. In that case any members not given initial values are set to zero by default. For example,

---

1. Older (non-ANSI) compilers may not allow the initialization of structures at the time of declaration. For more information about this see Chapter 8.

```
struct auto_part part4 = {"23L-t7"};
```

would define the variable `part4` and initialize the `id` member and set the `price` and `cur_inv` members to 0.

As with declarations of variables of other types in C, two or more variables can be declared in the same line of source code by placing the variable names in a comma separated list after the type. For example,

```
struct auto_part part1, part2;
```

declares two variables, `part1` and `part2`, that have type `struct auto_part`.

Another variation on structure and variable declarations allows the description of the structure to be combined with the declaration of variables of that type. For example,

```
struct auto_part {
        char  id[8];
        float price;
        int   cur_inv;
} part1, part2;
```

tells the compiler that a `struct auto_part` will be a structure with the stated three members, and declares the variables `part1` and `part2` to have that structure type.

Another variation on the declaration of these two variables might be to omit the tag, as in

```
struct {
        char  id[8];
        float price;
        int   cur_inv;
} part1, part2;
```

In this case the compiler would recognize `part1` and `part2` as structures having `id`, `price`, and `cur_inv` as members, but additional variables of this same type could not be declared later in the program.

When the tag is omitted, there is no way of referring to a structure of this type without redeclaring it. If it is redeclared, the compiler may not equate the two structure types. This issue is addressed in a set of Learning Activities.

There are very few restrictions on the types that the members of a structure may have. A member of a structure may not be a function, and it may not have type `void`. The only other restriction is that a structure may not nest a structure of its own type. For example, a `struct auto_part` may not have a member of type `struct auto_part`. It may have members that are structures of other types, and may have members that are pointers to a structure of the same type.

The individual fields of a structure can be accessed with the syntax

```
variable_name.member_name
```

For example, in a `struct auto_part`, the expression

        part1.id

is the name of the first member of `part1`; it is an array of 8 `char`s. The expression

        part1.price

is the name of the second member and is a quantity of type `float` while

        part1.cur_inv

is the name of the third member, an `int`. The type of each member of a structure determines the operations that may be performed on that member. All the operations associated with an `int` can be performed on `part1.cur_inv`, but only array operations are allowed on `part1.id`. Note that the individual cells in `part1.id` can be accessed either through the subscript notation, as in

        part1.id[3]

or through the pointer dereferencing notation, as in

        *(part1.id+3)

In Example 7-1 a variable of type `struct auto_part` is defined and initialized at the time of declaration. The program then displays the contents of the variable to the terminal. It shows basic structure handling.

Example 7-1: struct.c

```
/*              struct.c
 *
 *   Synopsis   - Declares and initializes a variable of type
 *                struct auto_part and displays its contents
 *                on the terminal screen.
 *
 *   Objective  - To illustrate declaring a structure and
 *                accessing its members.
 */

/* Include Files */
#include <stdio.h>
#include <string.h>

/* Type Descriptions */
```

```
struct auto_part {                                    /* Note 1 */
       char id[8];
       float price;
       int cur_inv;
};

void main( void )
{
                                                      /* Note 2 */
       struct auto_part part = { "J-145D", 4.79, 12 };

       printf( "Part-id:  %8s\n", part.id );          /* Note 3 */
       printf( "Price :  $%8.2f\n", part.price );     /* Note 3 */
       printf( "Quantity: %8d\n", part.cur_inv );     /* Note 3 */
}
```

 Running the Program

```
Part-id:    J-145D
Price :  $    4.79
Quantity:      12
```

This simple program consists of just the function `main()`. A variable of type `struct auto_part` is declared and initialized in the same line of code. Calls to `printf()` display the contents of this variable.

Note 1: The declaration of the type `struct auto_part` indicates that it is a structure with three members. The `id` member is an array of type `char` with 8 cells. The `price` member has type `float` and the `cur_inv` member has type `int`.

Note the position of this declaration. A common position for both function declarations and type descriptions is above `main()`. If there were many functions in this program, this description could be seen by any of the functions in the file.

Note 2: A variable named `part` of type `struct auto_part` is declared. The initial values of the members appear in a comma separated list inside a set of matching braces. When this variable is created, the initial values will be stored in the memory allocated to this variable.

Note 3: The members of the structure are accessed using the dot (`.`) notation in all of these calls to `printf()`. Note that the conversion specification in each control string applies to the type of the member being displayed. There is no conversion specification for a structure as a whole.

Learning Activities

1. Compile and execute struct.c to ensure that it works the same way on your system.

2. *C by Discovery*
   a. Add a new variable to struct.c with the same structure type. Experiment to determine where the declaration can appear. Can it be combined with the declaration of part? Can it appear on a separate line?
   b. Experiment by omitting the tag auto_part from the structure declaration and try to compile and execute the program again. What do you have to do to make the program work? Explain what happens in your own words.
   c. List some advantages of including a tag. When might the tag be omitted?

3. In the following code segment,

```
struct x {
        int     x1;
        char    x2;
        char * x3;
};

struct y {
        float y1, y2;
        char  y3;
        int   y4[5];
} structy1, structy2;

struct x   s1;
```

   a. What are the tags in the structure declarations? What are the members of the structures?
   b. Which lines allocate storage?
   c. Which of the following expressions are legal and which are illegal? For each of the legal expressions, state the type of the expression:

   i. s1.x   ii. structy1.y4   iii. structy2.y4[3]
   iv. s1   v. *(s1.x3)   vi. &s1.x2

4. Write a structure declaration that will hold the following information about a student: name, Social Security number, grade point average, total number of completed units, major code (a four-digit number).

5.   *C by Discovery*   Experiment to see if distinct identifiers must be used for structure tags, members, and variables. Similarly, experiment to see if members of different structure types need to have distinct member names. Summarize your findings and comment on the stylistic consequences.

7.2 Operations on Structures

Very few operations may operate on a structure as a whole. The following operations *are* allowed on structures:

1. The selection operators access a single member from the structure.
2. The assignment operator assigns the contents of one structure variable to another.
3. The address operator, &, can be used with a structure variable in most instances.
4. The sizeof() operator is usually defined for structures.

These are the only operations on structures that are specified in the ANSI standards. Therefore, the availability of other operators for structures may vary with different implementations of the language. For example, the comparison operators of == and != are generally not defined.

A Closer Look

When memory is allocated for a structure variable, space is allocated for each member. The members are stored in the same order as they appear in the member list in the structure declaration. However, there may be unused bytes or bits between structure members, since the computer system may require that certain quantities begin in certain positions in memory. One such common requirement is that an integer should begin on a word boundary in memory.

This is why comparison of two structures for equality is generally not supported. If unused bytes exist within the storage space for the structure, their contents cannot be determined. Therefore, any comparison that only compares bits will not be accurate. Since each different structure declaration may have different members, a single comparison operation for all structure types could not be easily implemented.

Example 7-2 demonstrates the storage of a structure in memory. It uses the sizeof() operator and the address operator on a variable of a structure type and displays information about its structure variables.

Example 7-2: stradd.c

```
/*                  stradd.c
 *
 *      Synopsis    - Displays the sizeof() a structure and the
 *                    addresses of two structure variables and
 *                    their members.
 *
 *      Objective   - To demonstrate the layout of a structure
 *                    in memory.
 */

/* Include files */
#include <stdio.h>

/* Type Descriptions */
struct empl {                                               /* Note 1 */
      char ssn[10];
      char initials[5];
      float rate;
      float hours;
};

void main ( void )
{
      struct empl employee1, employee2;
                                                            /* Note 2 */
      printf( "sizeof(struct empl) is %d.\n", sizeof( struct empl ) );
      printf( "employee1 is located at %p.\n", &employee1 );
      printf( "employee2 is located at %p.\n", &employee2 );
      printf( "\nIn employee1,\n" );                        /* Note 3 */
      printf( "\tssn is at %p.\n", &employee1.ssn );
      printf( "\tinitials is at %p.\n", &employee1.initials );
      printf( "\trate is at %p.\n", &employee1.rate );
      printf( "\thours is at %p.\n", &employee1.hours );

      printf( "\nIn employee2, \n" );
      printf( "\tssn is at %p.\n", &employee2.ssn );
      printf( "\tinitials is at %p.\n", &employee2.initials );
      printf( "\trate is at %p.\n", &employee2.rate );
      printf( "\thours is at %p.\n", &employee2.hours );
}
```

The program framework is simple. In the function `main()`, two variables of type `struct empl` are defined; the remainder of the code consists of `printf()` calls.

Note 1: Again, the declaration of the structure appears above any functions in this source file. Therefore any functions in the file would be able to access it. Often structure declarations like this one would be placed in a header file which would be included in the program source file with a `#include` preprocessor directive.

Note 2: The `sizeof()` a `struct empl` is displayed. Then the memory location of each of the structure variables is displayed. This demonstrates that both the `sizeof()` and address operator can be used with structures.

Note 3: The address of each member of the structure variables is displayed. The `&` operator can be used with the members of a structure also.

Learning Activities

6.   Find out if your system allows the use of the `sizeof()` and the address operators with structures in C. If it does, proceed with the next two problems.

7.   a.   Manually calculate the number of bytes in a `struct empl`. Then compile and execute stradd.c. Does the value displayed for `sizeof(struct empl)` match the value you calculated? If it doesn't, find out what was different and why.

   b.   Calculate the difference between the addresses of `employee1` and `employee2`. Does it equal `sizeof(empl)`?

8.   a.   Draw the layout of the two structures in memory. If there are any unused bytes, mark them.

   b.   Experiment by moving the two `float` members to the first members in the declaration of the structure and compile and execute the program again. Draw another memory map for the two variables in the modified program. Did the number or position of unused bytes differ?

9.   *C by Discovery*   Consider the following declarations:

```
struct a {
        char  a1;
        int   a2;
};

struct b {
        char  a1;
        int   a2;
};
```

The two structures declarations are very similar. Only the tag differs. Does your compiler recognize these similarities? Is it possible to assign a variable of type `struct a` to a variable of type `struct b`. Is it possible with a type cast? Write a short program to answer these questions.

10. *C by Discovery* Consider the following two structure declarations:

```
struct x {                        struct y {
        int a;                            float c;
        float b;                          int d;
};                                };
```

Write a program that declares variables of type `struct x` and `struct y`, initializes one of the variables and attempts to assign the contents of the initialized structure variable to the other variables. Note that this creates an error condition since the two variables have different types. How is this error handled by your system? If there are compile-time errors, add a type cast to the left-hand side of the assignment statement and compile the program again. Once the program compiles, display the members of the structures. Try to generalize what you've learned from this exercise.

7.3 Using Structures with Arrays and Pointers

In the previous sections we discussed the fundamentals of using structures. We saw how to declare them and access the members. We also discussed the operations that can be done on a structure. In this section, we discuss arrays of structures, pointers to structures, and structures as parameters to functions. These concepts lay the groundwork for the typical use of structures in C programs.

Arrays of Structures

In section 7.1 we saw that a member of a structure could be an array. In this section we will explore arrays of structures. Consider the declaration

```
struct auto_part inventory[4];
```

of an array of 4 elements where each element is of type `struct auto_part`. This definition has all properties of any array declaration. The only difference is that each cell is a structure. This is demonstrated in Figure 7.1

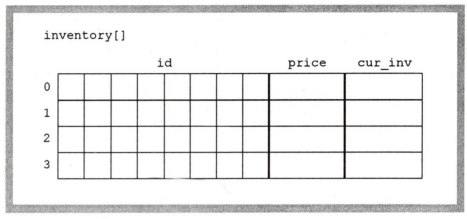

Figure 7-1

The expression

```
inventory
```

references the address of the first structure. The expression

```
inventory[2]
```

accesses the third structure (with index 2) in the array. The expression

```
inventory[2].cur_inv
```

accesses the cur_inv member of the structure in the third cell. The expression

```
inventory[2].id[3]
```

accesses the fourth character in the id member of the structure in the third cell.

Arrays of structures can be initialized by nesting the initial values for each structure as list elements in the braces enclosing the initial values for the array. For example,

```
struct auto_part inventory[4] = {  { "3bJ-4F", 1.35, 20 },
                                   { "4tH-2J", 0.89, 45 },
                                   { "89J-3K", 2.78, 12 }
                                };
```

will declare the array inventory and initialize the first three cells of the array. The remaining cell will be initialized with each bit set to zero.[1]

---

1. Compilers not supporting the ANSI C standards may not allow the initialization of variables with aggregate types (arrays or structures). See Chapter 8 for more information.

Pointers to Structures

In C, it is possible to declare a pointer to any type; this includes pointers to structures. The declaration

```
struct auto_part  *partptr;
```

declares a variable named `partptr` that is a pointer to a `struct auto_part`. Although a structure of the same type cannot be a member of a structure, a pointer to a structure *is* allowed. The following declaration should be rejected by the compiler since the second member nests a `struct node` within a `struct node`:

Illegal

```
struct node {
             int data;
             struct node y;
      };
```

However, both of the following two declarations are legal. The first is legal because the structure it contains is not a structure of the type being declared. The second is legal because it contains a *pointer* to a `struct node2` instead of a `struct node2`.

Legal

```
struct node1 {
      int data1;
      struct node2 data2;
};
```

Legal

```
struct node2 {
        struct auto_part data;
        struct node2 *next;
};
```

One example of the use of structures and pointers to a structure is a linked list. The following diagram depicts a linked list of auto parts. The definition for `struct node2` above is the basic structure declaration for this list.

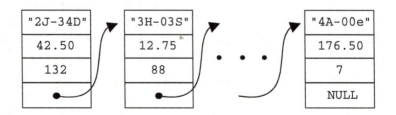

Some of the properties and code related to a linked list are presented in Chapter 11.

The concept of a pointer to structure is used so often in C that a special syntax was developed to reference the members of the target structure. If `partptr` is a variable of type `struct auto_part *` that has been initialized to point to a structure, the contents of the address in `partptr` can be accessed with two different notations, one using the dereference operator, `*`, in conjunction with the `.` selection operator for structures, and one using a new operator, `->`. The notation using the dereference operator, `*`, and the `.` selection for referencing the `price` member of the structure pointed to by `partptr` is

```
(*partptr).price
```

The parentheses are necessary in the above syntax because the dot selector, `.`, has higher precedence than the dereferencing operator, `*`. The quantity

```
(*partptr).price
```

has type `float`; any operation that is legal with type `float` can be performed on this quantity.

The following alternate syntax

```
partptr->price
```

also references the `price` member. The syntax consists of the variable name, a hyphen (`-`), and a greater than character (`>`), followed by the member name. The expression `partptr->price` is the same quantity of type `float` that is referenced by `(*partptr).price`. In existing C code, the `->` member selection notation is the more popular syntax with pointers to structures.

Passing Structures to and from Functions

Pointers to structures are also used to make structures available to functions.[1] When a pointer to a structure is passed to a function, the function can receive the information in the structure and can modify the information.

Example 7-3 illustrates a function that accepts input of information for a `struct auto_part`. It takes a single parameter that is a pointer to a `struct auto_part` and returns the information in that parameter. Since the purpose of the input routine is to change the value of a program variable, the address of that program variable is used as the parameter.

Two library functions are also introduced in Example 7-3. The function `atof()` takes a null terminated string containing the ASCII representation of a floating point number as its parameter; it converts the string to the corresponding value of type `float` and returns that value. The conversion stops at the first character in the array that could not be part of an ASCII floating point representation. The name `atof()` stands for "ASCII to `float`". For example, if the `char *` variable `float_string` has the following contents,

1	4	.	3	7	5		\0

---

1. Some of the older C compilers do not allow structures to be passed as parameters to functions, but a *pointer* to a structure can be a parameter in both ANSI C and non-ANSI C. Passing the pointer to a structure is generally more efficient than passing the structure itself. Similarly, some but not all compilers allow a function to return a structure as its return value, but all C compilers should allow a function to return a pointer to a structure.

the function call `atof( float_string )` returns the value `14.375` as type `float`.

The function `atoi()` is similar; its name stands for "ASCII to `int`". Its parameter is a null terminated string containing the ASCII representation of an integer. The return value is the corresponding value of type `int`. The function declarations of these library functions appear in the standard header file stdlib.h. This file should be `#include`'d in the program or, alternatively, just the declarations of the functions could be given.

The use of these functions allows the input of both numeric and character data to be done with the library function `gets()`. The advantage to using `gets()` is that `gets()` will read input through to a newline character. When `scanf()` reads an integer value from standard input, it is also reading a string of decimal digits (with an optional -), and converting the string to the corresponding integer value. In contrast to `gets()`, `scanf()` stops reading when it finds a character that is not part of the integer; in particular it leaves the newline in the buffer and a function call to do character input would read that newline instead of the desired input.

Example 7-3 getpart.c

```
/*                    getpart.c
 *
 *    Synopsis    - Accepts input of a struct auto_part from
 *                  standard input and returns the input values
 *                  in its parameter.
 *
 *    Objective   - Illustrates a function that takes a pointer
 *                  to a structure as a parameter.
 */

/* Include Files */
#include <stdio.h>
#include <string.h>
#include <stdlib.h>

/* Constant Declarations */                              /* Note 1 */
#define GOT_ONE        1
#define NONE_ENTERED   0
#define ID_SIZE        8

/* Type Descriptions */
struct auto_part {
        char id[ID_SIZE];
        float price;
        int cur_inv;
};
```

```
int get_part( struct auto_part *partptr )                    /* Note 2 */
{
     char instring[512];
     printf( "Enter the part number :" );
     gets( instring );
     if ( strlen( instring ) > 0 ) {                         /* Note 3 */
                                                             /* Note 4 */

          strncpy( partptr->id, instring, ID_SIZE-1 );
          partptr->id[7] = '\0';                            /* Note 5 */

          printf( "Enter the price: " );
                                                             /* Note 6 */
          partptr->price = atof( gets( instring ) );

          printf( "Enter the amount in inventory : " );
                                                             /* Note 7 */
          partptr->cur_inv = atoi( gets( instring ) );
          return( GOT_ONE );
     }
     else
          return( NONE_ENTERED );
}
```

This is not a complete program. The function get_part() would need to be compiled with a function named main() before it can be executed. Example 7-4 provides a complete program using get_part().

Note 1: The constants GOT_ONE and NONE_ENTERED are defined to be used as return values for get_part(). If the user enters an immediate newline, it signals this function that no input is forthcoming, and get_part() returns NONE_ENTERED. If the user enters characters before the newline, those characters are stored as the id of the struct auto_part and get_part() prompts for the other members of the structure. In this case get_part() returns GOT_ONE.

Note 2: The parameter to get_part() is a pointer to (that is, an address of) a structure. On return from get_part() the referenced structure will contain the inventory information that was entered. The declaration of this structure must appear in the program file before the function heading.

Note 3: The length of instring is tested. If it is zero, the user has indicated that no values will be entered; the value NONE_ENTERED is returned. If the length of instring is greater than zero, the input is stored and the function prompts for the other members of the structure.

Note 4: The library function strncpy() copies exactly 7 characters from instring to the character array id. The syntax partptr->id

accesses the id member of the struct auto_part; it is an array of
8 characters. If one of the copied characters is a null character ('\0'),
the string will be terminated with the copied null. The copied string will
not terminate properly if a null character does not occur within the first 7
characters. Therefore, the next statement copies a null into the last cell of
the array to make sure that the string is terminated with a null character.

Note that instring is a large buffer. Having this much space allocated
for input should help prevent errors.[1] Passing a 7 as the third parameter
to strncpy() assures that the characters entered for part identification
will not overrun the array. If the input were read directly into part.id,
the bounds of the array would be overrun when the input consisted of
more than 7 characters.

Note 5: A null character is placed in the last cell of the id array to terminate the
string. If the user had entered fewer than 7 characters, this null is super-
fluous; the null in instring is already in the id array. If the user
entered 7 characters or more, this null will be needed to terminate the
string.

Note 6: The function atof() is called to convert the input string to a floating
point value. The parameter to atof() is the value returned by gets()
which is the address of instring (or NULL in the case end-of-file is
sensed). The float value is assigned to partptr->price, the
price member of the structure.

Note 7: The function atoi() will convert the string input by gets() to an
int. The int value is assigned to the cur_inv member of the structure.

In Example 7-4 the program defines a variable of type struct auto_part,
initializes it from the keyboard, and outputs the contents to the terminal. It shows
basic structure handling. The function get_part() from Example 7-3 is used to
do the input.

Example 7-4: struct1.c

```
/*              struct1.c
 *
 *   Synopsis    - Accepts input of an auto_part from standard
 *                 input and echoes it to standard output.
 *
 *
 *   Objective   - To illustrate a pointer to a structure and
 *                 passing a pointer to a structure and a
 *                 structure as parameters to a function.
 */
```

---

1. When efficient memory usage is a priority, this buffer could be cut in size. However, when allocating space,
   remember that gets() will overrun the bounds of an array when there are too many characters on an input line.

```
/* Include Files */
#include <stdio.h>
#include <string.h>
#include <stdlib.h>

/* Constant Declarations */
#define GOT_ONE         1                        /* Note 1 */
#define NONE_ENTERED    0
#define IDSIZE          8

/* Type descriptions */
struct auto_part {                               /* Note 2 */
        char id[8];
        float price;
        int cur_inv;
};

/* Function Declarations */
void put_part( struct auto_part );               /* Note 3 */
int get_part( struct auto_part * );              /* Note 4 */

void main( void )
{
    struct auto_part part;                       /* Note 5 */
    int retval;

    retval = get_part( &part );                  /* Note 6 */
    if ( retval == GOT_ONE )
          put_part( part );
}

/***************************** get_part()   ********************/
/*    Accepts input of a struct auto_part from standard input
 *    and returns input values in its parameter.
 */

int get_part( struct auto_part *partptr )        /* Note 4 */
{
    char instring[512];

    printf( "Enter the part number :" );
    gets( instring );
    if ( strlen( instring ) > 0 ) {
          strncpy( partptr->id, instring, 7);
          partptr->id[7] = '\0';
```

```
        printf( "Enter the price: " );
        partptr->price = atof( gets( instring ) );

        printf( "Enter the amount in inventory : " );
        partptr->cur_inv = atoi( gets( instring ) );
        return( GOT_ONE );
    }
    else
        return( NONE_ENTERED );
}


/***************************** put_part()   *******************/
/*   outputs contents of a struct auto_part to the terminal    */
void put_part( struct auto_part part )                    /* Note 3 */
{
    printf( "Part-id:  %8s\n", part.id );                /* Note 7 */
    printf( "Price :  $%8.2f\n", part.price );           /* Note 7 */
    printf( "Quantity: %8d\n", part.cur_inv );           /* Note 7 */
}
```

This program contains three functions: main(), get_part() and put_part(). The function main() is a driver. It calls the other functions.

Note 1: Three constants are defined to improve programming style. The constants GOT_ONE and NONE_ENTERED relate to the values returned by get_part(). They indicate whether the user has signaled that the inventory input is completed. The constant IDSIZE is included to ease program modifiability. The size of the id member may be subject to change. The program currently allows for a maximum of eight characters. If this value must be changed, it is a simple matter of changing the preprocessor constant.

Note 2: Note the position of this declaration of a struct auto_part. It is outside any block and above any functions in this source code file. Therefore, every function in the file will know about a struct auto_part.

A struct auto_part is declared to have three members, an id member, a price member, and a cur_inv member.

Note 3: The parameter to the function put_part() is a structure. Changes for efficiency or for older compilers that do not accept a structure as a parameter to a function would involve changing the type of the parameter to a struct auto_part * and accessing the members with the -> selection operator.

Note 4: The parameter to get_part() is a pointer to a structure. This is necessary since the input routine needs to be able to change the contents of the structure.

Note 5: This line illustrates the declaration of a local variable of type `struct auto_part`. The earlier declaration of a `struct auto_part` declared the members of this structure. The inclusion of the tag `auto_part` in the earlier declaration allows the reference to that type in the declaration of this variable.

Note 6: The parameter to `get_part()` is the address of the structure that was previously declared. The return value from `get_part()` is assigned to the value `retval`. If that value is `GOT_ONE` (1), the variable `part` will be populated with the information entered by the user. Then the call to `put_part()` will display the information that was entered.

Note 7: The members of the structure are accessed using the dot (`.`) notation in all of these statements.

Learning Activities

11. Compile and execute struct1.c to ensure that it works on your system. You may need to change the parameter to `put_part()` to be a pointer to a `struct auto_part`. If so, the syntax in the body of the function would need to be changed also.

12. Test the function `get_part()` by running struct1.c several times with different input. How does it react to an `id` that is longer than 7 characters? How does it react to alphabetic data being entered when the program prompts for the price? for the current inventory?

13. Try to design a solution to the problems presented in the last Learning Activity. Look at the manual page for `strtod()` and `strtol()`.

Example 7-5 is another extension of the program dealing with a `struct auto_part`. It declares an array of type `struct auto_part`, initializes the array and displays the contents of that array. It uses the function `get_part()` from the Example 7-3 and the function `put_part()` from Example 7-4. It might be a first step in writing an inventory program.

Example 7-5: struct2.c

```
/*               struct2.c
 *
 *   Synopsis   - Initializes an array of structures with input
 *                from the terminal and displays the total
 *                inventory on standard output.
```

```
 *
 *    Objective  - To illustrate arrays of structures, pointers to
 *                 structures, and passing structures to functions.
 */

/* Include Files */
#include <stdio.h>
#include <stdlib.h>
#include <string.h>

/* Constant Declarations */
#define GOT_ONE        1
#define NONE_ENTERED   0
#define ID_SIZE        8
#define MAXPARTS       4

/* Type Descriptions */
struct auto_part {
        char id[ID_SIZE];
        float price;
        int cur_inv;
};

/* Function Declarations */
int  get_part( struct auto_part * );
void put_part( struct auto_part );

void main( void )
{
    struct auto_part  parts[MAXPARTS];                    /* Note 1 */
    int j, num_parts = 0;

    printf( "Initializing Inventory\n" );
    printf( "------------ ---------\n\n" );

                                                          /* Note 2 */
    while ( get_part( parts+num_parts )
        && ++num_parts < MAXPARTS )
        ;
    if ( num_parts == MAXPARTS )                          /* Note 3 */
        printf( "Inventory full\n" );

    printf( "\n\nPrinting Inventory of Auto Parts\n" );
    printf( "-------- --------- -- ---- -----\n\n" );
    for ( j = 0; j < num_parts; j++ )
        put_part( parts[j] );
}
```

```
/***************************** get_part()  *****************/
/*    Accepts input of information about an auto part from
 *    standard input. Returns value GOT_ONE if no information is
 *    entered, returns NONE_ENTERED otherwise.
 */
int get_part( struct auto_part *partptr )
{
    char instring[512];

    printf( "Enter the part number :" );
    gets( instring );
    if ( strlen( instring ) > 0 ) {

        strncpy( partptr->id, instring, ID_SIZE-1 );
        partptr->id[7] = '\0';

        printf( "Enter the price: " );
        partptr->price = atof( gets( instring ) );

        printf( "Enter the amount in inventory : " );
        partptr->cur_inv = atoi( gets( instring ) );
        return( GOT_ONE );
    }
    else
        return( NONE_ENTERED );
}


/***************************** put_part()  *****************/
/*   Displays the information in a struct auto_part.
 */
void put_part( struct auto_part part )
{
    printf( "Part-id:  %8s\n", part.id );
    printf( "Price :   $%8.2f\n", part.price );
    printf( "Quantity: %8d\n", part.cur_inv );
}
```

The program consists of three functions: main(), get_part() and put_part(). The function main() consists of a while loop and a for loop. The while loop calls get_part() repeatedly to input the inventory information about an auto part. The for loop calls put_part() each time to output the information for a single auto part.

Note 1: An array of structures is defined. Each cell of the array has enough memory to contain a complete `struct auto_part`. The array is local to `main()`.

Note 2: The condition for the `while` statement consists of two tests combined with a logical and, `&&`. The first test looks at the value returned by `get_part()`. The value returned is 1 when the user has entered information about an inventory item and 0 when the user presses return at the prompt for the input of the `id` member. The second test assures that the bounds of the array are not overrun. Note that the parameter to `get_part()` is the address of one of the elements in the array.

Note 3: The conditional statement tests which condition caused the `while` loop to terminate. If the loop terminates because the array is full, the user is notified of that fact.

Learning Activities

14. a. Try to compile and execute struct2.c. Your compiler may not accept the form of the parameter to `put_part()`.

 b. Modify the function `put_part()` and the function call to `put_part()` so that the structure parameter is replaced with a pointer to a structure.

 c. If your compiler accepts both the original and your modified version of the program, compare the size to the executable code to see if there is a difference.

15. Modify the program struct2.c by declaring a pointer to a structure in the function `main()`. Make all necessary changes so that the new pointer variable is used as an argument to `get_part()`. (Hint: The pointer variable should be initialized to point to the first cell of the array. Then the pointer variable should be incremented to traverse the array.)

16. a. Compile and execute the following program to verify that pointer arithmetic with structures works as you think it should.

```
/*                      la16.c
 *
 *    Synopsis    - Displays the sizeof() a structure and
 *                  the values of two pointer arithmetic
 *                  expressions.
 *
 *    Objective   - To provide practice with pointer
 *                  arithmetic with pointers to structures.
 */
```

```
/* Include Files */
#include <stdio.h>

/* Type Descriptions */
struct auto_part {
     char id[8];
     float price;
     int cur_inv;
} part;

void main( void )
{
     struct auto_part * partptr = &part;

     printf( "sizeof( part ) %d\n", sizeof( part ) );
     printf( "partptr %d, partptr+1 %d\n", partptr, partptr+1);
}
```

  b. Predict the output of the following statement:

```
          printf("%d\n", (partptr+1) - partptr);
```

   Add the statement to the above program and verify your prediction. Explain the output and adjust any mistakes in your thinking.

17. *C by Discovery* Is it possible to have the field width spacing in the `printf()` calls in `put_part()` equal the constant `IDSIZE`? In other words, if `IDSIZE` replaces the field width 8 in the `printf()` control strings, will the preprocessor find it and substitute the value? Experiment to find out what happens. Explain every part of the output of these statements when the 8 is replaced by `IDSIZE`.

18. Write a function that returns a pointer to the first structure in an array of structures where the number of parts in the inventory is less than 5.

7.4 Bit Fields

C allows different members of a structure to be packed into one word of memory with a construct called a *bit field*. This construct is one that allows the programmer to have direct access to the bits as well as having some control over the memory allocation in a program.

If a bit field is included in a structure definition, the number of bits that a bit field should occupy is specified. Theoretically, the compiler will pack as many bit field members as possible into a single word of memory. The following declaration

```
struct bits {
        unsigned  a : 4;
        unsigned  b : 2;
} bitvar;
```

declares a structure with two members. Both members are bit fields. The member a will occupy 4 bits; the member b will occupy 2 bits. Bit fields are declared by following the name of the member with a colon and the number of bits the member is to occupy.

The ANSI C standards require that a bit field must be either an int, unsigned int, or signed int.[1]

Often bit fields are used to try to match a hardware or software feature of a computer system exactly. For example, consider an assembly language that supports several addressing modes. The instruction (opcode), the operands, and the addressing modes for the instruction might be packed together into a single word of memory. If a word consists of sixteen bits, one way to pack this information for an assembly language instruction that takes two operands is as shown in Figure 7-2.

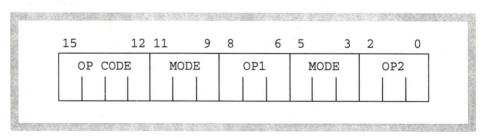

Figure 7-2

A structure defined to match that configuration exactly could be declared as follows:

---

1. Older compilers may limit the type of a bit field member to unsigned int.

```
struct two_ops {
        unsigned opcode    : 4;
        unsigned addr_mode1 : 3;
        unsigned operand1   : 3;
        unsigned addr_mode2 : 3;
        unsigned operand2   : 3;
} instruction;
```

In this structure, 4 bits would be allowed for the opcode and 3 bits would be allowed for each addressing mode and each operand. The structure could be packed into 16 bits. This configuration would allow for $2^4 = 16$ different instructions, $2^3 = 8$ different addressing modes, and $2^3 = 8$ different representations of the operands. The identifier `instruction` is a variable of type `struct two_ops`. Code that tests the value of the member `addr_mode1` in `instruction` is presented below. The action necessary to process addressing mode 3 is represented by a call to a function named `mode3()`.

```
if ( instruction.addr_mode1 == 3 )
     mode3( instruction );
```

Bit fields can also be used when memory is at a premium. For example, consider a system in which an integer occupies two bytes. Each variable of type `struct bits` that was defined above would occupy one byte of memory while a comparable structure with two members of type `unsigned int` that were not bit fields would occupy four bytes (two bytes for each member). The use of a variable of type `struct bits` would be even more space efficient on a system in which an integer occupies four bytes. The total amount of memory that is used might also depend on alignment requirements. These requirements might cause a variable's storage to begin on a word boundary and cut down the memory savings, but even so, bit fields offer the potential of using memory more efficiently.

A disadvantage of using bit fields lies in the lack of portability. The method with which bit fields are packed into words of memory can vary with the implementations of C. Therefore, programs that use bit fields may not port successfully to other implementations.

The program bitfld.c of Example 7-6 uses bit fields in an attempt to save memory. A structure that represents an employee is declared with two bit fields. The program demonstrates the assignment of values to a bit field and the accessing of those values.

Example 7-6: bitfld.c

```
/*               bitfld.c
 *
 *   Synopsis    - Declares a structure with bit fields, displays
```

```
*                    its size in bytes, initializes the structure
*                    and displays the contents of it.
*
*    Objective   - Provides an example of a structure with
*                    bit fields.
*/

/* Include Files */
#include <stdio.h>
#include <string.h>

/* Type Descriptions */
struct empl {
      char ssn[10];
      float rate;
      char initials[4];
      unsigned vested : 1;                              /* Note 1 */
      unsigned years_of_service : 6;                    /* Note 2 */
};

/* Function Declarations */
void put_empl( struct empl * );

void main( void )
{
    struct empl emp1;
                                                        /* Note 3 */
    printf( "sizeof( struct empl )  %d.\n", sizeof( struct empl ) );

    strcpy( emp1.ssn, "567624256" );
    emp1.rate = 7.50;
    strcpy( emp1.initials, "WLF" );
    emp1.vested = 1;                                    /* Note 4 */
    emp1.years_of_service = 17;
    put_empl( &emp1 );
}

/***************************** put_empl()  ******************/
/*   Displays contents of a struct empl on standard output     */
void put_empl( struct empl *emp )
{
    printf( "SSN:    %12s\n", emp->ssn );
    printf( "Rate:   $%12.2f\n", emp->rate );
    printf( "Initials%12s\n", emp->initials );
    printf( "vested  %12d\n", emp->vested );            /* Note 5 */
    printf( "years of service %3d\n", emp->years_of_service );
}
```

Running the Program

```
sizeof( struct empl )   19.
SSN:          567624256
Rate:  $         7.50
Initials          WLF
vested              1
years of service   17
```

The program consists of the functions `main()` and `put_empl()`. The function `main()` contains a `printf()` call to display the number of bytes occupied by a `struct empl`. It also contains calls to `strcpy()` and assignment statements to initialize the structure. Finally, a call to `put_empl()` displays the contents of the structure. The function `put_empl()` displays the contents of the parameter with calls to `printf()`.

Note 1: The declaration of `struct empl` contains two bit field members and three members that are not bit fields. The member `vested` is a bit field that occupies one bit. The bit would be set to one to indicate that the employee is vested in the retirement plan and cleared to indicate lack of vesting.

Note 2: The field `years_of_service` consists of six bits. The allowable values are from 0 to 63 ($2^6 - 1$).

Note 3: The next call to `printf()` outputs the `sizeof()` a `struct empl`. Theoretically, the last two members of the structure should occupy only one byte.

Note 4: Assignments to the bit fields are done with unsigned expressions in ordinary assignment statements.

Note 5: The bit fields are output by the calls to `printf()`. Again, the access is the same as for other members of the structure. The `%d` conversion specification can be used, as could the `%o`, `%x`, and `%u`.

Learning Activities

19.   Compile and execute bitfld.c to make sure that it works correctly on your system.

   a.   Is the value displayed for

```
      sizeof( struct empl )
```

   consistent with the concept of packing the two bit fields into one byte?

b. Modify the definition of a `struct empl` by making one of the bit fields the first member of the structure and leaving the other one at the end of the structure. When you run the program with this configuration, has the `sizeof( struct empl )` changed?

20. Modify the function `put_empl()` so that the Social Security number is output in the form `567-62-4256`.

21. Experiment to see if your system will allow types other than `unsigned int` for a bit field member of a structure. Explain your findings. What types are allowed?

22. Try to have the program display the address of the bit field members of `empl`. This should cause an error. Is it flagged as a compile-time error, a runtime error, or is it not flagged as an error at all?

23. Create an error condition by assigning values that take more memory than allocated in the bit fields to the members `vested` and `years_of_service`. Assign a value greater than 1 to `vested` and assign a value greater than 63 to the member `years_of_service`. Is this error caught at compile time? At runtime? Not at all?

24. Experiment by changing the size of the bit field `years_of_service` to see if your compiler imposes a maximum number on the bits in a bit field. Describe the results of your experiment.

Cautions with Bit Fields

We mentioned previously that programs using bit fields may not be portable. This is because bit fields must be stored sequentially in words of memory, and some computer systems store them from left to right while others store from right to left. This makes source code that accesses the bits by position, as with a bit mask, a potential portability problem.

The address operator, `&`, cannot be used with bit fields so that location of the fields in memory cannot be ascertained. Similarly, a pointer cannot be assigned to point to a bit field member of a structure. Both restrictions occur because a bit field is not required to start on a boundary of a byte or a word and therefore may not be able to be addressed. The method of storing the bit fields in memory should be documented in the compiler manual. Consult this manual before programming with bit fields.

Many implementations of C restrict the maximum number of bits that can be contained in a bit field. That maximum is usually the number of bits in a word of memory and can vary with different hardware systems.

Sometimes you may wish to access both the bits and the bytes in the same quantity. Program bitfld2.c in Example 7-7 illustrates one possibility for doing that. Two different structures containing bit fields are declared for the purpose of accessing the bits and the bytes in a word of memory. Structure pointers are initialized to point to a variable of type short   int that contains the quantity in question. This allows both bit and byte access.

Example 7-7: bitfld2.c

```
/*                bitfld2.c
 *
 *    Synopsis   - Displays the values of the bits and the bytes
 *                 in a short int.
 *
 *    Objective  - To illustrate the use of bit fields in
 *                 accessing the bits and bytes of a quantity.
 */

/* Include Files */
#include <stdio.h>

void main( void )
{
      struct bits {                                        /* Note 1 */
            unsigned first : 1;
            unsigned second : 1;
            unsigned third : 1;
            unsigned fourth : 1;
            unsigned fifth : 1;
            unsigned sixth : 1;
            unsigned seventh : 1;
            unsigned eighth : 1;
            unsigned ninth : 1;
            unsigned tenth : 1;
            unsigned eleventh : 1;
            unsigned twelfth : 1;
            unsigned thirteenth : 1;
            unsigned fourteenth : 1;
            unsigned fifteenth : 1;
            unsigned sixteenth : 1;
      } *bit_access;
```

```
struct bytes {                                          /* Note 2 */
      unsigned first:8;
      unsigned second :8;
} *byte_access;

unsigned short twobytes;                                /* Note 3 */

                                                        /* Note 4 */
printf( "sizeof( struct bits )  %d.\n", sizeof( struct bits ) );
printf( "sizeof( struct bytes ) %d.\n", sizeof( struct bytes ));
printf( "sizeof( twobytes )     %d.\n\n", sizeof( twobytes ) );

twobytes = 0x1248;                                      /* Note 5 */
byte_access = ( struct bytes * ) &twobytes;             /* Note 6 */
bit_access  = ( struct bits * )  &twobytes;

                                                        /* Note 7 */
printf( "first byte %x, second byte %x.\n\n",
                byte_access->first, byte_access->second );
                                                        /* Note 8 */
printf( "Bits:\tfirst        %x,    second        %x,\n",
          bit_access->first, bit_access->second );
printf( "\tthird        %x,    fourth        %x,\n",
          bit_access->third, bit_access->fourth );
printf( "\tfifth        %x,    sixth         %x,\n",
          bit_access->fifth, bit_access->sixth );
printf( "\tseventh      %x,    eighth        %x,\n",
          bit_access->seventh, bit_access->eighth );
printf( "\tninth        %x,    tenth         %x,\n",
          bit_access->ninth, bit_access->tenth );
printf( "\televenth     %x,    twelfth       %x,\n",
          bit_access->eleventh, bit_access->twelfth );
printf( "\tthirteenth %x,    fourteenth %x,\n",
          bit_access->thirteenth, bit_access->fourteenth );
printf( "\tfifteenth   %x,    sixteenth    %x\n",
          bit_access->fifteenth, bit_access->sixteenth );
}
```

 Running the Program

```
sizeof( struct bits )  2.
sizeof( struct bytes ) 2.
sizeof( twobytes )     2.
```

first byte 48, second byte 12.

```
Bits:   first        0,   second       0,
        third        0,   fourth       1,
        fifth        0,   sixth        0,
        seventh      1,   eighth       0,
        ninth        0,   tenth        1,
        eleventh     0,   twelfth      0,
        thirteenth   1,   fourteenth   0,
        fifteenth    0,   sixteenth    0
```

The program consists of the single function `main()`. Besides the structure declarations, the code consists of three assignment statements and numerous calls to `printf()`.

Note 1: A structure is declared that consists of sixteen bit fields. Each bit field contains one bit. The variable `bit_access` is a pointer to a quantity of type `struct bits`.

Note 2: A structure is declared that consists of two bit fields. Each bit field contains eight bits (one byte on most computer systems). The variable `byte_access` will point to a quantity of type `struct bytes`.

Note 3: A variable named `twobytes` of type `short int` is declared. The intent is that both structures take up the same number of bytes as this variable. If that is not true on your computer system, some adjustment may be needed for this program to work properly. The order in which your computer stores the bytes may also cause a problem with this program.

Note 4: The `sizeof()` each of the three quantities in question is output. If they do not agree with each other, adjust the declarations so that they do.

Note 5: A hexadecimal value is assigned to the variable `twobytes`. The value was written in hexadecimal for ease of checking the value of each bit and byte.

Note 6: Each of the pointer variables is assigned to point at `twobytes`. A type cast is used in each case to force the address of `twobytes` to be interpreted as the address of the relevant structure.

Note 7: The value of each byte is displayed.

Note 8: The value of each bit is displayed.

Learning Activities

25. a. Predict the output of bitfld2.c.

     b. Execute it to check your prediction. Resolve any differences between your prediction and the actual output.

    c. Is your concept of the first and second byte the same as the computer's?

    d. Notice the order in which your computer stores the bit fields in a word of memory. Is that what you expected?

26. Experiment by assigning different values to `twobytes` to make sure that the program works similarly with different values.

27. Experiment further with bitfld2.c by attempting some of the things mentioned under cautions. For example, try to display the address of a bit field and discover what type of error, if any, is reported. Try to port this program to a different computer system to see if the bit packing mechanism works the same.

Unnamed Bit Fields

Bit fields can be specified in a structure declaration without a name, as in this example:

```
struct unnamed {
        unsigned f1 : 5;
        unsigned    : 3;
        unsigned f3 : 7;
};
```

The second member does not have an identifier specified as the member name. The field serves as padding, and will force the third member to begin on the boundary of a byte. In this case, the second member cannot be accessed and its contents cannot be specified.

A special case of unnamed bit fields allows an unnamed bit field to be declared with zero bits specified, as in

```
struct unnamed {
        unsigned f1 : 5;
        unsigned    : 0;
        unsigned f3 : 7;
};
```

This is a signal to the compiler that the programmer wants the field `f3` to begin at the next "appropriate" spot in memory. That could be at a word or a byte boundary, depending on the underlying hardware and addressing modes.

7.5 Enumerated Types

Enumerated types are scalar types in C. They are presented in this chapter because they are often used in conjunction with structures and unions. Enumerated types are used to declare a set of integer constants in C. A declaration like

```
enum boolean {
      FALSE, TRUE
};
```

would be roughly equivalent to the two preprocessor directives

```
#define FALSE  0
#define TRUE   1
```

Without further specification in the `enum` declaration, `FALSE` would have the value `0` and `TRUE` would have the value `1`. The word `enum` is a keyword. One of the differences between the two constructs is that after defining `enum boolean`, it is possible to define variables of that type. For example,

```
enum boolean  correct;
```

would define a variable named `correct` that is legally supposed to accept only the values `FALSE` and `TRUE`. Note that compilers are not required to check that an assigned value is in the declared list, and assignments such as

```
correct = 7;
```

may be accepted.[1]

A declaration of type `enum` has the following syntax: the keyword `enum`, an optional tag, an open brace, a comma-separated list of identifiers, and a close brace. In the declaration

```
enum trees {
      oak, maple, cherry, spruce, pine
};
```

the type `enum  trees` and five constants have been declared. The identifier `trees` is the optional tag. The pair `enum trees` refers to this type declaration. No variables have been declared yet. A declaration

```
enum trees    tree1;
```

would define a variable named `tree1` that can legally assume any of the values in the identifier list. This variable declaration could have been combined with the type declaration as in the following:

```
enum trees {
      oak, maple, cherry, spruce, pine
} tree1;
```

---

1. On a UNIX system, the `lint` program may catch errors of this type.

The default values assigned to the identifiers are as follows: The first identifier, `oak` in this example, has the value 0, the second identifier, `maple`, has the value 1, and so on. By default, 0 is assigned to the first identifier in an `enum` definition, and each succeeding identifier is assigned successive integer values. The values assigned to these identifiers are constant. They cannot be changed.

The main reason for using enumerated types is to improve the readability and maintainability of C source code. For example, in a graphics program, the colors may be implemented with an enumerated type.

Other advantages of enumerated types include the automatic assignment and accounting of values. Enumerated types may not be fully implemented on a compiler that does not meet the ANSI C standards. The program boolean.c in Example 7-8 demonstrates a simple use of an enumerated type variable to simulate Boolean variables. Two sample outputs are given: one for an input value of 90, and one for an input value of 101.

Example 7-8: boolean.c

```
/*                boolean.c
 *
 *    Synopsis   - Accepts input of a positive integer and
 *                 displays all its factors.
 *
 *    Objective  - Illustrates the use of the enumerated type to
 *                 create a variable that takes values TRUE and
 *                 FALSE.
 */

/* Include Files */
#include <stdio.h>
#include <stdlib.h>

/* Type Descriptions */
enum boolean { FALSE, TRUE };                              /* Note 1 */

void main( void )
{
    enum boolean prime;                                   /* Note 2 */
    int num, divisor;
    char inarray[80];

    printf( "Enter a positive integer to be tested: " );
    num = atoi( gets( inarray ) );
```

```
    if ( num <= 0 ) {
        printf( "Sorry, that number wasn't positive.\n" );
        exit( 1 );
    }

    prime = TRUE;                                          /* Note 3 */
    printf( "List of divisors: 1 " );

    for ( divisor = 2; divisor < num; divisor++ )
        if ( !( num % divisor ) ) {
            printf( " %d ", divisor );
            prime = FALSE;                                 /* Note 4 */
        }

    if ( num != 1 )
        printf( " %d\n", num );
    else
        prime = FALSE;                                     /* Note 5 */

    if ( prime )                                           /* Note 6 */
        printf( "%d is a prime number\n", num );
}
```

Running the Program

```
Enter a positive integer to be tested: 90
List of divisors: 1  2  3  5  6  9  10  15  18  30  45  90
```

Running the Program

```
Enter a positive integer to be tested: 101
List of divisors: 1   101
101 is a prime number
```

The program consists of the single function main(). It does its input with gets() and converts the input to type int with atoi(). A for loop is used to test for and output all possible factors of num. The final factor is output for values of num that are greater than 1, with an added message when num is prime.

Note 1: The type enum boolean is declared. In this example, FALSE will have the value 0 and TRUE will have the value 1. These values agree with the usual interpretation of 0 and 1 by the C language. No variables have been declared yet, and no space has been allocated. The declaration appears above the function main() and therefore would be known by any functions in this source code file.

Note 2: A variable named prime of type enum boolean is declared. The only values that prime can take on are TRUE and FALSE.

Note 3: The variable prime is initialized to TRUE. It will be assigned the value FALSE if and when a divisor of num is found.

Note 4: The variable prime is assigned the value FALSE since the expression num % divisor was zero, which indicated that divisor divided num evenly. This suppresses the final message.

Note 5: The integer 1 is a special case. The factor 1 has already been displayed and should not be displayed again. Also, 1 is not a prime, but the previous for loop did not test that value. Here prime is set to FALSE if num is 1.

Note 6: The value of prime is tested to determine whether or not to issue the final message.

Learning Activities

28. Compile and execute boolean.c and make sure that you understand how it works. Test it with several different input values.

29. Modify boolean.c by adding a printf() call to output the value of prime as a decimal integer (%d conversion specification) at the end of the program. Test this modified program with both a prime and a composite integer as input. Are the values output the ones that you expected?

30. Modify boolean.c by declaring a variable named done of type enum boolean. Initialize done to FALSE and use it to drive a while loop that will allow a user to test many values without rerunning the program. Most of the existing program should be inside the while loop. You will also need to provide a way for the user to signal when there are no more integers to test. In this case, done should be set to TRUE and the while loop should terminate.

31. Write a program that accepts the input of an integer and issues a message indicating whether or not it is prime. You can use this program as a basis, but try to improve its efficiency. All your program needs to do is to determine whether or not its input is prime, so there is no need to test every factor.

A Closer Look

The default values of 0 for the first identifier in an enumerated type, 1 for the second, and so on can be overridden with specific assignment of values. In the declaration

```
enum trees {
     oak=5, maple=3, cherry, spruce=1, pine=1
};
```

oak is given the value 5, maple is given the value 3, spruce is given the value 1, and pine is given the value 1. Notice that two different identifiers can be assigned the same value. Also notice that cherry was not explicitly assigned a value. The compiler automatically assigns the value 4 to cherry, since it appears in the list immediately after maple, which was assigned the value 3.

Operations with the enum types are limited. The values represented by the identifier list are treated as constants of type int by the compiler and can appear anywhere in the syntax that any int constant can. After declaration of a variable of an enum type, values from the identifier list can be assigned to it, as in the following statement:

```
tree1 = oak;
```

Also, values can be tested for equality, as in

```
if (tree1 == spruce)
     dosomething();
```

Other than assignment and equality tests, no other operations must be supported by an ANSI C compiler. However, on many compilers, a variable of an enum type is treated as an int and other comparisons and operations can be done. Code using these extended features may not be portable; therefore their use is discouraged.

The program enumindx.c in Example 7-9 makes use of the fact that the enumerated types are based on type int. It uses an enumerated type variable as an index into an array. This use depends on the first identifier in the type declaration having value 0, the second having value 1, and so on. These values match those used for array indices.

The enumerated type is used in this program for readability. Instead of the reader having to remember that salesrecord[0] is the number of jade items sold and that salesrecord[1] is the number of navy items sold, the program could refer to salesrecord[jade] and salesrecord[navy]. The routines get_sales() and print_sales() are utility functions that accept input of and display the contents of the array salesrecord. These utility functions could be used in a program for a manufacturing or mail order firm that keeps sales and inventory records.

Example 7-9: enumindx.c

```
/*                    enumindx.c
 *
 *    Synopsis   - Accepts input of the number sold of each color
 *                 of an item, stores the number in an array and
 *                 displays the contents of the array.
 *
 *    Objective  - Illustrates the use of enum types for indexing
 *                 an array and the underlying connection between
 *                 enum types and ints.
 */

/* Include Files */
#include <stdio.h>
#include <string.h>

/* Type Descriptions */
enum color { jade, navy, white, coral, maize };           /* Note 1 */

/* Function Prototypes */
void makestring( enum color, char * );                    /* Note 2 */
void print_sales( int[] );
void get_sales( int * );

void main( void )
{
    int salesrecord[5];

    get_sales( salesrecord );
    print_sales( salesrecord );
}

/****************************** makestring()  *****************/
/*   Creates a string containing the color currently
 *   contained in item_color.  Used to aid output.
 */
                                                          /* Note 3 */
void makestring( enum color item_color, char *string )
{
    switch ( item_color ) {                               /* Note 4 */
        case jade:    strcpy( string, "jade" );
                      break;
```

```
                case navy:      strcpy( string, "navy" );
                                break;
                case white:     strcpy( string, "white" );
                                break;
                case coral:     strcpy( string, "coral" );
                                break;
                case maize:     strcpy( string, "maize" );
        }
}

/***************************** print_sales()  **************/
/*   Will display the color and contents of each cell of
 *   sales[]. Uses the integer representation of the
 *   colors.
 */
void print_sales( int sales[] )
{
        int i;
        char colorstr[6];

        printf( "The sales record shows the following " );
        printf( "sales by color.\n" );

        for( i = 0; i < 5; i++ ) {
                makestring( i, colorstr );                      /* Note 5 */
                printf( "%5s : %d\n", colorstr, sales[i] );
        }
}

/***************************** get_sales()  ****************/
/*   Accepts input of the number sold of each color item from
 *   standard input. Uses the identifier form of the color.
 */
void get_sales( int *salesrecord )
{
        enum color d_color;
        char colorstr[6];

        printf( "Enter the number of each color sold:\n" );
                                                                /* Note 6 */
        for ( d_color = jade; d_color <= maize; d_color++ ) {
                makestring( d_color, colorstr );                /* Note 7 */
                printf( "%5s : ", colorstr );
                                                                /* Note 8 */
                scanf( "%d", &salesrecord[d_color] );
        }
}
```

This program contains four functions: main(), makestring(), get_sales() and print_sales(). The function main() is a driver; it calls get_sales() to accept input of the sales record from the terminal and print_sales() to display the sales record. The function makestring() provides a connection between the identifiers used in the enumerated type and the corresponding string. For example, if the enumerated type value jade is passed in item_color, the string "jade" is passed back in string. The functions get_sales() and print_sales() both call makestring().

Both of the functions, get_sales() and print_sales(), contain a for loop to access the cells of the array holding the inventory, but both functions use a different syntax in doing so. In get_sales(), a variable d_color of type enum color is declared and used as an index to the array of ints; this variable is passed as a parameter to makestring(). In print_sales() an int variable is used as the index to the array of ints and passed to makestring().

Note 1: The type enum color is declared. The value of jade will be 0, the value of navy will be 1, and so on.

Note 2: The functions makestring(), get_sales(), and print_sales() are declared with type void. Since these declarations are above all function blocks, it is valid until the end of this source file.

Note 3: The parameters to makestring() are declared in the syntax of ANSI C. If you do not have an ANSI C compiler, you will need to change the function declarations before running this program.

The first parameter is declared to be of type enum color. An integer in the range 0 through 4 could be passed as the actual parameter.

Note 4: The parameter is used as the expression in the switch statement. Because the identifiers jade, navy, white, coral, and maize are integer constants, they can be used in the case labeled statements.

Note 5: In this call to makestring() an integer in the range 0 to 4 is passed as the actual parameter. This same parameter is also used to index the array salesrecord[].

Note 6: The enumerated type variable d_color is used to drive this for loop. In the expression that is evaluated at the bottom of the loop, d_color is incremented as if it had type int. Note that the relational operator <= was used with the enumerated type. The operations of incrementing and using the relational operator with enumerated types may not be supported on all compilers.

Note 7: In this call to makestring(), the parameter has type enum color. This could be replaced with an int, as in the call referenced by **Note 5**.

Note 8: The variable d_color can be used to index the array salesrecord[].

Learning Activities

32. Compile and execute enumindx.c. Test it with several different inputs.

33. Write a program that allows the user to request the number of items sold of any color. The program should first call `get_sales()` to initialize the array and then ask the user for a color. It should then display the contents of the corresponding element of the array.

34. Given the declaration

```
enum languages {
      french=12, english, russian, chinese=4, C, swedish
};
```

what is the value of each of the following constants?

```
english          _____
russian          _____
C                _____
swedish          _____
```

35. Assume the following declaration:

```
enum languages  spoken;
```

Which of the expressions involve standard operations with the enumerated type `enum languages`? Which may cause portability problems?

Expression	*Legal or Illegal?*
`spoken = C;`	_____
`french <= russian`	_____
`spoken++;`	_____
`french + english`	_____
`french + 15`	_____
`spoken == chinese`	_____

7.6 Unions

A union is another aggregate data type that is designed to hold members of different types. It is like a structure in that a list of members is declared. However, it differs from a structure in that a union will only contain one of its members at any instant. When a union is declared, enough storage is allocated for the member requiring the greatest amount of memory. When a value is assigned to any member of a union, it will overwrite any data previously stored in the union.

"A union will only contain one of its members at any instant." From the painting *The Proposal* by William Powell Frith, 1877.

The declaration of a union is like that of a structure. It has the general form

```
union tag { member list };
```

where `union` is a keyword and the tag is an optional identifier. The member list appears inside the matched braces and members are declared in a manner identical to the declaration of members in a structure declaration. For example,

```
union rate {
        float per_hour;
        int per_week;
};
```

declares a type that can later be referred to as `union rate`. It contains the two members, `per_hour` of type `float` and `per_week` of type `int`. Only one of those members can be occupied at any one time.

The rules for declaring unions are the same as those for declaring structures. The members of a union can be any type except `void` or a function type. A union may not contain a union of its own type as a member. Members of a union may be a pointer to a union of the same type or a pointer to a function.

As with structures, it is possible to have arrays of unions and pointers to unions. Also, arrays and pointers can be members of unions. Moreover, the members of a union can be accessed directly with the dot selector or through a pointer variable with the `->` member selection method. For example, consider the following declarations:

```
union rate  payrate,
            *ptr_rate = &payrate;
```

The variable `payrate` is a variable of type `union rate`. The variable `ptr_rate` is a pointer to a `union rate`; it has been initialized to point to `payrate`.

The assignment

```
payrate.per_hour = 10.85;
```

gives a value to the `per_hour` member of `payrate`. The statement

```
ptr_rate->per_hour += 1.50;
```

is a compound assignment that adds `1.50` to the `per_hour` member. The expression `ptr_rate->per_hour` refers to the `per_hour` member of the contents of `ptr_rate`. It is a quantity of type `float`. A subsequent assignment of

```
ptr_rate->per_week = 950;
```

initializes the `per_week` member of `payrate` (or `*ptr_rate`). At this point, the `per_hour` field no longer contains meaningful data. It has been overwritten.

There is no automatic mechanism to determine which member of a union is in use at any time. It is up to the programmer to keep track. Often an enumerated type is used with a union to establish which member is being used.

Unions are frequently included as part of a structure. The program unions.c in Example 7-10 includes a member of type `union rate` in a structure designed to hold information about an employee. A member of type `enum paytype` with the values `hourly` and `salaried` is also included to indicate which union member is in use.

Example 7-10: unions.c

```
/*                  unions.c
 *
 *    Synopsis   - Accepts input of and displays information for
 *                 one employee.
 *
 *    Objective  - To demonstrate use of enum types to keep track
 *                 of the contents of a union.
 */

/* Include Files */
#include <stdio.h>
#include <stdlib.h>

/* Type Descriptions */
enum paytype { hourly, salaried };                        /* Note 1 */

union rate {                                              /* Note 2 */
      float per_hour;
      int   per_week;
};

struct employee {
      char   name[20];
      char   ssn[12];
      enum   paytype paytype;                            /* Note 3 */
      union  rate payrate;
};

/* Function Prototypes */
void reademp( struct employee * );
void printemp( struct employee );

void main( void )
{
    struct employee emp;

    reademp( &emp );
    printemp( emp );
}
```

```
/****************************** reademp()  *******************/
/*    Accepts input information from the keyboard and stores it *
 *    in a struct employee                                     */

void reademp( struct employee *emptr )
{
     char instring[80];

     printf( "Enter the information for an employee.\n" );
     printf( "Name : " );
     gets( emptr->name );
     printf( "Social Security Number: " );
     gets( emptr->ssn );
     printf( "Hourly or salaried (h or s) : " );
     gets( instring );


                                                     /* Note 4 */
     if ( ( *instring == 'h' ) || ( *instring == 'H' ) )
          emptr->paytype = hourly;
     else if ( ( *instring == 's' ) || ( *instring == 'S' ) )
          emptr->paytype = salaried;
     else {
          printf( "Illegal paytype, program terminated.\n" );
          exit( 1 );                                 /* Note 5 */
     }
     if ( emptr->paytype == hourly ) {               /* Note 6 */
          printf( "Enter the hourly rate: " );
          emptr->payrate.per_hour = atof( gets(instring) );
     }
     else {
          printf( "Enter the weekly salary: " );
          emptr->payrate.per_week = atoi( gets(instring) );
     }
}

/****************************** printemp()  *******************/
/*    Displays the contents of the struct employee parameter    */

void printemp( struct employee emp )
{
     printf( "Name :    %s\n", emp.name );
     printf( "Social Sec. No. : %s\n", emp.ssn );
     if ( emp.paytype == hourly )                    /* Note 7 */
          printf( "Hourly rate   :$%7.2f\n", emp.payrate.per_hour );
     else
          printf( "Weekly Salary :$%7d\n", emp.payrate.per_week);
}
```

The program consists of the functions `main()`, `reademp()`, and `printemp()`. A variable of type `struct employee` is declared in `main()`; `main()` calls `reademp()` to read data from the keyboard and store it in the structure variable and then calls `printemp()` to display the data. The program might be a first step in developing a larger payroll program. Note that the ANSI C prototype has been used when declaring the functions `reademp()` and `printemp()`. You may need to modify this if you do not have an ANSI compiler.

Note 1: The type `enum paytype` is declared. It will be used to keep track of the active member of the union.

Note 2: The type `union rate` is declared. If the employee is paid by the hour, the pay rate is stored in type `float`. However, for an employee who is paid by the week, the pay rate is stored in an `int`.

Note 3: The type `struct employee` contains both a member of type `enum paytype` and a member of type `union rate`. Note that the identifier `paytype` can be used both as a tag in the declaration of the `enum` type and as the name of a member in the structure without conflict. Even though this double use of an identifier is discouraged, the compiler is able to distinguish the different contexts.

Note 4: To process the answer to the query `"Hourly or salaried (h or s) : "`, the following compound `if-else` statement inspects the first character of the input string. The appropriate value is assigned to the `paytype` member of the `struct employee` variable.

Note 5: The program is terminated in the case of incorrect input. This is a little extreme. Instead, the user could be given a chance to re-enter the `paytype`.

Note 6: The value of the `paytype` member is checked before access to the `payrate` member. In this way the correct member of the union can be accessed.

Note 7: Again the value of the `paytype` member is tested before accessing the union member. One way to keep track of which member of the `union rate` is active is to set the `paytype` member every time the union member is set, and to evaluate the `paytype` member before every access to the member of type `union rate`.

Learning Activities

36.   In the program unions.c, rewrite the error check on the `paytype`. Give the user another chance to enter the `paytype` correctly instead of terminating the program. If necessary, modify any other references to the `paytype` member so that a user can be sure that the `paytype` member has been set correctly at any time.

37.   Note that no error check is done on the input of `name` or `payrate`.
      a.   Can you think of any appropriate error check for the `name` input?

b. What might be an appropriate error check for the input of `payrate`? Implement it.
38. Must the parameter to `reademp()` be a pointer? Why or why not?
39. What happens when one union member is active and the other is accessed in the program? Modify the program by having the function `printemp()` always output an hourly salary. Compile and execute the program and enter the data for a salaried employee. Does the program execute properly? Explain what you think happens.

A Second Example with a Union

The fact that the C language does not keep track of which member of a union is active can sometimes be used to advantage. Programmers can assign a value to one union member and access other union members to obtain or create different data. However, programs written using that technique may not be portable.

The program union2.c in Example 7-11 illustrates a second method of accessing both bits and bytes in a quantity. It is very similar to the program bitfld2.c except that it uses a union in conjunction with bit field members of structures. The same two structures are declared with the bit fields representing the bits and the bytes in a quantity of type `short`, which is assumed to contain 16 bits or two bytes. However, this time a union is defined with three members, one that references the whole quantity, one of type `struct bytes`, and one of type `struct bits`. These latter two members are used to access the bytes and the bits, respectively, of the quantity.

Example 7-11: union2.c

```
/*              union2.c
 *
 *   Synopsis   - Displays the values of the bits and the bytes
 *                in a short int.
 *
 *   Objective  - To illustrate the use of bit fields and unions
 *                in accessing the bits and bytes of a quantity.
 */

/* Include Files */
#include <stdio.h>
```

```
void main( void )
{
     struct bits {                                        /* Note 1 */
          unsigned first      :1;
          unsigned second     :1;
          unsigned third      :1;
          unsigned fourth     :1;
          unsigned fifth      :1;
          unsigned sixth      :1;
          unsigned seventh    :1;
          unsigned eighth     :1;
          unsigned ninth      :1;
          unsigned tenth      :1;
          unsigned eleventh   :1;
          unsigned twelfth    :1;
          unsigned thirteenth:1;
          unsigned fourteenth:1;
          unsigned fifteenth  :1;
          unsigned sixteenth :1;
     } ;

     struct bytes {                                       /* Note 2 */
          unsigned first :8;
          unsigned second:8;
     } ;

     union access {                                       /* Note 3 */
          short whole;
          struct bits bit_access;
          struct bytes byte_access;
     } testvar;

                                                          /* Note 4 */
     printf( "sizeof(struct bits)  %d.\n", sizeof( struct bits ) );
     printf( "sizeof(struct bytes) %d.\n", sizeof( struct bytes ) );
     printf( "sizeof(union access) %d.\n\n", sizeof(union access) );

     testvar.whole = 0x1248;                              /* Note 5 */

                                                          /* Note 6 */
     printf( "first byte %x, second byte %x.\n\n",
          testvar.byte_access.first, testvar.byte_access.second );
                                                          /* Note 7 */
     printf( "Bits:\tfirst        %x,    second        %x,\n",
          testvar.bit_access.first, testvar.bit_access.second );
```

```
        printf( "\tthird        %x,    fourth       %x,\n",
               testvar.bit_access.third, testvar.bit_access.fourth );
        printf( "\tfifth        %x,    sixth        %x,\n",
               testvar.bit_access.fifth, testvar.bit_access.sixth );
        printf( "\tseventh      %x,    eighth       %x,\n",
               testvar.bit_access.seventh, testvar.bit_access.eighth );
        printf( "\tninth        %x,    tenth        %x,\n",
               testvar.bit_access.ninth, testvar.bit_access.tenth );
        printf( "\televenth     %x,    twelfth      %x,\n",
                    testvar.bit_access.eleventh,
                    testvar.bit_access.twelfth );
        printf( "\tthirteenth   %x,    fourteenth   %x,\n",
                    testvar.bit_access.thirteenth,
                    testvar.bit_access.fourteenth );
        printf( "\tfifteenth    %x,    sixteenth    %x\n",
                    testvar.bit_access.fifteenth,
                    testvar.bit_access.sixteenth );
}
```

 Running the Program

```
sizeof(struct bits)   2.
sizeof(struct bytes)  2.
sizeof(union access)  2.

first byte 48, second byte 12.

Bits:   first        0,   second      0,
        third        0,   fourth      1,
        fifth        0,   sixth       0,
        seventh      1,   eighth      0,
        ninth        0,   tenth       1,
        eleventh     0,   twelfth     0,
        thirteenth   1,   fourteenth  0,
        fifteenth    0,   sixteenth   0
```

The program consists of the single function main(). The executable code consists of a single assignment statement and calls to printf().

Note 1: A structure is declared that consists of sixteen bit fields. Each bit field contains one bit.

Note 2: A structure is declared that consists of two bit fields. Each bit field contains eight bits or one byte on most computer systems.

Note 3: A union with three members is declared. If a `short int` occupies two bytes, all three members should occupy the same amount of space. The hope is that the member of type `short int` can be initialized and the structure members can be accessed. This should allow access to the bytes of the `short int` with the `byte_access` member and access to any specific bit with the `bit_access` member. A portability problem may occur since the bit fields may be packed in the 16 bits in either order, but the code should be workable for any one system. The method of packing the bit fields should be apparent from running this program.

Note 4: The `sizeof()` each of the three quantities in question is displayed. If they do not agree with each other, adjust the declarations so that they do before interpreting the results of the program.

Note 5: A hexadecimal value is assigned to the variable `testvar`. The value was written in hexadecimal for ease in checking the value of each bit and byte.

Note 6: The value of each byte is output.

Note 7: The value of each bit is output.

Learning Activities

40. a. Predict the output of union2.c. Execute it to check your prediction. Resolve any differences between your prediction and the actual output.
    b. Are the results consistent with the execution of the program bitfield2.c? Why or why not?

41. List any problems that you think might occur with this approach for accessing the bits and the bytes of a quantity.

42. Experiment with types other than `short int`.

43. If you have access to a C compiler on a significantly different computer system, try to execute this program on a second system. Do you get the same results? If something is different, try to find out why.

44. Describe the result of the `sizeof()` operator used on a union.

45. *C by Discovery* Can a member of a union be a structure? A bit field? Experiment to find out.

A Closer Look

When a union is declared, only enough space for the largest member is allocated. Every member is stored at the beginning of the union. Subsequent assignments overwrite the existing members in the union. Any member of a union can be accessed at any time; however, the contents of a member may not be meaningful, if another member was most recently assigned.

The program union3.c in Example 7-12 is designed for experimenting with different types of members in a union and exploring the memory allocation. The experience gained with this experimentation should help you when writing other programs dealing with unions. Only one member of the union is assigned. The sizeof(), contents, and the address of the other members are output.

Example 7-12: union3.c

```
/*                union3.c
 *
 *    Synopsis    - Declares and initializes a union and displays
 *                  information about its addresses and contents.
 *
 *    Objective   - To illustrate the properties of memory
 *                  allocation with unions.
 */

/* Include Files */
#include <stdio.h>

void main( void )
{
    union x {                                          /* Note 1 */
          int intmem;
          float floatmem;
          unsigned bitmem:4;
          char stringmem[20];
    } tryit;

    tryit.intmem = 0x1248;                             /* Note 2 */
                                                       /* Note 3 */
    printf( "Sizeof the union and its members.\n" );
    printf( "---------------------------------\n" );
    printf( "sizeof(union x)  %d\n", sizeof( union x ) );
    printf( "sizeof(tryit.intmem) %d\n", sizeof(tryit.intmem));
    printf( "sizeof(tryit.floatmem) %d\n", sizeof( tryit.floatmem ));
    printf( "sizeof(tryit.bitmem) %d\n", sizeof( tryit.bitmem ));
    printf( "sizeof(tryit.stringmem) %d\n\n",
                          sizeof( tryit.stringmem ));
                                                       /* Note 4 */
    printf( "Addresses of the union and the members.\n" );
```

```
    printf( "-------------------------------------\n" );
    printf( "&tryit   %x.\n", &tryit );
    printf( "&tryit.intmem   %x\n", &(tryit.intmem) );
    printf( "&tryit.floatmem %x\n", &(tryit.floatmem) );
    printf( "&tryit.bitmem %x\n", &tryit.bitmem );
    printf( "tryit.stringmem   %x.\n\n", tryit.stringmem );
                                              /* Note 5 */
    printf( "Contents of members of the union.\n" );
    printf( "--------------------------------\n" );
    printf( "intmem = %x.\n", tryit.intmem );
    printf( "tryit.floatmem %5.2f\n", tryit.floatmem );
    printf( "tryit.bitmem %x\n", tryit.bitmem );
    printf( "tryit.stringmem[0] %x\n", tryit.stringmem[0] );
    printf( "tryit.stringmem[1] %x\n", tryit.stringmem[1] );
    printf( "tryit.stringmem[2] %x\n\n", tryit.stringmem[2] );
}
```

The executable code in the function main() consists of one assignment statement and many calls to printf(). Note that the value of the intmem member of the union x type variable is the only member assigned even though the program accesses all the members.

Note 1: A union named union x is declared. Its members include a bit field and an array for the purpose of experimentation.

Note 2: The member intmem is assigned a hexadecimal value so the calculation of the value of each bit is easy.

Note 3: The sizeof() operator is applied to the union itself as well as to its members.

Note 4: The address of each member is displayed. Note that the address of the array member is accessed with the array name. All members should start at the same location.

Note 5: The values of the members of the union are output. Note that only the member intmem was initialized. When another member is accessed, an attempt is made to interpret the contents as the appropriate type for that member.

Learning Activities

46.   The program union3.c will not compile as is. Without help from the compiler, try to find the compile error. Take out the offending statements and explain why they are incorrect.

47.   a.   Predict the sizeof() each of the members.

       b.   Given that the address of tryit is 0xce (hexadecimal), pre-

> dict the addresses of each member of `tryit`.
>
> c. Predict the contents of each member. Use your experience from the other bit field problems to predict the output of the bit field member.
>
> d. Execute the program to check your prediction. Reconcile any difference in the execution output and your prediction. Try to explain what the compiler does when the different members are referenced.
>
> 48. Are the two expressions `&(tryit.intmem)` and `&tryit->intmem` the same or different? What (if anything) is referenced by each syntax?

Language Elements Introduced in This Chapter: A Review

✓ **Enumerated Types**
  • Declaration

```
enum boolean {
        FALSE, TRUE
};
```

✓ **Functions**
  • Functions may return a pointer to a structure.
  • ANSI C functions may return a structure.
  • Functions may return unions or enumerated types.

✓ **Library Functions**

`strncpy()`	Copies a specified number of characters from one string into an array of chars.
`atoi()`	Converts a string of digits into the corresponding integer.
`atof()`	Converts a string representation of a floating point number to type `float`.

✓ **Operators**
  • Operators allowed with structure and union variables:
    assignment
    `sizeof()`
    address operator
  • Operators that can be used with `int`s can be used with enumerated types.

✓ **Parameters to Functions**
- Structures or pointers to structures can be parameters to functions in ANSI C.
- Unions and pointers to unions can be parameters to functions.
- Enumerated types and pointers to enumerated types can be parameters to functions.

✓ **Structures**
- Declaring a structure type:

```
struct tag {
    char namearray[20];
    int  intval;
    float floatval;
};
```

- Declaring a structure variable:

```
struct tag structvar;
```

- Accessing elements:

```
structvar.member
structptr->member
```

- Initializing:

```
struct tag structvar = { "NAME", 5, 1.47 };
```

✓ **Types**
- bit fields
- enumerated types
- structure types
- union types

✓ **Unions**
- Declarations:

```
union tag {
    char arrayfield[20];
    int  intfield;
    double doublefield;
};
```

- Accessing elements:

```
unionvar.fieldname
unionptr->fieldname
```

✓ **Variable Declarations**
- An array of structures:

```
struct tag structarray[20];
```

- A pointer to a structure:

```
struct tag *structptr;
```

- A structure with bit fields:

```
struct a {
        unsigned a:4;
        unsigned b:2;
};
```

- An enumerated variable:

```
enum boolean flag;
```

- A union:

```
union tag unionvar;
```

- A pointer to a union:

```
union tag *unionptr;
```

Things to Remember

1. A structure in C is an aggregate type that can hold multiple data values of different types at the same time.
2. Including a tag with a structure declaration allows variables of that structure type to be declared later in the program by referencing a `struct tag`.
3. A structure cannot contain a member that is a structure of the same type.
4. A structure can contain a member that is a pointer to a structure of the same type.
5. Different members of a structure can be packed into one word of memory with a construct called a bit field.
6. In ANSI C, a bit field must have type `int`, `unsigned int`, or `signed int`. Older compilers may limit the type of a bit field member to `unsigned int`.
7. Bit fields could be used to match hardware configuration or to save memory.
8. A disadvantage of using bit fields lies in the lack of portability.
9. The address operator, `&`, cannot be used with bit fields.
10. Many implementations of C restrict the maximum number of bits that can be contained in a bit field.
11. Bit fields can be specified in a structure declaration without a name. Such a bit field cannot be accessed and its contents cannot be specified. It may be used to force data alignment.
12. An enumerated type consists of a set of integer constants.
13. An enumerated type is primarily used to aid readability by giving readable names to numeric quantities.

14. A union is designed to hold members of different types. It will only contain one of its members at any instant.

15. There is no automatic mechanism to determine which member of a union is in use at any time. It is up to the programmer to keep track.

16. An enumerated type can be used with a union to establish which member is being used.

Exercises and Programming Problems

1. Write a program to figure the monthly salary for both hourly and salaried employees. Use the type `struct employee` that was illustrated in program unions.c of Example 7-8. Have the user enter the employee information with either the number of hours or the number of weeks worked, and have the program prepare a payroll report.

2. a. Write a structure (`struct card`) that will represent a card in a standard deck of playing cards. You will need to represent both the suit (clubs, diamonds, hearts or spades) as well as the rank (A, K, Q, J, 10, 9, 8, 7, 6, 5, 4, 3, 2) of each card. Note that a deck of playing cards can be represented as an array declared as

   •
   ```
   struct card deck[52];
   ```

   b. Write a function that will perform a perfect shuffle on a deck of cards represented using the data structures from part a. In a perfect shuffle, the deck is broken exactly in half and rearranged so that the first card is followed by the 27th card, followed by the second card, followed by the 28th card, and so on.

   c. Write a program that tests how many perfect shuffles are necessary to return the deck to its original configuration.

3. a. The game of bridge is played with a 13-card hand. Write a data structure to represent a bridge hand.

   b. Write a function to rearrange a bridge hand with all cards of each suit together and with the cards of each suit arranged from high rank to low rank.

   c. Write a function to display a bridge hand in the following form.

   ```
   Clubs:        A, K, J
   Diamonds:     Q, 10, 8, 7, 6, 4, 2
   Hearts:       void
   Spades:       A, 10, 8
   ```

   (In the context of a bridge game, the designation "void" means that the hand has no cards in that suit.)

    d. Write a function to calculate the points in a bridge hand according to the following rules:

        4 points for each Ace in the hand
        3 points for each King in the hand
        2 points for each Queen in the hand
        1 point for each Jack in the hand
        3 points for each void suit in the hand
        2 points for each one-card suit in the hand
        1 point for each two-card suit in the hand

    The points in the hand are calculated as the sum of the points above as they apply. For example, the hand represented in part c has 17 points:

2 Aces	+ 1 King	+ 1 Queen	+ 1 Jack	+ 1 void suit	=
2 * 4	+ 1 * 3	+ 2 * 1	+ 1 * 1	+ 3	= 17

4. In mathematics, a rational number is defined as a quotient of two integers where the denominator is not equal to zero. For example, 1/2, 6/1, -5/4, 12/3, and 468/(-325) are all rational numbers as are all fractions where the numerator and denominator are integers and the denominator is not equal to zero.

    a. Declare a data structure that will contain a rational number.

    b. Write functions that will add, subtract, multiply and divide rational numbers. In all functions, pass in three parameters, each pointing to a data structure of the type you declared in part a. Use two of the parameters for the operands, and the third for the result.

    c. Write a function that takes a pointer to your data structure as a parameter and returns the greatest common divisor of the numerator and denominator.

    d. Use your function from part c to write a function that will reduce a fraction (rational number) to lowest terms. Pass in a pointer to the fraction and have the fraction modified by the function.

    e. Write input and output functions so that a user can enter a fraction in the form

        2/3,   -5/6,   4/-5,   or   -12/-33

    and the output is in the same form. Have your input function check for errors in the input and return a value of -1 in case an error was sensed. The error might consist of a zero denominator as in 3/0, or an error in form as in 4a/5 or 4%5. Both the input function and the output function should take a single pointer to your data structure from part a as a parameter.

    f. Combine your functions from parts b through e to write a program that will perform rational number arithmetic for the user. The user should be allowed to enter any number of problems, and the program should output the answer in lowest terms. A sample dialogue is below. The user's input is in **boldface.**

```
FRACTION ARITHMETIC PROGRAM
-------- ---------- -------
Enter your problem:   2/3 + 1/5
The answer is 13/15.      Another problem (y/n)? y
Enter your problem:   4/2 - 5/0
Illegal input!!          Another problem (y/n)? y
Enter your problem:   2/9 * 3/4
The answer is 1/6.       Another problem (y/n)? n
Goodbye and thank you.
```

5. A state college charges state residents a flat fee of $300 for a semester's tuition. It charges nonresident students $85 per credit unit.

   a. Write a data structure using structures, unions, and enumerated types that will hold the following information about a student: name, Social Security number, resident/nonresident status, current semester units, and fee charged.

   b. Write a function that takes a pointer to your data structure as an argument and assigns the correct fee to the appropriate member of the structure. Assume that the remainder of the members in the structure are properly initialized.

   c. Write a function to accept input of the name, Social Security number, resident status, and current semester units for a student. Have your input function call the function you wrote in part b to calculate the fee to be charged.

   d. Write an output function to output the information about a student.

   e. Incorporate parts a through d above into a program that requests and accepts input of information about students and prepares a report with the student information and the total revenue from those students.

6. Expand the program struct2.c of Example 7-3 by adding a menu allowing a user to

   a. Insert an `auto_part` into the inventory.

   b. Delete an `auto_part` from the inventory.

   c. Find those parts whose current inventory are below a certain value.

   d. Change the inventory amount for an `auto_part` after a sale or receipt of an order.

   Write functions to implement each of the menu choices.

7. Use a bit field representation like that in program union2.c of Example 7-9 in a program that will input a value of type char and output its binary representation.

8. A string could be viewed as an array of characters with a specific length. This type of string could be implemented as a structure with a character array member and an int member for the length.

    a. Write a structure declaration (struct string) in C for a string implemented this way. The fields should be named chars and length.

    b. Write a version of the strlen() function for a string with this implementation. Call it mystrlen().

    c. Write a version of the strcat() function for a string with this implementation. Call it mystrcat().

    d. Write a function print_string() that takes a struct string as a parameter and outputs the meaningful characters to the terminal screen (a version of puts() for this implementation).

    e. Put your code for parts a, b, c and d in a file named mystring.h, and make sure your code will work with the following program:

```
/*                        epp8.c                        */

/* Include Files */
#include <stdio.h>
#include "mystring.h"

void main( void )
{
        struct string str1,
                        str2 = { "how now brown cow", 17 };

        str1.length = 0;
        printf( "Length of str1 - %d\n", mystrlen( str1 ));

        mystrcat( str1, str2 );
        print_string( str1 );
        printf( "\nLength of str1 - %d\n", mystrlen( str1 ));
}
```

9. a. There are three major types of banking transactions for a personal checking account: a deposit, a withdrawal, and a check. Write an enumerated type declaration for the three types of banking transactions.

    b. Write a declaration in C for a data type that will hold a date (month, day and year).

c. A bank transaction needs the following information: date, type of transaction, check number (when appropriate), payee for a check or memo for the other two types, and the amount. Write a C structure declaration to hold the information for a single banking transaction. Try to use a union within the declaration in an appropriate way.

d. Write a function that allows a user to enter the information about a banking transaction from the keyboard. Your function should take the address of a transaction structure as a parameter.

e. Write a function that displays the contents of a transaction to the terminal. Your function should take a transaction structure as a parameter.

f. Write a driver program that calls the input function and then the output function to test your functions.

10. The information kept about a student includes last name, first name, major code (four digits), year in school (freshman, sophomore, junior, senior or graduate), number of units completed, and grade point average.

a. Write a C type declaration for a data structure that will hold the information about a student.

b. Write a function that performs the input of the information about a single student from the keyboard. Your function should take a pointer to the type you declared in part a as a parameter.

c. Write a program that allows a user to enter student information for up to a maximum of 30 students from the keyboard. When the user is done, the program outputs a report about the students. The list of students should be in alphabetical order by last name, and the student information should be nicely formatted. Problems that should be addressed include the data structure necessary to hold all the students and the method of getting the students in alphabetical order by last name.

Chapter 8

Intraprogram Communication

8.1   **Introduction**
8.2   **Automatic versus Static Variables**
8.3   **Global versus Local Variables**
8.4   **Modules and External Variables**
8.5   **Typedefs**
8.6   **Function Definitions**
8.7   **Function Declarations and Calls**
8.8   **Pointers to Functions**

8.1 Introduction

When writing structured modular code in C, the programmer must set up effective communication between the different parts of the program. In this chapter we will consider topics that control this communication.

A structured program is composed of separate subprograms. Different parts of the same program may reside in separate modules or files. Prewritten software tools like the C library functions, data structure implementations, or functions written by programmers to fill a specific need can be incorporated into a program. For example, a software tool written to count the number of English words in an input string ideally should be able to work unchanged in many programs and not be dependent on the variable names used in the program for which it was originally written. To use tools and modules effectively, communication between the separate parts of a program must be understood.

The communication in C is accomplished through several mechanisms. We will discuss types, storage classes, scope of identifiers, function types, return values, and linkage in this chapter.

The *scope* of an identifier determines which program parts will know about the identifier and be able to use it. We saw an example of this in Section 2.2, where variables declared inside of blocks were unknown outside the blocks. The

399

scope of these variables started at the point of declaration and went to the end of their block. These variables could only be accessed inside the block.

A variable's storage class indicates its life span. The storage class of an identifier determines whether it exists for the duration of program execution or only for part of the execution time. A related issue is when a variable is initialized: every time the variable is accessed or only once during program execution.

Other techniques for passing information deal with functions and their parameters. Functions that are written with parameters make better tools. They can be used in more programs without change.

Another way that a function can communicate with the surrounding code is through its type and return value. The syntax of the `return` statement was discussed in Chapters 1 and 6. Some of the implications of the use of this statement in terms of communication between parts of a program will be discussed here.

Another mechanism we will consider is separating the source code into separate files, compiling each file separately, and linking the resulting object code files together to form an executable program. When this is done, the functions in one file may need to access some variables or functions in another file. We will study the linkage properties of the identifiers to determine how this can be used.

8.2 Automatic versus Static Variables

The keywords `auto` and `static` refer to two different storage classes in C. They specify the time span that a variable exists. The storage class `register` will also be discussed in this section. The other storage class specifiers include `extern`, which will be discussed in Section 8.4, and `typedef`, which will be discussed in Section 8.5.

Automatic Variables

Prior to this chapter we used the default storage class for all variables. If a variable is declared inside a function block and its declaration does not specify otherwise, it has the default storage class automatic or `auto`. An automatic variable is created each time its function is called and destroyed when the execution of its function terminates. If an automatic variable is declared inside the function `main()`, it is created when the program starts executing and destroyed at the end of execution. (The execution of the function `main()` does not terminate until the program finishes executing.)

The declaration of an automatic variable can be done in two ways. The keyword `auto` can precede the declaration, as in

```
auto int counter;
```

However, since the storage class automatic is the default for local variables, the above declaration is equivalent to

```
int counter;
```

All variables that we saw prior to this section were automatic variables.

When an automatic variable is created without an initializer, it is not given any initial value. It may contain garbage values. When accompanied by an initializer, as in

```
int counter = 1;
```

the initialization is done each time the variable is created. That is, the variable is reinitialized each time a function is called. Example 8-1 illustrates that concept.

Example 8-1: automatc.c

```
/*                  automatc.c
 *
 *    Synopsis    - Displays two integer values.
 *
 *    Objective   - Illustrates automatic variables.
 */

/* Include Files */
#include <stdio.h>

/* Function Prototypes */
int increment( void );

void main( void )
{
    printf( "%d\n", increment() );                          /* Note 2 */
    printf( "%d\n", increment() );
}


/***************************** increment()  *****************/
/*    increment() - Increments an automatic local variable and
 *                  returns its incremented value.
 */
int increment( void )
{
    int number = 0;                                         /* Note 1 */

    return ( ++number );
}
```

Running the Program

1
1

Two functions make up this program. The function `main()` consists of two calls to `printf()`. Each time, the value returned by the function `increment()` is displayed. The function `increment()` contains the declaration of an automatic variable named `number`, which is initialized to zero. The function `increment()` increments this variable and returns the incremented value.

Note 1: The declaration of `number` does not contain a storage class specifier. Since it is declared inside the function block of `increment()`, it has storage class automatic, by default. This means that `number` is created and initialized each time `increment()` is called. The value of `number` will be dependably zero each time `increment()` starts executing.

Note 2: These `printf()` calls display the value returned by the function `increment()`. Since the variable `number` is always zero at the start of execution of `increment()`, the value displayed will be the same in both `printf()` calls.

Static Variables

The concept of an automatic variable contrasts with that of a static variable. Whereas an automatic variable is in existence only when its function is executing, a static variable is in existence the whole time the program is executing. Its memory space has been allocated by the time the program starts executing and is not deallocated until the program terminates.

To declare a static variable, begin with the keyword `static`. For example,

```
static int counter;
```

Without explicit initialization, a static variable will be given the default initial value of `0`. However, an initializer can be added to the above declaration as in the following:

```
static int counter = 1;
```

In either case the variable `counter` would be initialized once at the beginning of program execution. In consequence, a static variable retains its value from one use to the next.

Consider the situation in which the `static` variable `counter` is declared inside a function block. Suppose the function is called, the value of `counter` is changed during function execution, and then the function is called again. The value of `counter` on each entry to the function would be the same as when exiting the function the previous time.

Example 8-2 illustrates this concept. Note the similarity between this program, static.c, and the previous program, automatc.c. Note also that the output is different. Understanding this difference is the key to understanding the difference between automatic and static variables.

Example 8-2: static.c

```
/*                static.c
 *
 *    Synopsis    - Outputs two integer values.
 *
 *    Objective   - Illustrates static variables.
 */

/* Include Files */
#include <stdio.h>

/* Function Prototypes */
int increment( void );

void main( void )
{
    printf( "%d\n", increment() );                    /* Note 2 */
    printf( "%d\n", increment() );
}

/***************************** increment()   *****************/
/*    Increments a static local variable and returns its
 *    incremented value.
 */
int increment( void )
{
    static int number = 0;                            /* Note 1 */

    return ( ++number );
}
```

Running the Program

1
2

This program is almost identical to the previous example program. It consists of two functions. The function `main()` consists of two `printf()` calls. Each time, the value returned by the function `increment()` is displayed. The function `increment()` contains a local variable named `number`, which is initialized to zero. The function `increment()` increments this variable and returns the incremented value.

Note 1: The variable `number` in this example has been declared with storage class `static`. It is in existence the whole time the program executes. It is only initialized once and holds its value between calls to `increment()`.

Note 2: These `printf()` calls display the value returned by `increment()`. Since the value of `number` at the start of execution of `increment()` is not always the same, different values are displayed by each statement.

Learning Activities

1. Execute automatc.c and static.c on your system to verify that the results are those shown.

2. a. Modify both automatc.c and static.c by adding the following call to `printf()` inside the function `increment()`:

   `printf("The address of number is %x.\n", &number);`

   b. Compile and execute both programs again. Note the results. Was the address of `number` the same in both programs? If not, were the two addresses close in value, or were they significantly different? Many compilers store static and automatic variables in different sections of memory. Does that appear to be the case with your compiler?

Register Variables

The third storage class that we will discuss is `register`. The designation of a variable as a register variable is a request by the programmer that a variable be placed in a register. The declaration of a register variable is usually an indication that the variable will be used often; it might be done in an attempt to improve the speed and performance of a program. The specifications for the C language do not guarantee that a variable will be placed in a register when one is requested; however, the knowledge that a register was requested may allow the compiler to optimize the code for efficiency.

The keyword `register` begins the declaration of a register variable. For example,

```
register int counter;
```

declares a register variable with type `int` and name `counter`. Register variables have the same properties as automatic variables. They exist only while their function is executing; they are created and initialized every time the function is entered, and are destroyed at termination of their function.

Variables that could be considered for the `register` storage class include array indices and loop counters. If a pointer variable is used to traverse an array, it might be given `register` storage class also. The number of `register` variables in a program that will be actually assigned to a register differs with different implementations of C and especially on the underlying hardware.

Example 8-3 illustrates the properties of register variables. The program register.c is very similar to the previous programs in this section, but the register variable is used more heavily.

Example 8-3: register.c

```
/*                register.c
 *
 *    Synopsis    - Displays two integer values.
 *
 *    Objective   - Illustrates register variables.
 */

/* Include Files */
#include <stdio.h>

/* Function Prototypes */
int increment_a_lot( void );

void main( void )
```

```
{
     printf( "%d\n", increment_a_lot() );
     printf( "%d\n", increment_a_lot() );
}

/****************************** increment_a_lot()  *************/
/*    Increments a register local variable 1000 times and
 *    returns the incremented value.
 */
int increment_a_lot( void )
{
     register int number = 0;                              /* Note 1 */

     for ( ; number < 1000; number++ )                     /* Note 2 */
     ;
     return ( number );
}
```

The similarities between this program and the previous example programs in this section should be noted. This program consists of two functions, main() and increment_a_lot(). The function main() is very similar to its counterpart in the previous examples; it consists of two calls to printf(). Each printf() call displays the value returned by the other function. The function increment_a_lot() has a register variable that is initialized to zero. The function returns the value of the variable after it has been incremented. The only difference is that the variable is incremented many times through use of a for loop.

Note 1: The declaration of number contains a storage class specifier of register. This is a request by the programmer that this variable be put in a register. The register variable is similar to an automatic variable in that it is created and initialized each time the function is called.

Note 2: The variable number is used to drive this for loop. Since the for loop is executed 1000 times, the variable is accessed 1000 times when the function is executed. Note that the initialization expression of the for loop can be omitted, because the variable number is dependably equal to zero at the start of the function execution.

Two final points about register variables should be considered before concluding this section. First, since the value of the variable might be stored in a register, it is illegal to use the address operator, &, with the name of a register variable. Second, different implementations of C might impose restrictions on the number and type of register variables it honors (assigns to a register). In fact, in some implementations of C, the storage class indicator is simply ignored; in others, the restrictions are dependent on the underlying hardware for the implementation.

Learning Activities

3. Predict the output of register.c and execute it to verify your predictions.

4. a. Determine if it is possible to look at the assembly code generated by the compiler on your implementation of C. Find out how it is done.

    b. If it is possible, stop compilation of register.c at that phase and inspect the assembly code. Can you tell where the variable `number` is stored? Was it allocated a register?

    c. Omit the storage specifier `register` in the program and repeat the process described in part b. Look to see if this omission made a difference in the assembly code. If it didn't, try to find out how your implementation of C handles register variables.

    d. Change the storage class specifier to `static` and compile the code to assembly language again. What are the changes this time?

8.3 Global versus Local Variables

The distinction between local and global variables deals with the *scope* of variables. The scope of a variable is the part of the program in which the variable can be referenced. A local variable is local to a block. The block can be a function block or a compound statement block. It is declared inside the braces for the block and can only be referenced inside its block. In contrast, a global variable is declared outside all function blocks. It is possible to access a global variable in more than one function. We will discuss local variables first.

Local Variables

Up to this point in the text, most of the variables have been local variables. They were known only inside the function block or compound statement block in which they were defined.

A local variable is declared inside a pair of matching braces that delimits a compound statement or a function block. It can be legally referenced at any point from its declaration to the closing brace for that block or function. Another way of saying this is: a local variable's scope is from its point of declaration to the end of the block in which it was declared. In C, the local variable declarations must appear before any code in the block.

As we saw in Section 8.2, the storage class specifiers `auto` and `static` can be used with local variables. The storage class specifier used with a local variable affects the life span of the variable and its initialization properties but does not change the scope of the variable.

Example 8-4 illustrates the fact that a variable declared inside a block will not be known outside the block. The program will not compile.

Example 8-4: error.c

```
/*              error.c
 *
 *    Synopsis   - This code contains compile time errors. Its
 *                 intent is purposely vague.
 *
 *    Objective  - To illustrate the compiler's understanding of
 *                 local variables and their scope.
 */


/* Include Files */
#include <stdio.h>

/* Function Prototypes */
int addit( void );

void main( void )
{
    int counter;                                        /* Note 1 */

    for ( counter = 1; counter < 5; counter++ ) {
        int i;                                          /* Note 2 */
        i = counter;                                    /* Note 3 */
        i = i + 5;
        addit();
    }
                                                        /* Note 4 */
    printf( "i was %d; addit() returned %d.\n", i, addit() );
}


/***************************** addit()  *********************/
/*    Attempts to add sum to counter.  Has syntax errors.
 */
```

```
int addit( void )
{
      int sum = 0;                                      /* Note 5 */

      sum = sum + counter;                              /* Note 6 */
      return ( sum );
}
```

The program consists of the function `main()` and a function `addit()`. In `main()`, the variable `counter` is declared and used to drive a `for` loop. The block that forms the body of the `for` loop contains the declaration of the variable `i`, two assignment statements, and a call to `addit()`. A final `printf()` call ends `main()`. The function `addit()` contains the declaration of `sum`, a single assignment statement, and a `return` statement.

Note 1: The variable `counter` is declared. Because it is declared inside the function block for `main()`, it is local to `main()`. It can be legally referenced only inside `main()`.

Note 2: The variable `i` is declared inside the braces delimiting a compound statement. Its scope is limited to that compound statement.

Note 3: The variable `counter` can be referenced anywhere inside `main()`. The assignment to `counter` inside the block will not cause any compile errors.

Note 4: The `printf()` call lies just outside the compound statement and references the variable `i`. Since `i` is local to that compound statement and the `printf()` call is outside the scope of the variable `i`, this reference will cause a compilation error.

Note 5: The variable `sum` is local to the function `addit()`. It will be initialized to zero every time the function is called.

Note 6: This assignment statement references the variable `counter`. Since `counter` is local to `main()`, this reference is outside `counter`'s scope. This causes another compile-time error in this program.

Learning Activity

5.   Make the following changes to the program error.c.
   a.   Remove the reference to the variable `i` in the `printf()` call. (For example, `printf()` could just report the value returned by `addit()`.)
   b.   Make `counter` a parameter to the function `addit()`. You will need to change the call to `addit()` and the function heading in the definition of `addit()`, and the function prototype.

> c. Compile the program error.c. Make any necessary changes so that it will compile.
>
> d. Predict the output of your modified program. Then run the program to verify your prediction. Reconcile any differences between your prediction and the actual output for the program.

Global Variables

A global variable (also called an external variable) is a variable that can be referenced by more than one function. It is defined outside function or compound statement blocks.

If a variable is declared before all the functions in a source code file, it can be referenced by all the functions in that file. A reference to a variable consists of using its name in an expression. The scope of a variable declared either before the functions in a file or between two functions in a file is from its point of declaration to the end of the file.

A global or external variable is in existence during the full execution time of the program. By default, a global variable is initialized to zero. An initializer can be included in the declaration to defeat the default. For example, if the declarations

```
int a, b = 5;
```

appear outside of any function block, the value of a will be 0, and the value of b will be 5. The keyword `static` has a special meaning with global variables. This will be discussed in Section 8.4.

The program global.c in Example 8-5 illustrates the difference between local and global variables.

Example 8-5: global.c

```
/*              global.c
 *
 *    Synopsis    - Assigns values to some variables and displays
 *                  those values.
 *
 *    Objective   - Illustrates the difference between global and
 *                  local variables.
 */

/* Include Files */
#include <stdio.h>
```

```
/* Global Variables */
int globalvar;                                              /* Note 1 */
int same_name = 3;                                          /* Note 1 */

/* Function Prototypes */
void sub_fcn( void );

void main( void )
{
    int localvar;                                          /* Note 2 */

    globalvar = 2;                                         /* Note 3 */
    localvar = 3;                                          /* Note 4 */
    printf( "Starting in main, " );
    printf( "globalvar is %d, localvar is %d.\n",
                                  globalvar, localvar );

    sub_fcn();

    printf( "\nAfter returning to main, " );
                                                           /* Note 9 */
    printf( "globalvar is %d, localvar is %d,\n",
                                  globalvar, localvar );
    printf( "and same_name has value %d.\n", same_name );
}
/***************************** sub_fcn()  *******************/
/*   Assigns values to local and global variables and displays
 *   the values.
 */

void sub_fcn( void )
{
    int localvar;                                          /* Note 5 */
    int same_name;                                         /* Note 6 */

    globalvar = 4;                                         /* Note 7 */
    localvar = 5;                                          /* Note 8 */
    same_name = 127;
    printf( "\nIn sub_fcn, " );
    printf( "globalvar is %d, localvar is %d,\n",
                                  globalvar, localvar );
    printf( "and same_name has value %d.\n", same_name );
}
```

Running the Program

```
Starting in main, globalvar is 2, localvar is 3.

In sub_fcn, globalvar is 4, localvar is 5,
and same_name has value 127.

After returning to main, globalvar is 4, localvar is 3,
and same_name has value 3.
```

This program consists of two functions, main() and sub_fcn(). Two variables, globalvar and same_name, are declared before the beginning of main(). The function main() consists of assignment statements, calls to printf(), and a call to sub_fcn(). The function sub_fcn() consists of assignment statements and printf() calls. The variables and their values are of specific interest.

Note 1: The variables globalvar and same_name are global variables. They can be accessed by any function in this source file. These global variables are declared before the declaration of any functions in the file. The variable globalvar will have the default initial value of 0; same_name will be initialized to 3 before execution of main() begins.

Note 2: The variable localvar is local to the function main(). Local variables are declared inside function blocks.

Note 3: A value is assigned to globalvar. This variable can be referenced by any function in this source code file. The function need only mention the variable's name.

Note 4: A value is assigned to localvar.

Note 5: A local variable named localvar is declared. This variable has no connection with the variable in the function main(); this variable is local to sub_fcn() and can only be referenced there.

Note 6: A local variable named same_name is declared. Note that the name of this variable conflicts with the name of a global variable previously defined. This is legal in C, but any reference to same_name inside sub_fcn() will always access the local variable with that name. It is impossible for sub_fcn() to reference the global same_name directly.

Note 7: A value is assigned to globalvar. The variable will retain this new value even after sub_fcn() has terminated. The action of changing the value of a global variable by a function is called a side effect. Side effects should be kept to a minimum for ease of reading, debugging, and maintaining a program.

Note 8: Assignment statements change the values of `localvar` and `same_name`. In both cases, the value of the local copy of the variable is changed. The value of `localvar` in `main()` is not changed. The value of the global variable `same_name` remains unchanged also. The following `printf()` call reflects the results of these assignment statements.

Note 9: After `sub_fcn()` executes, the values of `globalvar`, `localvar`, and `same_name` are output. Note that `sub_fcn()` made assignments to three variables with those names; however, not all of the values have been changed. The value of `globalvar` was changed by `sub_fcn()` since both functions could access the same global variable. The values of `localvar` and `same_name` were not changed. This `localvar` is local to `main()` and cannot be accessed outside `main()`. The reason that `same_name` was not changed is that `sub_fcn()` has its own variable named `same_name` and therefore can not access the global variable with that name.

"Execute the program to verify your prediction. Correct any errors in your thinking."
Based on *The Bull Hunt* by Antoine-Louis Barye, 1834.

Learning Activities

6.   a. Execute the program global.c to make sure it has the same result on your system.

        b. Make the following changes to global.c. Predict what will occur in each case and then execute the program to verify your prediction. Correct any errors in your thinking.

    i. Add a printf() call to main() to display the value of globalvar before the value 2 is assigned to it.

    ii. Add an assignment to the variable same_name to main(). Have that value displayed by a call to printf().

7.   a. Modify the program global.c by having it display the address of each variable in each function. Compile and execute the program again. Inspect the addresses when they are displayed. Do you see a similarity between the addresses of the local variables? Are they close to each other in memory or distant? What about the global variables? Are they close to the local variables or are they distant?

     b. Add a parameter to sub_fcn() and have the address of the formal parameter displayed also. Use localvar as the actual parameter to sub_fcn(). Compile and execute the program. Note the results.

     c. Modify the program once more to use globalvar as the actual parameter to sub_fcn(). Compile and execute the program again. Are the results the same?

     d. Explain your results. Can you conclude anything about the location in memory of global and local variables? What about parameters to functions? Do they seem to be handled more like global variables or local variables?

8.   Global variables cannot be referenced in functions that are declared before their point of declaration. Convince yourself of that fact by moving the declaration of globalvar to a spot between main() and sub_fcn() and try to execute it again. Do you get a compilation error, a runtime error, or no error at all?

9.   Consider the following program.

```
/*                              la9.c                        */

/* Include Files */
#include <stdio.h>

/* Global Variables */
int a, b, c;

/* Function Prototypes */
void f1( void );
void f2( void );

void main( void )
{
    int a;
    a = 5;
    b = 3;
```

```
        c = 7;
        printf( "%d, %d, %d\n", a, b, c );
        f1();
        printf( "%d, %d, %d\n", a, b, c );
}

int d = 4;

void f1( void )
{
        char c = 'A';

        a = 3;
        b++;
        printf( "%d, %d, %d, %d\n", a, b, c, d );
        f2();
        printf( "%d, %d, %d, %d\n", a, b, c, d );
}

void f2( void )
{
        int d = 45;

        a += 4;
        b = 7;
        c = d + a;
        printf( "%d, %d, %d, %d\n", a, b, c, d );
}
```

   a. List the variables that can be referenced by the function `main()`.

   b. List the variables that can be referenced by the function `f1()`.

   c. Predict the output from this program and then execute it to verify your prediction. Correct any mistakes in your thinking.

10. We mentioned that global variables act like static variables in the sense that they are in existence for the full execution time of the program.

   a. Would it be theoretically possible to have an automatic global variable? What would this mean? When would it exist? When would it be initialized? Which functions would be able to access it?

   b. Experiment with the program above to see if automatic global variables are allowed. What happens? Did everything work as you expected?

A Word about Style

Global variables should be used with discretion. A structured program should effect most of its communication through the use of function parameters and return values rather than by accessing global variables.

When a program's variables all are global, all functions may access them and change their values. This change of value of a global variable by a function is referred to as a *side effect*. Side effects cause problems in debugging because if the value of a global variable is incorrect, a detailed search through all the functions in the program for access to the variable must be made. This often involves a painstaking execution trace to find the instance where the offending value was assigned.

The same problem occurs with program maintenance. If a proposed change involves a global variable, a trace must be made to see what effect the change will have on the whole program. However, if the variable is local to a function, only that function needs to be examined.

8.4 Modules and External Variables

A source module might consist of the source code for all functions performing related tasks. In a C program, each module could be placed in a separate file. For example, all functions dealing with input and output might comprise one module while all arithmetic processing would be in a separate module. A third module might contain a driver, a function that does nothing more than call the other modules.

Each source module can be compiled separately. This would produce a corresponding object code module. Before executing the program, the object modules must be linked together. The ability to compile and link the code from source in different files is a feature of most C compilers.

The advantages of using separate source files include ease of editing and compiling shorter files. This organization also allows for teamwork in programming projects. Different members of the team could work on different modules.

It is often necessary for the functions in different modules to access the same variables. This can be accomplished in the following way: the variable could be declared in one module as a global (external) variable; in the other modules, it would be referenced with a declaration using the keyword `extern`.

To discuss the concept of external variables and the use of the keyword `extern`, we need to recall the distinction between declarations and definitions. The declaration of a variable states the type and name of the variable. The definition of a variable states its type and name and causes memory to be allocated for that variable. Any definition is a declaration, but there are declarations that are not definitions.

When a global variable is defined, it is known from its point of declaration to the end of the source file. Another property of global variables is that they have *external linkage*; this means that they can also be referenced in other source code files as well as in functions below their point of definition. Code in other source code files can declare (but not define) this same variable and give it the storage class `extern`. For example, if a source code file, containing the function `main()`, defined an external variable, it might have the following structure:

```
int globalvar;
main()
{
    . . .
}
```

In this example, the code

```
int globalvar;
```

would usually be taken as the definition of the variable `globalvar`; storage would be allocated. If functions `f1()` and `f2()` in another source code file needed to access the variable `globalvar`, they could include an `extern` declaration at the top of the source file.

```
extern int globalvar;

f1()
{
    . . .
}

f2()
{
    . . .
}
```

The keyword `extern` is used with declarations, but not with definitions of variables. It indicates that the variable is defined elsewhere; references to this variable should be resolved during the link phase of compilation.[1] Note that an external definition of a variable and an `extern` declaration are different.

Since global variables can be linked to other source files, there may be additional restrictions on the identifiers used. The allowed maximum length of the identifier could be shorter if it has external linkage, and distinction between uppercase and lowercase may not be made. This is not specified by the ANSI standards, so it needs to be researched for each compiler.

As a very simple example of a program with its source split between different files, suppose that a program is to (1) display the value of a variable, (2) increment that variable, and (3) display the value of that variable again. To illustrate modular programming, this simple program will be broken down into three separate mod-

---

1. On some compilers, the keyword `extern` is not necessary. The linker takes the first declaration as the definition. The method illustrated in this text should work with most compilers.

ules: one to output the variable, one to increment the variable, and one, the driver module, to call the other two modules. The variable will have the name x.

The output module will be named output.c and will contain a single function named `output()` that displays the current value of x. The increment module will be named incr.c and will contain a single function named `incr()` that increments the value of x. The driver module will be named driver.c and will contain the single function `main()`. Execution of the program will start at the beginning of the function `main()`. The function `main()` will call `output()`, `incr()`, and `output()` in that order.

The variable x needs to be known to `incr()` and to `output()`, but not necessarily to `main()`. However, by stylistic convention, most global variables for a program are declared either in an include file or in the module containing `main()`. Therefore, the variable x will be declared in driver.c.

Example 8-6 shows the driver module in the file driver.c.

Example 8-6: driver.c

```
/*              driver.c
 *
 *   Synopsis   - Displays the value of a variable, increments it,
 *                and displays it again.
 *
 *   Objective  - To demonstrate a very simple modular program
 *                with a variable declared externally.
 */

/* Global Variables */
int  x = 5;                                          /* Note 1 */

/* Function Prototypes */
extern void output( void );                          /* Note 2 */
extern void incr( void );

void main( void )
{
    output();                                        /* Note 3 */
    incr();
    output();
}
```

This file contains a single function named `main()`. When the program is executed, execution begins with the function `main()`. A single global variable named x is declared. The code for `main()` consists of three function calls. The source for the called functions appears in other source modules.

Note 1: The variable x is declared as a global variable in this file. It will be accessed by the functions in the other files. The initialization takes place before the program begins execution. The variable x is not accessed in this file, and could have been defined in one of the other modules just as well.

Note 2: The functions that do not appear in this source code file are declared here. Just as with variables, the keyword extern indicates that the functions are defined in another file and will be linked to the executable file. This declaration is not necessary with all compilers.

Note 3: The code in main() consists of calls to functions that are not in this file. When the program is compiled for execution, the code for these functions must be found in other files. This is usually done in the last phase of compilation which is known as linking. The names of all the object files must be supplied to the linker.

The contents of the file output.c are shown in Example 8-7.

Example 8-7: output.c

```
/*                  output.c
 *
 *      Synopsis   - The function output() displays the value of
 *                   the variable x.
 *
 *      Objective  - Part of a simple modular program that
 *                   illustrates variables that are externally
 *                   declared.
 */

/* Include Files */
#include <stdio.h>                                      /* Note 1 */

/* External Variable Declarations */
extern int x;                                           /* Note 2 */

void output( void )
{
    printf( "The value of x is %d.\n", x );
}
```

This file consists of the single function output(). The function main() is in a different module. The code in output() consists of a single printf() call.

Note 1: The file stdio.h is included here by a preprocessor directive. Since the call for output is in this file, it is the only one with use for the information in stdio.h. No preprocessor statements are necessary in the other files.

Note 2: This line contains a reference to the variable x. The keyword `extern` indicates that this variable is defined in a different file. All references to x in this module will refer to that externally defined variable. The address of x is resolved in the link phase of compilation.

The module incr.c is shown in Example 8-8.

Example 8-8: incr.c

```
/*                  incr.c
 *
 *    Synopsis    - The function incr() increments the variable x.
 *
 *    Objective   - Part of a very simple modular program
 *                  illustrating variables declared externally.
 */

/* External Variable Declarations */
extern int x;                                               /* Note 1 */

void incr( void )
{
      x++;
}
```

This file contains the single function `incr()`. The code for `incr()` incre-ments the variable x.

Note 1: The variable x is referenced in this file also. Again, the keyword `extern` indicates that x has been defined in a different file but will be referenced here. The external reference will be resolved at link time.

Learning Activities

11.   Find out if separate compilation of source files is possible with your implementation of C. If it is,

a.   Compile, link, and execute the program consisting of the files driver.c, output.c, and incr.c.

b. *C by Discovery*   Experiment with the placement of the declaration and external declaration of the variable x. Determine the answers to the following questions.

    i.   Can the declaration for x be omitted from driver.c?

    ii. Can the external reference to x in output.c be moved from the top of the file to a position inside the function? Can it be moved to the bottom of the file? Try these modifications to get the answer.

    iii. What happens if the word `extern` is omitted from the file output.c? Try it.

c. Explain the general concept illustrated by each of the above experiments.

12. In the above program, the variable x is initialized in the file driver.c. Modify the program so that a user can input the initial value rather than having it initialized in the source code. Modify it by creating a fourth source file named input.c that will access the variable x correctly and do the input. You will also need to modify the function `main()`.

The Static Storage Class with External Variables

Earlier in this section, we saw that global variables can be linked with variables declared externally in other modules. It is possible to have a situation in which a variable needs to be accessed by many functions in one module but should not be available to any other modules. The information it contains may need to be hidden from the other modules. That is, we want the variable to be global in its own source code file, but not to have external linkage.

We have seen that by default, a variable that is defined outside any function in a source code file has external linkage. This default can be defeated by declaring the variable to have storage class `static`. It can then be accessed by any function below its point of declaration in its source code file, but it will be unknown in other source code files. This `static` declaration affords a measure of privacy when needed.

Learning Activity

13. Consider again the modular example presented in this section. The variable x was defined as a global variable in the file driver.c. It was declared externally in both of the other files, output.c and incr.c.

Modify the module driver.c by changing the line

```
int x = 5;
```

to

```
static int x = 5;
```

Now try to compile the files again and link the three object files together. Did you get an error? If so, try to determine which phase of the compile-link phase reported the error.

A Word about Style

Note that the previous example had the sole purpose of demonstrating a modular program. It was extremely simple so that the elements of communication between the modules would be evident. However, it was not a model for a well-designed program. A program that simple would not need to be modularized. Also, the side effect caused when incr() changes the global variable x could easily be avoided by writing incr() to accept x as a parameter. If this was done, incr() would be more like a software tool. It would work in any program and would not depend on the program having a variable named x.

8.5 Typedefs

The typedef storage class is used to associate an identifier with a type. Unlike other storage classes, a typedef declaration does not cause any storage to be allocated. The word typedef is a key word in C; it appears in declarations. For example,

```
typedef long big_int;
```

will associate the identifier big_int with the type long.

A typedef can be viewed as similar to a #define preprocessor directive with the following differences: a typedef is processed by the compiler and is limited to data types; a #define directive is processed by the preprocessor and can be used to define constants, macros, and other entities as well as data types.

The syntax of using a typedef is:

```
typedef old_type new_type;
```

where new_type is the identifier being declared and old_type is a type declaration.

After a `typedef`, the new identifier can be used to declare variables of that type. For example,

```
typedef struct {
        float radius;
        float x_center;
        float y_center;
} CIRCLE;
```

might be declared to provide a data structure to hold information about a circle. This statement does not allocate any storage, it just associates the identifier `CIRCLE` with that particular structure. Later in the program, variables `c1` and `c1` can be defined with a declaration like

```
CIRCLE c1, c2;
```

where the identifier `CIRCLE` serves as the data type in the declaration. Since a `CIRCLE` is declared as a structure, the `radius` member of `c1` can be referenced with the syntax

```
c1.radius
```

Portability Considerations

`Typedef` declarations are often put in header files. They are used for readability and for portability. For example, suppose a program must be ported to many different computer systems on which word sizes vary. If a program needs the size of a certain type to be two bytes, a new type named `twobytes` might be defined with a `typedef`. The main program source code might make reference to the type `twobytes`. When this program is distributed, several header files might be supplied with the source. In one header, the definition might be

```
typedef int twobytes;
```

In another, the definition might be

```
typedef short twobytes;
```

When the program is configured for a certain system, the appropriate header file with the definitions that match the hardware and implementation of C would be included with a preprocessor directive and the program would be configured properly.

One specific example of this type of configuration is in the ANSI additions to the C compiler. In earlier compilers, the return value of many of the library functions was of type `int`. For example, consider the library function `strlen()` that calculates the length of a string. Since the number of bytes in an `int` varies on different computer systems, the type `int` as a return value poses a portability problem. With ANSI C, the return value of `strlen()` is defined to be of type `size_t`. The identifier `size_t` is declared in one of the standard header files supplied with an ANSI C compiler; the type `size_t` is generally one of the unsigned integer types. When any program declaring `strlen()` to be of type `size_t` is ported to a different ANSI C compiler, the type of the `strlen()` function will be automatically adjusted. In contrast, if `strlen()` is declared to return type `int` and the program is ported from a computer in which an `int` occupies two bytes to one in which an `int` occupies four bytes, a potential portability problem exists.

An Example of typedefs and Data Types

A `typedef` declaration can be used in the implementation of a data type. A data type would be declared with a `typedef`, and the specific operations for the data type would be implemented as C functions. After the declaration, a programmer would be able to use the data type without depending on the specifics of the implementation. The implementation could be changed to better match the specific application without causing the main program to be modified.

As an example, a stack is a data type that is defined as a list where all additions and insertions take place at the same end of the list. It is often called a *LIFO* (last in, first out); one familiar model is that of a stack of cafeteria trays. Trays are taken off the top, and additions to the stack of trays are added to the top.

The basic operations are to *push* (or add) a value to the top of the stack or to *pop* (or remove) a value from the top of the stack. A stack could be implemented as an array or a linked list. The basic operations would be implemented as functions in C. The functions `push()` and `pop()` would be written to access the underlying data type, but their functionality would remain the same in either case.

Examples 8-9, 8-10, and 8-11 illustrate an array implementation of a stack, using many of the concepts in this chapter and the previous one. The example consists of three files. The function `main()` appears in the file stackex.c; it is a driver and has the single purpose of testing the other code. The file stack.h is a header file; it contains the `typedef` declaration of a STACK and the ANSI prototype declarations of the stack utility functions.

The file stack.c is the stack utility module that contains the C source code for the functions `push()` and `pop()` that perform the major operations on the STACK. Three other functions have been included also. The function `is_empty()` checks to see if there is valid data in the stack; it returns a value of 1 if the STACK is empty and 0 otherwise. The function `is_full()` returns 1 if there is no room for additional data in the STACK and 0 otherwise. The function `init_stack()` initializes a STACK to the state where `is_empty()` tests true.

Before looking at the source code, we need to understand how these functions will work. The STACK is implemented as a structure with two members. The actual data is kept in the array member with the name `elts`, which has MAX elements. This STACK will contain elements of type `char`. The type could be modified for other use. The second member is an `int` named `top`. It will serve as an index into the array that indicates the element on the top of the stack.

After initialization by a call to `init_stack()`, a stack would have the configuration shown in Figure 8-1.

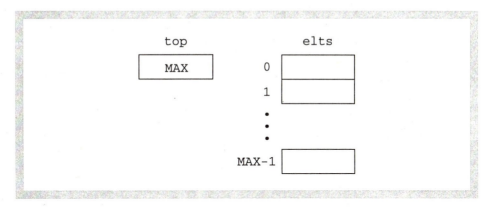

Figure 8-1

The index `top` would be set to one position beyond the bottom of the array to indicate that there is no meaningful data in the STACK.

A call to `push()` will put an element on the STACK. The element is put in the last available position in the array and the index `top` is adjusted to point to the element at the top of the array. The function `push()` takes two parameters, a pointer, S, indicating which STACK to access and the element to be pushed on the STACK. After the following three calls to `push()`,

```
push ('a', S);
push ('b', S);
push ('c', S);
```

the stack pointed to by S has the contents shown in Figure 8-2. The member `top` contains the index of the last element pushed on the stack.

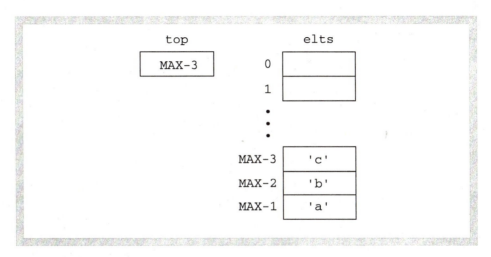

Figure 8-2

The function `pop()` takes a single parameter, a pointer to the STACK to be popped. After the call

    pop(S)

the STACK pointed to by S has the contents shown in Figure 8-3. Note that the element was not actually removed from the stack. The index `top` was adjusted instead. The function `pop()` returns the value that was at the top of the stack, the `'c'` in this case.

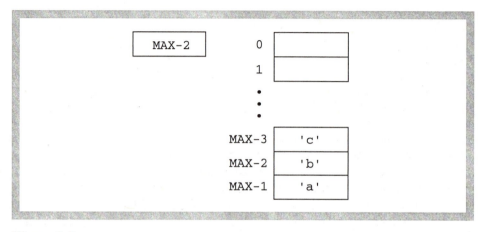

Figure 8-3

We start by examining the header file stack.h in Example 8-9. Note that ANSI C function prototypes are declared, which may need to be changed for older compilers.

 Example 8-9: stack.h

```
/*              stack.h
 *
 *    Contains the declaration of the data type STACK and the
 *    declarations of the stack utility functions. This header
 *    file should be included in every C source file that
 *    references a STACK or any of its utility functions.
 */

/* Constant Declarations */
#define MAX     8                                    /* Note 1 */

/* Type Descriptions */
```

```
typedef  struct {
         char  elts[MAX];
         int   top;
} STACK;                                               /* Note 2 */

/* Stack Utility Function Prototypes */
int push( char item, STACK *s_ptr );                   /* Note 3 */
int pop( STACK *s_ptr );
void init_stack( STACK *s_ptr );
int  is_empty( STACK s );
int  is_full( STACK s );
```

This file contains the `typedef` declaration of a STACK and the declarations of the associated utility functions. The file should be included with the `#include` preprocessor directive in every source code file that needs to declare a STACK.

Note 1: Currently, the constant MAX is set to 8. This is the maximum number of items that are allowed in a STACK. The choice of 8 makes it easy to test for things like overflow and underflow, but in a practical application, the number would probably be increased.

Note 2: The data type STACK has been declared with a `typedef`. In the program source code, reference can be made to a STACK instead of having to specify the contents of this structure. The stack contains an array, `elts`, that will hold the elements on the stack, and an integer, `top`, that acts as an index into that array and keeps track of the top of the stack.

Note 3: The next five lines of source code contain declarations of the five STACK utility functions. When this header file is included in a program, a programmer will not have to make additional declarations about the function types.

The second file to be discussed, stack.c, is listed in Example 8-10. It contains the declarations of the stack utility functions.

Example 8-10: stack.c

```
/*                  stack.c
 *
 *    Synopsis    - Not a full program!  This file contains the
 *                  stack utility functions push(), pop(),
 *                  init_stack(), is_empty(), and is_full().
 *
 *    Objective   - To illustrate use of typedef to create
 *                  a data structure.
 */
```

```c
/* Include Files */
#include "stack.h"                                            /* Note 1 */

/***************************** init_stack()  ****************/
/*    Initializes a stack to an empty state by setting         *
 *    top beyond the end of the array.                         */

void init_stack( STACK *s_ptr )                              /* Note 2 */
{
    s_ptr->top = MAX;                                       /* Note 3 */
}


/***************************** is_empty()  ****************/
/*    Returns 1 if the STACK is empty and 0 if not.          */

int is_empty( STACK s )
{
    if ( s.top >= MAX )                                     /* Note 4 */
        return ( 1 );
    else
        return ( 0 );
}


/***************************** is_full()  ****************/
/*    Returns 1 if the STACK is full, and 0 if not.          */

int is_full ( STACK s )
{
    if ( s.top <= 0 )                                       /* Note 5 */
        return ( 1 );
    else
        return ( 0 );
}


/***************************** push()  ****************/
/*    Puts a new item on the stack and adjusts top.          */

int push( char item, STACK *s_ptr )
{
    if ( is_full( *s_ptr ) )                                /* Note 6 */
        return ( -1 );
    else {
        s_ptr->top--;                                      /* Note 7 */
        s_ptr->elts[ s_ptr->top ] = item;
        return ( 0 );
```

```
    }
}

/*************************** pop()  ********************/
/*    Removes an item from the top of the stack, adjusts top,    *
 *    and returns the removed item, or -1 if the stack was       *
 *    empty.                                                      */

int pop( STACK *s_ptr )
{
    if ( is_empty( *s_ptr ) )                        /* Note 8 */
        return ( -1 );
    else {
                                                     /* Note 9 */
        return ( s_ptr->elts[ s_ptr->top++ ] );
    }
}
```

This module contains the five utility functions for a STACK. It needs to be linked with a function main() in order to execute.

Note 1: The header file stack.h is included here so that the declaration of STACK is known to all functions in this file.

Note 2: The identifier STACK is used in this declaration because it now represents a type. The parameter s_ptr is a pointer to a STACK. The function init_stack() will change the contents of the STACK pointed to by s_ptr. Even though the formal parameter is declared as type STACK *, the actual use in the function indicates that a more accurate description of the parameter type is *address of a* STACK. In use, a STACK should be declared in the calling function and the address of that variable should be passed to init_stack().

Note 3: To establish an empty STACK, the index, top, is set to one position beyond the bottom of the array of elements.

Note 4: The function is_empty() checks the index top to determine if the STACK is empty or not. A value of MAX indicates an empty STACK.

Note 5: Similarly, the function is_full() checks the index top to determine if there is still space in the STACK. A value of 0 for top indicates that the STACK is full.

Note 6: The function push() checks for overflow before pushing a new element on the STACK. If it is full, a value of -1 is returned to indicate that the attempt to push the element on the STACK was not successful.

Note 7: If space is still available in the elts array, the value of top is adjusted and the element is placed in the array. The return value of 0 indicates success. Note that the actual parameter to push() should be the address of a STACK instead of an uninitialized STACK * variable.

Note 8: The function pop() checks for underflow before popping an element from the STACK. The value −1 is returned if the STACK is empty. Because STACK has been implemented as an array of type char and the popped value is returned by pop(), a value that could not possibly be part of the array must be returned in case of failure to pop a value. Since the value −1 is not a char value, it was chosen as the return value in case of error.

Again the parameter to pop() should be the address of an existing STACK. The fact that pop() changes the contents of its parameter indicates this.

Note 9: All that is necessary to pop a value from the STACK is to increment the index top. The return statement returns the value at the cell in the elts array that is indexed by the old value of top and increments top.

The last module, stackex.c in Example 8-11, is the one containing the test program. It will simply read one line of input from the terminal and echo it back to the terminal with the characters reversed.

Example 8-11: stackex.c

```
/*                  stackex.c
 *
 *    Synopsis    - A driver program to test the stack utilities.
 *                  This program accepts a line of input from
 *                  standard input and displays the characters
 *                  in reverse order to standard output.
 *
 *    Objective   - To demonstrate and test the stack utilities.
 */

/* Include Files */
#include <stdio.h>
#include "stack.h"                                       /* Note 1 */

void main( void )
{
    char inbuff[80];
    int index;
    STACK st;                                            /* Note 2 */

    printf( "Enter a line of characters : " );
    gets( inbuff );

    init_stack( &st );                                   /* Note 3 */
    for ( index = 0; inbuff[index] != '\0'; index++ ) {
```

```
        push( inbuff[index], &st );
}

while ( !is_empty( st ) ) {
        putchar( pop( &st ) );
}
putchar( '\n' );
}
```

The function `main()` is in this source file. It is designed as a driver function to test the STACK utility functions. Note that no reference is made to the specifics of the implementation of a STACK. The constant MAX, the elts array, and the index top are not mentioned. The program is written using the identifier STACK and the STACK utility functions.

Note 1: The header file stack.h must be included to provide the declaration of a STACK.

Note 2: The identifier STACK is used as the type name in this declaration of a variable of type STACK.

Note 3: The address of the variable st is passed to those STACK utility functions that need a parameter of type STACK *. Since the functions change the contents of a STACK, it is not enough to pass in a pointer to a STACK; the address of a STACK declared in the program should be the actual parameter.

Learning Activities

14. If your compiler supports linking code from separate source files, compile and link the files stackex.c and stack.c. Execute the program with several different lines of input to ensure that it works properly.

15. If your compiler does not support separate source modules, you can make this program work by combining the files stackex.c and stack.c into one source code file. The second occurrence of the line

    ```
    #include "stack.h"
    ```

    should be omitted from your file before compiling it. Test the program with several different lines of input.

16 a. What happens if more characters are put into the stack than there is room for in the buffer? Do the stack utility functions allow you to overwrite the end of the array? Why or why not?

    b. Modify `main()` to output a diagnostic message when an attempt is made to overrun the array. The modification should not reference the constant MAX, the array elts, or the index

top, since those are part of the specifics of the STACK implementation. Instead, the values returned by the STACK utility
functions should be examined to provide the needed information.

17. Test stackex.c by entering a carriage return immediately after the
prompt. Does this cause any problems? Trace the execution of the
program by hand for this case.

18. *C by Discovery*   With the following declarations,

```
typedef int INTEGER;
int x;
INTEGER y;
```

will x and y be recognized as the same type? Write a short program to
test this. Your program will not need to do any more than declare and
initialize the variables and try to test them for equality, or to assign
one variable to the other to see if the compiler will allow the mixing
of these types.

8.6 Function Definitions

As with variables, there is a distinction between function definitions and function
declarations. We will discuss function definitions here. Declarations will be discussed in Section 8.7. Many examples of functions have appeared earlier in the
text. The information communicated by the function definition includes the function type, the function name (an identifier), the names, types and number of formal
parameters, and the executable statements for the function. The syntax for defining
the functions and the formal parameters will be reviewed here.

Formal Parameters in ANSI C

The parameters that appear in the heading in the function definition are called formal parameters. The parameters that appear in function calls are known as actual
parameters. The list of formal parameters must appear inside the parentheses that
follow the name of the function in the heading. The formal parameter list is a
comma-separated list of formal parameter declarations. The order of the parameter
declarations must match the order of the actual parameters in a function call. Each
formal parameter declaration consists of the type of the parameter followed by the
name by which it will be referenced in the function code. An example of the declaration of the formal parameters for a function appears below.

```
type function_name ( int param1, char *param2, int param3)
{
        /* function code goes here */
}
```

The function in the example takes three parameters named `param1`, `param2`, `param3`. Both `param1` and `param3` are of type `int`, while `param2` is a pointer to a `char`. The function code will reference these parameters by their names.[1]

If a function does not take any parameters, the formal parameter list should consist of the single keyword `void`, as in the following example.

```
type funct_name( void )
{
        /* function code */
}
```

Function Types

Another way that functions communicate with other parts of the program is through their return value and its type. When a function is defined, the function type appears first in the definition. The default type for a C function is type `int`. Any other type must be explicitly defined. Other possible function types include any of the integer or floating point types, pointers, structures, and unions. A function may not return an array or another function. The type of a function matches the type of the expression associated with its `return` statement.

If a function does not return a value, type `void` should be indicated in its definition. There are two ways in which a function will not return a value. First, a function may not contain a `return` statement. In this case, the function would terminate execution at the closing braces for the function block. Second, the `return` statement may be used without an accompanying expression.

If an expression accompanies the `return` statement, the value of the expression becomes the value of the function and the type of the expression becomes the function's type. In C, the function value can be assigned to a variable, as in the statement

```
total = sum(n1, n2, n3);
```

This assignment is optional. If the function does tasks other than simply returning

---

1. For older compilers, just the formal parameter names appear between the parentheses in the function heading. The declarations of the parameter types are like variable declarations except that they are placed between the function heading and the opening brace for the function block. An example of a function declaration in a non-ANSI compiler would be

```
type function_name ( param1, param2, param3 )
int param1, param3;
char *param2;
{
    /* function code goes here */
}
```

a value, it could be called without assigning the return value.

For example, a function could be written to find the end of a sentence in input. If it is known that every sentence in the input ends with either a period, a question mark, or an exclamation point, the code might be written as shown in Example 8-12.

Example 8-12: endofsen.c

```
/*                  endofsen.c
 *
 *    Synopsis    - A function that finds the end of a sentence if
 *                  it ends in '.', '?', '!'.  Returns 1 for
 *                  success, 0 for end-of-file.
 *
 *    Objective   - To illustrate a use for the return statement.
 */


/* Include Files */
#include <stdio.h>

int endofsen( int * punctptr )                              /* Note 1 */
{
    int iochar;
    while ( ( iochar = getchar() ) != EOF )
        if (( iochar == '.' ) || ( iochar == '?' )
                                || ( iochar == '!' )) {
            *punctptr = iochar;                             /* Note 2 */
            return 1;                                       /* Note 3 */
        }
    return 0;                                               /* Note 4 */
}
```

This is a single function, not a whole program. The input is read character by character in a while loop with getchar(). Each input character is tested against the given punctuation. The function will terminate its execution if getchar() reads one of the given punctuation marks or senses end of input (EOF).

Note 1: The parameter to endofsen() is punctptr. The punctuation mark that terminates the current input sentence will be passed back to the calling function in the parameter. Since a value of a variable in the calling function is to be changed, a pointer to that variable is passed into endofsen().

Note 2: If one of the punctuation marks is read, its value is assigned to the contents of the address in punctptr.

Note 3: If one of the given sentence terminators is read, the function returns the
value 1.

Note 4: This line will only be executed when end of input is sensed before one of
the stated punctuation marks. The return value is zero to indicate this situation.

This function might be used in a program to analyze English sentences and
classify them as questions, statements, or exclamations. In this case it would be
necessary to check the value of the parameter upon return from the function. However, if the program reads to the end of input without encountering one of the
specified punctuation marks, that fact should be checked by the program too. A
program to do that is shown in Example 8-13.

Example 8-13:   classify.c

```
/*                    classify.c
 *
 *    Synopsis    - Reads through English sentence input and counts
 *                  each sentence that ends with '.', '?', or '!'
 *                  as a statement, a question, or an exclamation.
 *
 *    Objective   - To illustrate checking the return value of a
 *                  function as well as the value of a parameter.
 */

/* Include Files */
#include <stdio.h>

/* Function Prototypes */
extern int endofsen( int * );

void main( void )
{
     int punct;
     int statementcounter = 0,
         questioncounter  = 0,
         exclaimcounter   = 0;

     printf( "Enter English sentences as input.  " );
     printf( "Terminate input with an End of File mark.\n" );

     while ( endofsen( &punct )) {                        /* Note 1 */
          if ( punct == '.' )                             /* Note 2 */
                  statementcounter++;
```

```
        else if ( punct == '?' )
                questioncounter++;
        else if ( punct == '!' )
                exclaimcounter++;
    }
    printf( "%d statements, %d questions, ",
                        statementcounter, questioncounter );
    printf( "and %d exclamations.\n",  exclaimcounter );
}
```

This program will need to be linked with the object code from the file endofsen.c. The linker will take care of the unresolved reference to the function `endofsen()` that appears in the `while` loop expression. Other than variable declarations, initializations, and calls to `printf()`, the code consists of a compound `if-else` statement nested inside a `while` loop.

Note 1: The `while` loop tests the value returned by `endofsen()`. If it is 1 (true), the loop will be entered because the end of a sentence was found. If it is 0 (false), the `while` loop will terminate because end of input was sensed.

Note 2: The value of `punct` is checked in the compound `if-else` statement. This statement is only executed when the end of a sentence is found, and in that case, `punct` contains the sentence-terminating punctuation mark. The classification of the sentence depends on this value.

Learning Activities

19.   Test classify.c with several different input streams.

a.   Does it work correctly with input consisting of English sentences that end in the characters '.', '?', '!'? (Does it work for the input for which it was designed?)

b.   If the input stream consists of the characters in the boxes below,

what is the output of the program? How many times would the function `endofsen()` be called?

c.   Does the program handle end-of-file correctly? Test it with empty input. Test it with the end of the last sentence coinciding with the end of the input stream. Test it with the input stream ending in mid-sentence without any punctuation.

d. Obviously this program would not behave correctly if there
were real numbers (containing decimal points) in the input
stream. List several other types of input that would cause the
program to misbehave.

Another use of the function `endofsen()` might be to simply position the
input pointer after the current sentence so that other input processing could take
place. As long as the other input processing would be doing its own checking on
the end of input, neither the parameter nor the return value of the function need be
checked. The program in Example 8-14 implements this situation. The function
that does the other input processing is written as a stub.

Example 8-14: position.c

```
/*              position.c
 *
 *   Synopsis   - Program calls endofsen() to read input up to
 *                the first occurrence of '.', '?', or '!' and
 *                then calls a stub function (that needs to be
 *                completed) to process the remaining input.
 *
 *   Objective  - To illustrate calling of a function for the
 *                tasks it performs and not for its return value
 *                or its parameter value.
 */

/* Include Files */
#include <stdio.h>

/* Function Prototypes */
extern int endofsen( int * );
void processinput( void );

void main( void )
{
    int dummy;

    printf( "Enter your input now.  Terminate by " );
    printf( "signaling end of file.\n" );

    endofsen( &dummy );                              /* Note 1 */
```

```
        processinput();
}

/***************************** processinput()  ***********/
/*   A stub function.   It reads to end of input.
 */

void processinput( void )
{
        int iochar;

        while (( iochar = getchar() ) != EOF ) {            /* Note 2 */
            /* code for processing would go here */
        }
}
```

Two functions, `main()` and `processinput()`, make up this file. The object code from this module would be linked with the object code from `endofsen()` before execution. The function `main()` simply prompts for input and calls the other two functions. The function `processinput()` is a stub. A `while` loop reads through input to end of file.

Note 1: This call to `endofsen()` is different from the call in classify.c. The return value is not assigned to any variable or checked in any way. The parameter is simply a place holder. Its value upon return from the function is not checked either.

Note 2: Because the return value from `endofsen()` was not checked, it is imperative that `processinput()` check for end of input. Depending on the processing to be done and what is known about the form of input, the technique for checking may change.

Learning Activities

20. Test position.c with several different input streams.
21. Make a list of input situations in which the program would not behave correctly.
22. Comment on the practice of ignoring the information passed back by a function in its return value and in its parameter. Rewrite the program to meet your criteria.

8.7 Function Declarations and Calls

When a function is called, an execution environment is created for the function and control passes to its code. The execution environment contains memory for the parameters to the function and any local variables. When the function terminates execution, the memory space occupied by the execution environment is returned to the system for other use. The space occupied by the local variables and parameters is not guaranteed to retain their contents.

A function call consists of the function name and a pair of parentheses enclosing a list of the actual parameters. The actual parameters (also called the arguments) to a function are those expressions that appear in a call to that function. The program communicates with the function through the actual parameters in the function calls.

If a parameter is passed by value, as it is in C, the current values of the actual parameters are copied to a special place in memory (usually a stack) where the function will access them. This occurs every time the function is called. In the function, changes to parameters are made to these copies. The values of the actual parameters are not touched. Diagrams indicating the execution environment for the program param.c appeared in Section 4.4.

Declarations (Prototypes) of Functions in ANSI C

A feature that is new with the ANSI Standards for C is that of function prototyping. This new syntax for a function declaration consists of the return type of a function, the function name and a list of the types of the formal parameters inside a pair of parentheses. The number and types of the parameters in the prototype declaration should match the number and types of the parameters in the function heading and the function call. As an example, the prototype declaration for the function strcpy() is given here.

```
char *strcpy( char *, const char * );[1]
```

The information communicated by this declaration includes the number and the type of the parameters as well as the type returned by the function. The declaration could appear either in an external position (outside a function) above the position where strcpy() was called, in an included header file, or in the function block where the call to strcpy() appears.

Function prototype declarations allow the C compiler to check the type and number of parameters. This was not a possibility in earlier C compilers.

In an older C compiler, if a function returned a value with type other than int, a declaration that could be seen by the calling function was necessary so that the program would set up correctly for the return value. The information contained in that declaration consisted of just the function's type and its name. For example, an old-style declaration of strcpy() would be

---

1. The keyword const is new in ANSI C. It is a type qualifier and indicates that the second parameter will not be changed. It is added in ANSI C for additional optimization possibilities.

```
char *strcpy();
```

ANSI compilers will accept the old-style function declarations for a transition period. For this reason, the syntax

```
char *strcpy();
```

is taken to mean that the compiler can make no assumptions about parameters to `strcpy()`. It turns off type checking; it does *not* mean that `strcpy()` does not take any parameters. If a function does not take any parameters, its prototype declaration would contain the keyword `void` between the parentheses. For example,

```
char *f1( void );
```

declares `f1()` as a function that does not take parameters and returns a `char *` value.

Currently, the old-style declarations are more portable because not every system has an ANSI C compiler. However, if you do have an ANSI C compiler, you should use the new prototype declarations. The ability of the compiler to do parameter checking is very desirable.

A Closer Look

In the old style of function parameter declaration, a difficulty with type checking arose from the fact that different source files were compiled separately. There was no mechanism for communicating the type and number of parameters to a C function across the different files. The verification of the number and type of the parameters to a function was left to the programmer. Now the ANSI C prototype declarations include the function type and the number and type of the formal parameters.

With ANSI C prototyping, the declared type of a parameter is explicit; the compiler will expect the declared type. An actual parameter may be converted to the expected type by the usual conversion rules in C, but the converted value must match the formal parameter in type. It is still possible to pass an actual parameter that does not match the declared parameter type in the function; however, it is now necessary to explicitly cast the actual parameter to the declared type.

Scope of Function Declarations

Since the function name in a function definition is outside a function block, functions will have external linkage by default. This default can be defeated by defining the function with the `static` storage class. As with `static` variables defined externally to a function block, a `static` function will not be known outside its source file.

When a function is called whose code does not appear in the source file, the function is assumed by the compiler to have external linkage. An attempt to resolve the reference will occur during the link phase of the compilation. The linker will search other specified object files as well as the standard or specifically named libraries for the function definition. An error is reported only if the function is not found.

An Example

The program avg.c in Example 8-15 illustrates the syntax for declaring and defining functions that return values other than int. The ANSI C prototype is used. The program calculates the mean or average of a collection of integers.

Example 8-15: avg.c

```
/*                  avg.c
 *
 *    Synopsis    - Computes and displays the average of
 *                  a set of up to 100 integers.
 *
 *    Objective   - To illustrate the syntax of a function returning
 *                  a noninteger value. Also illustrates the use of
 *                  the value returned by scanf().
 */

/* Include Files */
#include <stdio.h>

/* Constant Declarations */
#define MAX 100

/* Function Prototypes */
float average( int[], int );                              /* Note 1 */
int getinputvalues( int[] );

void main( void )
{
    int count;
    int values[MAX];

    printf( "Enter your data now. " );
    printf( "Enter one integer per line.\n" );
    printf( "Enter 'Q' when you want to quit.\n" );

    count = getinputvalues( values );                     /* Note 2 */
                                                          /* Note 3 */
    printf( "The average is %5.2f.\n", average( values, count ));
}
```

```
/***************************** getinputvalues()  *************/
/*   Reads integers from the keyboard until a noninteger is
 *   found. Puts the input into an array. Returns the number of
 *   integers input.
 */

int getinputvalues( int *valarray )                    /* Note 4 */
{
     int i = 0;

     printf( ">  " );
                                                       /* Note 5 */
     while ( i < MAX && scanf( "%d", valarray + i )) {
          i++;
          printf( ">  " );
     }
     return ( i );
}


/***************************** average()  *********************/
/*   Calculates and returns the average of the integers in
 *   the array intarray.
 */

float average( int *intarray, int count )              /* Note 6 */
{
     int i, sum = 0;

     if ( count != 0 ) {
          for ( i = 0; i < count; i++ )
               sum += intarray[i];
          return ( ( float ) sum / count );            /* Note 7 */
     }
     else
          return ( 0.0 );                              /* Note 8 */
}
```

The program consists of three functions, main(), getinputvalues(), and average(). The function main() makes its declarations, prompts for input, and calls the other functions. The function getinputvalues() reads the integers that are entered. It uses a while loop and stores the input into an array. It also keeps track of how many integers are entered. The function average() calculates the sum and returns the average.

Note 1: The function average() returns a noninteger value. It must be declared. The ANSI C prototype also gives the type and the number of parameters to `average()`.

Note that names for the parameters could be optionally included in the prototype. These names do not have to match either the names of the formal parameters in the definition of `average()` or the names of the actual parameters in any call. As an example, these prototype declarations could be given as

```
float average( int x[], int y );
int getinputvalues( int z[] );
```

More often the names are be omitted entirely as in this program.

The prototype declaration of `getinputvalues()` appears on the next line. Since this function returns a value of type `int`, it was not absolutely necessary to declare it. However, without this declaration, the parameter checking would not be done.

Note 2: In this call to `getinputvalues()`, the actual parameter is the array `values`. The function `getinputvalues()` is to fill up the array, so the array must be declared in the program to allocate the space properly. The address of the first cell in the array is passed to the function. The function will return the number of cells into which it placed a value.

Note 3: The function `average()` returns a value of type `float`. This is converted by `printf()` to the `%f` format. It will use a minimum field width of five spaces with two decimal places.

Note that `printf()` is an example of a function whose code does not appear in this source code file. The compiler assumes that `printf()` has external linkage and the reference is resolved by the linker.

Note 4: The function `getinputvalues()` returns an `int`; the inclusion of the return type is optional here. The parameter is declared to have type `int *`. This type is compatible with the type in the prototype declaration above `main()`. Note that it is important to know what this function does with its parameter. An unknowledgeable programmer might call this function by passing it an uninitialized `int *` variable instead of the address of an array. If the space for the array has not been allocated properly, the program may have unexpected results.

Note 5: Two conditions control this `while` loop. First the index into the array is checked to insure that the array bounds are not overrun. Then the value returned by `scanf()` is checked.

In this case, `scanf()` reads the sequence of digits on the input line, converts them to a value of type `int`, and stores this result in the array. The function `scanf()` returns the number of successful conversions. In this case, 1 would be returned if a conversion was made and 0 would be returned if noninteger characters were encountered before any conversion took place.

A sequence of input digits would cause a successful conversion and the `while` loop would be entered. When an alphabetic character such as `'Q'` is entered, `scanf()` would return 0 and the `while` loop would terminate.

Note that scanf() is another example of a function in which external linkage is assumed. The code for scanf() will be found by the linker when the C library is searched. A prototype declaration for scanf() is usually in the file stdio.h.

Note 6: The function average() returns a float and takes two parameters, the address of the first cell in an array of type int, and an int. The array contains the integers that were entered and the int indicates the number of meaningful elements in the array.

Note 7: The return value is (sum / count). Since both sum and count are variables of type int, the result of this operation would be of type int also. The variable sum is cast to type float to preserve the fractional part of this quotient.

Note 8: The function average() returns a value of 0.0 when the number of elements entered was 0. It might be desirable to choose a more appropriate return value since the average of a set of input integers could be 0.0.

Learning Activities

23. Execute avg.c to make sure it runs as you expected.

24. Modify avg.c in the following ways. After each modification, recompile the program, and if that is successful, test the program by entering the integers 1, 2, 3, 4. The result should be 2.50.

   a. Move the declaration of average() from above main() to a position with the declaration inside main(). What happens when you test it?

   b. Remove the declaration of average() from the new position inside main(). What happens when you test it this time?

   c. Remove the keyword float from the first line of the function definition. At this point the type of the function should not be mentioned in your modified version of the program. What happens when you test the program this time?

   d. Now add both declarations of average() as type float to their original positions. Remove the cast, (float), from the return statement in average(). What happens when you test the program?

   e. Try to generalize from these experiences about the types of functions, their declarations, and their return values.

> 25.   Experiment with `scanf()`. Try entering different input to see what
> the action is. What happens when you signal end of input? What hap-
> pens for the other control characters? The alphabetics? The punctua-
> tion marks? If you have access to the documentation for `scanf()`,
> read about its return value. Did `scanf()` behave as the documenta-
> tion specified?

8.8 Pointers to Functions

When a C program is compiled and loaded into memory, the executable code is
organized in such a way that an address is associated with every identifier with
either external linkage or `static` storage class. This is true of identifiers that represent variables, as well as identifiers that name functions.

When the name of a function is mentioned in C source code, it is interpreted as
the address of the code for that function in memory. This is analogous to the use of
an array name to mean the address of the first cell of the array.

In C it is possible to declare a variable that is a pointer to a function returning
any legitimate type. The values that can be assigned to such a variable are the
addresses of functions in the source code.

An example of an ANSI C prototype of a pointer to a function returning an `int`
is

```
int ( *fnptr )( char *s, int i );¹
```

Notice that the type and number of the parameters to the function are specified
also. To decode this declaration, we note first that anything of the form

```
(*fnptr)( ____, ____ )
```

is an `int`. Also we note that the parentheses around `*fnptr` serve to bind the `*`
more closely to the identifier `fnptr` than the pair of parentheses. Removing the
parentheses next, we see that `(*fnptr)` is a function returning an `int` and taking
two parameters, a `char *` and an `int`. The final step removes the dereferencing
operator, `*`, and tells us that `fnptr` is a pointer to the function returning an `int`
and taking a `char *` and an `int` as parameters.

In the declaration

```
float (*fn (int y, float z)) (char *x);
```

`fn` is a function that takes two parameters: `y` of type `int` and `z` of type `float`.
The value returned by `fn()` is a pointer to a function that returns a `float` and
takes a single parameter of type `char *`. This declaration and other C declarations

---

1. In the older style of declaration, a pointer to a function returning an `int` would have the following form:
   `int ( *fnptr )();`

can be decoded in the same way as the previous example. Each set of tokens can be removed in the order dictated by precedence and parentheses and the type of the resulting expression can be determined. Gaining this skill takes practice.

To illustrate this concept, we will use the `signal()` library function. In certain instances, when a software error or some external event occurs, a signal can be sent from the operating system to a running program. For example, a user who wants to abort a running program might press a sequence of keys to request the operating system to abort that program. The operating system then sends a special signal to the program to cause it to terminate. Other cases when a signal might be sent are when a program encounters a floating point error, an overflow condition, or an illegal memory reference. Each of these conditions might cause the operating system to "signal" the program to terminate.

In contrast, the user might notice that the same sequence of keys pressed to abort a running program has a totally different effect when in an editor program. This is due to the signal-handling properties of the editor program. When the interrupt sequence of keys is pressed, the operating system will still send the signal to the editor program, but the editor program handles the signal differently. This signal handling can be done with the `signal()` library function. It is a part of the standard C library that is delivered with ANSI C compilers.

The purpose of the `signal()` library function is to specify how a particular signal is to be handled. It takes two parameters, the signal number that is to be handled and the address of the function that should be executed when a signal occurs. The type of the second parameter is pointer to function.

An ANSI C implementation should provide a header file, signal.h, that contains the relevant signal numbers for each system. Each signal has a specific meaning and a specific default action set by the system. When the `signal()` library function is called, the default action can be changed.

The function `signal()` also returns a pointer to a function. Its value could be the address of the previous signal-handling routine, a representative of the default, or a system-provided signal-handling routine. The program signal.c in Example 8-16 illustrates signal handling and the use of a pointer to a function.

The example is very simple in concept. An infinite loop is started. The only way out of this program would be to press the keys on the keyboard to signal an interrupt. Usually, when those keys are pressed, the program would terminate quietly. Any messages would be issued by the operating system. With this new signal handling, the program will output the message "`You got me!`" before terminating.

Example 8-16: signal.c

```
/*              signal.c
 *
 *   Synopsis    - Changes the interrupt signal handling to display
```

```
*                  a message before terminating the program.
*
*    Objective  - To illustrate a use for a pointer to a function.
*/

/* Include Files */
#include <stdio.h>
#include <stdlib.h>
#include <signal.h>                                          /* Note 1 */

/* Function Prototypes */
void printit( void );

void main()
{
    signal( SIGINT, printit );                               /* Note 2 */
    while ( 1 )
        printf( "Still looping.\n" );
}

/****************************** printit()  *****************/
/*    Displays a message and terminates the program.
 */

void printit( void )
{
    printf( "You got me!\n" );
    exit( 0 );
}
```

The program consists of the functions `main()` and `printit()`. The code for `main()` consists of a call to `signal()` and an infinite loop. The code for `printit()` consists of a call to `printf()` and a call to `exit()`.

Note 1: The file signal.h is included. It contains the list of signal numbers and the proper declaration of the `signal()` library function. As an example, the signal.h header file from one ANSI C compiler contains the following prototype declaration of `signal()`:

```
void (*signal(int sig, void (*sighandler)(int)))(int);
```

This gives the following information about `signal()`:

a. It returns a pointer to a function that does not return any value and takes a single parameter of type `int`.

b. The parameters to signal are a value of type `int`, and a pointer to a function that does not return any value and takes a single parameter of type `int`. The return value from signal is the address of the previous signal handler, and the second parameter is the address of the new signal handler.

Note 2: In this call to signal (), the signal being handled is SIGINT, the interrupt signal. The function to be executed when an interrupt occurs is printit (). The return value from signal () is ignored.

Be aware that in this section, the example of signal handling was used to show a use for pointers to functions. This section did not provide a complete discussion of signal handling. Much of the signal handling is dependent on the specific operating system and hardware. This discussion is beyond the scope of this text.

Learning Activities

26. a. If the signal-handling functions are available on your system, run the program signal.c to see how it works.

   b. Modify signal.c by removing the call to exit () in printit (), and run the program again. Explain what you think happened this time.

27. Decode the following declarations. When one of the identifiers is a function or a pointer to a function, state the return type of the function and the type of the parameters.

   a. In the declaration

   ```
   int (*compare)(void * val; void * datum);
   ```

   state the types of compare, val, and datum.

   b. In the declaration

   ```
   float (*what ( char *x, int (*y)(char *z))) (int w);
   ```

   state the types of what, w, x, y, and z.

Language Elements Introduced in This Chapter: A Review

✓ ANSI Function Definitions

```
• type function_name( int param1, char *param2,
                                    int param3)
{
   /* function code goes here */
}
```

✓ **ANSI Function Prototype Declarations**

- ```
  type function_name( int param1, char *param2,
                                 int param3 );
  ```

- ```
  char f1( void );              /* No parameters */
  ```

✓ **Pointers to Functions**

- ```
  int ( *fnptr )( char *s, int i );  /* ANSI C */
  ```

- ```
  int ( *fnptr )();    /* old style */
  ```

✓ **Storage Class Specifiers**

- `auto`
- `static`
- `register`
- `extern`
- `typedef`

✓ **Types**

- ```
  typedef old_type  new_type;
  ```

✓ **Variable Declarations**

- ```
  auto int counter;
  ```

- ```
  static int counter;
  ```

- ```
  register int counter;
  ```

- ```
  extern int x;
  ```

Things to Remember

1. `auto` and `register` variables are created each time their function is called.
2. External and `static` variables are in existence during the full time of program execution.
3. It is illegal to use the address operator, &, with the name of a register variable.
4. Different implementations of C might impose restrictions on the number and type of `register` variables allowed.
5. Local variables are declared inside a function or block. They can only be accessed in that function or block and are unknown outside it.
6. Global (external) variables are declared outside function blocks and can be referenced by any function in the file that occurs after the declaration of the variable.
7. If a local variable in a function has the same name as a global variable, all ref-
  ```

erences to that name will access the local variable.

8. A side effect is produced when a function modifies the value of a global variable. Side effects should be kept to a minimum and clearly documented with comments.

9. A source module consists of source code related to a single task. In C each source module can be put in a separate file and compiled separately. The corresponding object modules must be linked together before the program can be executed.

10. By default, external variables have external linkage. This default is overridden by declaring an external variable with `static` storage class.

11. `typedefs` associate an identifier with a type.

12. `typedefs` are used for readability and portability. They are often put in header files.

13. A stack is a data type defined as a list in which all additions and insertions take place at the same end of the list. The basic operations are to push (or add) a value to the top of the stack and to pop (or remove) a value from the top of the stack.

14. The parameters as they appear in the definition of the function are called formal parameters. The parameters that appear in function calls are known as actual parameters.

15. ANSI compilers will accept the old-style function declarations for a transition period.

16. In ANSI C, the syntax `char *f_name();` is taken to mean that the compiler can make no assumptions about parameters to `f_name()`.

17. The ANSI C prototype declarations allow the compiler to check the type and number of the parameters in a function call. This was not possible with older compilers.

18. Functions have external linkage by default. This default can be defeated by defining the function with the `static` storage class.

19. When the name of a function is mentioned in C source code, it is interpreted as the memory address of the code for that function.

Exercises and Programming Problems

1. Write two versions of a program that displays the following table:

X	X cubed
1	1
2	8
3	27
4	64
. . .	

Have the table continue until x is 20.

   a. For the first version, write a function to do the cube calculation that takes a single parameter. If the parameter is 2 on entry to the function, the parameter should have the value 8 on exit from the function. That is, implement a "pass by reference" on the function's parameter and have the cubed value passed back in the parameter.

   b. For the second version, write a function that does the cubing, but, have the cubed value passed back to the main program as the return value of the function.

2. Write a function that interchanges two values of type int. Write a driver program to test your function.

3. Write a program that accepts input of the date in the form

```
1/14/94
```

and outputs it in the form

```
January 14, 1994
```

Write the program in a structured style, and plan the communication between parts of the program before you start coding.

4. Write a program that reads from standard input and displays the number of characters, words, and lines that it reads. For this problem, a word will be defined as a sequence of characters delimited by whitespace (a blank, ' ', a tab, '\t', or a newline, '\n'). Use the communication concepts in this chapter.

5. Predict the output of the following program by filling in the blanks below.

```c
/*                          epp5.c                          */

/* Include Files */
#include <stdio.h>

/* Global Variables */
int   W, X, Y, I;

/* Function Prototypes */
void demonstrate( int *y, int v );

void main( void )
{
    W = 3;
    X = 2;
    Y = 1;
    I = 2;
```

```
        demonstrate( &W, Y );
        printf( "%d, %d, %d, %d\n", W, X, Y, I );

        demonstrate( &I, X );
        printf( "%d, %d, %d, %d\n", W, X, Y, I );

}

void demonstrate( int* Y, int V )
{

    int    W, X;

    X  = (*Y) * V;
    W  = X / 2;
    *Y = W - V;
    I++;
    printf( "%d, %d, %d, %d\n",  V, W, X, *Y );
}
```

Output: ___, ___, ___, ___
       ___, ___, ___, ___
       ___, ___, ___, ___
       ___, ___, ___, ___

6. Predict the output of the following program by filling in the blanks below.

```
/*                          epp6.c                          */

/* Include Files */
#include <stdio.h>

/* Global Variables */
int int1 = 7,
    int2 = 8,
    int3 = 9;

/* Function Prototypes */
void p1( int *x, int y );

void main( void )
{
    int int3, int4, int5;

    int1 = 1;
    int2 = 2;
    int3 = 3;
```

```
        int4 = 4;
        int5 = 5;
        p1( &int3, int4 );
        printf( "int1 %d, int2 %d, int3 %d, int4 %d, int5 %d\n",
                        int1, int2, int3, int4, int5 );

        p1( &int2, int5 );
        printf( "int1 %d, int2 %d, int3 %d, int4 %d, int5 %d\n",
                        int1, int2, int3, int4, int5 );
}

void p1( int *x, int y )
{
    static int int2 = 5;
            int int1 = 2;

    *x = *x + 3;
    y  = y - 4;
    int1 *= 2;
    int2 += 5;
    int3 -= 1;

    printf( "int1 %d, int2 %d, int3 %d, *x %d, y %d\n",
                    int1, int2, int3, *x, y );
}
Output:  int1 ____, int2 ____, int3 ____, *x ____, y ____
         int1 ____, int2 ____, int3 ____, int4 ____, int5 ____
         int1 ____, int2 ____, int3 ____, *x ____, y ____
         int1 ____, int2 ____, int3 ____, int4 ____, int5 ____
```

7. Write a program to do fraction arithmetic. A sample run follows:

```
Welcome to the Fraction Arithmetic program.
------------------------------------------
Your problems with fractions can be solved here. Enter a
fraction arithmetic problem (Example 2/5 - 4/7).  1/2 + 1/4
The answer is 6/8.
```

Your program should handle the operations of addition, subtraction, multiplication and division. The answer does not have to be in lowest terms for this version of the program.

Plan your program so that it is modular. Have the input done in one module, the output done in a second module, and the calculation done in a third. Put each module in a separate source code file. The function main() should reside in its own module and be a driver program. If possible, try to write the program without using any global variables.

8. Write a program that will simulate a soft drink machine that dispenses four

types of soft drinks. The program will accept character input only. The symbols `'C'`, `'O'`, `'L'`, and `'S'` will stand for the drinks (Cola, Orange, Lemon, and Spritzer). The symbols `'N'`, `'D'`, and `'Q'` will stand for the coins (nickel, dime, and quarter). No other coins will be accepted. The character `'R'` when read as input will stand for the coin return. Any time that an `'R'` is input, all money should be returned to the user.

The program will output messages that simulate the output from the soft drink machine. For example, `"Cola    dispensed,"`   `"30    cents returned,"` `"Sorry, out of Spritzer,"` or `"Your change is 10 cents."`

In addition to accepting input of the money and drink selections, and displaying messages to the user, the program will internally keep track of the amount of change, and the inventory of each drink. A sample run follows.

```
Enter 65 cents for a drink > Q
 25 cents received          > D
 35 cents received          > D
 45 cents received          > Q
 70 cents received
Make your drink selection now  > O
Orange drink dispensed
5 cents in change given

Enter 65 cents for a drink > Q
25 cents received              > Q
50 cents received              > C
Sorry, insufficient funds entered
Please enter additional 15 cents > R
50 cents returned

Enter 65 cents for a drink >
```

Write your program in a modular structured style with the different modules in separate source files. Plan the communication between the different parts of the program. Minimize your use of global variables.

9. The data structure stack was discussed in Section 8-5. A queue is another specialized list in which insertions are done at one end (the rear) of the list and deletions are done at the other (the front of the list). For example, a supermarket check-out line operates on the queue principle. Like a stack, a queue can also be implemented with an array. In addition to the array to hold the elements, two additional values must be stored, the index of the front of the list and the index of the rear of the list. Note that a queue can start and end at any position of the array. For example, if the array contains 8 cells, consider the configuration after 8 additions to the queue and 3 deletions, as shown in Figure 8-4.

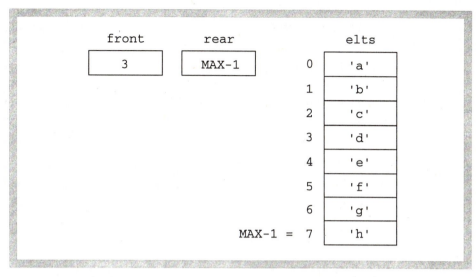

Figure 8-4   After Inserting a, b, c, d, e, f, g, h and Deleting a, b, c

The next addition to the queue would not fit at that end of the array but could be stored in the cell with index 0 in a wraparound or circular fashion. The resulting configuration is shown in Figure 8-5.

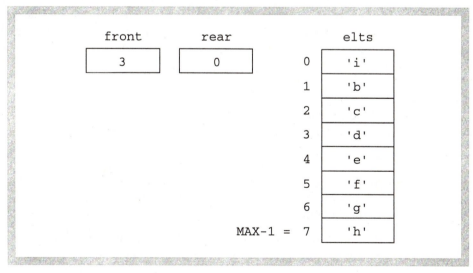

Figure 8-5   After Inserting i

a. Write a declaration of a data structure to store a queue where the elements are of type `char`.

b. To add an element to the rear of a queue is to enqueue the element. Write a function `enqueue()` that takes the following parameters: an element of type `char` that is to be enqueued, and a pointer to the queue that will receive the addition. Have the function return 1 for success and 0 for failure in case the queue is already full.

c. To delete an element from the queue is to "dequeue" an element. Implement the function `dequeue()`. Have it take a single parameter, the queue, and have it return the value dequeued or -1 in case of error (the queue was empty).

d. Write the utility functions `is_full()`, `is_empty()`, and `init_queue()` to complete your queue implementation.

10. Consider the following `typedef` declaration of a different implementation of a string. This should be similar to your declaration for problem 8 of Chapter 7.

```
typedef struct {
        char word[80];
        short length;
} STRING;
```

a. Write a conversion function with the ANSI C prototype

```
STRING *strconv( STRING *newform, char * oldform );
```

that will take C's usual representation of a string and convert it to a value of type `STRING` which is stored in the contents of newform. Have your function report an error by returning a `NULL` pointer if the string `oldform` does not fit correctly in `newform->word`. What should be the value returned in the member `newform->word` in case of buffer overflow?

b. Write a version of the string copy function that will copy one element of type `STRING` to another.

c. Modify your version of the string concatenation function. It should have ANSI C prototype

```
STRING *strconcat( STRING *s1, STRING *s2 );
```

and should concatenate s2 onto the end of s1. Have your function report an error by returning a `NULL` pointer if the concatenated string would overflow the buffer.

11. The package for the data type stack was written with an array implementation. Rewrite this package using a linked list implementation.

a. Use a `typedef` to declare a `node` that has space for a data element and a pointer to the next `node`. Your stack will be represented by a pointer to a node. After the elements `'a'`, `'b'`, and `'c'` are pushed on, in that order, a stack s would have the following representation:

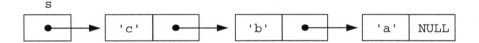

After a `pop()` operation, the stack s would have the following configuration:

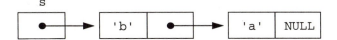

b. Write C functions for the operations `push()`, `pop()`, `is_full()`, `is_empty()` and `init_stack()`. These functions should take the same parameters and return the same values and types as the functions in the text. You will need to read the documentation for the C library functions `malloc()` and `free()` and dynamically allocate each addition to the linked list.

c. Put the `typedef` declarations and the function declarations in a header file stack.h and the function definitions in a file stack.c. (You may want to save your other versions of stack.h and stack.c first.) Test your package with the program stackex.c. It should run properly without any changes to stackex.c.

Multidimensional Arrays and Double Indirection

9.1 Two-Dimensional Arrays

A two-dimensional array can be thought of as a matrix or rectangle of elements. For example,

	Col 0	Col 1	Col 2	Col 3
Row 0	3.1	7.6	9.4	2.2
Row 1	5.3	8.2	1.4	2.7
Row 2	6.0	4.2	7.8	5.1

This depicts a two-dimensional array with base type `float`. It has three rows and four columns. Indices are used to access the elements in each cell of the array. In this array, the row indices start at 0 and terminate at 2 and the column indices start at 0 and terminate at 3. The element 4.2 is in the position with row index 2 and column index 1. This could be referred to as the `[2][1]` position.

    A two-dimensional array is declared by stating the type of its elements, the variable name, and both dimensions in brackets (`[]`). The following line of code declares a two-dimensional array of `float` elements. The name of the array is

459

two_d and it will have 3 rows and 4 columns. It would serve to declare the array depicted above.

```
float two_d[3][4];
```

The expression two_d[2][3] would reference the element in the [2][3] position, with row index 2 and column index 3. Its value is 5.1.

A two-dimensional array in C is more accurately described as an array of arrays. An equivalent declaration of the variable two_d is

```
float (two_d[3])[4];
```

which indicates that two_d is an array of 3 elements and each element is an array of 4 floats. This concept is discussed in more detail in the **A Closer Look** part of Section 9.4.

The program determ.c[1] in Example 9-1 gives an illustration of declaring and accessing the elements in a two-dimensional array. A 2 x 2 array of type float is declared, and its determinant is calculated.

Example 9-1: determ.c

```
/*                  determ.c
 *
 *   Synopsis   - Accepts input of elements for a 2 x 2 matrix
 *                and calculates its determinant.
 *
 *   Objective  - To show the basics of two-dimensional arrays.
 */

/* Include Files */
#include <stdio.h>

void main( void )
{
    int i, j;
    float m[2][2], determinant;                      /* Note 1 */

    printf( "Calculate the determinant of a 2x2 matrix.\n" );
    printf( "--------- --- ----------- -- - --- -------\n" );

    printf("\nEnter the matrix now.\n");
                                                     /* Note 2 */
```

---

1. This program finds a bug in some versions of one of the C/C++ compilers on a microcomputer. If the program terminates abnormally without allowing the user to enter a value, you will need to consult the documentation supplied with the compiler and add the code suggested there in order for the program to execute properly.

```
for ( i = 0; i <= 1; i++ )
    for ( j = 0; j <= 1; j++ ) {
        printf( "\tPosition %d,%d: ", i+1, j+1 );
        scanf( "%f", &m[i][j] );                    /* Note 3 */
    }
                                                    /* Note 4 */

determinant = m[0][0] * m[1][1] - m[0][1] * m[1][0];

printf( " The determinant is %8.2f\n", determinant );
}
```

The program consists of the single function `main()`. Calls to `printf()` are used to prompt the user for input and give the result. A call to `scanf()` inside a set of nested `for` loops does the input. Calculation of the determinant is done with a single assignment statement.

Note 1: The variable `m` is a two-dimensional array of `float` values. It has two rows and two columns. Both the row and column indices will go from 0 to 1.

Note 2: The following nested `for` loops are used to access each element in the two-dimensional array. The outer `for` loop works through the rows of the array. The inner `for` loop works through the elements in a row. Each row will be indexed by the variable `i` and each column by `j`.

Note 3: Accessing an element of the array `m` requires two subscripts. The expression `m[i][j]` is the element in the ith row and j^{th} column; `&m[i][j]` is the address of that cell and is passed as the parameter to `scanf()`. Recall that `scanf()` requires an address.

Note 4: The determinant is calculated by multiplying the elements in the `[1][1]` and `[2][2]` positions and subtracting the product of the elements in the `[1][2]` and `[2][1]` positions. The array name followed by two indices is used to access each element.

Learning Activities

1. Declare a two-dimensional array of type `int` with 3 rows and 3 columns.

2. Write a program to accept the input for the elements and calculate the determinant of a 3x3 matrix of integers. If the matrix is given by

$$\begin{pmatrix} a_{11} & a_{12} & a_{13} \\ a_{21} & a_{22} & a_{23} \\ a_{31} & a_{32} & a_{33} \end{pmatrix}$$

the determinant can be calculated using the formula:

```
a11*a22*a33 + a12*a23*a31 + a21*a32*a13
- a12*a33*a21 - a11*a23*a32 - a13*a22*a31
```

9.2 Storage Class and Scope of Multidimensional Arrays

Multidimensional arrays follow the same rules regarding storage class, scope, and initialization properties as variables of other types.

If the previous declaration of two_d appeared inside a function, the variable two_d would have the default storage class of auto, would be created when the block starts executing and destroyed when the block finishes execution, would be known only inside its block, and would have no initialization done. Inserting the word static at the beginning of the declaration, as in

```
static float two_d[3][4];
```

would change the storage class and initialization properties. In this case, two_d would be in existence during the full execution time of the program, and would be initialized with zero values for every cell. The initialization would only be done once, at the beginning of program execution.

Had two_d been declared outside of all functions, it would be known from point of declaration to the end of the file, would be able to be accessed by other source modules, would be in existence during program execution, and would be initialized with all zero values.

Static and external arrays can be given initial values at the time of declaration. To give two_d the values in the array pictured above, the declaration would be either

```
static float two_d[3][4] = { { 3.1, 7.6, 9.4, 2.2 },
                             { 5.3, 8.2, 1.4, 2.7 },
                             { 6.0, 4.2, 7.8, 5.1 }
                           };
```

or

```
static float two_d[][4] =  { { 3.1, 7.6, 9.4, 2.2 },
                             { 5.3, 8.2, 1.4, 2.7 },
                             { 6.0, 4.2, 7.8, 5.1 }
                           };
```

Each of the element lists in the three inner sets of braces is used to initialize one row of the array. The reason that the first dimension can be omitted and the second dimension must be included will be discussed later.

As an example of the use of arrays, an investor is following six stocks that he owns. He wants a program that will compare the current prices of his six stocks with the price at which he bought them. He wants to have the original prices stored in the program and he will enter the current prices.

We could use a two-dimensional array for the stock prices. The array might have 2 rows and 6 columns. The first row (index 0) would be initialized with the original prices of the six stocks. The second row would be entered at time of execution. Each column in the array would store the two relevant prices of one of the stocks.

In Example 9-2, the program has been blocked out and the input function has been written. The functions process() and output_results() have been left as stubs and will appear as exercises. The library function, atof(), is used to aid in the input. Its basic functionality was explained in Chapter 7; the *Programmer's Handbook* should be consulted for error handling and other details.

Example 9-2: stocks.c

```
/*                  stocks.c
 *
 *    Synopsis    - Accepts the input of six stock prices into a
 *                  two-dimensional array.
 *
 *    Objective   - Illustrates the declaration, initialization, and
 *                  accessing of elements of two-dimensional arrays.
 */

/* Include Files */
#include <stdio.h>
#include <stdlib.h>
#include <string.h>
/* Function Prototypes */
void input_prices( void );
void process( void );
void output_results( void );

/* Global Variables */                                    /* Note 1 */
float stock_prices[2][6] = { { 12.5,   76.125,   34.875,
                               112,     43.25,    88      } };

void main( void )
{
    printf( "STOCK INFORMATION PROGRAM\n" );
    printf( "------------------------\n" );
```

```
        printf( "This program will give information about the " );
        printf( "prices of \nsix specific stocks. You are " );
        printf( "to enter the current prices of\nthe stocks. " );
        printf( "A comparison will be made with the buying " );
        printf( "prices\nof the stocks.\n\n" );

        input_prices();
        process();
        output_results();
}

/****************************** input_prices()  ***************/
/*    Accepts input of 6 quantities of type float to be stored in
 *    the second "row" of the global array stock_prices.  The
 *    combination of library functions gets() and atof() is used
 *    to perform the input of the float values.
 */
void input_prices( void )
{
        int i;
        char instring[20];

        printf( "Please enter the current stock prices now.\n" );
        printf( "Stock\tBuying price\tCurrent price\n" );
        printf( "-----\t------------\t-------------\n" );
        for ( i = 0; i < 6; i++ ) {
                                                        /* Note 2 */
                printf( "#%d: \t%6.2f   \t   ", i+1, stock_prices[0][i] );
                                                        /* Note 3 */
                stock_prices[1][i] = atof( gets( instring ) );
        }
        printf( "Thank you!\n" );
}

/****************************** process()   *******************/
/*    Function process() - a stub
 */

void process( void )
{
        printf( "process() stub entered.\n" );
}

/****************************** output_results()  *************/
/*    Function output_results() - a stub
 */
```

```
void output_results( void )
{
     printf( "output_results() stub entered.\n" );
}
```

The program stocks.c consists of four functions, `main()`, `input_prices()`, `process()`, and `output_results()`. The two functions `process()` and `output_results()` are simply stubs. They will be completed in the exercises. The function `main()` is a driver program. It issues some messages and then calls the other functions. The meaningful code is in the function `input_prices()`, which consists of a `for` loop. Notice that the array was declared globally since the passing of multidimensional arrays as parameters will not be discussed until the next example program. This program could be modified at that time.

Note 1: This illustrates the declaration of a two-dimensional array. This array will be in existence during the total execution time of the program and can be accessed by any of the functions in this source code file. The array is partially initialized at the time of declaration. The outer braces define the two-dimensional array. The inner set of braces delimit the values for the first row of the array. No initial values were provided for the second row; therefore each cell will be given values of `0.0`.

Note 2: The elements in the array are accessed using the subscript notation. An element in the first row (first index `0`) of the array is displayed by this call to `printf()`. As with one-dimensional arrays, the pointer notation can be used with more efficiency. The pointer notation for the cell `stock_prices[0][i]` would be

$$*(*(stock\_prices + 0) + i)$$

The rationale for this is presented later.

Note 3: The library function `gets()` will accept input of a string of characters and store it in `instring`. The address of `instring` is returned and passed to `atof()`; then `atof()` converts the ASCII characters in the string to a `float` value. That value is assigned to a cell in the second row (first index `1`) of the array.

Learning Activities

3.   Extend the stub for `output_results()` so that it displays the contents of both rows of the array. For the input

    `15 <CR> 75.5 <CR> 36.25 <CR> 98.5 <CR> 55 <CR> 87.5`

    the output should be

    ```
    Buying price:    12.50   76.12   34.87   112.00   43.25   88.00
    Current price:   15.00   75.50   36.25    98.50   55.00   87.50
    ```

Problem 1 at the end of the chapter gives specifications for the function `process()` and the completion of this program.

4. a. Execute stocks.c and convince yourself that it works. Experiment with erroneous input and see how the combination of `atof()` and `gets()` handles the errors.

    b. Look up `atof()` in the *Programmer's Handbook*. Are the errors in input handled by your system as stated in the handbook?

5. The program stocks.c uses subscript notation to access the elements of the two-dimensional array. Change this notation to the equivalent pointer notation as described in **Note 3** and test it to make sure that it works.

9.3 Multidimensional Arrays as Parameters to Functions

In the previous example, the array `stock_prices` was declared externally to any function so that it could be accessed by all functions. It is better programming style to pass the array into the functions as a parameter. When a multidimensional array is passed as an argument to a function, every dimension except the first must be known to the function. As with one-dimensional arrays, the address of the array is actually passed to the function, but the dimensions must be declared so that the function can properly find elements in specific locations. For example, if the array were to be passed as a parameter to `input_prices()` in the last example, the ANSI C definition of the function would have either of the following two forms:

```
void input_prices( float pricearray[][6] )
{
     /* function code */
}
```

or

```
void input_prices( float ( *pricearray )[6] )
{
     /* function code */
}
```

The second form makes use of the fact that a copy of the address of the array is actually passed in; this address can be treated as a pointer.[1]

---

1. For older compilers the first line of the function definition would be replaced by either
```
void input_prices( pricearray )     or  void input_prices( pricearray )
float pricearray[][6];                  float ( *pricearray )[6];
```

Example 9-3 prints a multiplication table for the nonnegative integers through the product 3*4. The products are stored in a two-dimensional array.

The ?: construction is also introduced in this program; it is used in the output routine. The ?: construct has the following syntax

```
expression1 ? expression2 : expression 3
```

This construct is known as the conditional expression. When it is evaluated, expression1 is evaluated first. If it evaluates to 0, then expression3 is evaluated and becomes the value of the conditional expression. If the value of expression1 is nonzero, then expression2 becomes the value of the conditional expression. For example, the value of the conditional expression

```
(i > 0) ? 3 : 5
```

is either 3 or 5. If the value of i is positive, the value is 3; otherwise it is 5. Two additional ?: constructs appear in the program multi.c

Example 9-3: multi.c

```
/*                multi.c
 *
 *    Synopsis    - Displays a multiplication table for positive
 *                  integer products between 0*0 and 3*4.
 *
 *    Objective   - Demonstrates multidimensional arrays and
 *                  the ?: construct.
 */

/* Include Files */
#include <stdio.h>

/* Function Prototypes */
void printab( int, int, int[][5] );                        /* Note 1 */

void main( void )
{
      int multiarray[4][5],                                /* Note 2 */
          row, column;

      for ( row = 0; row < 4; row++ )                      /* Note 3 */
          for ( column = 0; column < 5; column++ )
```

```
                    multiarray[row][column] = row * column;

        printab( 4, 5, multiarray );
}


/****************************** printab()  ********************/
/*    An output routine. Displays the contents of an array of
 *    type int. The array is passed as a parameter along with
 *    the number of rows and columns to be displayed.
 */
                                                        /* Note 4 */
void printab( int rows, int columns, int array[][5] )
{
        int i = 0, j = 0;

        while ( i < rows ) {
                printf( "%d%c", array[i][j],                /* Note 5 */
                        ( j == columns-1 ) ? '\n' : '\t' );
                                                            /* Note 5 */
                ( j == columns - 1 ) ? i++,j=0 : j++;
        }
}
```

 Running the Program

```
0    0    0    0    0
0    1    2    3    4
0    2    4    6    8
0    3    6    9    12
```

Two functions, `main()` and `printab()`, make up this program. Variables are declared inside `main()`. The code consists of a set of nested `for` loops and a call to `printab()`. The function `printab()` uses a `while` loop to display the contents of the array in tabular form.

Note 1: The function prototype for `printab()` indicates that the first two parameters are of type `int`. The third parameter is a two-dimensional array of type `int` with 5 columns. The compiler needs to know the number of columns so that it can access the elements correctly.

Note 2: The two-dimensional array is declared. No initialization is done.

Note 3: A set of nested `for` loops are used to assign values to each cell of the array. Individual cells are accessed with the subscript notation.

Note 4: Three parameters are passed to `printab()`. The parameters `rows` and `columns` inform the function of the shape of the array. The array itself is also passed in as the address of the first element. The declaration must include the second dimension of this array; this value must be a constant.

Note 5: The two `?:` expressions are used to aid in the output format. The first tests the value of `j` to see if the last element in a column is being output. If so, a newline is placed in the output buffer instead of a tab character. The second `?:` expression makes the same test and uses the result to determine when to update `i` and `j` for a new row.

Learning Activities

6.   a. Execute multi.c.

      b. Modify multi.c so that the row and column of zeros in the table are eliminated and the products go from `1*1` to `4*5`. Do this without changing the size of the array.

      c. Modify multi.c again so that the output looks like this:

```
*  |  1        2        3        4        5

-------------------------------------------

1  |  1        2        3        4        5
2  |  2        4        6        8        10
3  |  3        6        9        12       15
4  |  4        8        12       16       20
```

        Use a hyphen (–) for the horizontal line and the vertical bar (|) for the vertical line. Make the spacing as even as possible.

7.   Modify multi.c so that it requests the upper limits on the multiplication table as input from a user and outputs a table containing the products from `1*1` to `upper*upper` where `upper` is the value entered by the user. For practical purposes, do not allow the user to input a value greater than `10`.

8.   Modify the program stocks.c from the last example so that the array is passed as a parameter to all three functions.

9.4 Arrays with More Than Two Dimensions

The extension to more than two dimensions is straightforward. For example,

```
double three_d[2][3][4];
```

declares a three-dimensional array with base type `double`. The element in the position with first index 1, second index 2, and third index 0 is accessed with the expression

```
three_d[1][2][0]
```

Such arrays have the same concepts of storage class, scope, and initialization properties as other variables.

Initializing `three_d` at the time of declaration would be done as follows:

```
double three_d[2][3][4] = {
                        { {0.0,  0.1,  0.2,  0.3},
                          {1.0,  1.1,  1.2,  1.3},
                          {2.0,  2.1,  2.2,  2.3}      },
                        { {10.0,  10.1,  10.2,  10.3},
                          {11.0,  11.1,  11.2,  11.3},
                          {12.0,  12.1,  12.2,  12.3} }
                      };
```

The syntax for the initialization of this three-dimensional array indicates that, in C, `three_d` is actually an array of arrays of arrays of type `double`. See the **A Closer Look** discussion for more detail. Arrays of four, five, or even more dimensions can be declared and initialized in a similar fashion. Accessing the elements is also done analogously.

A three-dimensional array could be visualized as a rectangular solid of values,

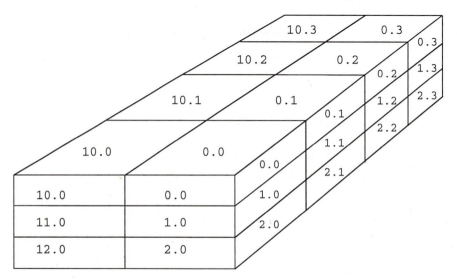

but is more often thought of as multiple two-dimensional arrays. To illustrate this, the program threedim.c in Example 9-4 outputs the elements of three_d as two 3 x 4 arrays.

Example 9-4: threedim.c

```
/*              threedim.c
 *
 *   Synopsis   - Displays the contents of a three-dimensional
 *                array as a pair of two-dimensional arrays.
 *
 *   Objective  - Illustrates declaration, initialization, and
 *                element access in a three-dimensional array.
 */

/* Include Files */
#include <stdio.h>

void main( void )
{                                                          /* Note 1 */
    double three_d[2][3][4] = {                            /* Note 2 */
            { { 0.0, 0.1, 0.2, 0.3 },
              { 1.0, 1.1, 1.2, 1.3 },
              { 2.0, 2.1, 2.2, 2.3 }
            },
            { { 10.0, 10.1, 10.2, 10.3 },
              { 11.0, 11.1, 11.2, 11.3 },
              { 12.0, 12.1, 12.2, 12.3 }
            }
    };
    int i, j, k;

    for ( i = 0; i < 2; i++ ) {
        for ( j = 0; j < 3; j++ ) {
            for ( k = 0; k < 4; k++ ) {                    /* Note 3 */
                printf( "%5.1f\t", three_d[i][j][k] );
            }
            printf( "\n" );
        }
        printf( "\n\n" );
    }
}
```

Running the Program

```
0.0    0.1    0.2    0.3
1.0    1.1    1.2    1.3
2.0    2.1    2.2    2.3



10.0   10.1   10.2   10.3
11.0   11.1   11.2   11.3
12.0   12.1   12.2   12.3
```

The program consists of the single function named main(). The array is declared and initialized. The executable code consists of nested for loops. One for loop is needed for each dimension of the array.

Note 1: The declaration of a three-dimensional array. The type is specified and followed by the array name and the three dimensions in brackets.

Note 2: The initialization of the array follows. The contents of each array must be in a comma-separated list enclosed in braces. Since this is actually an array of arrays of arrays, this initialization consists of three nested comma-separated lists enclosed in braces.

Note 3: The elements of the array are accessed with the appropriate subscripts enclosed in brackets.

Learning Activities

9. Execute threedim.c to understand how it works.

10. *C by Discovery*   With the declaration of one-dimensional arrays, the dimension could be omitted from between the braces when the array was initialized. Experiment with the declaration of the variable three_d to see if that is true with three-dimensional arrays. Which (if any) of the dimensions can be omitted?

11. In threedim.c rewrite the statement with the call to printf() using pointer notation instead of subscript notation to access the elements.

12. Modify threedim.c so that the current values of i, j, and k are output with the two arrays. That is, make the output match the following:

```
              k =    0      1      2      3
    i=0
         j=0         0.0    0.1    0.2    0.3
         j=1         1.0    1.1    1.2    1.3
         j=2         2.0    2.1    2.2    2.3


    i=1
         j=0        10.0   10.1   10.2   10.3
         j=1        11.0   11.1   11.2   11.3
         j=2        12.0   12.1   12.2   12.3
```

"A closer look at the discovery of C." From the Naval Museum in Pegli. The reference reads **"Amerigo Vespucci, after whom the American continents are named."** Artist unknown, date unknown.

A Closer Look

Recall that in C, an array of almost any type can be declared. The concept of multidimensional arrays is built on this fact. A two-dimensional array is an array of one-dimensional arrays. A three-dimensional array is an array of two-dimensional arrays, and so on.

The syntax for declaring a two-dimensional array is that of declaring an array of arrays. The declaration

```
int two_d[3][4];
```

is equivalent to

```
int (two_d[3])[4];
```

Analyzing the above declaration, we see that the expression two_d[3] is an array of 4 ints; the expression two_d is an array of 3 elements where each element is an array of 4 ints. The fact that a two-dimensional array is really an array of arrays has several consequences. The first is the meaning of the expressions involving the array name two_d.

The value of the expression two_d itself is the address of the first of its three elements or the address of the first array of 4 ints.

The expression *two_d is an array of 4 ints. The expression *two_d evaluates to the address of the first element in that array.

The following list gives the meanings of other expressions

two_d[0]	The same as *two_d.
**two_d	The first element in the array. Actually, it is the first int in the first array of four ints.
two_d[0][0]	The same as **two_d.
two_d + 1	The address of the second element in two_d or the address of the second array of four ints.
*(two_d + 1)	The second array of four ints. Its value is the address of that array.
(two_d + 1)[0]	The same as *(two_d + 1).
**(two_d + 1)	The first element in the second array of four ints. It is synonymous with two_d[1][0].

The following diagram indicates the three levels of expressions in the list above.

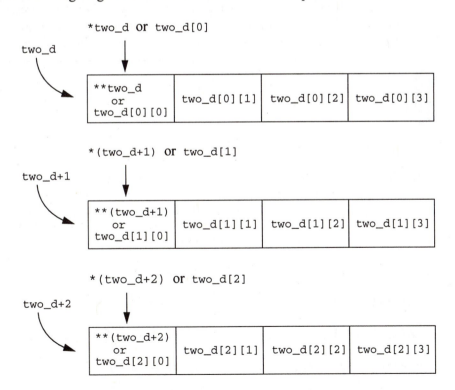

Notice that the address of the first array of 4 `ints` is the same as the address of the first element in that array. Numerically, the values of `two_d` and `*two_d` are identical. However, the two expressions have different types. This can be seen by inspecting the value of the `sizeof()` operator applied to the two expressions. The expression `sizeof(two_d)` is the total number of bytes in the whole array while `sizeof(*two_d)` is the number of bytes in the first of the three arrays of four `ints`.

Second, the concept of a multidimensional array as an array of arrays leads to the fact that the elements of multidimensional arrays are stored contiguously and in row major form (that is, all elements with first subscript 0 will be stored first, followed by all elements with first subscript 1, and so on). For example, for the array `two_d` declared previously, the elements actually are stored in memory in the following pattern:

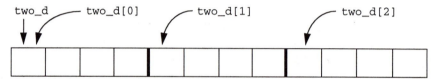

The program in Example 9-5 illustrates the meaning of some of the expressions related to a two-dimensional array by displaying their values. It also displays the result of the `sizeof()` operator applied to several of the expressions to illustrate that the types are different even when the values are the same. Third, it displays the addresses of elements in the array to illustrate the contiguous storage.

Example 9-5: md.c

```
/*                      md.c
 *
 *    Synopsis    -  Displays information about a 2 x 3 array of
 *                   characters.
 *
 *    Objective   -  To illustrate the relationship between different
 *                   expressions related to an array.
 */

/* Include Files */
#include <stdio.h>

void main( void )
{
        static char t[2][3] = { { 'a', 'b', 'c' },
                                { 'd', 'e', 'f' }  };
```

```
    printf( "sizeof( char )    %d\n", sizeof( char ) );

    printf( "   2 X 3 array\n" );
    printf( "-------------------\n" );
    printf( "t                   %p\n", t );              /* Note 1 */
                                                          /* Note 2 */
    printf( "sizeof(t)           %d\n\n", sizeof(t) );

    printf( "  First 1 X 3 array\n" );
    printf( "-------------------\n" );
    printf( "*t                  %p\n", *t );             /* Note 1 */
                                                          /* Note 2 */
    printf( "sizeof(*t)          %d\n\n", sizeof(*t) );

    printf( "First element in array\n" );
    printf( "----------------------\n" );
    printf( "&t[0][0]            %p\n", &t[0][0] );       /* Note 1 */
                                                          /* Note 2 */
    printf( "sizeof(&t[0][0]) %d\n",
            sizeof( &t[0][0] ) );
    printf( "t[0][0]             %c\n", t[0][0] );        /* Note 3 */
    printf( "sizeof (t[0][0]) %d\n", sizeof( t[0][0] ) );
    printf( "**t                 %c\n\n", **t );          /* Note 3 */

    printf( "Second 1 X 3 array\n" );
    printf( "-------------------\n" );
    printf( "t+1                 %p\n", t+1 );            /* Note 4 */
    printf( "sizeof(t+1)         %d\n", sizeof( t+1 ) );
                                                          /* Note 4 */
    printf( "*(t+1)              %p\n", *( t+1 ) );
    printf( "sizeof (*(t+1))     %d\n", sizeof( *( t+1 ) ) );
                                                          /* Note 5 */
    printf( "*(t+1) +2           %p\n", *( t+1 ) + 2 );
    printf( "*(*(t+1) +2)        %c\n", *( *( t+1 ) + 2 ) );
}
```

 Running the Program

```
sizeof( char )    1
   2 X 3 array
-------------------
t                 00A8
sizeof(t)         6
```

```
First 1 X 3 array
--------------------
*t                  00A8
sizeof(*t)          3

First element in array
--------------------
&t[0][0]            00A8
sizeof(&t[0][0])  2
t[0][0]             a
sizeof (t[0][0])  1
**t                 a

Second 1 X 3 array
--------------------
t+1                 00AB
sizeof(t+1)         2
*(t+1)              00AB
sizeof (*(t+1))    3
*(t+1) +2           00AD
*(*(t+1) +2)        f
```

The program consists of the single function, `main()`. A 2 x 3 array of characters is declared and initialized. The remainder of the code consists of calls to `printf()` to display information about the array. The program output, displayed above, was obtained by compiling and executing this code on a microcomputer. Refer to the output shown or the output from your computer while you read the program discussion. In this program, **Note 1** is associated with more than one statement. The discussion will refer to all of the statements.

Note 1: This note refers to the `printf()` calls where values of t, *t, and &t[0][0] are displayed. Check these values in the output. All of the values are identical since they all refer to the address of the array or the first cell of the array.

Note 2: This note refers to the `printf()` calls where the values of `sizeof(t)`, `sizeof(*t)`, and `sizeof(&t[0][0])` are displayed. These values should be different from one another since the three quantities that had the same value in the **Note 1** statements all have different types. The expression t refers to a 2 x 3 array of characters which can also be thought of as two 1 x 3 arrays; its size should be that of a buffer that will store 6 characters. The expression *t refers to the first of the 1 x 3 arrays. Its size reflects that of a buffer to hold 3 `chars`. The expression &t[0][0] is the address of the first character in the array. It should have the "sizeof" an address on your system.

Note 3: This note refers to `printf()` calls where `t[0][0]` and `**t` are displayed. Both expressions are synonyms for the first character in the array.

The expression `**t` uses "double indirection" to access an element of the array. Recall that `*` is the dereferencing operator. When used with an address, it refers to the contents of the address. In this example, `t` is the address of the 2 x 3 array of `chars`, `*t` is the first array of three `chars` (it evaluates as the address of the first `char`), and `**t` is the first `char` value. It is equivalent to `t[0][0]`.

Note 4: The next four statements demonstrate the relationship between `t` and `*t`. The expression `t + 1` evaluates to the address of the second 1 x 3 array. It is an address and should have the "sizeof" an address. The value of the expression `*(t + 1)` should be identical, but its "sizeof" is different since it has a different type. (Determine its type.)

Note 5: The next two statements involve the last element in the array. The expression `*(t + 1) + 2` refers to the address of the last element. It should be `2 * sizeof(char)` beyond the address `t + 1`. The expression `*( *( t+1 ) +2 )` refers to the value of last element in the array. It should be an `'f'`.

Learning Activities

13.   As you read the above discussion, questions about other expressions may have occurred to you. If so, modify md.c to output the values of those expressions. Try to reconcile the results of the execution with your understanding of the concepts.

14.   a.   What would be output by the call

```
printf( "%x\n", &t[1][0] );
```

  b.   What does the expression

```
*( *t+2 )
```

  reference?

  c.   What does the expression

```
**( t+1 )
```

  reference?

15.   Predict the output from the program md.c if both of the following changes were made.

  a.   Change the declaration to read

```
static double t = { {1.0, 2.0, 3.0},
                     {4.0, 5.0, 6.0}
                   };
```

  b.   Change every `%c` output specification to `%f`. You may have to determine `sizeof(double)` before you can answer accurately. You will not be able to predict the address of the first element in the array.

16. In the expression `**( two_d + 1 )` convince yourself that the parentheses are necessary. Consult the precedence chart in the *Programmer's Handbook* to find the relative precedence of `*` and `+`.

9.5 Arrays of Pointers

The following type of declaration is very useful and often seen in C code:

```
char *ptrarray[4];
```

Analyzing this declaration, we see that an expression of the form `*ptrarray[x]` is a `char`.[1] Since the `[]` have higher precedence than the indirection operator, `*`, the next step in the analysis indicates that the type of any expression of the form `ptrarray[x]` is `char *`, and that `ptrarray` is an array of four elements of that type. In other words, `ptrarray` is an array of four pointers to elements of type `char` and is the construct used in C for an array of strings. When the identifier `ptrarray` appears in a program, it refers to the address of the first element of that array. This data structure can be pictured as shown below.

ptrarray

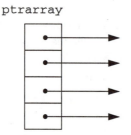

To see the concept of an array of pointers in use, consider the code in Example 9-6, which might be part of a text processing program. Assume that a word is defined as a sequence of nonblank characters delimited by blanks. A line of text consisting of a sequence of these words is entered from the keyboard and stored in a one-dimensional array.

The program ptrarray.c uses an array of type `char *` to keep track of the beginning of each word. It counts the words and displays them to the terminal in reverse order.

---

1. This type of declaration analysis has been demonstrated in some simple examples earlier in the text. It becomes more useful as the declarations become more complicated. It will be discussed in detail in Section 9.6

Example 9-6: ptrarray.c

```
/*                ptrarray.c
 *
 *    Synopsis    - Accepts a line of text as input from the key-
 *                  board. Finds the individual words in the input
 *                  text, counts them, displays the count, and
 *                  displays the words in reverse order.
 *
 *    Objective   - Illustrates use of an array of pointers to char.
 */

/* Include Files */
#include <stdio.h>
#include <string.h>

void main( void )
{
      char instring[512];
      char *words[50],                                      /* Note 1 */
           *current;
      int  i = 1;

      printf( "Enter text with words delimited by blanks:\n" );
      gets( instring );

      words[0] = current = instring;                        /* Note 2 */
                                                            /* Note 3 */
      while ( ( current = strchr( current, ' ' )) != NULL ) {
            *current++ = '\0';
            words[i++] = current;                           /* Note 4 */
      }

      printf( "There were %d words in that line.\n", i );
      printf( "In reverse order they are :\n" );
      for ( --i; i >= 0; i-- )
            printf( "%s\n", words[i] );                     /* Note 5 */
}
```

There is one function, main(). Input is done by a call to gets(). A while loop is used to work through the line of input to find the beginning of each word and store its address in an array of type char *. A for loop displays the words in reverse order.

Note 1: An array of 50 pointers to `char` is defined. No initialization is done.

Note 2: The first element in the array is initialized to point to the beginning of the input line. The auxiliary variable `current` is assigned to point there also.

Note 3: In each pass through the following `while` loop, `strchr()` looks for a blank that delimits the end of a word. The blank is then replaced by a `'\0'` and `current` is incremented to point to the beginning of the next word. If a blank is not found, `strchr()` returns `NULL` and the loop terminates.

Note 4: The next element in the array is assigned to point to the beginning of the next word, and the index into the array is incremented. Assume that the input line is `"Frick and Frack"`. After the `while` loop has terminated, the memory configuration would be represented as follows:

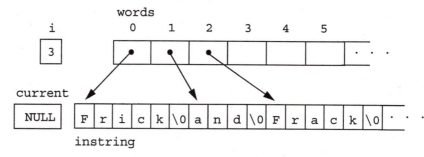

Note 5: The individual words are displayed on separate lines. The index `i` goes from the number of words back to zero so that the words are displayed in reverse order.

The useful part of this program is the set up of the memory configuration discussed and illustrated in **Note 4**. Once that configuration is set up, the individual word of input can be accessed easily for any need.

Learning Activities

17. Compile and execute ptrarray.c. Test it with several different input strings to see how it behaves. What happens when there are no blanks in the input? What happens when there are two blanks between one word and the next? If either of these behaviors is not acceptable, modify the program accordingly.

18. When a single carriage return is entered in response to the prompt, the word count is reported to be one. Fix this bug in the program so that it counts zero words correctly.

19. When more than fifty words are entered, an error condition occurs.

Fix this bug by having the program check on the number of words and not process more than fifty words even if more exist on the input line.

20.   Modify ptrarray.c so that it displays the words in the same order that they were entered.

A Closer Look

An array of pointers shares properties with other arrays. In particular, an expression consisting of the array name itself is evaluated as the address of the first element of the array. Therefore, since it is an address, the pointer notation can be used for it.

If an array of strings was created as in the last program, then the data structure could be thought of as having two dimensions, as illustrated in the following diagram for the input "Frick and Frack".

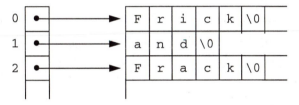

This data structure is similar to a two-dimensional array of characters, but each row of the structure can have a different number of elements. However, the array subscript notation can be used to reference elements in arrays of pointers also.

In each of the following examples, the expressions are equivalent:

> words[0]
>
> and
>
> *words

⎫ both refer to the first word in the input string, "Frick".

> *words[0]
>
> and
>
> **words
>
> and
>
> words[0][0]

⎫ all refer to the first letter in that string, "F".

```
* (words[0]+3)
```

and

```
* (*words + 3)
```

and

```
words[0][3]
```

all refer to the fourth letter in that string, `"c"`.

```
* (words[2]+1)
```

and

```
* (* (words+2) +1)
```

and

```
words[2][1]
```

all refer to the second letter, `"r"`, in the input string `"Frack"`.

9.6 Double Indirection

Since any type in C can have a pointer to it, we can declare a pointer to a pointer. For example, we can declare a pointer to a pointer to an `int`. The declaration would be

```
int **ptr;
```

Interpreting the declaration, we see that the expression `**ptr` is of type `int`. Therefore, `*ptr` is the address of (that is, a pointer to) an `int`, and `ptr` itself is the address of (a pointer to) a pointer to an `int`.

Consider the following declarations:

```
int   r = 3,
     *q = &r,
    **p = &q;
```

The variable `r` has type `int` and has been initialized to 3. The variable `q` has type pointer to `int` and has been initialized to point to `r`. That means that it contains the address of `r`. The variable `p` has type pointer to pointer to `int`. It has been initialized to point to `q`. That means that the following relationships hold:

   `p` contains the address of `q` and is said to point to `q`.
  `*p` is equivalent to `q` and therefore points to `r`.
`**p` is equivalent to both `*q` and `r` and has the value 3.

The relationships are illustrated in the following figure.

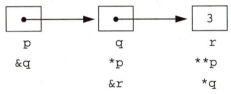

C does not put a limit on the number of levels of indirection. It is possible to declare

```
float ***f;
```

which is a pointer to a pointer to a pointer to a `float`, or even

```
char ****w;
```

where w would be a pointer to a pointer to a pointer to a pointer to a `char`. Typically, the level of indirection is kept low for ease of understanding the code.

The program ptrptr.c in Example 9-7 explores the relationship between an array of pointers and a pointer to a pointer.[1] It also shows techniques for accessing strings and individual characters using either an array of pointers to `char` or a variable of type `char **`. The variable with type `char **` is used to traverse the array of type `char *`. This is a major use of `char **` variables in C.

Example 9-7: ptrptr.c

```
/*                 ptrptr.c
 *
 *     Synopsis    - Outputs information, strings, and individual
 *                   characters in an array of pointers to type char.
 *
 *     Objective   - To illustrate double indirection and use the
 *                   pointer to a pointer to traverse an array of
 *                   pointers.
 */


/* Include Files */
#include <stdio.h>
#include <string.h>


void main( void )
{
```

---

1. The phrase in this program is the one my father-in-law used to remember the spelling of "geography."

```
        char *ptrarray[] = { "George",
                             "Elliot's",
                             "Oldest",
                             "Girl",
                             "Rode",
                             "A",
                             "Pig",
                             "Home",
                             "Yesterday",
                             ""                           /* Note 1 */
                  };

    char **ptrptr = ptrarray;                            /* Note 2 */


                                                         /* Note 3 */
    printf( "sizeof( ptrarray )  %d,\tsizeof( ptrptr )  %d\n",
                        sizeof( ptrarray ), sizeof( ptrptr ));
    printf( "ptrarray           %p,\tptrptr           %p\n",
                        ptrarray, ptrptr );
    printf( "ptrarray[0]        %p,\t*ptrptr          %p\n\n",
                        ptrarray[0], *ptrptr );


                                                         /* Note 4 */
    printf( "ptrarray[0]   %s,\t*ptrptr         %s\n",
                        ptrarray[0], *ptrptr );
    printf( "ptrarray[1]   %s,\t*( ptrptr+1 ) %s\n\n",
                        ptrarray[1], *( ptrptr+1 ));


                                                         /* Note 5 */
    printf( "*ptrarray[0]       %c,\t**ptrarray        %c\n",
                        *ptrarray[0], **ptrarray );
    printf( "ptrarray[0][4]     %c,\t*(*ptrarray + 4) %c\n\n",
                        ptrarray[0][4], *( *ptrarray+4 ));


                                                         /* Note 6 */
    for (   ; strcmp( *ptrptr, ""); ptrptr++ )
         printf( "%s ", *ptrptr );
    printf( "\n" );
                                                         /* Note 7 */
    for ( ptrptr = ptrarray; strcmp( *ptrptr, "" ); ptrptr++ )
         printf( "%c", **ptrptr );
    printf( "\n" );
}
```

Running the Program

```
sizeof( ptrarray )  20,sizeof( ptrptr )  2
ptrarray            FFE2,ptrptr         FFE2
ptrarray[0]         00BC,*ptrptr        00BC

ptrarray[0]   George,  *ptrptr          George
ptrarray[1]   Elliot's,*( ptrptr+1 ) Elliot's

*ptrarray[0]        G,  **ptrarray         G
ptrarray[0][4]      g,  *(*ptrarray + 4) g

George Elliot's Oldest Girl Rode A Pig Home Yesterday
GEOGRAPHY
```

In the one function, main(), the executable code consists primarily of calls to printf(). Two for loops are used to display the strings and the first character of each string.

Note 1: An array of pointers is declared and initialized. The initial values for the array are the addresses of the given strings. They must be in a comma-separated list enclosed in braces. A null string is placed as the array terminator. The picture is as follows:

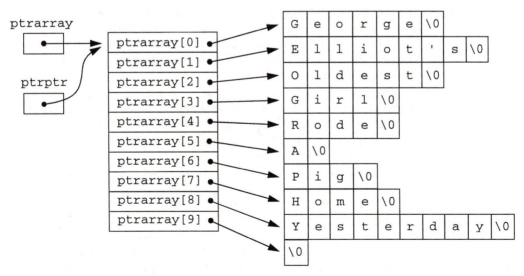

Note 2: A pointer to a pointer to a char variable is declared and initialized to point to the first element in the array of pointers.

Note 3: Information about the values of expressions involving ptrptr and ptrarray is displayed in the next three printf() calls. The first printf() call displays the sizeof() both ptrptr and ptrarray to point out the fact that these two expressions have different types. The expression sizeof(ptrarray) gives the total number of bytes in the array while the expression sizeof(ptrptr) should be that of a pointer to (address of) a char. In the next two printf() calls, each expression involving ptrptr should have a value identical to the one involving ptrarray. The expressions ptrptr and ptrarray both refer to the address of the first of the pointers, and the expressions ptrarray[0] and *ptrptr both refer to the contents of the first element in the array of pointers or the address of the first string.

Note 4: The next two calls to printf() illustrate how to access the strings in the array. They can be accessed either through the array subscript notation or through the pointer notation. Notice that the first of these printf() calls has exactly the same arguments as the previous call to printf(). This emphasizes the fact that the expressions ptrarray and ptrptr evaluate to addresses. They can be accessed either numerically with the %p conversion specification or as a string with the %s conversion specification.

Note 5: The technique of accessing individual characters is demonstrated by the next two calls to printf(). The first printf() call contains two expressions that access the 'G' in "George". Note that either subscript notation, pointer notation, or a combination of the two can be used. The second call to printf() illustrates two ways of accessing the 'g' in "George".

Note 6: This for loop will display all the strings in the array of pointers. The variable ptrptr, of type char **, is used to traverse the array. In particular, notice the test for continuing the for loop. The loop will continue until the strcmp() function returns a zero (in other words, until ptrptr points to the null string).

Note 7: This for loop will display the first character in each of the strings. The variable ptrptr needed to be reassigned to point to the array since it was changed in the last for loop. The test for continuing or terminating the for loop is the same as in the last loop.

Learning Activities

21. Write C expressions involving ptrarray from ptrptr.c that reference the word "Pig", the 'P' and the 'g'. Add calls to printf() to the program ptrptr.c so that you can check your answers.

22.   Modify the first `for` loop in ptrptr.c so that the strings are output in reverse order.

23.   Modify ptrptr.c so that the last character in each of the strings is displayed by the second `for` loop.

24.   After the assignment `ptrptr = ptrarray`, state the meaning of each of the following expressions from the last program. Two have been done for you.

   a. `ptrptr ==` address of the first element in the array of pointers.

   b. `*ptrptr`

   c. `**ptrptr`

   d. `ptrptr+1`

   e. `*(ptrptr+1)`

   f. `**(ptrptr+1)   ==   'E'`

   g. `*(*(ptrptr+1)+2)`

   h. `**ptrptr + 1`

   i. `*ptrptr + 1`

   j. `*ptrptr[1]`

   k. `*(*ptrptr + 2)`

Reading C Declarations

Before proceeding, we will review some of the symbols used in C declarations and see how they can be combined. The symbols we will discuss are brackets, `[]`, parentheses, `()`, and the asterisk, `*`. The precedence of these operators is important.

Parentheses have the highest precedence when they are used to group elements of an expression. They can also be used in a declaration to declare a function. Brackets are next in precedence and the asterisk has the lowest precedence of the three symbols.

To read a C declaration, remove the operator with lowest precedence from the declared expression and determine what the remaining expression must represent. Continue this process until only the identifier remains.

We will start with an example for which we know the answer to illustrate the process. Consider the declaration

```
int  *x[8];
```

The expression `*x[8]` must represent an `int`. Since `*` has lower precedence than `[]`, the declaration could be written equivalently as

```
int   *(x[8]);
```

This implies that the expression x[8] (or any expression of the form x[i]) has type int *. Therefore, x is an array of 8 elements of type int *; that is, x is an array of 8 pointers to int.

In contrast, the declaration

```
int   (*y)[8];
```

indicates that the expression *y is an array of 8 ints so y is the address of a pointer to an array of 8 ints.

Consider the following declaration as another example:

```
int   (*z[5])();
```

The expression (*z[5])() is an int; therefore, *z[5] is a function returning an int. Again * has lower precedence than [] so that the * is removed first to get the expression z[5], which is the address of (a pointer to) a function returning an int. Finally, z is an array of 5 pointers to functions returning ints.

Learning Activity

25. Determine the legality or illegality of each of the following declarations. If the declaration is legal, state the type of the variable what.

  a. `float   (what[3])();`   b. `float   what[3]();`

  c. `char    (*what)();`   d. `char    *what();`

  e. `double  (*what())[3];`   f. `double  *(what()[3]);`

  g. `int     **what[3];`   h. `int     **what();`

  i. `int     (**what)[3];`   j. `int     *(*what)[3];`

9.7 Command Line Parameters

Most computer systems have a facility for passing information to a C program at execution time. This information takes the form of a sequence of strings that are known as command line parameters. They appear as strings on the command line after the name of the program when it is executed. These strings are separated by blanks, tabs, or other allowed whitespace. The command line parameters are available throughout the time that the program is executing.

Command line parameters can be used in many ways. For example, many operating system utilities need this facility. An editor might take the name of the file to edit as a command line parameter. A program that makes a copy of a file might take the name of the existing file and the name of the future copy as command line parameters. A debugger might take identification of a running process as a command line parameter. The possibilities are endless.

A C program can be structured to access command line parameters by declaring arguments to `main()` in the form of an ANSI C prototype.[1]

```
main( int argc, char *argv[] )
```

The parameter names, `argc` and `argv`, are traditionally used by C programmers, but like parameter names in other functions, they are not specified by the language.

The parameter `argc` contains the **count** (number) of parameters on the command line. The name of the program being executed is the first command line parameter and is part of the count so that `argc` is always at least one. Examples appear below.

The parameter `argv` is a "vector" of the actual command line parameters. It is an array of pointers to `chars`. In this case the pointers point to the strings that appeared on the command line. The array is indexed by the integers from 0 to `argc-1` and terminated with a `NULL` pointer.

Suppose that the operating system prompt is "# " and consider a program named `sample`. When `sample` is executed, its name would appear on the command line as

```
# sample
```

With this program invocation, `argc` would be 1 and `argv` would have the following configuration:

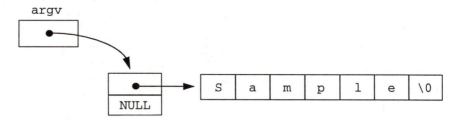

With the invocation

```
# sample   p1   p2   p3
```

`argc` would be 4 and `argv` would look like the following:

---

1. For older compilers, the prototype would be replaced with the three lines
```
main( argc, argv )
int argc;
char *argv[];
```

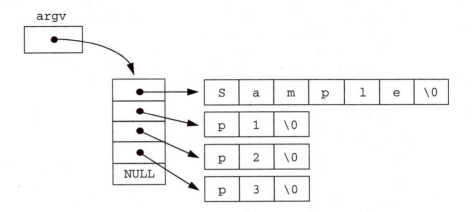

The program cmdline.c in Example 9-8 illustrates the declaration of the parameters argc and argv to the function main() so that the command line parameters can be accessed. It simply displays the value of argc and demonstrates techniques for accessing the strings in argv.

Example 9-8: cmdline.c

```
/*                    cmdline.c
 *
 *    Synopsis    - Prints the value of argc and the command
 *                  line parameters.
 *
 *    Objective   - To illustrate how command line parameters work
 *                  and to demonstrate two techniques for accessing
 *                  the arguments passed to a program on the command
 *                  line.
 */

/* Include Files */
#include <stdio.h>

void main( int argc, char *argv[] )                        /* Note 1 */
{
      int index ;

      printf( "There were %d arguments on the command line.\n",argc );
      printf( "They are :\n" );

      for ( index = 0; index < argc; index++ )             /* Note 2 */
```

```
        printf( "\t%p \t%s\n", argv[index], argv[index] );
printf( "\n\n" );
                                                       /* Note 3 */
printf( "Terminating char * value in argv, %p\n", argv[argc] );
printf( "\n" );

while ( argc-- > 0 )                                   /* Note 4 */
        printf( "    %s ", *argv++ );
printf( "\n\n" );
}
```

The function `main()` consists of `printf()` calls and two loops that display the command line parameters. The `for` loop displays the command line parameters as an address and as a string. The `while` loop again displays the command line parameters but uses a different syntax to reference them. One auxiliary variable `index` was declared.

Note 1: The parameters `argc` and `argv` are declared inside the parentheses for `main()`. The parameter `argc` is of type `int` and `argv` is an array of type `char *`. The address, `argv`, of the array of pointers is passed into `main()`. Each value in the array is the address of one of the parameter strings on the command line.

Note 2: Each time through the `for` loop, one of the command line parameter strings is displayed. The string can be accessed with subscript notation used with `argv`. The value in one cell of the array is the address of the first character in the string. It can be accessed as a numerical quantity with the `%p` conversion specification or as a string with the `%s` conversion specification. Both values are displayed.

Note 3: The strings on the command line occupy the first `argc` cells in the array with indices 0 through `argc-1`. The next cell contains a terminating `NULL` pointer. This call to `printf()` outputs the `NULL` as a pointer value.

Note 4: The `while` loop uses a different syntax to display the strings on the command line. Note that `argc` is decremented each time the control expression for the `while` loop is evaluated. The strings can be accessed using the `*` to reference the contents of address `argv`. After one parameter string is displayed, `argv` is incremented to point to the next address of a parameter string. Note that after the `while` loop terminates, both the count and location of the command line arguments have been destroyed. This program would not be able to access these arguments again.

Learning Activities

26. Find out if you are able to use command line arguments with a C program on your system and what, if anything, needs to be done to use them.

27. If you can use command line arguments, compile and execute cmdline.c with several different sets of command line arguments.[1]

    a. Test the program with no command line arguments other than the program name. What happens?

    b. Test to see if you can find a reasonable limit for the number of command line arguments. Test the program with a large number of short command line arguments. Do not press the Return key until you have entered all the parameters.

    c. Test to see if you can find a reasonable limit for the length of a command line argument. Test the program with the program name and one very long argument string.

The program count.c in Example 9-9 gives a simple use of command line parameters. It takes three command line parameters after the program name. Assume that the executable version of the program is in a file named "count". If the invocation to count is

        count   3   20   5

the program will count from 3 to 20 by fives. The output would be

        3   8   13   18

Example 9-9: count.c

```
/*              count.c
 *
 *   Synopsis    - Takes values of initial, final, and step from
 *                 the command line arguments. Counts from the
 *                 low value of initial to the high value of
 *                 final with increments of step.
```

---

1. If you do not have an ANSI C compiler, you will need to replace the declaration of the parameters with the old-style declaration.

```
 *
 *    Objective   - To illustrate a use of command line arguments.
 *                  Also uses the library function atoi().
 */

/* Include Files */
#include <stdio.h>
#include <stdlib.h>

/* Function Prototypes */
void count( char ** );                                          /* Note 3 */

void main( int argc, char *argv[] )
{
     if ( argc != 4 ) {                                         /* Note 1 */
          printf( "Usage: count start stop step\n" );
          exit( 1 );
     }

                                                                /* Note 2 */
     printf( "Counting from %s to %s by %s's.\n",
                      *(argv+1), *(argv+2), *(argv+3) );
     count( argv );
}
/***************************** count()   *********************/
/*   Displays integer values from argv[1] to argv[2] in
 *   increments of argv[3].
 */
void count( char **args )                                       /* Note 3 */
{
     int result, initial, final, step;

     initial = atoi( args[1] );                                 /* Note 4 */
     final   = atoi( args[2] );
     step    = atoi( args[3] );

     for ( result = initial; result <= final; result += step )
          printf( "%d\t", result );
     printf( "\n" );
}
```

The program code consists of two functions, main() and count(). In main(), an if statement checks for the correct number of command line parameters. If the proper number of command line parameters were issued, main() calls count() to do the counting. In count(), several assignment statements convert the command line parameters to type int, and a for loop does the counting. The auxiliary variable `result` is used to drive the `for` loop and its current value is displayed in each iteration of the `for` loop.

Note 1: The value of `argc` is checked to see that the program was invoked correctly. If it was not invoked with the correct number of command line arguments, execution terminates after an error message is issued.

Note 2: The call to `printf()` accesses the command line arguments as strings using pointer arithmetic to obtain the address of each separate argument.

Note 3: The parameter to `count()` will be `argv`, the address of the first cell in an array of type `char *`. The declaration of the parameter to `count()` could either be

```
char *args[];
```

or

```
char **args;
```

Note 4: The address of the vector of command line arguments is passed in as a parameter to `count()`. The command line parameters should be strings of digits. The digits must be converted to type `int` for counting. The standard library function `atoi()` is used for the conversion. Each command line parameter is used as an argument to `atoi()`. The equivalent integer value is returned.

Learning Activities

28. a. If your system implements command line arguments, execute the program with several different sets of command line parameters. Does the check on the number of parameters seem to work?

    b. What happens when nondigits are used as command line arguments, as in

    ```
    count two  twentyseven  three.
    ```
    What do you think happened?

29. Read about the library function `atoi()` in your documentation. Does this shed any light on the happenings in your question 28b experiment? Explain what happened in view of this.

30. Add an error check to count.c to ensure that each command line argument consists of digits only. Have the program terminate execution if a nondigit is found. (Hint: Look up the function `isdigit()` in your compiler documentation or the *Programmer's Handbook*. It might be handy for this problem.)

31. Modify count.c so that the format of the output is changed to 8 columns of numbers per line. For example, with the invocation

```
        count   4   49  5
the output should be
            4    9    14    19    24    29    34    39
        44    49
```

A Closer Look

The address of the array of strings is passed to `main()` in `argv`; therefore, `argv` is a pointer to a pointer to a `char`. It could be declared as

```
char **argv;
```

In most implementations of C, the command line arguments are put on a stack and the address of each argument is recorded. The list of addresses is terminated with a NULL pointer. The address of the list of addresses is the initial value of `argv`. For example, assume that the invocation of the program `count` above is

```
count   34    158   23
```

Then, assuming it takes 2 bytes to represent an address, a hypothetical configuration of memory might be as follows.

Name	Hexadecimal address	Contents
argv	FFD6	FFDA
argv[0]	FFDA	FFE4
argv[1]	FFDC	FFF1
argv[2]	FFDE	FFF4
argv[3]	FFE0	FFF8
argv[4]	FFE2	0(NULL)
	FFE4	C:\COUNT.EXE
	FFF1	34
	FFF4	158
	FFF8	23

Language Elements Introduced in This Chapter: A Review

✓ **Multidimensional Arrays**

- Accessing elements

```
two_d[2][3]
three_d[1][2][0]
```

- Initializing

```
static float two_d[3][4] = {  { 3.1, 7.6, 9.4, 2.2 },
                              { 5.3, 8.2, 1.4, 2.7 },
                              { 6.0, 4.2, 7.8, 5.1 }
               };

static float two_d[][4] =  {  { 3.1, 7.6, 9.4, 2.2 },
                              { 5.3, 8.2, 1.4, 2.7 },
                              { 6.0, 4.2, 7.8, 5.1 }
               };

double three_d[2][3][4] ={
                          { { 0.0, 0.1, 0.2, 0.3 },
                            { 1.0, 1.1, 1.2, 1.3 },
                            { 2.0, 2.1, 2.2, 2.3 }
                          },
                          { { 10.0, 10.1, 10.2, 10.3 },
                            { 11.0, 11.1, 11.2, 11.3 },
                            { 12.0, 12.1, 12.2, 12.3 }
                          }
               };
```

✓ **Parameters to Functions**

- To pass a two dimensional array as a parameter to a function, pass address and second dimension,
  e.g., function declaration

```
funct( float two_d[][4] )
```
    or
```
funct( float *two_d[4] )
```
    or pass in as a pointer to a pointer
```
funct( float **two_d )
```
  e.g., function call
```
float array[4][5];

    ...
funct( array );
```

• Parameters to `main()` access the command line parameters

```
main( int argc, char *argv[] )
```

✓ **Variable Declarations**

• Multidimensional arrays

```
float two_d[3][4];
double three_d[2][3][4];
```

• Arrays of pointers

```
char *ptrarray[4];
```

• Pointers to pointers

```
int **ptr;
```

Things to Remember

1. Multidimensional arrays share the same storage class, scope, and initialization properties as one-dimensional arrays and variables of other types.

2. A two-dimensional array is an array of one-dimensional arrays.

3. A three-dimensional array is an array of two-dimensional arrays, and so on.

4. Given the declaration `int two_d[3][4];`
   a. the value of the expression `two_d` is the address of the first array of 4 `int`s.
   b. the expression `*two_d` evaluates to the address of the first element in the first array of 4 `int`s.

5. The elements of multidimensional arrays are stored contiguously and in row major form.

6. With the declaration

```
static char t[2][3];
```

   the expressions `t`, `*t`, and `t[0]` all have the same numerical value but are of different types.

7. There is no limit on the number of levels of indirection.

8. To decode a C declaration, look at the types of the elements of a sequence of expressions. Start with the declaration and continually peel off the operator with the lowest precedence until you can determine the type of the identifier alone.

9. Pointers to pointers can be used to traverse an array of strings and to access individual strings and characters.

10. Command line parameters appear as strings on the command line after the name of the program when it is executed.

11. The parameter `argc` contains the count of the parameters on the command

line. The parameter `argv` is the vector of the actual command line parameters.

12. The command line parameter `argv` can be used with either the array subscript or the pointer * notation.

Exercises and Programming Problems

1. Complete the function `process()` from the program stocks.c of Example 9-2 so that it calculates and stores the net change in price for each stock. Modify `output_prices()` so that it displays the buying price, the current price, and the net change in price for each stock.

2. Write a program that will produce a report about the activity of stocks traded on the New York Stock Exchange for a week's time. The program should ask for and accept input of the name of the stock and its closing price for each day of the week. The report should include the name of each stock, the high and low prices, and the net change for the week. A sample run appears below. The user's response is in **boldface**.

```
            STOCK INFORMATION PROGRAM
            ----- ----------- -------


This program will create a report on the weekly activity
of any stocks that you wish. You need only enter the stock
name and the closing prices for Monday through Friday.
Press Return at the stock name prompt when you are
through.

Ending date of the week of this report: 11/30/90

Stock name (Press Return when done):  AT&T
Monday's close:      40.5
Tuesday's close:     41
Wednesday's close: 40.875
Thursday's close:  41.125
Friday's close:      41

Stock name (Press Return when done):  IBM
Monday's close:      116.25
Tuesday's close:     114
Wednesday's close: 117.875
Thursday's close:  116.25
Friday's close:      115.875

Stock name (Press Return when done): <Ret>
```

```
                    STOCK ACTIVITY REPORT
                 Week Ending Friday 11/30/90

      -------------------------------------------------
      Stock     |   High   |  Low   |  Final  | Net Change
      -------------------------------------------------
      AT&T      |  41.125  |  40.5  |  41     |   0.5
      IBM       | 117.875  |  114   | 115.875 |  -0.375


                       END OF REPORT
```

3. Write a program that will help a teacher keep track of a class of students. The teacher wants to create a report with the students' initials, the grades on three tests, the total of the three test scores and the final letter grade for each student. A sample run follows. The user's response is in **boldface**.

```
                   SEMESTER GRADE REPORT
                   -------- ----- ------


      You will need the class identification, the initials of
      and the three test scores for each student, and the low
      cutoff score for a grade of  'A', 'B', 'C', and 'D'.

      When you have entered the scores for the last student,
      press Return at the initials prompt.

      Press Return when you are ready to proceed:

      Fall or Spring semester?  (F or S):  F
      Year: 1994
      Which class:  Math 101
      Low score for an 'A' (out of 300) : 270
      Low score for a  'B' (out of 300) : 230
      Low score for a  'C' (out of 300) : 190
      Low score for a  'D' (out of 300) : 160
      Student's initials: MHN
      Scores:
           Test #1: 78
           Test #2: 85
           Test #3: 87

      Student's initials: ATR
      Scores:
           Test #1: 88
           Test #2: 65
           Test #3: 58
```

```
Student's initials:  GJW
Scores:
     Test #1: 63
     Test #2: 68
     Test #3: 92

Student's initials: WLF
Scores:
     Test #1: 95
     Test #2: 93
     Test #3: 89


Student's initials: <Ret>


               SEMESTER GRADE REPORT
               -------- ----- ------
            Semester:  Fall, 1991
                Class: Math 101
        Number of students completing course: 4


-------------------------------------------------------
STUDENT | TEST 1 | TEST 2 | TEST 3 | TOTAL | GRADE
-------------------------------------------------------
MHN     |   78   |   85   |   87   |  250  |  B
ATR     |   88   |   65   |   58   |  211  |  C
GJW     |   63   |   68   |   92   |  223  |  C
WLF     |   95   |   93   |   89   |  277  |  A
```

4. The following program is a modification of the program stocks.c from Example 9-2. Again, the buying price for six stocks is stored in the program. The user enters the current price. The program is intended to output the percentage change of the current price from the buying price.

   a. Execute the program to see how it works.

   b. Draw diagrams like those in the text that represent the variables stock_prices from main() and new and old from output_change(). Include the contents of the arrays.

```
/*                          epp4.c
 *
 *   Synopsis   - Accepts input of 6 stock prices into a
 *                two-dimensional array and should output
 *                the percent change from the old prices.
 *                Has a syntax error.
 *
```

```
 *   Objective  - To provide practice with the C syntax and
 *                the relationship between different
 *                expressions.
 */

/* Include Files */
#include <stdio.h>
#include <stdlib.h>

/* Global Variables */
double stock_prices[2][6] = { { 12, 80, 30,
                                100, 40, 50  } };

/* Function Prototypes */
void output_change( double *new, double *old );
void input_prices( void );

void main( void )
{
    printf( "STOCK INFORMATION PROGRAM\n" );
    printf( "------------------------\n" );
    printf( "This program will give information about the " );
    printf( "prices of \nsix specific stocks. You are to " );
    printf( "enter the current prices of \nthe stocks. The " );
    printf( "percent change from the buying prices\n" );
    printf( "will be displayed.\n\n" );

    input_prices();
    output_change( *stock_prices, *( stock_prices+1 ) );
}

/*********************** input_prices()  *************/
/*  Accepts input of 6 quantities of type float to be
 *  stored in the second "row" of the array. The
 *  combination of library functions gets() and atof() is
 *  used to input the float value.
 */

void input_prices( void )
{
    int i;
    char instring[20];

    printf( "Please enter the current stock prices now.\n" );
    printf( "Stock\tBuying price\tCurrent price\n" );
    printf( "-----\t------------\t-------------\n" );
```

```
        for ( i = 0; i < 6; i++ ) {
                printf( "#%d: \t%6.2f    \t   ",
                                     i+1, stock_prices[0][i] );
                stock_prices[1][i] = atof( gets( instring ));
        }
        printf( "Thank you!\n" );
}


/*********************** output_change()  ************/
/*  Outputs the percentage change of the new prices in
 *  comparison with the old.
 */
void output_change( double *old, double *new )
{
        double change;
        int i;

        printf( "\nPercent change of each stock:\n" );
        for ( i = 0; i < 6; i++ ) {
                printf( "Stock #%d: ", i );

                /* Calculate the percent change */
                change = ( *new++ / *old++ - 1 ) * 100;
                printf( "Percent change is %3.0f%%.\n", change );
        }
}
```

5. El Cilantro Tacos has stores in three locations. They sell burritos, tacos, tosta-
   das and taquitos. The owner wants a program that will keep track of sales and
   calculate the profit for each item, for each store, and the total profit. He
   expects to enter each store's number, the profit margin for each item, and the
   quantity of each item sold at each store. He would like the program to output a
   full report summarizing each store's activity and profits. An example of a
   report is below.

```
                          El Cilantro Tacos
                          -- -------- -----

                  Burritos   Tacos  Tostadas  Taquitos  Store Totals
                  --------   -----  --------  --------  ------------
Store #1     |        134     345        87       240           806
Store #2     |        578     623       400       397          1998
Store #3     |        436     421       258       376          1491
                  --------   -----  --------  --------  ------------
Item totals          1148    1389       745      1013          4295

Profit
Margin                 .74     .38       .53       .26
                                                          Total Profit
Item Profit         849.52  527.82    394.85    263.38         2035.57
```

6. Write a statistical program that uses command line parameters to input the data. The program will sort the data and output the sorted data and its maximum, minimum, mean, and variance. For example, if the executable version of the program is in a file named "stats" and the call to the program is

```
stats 12 3 6 5
```

the output would be

```
Data:    3   5   6 12
Maximum:   12
Minimum:   3
Mean:      6.5
Variance: 11.25
```

7. Write a program that will output the graph of $y = 1/(x^2 + 1)$. To do this, declare a two-dimensional array of type char whose dimensions match the number of character positions on the monitor. For example, many monitors will hold 23 rows of 80 characters each. For this graph, let each character in the vertical direction represent 1/20 of a unit, and let each character in the horizontal direction represent 1/10 of a unit. The elements of your array that lie on the graph could contain the asterisk, '*'. The horizontal axis could be represented by the hyphen, '-', and the vertical axis could be the vertical bar, '¦'. The rest of the array could be filled with blank characters. You will need to decide the placement of your graph for the best viewing and calculate and fill in each element in the array. Then the graph could be displayed by simply printing the contents of the array.

8. Write a program that will search its input for and count the number of occurrences of a given character. The character should be given as a command line argument. Suppose that the executable version of the program is in the file count. A sample run of a similar program is below. The user's input is in **boldface**.

```
# count s
Counting s's. Enter your input now. Press return to finish.
> She sells sea shells down by the sea shore.
There were 8 s's in that text.
```

9. Write a function in C that takes three parameters: the address of a two-dimensional array of type int, the number of rows in the array, and the number of columns in the array. Have the function calculate the sum of the squares of the elements. For example, for the array nums that is pictured below,

```
23   12   14    3
31   25   41   17
```

the call to the function might be

```
sumsquares( nums, 2, 4 );
```

and the value returned would be 4434. Write a short program to test your function.

10. Modify the program for exercise 5 in Chapter 7 by allowing the user to specify both the flat fee for state residents and the nonresident student fee for each credit unit as command line parameters.

11. Modify the program for exercise 3 in Chapter 8 by having the user enter the original form for the date as a command line parameter.

Chapter 10

Input and Output

10.1 Review of Input and Output

Up to this point in the text, we have worked with terminal input and output only. In this chapter, we will study it more closely and also explore file handling in C.

Input and output are not included as part of the C language. They are accomplished by the use of the library functions, which in turn make system calls to interact with each specific operating system. A set of standard specifications for these functions is included in ANSI C so that programs using them will port to other implementations of ANSI C. Most of the functions discussed in this chapter are available in non-ANSI compilers also and, in addition, some compilers may have functions that are not defined in ANSI C. A full list of the ANSI C input and output functions appears in the *Programmer's Handbook*.

A variety of different library functions exists for different input and output situations. We have seen the use of `printf()` to perform formatted output, `scanf()` to perform formatted input, `getchar()` to read a single character at a time from the keyboard, `putchar()` to write a single character at a time to the terminal, `gets()` to read a string from the keyboard, and `puts()` to write a string to the terminal.

With many compilers, the above functions do buffered input and output. That is, if input is performed in a C program, the input characters are usually kept in a buffer until the user presses <Enter>. Then the input buffer can be processed by the C program. Similarly, output characters are kept in an output buffer until some event causes the buffer to be flushed to the screen.

Usually, both standard input and standard output are *line buffered*; each holds a line of text at a time. A buffer for standard output is flushed in case of five separate events: when a newline character is placed in the buffer, when the buffer becomes full, when the system must prepare to do input, when the program terminates, or when the library function `fflush()` is called with `stdout` as its argument. An input buffer is flushed when a user presses the <Enter> key, when the program terminates, and when all the input has been read and the program needs to do more input. (As we have seen before, the identifiers `stdin` and `stdout` usually refer to terminal input and output.)

In many situations a programmer needs to be aware of the buffering of standard output. For example, if output statements are used to trace execution of a program, they must be concluded with a newline character if the programmer wants the output to appear when the output statement is executed. Otherwise, the output either may appear considerably after the statement was executed, or may not appear at all in case of a program crash.

In the following sections we will look at the C library functions that do file handling, and study the functions mentioned above and their counterparts for files.

10.2 An Introduction to Files in C

A file is viewed as a stream of bytes by a C program. Any structure put on a file is put there by the programmer.

When a C program is executed, three files are automatically opened:

1. Standard input, which is usually input from the keyboard.
2. Standard output, which is usually output to the monitor screen.
3. Standard error, which is also usually associated with terminal output.[1]

These three files are referenced with the identifiers `stdin`, `stdout`, and `stderr`, respectively. The identifiers have `FILE *` type. The identifier `FILE` is declared in the file stdio.h with a `typedef` declaration. A `FILE` is a structure in which C keeps information about a file. The `FILE` structure is discussed in more detail in Section 10.8.

When an external file is to be opened for use in a program, the programmer must declare a new variable of type `FILE *`. Therefore, the header file stdio.h must be included in programs using external files. For example, the declaration below declares two variables of type `FILE *`:

```
FILE *infile, *outfile;
```

After this declaration, `infile` and `outfile` need to be connected with file on the disks. This connection is made by using the C library routine `fopen()` to open

---

1. On many computer systems the programmer can manipulate these three files so that they are not associated with the terminal. This is done with operating system commands. However, association with the terminal is the default.

the files. The function `fopen()` makes a file available for use by the program. A typical call to `fopen()` is

```
infile = fopen( "fname", "r" );
```

In this call, the value returned by `fopen()` is of type `FILE *`. It is assigned to the `FILE *` variable `infile`. There are two parameters to `fopen()`; the first is the pathname of the file to be opened and the second is the mode for the file. The `fopen()` library function will form a connection between the program and the file named in the first parameter so that the program can then use the identifier `infile` to refer to the file.

The mode of a file determines whether the file is opened for reading, writing, or a combination of the two. The mode `"r"` indicates that the file is opened for reading only. A file can be opened with any of the following modes:

`"r"`	open an existing file for reading only
`"w"`	open a new file for writing only
`"a"`	open a file for appending (writing at the end of the file)
`"r+"`	open an existing file for update (reading and writing)
`"w+"`	open (create) a new file for update
`"a+"`	open a (new or existing) file for reading and appending

At the end of a program execution, the connection between the file and the program should be broken. This is done by closing the file with the C library function, `fclose()`. The call to `fclose()` to close `infile` would be as follows:

```
fclose (infile);
```

The parameter to `fclose()` is the `FILE *` variable that references the file to be closed. The function `fclose()` returns an integer.

The program fopen1.c in Example 10-1 simply opens a file named `"info"` and then closes it. It illustrates the simplest use of the C library functions `fopen()` and `fclose()`.

Example 10-1: fopen1.c

```
/*              fopen1.c
 *
 *   Synopsis   - Opens a file for reading and then closes it.
 *
 *   Objective  - To present the most basic file handling.
 */

/* Include Files */
#include <stdio.h>                                    /* Note 1 */
```

```
void main( void )
{
      FILE *fp;                                              /* Note 2 */

      fp = fopen( "info", "r" );                             /* Note 3 */

      /* Other code to process the file might
       * be placed here.
       */

      fclose( fp );                                          /* Note 4 */
}
```

This program is very simple. It opens a file and then closes it. The program consists of two lines of executable code. Additional code to check on file handling errors and to process the file should be added.

Note 1: The file stdio.h must be included since the `typedef` declaration of a FILE is in that file. The prototype declaration of `fopen()` is also included in stdio.h.

Note 2: In preparation for opening a file, a variable `fp` of type FILE `*` is declared.

Note 3: The standard library function `fopen()` will attempt to open a file. The name of the file is the first parameter to `fopen()` and the mode is the second. In this example, the function `fopen()` attempts to open a file named `"info"` for reading (`"r"`). If the file is opened successfully, `fopen()` will return a pointer to a FILE structure that will contain the current information about the file. A NULL pointer is returned in case of error.

Note 4: The standard library function `fclose()` will attempt to close the file. The parameter to `fclose()` is the FILE `*` value that was returned earlier by `fopen()`.

Learning Activities

1. Create a file named `"info"` and then compile and run this program.

2. Now delete or rename `"info"` and execute the program again. Since the program was trying to open `"info"` and there was no file by that name, an error condition was created. Was there any notification by the compiler or the system of the error?

3. Get a copy of the header file stdio.h from your system. Look at it briefly to get a feeling for its contents. In particular, look at the declaration of a FILE in stdio.h. See if `fopen()` and `fclose()` were declared.

Error Handling with fopen() and fclose()

In the last Learning Activities, an error condition was created. Most systems would not have reported the error condition. In a longer, more complicated program, the error would probably cause either a program crash or, at least, unreliable output at some other point in the program. The library function `fopen()` has facilities for reporting the error when it occurs. It is up to the programmer to access the facilities.

In case no error occurs, the C library function `fopen()` returns a pointer to the `FILE *` structure that is created by the system when the file is opened. In case an error occurs while opening the file, a `NULL` pointer is returned instead. The value of the pointer returned by `fopen()` should be checked for the indication of an error.

Similarly, the return value from `fclose()` will signal an error condition. If the function `fclose()` is successful in closing a file, the value `0` is returned. Otherwise `EOF` is returned to signal the error.

The program fopen2.c in Example 10-2 is a slight modification of fopen1.c from the previous example. The program still attempts to open the file `"info"` and to close it, but now the program also reports on error conditions and terminates the program if the file cannot be opened.

Example 10-2: fopen2.c

```
/*                  fopen2.c
 *
 *   Synopsis    - Opens a file named info and closes it.
 *
 *   Objective   - Demonstrates elementary error handling with
 *                 fopen() and fclose().
 */

/* Include Files */
#include <stdio.h>
#include <stdlib.h>

void main( void )
{
    FILE *fp;
                                                    /* Note 1 */
    if (( fp = fopen( "info", "r" )) == NULL ) {
        printf( "Input file could not be opened\n" );
        exit( 1 );
    }
```

```
/* Other code to process the file might
 * be placed here.
 */

if ( fclose( fp ) == EOF )                              /* Note 2 */
      printf( "File couldn't be closed\n" );
}
```

This program has essentially the same functionality as fopen1.c; however, now some error handling has been added. Since the program attempts to open and close a file, the file stdio.h has been included and fp was declared. The calls to fopen() and fclose() are now embedded in if statements. The return value from each function is checked for indication of error.

Note 1: In the expression for this if statement, a call to fopen() is made to open the file "info" for reading ("r"). The value returned by fopen() is tested. If that value is NULL, an error occurred while opening the file. In that case, an error message is issued and the program terminates.

Note 2: The program will only reach this if statement if the file was opened successfully. The function fclose() is called to close the file. The value returned by fclose() is tested to see if an error occurred. If the value is zero, no error occurred; the value EOF signifies an error. Not many errors occur when attempting to close a file. Therefore, in C programming, testing the return value of fclose() is not done as often as testing the return value of fopen().

Learning Activities

4. Test fopen2.c in the three following situations:
   a. The file "info" exists and contains information.
   b. The file "info" does not exist.
   c. The file "info" exists and is empty.
   Explain what happens in each case.

5. a. Modify the call to fopen() to open the file "info" for writing.
   b. Execute the program without an available file named "info". Does this cause an error? Check on the status of "info" after running the program. Does it exist now? What are its contents?
   c. Execute the modified program when the file "info" exists and has some unimportant contents. Check on the contents of "info" after executing the program. Did the contents change?
   d. Give a general explanation of the effect of the fopen() call on the status of a file when fopen() is called to open a file for writing.

6. Check the documentation that was supplied with your compiler to see what conditions might cause a call to `fopen()` to fail. Test those conditions on your system and report on the results of your experiment. Do the same for `fclose()`. Try to create a situation where `fclose()` fails.

7. The action to be taken when an error occurs in a program should be carefully considered. Program termination may not always be appropriate. What other actions might be appropriate when a file cannot be successfully opened or closed?

"Action to be taken when an error occurs in a program should be carefully considered." Based on an illustration in *Harpers Weekly*, 1884 (artist unknown).

10.3 Character Input and Output

The utility `getchar()` is used to read a single character from standard input; the utility `putchar()` is used to write a single character to standard output. Both `getchar()` and `putchar()` are specialized versions of other utilities. The utility `getchar()` is defined in the file stdio.h.

The utility `getc()`, a generalized version of `getchar()`, takes a parameter of type FILE *. Before using `getc()`, a call to `fopen()` should be made to open a file for reading; the return value is a pointer to a FILE structure containing information about a file that has been opened for reading; this return value would be used as the parameter to `getc()`. A typical call to `getc()` is

        getc(fp);

where fp is the parameter of type FILE *. The value returned by `getc()` is the next byte in the input buffer. It is returned as a value of type int. When the end of the input file is sensed, `getc()` returns EOF, a preprocessor-defined value in stdio.h. The facility `getchar()` that reads from `stdin` is a specialized version of `getc()`.

Similarly, `putc()` is the generalized version of `putchar()`; `putc()` will write a single byte to a file. The parameters to `putc()` are a value of type int that holds the byte to be written, and the FILE * value indicating the file that will receive the output. A typical call to `putc()` is

        putc(charval, fp);

where `charval` is of type int and fp is a FILE * value that was returned by `fopen()`. The corresponding file must have been opened for writing.

The program cp.c in Example 10-3 makes a copy of a file. Both the input and the output file are opened with calls to `fopen()`. The contents of the input file are read with `getc()`; output is done with calls to `putc()`. The names of the original file and the new copy are passed to the program with command line arguments. Note that the command line arguments are declared with ANSI C prototypes. If you do not have an ANSI C compiler, these declarations may have to be changed.

Example 10-3: cp.c

```
/*              cp.c
 *
 *   Synopsis    - Makes a copy of a file. The names for the original
 *                 file and the copy are on the command line.
 *
 *   Objective   - To illustrate file handling.
 */
```

```
/* Include Files */
#include <stdio.h>                                   /* Note 1 */
#include <stdlib.h>
void main( int argc, char *argv[] )
{
     FILE *fpin, *fpout;                             /* Note 2 */
     int iochar;

     if ( argc != 3 ) {
          printf( "Usage: cp oldfile newfile\n" );
          exit( 1 );                                 /* Note 3 */
     }

     if (( fpin = fopen( argv[1], "r" )) == NULL ) {
                                                      /* Note 4 */
          printf( "Can't open input file.\n" );
          exit( 1 );
     }

     if (( fpout = fopen( argv[2], "w" )) == NULL ) {
                                                      /* Note 5 */
          printf( "Can't open output file.\n" );
          exit( 1 );
     }

     while (( iochar = getc( fpin )) != EOF )         /* Note 6 */
          putc( iochar, fpout );

     fclose( fpin );
     fclose( fpout );
}
```

This program consists of the single function named `main()`. The executable code consists of three `if` statements and a `while` loop.

Note 1: The header file stdio.h must be included in this program for the declaration of the `FILE` structure and the definitions of `getc()` and `putc()`.

Note 2: Two variables of type `FILE *` are declared. The variable `fpin` will denote the input file and the variable `fpout` will denote the output file.

Note 3: The program is designed to be invoked with the command

```
cp oldfile newfile
```

The executable version of this program is expected to be in a file named cp. The number of arguments on the command line is checked as an indication of the correct invocation of the program. If the program was invoked with the wrong number of command line arguments, a message as to the correct usage of the program is issued and the program is terminated.

Note 4: If the number of arguments is correct, an attempt to open file with the name that appears as the second command line argument (`argv[1]`) is made with a call to `fopen()`. The return value from `fopen()` is examined to detect an error. If one is found, an error message is issued and the program is terminated.

Note 5: If no error is encountered in opening the input file, an attempt is made to open a file with the name that appears as the third command line argument. Again, if an error is encountered, a message to that fact is issued and the program is terminated. The `exit()` library function is called to terminate the program. One of its features is to close all open files properly. Otherwise, any file that had previously been opened would need to be specifically closed.

Note 6: If all the files have been successfully opened, the contents of the input file are copied to the output file with this `while` loop. The facility `getc()` is used to read a byte at a time from the input file, and `putc()` is used to write a byte at a time to the output file. There is no error handling available with `getc()` and `putc()`.

Learning Activities

8. Test cp.c for the following situations.

    a. A nonexistent input file.

    b. An empty input file and an existent nonprotected output file.

    c. An existent input file and an existent output file that does not have write permission for users.

    d. An existent input file and a nonexistent output file.

    Generalize the findings from your tests.

9. In cp.c, would it be appropriate to open the output file with the mode `"a"`, `"a+"`, or `"w+"`? Why or why not?

10. Some compilers will allow you to stop the compilation process after the preprocess phase. If you can look at the code generated by the preprocessor, stop the compilation after the program has been preprocessed. Find the previous locations of `getc()`, `putc()`, and `EOF` and inspect the code that has been placed there. Try to interpret this code. (It consists of C expressions or statements.)

A Word of Warning

The facilities getc() and getchar() return values of type int; the value stored in the int represents a single byte of input. A typical mistake for beginning C programmers is to declare a variable of type char to hold the value input by one of these utilities. This will work correctly for most of the input, but in case the default char type on your implementation of C is that of unsigned char, the usual test for end-of-file will not work correctly. For example, the program filerr.c in Example 10-4 is a modification of cp.c of Example 10-3. It attempts to make a copy of a file named on the command line. Be advised that it may hang your system if you are using a microcomputer.

Example 10-4: filerr.c

```
/*                  filerr.c
 *
 *    Synopsis   - Attempts to make a copy of a file.  Designed to be
 *                 invoked with the file names on the command line.
 *
 *    Objective  - To illustrate the need for storing the return
 *                 value from getchar() in a variable of type int.
 */

/* Include Files */
#include <stdio.h>
#include <stdlib.h>

void main( int argc, char *argv[] )
{
    FILE *fpin, *fpout;
    unsigned char iochar;

    if ( argc != 3 ) {
        printf( "Usage: cp oldfile newfile\n" );
        exit( 1 );
    }

    if (( fpin = fopen( argv[1], "r" )) == NULL ) {
        printf( "Can't open input file.\n" );
        exit( 1 );
    }

    if (( fpout = fopen( argv[2], "w" )) == NULL ) {
        printf( "Can't open output file.\n" );
```

```
        exit( 1 );
    }

while (( iochar = getc( fpin )) != EOF )              /* Note 1 */
        putc( iochar, fpout );

fclose( fpin );
fclose( fpout );
}
```

This program is almost identical to cp.c of Example 10-3. The only change in the code is in the declaration of the variable iochar. It was of type int in cp.c. Here it is of type unsigned char.

Note 1: The program will execute almost identically to cp.c. The only exception is the test for end-of-file in the while loop. Here the return from getc() is stored in a variable of type unsigned char. When end-of-file is sensed, getc() will return EOF, which is usually defined to be -1 in stdio.h. This value was chosen to represent EOF because it is impossible to type from the keyboard as a single char and it is outside the range for an ASCII character. Normally, when EOF is returned by getc() and stored in type int, a loop like this one would terminate. However, in this case, the -1 (EOF) is stored in type unsigned char. When this value is tested against the EOF in the while loop expression, the type unsigned char is promoted to integer by C's automatic conversion feature. When this promotion takes place, the extra bits are set to zero so that the promoted value will not test equal to -1. This causes an infinite loop.

It would be unlikely that a programmer would purposely choose a variable of type unsigned char to store the input from getc(), but a variable of type char on some computer systems can be either signed or unsigned char by default. For maximum portability, type int should be used.

Learning Activities

11. Run filerr.c as it is with an existent input file. Does it terminate normally? (Be sure to use the proper command line parameters.)

12. Change the declaration of iochar to type signed char and execute filerr.c again. Does it behave better this time?

13. Omit the keywords signed and unsigned from filerr.c and execute it again. Can you tell if the default char type on your system is unsigned or signed? Explain your conclusion.

The Utility ungetc()

The C library provides a facility, `ungetc()`, for putting a single character back in an input stream. Then the character will be the first character read in the next input statement. The parameters to `ungetc()` are the character to be returned to the input buffer and the `FILE` pointer associated with the file. Note that the first parameter is of type `int`.

Certain restrictions exist for the use of `ungetc()`. Only one character can be returned to each `FILE` and `EOF` cannot be returned.

The program ungetc.c in Example 10-5 illustrates the use of the `ungetc()` facility. The program seeks out all strings of alphabetic characters and strings of digits. This is done with `while` loops where the input value is tested by character processing facilities that are defined in the standard header file ctype.h. The facility `isalpha()` returns a nonzero value if its argument is an alphabetic character and zero otherwise. Similarly `isdigit()` returns nonzero if its argument is a decimal digit and zero otherwise. Both `isalpha()` and `isdigit()` are defined in the header file ctype.h.

The standard function `feof()` is also introduced in this program. It takes a single argument of type `FILE *`, and returns a nonzero value if the current file position is at the end of the file. A zero is returned when the current position in the file is not at the end.

The `ungetc()` facility that appears after the termination of the `while` loop that finds a string of alphabetic characters is used since exit from that `while` loop occurs when the character read is not alphabetic. It may be a digit that needs to be tested for a string of digits. A separate test could be written for that character, or it could be returned to the input buffer with `ungetc()` as it is here. Similar reasoning applies to the other calls to `ungetc()`.

Example 10-5: ungetc.c

```
/*              ungetc.c
 *
 *    Synopsis    - Picks out all strings of alphabetic characters
 *                  and all strings of digits from "text" and prints
 *                  each on a separate line of terminal output.
 *
 *    Objective   - Illustrates the use of the file facilities
 *                  ungetc(), feof() and the character typing
 *                  facilities isalpha() and isdigit().
 */

/* Include Files */
#include <stdio.h>
```

```
#include <ctype.h>                                          /* Note 1 */
#include <stdlib.h>

void main( void )
{
     FILE *fp;
     int iochar;

     if (( fp = fopen( "text", "r" )) == NULL ) {
          printf( "text couldn't be opened\n" );
          exit( 1 );
     }

     while ( !feof( fp )) {                                 /* Note 2 */
                                                            /* Note 3 */
          while ( isalpha( iochar = getc( fp )))
                putchar( iochar );
          putchar( '\n' );
          ungetc( iochar, fp );                            /* Note 4 */
                                                            /* Note 5 */
          while ( isdigit( iochar = getc( fp )))
          putchar( iochar );
          putchar( '\n' );
          ungetc( iochar, fp );                            /* Note 6 */
                                                            /* Note 7 */
          while ( !isalpha( iochar = getc( fp )) &&
                ( !isdigit( iochar )) &&
                ( !feof( fp )))

          ;
          ungetc( iochar, fp );                            /* Note 8 */
     }
     fclose( fp );
}
```

The program consists of the single function main(). A file named "text" is opened. Nested while loops direct the reading of the contents of "text". After each while loop, the program uses ungetc() to set up for the next while loop.

Note 1: The utilities isdigit() and isalpha() are defined in ctype.h.

Note 2: The function feof() will return a zero while there is more input to be processed. Its declaration is in stdio.h. When the end-of-file associated with fp is reached, feof() will return 1 and the expression !feof(fp) will test false and terminate the outer while loop.

Note 3: Input is done with a call to getc() and the return value is tested by isalpha(). If either an uppercase or lowercase alphabetic character was read, isdigit() will return a nonzero value. A zero value indicates a nonalphabetic character and terminates the `while` loop.

Note 4: Since the character just read may have been a digit, it is put back into the input stream so that it will be read and tested in the next `while` loop.

Note 5: Again input is done by `getc()` and the input character is tested. If the character input is a digit, `isdigit()` returns a nonzero value and the next character is read. A nondigit will terminate the `while` loop.

Note 6: The nondigit character may have been an alphabetic so it is put back in the input stream to be read and tested again.

Note 7: This `while` loop will skip over all nondigits and nonalphabetics. It terminates if either a digit or an alphabetic character is read or if end-of-file is reached.

Note 8: Again, since the read that terminated the previous `while` loop may have been a digit or alphabetic character, that character is put back in the input stream to be read and tested again. If end-of-file is reached, the `ungetc()` call will not push anything back. In that case, the program is terminated in the `feof()` call at the top of the outer `while` loop.

Learning Activities

14. a. Create a file named `"text"` with good test material for ungetc.c. For example, input like

```
NOW123is 456   789the   time .
```

has several combinations of data: alphabetic strings delimited by both strings of digits and strings of nondigits. Incorporate as many test situations for this program as you can into `"text"`.

   b. Test ungetc.c with your file `"text"`. Write up any bugs that you find and try to fix them.

   c. The program ungetc.c tests for end-of-file twice. Is this necessary? Write up your conclusion.

15. a. Modify ungetc.c to get the name of the file to be processed from the command line so that the program becomes more of a tool.

   b. Will your modified program find strings of alphabetic characters in object code? Test it with the object code from the program ptrptr.c of Section 9.6.

10.4 String Input and Output

In Chapter 5, we discussed the use of the function `gets()` to accept input of a line of text from standard input and store it as a string. We also discussed the use of `puts()` to display a string on standard output as a line of text. These functions work with standard input and output only. In this section we will consider the C library functions `fgets()`, which was designed to read a line of text from a file, and `fputs()`, which was designed to write a string to a file.

The function `fgets()` takes three parameters: the address of a buffer where the input text will be stored, the maximum number of characters to be read, and a `FILE *` value that references the file that contains the input. For example, the call

```
fgets( buffer, 80, fp );
```

instructs `fgets()` to read characters from the file associated with `fp` and store them in `buffer`. Note that `buffer` should be the address of an array declared in the program. The function `fgets()` will read characters until one of three things happens: a newline character is read, `79` characters have been read, or the end-of-file is encountered. The input text is stored in the array addressed by `buffer` and is terminated by a null character (`'\0'`). The newline character, if read, is stored in `buffer` also. If the input proceeded without error, `fgets()` returns `buffer` or the address of the first character it stored. If either an error occurred or end-of-file was encountered before any characters were read, a `NULL` pointer is returned and `buffer` may contain invalid data.

The function `fputs()` takes two parameters, the address of the string to be written and the `FILE *` value associated with the output file. For example, the call

```
fputs( buffer, fp )
```

will write the data in `buffer`, starting with the first character and stopping with the first null (`'\0'`) character, to the file associated with `fp`. An error is indicated by the return of `EOF` by `fputs()`.

The program in Example 10-6 gives a use of `fgets()` and `fputs()`. The program is a simplified version of the UNIX utility `nl`. It reads a file named on the command line and displays each line of the file preceded by a line number. To make the error message meaningful, the executable version of this program should be in a file named `nl`.

Example 10-6: nl.c

```
/*                    nl.c
 *
 *   Synopsis    - Opens a text file and copies the lines of the
 *                 file to standard output with each text line
```

```
*                      preceded by a line number.
*
*     Objective   - To illustrate the use of fgets() for input and
*                   fputs() for output.
*/

/* Include Files */
#include <stdio.h>
#include <stdlib.h>

/* Constant Declarations */
#define NUMCHARS 512

void main( int argc, char *argv[] )
{
      char inarray[NUMCHARS];                              /* Note 1 */
      int linecount = 1;
      FILE *fp;

      if ( argc < 2 ) {
            printf( "Usage:  nl  filename\n" );
            exit( 1 );
      }
      else if (( fp = fopen( argv[1], "r" )) == NULL ) {
            printf( "Unable to open file %s.\n", argv[1] );
            exit( 1 );
      }
                                                           /* Note 2 */
      while ( fgets( inarray, NUMCHARS, fp ) != NULL ) {
            printf( "%d\t", linecount++ );
            fputs( inarray, stdout );                      /* Note 3 */
      }
      fclose( fp );
}
```

The program consists of the single function main(). The executable code begins with an if-else statement that checks for the correct number of command line parameters and attempts to open the file named as the second command line parameter. An error message is issued and the program is terminated if an error is found in either case. The while loop will read and process the lines in the text file.

Note 1: The array inarray is declared to have the same number of cells as the second parameter to fgets() which is one more cell than the maximum number of characters that will be read by fgets(). This will allow room in the array for the terminating '\0'.

Note 2: The standard library function fgets() is used to do the input. It will return a NULL pointer in the case of either an error or the end of the input file; it returns a pointer to the input buffer, inarray, if no error is encountered. The parameters to fgets() are the address of the input buffer, the number of characters in the buffer, and the FILE pointer for the input file. fgets() will stop reading either when it reads a newline character or when it has filled the buffer and terminated the string with a null character.

Note 3: A call to fputs() outputs each line. It takes two parameters, the address of the buffer to be output and the FILE pointer for the output file.

Learning Activities

16. Compile and run nl.c to ensure that it works on your system. Test the program with several different sets of input.

17. This program accepts input of a line of text into an array of 512 characters. If the file is a text file, it would be unusual for a line of text to contain more characters than the space allocated in the array, but, depending on the system and the input file, it still might be possible. Note that fgets() ensures that the bounds of the array will not be overrun. To see how the program behaves if the input lines contain more characters than the buffer, change NUMCHARS to 8, compile and run the program, and use a file with lines longer than 8 characters as input. Describe how fgets() works in this case.

18. If nl.c misbehaves with a buffer shorter than the length of the lines in the file, change the program so that it behaves as follows:

    a. Lines with 70 characters or less are displayed in their entirety.

    b. The first 70 characters of longer lines are displayed.

    c. The end of long lines (more than 70 characters) will be truncated.

    d. The program only assigns one line number to a line.

    How many cells were declared in your array? Why did you make that choice?

19. Modify nl.c to display the numbered lines to either a file or standard output. If the output is to go to a file, that file will be named as the third command line parameter. If there is no third command line parameter, the output should go to standard output.

10.5 Reading Blocks of Data at a Time

The C library provides the functions `fread()` and `fwrite()` to read and write blocks of data. The function `fread()` takes four parameters:

```
fread( buffer, size, number, fp );
```

The first parameter, `buffer`, is the address of an array or area of memory where the input data will be stored. The memory must be allocated in the program. The second parameter, `size`, indicates the size of the elements to be read; its type coincides with the type returned by `sizeof()` (`size_t` in ANSI C, and one of the integer types, usually `unsigned int`, in earlier versions of C). The third parameter to `fread()` is the `number` of elements to read; its type will be either `size_t` (in ANSI C) or an integer type. The product of the values passed in the second and third parameters gives the total number of bytes to be read. The final parameter is of type `FILE *`; it is associated with the file from which the input data is to come. The parameters to the library function `fwrite()` are analogous to those of `fread()`.

Both of these functions will return the number of elements actually read or written. If no error occurs, the number returned should agree with the third parameter in the function call. If the value returned is less than the third parameter, then an error has occurred or end-of-file was encountered by the call to `fread()`.

These functions do not expect any particular type of data nor do they do any conversions. They simply attempt to read or write the requested number of bytes. For the following examples, consider the declarations below:

```
char ch, chararray[10];
int intgr;
struct emp {
     char name[30];
     float salary;
} staff[30];
```

The call

```
fread( &ch, sizeof( ch ), 1, stdin );
```

would read a value for `ch`. It reads a single byte from standard input. The expression `&ch` is used as the address of a one-byte "buffer" in memory.

The call

```
fwrite( &intgr, sizeof( int ), 1, fp );
```

writes a value of type `int` that is stored in `intgr` to the file associated with `fp`. The function `fwrite()` will store binary data in the file. Conversion to ASCII digits is not done by this output function.

The call

```
fread( staff, sizeof( struct emp ), 30, fp );
```

would attempt to read a block big enough to contain thirty structures of type struct emp from the file associated with fp. The structures would fill up the array staff. Recall that the name staff is the address of the array buffer in memory. Again, binary data is expected for the salary member of this structure.

The program fwrite.c in Example 10-7 is a first step in a program to manage a checking account. It reads information about checking account transactions from the keyboard and stores it in a file. A structure is used to hold the transaction information. The first member of the structure, t_type, indicates the type of the transaction. It will hold the value 'W' when the transaction is a withdrawal, 'D' when the transaction is a deposit, or the check number for a check. The second member, payee_memo, will hold either the name of the person to whom a check is written or a memo describing a transaction. The third and fourth members are bit fields. The tax_deduct member will be 1 when the entry is tax deductible and zero otherwise. Similarly, the cleared member will be set to 1 when an entry has cleared the bank; it will be zero otherwise.

Example 10-7: fwrite.c

```
/*              fwrite.c
 *
 *    Synopsis    - Accepts input of information about banking
 *                  transactions and stores the information in
 *                  a file.
 *
 *    Objective   - To illustrate the use of fwrite() to do block
 *                  output of a structure.
 */

/* Include Files */
#include <stdio.h>
#include <ctype.h>
#include <stdlib.h>

/* Constant Declarations */
#define TRUE        1
#define FALSE       0
#define BUFFSIZE    50
```

```c
/* Type Descriptions */
struct trans {                                          /* Note 1 */
        int t_type;
        char payee_memo[BUFFSIZE];
        float amount;
        unsigned tax_deduct:1;
        unsigned cleared:1;
};
/* Function Prototypes */
int get_type( void );
void get_trans( struct trans * );
void put_trans( struct trans *, FILE * );

void main( void )
{
    struct trans transact;
    FILE *fp;
                                                        /* Note 2 */
    if (( fp = fopen( "transact", "a+" )) == NULL ) {
        printf( "Transaction file couldn't be opened.\n" );
        exit( 1 );
    }

    /*  The following while loop will continue until the
     *  user types a 'Q' for the transaction type.  Each
     *  time the loop is executed, one transaction is input
     *  and stored in the file.
     */
    while (( transact.t_type = get_type() ) != 'Q' ) {
        get_trans( &transact );
        put_trans( &transact, fp );
    }
    fclose( fp );
}
/****************************** gettype()  ********************/
/*  Requests and accepts input of the transaction type from the
 *  keyboard. Any letter entered is converted to uppercase
 *  before returning, and a string of digits is converted to
 *  type int. Ensures that a correct transaction type is returned.
 */
int get_type( void )
{
    char buffer[80];
    int correct = FALSE, t_type;

    while ( !correct ) {
        printf( "D=deposit, W=withdrawal, or Check #\n" );
```

```
                        printf( "Enter transaction type ('Q' to quit): " );
                        gets( buffer );
                        if ( isdigit( *buffer )) {
                                /* convert string of digits to
                                 * type int
                                 */
                                correct = TRUE;
                                t_type = atoi( buffer );
                        }
                        else {
                                /* Translate any alphabetic character
                                 * to uppercase for testing and storage.
                                 */
                                t_type = toupper( ( int ) *buffer );
                                if (( t_type !='D' )&& ( t_type !='W' )
                                                    && ( t_type != 'Q' ))
                                        printf( "Incorrect, try again\n" );
                                else
                                        correct = TRUE;
                        }
                }
        return( t_type );
}
/****************************** get_trans()   *****************/
/*    Accepts input of a single transaction from the terminal.
 */
void get_trans( struct trans *trans_ptr )
{
        char inbuf[80];

        printf( "Amount: $" );
        trans_ptr->amount = atof( gets( inbuf ));

        switch ( trans_ptr->t_type ) {
                case 'W':
                case 'D':printf( "Memo: " );
                        fgets( trans_ptr->payee_memo, BUFFSIZE, stdin );
                        break;
                default: printf( "Payee: " );
                        fgets( trans_ptr->payee_memo, BUFFSIZE, stdin );
        }

        printf( "Tax_deductible? (y/n) : " );
        gets( inbuf );
        if (( *inbuf == 'y' ) || ( *inbuf == 'Y' ))
                trans_ptr->tax_deduct = 1;
        else
```

```
            trans_ptr->tax_deduct = 0;

     printf( "Cleared? (y/n) : " );
     gets( inbuf );
     if (( *inbuf == 'y' ) || ( *inbuf == 'Y' ))
          trans_ptr->cleared = 1;
     else
          trans_ptr->cleared = 0;
}


/***************************** put_trans()   *****************/
/*    Writes the contents of the structure pointed to by
 *    trans_ptr to the file associated with fp.
 */
void put_trans( struct trans *trans_ptr, FILE *fp )
{
                                                /* Note 3 */
     fwrite( trans_ptr, sizeof( struct trans ), 1, fp );
}
```

The program consists of the functions main(), get_type(), get_trans(), and put_trans(). The function main() opens the file and handles file-opening errors. A while loop calls the other functions to get the information about the transactions and store the transaction information in a file. The function get_type() will always return a valid transaction type or a 'Q' to stop execution of the program. The functions get_trans() and put_trans(), respectively, accept input of information for a single transaction from the keyboard and write it to the file.

Note 1: The structure for a bank transaction is declared. The sizeof() this structure will be used in the call to fwrite() when the information is written to a file.

Note 2: The call to fopen() opens the file with the mode "a+". This would allow both reading the file and writing at the end of the file (appending). In this program, we will just be writing to the file, but these routines might well be used in a program that would both read and write to a file.[1]

Note 3: This call to fwrite() will write the information about a single transaction to the file. The first parameter to fwrite() is the address of the buffer where the information to be written resides. In this case, the buffer is the structure itself, and the address is passed to fwrite() by the pointer trans_ptr. The next two fields combine (multiply) to give the total number of bytes to be written. In this case, one structure is being written so that the number of bytes is given by sizeof(struct trans) * 1. The final parameter indicates the file where the output is to be stored.

---

1. Some of the microcomputer compilers have special modes to open files that will contain binary data. For example, if this program is to be executed on a microcomputer, the mode for opening this file would be "ab+". The modes for opening files with binary data on a microcomputer are "rb", "wb", "ab", "rb+", "wb+", "ab+". They have the same meaning as the corresponding modes without the 'b'.

Learning Activities

20. a. Compile and run fwrite.c. Make up three or four transactions to enter.

    b. After you have completed part a, you should have a file named "transact" in your directory. This file will contain both binary and ASCII data. Inspect the contents of the file with a dump program if your system has one.

21. The function fwrite() returns the number of items actually written. If this number is less than the third argument to fwrite(), an error has occurred. The program fwrite.c does not currently check on the value returned by fwrite(). Modify fwrite.c to check on this return value and to handle any errors that may occur.

22. Give a single call to fwrite() that would write an array of type struct trans to a file. Assume that the array has five entries.

The program fread.c in Example 10-8 is a companion program to fwrite.c. It reads a file created by fwrite.c and displays the contents of each transaction record to standard output.

Example 10-8: fread.c

```
/*                    fread.c
 *
 *    Synopsis    - Reads transactions (elements of type struct
 *                  trans) from a file and displays them on
 *                  standard output.
 *
 *    Objective   - To illustrate the use of fread() with structures.
 */

/* Include Files */
#include <stdio.h>
#include <stdlib.h>

/* Constant Declarations */
#define BUFFSIZE  50
```

```
/* Type Descriptions */
struct trans {
        int t_type;
        char payee_memo[BUFFSIZE];
        float amount;
        unsigned tax_deduct:1;
        unsigned cleared:1;
};

/* Function Prototypes */
void print_trans( struct trans * );
int read_trans (struct trans *, FILE * );

void main( void )
{
    struct trans transact;
    FILE *fp;

    if (( fp = fopen( "transact", "r" )) == NULL ) {
            printf( "Transaction file couldn't be opened.\n" );
            exit( 1 );
    }

    while ( read_trans( &transact, fp ))              /* Note 1 */
            print_trans( &transact );
    fclose( fp );
}
/***************************** read_trans()  *****************/
/*   Reads a single transaction from the file associated with fp.
 *   Stores it in the structure pointed to by trans_ptr.
 */
int read_trans( struct trans *trans_ptr, FILE *fp )
{
    int retval;
                                                       /* Note 2 */
    retval = fread( trans_ptr, sizeof( *trans_ptr ), 1, fp );
    return ( retval );
}
/*********************************  print_trans()   *******/
/*   Displays the contents of the structure pointed to by outtrans
 *   on standard output.  Each field is separated with a vertical
 *   bar character.
 */
void print_trans( struct trans *outtrans )
{
```

```
    /* Cleared field */
    if ( outtrans->cleared )
         printf( "C ¦ " );
    else
         printf( "  ¦ " );

    /* Transaction type */
    if (( outtrans->t_type =='D' )
                    ¦¦ ( outtrans->t_type == 'W' )
                    ¦¦ ( outtrans->t_type == 'I' ))
         printf( "%4c ¦ ", outtrans->t_type );
    else
         printf( "%4d ¦ ", outtrans->t_type );

    /* tax_deduct field */
    if ( outtrans->tax_deduct )
         printf( " T ¦ " );
    else
         printf( "   ¦ " );

    printf( "%10.2f ¦ ", outtrans->amount );
    printf( "%s", outtrans->payee_memo );
}
```

The program consists of the functions main(), read_trans() and print_trans(). The declaration of a struct trans is made globally. This declaration is exactly the same as the one in the program fwrite.c of Example 10-7. In the function main(), a file is opened and a while loop is executed. The functions read_trans() and print_trans() are called within the while loop. The function print_trans() displays the members of the structure pointed to by its parameter. In the output, the members are separated with a ' ¦ ' character.

Note 1: In evaluating the expression for the while loop, a call is made to the function read_trans(). The value returned by read_trans() is 1 if a transaction has been read successfully and 0 if either the end-of-file was encountered or if an error occurred.

Note 2: A call to fread() reads a block of data to fill a variable of type struct trans. The address of a struct trans, trans_ptr, is passed in as the first parameter to fread(). It serves as a buffer to be filled by fread(). The product of the next two parameters indicate the total number of bytes to read. The final parameter is the FILE * variable associated with the input file. The value returned by fread() is the number of objects actually read. This value is passed back to the calling function. When the value is zero, no elements have been read and the while loop in main() terminates.

Learning Activities

23. Execute fread.c with the file created by fwrite.c to ensure that it displays the correct data[1]
24. Modify the program by having the value returned by `fread()` displayed before it is returned by `read_trans()`. Is the number of characters read on successful calls to `fread()` a constant value?
25. The function `read_trans()` can be shortened. Rewrite `read_trans()` as a single statement that combines the `return` with the call to `fread()`.
26. Modify the program once again by rewriting the `if-else` statements in `print_trans()` as `?:` expressions.

10.6 Formatted Input and Output

The functions `printf()` and `scanf()` do formatted input and output to and from the terminal (standard output and input). The C library contains counterparts, `fprintf()` and `fscanf()`, that perform the same type of output and input to and from a file. Similar functions, `sprintf()` and `sscanf()`, write and read to and from a string.

The first parameter to `fscanf()` and `fprintf()` is an expression of type `FILE *` that is associated with the file for the input or output. The second parameter is the control string, and the remainder of the parameters have the same meaning as for `scanf()` and `printf()`. Typical calls to these functions would be

```
fscanf( fp1, "%d", &intvar );
```

to read a decimal value from the file associated with `fp1` and store it in the variable `intvar`. Also,

```
fprintf( fp2, "That value was %d.\n", intvar );
```

will write the control string with the `%d` replaced by the decimal value of `intvar` to the file associated with the `FILE *` value `fp2`.

The functions `sscanf()` and `sprintf()` have the address of a memory buffer as their first parameter. Otherwise, their parameters are the same as their companion functions `printf()` and `scanf()`. In the case of `sscanf()`, the contents of the buffer are scanned for characters that match the conversion specifica-

---

1. If you are working on a microcomputer, you may have to change the mode in the `fopen()` call to `"rb"` since the file will contain binary data.

tions contained in the control string. In the case of `sprintf()`, the control string with the indicated conversions performed is written to the buffer. Take care to ensure that the memory buffer is large enough to hold the string that will be written to it.

The program in Example 10-9 illustrates some of these functions. It reads a text file that is composed of student information. Each line of the file should contain the information about one student, a first name, a last name, and the grade point average. The names are made up of alphabetic characters and possibly a single quote; the grade point average is a `float` value. The first and last names are separated with spaces. The grade point average is separated from the names with some spaces also. The program will create two new files; one file will contain only the student names, written with the last name first; the second file will contain only the grade point averages. For example, if the input file contains the information

```
Albert Einstein 3.47
Alfred Neuman 2.29
Donald Knuth  3.79
```

after running the program, the file `names` will contain

```
Einstein, Albert
Neuman, Alfred
Knuth, Donald
```

and the file `gpas` will contain

```
3.47
2.29
3.79
```

The program uses `fgets()` to read a line from the file into an array `inbuff`. The function `sscanf()` scans `inbuff` to find the first name, the last name and the grade point average of each student. Then the function `fprintf()` is used to write the information to the files `names` and `gpas`.

Example 10-9: prntscan.c

```
/*              prntscan.c
 *
 *  Synopsis    - Opens a file of student names and grade point
 *                averages, reads the file, and puts the names in
 *                one file and the grade point averages in another.
 *
 *  Objective   - To demonstrate some of the printf(), scanf()
 *                family of functions. In particular to demonstrate
```

```
 *                  sscanf() and fprintf().
 */

/* Include Files */
#include <stdio.h>
#include <stdlib.h>

void main( void )
{
     FILE *fp, *name_fp, *gpa_fp;
     char first[15], last[15], inbuff[80];
     double gpa;
     if (( fp = fopen( "studinfo", "r" )) == NULL ) {
          printf( "Unable to open input file.\n" );
          exit( 1 );
     }

     /* Open output files and report any errors.   */
     if (( name_fp = fopen( "names", "w" )) == NULL ) {
          printf( "Unable to open names file.\n" );
          exit( 2 );
     }

     if (( gpa_fp = fopen( "gpas", "w" )) == NULL ) {
          printf( "Unable to open gpa file.\n" );
          exit( 3 );
     }

     while ( fgets( inbuff, 80, fp ) != NULL ) {
                                                          /* Note 1 */
          sscanf( inbuff, "%s %s %f%*c", first, last, &gpa );
                                                          /* Note 2 */
          fprintf( name_fp, "%s, %s\n", last, first );
          fprintf( gpa_fp, "%4.2f\n", gpa );
     }
     fclose( fp );
     fclose( name_fp );
     fclose( gpa_fp );
}
```

This program consists of a single function, main(). The three if statements open the input file, studinfo, and the two output files, names and gpas. If an error occurs while opening any of the files, an error message is issued and the program terminates. The while loop processes the contents of the input file. Each iteration of the loop processes one line of the file, the information about one student. The input is done with fgets(), which reads a line of the file at a time.

Note 1: The array `inbuff` contains one line of the file and is terminated with a null character (`'\0'`). The function `sscanf()` will look for two strings delimited by whitespace (blanks, tabs, and so on), and a string of digits with a possible decimal point that will be converted to a `float` value.[1] The addresses of the memory locations where the strings and the `float` value will be stored are given as additional parameters.

Note the fourth conversion specification, `%*c`, in the control string for `sscanf()`; it demonstrates the use of the conversion suppression flag, `*`. This tells `sscanf()` to read an extra character, but not to convert or store it. With this syntax in the control string, `sscanf()` will read past the newline character.

Note 2: The library function `fprintf()` is used to write both the student name to the `names` file and the grade point average to the `gpas` file. The `FILE *` variable that is associated with each of the output files is used as the first parameter. The remainder of the parameter list could be used with a `printf()` statement. Note that the student name is written with the last name first, followed by a comma and the first name.

Learning Activities

27.   a.   Create an input file named "studinfo" with data in the form

       `LAST<space>FIRST<space>GPA`

on each line.

    b.   Compile and run prntscan.c with this input file to see how it executes.

    c.   Experiment by putting a variable number of spaces and/or tab characters between the names and the grade point average. Run the program again. Does the new format change the result? Why or why not?

28.   In the `sscanf()` statement, the `*` before the `c` in the control string tells `sscanf()` that there will be an additional character, the newline character, `'\n'`, and that it should not be converted and stored. Is this conversion specification necessary? Experiment with the following cases.

    a.   Omit the `*` from the `%*c` and attempt to run the program again. If the results are not correct, explain why.

    b.   Omit the whole conversion specification, `%*c`, and run the program again. Explain what happens.

---

1. The function `sscanf()` has been used here without properly checking on its return value. You will be asked to modify this program to provide this check in the Learning Activities after the next example program.

c. Run the program in its original form, but change the input file by adding some blank characters at the end of each line. Does this cause an error? Explain what you think happens.

d. Modify the input file again by placing some alphabetic characters at the end of each line. Run the program with this modified input file and explain what happens.

29. In prntscan.c, the input from the terminal was read with `fgets()` and then `sscanf()` was called to scan the input string. Could `fscanf()` have been used directly on the input file instead of using `fgets()` on the file and `sscanf()` on the resulting string? Experiment to find out.

Error Detection with the printf() and scanf() Families

We have mentioned before that `printf()` and `scanf()` are powerful, flexible functions. The same is true for `fprintf()`, `fscanf()`, `sprintf()`, and `sscanf()`.

The input functions, in particular, may give unexpected results when the actual input is not formatted the way that the control string parameter to the function specifies. When this happens, the function does not terminate the program as might happen with general-purpose input routines in other programming languages. The program continues with possibly invalid data in the input variables. Therefore, if the conversion values are not validated by the program, erroneous results may occur.

Values are returned by `printf()`, `scanf()`, and the related functions. The `printf()` family will return an int value indicating the total number of characters written by each particular call. The `scanf()` family also returns a value of type int; it returns the number of conversions that were made matching the conversion specifications in its control string. If the number of actual conversions made is less than the number requested, an error in input has occurred.

The program in Example 10-10 examines the values returned by `printf()` and `scanf()`. It is designed to be used solely as a learning aid. It should be tested with different forms of input, and the resultant values should be studied with the goal of fully understanding when and what conversions are made by `scanf()` with different input values.

Example 10-10: retval.c

```
/*              retval.c
 *
 *   Synopsis   - Requests and accepts input of a string, an int, a
 *                char, and a float.  Echoes those quantities and
 *                displays return values of printf() and scanf().
 *
 *   Objective  - To allow the reader to experiment with input to
 *                scanf() to get a feel for when and how conversions
 *                are made and what feedback is provided by scanf().
 */

/* Include Files */
#include <stdio.h>

void main( void )
{
     char charvar, buff[80];
     int intvar, printret, scanret;
     float floatvar;

     printf( "Enter a string, an int, a character, and a float: " );
                                                       /* Note 1 */
     scanret = scanf( "%s%d%c%f", buff, &intvar,
                                    &charvar, &floatvar );
                                                       /* Note 2 */
     printret = printf( "Values : %s, %d, ¦%c¦, %5.3f\n",
                              buff, intvar, charvar, floatvar );
     printf( "printret %d, scanret %d\n", printret, scanret );
}
```

The executable code consists of three printf() calls and a call to scanf(). The return values from the scanf() call and one of the calls to printf() are stored and displayed on standard output.

Note 1: When scanf() finishes executing, it returns the number of successful conversions it made; it will read until it completes the required number of conversions or it encounters a character that cannot be converted.

Note 2: The value returned by printf() is the number of characters it placed in the output buffer. It will vary with the data, but if successful output has occurred this value will be greater than or equal to a calculated minimum.

Learning Activities

30. Predict the output of retval.c with each of the following sets of input.

    a. `hi 7r4.5`

    b. `hi 7 r 4.5`

    c. `hi 7r 4.5`

    d. `hi`
       `7`
       `r`
       `4.5`

    e. `hi`
       `7r`
       `4.5`

    f. `hi there`

    Explain what you think happens with each set of input values.

31. Compile and execute retval.c to test your predictions. Correct any mistakes in your thinking. Execute the program with several additional sets of input to test any concept questions that may have occurred to you. Continue to experiment until you are sure you understand the way that `scanf()` operates.

32. Answer the following questions.

    a. Why does `scanf()` sometimes read past carriage returns and sometimes appear to terminate when the carriage return is pressed?

    b. What difference does a space make
       i. between the `hi` and the `7` in 30a and 30b?
       ii. between the `7` and the `r` in 30b?
       iii. between the `r` and the `4.5` in 30c?

33. If the value returned by `scanf()` is less than 4, an error has occurred since 4 conversions were requested. Modify the program to display an error message and terminate the program in that case.

34. In retval.c, what is the minimum value that can be returned by `printf()` without the occurrence of an error in output? Allow the possibility that errors were encountered by `scanf()`. Determine a set of input that will produce that minimum return value.

35. a. Read your documentation to discover the meaning of the value returned by `sscanf()`.

    b. Modify the program prntscan.c of Example 10-9 to check the value returned by `sscanf()` and take appropriate action.

10.7 Random versus Sequential Access in Files

So far, we have discussed sequential access to files. When a file is opened, reading (or writing) starts at the beginning of the file and proceeds through the file in a sequential manner. The current position in the file is recorded in something we will loosely refer to as the file pointer. Whenever a read is done, the file pointer then moves to point to the next element in the file to be read.

Consider the file "transact" created by fwrite.c of Example 10-7. The file was written sequentially; the first write took place at the beginning of the file and subsequent writes appended information to the end of the file. The program fread.c of Example 10-8 reads the records in sequential order from the first record in the file to the last. In sequential access, reading the nth record requires first reading the $n - 1$ previous records.

In contrast to sequential access, random access allows the reading of the records in any order. For example, the third record could be read, then the fifteenth record, and then the first record. Two library functions in the standard C library help with random access of files. These functions are `fseek()` and `ftell()`.

The function `fseek()` moves the file pointer to any byte position in the file. It takes three parameters. A typical call to `fseek()` might be

```
fseek( fp, offset, start );
```

where `fp` is the `FILE *` variable associated with the file whose pointer is to be moved. The parameter `offset` is a variable of type `long` that represents the byte offset or number of bytes that the pointer is to be moved. The parameter `start` indicates the beginning position for the file pointer. The legal values for `start` are `0`, `1`, and `2`. A value of `0` requests `fseek()` to move the file pointer `offset` bytes from the beginning of the file; a value of `1` requests that the seek movement start from the current position in the file; and a value of `2` requests a seek from the end of the file. (In ANSI C the constant values `SEEK_SET` for `0`, `SEEK_CUR` for `1` and `SEEK_END` for `2` have been defined in stdio.h for use with the `fseek()` function. They may be used to make the code more readable.)

The function `ftell()` returns the current byte offset from the beginning of the file. It takes a `FILE *` parameter that indicates the relevant file. For example, the code

```
fseek( fp, ( long ) 0, 0 );
```

positions the file pointer at the beginning of the file. The code

```
fseek( fp, ( long ) 0, 2 );
length = ftell( fp );
```

first positions the file pointer at the end of the file; `ftell( fp )` then returns the byte offset from the beginning of the file and stores it in `length`. The value of `length` will be the number of bytes in the file. The call

```
fseek( fp, 2*sizeof( struct trans ), 0 );
```

should position the file pointer at the beginning of the third record of type `struct trans` in the file.

The program fseek.c in Example 10-11 allows a user to view any record in the file "transact" that was created by fwrite.c of Example 10-7. The user enters record numbers corresponding to the position of the record in the file, `0` for the first record, `1` for the second, and so on, and the program displays the requested records on the screen.

Example 10-11: fseek.c

```
/*                 fseek.c
 *
 *    Synopsis    - Opens a file and displays records at a user's
 *                  request.
 *
 *    Objective   - To introduce the standard library functions
 *                  fseek() and ftell().
 */

/* Include Files */
#include <stdio.h>
#include <stdlib.h>

/* Constant Declarations */
#define BUFFSIZE   50

/* Type Declarations */
struct trans {
        int t_type;
        char payee_memo[BUFFSIZE];
        float amount;
        unsigned tax_deduct:1;
        unsigned cleared:1;
};
```

```
/* Function Prototypes */
void print_trans( struct trans * );
void browse( FILE *, long );
int read_trans( struct trans *, FILE * );
long int getnumrecs( FILE * );

void main( void )
{
     FILE *fp;
     long int totalrec;
                                                      /* Note 1 */
     if (( fp = fopen( "transact", "r+" )) == NULL ) {
          printf( "Transaction file couldn't be opened.\n" );
          exit( 1 );
     }
     totalrec = getnumrecs( fp );
     if ( totalrec == -1L ) {
          fprintf( stderr, "Error with transaction file\n" );
          exit( 1 );
     }

     printf( "Transaction Browser\n" );
     printf( "Enter the record number you want to see " );
     printf( "or 'Q' to quit.\n" );
     browse( fp, totalrec );
}

/***************************** read_trans()   *****************/
/*   Reads a single transaction from the file associated with fp.
 *   The information read is stored in the structure pointed to
 *   by trans_ptr.
 */
                                                      /* Note 2 */
int read_trans( struct trans * trans_ptr, FILE * fp)
{
     int retval;

     retval = fread( trans_ptr, sizeof( *trans_ptr ), 1, fp );
     return ( retval );
}

/***************************** print_trans()   *****************/
/*   Displays the contents of the structure pointed to by outtrans
 *   to standard output.  Each field is separated with a vertical
 *   bar character.
```

```
    */
void print_trans( struct trans * outtrans )                    /* Note 3 */
{
    /* Cleared field */
    if ( outtrans->cleared )
        printf( "C ¦ " );
    else
        printf( "  ¦ " );

    /* Transaction type */
    if (( outtrans->t_type =='D' )
                                ¦¦ ( outtrans->t_type == 'W' )
                                ¦¦ ( outtrans->t_type == 'I' ))
        printf( "%4c ¦ ", outtrans->t_type );
    else
        printf( "%4d ¦ ", outtrans->t_type );

    /* tax_deduct field */
    if ( outtrans->tax_deduct )
        printf( " T ¦ " );
    else
        printf( "   ¦ " );

    printf( "%10.2f  ¦ ", outtrans->amount );
    printf( "%s", outtrans->payee_memo );
}

/***************************** browse()   ********************/
/*   Accepts input of record numbers, finds and displays the
 *   records until the user signals quit with a 'Q'.
 */
void browse( FILE *fp, long numrecs )
{
    int recnum;

    struct trans transact;

    printf( "Transaction number: " );
    while ( scanf( "%d", &recnum )) {                          /* Note 4 */
        if ( recnum >= numrecs )
            printf( "Enter a number between 0 and %d\n",
                                            numrecs-1 );
        else {
                                                              /* Note 5 */
            fseek( fp, ( long ) recnum*sizeof( transact ), 0 );
            if ( read_trans( &transact ,fp ))
```

```
                              print_trans( &transact );
                  else
                              printf( "Transaction %d not found.\n", recnum );
            }
            printf( "Next transaction Number: " );
      }
}


/****************************** getnumrecs()   *****************/
/*    Calculates the number of records in the file by getting
 *    the total length of the file and dividing by the number
 *    of bytes in a record.
 */
long int getnumrecs( FILE *fp )
{
      long int numbytes;

      fseek( fp, ( long ) 0, 2 );                           /* Note 6 */
      numbytes = ftell( fp );                               /* Note 7 */
      if ( numbytes != -1 )
            return ( numbytes/sizeof( struct trans ));
      else
            return ( -1L );
}
```

This program consists of the functions main(), read_trans(), print_trans(), browse(), and getnumrecs(). The function main() opens the file "transact", calls getnumrecs() to calculate the number of records in the file, issues some messages to the user and calls the function browse() to browse through the file.[1]

Note 1: In this call to fopen(), the file "transact" is opened with mode "r+"; this allows both reading and writing to the file. The file contents are left intact when the file is opened. The modes "w+" and "a+" also allow both reading and writing; with "w+", any existing file contents are destroyed when the file is opened, and with "a+", writes to the file are only done at the end of the file.

Note 2: The function read_trans() is exactly the same as the one that appeared in the program fread.c of Example 10.8.

Note 3: The function print_trans() is also taken from fread.c. Both of these functions could be kept in a separate utilities file and linked in during the link step of the compilation process.

Note 4: The expression in this while loop exploits the behavior of scanf(). When a 'Q' is entered, scanf() will not be able to make a conversion

---

1. If you are working on a microcomputer, remember to change the mode in the call to fopen() to "rb+".

to type int and will therefore return 0. The value of 0 will stop the execution of the while loop.

Note 5: The function fseek() is called to position the file pointer at the beginning of the correct record. The offset value is the total number of bytes from the beginning of the file that must be skipped to position the file pointer at the beginning of the record with record number recnum. This assumes that the user knows that record numbering begins with 0.

Note 6: This call to fseek() will position the file pointer at the end of the file.

Note 7: The function ftell() returns the byte offset from the beginning of the file. This number is stored in numbytes, and used to calculate the number of records in the file.

Learning Activities

36. Run fseek.c using the file created by fwrite.c of Example 10-7 as input.

a. If it does not work correctly, modify fwrite.c to open the file with the mode "ab+", compile and execute it again to recreate the data file. Then modify fseek.c to open the file with mode "rb+", compile and execute it again with the new data file.

b. If it does not work correctly, modify the program fread.c to display the offset of each record before it reads it. Check to see if the records are evenly spaced within the file. If so, modify fseek.c to seek the correct distance to find each record and run the program again. If the records are not evenly spaced within the file, it may not be possible to make this program work without major modifications.

37. Modify fseek.c to allow a user to start counting records with 1. That is, 1 should refer to the first record in the file, and the number returned by getnumrecs() should refer to the last record.

10.8 A Closer Look at stdio.h

The file stdio.h contains facilities for input and output. This file differs on different implementations of C because most of the input and output library functions are redesigned for each computer system. Here we will examine the contents of a typical stdio.h file.

Preprocessor-defined constants are defined with a #define in stdio.h. We have used the constants EOF and NULL. Another constant typically defined in stdio.h is BUFSIZ. Input and output from files are generally buffered, and BUFSIZ is the size of the default buffer.

As mentioned earlier in this chapter, a typedef declaration of the identifier FILE also appears in stdio.h. A FILE is declared to be a C structure that is used by the library functions and the operating system to keep information about a file. Typically, a FILE contains at least three members, a member that counts the number of characters still to be processed before the buffer needs to be refreshed, the address of the buffer, and the pointer into the current position in the buffer. A partial example of the declaration of a FILE is below.

```
typedef  struct {
        short count;     /* number of unprocessed characters
                          * (cells) in the buffer */
        char *bufaddr;  /* the address of the buffer */
        char *curptr;   /* pointer to the current position
                         * of the buffer */
            .
            .
            .
    } FILE;
```

Different compilers may implement the FILE structure with different members or different names for these members, but the existence of three members with the uses mentioned above is typical. Additional members might include flags that indicate whether the file is opened for reading, writing, or a combination; an indication if end-of-file has been encountered; an error indicator; and a member by which the operating system keeps track of the file.

One FILE structure is kept up to date for every open file in the program. The operating system updates the current information in the FILE every time the status changes.

The program stdio.c in Example 10-12 displays the values of the members in the FILE structure for stdin and stdout as changes occur. Input and output are done by calls to getchar() and putchar(). The program is a modification of inout2.c from Example 2-13. The names of the FILE members are those used in Borland's Turbo C/C++ compiler. If you are not using this compiler, the program will have to be modified to run correctly on your system. It will require the examination of the declaration of a FILE in stdio.h and the adjustment of at least the names of the members of the FILE structure in the program to match those in your stdio.h file.

Example 10-12: stdio.c

```
/*                stdio.c
 *
 *    Synopsis    - Echoes its input to its output and displays
 *                  information about contents of stdin and stdout.
 *
 *    Objective   - To provide a vehicle for studying the changes
 *                  in the FILE structure.
 */

/* Include Files */
#include <stdio.h>

/* Function Prototypes */
void FILEinfo( FILE *fp, char *fn );

void main( void )
{
    int iochar;

    printf( "Enter text - signal EOF to quit.\n" );
    while (( iochar = getchar() ) != EOF ) {
        FILEinfo( stdin, "stdin" );                      /* Note 1 */
        putchar( iochar );
        FILEinfo( stdout, "stdout" );                    /* Note 2 */
    }
}

/***************************** FILEinfo()  *******************/
/*   Displays the current information from a FILE structure.
 *   Names taken from Borland Turbo C++/C stdio.h.  May need
 *   to be changed for other compilers.
 */
void FILEinfo( FILE *fp, char *FILEname )
{                                                        /* Note 3 */
    fprintf( stderr,"%s : level %d, buffer %x, ",
                        FILEname, fp->level, fp->buffer );
    fprintf( stderr,"curp %x, *curp %x, previous %x.\n",
                        fp->curp, *( fp->curp ), *( fp->curp-1 ));
}
```

The program consists of the function `main()` and a subfunction `FILEinfo()`. The function `main()` consists of a `while` loop that reads from standard input and writes to standard output until the end of the input file. After each input and output call, a call to `FILEinfo()` displays the information in the FILE structures.

Note 1: The first parameter to `FILEinfo()` is a pointer to the FILE structure from which the information is to be displayed and the name of the FILE pointer as a string so that it can be identified in the output.

Note 2: The information displayed by this call to `FILEinfo()` may not change as the program is executing. This could be because both `stdout` and `stderr` refer by default to terminal output and the terminal output may be flushed with every output statement.

Note 3: The information displayed is the name of the FILE * variable being referenced; the value of `level` (which is a reference to the number of processed or unprocessed characters in the buffer); the value of `buffer` (the address of the buffer); the value of `curp` (the address of the current position in the buffer); and the contents of `curp` (the actual character). Note that all values except the name of the FILE * variable being referenced are all displayed in numeric quantities to avoid unprintable characters messing up the terminal screen.

Learning Activities

38. Obtain a copy of stdio.h from your system. Modify the names of the FILE structure members throughout stdio.c to match those in the definition of the FILE in your stdio.h.

39. Compile and execute stdio.c. Feed it very short lines of input. Try a line with 0 characters before the newline (`'\n'`), with one character before the newline, with two characters before the newline, etc.

40. Describe what happens to the members of the FILE structure pointed to by `stdin`, and what happens to the corresponding members of the FILE structure pointed to by `stdout`. How do these changes differ? How are they the same?

41. If the values displayed for `stdout` do not change, try removing the `'\n'` character in the `fprintf()` call in `FILEinfo()`. Since this will make reading the output difficult, it should only be done as a last resort. However, it may show some of the changes in `stdout`.

Language Elements Introduced in This Chapter: A Review

✓ **File Opening Modes**

`"r"`	`("rb")`	open a (binary) file for reading
`"w"`	`("wb")`	open a new (binary) file for writing only
`"a"`	`("ab")`	open a (binary) file for appending (writing at the end)
`"r+"`	`("rb+")`	open a (binary) file for update (reading and writing)
`"w+"`	`("wb+")`	open a new (binary) file for update
`"a+"`	`("ab+")`	open a (binary) file for reading and appending

✓ **Header Files**

stdio.h

✓ **Library Functions**

`fopen()`	opens a file
`fclose()`	closes a file
`fgets()`	reads a line of text from a file and stores it as a string
`fputs()`	outputs a string to a file
`fread()`	reads a block of bytes from a file
`fwrite()`	writes a block of bytes to a file
`fprintf()`	does formatted output to a file
`fscanf()`	does formatted input from a file
`fseek()`	moves the file pointer to an indicated position in the file
`ftell()`	returns the byte offset of the current position from the beginning of a file
`sprintf()`	does formatted printing to a string
`sscanf()`	scans a formatted string and converts embedded values

✓ **Utilities in stdio.h**

`getc()`	inputs a single character from a file
`putc()`	outputs a single character to a file
`ungetc()`	pushes a single character back onto an input stream

✓ **Types**

FILE
FILE *

✓ **Variable Declarations**

FILE *infile, *outfile;

Things to Remember

1. Input and output may be either buffered or line buffered.
2. A file is a stream of bytes to a C program. Any structure put on a file is put there by the programmer.
3. When a C program is executed, three files are automatically opened: standard input, standard output, and standard error.
4. The return value from a call to a library function usually indicates when an error has occurred.
5. The utilities `getc()` and `getchar()` return a value of type `int`. Using type `char` will, at best, produce nonportable code.
6. A `FILE` is a structure that C uses to keep track of the current position in a file. One `FILE` structure is kept up to date for every open file in the program.

Exercises and Programming Problems

1. The program cp.c makes a copy of a file. It uses `getc()` and `putc()` to do the input and output. Write four new versions of a file copy program. Each of the programs should have the same functionality as cp.c.

   a. In the first version, use `fgetc()` to do the input and `fputc()` to do the output.

   b. In the second version, use `fgets()` to do the input and `fputs()` to do the output.

   c. In the third version, use `fread()` to do the input and `fwrite()` to do the output.

   d. In the fourth version, use `fscanf()` to do the input and `fprintf()` to do the output.

   e. Compare the sizes of the object code from all five versions of the file copy programs. If facilities for testing execution efficiency are available on your system, test the efficiency of each version. Report on your findings.

2. Write a program that will open a file and report on the number of lines, characters, and words in a file. Have the name of the file to be opened appear as a command line argument. You will need to find out what characters your computer system uses to mark the end of lines. For this program, assume that words are sequences of printable characters that are delimited by either whitespace or unprintable characters.

3. Write a program that searches for every occurrence of a string in a text file and displays every line in which it finds the string. Have the string appear as the first command line parameter after the executable program name, and the filename appear as the second command line parameter.

4. a. Write a program that will create an inventory file for a `struct auto_part` (from Section 7.1). Have the inventory information for each auto part entered from the terminal and stored in a file. Use `fwrite()` to write the structure to the file.

    b. Write a program that will read a file like the one created by the program in part a and write the inventory information about each of the auto parts in the file to the terminal screen.

    c. Write a program that will read a file like the one created by the program in part a and report the part identification for each automobile part for which there are less than 5 items in the inventory.

5. Write a C program that will change every occurrence of one string in a text file to another string. Both strings and the name of the file should appear as command line arguments. If the program is named `change`, the invocation

    ```
    change Smith Johnson namefile
    ```

    should open the file `namefile` and change every occurrence of the string `"Smith"` to the string `"Johnson"`.

6. Write a C program that reads a file and displays it on the terminal screen with a header for each page. Have the name of the file and the number of lines in a page entered as command line parameters. The header should consist of a blank line, a line with the file name and the page number, and another blank line. For example, if the program is named `prfile`, the invocation

    ```
    prfile 6 filename
    ```

    should produce a header like this:

    ```
    File : filename                         Page Number 1
    ```

    There should be three lines of text on each page. (Note that the 6 lines per page includes the three lines of the header as well as three lines of text.)

7. Write a C program that compares two files and issues the message

    ```
    file1 and file2 are identical
    ```

    when the files are the same or issues the message

    ```
    file1 and file2 :  first difference in byte number ____.
    ```

    when they are different. The names of the two files should appear as command line parameters.

8. Write a C program that will copy the contents of a text file to the terminal screen and pause for instructions after each screen of text has been displayed. After a pause, the user may press different keys to signify different actions to the program:

   a. Pressing <Return> will be the signal to display the next page.

   b. Pressing a 'q' and then <Return> will be the signal to quit displaying the file and terminate the program.

   c. Pressing a 'd' followed by a <Return> will be the signal to display 11 more lines.

9. Write a C program designed to open and read a binary file and display all null-terminated strings of ASCII characters in the file that consist of alphabetic, numeric, whitespace or punctuation characters and have length greater than 1. Display the hexadecimal representation of the byte offset of the string within the file and the string itself on a single line of output. Sample output might be:

```
Byte Offset              String

-----------              ---------
30a2                     Flat as a flounder
3182                     Not a patch on you
452e                     Running at rovers
534c                     In my mind's eye
```

if those strings were in the file. Again, the file name should be given as a command line argument. To test your program, write a simple C program that calls printf() to display the four strings above. Compile the program and use the compiled version as the input file to test your program. Your program should find and display the four strings above as well as many other strings. Note that many of the strings will be meaningless.

C Library and
Preprocessor Facilities

11.1   Introduction to the C Library

A library is a collection of functions that can be easily used in different programs. A function might be placed in a library because it provides a standard method for accessing parts of the hardware in a computer. Such functions usually interface with an operating system. The input and output functions and file handling functions are examples of functions that are placed in a library for that reason. Functions may also be placed in a library because they do standard tasks that are often necessary in a program. The string library functions are examples of this type of function.

A C library is usually provided with a C compiler. The selection of functions included in a library evolves with the different uses of the C language, and changes from installation to installation. Functions may be added that have proved useful for a specific operating system. For example, the C library developed for the UNIX operating system is especially rich and varied. A C library for a microcomputer might also contain graphics routines. However, in all C libraries, a common core of functions are usually included. The specification of the ANSI C language includes specifications for the functions that must be included with an ANSI C compiler.

The standard library as defined by ANSI includes functions on the following topics: file handling, formatted input and output, character input and output, block input and output, error handling and diagnostic functions, character testing, string

553

handling, mathematical functions, general utility functions, and date and time functions.

Earlier in this text we have seen uses of library functions dealing with files, input and output, and string handling as well as some of the general utility functions like `atof()` and `atoi()` to convert ASCII strings to numeric quantities. This chapter will introduce some of the other library functions like those to dynamically allocate and deallocate memory, do mathematical calculations, and manipulate characters. Additional library functions specified in the ANSI Standards for C are included in the *Programmer's Handbook*.

Other topics that are introduced in this chapter are the preprocessor facilities of conditional compilation and macros. Utilities like `getchar()`, `putchar()`, and the character typing facilities like `isdigit()` and `isalpha()` look like functions in C source code, but act differently; they are handled by the preprocessor and expanded in place before being translated into assembly or object code. These utilities are called macros. Examples of writing and using macros appear in Section 11.7 and examples of conditional compilation are done in Section 11.8.

The Time and Date Functions

We will look at some of the functions that allow a program to know the current time and date. The functions that we will consider are `time()`, `ctime()`, and `localtime()`. These functions are specified as a part of the ANSI C library.

The function `time()` returns a measure of the current time. The actual implementation of the `time()` function and what is meant by calendar time will differ with different computer systems. One popular method is to have `time()` return the total number of seconds since some predetermined date.

The return value from `time()` is defined as type `time_t` in the header file time.h. This hides the differences in implementations on different computer systems. A return value of -1 indicates an error. The parameter to `time()` is the address of a quantity of type `time_t`. If variables `t1` and `t2` have been declared as type `time_t`, a typical call to `time()` might be

```
t1 = time( &t2 );
```

On return from this function call, the measure of the current time would be both assigned to `t1`, and placed in `t2`. The duplication of the return values can be avoided with the following two calls to `time()`:

```
time( &t2 );
```

or

```
t1 = time( (time_t *) 0 );
```

In the first call, the measure of the current time is put in the variable `t2` and the value returned by `time()` is ignored. In the second call, the return value is assigned to the variable `t1`. The parameter in this call is 0 which has been cast to type `time_t *` to conform to the parameter type expected by `time()`. Passing a zero value as the parameter to time() suppresses the return of the current time in the parameter.

As mentioned above, the type of the value returned by time() may differ with different computer systems; it is unlikely that it is in a useful form. The C library functions ctime(), localtime() and others transform that value to a usable form. The function ctime() accepts the address of the value returned by time() as its parameter; it returns a char * value that references a string with the date in a readable form. For example, the return value from ctime() might point to the string

```
Sun Dec 5   17:35:54   1993\n
```

If timestr is declared to be of type char *, a typical call to ctime() might be

```
timestr = ctime( &t );
```

where t was returned by time(). Note that timestr should not be an array.

The function localtime() gives the programmer another method of working with the time and date. The parameter to localtime() is again the address of the value returned by time(); however, the value returned by localtime() is a pointer to a struct tm structure. A struct tm structure is declared in time.h and contains the following fields:

```
struct    tm    {
          int    tm_sec;          /* 0 - 59 */
          int    tm_min;          /* 0 - 59 */
          int    tm_hour;         /* 0 - 23 */
          int    tm_mday;         /* 1-31, the month-day */
          int    tm_mon;          /* 0 - 11 */
          int    tm_year;         /* since 1900 */
          int    tm_wday;         /* 0(Sunday) - 6*/
          int    tm_yday;         /* 0(Jan 1) - 365 */
          int    tm_isdst;        /* 1 if Daylight
                                   * Savings Time,
                                   * 0 if not */
     };
```

This structure allows the programmer to access any part of the date separately and allows manipulation of the structure and output of the date in different forms.

The program timex.c in Example 11-1 shows the use of these three functions to display some dates. It also demonstrates the library function clock() which is included in the ANSI C library. A measure of the processor time used by the program since the beginning of execution is returned by clock(). Again to overcome the differences between computer systems, the value returned by clock() is type clock_t which is defined in the file time.h; clock() does not take a parameter.

Example 11-1: timex.c

```c
/*                   timex.c
 *
 *    Synopsis   - Displays today's time and date, the date
 *                 tomorrow, and the processor time used by
 *                 the program.
 *
 *    Objective  - To introduce the time and date library
 *                 functions.
 */

/* Include Files */
#include <time.h>                                          /* Note 1 */
#include <stdio.h>

void main( void )
{
    time_t t1;                                             /* Note 2 */
    struct tm *tptr;
    clock_t ticks;                                         /* Note 2 */
    char *s;
                                                           /* Note 3 */
    if ( ( t1 = time(( time_t * ) 0 )) != ( time_t )-1 ) {
        s = ctime( &t1 );                                  /* Note 4 */
        printf( "currentdate is %s", s );
        tptr = localtime( &t1 );                           /* Note 5 */
        printf( "Tomorrow is %d/%d/19%d.\n",               /* Note 6 */
                            tptr->tm_mon+1,
                            tptr->tm_mday+1,
                            tptr->tm_year );
    }
    else
        printf( "Error with the time() function\n" );

                                                           /* Note 7 */
    if (( ticks = clock() ) != ( clock_t )-1 )
        printf( "%4.2f seconds used by the processor.\n",
                            ticks/CLK_TCK );               /* Note 8 */
    else
        printf( "Error with the clock() function\n" );
}
```

The program consists of the single function `main()`. The executable code consists of two `if` statements: one to demonstrate the calls to `time()`, `ctime()`, and `localtime()`, and one to demonstrate the library function `clock()` and display the processor time used by the program.

Note 1: The file time.h must be included. It contains type declarations, constant declarations, and function prototypes for the time and date functions. In particular, the declarations of the types `time_t`, `clock_t`, and `struct tm` are included.

Note 2: The variable `t1` must be declared of type `time_t` since it will hold the value returned by `time()`. The variable `ticks` is declared to be type `clock_t` to agree with the value returned by `clock()`. The variable `tptr` will point to the value returned by `localtime()`.

Note 3: The function `time()` is called with 0 as the actual parameter. This value has been cast to type `time_t` to match the parameter type required by `time()`. In this case, the calendar time is returned by the function and assigned to `t1`. If a legal pointer value had been passed to `time()`, the function would have placed a copy of the calendar time in the location pointed to by the parameter as well as return the value. The return value is tested against −1 (which has also be cast to type `time_t` to match the return type of `time()`) to ensure that the call is completed successfully.[1] If `time()` returns a −1, an error has occurred and the steps to convert the form of time and display the current time are skipped.

Note 4: The function `ctime()` takes the value returned by `time()` as its parameter and converts it to a string that contains the local time in a format suitable for output. It returns a pointer to the first character in the string. That string is displayed by the next `printf()` call.

Note 5: This call to `localtime()` also converts the value returned by `time()` to local time. However, `localtime()` returns a pointer to a quantity of type `struct tm`. The individual members of the `struct tm` quantity have been populated with the correct values representing the local time. This structure is used to display tomorrow's date in a different format. The return of a pointer to a `struct tm` gives the `localtime()` library function much flexibility in use.

Note 6: The `printf()` function call displays tomorrow's date in the form `10/31/94`. The individual members of the `struct tm` referenced by the return value from `localtime()` give the month, day, and year.

Note 7: The function `clock()` returns a measure of the processor time used by this program's execution. It returns −1 if an error occurs. To test for an error, the value returned by `clock()` is compared to −1 which has been cast to type `clock_t`.

Note 8: The constant CLK_TCK is defined in time.h. The expression

`ticks/CLK_TCK` represents the number of seconds of processor time.

---

1. Type casts are commonly used with the C library functions to make parameter and return types match those specified by the library functions.

Learning Activities

1. If you have an ANSI C compiler, compile and run timex.c to make sure that it works correctly on your system. If your compiler is not yet fully ANSI C compatible, you may have to comment out some of the function calls.

2. The implementation of the `time()` function may differ with different C compilers. Look at the include file, time.h, and your compiler documentation to try to determine how time is recorded by your compiler. Have the value returned by `time()` displayed and try to do the conversion yourself to verify the results of your research.

3. Modify timex.c so that it displays the time in a different time zone. For example, if you live in New York, have the program display the time in Hawaii.

4. Look in the manual that comes with your compiler to see the other functions that provide information about the time and date on the system. Write a sample program to test some of the functions.

11.2 Error Handling with the ANSI C Library

Many of the C library functions indicate through their return value when an error has occurred. For example, we have seen that `fopen()` returns a NULL pointer when an error occurs in opening a file. Many of the string functions do also. The function `fseek()` returns a nonzero value when it discovers an error and 0 otherwise; `ftell()` returns -1 on error.

ANSI C specifies an additional error handling device. An external variable `errno` is provided that indicates more precisely which error has occurred. When an error occurs, `errno` is given a value that corresponds to the error. Each error is also associated with an implementation-dependent error message. The variable `errno` is declared in the standard header file errno.h. A C program may access its value after any error.

Some error handling functions are also provided in the ANSI C library. The functions `ferror()` and `clearerr()` deal with errors that occur when reading or writing with a file. Both take a FILE * parameter that is associated with the file. The call

```
ferror( fp );
```

checks to see if an error has occurred on the file associated with `fp`. If it has, `ferror()` returns a nonzero value; otherwise, it returns zero. The call

        clearerr(fp);

explicitly clears the error condition for the file associated with `fp`. Without this call, any subsequent call to `ferror()` would always return an error.

The function `perror()` checks on and reports more general errors. The parameter to `perror()` is a `char *` value that holds the address of the first character in a string to be displayed. The call

        perror(s);

will display the string `s` followed by a colon, a space, and an error message. The error message chosen by `perror()` is based on the current value of `errno`.

As an example of these three functions in action, consider the program perror.c in Example 11-2. The program attempts to open a file and read through the file. It uses `perror()` to report on any errors it encounters. The functions `ferror()` and `clearerr()` are used to detect errors associated with reading from the file. The values returned by `fopen()` and by `fread()` are inspected for error indications also.

Example 11-2: perror.c

```
/*              perror.c
 *
 *   Synopsis   - Checks for the correct number of command line
 *                parameters, opens the file in argv[1], reads
 *                through the file and reports on any errors found.
 *
 *   Objective  - To demonstrate the use of some of the error
 *                handling functions.
 */

/* Include Files */
#include <stdio.h>                                    /* Note 1 */
#include <stdlib.h>

/* Function Prototypes */
void processit( void );

void main( int argc, char *argv[] )
{
    FILE  *fp;
    char  buf[100];
```

```
     if ( argc < 2 ) {
          printf( "Usage: perror file\n" );
          exit( 1 );
     }

     if (( fp = fopen( argv[1], "r" )) == NULL ) {
          perror( "fopen error" );                          /* Note 2 */
     }

     while ( fread( buf, sizeof( char ), 100, fp ) > 0 ) {
          processit();
     }
     if ( ferror( fp )) {                                   /* Note 3 */
          perror( argv[1] );                                /* Note 4 */
          clearerr( fp );                                   /* Note 5 */
     }

     /* Processing may continue */
}
/***************************** processit()   ******************/
/*    Stub Function to indicate file processing
 */
void processit( void )
{
     printf( "File processing stub.\n" );
}
```

The program consists of two functions, main() and processit(). The function processit() is a stub. It symbolizes processing that might be done on each block of characters from the file. The function main() uses if statements to check for the correct number of command line arguments, open the file, and check for errors. A while loop reads through the contents of the file.

Note 1: The functions perror(), clearerr(), and ferror() are declared in the header file stdio.h. Both perror() and clearerr() are of type void; ferror() returns type int. The parameter to perror() is a string; the parameter to both clearerr() and ferror() is a FILE   * variable that had previously been initialized with a call to fopen().

Note 2: The function perror() is called in case an error occurs while opening the file. The function will display the string "fopen error" followed by the reason for the error. These reasons are implementation dependent. They could be different on different computers.

Note 3: When the previous while loop terminated, the return value from fread() was either 0 or negative. This call to ferror() determines whether or not an error occurred while reading from the file. The function `ferror()` returns a nonzero value when it senses an error and 0 otherwise.

Note 4: In the case that an error occurred with the file associated with `fp`, a call to `perror()` will display the name of the file and an error message.

Note 5: The function `clearerr()` is called to explicitly clear the error condition associated with the file referenced by `fp`. Now processing can continue and `ferror()` can be used again to check on errors. Without this call, `ferror()` would continue to report an error when called.

Learning Activities

5.   If you have an ANSI C compiler or work on a UNIX system, compile and run perror.c. (You may need to change the function prototypes if you don't have an ANSI C compiler.)

    a.   Test it without command line parameters.

    b.   Test it with `argv[1]` naming a file that does not exist.

    c.   Test it with the name of a relatively short file in `argv[1]`. Is reading at the end-of-file considered an error?

6.   In the documentation for your compiler, look up other error conditions. Try to devise tests to see how this program handles these errors. If necessary, rewrite the program to test for the other error conditions.

11.3 Using Mathematical Functions

Many mathematical functions are included with the C library: the trigonometric functions, inverse trigonometric functions, hyperbolic functions, exponents, logs, powers, and square roots, among others. A list of many of the mathematical functions specified in ANSI C appears in the *Programmer's Handbook*.

Most of the mathematical functions return a value of type `double`. They are declared in the header file math.h which also contains type declarations, constants, and some utilities used by the mathematical functions. If that file is not included in a program, then an explicit declaration of the function should be included.

On some systems, UNIX for example, the mathematical functions are kept in a separate library which must be explicitly searched at link time. This usually involves a modification of the compiler call so that the linker will know to search the different library. In some other systems, all of the libraries are automatically searched at link time.

The use of the mathematical functions in the C library is illustrated in the program polar.c of Example 11-3. This program converts Cartesian coordinates of a point to polar coordinates. The Cartesian coordinates and the polar coordinates of a point are illustrated in Figure 11-1.

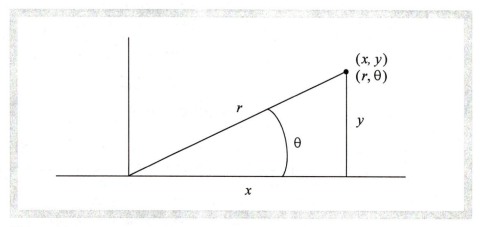

Figure 11-1

The Pythagorean theorem gives the conversion formula for obtaining the radius, r, of the polar coordinates from the Cartesian coordinates x, y. It is illustrated in Figure 11-2.

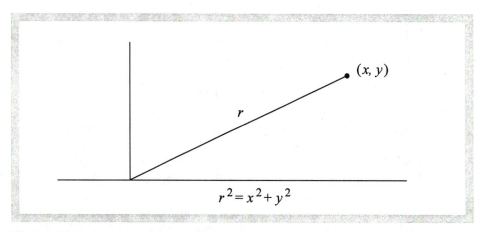

Figure 11-2

The angle is obtained by applying the arctangent to the expression $\frac{y}{x}$. This is illustrated in Figure 11-3.

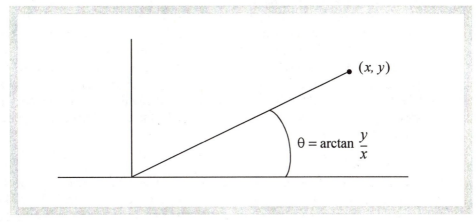

Figure 11-3

In the program, the Cartesian coordinates and the polar coordinates of a point are stored in C structures. They are declared before the function `main()` so that the structure declaration will be visible throughout the program. Both structures are composed of two members of type `double`, but the names of the members reflect the different coordinates.

The mathematical functions from the C library used in this program are `sqrt()`, `pow()`, and `atan2()`. The `sqrt()` function takes a parameter of type `double` and returns the square root of its argument. The return value is of type `double` also. Passing a negative parameter to the `sqrt()` function causes an error condition.

The `pow()` function takes two arguments of type `double` and returns a value of type `double`. For example, the call

```
pow( x, y );
```

will return the value x^y. Errors will occur with the `pow()` function when either

```
x is zero and y is negative
```

or

```
x is negative and y is not an integer
```

The function `atan2()` takes two arguments of type `double` and returns an angle between `-PI` and `PI`; the angle is measured in radians. For example, the call

```
atan2( y, x );
```

will return the angle between the positive x axis and the line from the origin through the point (x, y) in Cartesian coordinates. A second library function, `atan()`, in the C library also calculates the arctangent of a value. This function takes a single argument and returns a value between $-PI/2$ and $PI/2$; it would require the program to adjust for the angle in different quadrants. The function atan2() has this functionality built in.

Another utility function, strtod(), is used in this program. It will convert a string of ASCII characters that represents a floating point value to a numeric value of type double. The name strtod() stands for string to double. It takes two parameters. The first is a pointer to the first character in the string. The second is a pointer to a pointer to a character. The function will convert as many elements in the string as possible to type double, return that value, and set the contents of its second parameter to point to the unconverted remainder of the string. For example, if the call to strtod() was

```
strtod( "123.4abc", remainder );
```

the value 123.4 will be returned as type double and *remainder will point to the 'a'. In this program, we will not need to look at the remainder of the string after conversion so we can suppress this part of the functionality by passing a NULL value as the second parameter to strtod().

Example 11-3: polar.c

```
/*                  polar.c
 *
 *    Synopsis    - Converts sets of points in Cartesian coordinates
 *                  to polar coordinates.
 *
 *    Objective   - Illustrates the use of some of the mathematics
 *                  in the ANSI C library.
 */

/* Include Files */
#include <stdio.h>
#include <math.h>                                      /* Note 1 */
#include <stdlib.h>

/* Constant Declarations */
#define PI     3.14159

/* Type Descriptions */
struct cartesian {
        double x;
        double y;
};
```

```
struct polar {
        double radius;
        double angle;
};

/* Function Declarations */
struct polar *to_polar( struct cartesian * );
double get_c_coord( char * );

void main( void )
{
     struct cartesian cpoint;
     struct polar     *ppoint;
     char             buff[80];
     int              more = 1;

     printf( "Conversion: Cartesian to polar coordinates.\n" );
     while ( more ) {
             cpoint.x = get_c_coord( "x" );
             cpoint.y = get_c_coord( "y" );
             ppoint = to_polar( &cpoint );
             printf( "Polar coordinates: " );
             printf( "radius %5.2lf, angle %5.2lf\n",
                                 ppoint->radius, ppoint->angle );
             printf( "Another one? (y/n) " );
             gets( buff );
             if ( buff[0] != 'y' )
                   more = 0;
     }
}

/***************************** get_c_coord()   ***************/
/*   Accepts input of a string from standard input. The string
 *   should contain a representation of a floating point value.
 *   The function returns the double value.
 */
double get_c_coord( char *s )
{
     char buffer[80];

     printf( "Enter the %s value: ", s );
     gets( buffer );
     return( strtod( buffer, ( char ** )NULL ) );        /* Note 2 */
}
```

```
/****************************** to_polar()  *****************/
/*    Converts a point from Cartesian coordinates to polar
 *    coordinates.
 */
struct polar *to_polar( struct cartesian *cart )
{
      static struct polar p;
      double temp;

      temp = pow( cart->x, 2 ) + pow( cart->y,2 );        /* Note 3 */
      p.radius = sqrt( temp );                            /* Note 4 */
      p.angle = atan2( cart->y, cart->x );                /* Note 5 */
      if ( p.angle < 0 )
            p.angle += 2 * PI;
      return ( &p );
}
```

The program consists of the three functions main(), get_c_coord(), and to_polar(). The function get_c_coord() takes care of input. A value is entered as a string of characters, and is converted to type double and returned. The function to_polar() takes a pointer to a struct cartesian and returns a pointer to a struct polar that contains the polar coordinates of the point. In every pass through its while loop, the function main() calls get_c_coord() to get the values of a point in cartesian coordinates from standard input, calls to_polar() to convert it to polar coordinates, and calls print() to display the result.

Note 1: The header file math.h should be included whenever functions from the mathematics portion of the C library are used. The declarations of the functions and declarations of relevant constant values and types are in that file.

Note 2: The function strtod() is called to convert the input string to a value of type double. The first parameter points to the first character in the string. In this case, the second parameter is NULL since the unconverted part of the string is not of interest in this program. The function strtod() was declared of type double in stdlib.h.

Note 3: The function call pow(val, 2) will compute the square (power 2) of val. The sum of the squares of the x and y coordinates is calculated in this statement.

Note 4: The C library function sqrt() is called to compute the square root of the sum of the squares of the x and y coordinates which is the distance of the point from the radius. This call completes the computation of the radius coordinate.

Note that the variable p has been declared static; this ensures that its value will be preserved and available to be accessed through the pointer returned by to_polar() to main().

Note 5: The function `atan2()` was chosen to calculate the angle, given the `x` and `y` coordinates of the point. This function was chosen over `atan()` since it will give values from `-PI` to `PI` instead of the smaller interval from `-PI/2` to `PI/2`. (The latter interval refers only to the first and fourth quadrants of the plane.) Note that a zero value for the `x` coordinate is not an error in this expression. In the next statement, a negative angle is converted to the corresponding value between 0 and 2 * `PI`.

Learning Activities

7. Compile polar.c. If error messages indicate that the functions `sqrt()`, `pow()`, and `atan2()` are not found, you may have to use a different compiler call to tell the linker to search the mathematics library to resolve those references. If that is the case, find out how to link the mathematics library functions and compile the program again.

8. Run polar.c with different input values. Hand calculate the expected answers to verify that the program is correct.

9. Many people expect the angles to be given in degrees instead of radians. Modify polar.c to output the angle in degrees.

Error Handling with the Mathematical Functions

When an error occurs in a mathematical function, the external variable `errno` is set to indicate the specific error. The errors are primarily of two types. An error can occur when the parameter passed to a mathematical function is not in the domain of that function. For example, such an error would occur when a negative number was passed to the function `sqrt()`. A constant value, `EDOM`, is defined in errno.h, and is placed in `errno` to indicate that a domain error has occurred.

A second type of error occurs when the calculated value is too large for the computer to handle. For example, the `pow()` function calculates powers. The call

```
pow( x,n )
```

calculates x^n. If both `x` and `n` were very large, the value x^n might cause an overflow error. In this case, the function `pow()` would return `HUGE_VAL`, and the value of `errno` would be `ERANGE` to indicate the error. Both `HUGE_VAL` and `ERANGE` are constants defined in errno.h that are used to indicate an error in the range of a mathematical function.

The program math.c in Example 11-4 is designed to allow you to experiment to find out how errors are handled with the mathematical functions.

Example 11-4: math.c

```
/*                  math.c
 *
 *    Synopsis    - Accepts input of values for x and n and displays
 *                  the calculated values from the pow(), sqrt() and
 *                  tan() functions.
 *
 *    Objective   - To illustrate error handling with the
 *                  mathematical functions in the ANSI C library.
 */

/* Include Files */
#include <math.h>
#include <stdio.h>
#include <errno.h>                                              /* Note 1 */
#include <stdlib.h>

/* Function Declarations */
void error( char * );

void main( void )
{
    double n, x, y;
    char buff[50];

    printf( "Enter a value for n: " );
    n = strtod( gets( buff ), NULL );
    printf( "Enter value for x: " );
    x = strtod( gets( buff ), NULL );
    printf( "x is %5.2f.\n", x );
    printf( "n is %5.2f.\n", n );
    y = sqrt( x );                                              /* Note 2 */
    error( "sqrt" );
    printf( "sqrt(%4.2f) is %5.2f\n",x, y );                    /* Note 3 */
    y = tan( x );                                               /* Note 4 */
    error( "tan" );
    printf( "tan(%4.2f) is %5.2f.\n", x, y );
    y = pow( x, n );                                            /* Note 5 */
    error( "pow" );
    printf( "pow(%4.2f, %4.2f) is %5.2f.\n", x, n, y );
}
```

```
/***************************** error()    ********************/
/*    Checks the value of errno, and if it is nonzero, issues
 *    an error message.
 */
void error( char *s )
{
    if ( errno )                                          /* Note 6 */
        perror( s );
    errno = 0;                                            /* Note 7 */
}
```

The program consists of two functions, main() and error(). The expression strtod(gets(buff), NULL) is used to get two double values from standard input. Then the mathematical functions sqrt(), tan(), and pow() are called with the input values as parameters. The function error() issues error messages by calling perror() when an error has occurred.

Note 1: The header file errno.h contains the declaration of the external variable errno and the codes for the different error messages.

Note 2: Domain errors could occur with the sqrt() function. For example, a negative number is not in the domain of the sqrt() function. When you run this program, you may notice that the mathematical functions issue their own version of the error messages.

Note 3: The value of y is displayed even when an error occurred. This should demonstrate that the value is meaningless in case of error. This output is done in this program for the other three functions also. Learning Activity 11 addresses this action.

Note 4: The tan() function excludes the value PI/2 from its domain. The function value is undefined when x is PI/2 or -PI/2.

Note 5: Errors occur with the pow() function when either x is 0 and n is negative or when x is negative and n is not an integer.

Note 6: The value of errno is checked before calling perror(). In most implementations, no error has occurred in cases where errno is zero.

Note 7: The value of errno is set to zero to clear the error condition.

Learning Activities

10.   If you have an ANSI C compiler or are working on a UNIX system, compile math.c and test it with different sets of input. Each suggestion should give at least one error. Try to find more combinations that give errors. Specifically, try

a.   a negative number for x and an int value for n.

b.   a huge number for both x and n.

c. a negative number for x and a fractional value for n.

d. the numerical value of PI/2 for x.

e. Modify math.c by commenting out the line errno = 0; and repeat parts a. through d. Can you explain the difference in the program output?

11. Note that the value returned by the function is always displayed; it is invalid if an error has occurred. Modify the function error() to return 1 if an error occurred and 0 otherwise and have the functional value displayed only in the case that no error occurred.

11.4 Character Manipulation

Facilities are available in C to test the properties of the character set. These facilities are declared in the standard header file ctype.h, which should be included in any program using these facilities.

The facilities are of two basic types: facilities to test the properties of a character, and facilities to perform conversions on a character. All the functions or macros take a single argument of type int.

Facilities to test the properties of characters all return a nonzero value if the character tested has the desired property and zero otherwise. They include

isalpha() which tests to see if its argument is an alphabetic character
isdigit() which tests to see if its argument is a digit
isspace() which tests to see if its argument is a whitespace character
isupper() which tests to see if its argument is an uppercase alphabetic character
ispunct() which tests to see if its argument is a punctuation character

A complete list appears in the *Programmer's Handbook*. Facilities to perform conversions on characters include

toupper() which converts any lowercase alphabetics to uppercase and leaves all other characters unchanged
tolower() which converts uppercase alphabetics to lowercase and leaves other characters unchanged

Other conversion routines may be provided with individual implementations of C, but the two above are specified in the ANSI C standards.

The program ctype.c in Example 11-5 provides an example of the use of many of the facilities that test for a specific property of a character. The program reads from a text file or from standard input and counts the number of alphabetics (uppercase and lowercase), digits, whitespace characters, punctuation, and control characters.

Example 11-5:   ctype.c

```
/*              ctype.c
 *
 *    Synopsis    - Counts the number of alphabetics, digits,
 *                  whitespace, punctuation and control characters
 *                  in its input. The input can come from a file
 *                  or the keyboard.
 *
 *    Objective   - To illustrate the use of the functions defined
 *                  in ctype.h.
 */
/* Include Files */
#include <stdio.h>
#include <stdlib.h>
#include <ctype.h>                                          /* Note 1 */

void main( int argc, char *argv[] )
{
    FILE *fp;
    int ch;
    int numlower = 0, numupper = 0, numdigit = 0,
        numspace = 0, numcntrl = 0, numalpha = 0,
        numpunct = 0;

    if ( argc < 2 )
        fp = stdin;                                         /* Note 2 */
    else if (( fp = fopen( argv[1], "r" )) == NULL ) {
        printf( "Can't open file %s.\n", argv[1] );
        exit( 1 );
    }

    while (( ch = getc( fp )) != EOF ) {
        if ( isalpha( ch ))  {                              /* Note 3 */
            numalpha++;
            if ( islower( ch ))                             /* Note 4 */
                numlower++;
            else
                numupper++;                                 /* Note 5 */
        }
        else if ( isdigit( ch ))                            /* Note 6 */
            numdigit++;
        else if ( isspace( ch ))                            /* Note 7 */
```

```
                    numspace++;
            else if ( ispunct( ch ))                           /* Note 8 */
                    numpunct++;
            else if ( iscntrl( ch ))                           /* Note 9 */
                    numcntrl++;
    }
    printf( "That data contained %d alphabetic characters ",
                                             numalpha );
    printf( "of which %d were uppercase \n", numupper );
    printf( "and %d were lowercase.  It also contained ",
                                             numlower );
    printf( "%d digits, %d whitespace", numdigit, numspace );
    printf( "characters,\n%d control characters, ", numcntrl );
    printf( "and %d punctuation characters.\n", numpunct );
}
```

This program consists of the single function named main(). The number of command line parameters determines whether the input will come from standard input or whether a file is to be opened. A while loop processes the input; it consists of a compound if-else statement. A sequence of printf() calls displays the results.

Note 1: The file ctype.h contains declarations of all the character typing facilities. Some of them may be macros defined in this file, and some may be implemented as functions.

Note 2: If no file is specified, the input will come from stdin. The variable fp will reference standard input in this case.

Note 3: The function isalpha() will return a nonzero value if its parameter is 'a', 'b', 'c', 'd',... 'z', 'A', 'B', 'C',..., or 'Z' and zero otherwise.

Note 4: The function islower() will return nonzero if its parameter is 'a', 'b', 'c',..., or 'z' and zero otherwise.

Note 5: Instead of calling the function isupper(), it is more efficient to simply increment the counter numupper since at this point, it has been determined that the character is an alphabetic character and is not lowercase. Therefore, the only other possibility is for it to be uppercase.

Note 6: If the character being tested is one of the digits, '0' to '9', isdigit() returns a nonzero value. It returns 0 otherwise.

Note 7: The function isspace() tests for spaces, formfeeds, newlines, carriage returns, tabs, and vertical tabs. It returns a nonzero value if it finds one of the whitespace characters.

Note 8: The function ispunct() tests for the punctuation characters. This includes exclamation points, quotes, periods, commas, parentheses, braces, brackets, slashes, and so on.

Note 9: Finally, the function iscntrl() tests for the presence of a control character and returns a nonzero value when one is found. The control characters are those at the beginning or at the very end of the ASCII sequence. Their decimal equivalents are 0 through 31 and 127.

Learning Activities

12.   Execute ctype.c with very simple input for which you can easily hand calculate the expected result. Verify that it works correctly on your system.

13.   Modify ctype.c by removing all the `else` keywords except the first from the program. Execute it with the same input to see if the output is the same or if some of the characters are counted twice.

    a.   For example, how is a tab counted? Is it a control character, a space, punctuation, or all three?

    b.   What about ^M (control-M)?

    c.   Which characters, if any, are counted in two categories?

14.   If your system has facilities to test the efficiency of execution of a program, test the version with the `else` keywords included against the version with them omitted. Which would you expect to be more efficient? Is there any noticeable difference with this short program?

Often the facilities that test a character for a specific property are used to validate the input to a particular routine. For example, the program convert.c in Example 11-6 converts a string of digits to an integer value. It provides much the same functionality as the library function `atoi()` and, if packaged as a function with a return value and some error handling added, might be used as a substitute for that library function. The facility `isdigit()` is used to validate the input to the conversion routine.

Example 11-6: convert.c

```
/*              convert.c
 *
 *   Synopsis    - Accepts the input of a string of digits and
 *                 converts those digits to a decimal integer.
 *
 *   Objective   - To show the use of the facility isdigit() in
 *                 validating input.
```

```
    */

/* Include Files */
#include <stdio.h>
#include <ctype.h>                                          /* Note 1 */

void main( void )
{
      int index = 0, num = 0;
      char inbuff[80];

      printf( "Enter a string of decimal digits: " );
      gets( inbuff );

      while ( isdigit( inbuff[index] ))                     /* Note 2 */
                                                            /* Note 3 */
            num = 10*num + inbuff[index++] - '0';

      printf( "That number is %d.\n", num );
}
```

The program consists of a single function, main(). A call to gets() accomplishes the input of the string of digits. A while loop converts the digits to type int, and a printf() call displays the result.

Note 1: The file ctype.h must be included. The definition or the declaration of isdigit() is included in this file.

Note 2: Each character in inbuff is passed to isdigit(). If the character is a digit, the return value will be nonzero and another iteration of the while loop will be executed. When the value returned by isdigit() is zero, the while loop is terminated since the character referenced is not a digit.

Note 3: This algorithm to convert from character to integer depends on the contiguity of the digits in the ASCII character set. The difference between any digit and '0' is the numerical value of that digit. For example, the digit '3' corresponds to the integer 51 in the ASCII collating sequence, and '0' corresponds to the integer 48. The expression '3' - '0' translates to 51 - 48, which evaluates to the integer 3, thus accomplishing the conversion of the character. The accumulation of the integer value is kept in the variable num.

Learning Activities

15. Hand execute convert.c for the following input strings

| 1 | 4 | w | \n |

and

| 2 | 5 | 8 | \n |

to make sure that you understand the conversion algorithm.

16. a. Execute convert.c to verify your prediction.

b. Predict the output for each of the following inputs and explain what happens.

   i.   A single carriage return is pressed.

   ii. Two spaces are typed before the string of digits is input.

   iii. The word "one" is entered and the carriage return is pressed.

   iv. The string "938492838747567345" is entered and the carriage return is pressed.

c. Explain the differences between the action of convert.c and the action of the following program for different input strings.

```
/*                          la16.c                        */

/* Include Files */
#include <stdio.h>

void main( void )
{
    int num;

    printf( "Enter a string of decimal digits: " );
    scanf( "%d", &num );
    printf( "That number is %d.\n", num );
}
```

11.5 Dynamic Allocation and Deallocation of Memory

The C library provides functions for dynamic allocation and deallocation of memory. The functions `malloc()` and `calloc()` allocate memory, and the function `free()` deallocates memory.

The declarations for the dynamic allocation functions are provided in a header file. In ANSI C, the declarations will be in the file stdlib.h.[1]

The function malloc() takes one parameter. In ANSI C, the parameter's type is size_t which is defined with a typedef in several header files. The parameter tells malloc() the number of bytes to allocate. The return value from malloc() is the address of the first byte in the newly allocated buffer; the address is typed as void *.[2] When the address of the space is returned, a type cast is used to convert it to the correct type. Examples of calls to malloc() with the appropriate variable declarations might be

```
char *string, buffer[50];
string = (char *) malloc( strlen(buffer) + 1);
```

The length of the string in buffer is tested with strlen() and one is added to allot space for the terminating '\0'. When the space is allocated, the return value is cast to type char * before assigning it to the variable string.

"Another look at testing the length of the string."From the painting *Childhood of Blondin*, Joseph Cornell, 1943.

---

1. Earlier compilers might keep these declarations in the header files alloc.h or malloc.h. The documentation provided with the compiler should give this information.
2. With older C compilers, the parameter's type will probably be one of the integer types and the type of the return value is usually char *.

Another example:

```
struct trans *transaction;
transaction = (struct trans *)malloc( sizeof(struct trans) );
```

In this example, `malloc()` will allocate the number of bytes necessary to store a value of type `struct trans`. The return value is cast to type `struct trans *` before being assigned to the variable `transaction`.

The function `free()` will deallocate space that was allocated by either `malloc()` or `calloc()`. Its parameter is a pointer to the space to be freed. It will have type `void *` on ANSI C compilers. If that pointer was cast to a different type on allocation, it must be recast on return. For example, the call

```
free(( void * ) transaction );
```

would deallocate the space that was obtained on the second call to `malloc()` above.

The program malloc.c in Example 11-7 gives an example of the use of `malloc()`. The program inputs a line of text from standard input into a buffer. It copies each word to a dynamically allocated buffer that will exactly fit the word, and prints the word on standard output.

Example 11-7: malloc.c

```
/*                   malloc.c
 *
 *   Synopsis    - Accepts input of a line of text, separates each
 *                 of the blank-separated words in the line, and
 *                 displays each word.
 *
 *   Objective   - To illustrate use of the malloc() function.
 */

/* Include Files */
#include <stdio.h>
#include <stdlib.h>                                      /* Note 1 */
#include <string.h>

void main( void )
{
        char instring[512], *currentpl, *endword, *word;

        printf( "Enter a line of text " );
        printf( "with words separated with blanks:\n" );
        gets( instring );
```

```
        currentpl = instring;
                                                                /* Note 2 */
        while (( endword = strchr( currentpl, ' ' )) != NULL ) {
                *endword = '\0';                                /* Note 3 */
                                                                /* Note 4 */
                word = ( char * ) malloc( strlen( currentpl ) + 1 );
                strcpy( word, currentpl );
                printf( "I read that as \"%s\".\n", word );
                currentpl = endword+1;                          /* Note 5 */
                free (( void * ) word );                        /* Note 6 */
        }
                                                                /* Note 7 */
        word = ( char * )malloc( strlen( currentpl ) + 1 );
        strcpy( word, currentpl );
        printf( "I read that as \"%s\".\n", word );
        free(( void * ) word );
}
```

The program consists of the single function `main()`. The variable `instring` is used to hold a line of input from standard input. The pointers `currentpl` and `endword` are used as pointers into `instring` to mark the beginning and the end of the individual words. The variable `word` will point to a separate buffer in memory where the individual words are to be copied. Input is done with a call to `gets()`. The `while` loop works through the line of input, picking out the end of each word with a call to `strchr()`. The last word in the buffer `instring` is processed after the `while` loop terminates.

Note 1: In ANSI C, the memory allocation functions are declared in the file stdlib.h. In earlier versions of C this filename may have to be changed.

Note 2: The string library function `strchr()` was first discussed in Section 5.6. This call to `strchr()` will return a pointer to the first blank character that it finds in the buffer pointed to by `currentpl`. It returns a NULL pointer if no blank is found.

Note 3: The blank character in the buffer is replaced with a '`\0`' to form a string referenced by `currentpl`. This allows the "word" to be accessed as a string by the string library function.

Note 4: The library function `malloc()` is called to dynamically allocate the correct amount of space for the string. The number of bytes is measured by the `strlen()` of the string plus one byte for the terminating null character ('`\0`'). In ANSI C, `malloc()` returns a `void *` value which must be cast to the correct type in order to be used properly. In this case the correct type is `char *`. With older C compilers, `malloc()` returns a value of type `char *` and the cast would not be necessary but including the cast with an older compiler would not cause an error and would allow the program to be ported with less work.

Note 5: The pointer `currentpl` is advanced to the position in the buffer immediately after the blank that terminated the previous word. This will set up the pointers for the next iteration of the `while` loop.

Note 6: The space pointed to by `word` is no longer needed and is therefore freed for possible reuse. It is a good idea to free dynamically allocated space that is no longer needed. Be aware that some implementations of C ignore this request.

Note 7: The last word in the input buffer was not processed by the `while` loop, and must be processed now.

Learning Activities

17. Compile and execute malloc.c. Test it with several sets of input.

18. What happens when multiple contiguous blanks exist in the input? If necessary, fix malloc.c so that this situation is handled correctly.

19. Note that the only delimiting characters allowed by malloc.c are blanks while in reality, in English text, words are delimited by blanks, tabs, and punctuation characters. The standard C library function `strtok()`, when called repeatedly, will find all "words" delimited by a user-defined set of characters.

    a. Read the information on `strtok()` in the *Programmer's Handbook* and in the documentation for your C compiler.

    b. Modify the program so that it finds "words" delimited by blanks, tabs, periods, and commas. If `strtok()` is available on your system, replace `strchr()` with an appropriate use of `strtok()` to make this modification.

    c. If `strtok()` is not available on your system, write your own version of `strtok()` to use for this purpose.

The library function `calloc()` is also used to allocate memory during a program's execution. One difference is that the memory allocated by `calloc()` is initialized to zero while the memory allocated by `malloc()` is uninitialized. Another difference is that `calloc()` takes two parameters. The first gives a number of items; the second gives the size of each item. The number of bytes of memory allocated is the product of the two parameters. Memory for arrays can be allocated with `calloc()`. For example, the call

```
trans_array = (struct trans *)calloc(20, sizeof(struct trans) );
```

will allocate enough space for twenty structures of type `struct trans`. Since array names signify the address of the buffer in memory, `trans_array` can be treated as an array in most situations. For example, `trans_array[0]` will access the first structure in the buffer, `trans_array[1]` will access the second structure, and so on.

The program calloc.c in Example 11-8 gives an example of `calloc()` in use. It will read the file that was created by the program fwrite.c of Example 10.7 where information for a `struct trans` value was entered from standard input and `fwrite()` was called to write the information to a file. In this program, the number of records in the file is calculated and `calloc()` allocates memory for the contents of the whole file. A single `fread()` will read the contents of the file and place it in the allocated buffer. The contents of that buffer is displayed one record at a time. The technique of reading the whole file in one disk access and allocating exactly the needed amount of memory is efficient in both memory use and execution time.

Example 11-8: calloc.c

```
/*                  calloc.c
 *
 *    Synopsis    - Reads transactions (elements of type struct
 *                  trans) from a file into a dynamically allocated
 *                  array and displays them on standard output.
 *
 *    Objective   - To illustrate the use of calloc() in allocating
 *                  space for an array of structures.
 */

/* Include Files */
#include <stdio.h>
#include <stdlib.h>

/* Constant Declarations */                              /* Note 1 */
#define BUFFSIZE   50

/* Type Descriptions */
struct trans {
        int        t_type;
        char       payee_memo[BUFFSIZE];
        float      amount;
        unsigned tax_deduct:1;
        unsigned cleared:1;
};

/* Function Declarations */
void print_trans(struct trans *outtrans);
```

```
void main( void )
{
     struct trans *t_array;
     FILE       *fp;
     int         i, nrecs;
     long       numbytes;

     if (( fp = fopen( "transactions", "r" )) == NULL ) {
         printf( "Transaction file couldn't be opened.\n" );
         exit( 1 );
     }

     fseek( fp, 0L, 2 );                                 /* Note 2 */
     numbytes = ftell( fp );
     nrecs = (int ) numbytes / sizeof( struct trans );

                                                         /* Note 3 */
     if (( t_array = ( struct trans * ) calloc( nrecs,
                         sizeof( struct trans ))) == NULL ) {
         printf( "Unable to get the space.\n" );
         exit( 1 );
     }

     fseek( fp, 0L, 0 );                                 /* Note 4 */
                                                         /* Note 5 */
     if ( !( fread( t_array, sizeof( *t_array ), nrecs, fp ))) {
         printf( "Error in reading the file\n" );
         exit( 2 );
     }

     for ( i = 0; i < nrecs; i++ )
         print_trans( &t_array[i] );
     fclose( fp );
}

/***************************** print_trans()   ***************/
/*   Displays the contents of the structure outtrans on standard
 *   output. Each field is separated with a vertical bar character.
 */
void print_trans( struct trans *outtrans )
{
     /* Cleared field */
     if ( outtrans->cleared )
         printf( "C ¦ " );
     else
```

```
        printf( "   ¦ " );
/* Transaction type */
if (( outtrans->t_type =='D' ) ¦¦ ( outtrans->t_type == 'W' )
                               ¦¦ ( outtrans->t_type == 'I' ))
        printf( "%4c ¦ ", outtrans->t_type );
else
        printf( "%4d ¦ ", outtrans->t_type );
/* tax_deduct field */
if ( outtrans->tax_deduct )
        printf( " T ¦ " );
else
        printf( "   ¦ " );
printf( "%10.2f  ¦ ", outtrans->amount );
printf( "%s", outtrans->payee_memo );
}
```

The functions `main()` and `print_trans()` make up this program. The function `print_trans()` is used unchanged from the program fread.c of Example 10-8. A call to `fopen()` opens the file `"transactions"` for reading; the program is terminated if the file cannot be opened. Next, the number of records in the file is calculated, space is allocated, the file is read into memory, and the contents of each `struct trans` entry is displayed.

Note 1: The file stdlib.h is included since the declaration of the function `calloc()` is included there. ANSI C specifies stdlib.h as one of the standard header files. In older versions of the compiler, the declaration of `calloc()` may appear in another file instead. For example, on UNIX systems, it might be included in the header file malloc.h. The declaration

```
        void *calloc( size_t nitems, size_t size );
```

for ANSI C compilers (or the declaration `char *calloc()` for older compilers) could take the place of the include file in this program.

Note 2: To calculate the number of records in the file, `fseek()` is called to seek to the end of the file, `ftell()` is called to return the number of bytes in the file, and then that number is divided by the `sizeof()` a `struct trans` to give the total number of records.

Note 3: Enough space to hold all the records in the file is allocated by the call to `calloc()`. The parameter `nrec` indicates the number of items for which memory is to be allocated, and the second parameter,

```
        sizeof( struct trans )
```

indicates the size of each item. The total number of bytes allocated would be

```
        nrecs * sizeof( struct trans )
```

An equivalent call to `malloc()` would be

```
        malloc( nrecs * sizeof( struct trans ));
```
The value returned by `calloc()` has type `void *` in an ANSI C compiler (or `char *` in an older compiler). It needs to be cast to the correct type for this application. In this case, it is cast to type `struct trans *` before assigning to the variable `t_array`.

Note 4: The file pointer is set back to the beginning of the file in preparation for the input of the file.

Note 5: The entire contents of the file are read with one call to `fread()`. The contents are placed in the memory allocated earlier and pointed to by `t_array`. From this point on, `t_array` can be treated almost as if it were an array of `struct trans` items.

Learning Activities

20.   Compile and run calloc.c with the sample file you created when you tested the program fwrite.c of Example 10-7. (You might need to change the mode to `"rb"` if you are using a microcomputer.)

21.   Does calloc.c work correctly if the file exists but is empty? What happens? What do you think should happen? Modify the program to work correctly if necessary.

11.6 A Linked List—The Theory and an Example

One of the uses of pointers and dynamic allocation is to create linked lists. The concept of a linked list is common in creating data structures to organize data. Many data structures can have either array or linked list implementations. In Section 8.5, we saw a simple implementation of a stack (a LIFO) with an array. A stack can also be implemented as a linked list.

To create a linked list we first need to declare the type of the items in the list. This can be anything from a `char` value to a more complicated structure. It would need to be changed for different applications, and is usually done with a `typedef`. For example,

```
    typedef _____ element;
```
where the blank would be filled in with the appropriate type. Each `element` in the list would be embedded in a node, which is declared as a structure as

```
struct node {
        element data;
        struct node *next;
    };
```

Each node has two members, the `data` member, which will hold a value of type `element`, and the `next` member, which points to the next node in the list. A node with a `NULL` pointer in the `next` member will signify the end of the list. The linked list itself is declared as a pointer to a node. For example,

```
struct node *list;
```

When the list is set up properly, it has the configuration depicted in Figure 11-4.

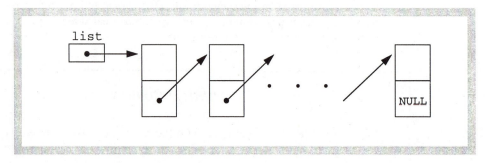

Figure 11-4 A Completed Linked List

One of the advantages of using a linked list is that unlike in an array, the number of items in the list does not have to be accurately approximated at compile time. Another advantage is that insertions and deletions in a linked list can be done by adjusting two pointers, while insertions and deletions in an array involve shifting data up or down to preserve the ordering. The steps necessary to insert a node in a linked list are shown in Figure 11-5.

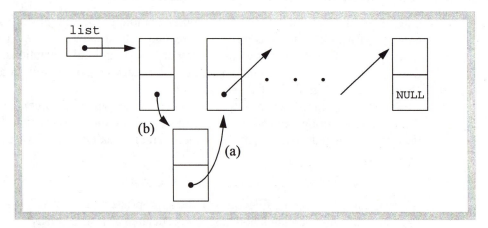

Figure 11-5   Inserting a Node in a Linked List

(a) Adjust the `next` member of the new node to point to its successor in the list.
(b) Adjust the `next` member of the previous node to point to the new node.

The program linklist.c in Examples 11-9 through 11-14 gives an example of a linked list. It essentially echoes its input to its output, but internally, each line of input is stored in a node of a linked list. Each node of the linked list contains two pointers as members. The first member is a `char *` value named `word` that will point to a dynamically allocated array of characters holding the input line as a string. The second member is the `next` field; it points to the next node in the list. For example, if the input to the program is

```
To bed
To bed
said
Sleepy Head
```

the internal linked list is shown in Figure 11-6.

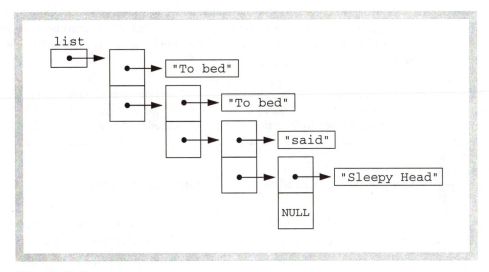

Figure 11-6

We will discuss each subfunction from the program linklist.c separately to see what each one does before putting them together in the program. To compile this program, all functions could be placed in the same file. If separate source files are desired, it will be necessary to include some header files.

Example 11-9: linklist.c: function get_node_space()

```
/***************************** get_node_space()  *************/
/*   Allocates the space for a single node and returns the
 *   pointer to the first byte of the space.
```

```
*/

struct node *get_node_space( void )
{
    struct node *temp_ptr;
                                                        /* Note 1 */
    temp_ptr = ( struct node * ) malloc( sizeof( struct node ));
    if ( temp_ptr == NULL ) {
        printf( "out of memory for nodes\n" );
        exit( 1 );
    }
    return ( temp_ptr );
}
```

The purpose of this function is to allocate the space for a node in the linked list. It calls malloc() to get the space and checks its return value to make sure that the space allocation was successful. The program is terminated if the space was not obtained. The pointer to the first byte of space is returned to the calling function.

Note 1: The parameter in the call to malloc() specifies that enough memory to store a struct node is requested. The cast to a struct node * must be used to force that address to be the address of a struct node.

 Example 11-10: linklist.c: function hook_it_up()

```
/***************************** hook_it_up()  ****************/
/*   Attaches new_node to the end of a list. The parameter
 *   old_list must point to the last node in the list.
 */
void hook_it_up( struct node *old_list, struct node *new_node )
{
    new_node->next = NULL;
    old_list->next = new_node;
}
```

The purpose of this function is to put the new node on the end of the linked list. The parameters are both pointers to nodes. On entry to the function, the first parameter, old_list, should point to the last node in the list. The second parameter, new_node, should point to the node to be added to the list. The configuration is illustrated in Figure 11-7.

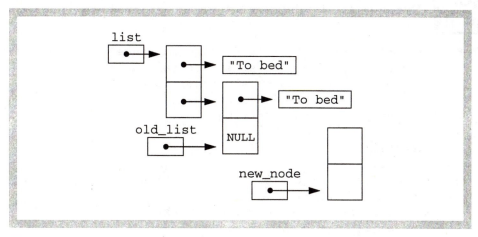

Figure 11-7

The code for the function consists of adjusting two pointers. The next member of new_node is set to NULL to signify the end of the list, and the next member of old_list points to new_node. The final configuration is shown in Figure 11-8.

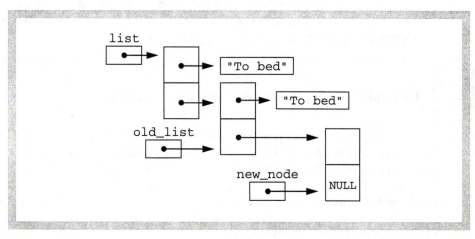

Figure 11-8

Example 11-11: linklist.c: function get_word_space( )

```
/***************************** get_word_space()  *************/
/*   Allocates space for the string contained in its
 *   first parameter. Returns a pointer to the first byte.
 */
char *get_word_space( char *string )
{
     char *temp;

     temp = ( char * ) calloc( strlen( string ) + 1, 1 );
     if ( temp == NULL ) {
          printf( "Out of memory for text.\n" );
          exit( 2 );
     }
     return ( temp );
}
```

This function dynamically allocates the memory needed for the string in its parameter `string`. The library function `calloc()` is used to obtain space for an array of `strlen( string )+1` elements of size one byte. The value returned by `calloc()` is checked to make sure that the memory allocation is successful. If it was not, the program is terminated with an error message. If it was successful, the address of the first byte of the buffer is returned.

Example 11-12: linklist.c: function release( )

```
/***************************** release()  *******************/
/*   Systematically deallocates the memory used by the list.
 *   Works from the front of the list to the back.
 */
void release( struct node **listptr )                      /* Note 1 */
{
     struct node *temp1, *temp2;

     temp1 = *listptr;
     while ( temp1->next != NULL ) {
          temp2 = temp1->next;
          free(( void * )temp1->word );                    /* Note 2 */
          free(( void * )temp1 );
```

```
        temp1 = temp2;
}
free(( void * )temp1->word );
free(( void * )temp1 );
*listptr = NULL;
}
```

This function does the job of memory deallocation. It moves through the list with the local variables, `temp1` and `temp2`. At each `node`, it first adjusts `temp2` to point to the next `node` in the list and then calls `free()` to release the space occupied by the `node` at which `temp1` points (see Figure 11-9). It first releases the space occupied by the string (Figure 11-10) and then the space occupied by the `node` itself (see Figure 11-11).

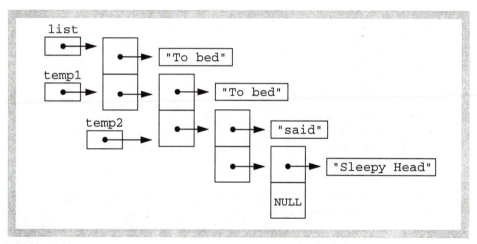

Figure 11-9

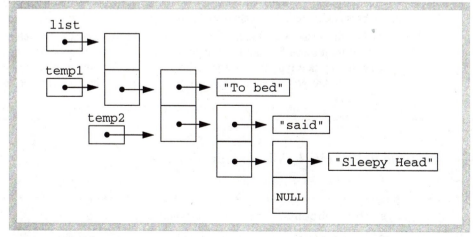

Figure 11-10

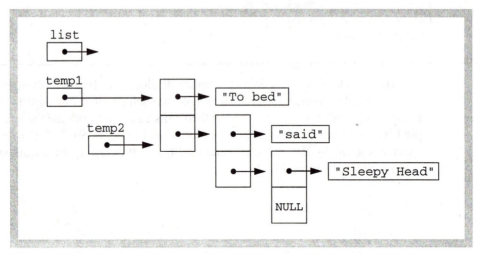

Figure 11-11

The while loop terminates when temp1 points to the last node in the list. The space it occupies still has to be deallocated. Finally, the contents of listptr are set to NULL. Note that the order of these steps is important. If things are done in a different order, some of the memory pointers might be lost and the attached memory could not be deallocated.

Note 1: The purpose of the function is to change the value of the pointer to the list. On entry a list of nodes exists; it will be represented by a pointer to the first node. On exit the list should be empty and the pointer should have been set to NULL. Since release() needs to change the list, a pointer to the struct node * value that represents the list must be passed in. In the body of the function, the parameter, listptr, is dereferenced so that the contents of the struct node * value representing the list are actually changed.

Note 2: When the space was obtained by calloc() or malloc(), the return value from those functions had type void *. That pointer was cast to the appropriate type for each specific use. Now that the space is to be released, the pointer should be recast to void * when it is passed to free().

Example 11-13: linklist.c: function print()

```
/****************************** print() ***********************/
/*    Displays the contents of the word member of nodes in
```

```
 *     the list.
 */
void print( struct node *ptr )
{
    while ( ptr->next != NULL ) {
        printf( "%s\n", ptr->word );
        ptr = ptr->next;
    }
    printf( "%s\n", ptr->word );
}
```

A `while` loop moves through the list and displays the string stored in each node. Note that auxiliary pointers are not necessary. The parameter `ptr` is used to move through the list. Since the parameter is passed by value, the changes to `ptr` in this function will not affect the value of the actual parameter in the rest of the program.

Now that we know what the utility functions do, we will study the driver function `main()` in Example 11-14 to see how it all works together.

Example 11-14: linklist.c: function main( )

```
/*                 linklist.c
 *
 *     Synopsis    - Echoes its input to its output, but keeps the
 *                   input in a linked list.
 *
 *     Objective   - Illustrates building a linked list of words
 *                   with dynamic allocation of memory.
 */

/* Include Files */
#include <stdio.h>
#include <stdlib.h>
#include <string.h>

/* Type Descriptions */
struct node {                                          /* Note 1 */
    char *word;
    struct node *next;
};

/* Function Declarations */
char         *get_word_space( char *s );
struct node  *get_node_space( void );
```

```
void      release( struct node ** );
void      print( struct node * );
void      hook_it_up( struct node *, struct node * );

void main( void )
{
    char          inputbuffer[512];
    struct node   *list, *lead_ptr, *follow_ptr;

    printf ( "Enter some text for the linked list.\n" );
    printf( "Terminate input by signaling end of file.\n" );
    if ( gets( inputbuffer ) != NULL ) {              /* Note 2 */
        list = get_node_space();                      /* Note 3 */
        list->next = NULL;                            /* Note 4 */
        follow_ptr = list;
                                                      /* Note 5 */
        list->word = get_word_space( inputbuffer );
        strcpy( list->word, inputbuffer );            /* Note 6 */
    }
    while ( gets( inputbuffer ) != NULL ) {
        lead_ptr = get_node_space();                  /* Note 7 */
        hook_it_up( follow_ptr, lead_ptr );           /* Note 8 */
        follow_ptr = lead_ptr;                        /* Note 9 */
                                                      /* Note 10 */
        lead_ptr->word = get_word_space( inputbuffer );
                                                      /* Note 11 */
        strcpy( lead_ptr->word, inputbuffer );
    }

    print( list );
    release( &list );                                 /* Note 12 */
}
```

An if statement calls gets() to get the first line of input and a while loop handles the remainder of the input. Finally, calls to print() and release() display the contents of the list and deallocate the space. The notes below and accompanying figures will trace through the execution of the program with the two lines

```
Tweedledee
Tweedledum
```

as sample input.

Note 1: A struct node is declared. It consists of two pointer values, and has the configuration shown in Figure 11-12.

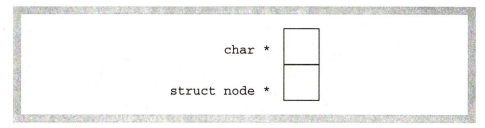

Figure 11-12

Note 2: The input to the program is done with calls to gets(). A NULL pointer returned by gets() signifies that either an error has occurred or end-of-file was sensed.

Note 3: The function get_node_space() is called to obtain the space for a node. The configuration is pictured in Figure 11-13.

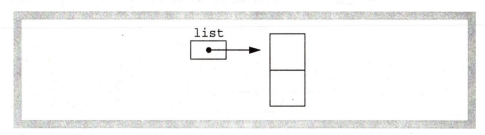

Figure 11-13

Note 4: Two pointers are adjusted. The next member of the node is set to NULL to signify the end of the list, and follow_ptr is set to point to the node in preparation for the next input. The configuration is shown in Figure 11-14.

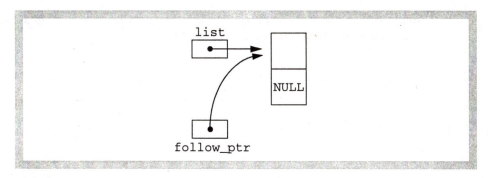

Figure 11-14

Note 5: The function `get_word_space()` will allocate the correct amount of space for the first line of input, `"Tweedledee"`. On return, the configuration is like that shown in Figure 11-15.

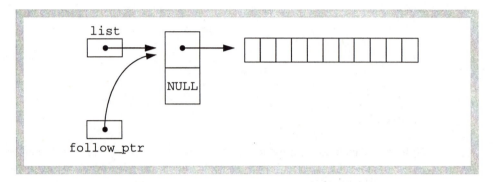

Figure 11-15

Note 6: The input is copied from `inputbuffer` to the `node`. The first line of input has been processed and the configuration is shown in Figure 11-16.

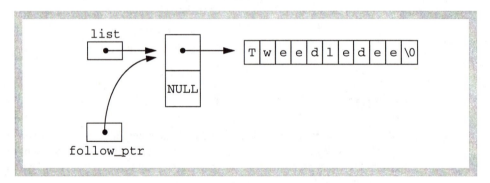

Figure 11-16

Note 7: After the second line of input, `get_node_space()` is called to allocate space for a new `node`. See Figure 11-17.

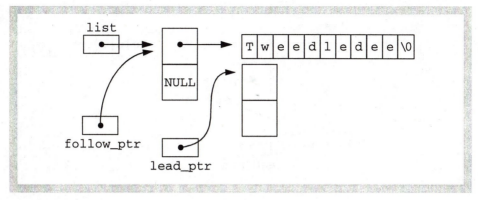

Figure 11-17

Note 8: The new node is hooked into the list by hook_it_up(). See Figure 11-18.

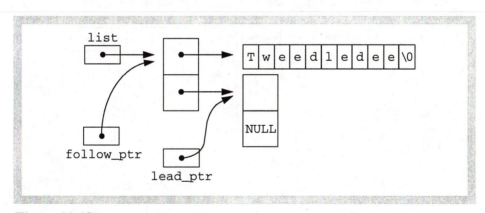

Figure 11-18

Note 9: The pointers are adjusted for the next input, if any. See Figure 11-19.

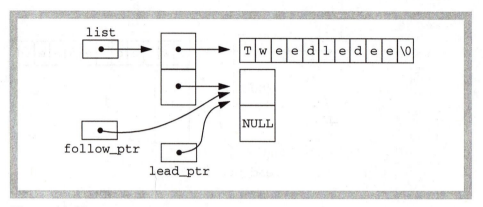

Figure 11-19

Note 10: Space is allocated for the string in `inputbuffer`. See Figure 11-20.

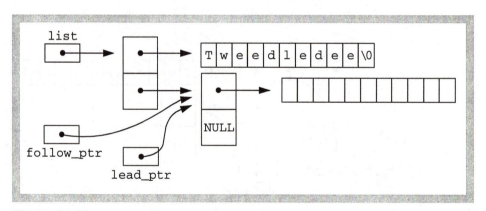

Figure 11-20

Note 11: The string in `inputbuffer` is copied into the new `node`, thus completing the construction of the linked list for these two lines of input (see Figure 11-21). The `while` loop will be exited when end-of-file is signaled on the next input attempt.

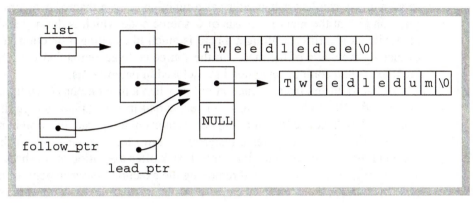

Figure 11-21

Note 12: After the list is displayed, `release()` is called to deallocate the memory used by the list. Because the program ends here, this step was not really necessary, but since a routine like this could be part of a larger program, deallocating memory would be necessary in that situation. See Figure 11-22 for the final configuration.

Figure 11-22

Learning Activities

22. Execute the program with several sets of input to make sure that it works. Try it with long lines and short lines, many lines and few lines. If you ran out of memory, did that seem reasonable for the amount of input you entered?

23. What happens when end-of-file is signaled immediately after the prompt? Does the program terminate properly? If it doesn't, what happens? If necessary, modify it so that it works correctly.

11.7 Defining Macros

In C, a utility can be written either as a function or as a macro. A macro is like a function in that the macro consists of C source code which is defined and associated with an identifier. Calling a macro is much like calling a function; it consists of placing the name of the macro in the source code accompanied with the actual parameters in a comma-separated list enclosed in parentheses.

A macro differs from a function in that when a program has been translated to object code, the code for the macro is expanded in every place where the macro was called, while the code for a function remains in a separate location in memory. Executing a function requires transferring control to a separate part of the object code in memory and transferring control back after execution is finished. There is other overhead in setting up and removing the execution environment for the function. In contrast, the code for the macro is expanded at the position of the call, and thus avoids the transfer of control and the overhead. In general, macros execute faster than functions, but take up more memory if they are called often.

In C, macros are handled in the preprocess phase of compilation. They are defined with the #define directive. For example, the directive

```
#define printit          printf( "it" );
```

at the top of a source code file would cause every occurrence of the identifier printit in the source code to be replaced with the statement

```
printf( "it" );
```

Note that the expression

```
printit;
```

would be replaced with

```
printf("it");;
```

since the semicolon is included in the macro expansion.

Macros can be declared with parameters, and the preprocessor will substitute the actual parameters for the formal parameters when it expands the macro. For example, the macro

```
#define pr( s )      printf( "The value is %d.\n", s );
```

would cause the expression

```
pr( counter );
```

to be replaced with

```
printf( "The value is %d.\n", counter );;
```

The preprocessor expects to find macro definitions contained on one line of source code. If it is necessary to continue the definition onto a second line, the character ' \ ' may be placed at the end of a line to indicate that the definition continues on the next line. For example,

```
#define pr( s )       printf( "The value is %d\n",\
                              s );
```

is equivalent to

```
#define pr( s )       printf( "The value is %d\n",s );
```

Some of the facilities available in the standard header files are macros. For example, `getc()`, `getchar()`, `putc()` and `putchar()` are implemented as macros. Many of the character handling utilities like `isalpha()`, `isprint()`, and so on are also written as macros.

The program macros.c in Example 11-15 uses the standard macros `getchar()` and `isdigit()` in its input/conversion routine `getint()`. A user-defined macro `MAX()` is called to calculate the maximum of the input values.

Example 11-15: macros.c

```
/*                  macros.c
 *
 *    Synopsis    - Accepts input of two integers from the keyboard
 *                  and displays the maximum of the two values.
 *
 *    Objective   - Will illustrate the expansion of macros by the
 *                  preprocessor.
 */

/* Include Files */
#include <stdio.h>                                    /* Note 1 */
#include <ctype.h>                                    /* Note 2 */

/* Macro Definitions */
#define MAX(a, b)        (a > b) ? a : b              /* Note 3 */

/* Function Declarations */
int getint( int * );

void main( void )
{
    int x, y;

    printf( "Calculating the maximum of two numbers.\n" );
    printf( "Please enter the first nonnegative number : " );
```

```
        getint( &x );
        printf( "Please enter the second nonnegative number : " );
        getint( &y );
        printf( "The maximum of %d and %d is %d.\n",
                                    x, y, MAX( x,y ));        /* Note 4 */
}


/***************************** getint()   *********************/
/*   Reads a line of input and converts input digits to a
 *   value of type int and stores the result in its parameter.
 *   Returns a 0 for success and a 1 if any nondigit is found.
 *   In the latter case, the contents of val are set to 0.
 */
int getint( int *val )
{
        int iochar, num;

        num = 0;
        while (( iochar = getchar() ) != '\n' ) {            /* Note 5 */
                if ( isdigit( iochar ))                       /* Note 6 */
                        num = 10*num + iochar - '0';
                else {
                        printf( "Illegal input - %c\n", iochar );
                                                             /* Note 7 */
                        while (( iochar = getchar() ) != '\n' )
                                ;
                        *val = 0;
                        return( 1 );
                }
        }
        *val = num;
        return ( 0 );
}
```

The functions main() and getint() comprise this program. Calls to getint() to process the input and calls to printf() for output make up main().

The function getint() reads an integer value from standard input and returns the value in the location pointed to by its parameter. It adds some error handling to the input routine. A while loop driven by calls to getchar() does the input. If digits are found, conversion to type int takes place. In case a nondigit is found in the input, an error message is issued, the input buffer is flushed, the contents of val are set to 0, and 1 is returned to indicate the error. If the while loop terminates normally, val gets the value of the converted integer and 0 is returned to indicate success.

Note 1: The macros getchar() and getc() are defined in stdio.h.

Note 2: The macro isdigit() is defined in ctype.h.

Note 3: This line has the definition of the macro MAX(). It is defined with a ?: conditional expression. First the expression a > b is evaluated. If it is true, the value returned by the macro is a; otherwise, the return value is b.

Note 4: The call to the macro MAX() appears as a parameter to this printf() call. The preprocessor will replace this call by the defining sequence above and substitute the actual parameters for the formal ones.

Note 5: The macro getchar() is called on this line. During preprocessing, this line will be modified by the macro expansion facility.

Note 6: The macro isdigit() on this line will also be expanded during the preprocess phase of compilation.

Note 7: Reading to the newline character is done to flush the input buffer. The macro getchar() will be expanded in this position also.

Learning Activities

24. a. Compile and run macros.c to make sure that it works correctly on your system.

  b. Test it several times with positive, negative, equal and unequal input values.

  c. What happens with negative values? Modify getint() so that it works for negative values also.

  d. What happens if either of the values entered is larger than the maximum int that can be handled by your system? How might you improve this performance? Does any change have to be made to the macro MAX()?

25. Look at the files stdio.h and ctype.h. Pick out the definition of the macros getchar() and getc() in stdio.h and isdigit() in ctype.h.

26. a. Compile macros.c again, but, if possible, stop the compilation after the preprocess phase and look at the preprocessed file.

  b. Locate the macro substitutions for getchar(), isdigit(), and MAX().

  c. Compare this code with the code in the header files and the definition of the source files.

  d. Explain the substitutions made by the preprocessor in macro expansion.

27. Write your own version of the macro isdigit(). Test it by removing the line

      #include <ctype.h>

  from the source in macros.c, and replace it with your macro definition.

28.   The function `getint()` returns 1 in case an error in conversion has occurred and 0 otherwise. Currently, the function `main()` ignores the return value. Therefore, if there is an error in the input, the output will be in error also. Modify the program to correct this deficiency. Have `main()` check the return value from `getint()` and repeatedly ask for input until the user gets the input correct.

A Word of Caution

The substitution for parameters in macros is exact. If the argument is `a++` or `a + 1`, that is what is substituted for the parameter in the macro. Many times this causes unexpected problems. Some of them are illustrated in the program squares.c of Example 11-16. In this program, a function and two macros are defined to perform the squaring operation on a value. The results of different calls to the functions and macros are displayed to illustrate some of the unexpected results.

Example 11-16: squares.c

```
/*                squares.c
 *
 *    Synopsis    - Displays results of the macros SQUARE(x),
 *                  SQR(x), SQR2(x) and the function square(x).
 *
 *    Objective   - To illustrate some of the differences between
 *                  macros and functions: how substitutions take
 *                  place and how macros are expanded.
 */

/* Include Files */
#include <stdio.h>

/* Macro Definitions */
#define SQUARE( x )           x * x                     /* Note 1 */
#define SQR( x )              (( x ) * ( x ))           /* Note 2 */

int SQR2_x;                                             /* Note 3 */
#define SQR2( x )             ( SQR2_x=( x ), SQR2_x * SQR2_x )

/* Function Declarations */
int square( int );
```

```c
void main( void )
{
    int a;

    a = 3;                                                          /* Note 4 */
    printf( "square( a ) is %d.\n", square( a ));
    printf( "SQUARE( a ) is %d.\n", SQUARE( a ));
    printf( "SQR( a ) is %d.\n", SQR( a ));
    printf( "SQR2( a ) is %d.\n", SQR2( a ));


                                                                    /* Note 5 */
    printf( "\nsquare( a+1 ) is %d\n", square( a+1 ));
    printf( "SQUARE( a+1 ) is %d.\n", SQUARE( a+1 ));
    printf( "SQR( a+1 ) is %d.\n", SQR( a+1 ));
    printf( "SQR2( a+1 ) is %d.\n", SQR2( a+1 ));

                                                                    /* Note 6 */
    printf( "\nsquare( a++ ) is %d, and ", square( a++ ));
    printf( "a is %d\n", a );

    a = 3;
    printf( "SQUARE( a++ ) is %d, and ", SQUARE( a++ ));
    printf( "a is %d\n", a );

    a = 3;
    printf( "SQR2( a++ ) is %d, and ", SQR2( a++ ));
    printf( "a is %d\n", a );

    a = 3;
    printf( "SQR( a++ ) is %d, and ", SQR( a++ ));
    printf( "a is %d\n", a );
}

/***************************** square()   ********************/
/*   Returns the square of its argument.
 */
int square( int x )                                                 /* Note 7 */
{
    return ( x * x );
}
```

 Running the Program

```
square( a ) is 9.
```

```
SQUARE( a ) is 9.
SQR( a ) is 9.
SQR2( a ) is 9.

square( a+1 ) is 16
SQUARE( a+1 ) is 7.
SQR( a+1 ) is 16.
SQR2( a+1 ) is 16.

square( a++ ) is 9, and a is 4
SQUARE( a++ ) is 12, and a is 5
SQR2( a++ ) is 9, and a is 4
SQR( a++ ) is 12, and a is 5
```

This program is very simple. Three macros, SQUARE(), SQR(), and SQR2(), and a function, square(), all have the purpose of squaring their arguments. The function main() displays the results of different calls to the macros and the function.

Note 1: The simplest way of squaring a value is defined by the macro SQUARE(). When the expression SQUARE(parm) is found in the source code, it will be replaced by parm * parm. As will be seen later in this program, this macro has some problems.

Note 2: A second form of a macro to square a value contains three sets of parentheses. Although SQR() works better than SQUARE(), it is not trouble free.

Note 3: The macro SQR2() uses the comma operator in its definition. The assignment of x to SQR2_x is done first and then SQR2_x is squared. The value of the expression is the square of SQR2_x. Notice that the variable SQR2_x must be declared in order to use this macro.

Note 4: The variable a is initialized to 3, and the values of the macros and the function are output with a as the actual parameter. All four results are correct.

Note 5: This sequence of printf() calls displays the values of both macros and the function when the actual parameter is a+1. The function square() and the macros SQR() and SQR2() return the correct value, but the macro SQUARE() does not. When a+1 is substituted for x in the macro definition, the macro expansion has the form

```
a+1 * a+1
```

Since multiplication has precedence over addition, the expression groups as

```
a + (1 * a) + 1
```

Since the value of a is 3, this evaluates to

```
3 + (1 * 3) + 1    or 7.
```

This is probably not the desired result.

Note 6: In the next sequence of statements, the value of the macros and the function is output with the argument a++. The value of a is reinitialized to 3 before each call. The value returned by the function is 9, or 3 squared, and the value of a has been incremented to 4. However, in two of the macros, the value returned is 12 and a has been incremented to 5. In SQUARE() the replacement of the formal parameter x with the actual parameter a++ results in the expression

```
a++  *  a++
```

In SQR(), it results in

```
(( a++ )  *  ( a++ ))
```

Both expressions evaluate to 12 since a gets incremented after the first factor is evaluated. Since it also gets incremented after the second factor is evaluated, the final value of a is 5.

Note that the macro SQR2_x() gave the correct value in both of these last two cases. Performing the assignment of x to SQR2_x in a separate step removed the problems in the other two macros.

Note 7: The function square() will always return the square of its parameter. The mechanism of passing parameters to functions is not sensitive to the ++ operator.

Learning Activities

29. In squares.c, change all the assignment statements of the form a = 3 to a = 7. Predict the output from the modified program, then compile and run the program to verify your prediction. Resolve any differences between your prediction and the actual output.

30. Look at the code produced by the preprocessor to verify the claims in **Note 5** and **Note 6**.

31. Try to write another macro that will return the square of its parameter correctly in all three cases in the program. Were you able to create one? Summarize your findings.

11.8 Conditional Compilation

Conditional compilation is a facility provided by the C preprocessor. It allows a choice of lines to be compiled based on the definition of certain symbols at compile time.

As an example, suppose a company is writing a software package to do billing for several commercial firms. One of the programs in the package is to accept input of a customer name, account number, and the transactions for that month, and write the information to a file for further processing by another program. Most of the firms that will use this program have a 16-character account number for their customers and an integer transaction code. However, ACME Electric has an 8-character account number and a 4-character transaction code. It is possible to handle both situations with a single program by using conditional compilation and compiling a different version for ACME. With conditional compilation, the structure holding the monthly transactions of a customer can be modified for ACME without doing any more than recompiling.

The preprocessor directives used for conditional compilation are:[1]

`#define`	used to define symbols to the compiler
`#ifdef`	tests whether a symbol is defined to the compiler
`#else`	provides an alternative to `#ifdef`
`#elif`	used to build compound conditional directives
`#endif`	signals the end of the body of an if directive
`#ifndef`	tests whether a symbol is not defined
`#if`	tests values of constant expressions
`defined`	used in conjunction with `#if` to replace `#ifdef`

In Section 11-7 and earlier, we have seen the use of the `#define` directive to define macros, which are then expanded during the preprocess phase of compilation. A second use is to make a symbol known to the compiler. A directive such as

```
#define  XYZ
```

makes the symbol XYZ known to the compiler, but does not require much macro expansion. (In this example, any occurrence of XYZ in the source code would be essentially removed by macro expansion.)

Other ways of defining symbols to the compiler may be available with a particular implementation of C. For example, in the UNIX system, the `-D` command line option for the compiler can be used to define symbols for a particular compilation without modifying the source code. In some of the windowing compiler environments on a microcomputer, a symbol can be defined with an option.

The directives

```
#ifdef XYZ        or      #if defined XYZ
```

can be used to test whether the symbol XYZ has been defined to the compiler. If it has, the lines following the directive until the occurrence of either `#else`, `#elif`, or `#endif` in the source code file will be included for compilation. If the symbol XYZ has not been defined to the compiler, the lines are omitted.

The directives `#else` and `#elif` work similarly to `else` or `else if` in a conditional statement. With them it is possible to choose which source lines to include.

The program ccomp.c of Example 11-17 is a start on a program to accept input

---

1. The directives `#elif` and `defined` may not be available with some older compilers.

of the customer's name and account number from standard input, and store them in
a file. The code to read and store the monthly transactions still needs to be added.

Example 11-17: ccomp.c

```
/*              ccomp.c
 *
 *   Synopsis    - Accepts input of information about a customer
 *                 from standard input, and stores the information
 *                 in a file named "transactions".
 *
 *   Objective   - To illustrate conditional compilation.
 */

/* Include Files */
#include <stdio.h>
#include <stdlib.h>

/* Type Descriptions */
struct statement {
    char name[30];
#ifdef ACME                                             /* Note 1 */
    char account[9];
#else
    char account[17];
#endif
    float balance;
    struct {
#ifdef ACME                                             /* Note 2 */
        char t_code[5];
#else
        int t_code;
#endif
        int quantity;
        float price;
    } transactions[50];
};

/* Function Declarations */
int get_customer( struct statement * );

void main( void )
{
    struct statement customer;
```

```
        FILE *fp;

        if (( fp = fopen( "statements", "w" )) == NULL ) {
            perror( "File Opening Error" );
            exit( 1 );
        }

        printf( "Enter your customer transactions now.\n" );
        printf( "Signal EOF when you are done.\n" );

        while ( get_customer( &customer ))
            fwrite( &customer, sizeof( customer ), 1, fp );

        printf( "Thank you, the statements will be prepared.\n" );
}


/****************************** get_customer()  **************/
/*   Accepts input of information for a single customer.
 */
int get_customer( struct statement *cust )
{
        printf( "Enter customer name: " );
        if ( fgets( cust->name, 30, stdin ) == NULL )
            return ( 0 );

        printf( "Enter customer account number: " );
#ifdef ACME                                                   /* Note 3 */
        fgets( cust->account, 8, stdin );
#else
        fgets( cust->account, 16, stdin );
#endif

        /* code to enter the transactions goes here */
        return ( 1 );
}
```

The program consists of main() and get_customer(). The function main() opens the output file and handles any resulting errors. It then enters a while loop to read and store the customer information. The function get_customer() will return a value of 1 when it has valid customer information and a value of 0 when it reaches the end of input. The code for get_customer() consists of printf() calls to prompt for input, and calls to fgets() to read the input.

Note 1: If the symbol ACME has been defined for a particular compilation, the size of the character array will be 9 (for the 8-character account number and a terminating null character). If ACME is not defined, the account array will hold a 16-character account number plus a terminating null character.

Note 2: For ACME, the t_code member will be able to store 4 characters plus a terminating null character. For other companies, it is declared to hold a value of type int.

Note 3: Since the account array has fewer cells when ACME is defined, a separate fgets() call could be used to input the account number for ACME.

Learning Activities

32. a. Find out how to define a value for a specific compilation with your C compiler.

   b. Compile the program but stop the compilation process after the preprocess phase and inspect the file to see which lines of source code have been included. Compile the program down to object code and execute it.

   c. Compile the program with the identifier ACME defined. Again, stop the compilation process and inspect the file after the preprocess phase. Compile this version to object code and test it also.

33. a. List two or more ways to verify that the compiler actually made the requested changes at compilation time.

   b. Implement at least two of these methods and test the two different compilations of the code.

   c. Summarize your findings from the tests.

Conditional Compilation in Program Development and Debugging

A popular use for conditional compilation is to provide a trace through a program and possibly display the values of some important variables. This use would occur as the program is being developed or possibly when modifications might be made in the program maintenance phase of the programming cycle.

The program recurs2.c in Example 11-18 illustrates this use. The program recurs.c of Chapter 6 has been modified by adding conditional compilation directives and source code to provide a trace of execution. The output is shown for the input value of 3.

Example 11-18:   recurs2.c

```
/*                  recurs2.c
 *
 *    Synopsis    - Accepts input of a positive integer, calculates
 *                  its factorial, and displays the result.
 *
 *    Objective   - Illustrates the use of conditional compilation
 *                  during program development and debugging.
 */

/* Include Files */
#include <stdio.h>
#include <ctype.h>
#include <stdlib.h>

/* Directives for Conditional Compilation */
#ifdef   DEBUG                                                 /* Note 1 */
int      nesting = 0;                                          /* Note 2 */
                                                               /* Note 3 */
#define ENTER(fn)  printf("\n%*s{ ENTER %s\n", ++nesting*4, "", fn)
#define EXIT(fn)   printf("\n%*s} EXIT  %s\n", nesting--*4, "", fn)
#else
#define ENTER(fn)                                              /* Note 4 */
#define EXIT(fn)
#endif

/* Constant Declarations */
#define BLANK          ' '
#define END_OF_LINE    '\n'

/* Function Declarations */
long factorial( long );
long convert( void );
void error( void );

void main( void )
{
    long n;
    ENTER("main");                                            /* Note 5 */
    printf( "Program to Calculate Factorials.\n" );
    printf( "------- -- --------- -----------\n" );
    printf( "\nEnter a positive integer value : " );
```

```
     n = convert();                                    /* Note 2 */

     printf( "\n%ld! is %ld.\n", n, factorial( n ) );
     EXIT( "main" );                                   /* Note 7 */
}

/***************************** factorial()   *****************/
/*   Uses a recursive algorithm to calculate the factorial
 *   of its argument.
 */
long factorial( long n )
{
     long temp;

     ENTER( "factorial" );
     if ( n == 0 ) {
          EXIT( "factorial - 1" );                     /* Note 3 */
          return ( 1 );
     }
     else {
          temp = n * factorial( n - 1 );
          EXIT( "factorial" );                         /* Note 7 */
          return ( temp );
     }
}

/***************************** convert()   *******************/
/*   Reads standard input until either a BLANK, an END_OF_LINE
 *   or a nondigit is found. If only digits are found, the
 *   function returns the converted value as type int. Otherwise,
 *   the function error() is called
 */
long convert( void )
{
     int    ch;
     long   sum = 0;

     ENTER( "convert" );
     while ((( ch = getchar() ) != BLANK ) && (ch != END_OF_LINE )) {
          if ( !isdigit( ch ) )
               error();
          sum = sum * 10 + ( ch - '0' );
     }
#ifdef DEBUG                                            /* Note 6 */
     printf( "Converted Value: %ld\n", sum );
```

```
#endif

    EXIT( "convert" );                                        /* Note 7 */
    return ( sum );
}

/***************************** error()  ********************/
/*  Displays an error message and terminates the program with
 *  exit value 1.
 */
void error( void )
{
    ENTER( "error" );
    printf( "Nondigit in input. Program terminated.\n" );
    EXIT( "Terminating Program" );                            /* Note 7 */
    exit( 1 );
}
```

 Running the Program

```
    { ENTER main
Program to Calculate Factorials.
------- -- --------- -----------

Enter a positive integer value : 3
        { ENTER convert
Converted Value: 3

        } EXIT  convert

        { ENTER factorial

            { ENTER factorial

                { ENTER factorial

                    { ENTER factorial

                    } EXIT  factorial - 1

                } EXIT  factorial

            } EXIT  factorial

        } EXIT  factorial
```

```
3! is 6.

    } EXIT  main
```

The basic program is very similar to recurs.c of Section 6.7. The only things that have been added are some preprocessor directives that control conditional compilation and a printf() call that will be conditionally included in the object code. The calculation of the value returned by factorial() has also been changed slightly.

Note 1: The symbol to be defined is DEBUG. It can be defined at the time of compilation by using the facilities of the compiler or it can be defined with the preprocessor directive

      #define DEBUG

which should appear above the #ifdef directives.

Note 2: The variable nesting will be declared when the symbol DEBUG is defined to the compiler. It will indicate the level of nesting of a particular function; that is, it keeps track of the number of functions that are active at any instant during execution of the program.

Note 3: ENTER() and EXIT() are preprocessor macros. When the symbol DEBUG is defined, they will expand to a call to printf(). The macro ENTER() will be called each time a function starts executing. The macro EXIT() will be called each time a function terminates. These macros also illustrate new forms of conversion specifications for printf().

Consider the first conversion specification, %*s. The asterisk, *, is in the position of the field width specifier, and indicates that the field width is variable. When the asterisk is present in this position, printf() evaluates its next argument, which should be of type int, to give the field width. In this case, the incremented value of nesting multiplied by 4 provides the minimum number of spaces for this field. The string to be displayed is the empty string so that this expression will cause the remainder of the output to be indented.

Note 4: When the symbol DEBUG is not defined to the compiler, the macros ENTER() and EXIT() will be replaced by a blank line. This way, the calls to ENTER() and EXIT() can remain in the finished source code without affecting execution. Then if the code needs to be modified or debugged, they can be reactivated by compiling the program again with DEBUG defined.

Note 5: The macro ENTER() is called as the first line of executable code for each function in the program. The parameter to ENTER() will be a string containing the name of the function. When the macro is the printf() call, this macro will announce that the function is being entered and the indentation will give an indication of the level of nesting. The code will have no effect on program execution in a version where DEBUG has not been defined at compile time.

Note 6: In the DEBUG version, the conversion routine is checked with a call to printf() to display the converted value.

Note 7: The macro EXIT() is called every time a function terminates. The parameter is a string consisting of the function name. In a version where DEBUG has been defined to the compiler, the macro announces that the function is exiting and gives the level of nesting. The nesting level should match that at the start of execution of the function. The macro EXIT() has no effect on program execution in a version where DEBUG is not defined to the compiler. The macros ENTER() and EXIT() will provide a trace of the execution of the program when they are activated.

Learning Activities

34. Compile recurs2.c without defining DEBUG and test it to make sure that it executes like recurs.c of Section 6.7.

35. Define the symbol DEBUG to the compiler, and compile recurs2.c again.

    a. Stop the process after the preprocess phase to see if the conditional code was included.

    b. Compile down to executable code with DEBUG defined to the compiler. Execute the program several times with different inputs. Make sure you see how the conditionally compiled statements provide a trace through the program. In particular, make sure you understand the purpose of the variable nesting and how the variable field width specification works.

Language Elements Introduced in This Chapter: A Review

✓ Header Files

```
time.h
math.h
ctype.h
stdlib.h
malloc.h (non-ANSI compilers)
```

✓ Standard Library Functions and Preprocessor Macros

`time()`	returns a measure of the current time
`ctime()`	works with `time()` to provide a character string representation of time and date
`localtime()`	works with `time()`; returns information about the time and date in a `struct tm`
`clock()`	returns a measure of time used by the processor
`ferror()`	reports on errors associated with a file
`clearerr()`	clears an error condition associated with a file
`perror()`	reports on general errors
`sqrt()`	returns the square root of its argument
`pow()`	raises a number to an integral power
`atan2()`	returns the angle between `-PI` and `PI` whose tangent is the quotient of the arguments to the function
`strtod()`	converts as many characters in its parameter string as possible to a double value
`isalpha()`	tests to see if its argument is an alphabetic character
`isdigit()`	tests to see if its argument is a digit
`isspace()`	tests to see if its argument is a whitespace character
`isupper()`	tests to see if its argument is an uppercase alphabetic character
`ispunct()`	tests to see if its argument is a punctuation character
`toupper()`	converts any lowercase alphabetics to uppercase and leaves all other characters unchanged
`tolower()`	converts uppercase alphabetics to lowercase and leaves other characters unchanged
`malloc()`	dynamically allocates memory
`calloc()`	dynamically allocates memory and initializes it to bytes of `NULL`
`free()`	releases dynamically allocated memory

✓ Preprocessor Directives

`#define`	used to define symbols to the compiler
`#ifdef`	tests whether a symbol is defined to the compiler

`#else`	provides an alternative to `#ifdef`
`#elif`	used to build compound conditional directives
`#endif`	signals the end of the body of an if directive
`#ifndef`	tests whether a symbol is not defined
`#if`	tests values of constant expressions
`defined`	used in conjunction with `#if` to replace `#ifdef`

✓ **Types**

`clock_t`	declared in time.h
`time_t`	declared in time.h
`struct tm`	declared in time.h
`size_t`	declared in stdlib.h and other header files.

Things to Remember

1. Many of the standard library functions provide built-in error reporting facilities through their return value.

2. Some libraries will not be searched by default. The compiler may have a switch that will allow the programmer to indicate which libraries other than the default to search.

3. Errors to the mathematical functions could occur if a parameter to a function is not in the domain of that function or when a calculated value is too large for the computer to handle.

4. The character manipulation facilities are implemented as functions or as macros.

5. The values returned from `malloc()` and `calloc()` need to be cast to appropriate types when they are assigned. The pointer arithmetic counts on the cast value.

6. When using `free()`, remember to cast the parameter to type `void *`.

7. A structure declaration such as

```
struct node {
        element data;
        struct node *next;
};
```

can be used for the nodes of a linked list.

8. A macro is a code segment that is expanded in the code at compilation time. It looks like a function, but is declared using the `#define` preprocessor directive.

9. The substitution for parameters in macros is exact. If the argument is `a++` or `a+1`, then that is what is substituted for the parameter in the macro.

10. Conditional compilation can be used to help customize software for a specific application or to help in the software development phase.

Exercises and Programming Problems

1. In the program linklist.c, the new nodes are always placed at the end of the linked list. Modify this program so that the new nodes are always placed at the beginning of the list. When your program is correct, the `print()` function will display the input lines in reverse order.

2. The data type stack was discussed in Section 8.5. It was implemented with an array there. For this problem, implement a stack as a linked list. Write a data structure for a STACK element and define a STACK as a pointer to the data structure. Note that the data structure should have a pointer field to link to the next element in the stack. Write the stack utility functions with the declarations below.

   ```
   int push( char item, STACK *s_ptr );
   int pop( STACK *s_ptr );
   void init_stack( STACK *s_ptr );
   int  is_empty( STACK s );
   int  is_full ( STACK s );
   ```

   Put the STACK declaration and declarations of the functions in a header file named stack1.h, put the function definitions in a separate module named stack1.c, and insert a line `#include "stack1.h"` at the beginning of stack1.c. To test your package, modify the program stackex.c of Example 8.9 by changing the line

   ```
   #include "stack.h"
   ```

   to

   ```
   #include "stack1.h"
   ```

   Now you should be able to compile the modules stackex.c and stack1.c and link them together. The results should be the same as those for stackex.c compiled with the array implementation of a stack that appears in the files stack.h and stack.c.

3. A queue was discussed in problem 10 of Section 8.9. In that problem you were asked to write an array implementation of a queue. Now write a linked list implementation of a queue. You will need to write a declaration of a node to hold a queue element. (A pointer to another node should be a member.) A data structure for the queue itself should contain a pointer to the first node and a pointer to the last. Write the functions `enqueue()`, `dequeue()`, `is_full()`, `is_empty()` and `init_queue()` with declarations identical to those in problem 9 of Chapter 8.

4. a. Look up the functions `rand()` and `srand()` in the *Programmer's Handbook*. The function `rand()` will return a "random" number between 0 and some implementation-defined maximum. The function `srand()` seeds the random number generator.

b. Use the data type you developed in problem 3 of Chapter 7 and write a function to deal bridge hands (13 cards of a standard deck) to four people.

c. Test your function by writing a program that incorporates your functions from parts b and c of problem 3 of Chapter 7 to display the bridge hands. Run your program several times. If the random number generator `rand()` has been seeded properly with `srand()`, you should almost certainly get different results each time.

5. Finish the function `get_customer()` in the program ccomp.c. Have the transaction code, quantity, and price input for each transaction. Have the user enter 0 for the transaction code to signal the end of the transactions. If the transaction code `"REFD"` for ACME and `11` for other companies signals a refund, have your function calculate the ending balance from the input transactions. (Every transaction other than a refund should indicate money collected.)

6. ACME wants the program to write a monthly balance report with each customer listed in the form

```
    Account No.              Name                Balance
```

while the other companies want their monthly balance report with each entry written in the form

```
    Name                Account No.             Balance
```

Write a single program to read the file `"statements"` and write a transaction report. Use conditional compilation to make sure that ACME's and the other companies' files are read correctly and that their transaction report has the desired form.

7. Modify your program written for exercise 6 by having the program print the date and time that the report was created as the first line of the report.

8. Write a program that displays a list in tabular form of each of the ASCII characters in the following categories: alphabetic, alphanumeric, control, decimal digit, hexadecimal digit, graphical, printable, punctuation, and whitespace. Use the macros defined in the standard header file ctype.h. (Non-printing characters could be displayed in either octal, hexadecimal or with a special character sequence like ESC for the escape character.)

9. a. Write a function `toint()` that takes a single character as a parameter and returns its decimal value. For example, `toint('9')` should return 9 and so on.

b. Rewrite the function in part a as a macro.

c. Use the code that you wrote in parts a and b to write a function `myatoi()` that takes a string of digits as a parameter and returns the decimal value of the ASCII string. For example, if the input string contains the characters `'1'`, `'2'`, `'3'`, `'\0'`, the function `myatoi()` should return the `int` value

123. Have your function handle strings with characters other than digits the same way that the library function `atoi()` does.

d. Test your function in a simple program that accepts input of a string of digits and displays the `int` value. Test it with both the function and macro version of `toint()` that you wrote in parts a and b of this problem. Test to see which version is more efficient.

10. Modify your program in problem 9 so that it assumes that the input string is a hexadecimal digit, and displays the conversion of the input hexadecimal string to a decimal integer. You will have to modify both versions of `toint()` as well as the function `myatoi()`.

11. Write a program that accepts input of an array of `ints` and displays them in sorted order. Use the standard library function `qsort()` to do the sorting. Look it up in the *Programmer's Handbook* and in the documentation for your compiler.

Programmer's Handbook

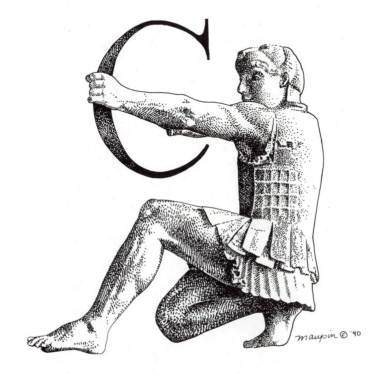

maupin © '90

A

Identifiers in ANSI C

ANSI C identifies two types of identifiers: those whose scope does not go beyond the end of the source module in which they are defined (those with internal linkage) and those that are available to be linked with other modules (those with external linkage). The rules for the two types of identifiers may differ, but both consist of alphabetic characters, digits, and underscores, and must begin with a letter or an underscore.

Identifiers with internal linkage can be any length. At least the first 31 characters will be significant. Uppercase and lowercase letters will be distinguished. Identifiers with internal linkage include local variables, function parameters, static global variables, and preprocessor-defined macro names.

The rules for identifiers with external linkage are implementation dependent and may be considerably more restrictive. They may be limited to as few as 6 characters, and uppercase and lowercase alphabetic characters may not be distinguished.

B

Keywords in C

`auto`	a storage class
`break`	control statement - breaks out of loops and switches
`case`	`case` labels used with `switch` statement
`char`	a data type
`const`*	a type qualifier - value will not be changed
`continue`	control statement - `continue` at top of loop
`default`	marks `default` case in switch statement
`do`	`do-while` loop control statement
`double`	a data type
`else`	`if-else` control statement
`enum`	enumerated data type
`extern`	a storage class
`float`	a floating point data type
`for`	`for` loop control statement
`goto`	control statement
`if`	`if` control statement
`int`	the default integer data type
`long`	as in `long int` and `long double` data types
`register`	a storage class
`return`	`return` control statement
`short`	as in `short int` data type
`signed`*	`signed`, `signed short`, `signed long`, `signed char` data type
`sizeof`	`sizeof` operator - gives number of bytes in a type
`static`	a storage class
`struct`	structure data type definitions and declarations

---

* These keywords are new with the ANSI standards.

switch	switch control statement
typedef	typedef declarations
union	union data type definitions and declarations
unsigned	unsigned, unsigned char, short or long data types
void	void data type
volatile[*]	type qualifier - suppress optimization
while	while loop and do-while loop control statements

---

* These keywords are new with the ANSI standards

C

Declarations in C

Each declaration of a single identifier in C has the following form. The brackets `[ ]` indicate that the enclosed item is optional.

```
[storage class] [qualifier] type  identifier [= initializer];
```

Declaration of multiple identifiers can be made within the same declaration in the form

```
[storage class] [qualifier] type  identifier-list;
```

where the identifier-list is a comma-separated list of entries of the form

```
identifier [= initializer]
```

Storage Class Specifiers

These were discussed in Chapter 8. The possible storage class specifiers are given in the list below.

```
auto
extern
register
static
typedef
```

Type Qualifiers

These are new with ANSI C. They include the keywords

`const`   indicates that the value will not be changed

`volatile` announces that the normal optimization should not be applied to this object as modification may be done by something outside of the program such as an interrupt routine or an I/O port as well as by the program.

Compilers may choose to ignore these qualifiers with the exception of flagging attempts to change a const identifier as an error. Note that an identifier declared with the type qualifier const differs from a preprocessor constant in that a memory location is allocated, and it is handled in the compiler phase rather than the preprocess phase.

Type Specifications

The scalar types (with the exception of enum) were discussed in Chapter 3, arrays were discussed in Chapter 4, and the structured types (struct and union) were discussed in Chapter 7. The possible type specifiers are listed below.

```
void
char
short
int
long
float
double
signed
unsigned
```
structure type specifiers
enum type specifiers
union type specifiers

Initializers

When initializing a variable at the time of declaration, the variable's identifier is followed by an equal sign, =, and an initializer. For scalar types, this initializer is an expression having the same type as the variable. For aggregate types (arrays and structures), the initial values are placed in a comma-separated list in a pair of matching braces.

For an array, each initial value goes in one cell of the array. Uninitialized cells will be set to zero. For older compilers, only static and external arrays can be initialized. In ANSI C, automatic arrays can be initialized with constant values.

For a structure, each initial value in the comma-separated list will be stored in the corresponding member of the structures. Uninitialized members will have all the bytes set to 0.

Reading C Declarations

The technique for interpreting C declarations was discussed in detail in Chapter 8. It will be reviewed here. The technique involves peeling off operators in inverse order of precedence and building up the type of the resulting expressions. A precedence table should be within reach during this process. For example, consider the declaration

```
float (*ident())[];
```

We will successively peel off the operators and determine the resulting type until we can conclude the type of the identifier `ident`.

	Expression	**Type**
Step 1:	`(*ident())[]`	`float`
Step 2:	`(*ident())`	array of `floats`
Step 3:	`ident()`	pointer to an array of `floats`
Step 4:	`ident`	function returning a pointer to an array of `floats`

For a second example, see Section 8.8.

D

Operators and Expressions

In the chart below, the U/B column indicates whether the operator is unary or binary. The result type for numeric operands is affected by the automatic conversion that takes place in C.

Name	U/B	Symbol	Operand Type	Result Type
Arithmetic Operators				
unary minus	U	–	numeric	same as operand
addition	B	+	numeric and enum	same as operands
subtraction	B	–	numeric	same as operands
multiplication	B	*	numeric	same as operands
division	B	/	numeric	same as operands, e.g., truncating division with `int`s
remainder	B	%	`int`	`int`
increment	U	++	scalar	same as operand
decrement	U	--	scalar	same as operand
Logical Operators				
negation	U	!	scalar	`int` (1 if operand is zero; 0 if operand not zero)
or	B	¦¦	scalar	`int` (0 or 1)
and	B	&&	scalar	`int` (0 or 1)

Name	U/B	Symbol	Operand Type	Result Type
Bitwise Operators				
negation	U	~	integral	integral
and	B	&	integral	integral
or	B	¦	integral	integral
xor	B	^	integral	integral
shift right	B	>>	integral	integral
shift left	B	<<	integral	integral
Assignment Operators				
assignment	B	=	arithmetic, pointer, enum, structure, union (also pointer = 0)	type of the left operand
compound assignment	B	+=, -=, *=, /= %= ^=, ¦=, &= <<=, >>=	arith. or (ptr += int) arithmetic integral integral integral	left operand type left operand type integral integral integral
Relational Operators				
equality	B	==	arithmetic, pointer, enum, pointer == 0	int (0 or 1)
not equal	B	!=	arithmetic, pointer, enum, pointer == 0	int (0 or 1)
less than	B	<	arithmetic, pointer, or enum	int (0 or 1)

Name	U/B	Symbol	Operand Type	Result Type
less than or equal to	B	`<=`	arithmetic, pointer, or `enum`	`int` (0 or 1)
greater than	B	`>`	arithmetic, pointer, or `enum`	`int` (0 or 1)
greater than or equal to	B	`>=`	arithmetic, pointer, or `enum`	`int` (0 or 1)
Miscellaneous Operators				
sizeof	U	`sizeof()`	expression any type	unsigned integral (`size_t` in ANSI)
address	U	`&`	lvalue or function (not with bitfield or register variable)	pointer to operand type
indirection	U	`*`	pointer to object	type of object
sequential	B	`,`	any expressions	type of right operand
. selector	B	`.`	structure . member	type of member
-> selector	B	`->`	structptr->member	type of member
cast	U	`()`	(type)expression	same as type

Operator Precedence Chart

A PRECEDENCE CHART FOR OPERATORS IN C

In the following chart, all operators on the same line have the same priority. The grouping order is indicated with each group.

Highest precedence

Type	Operator						Associativity
primary	( ) [ ] .			->			left to right
unary	++ -- sizeof (type name) ~ ! - & *						right to left
binary	* / % + - >> << < > <= >= == != & ^ | && || ?:						left to right
assignment	= += -= *= /= %= >>= <<= &= ^= |=						right to left
other binary	, (comma)						left to right

Lowest precedence

E

Control Statements in C

The break **Statement**

SYNTAX

```
break;
```

FUNCTIONALITY

Used to break out of a switch statement, a while loop, a do-while loop or a for loop. Causes control to be passed to the statement immediately following.

See examples in Section 6.4.

The Compound Statement or Block

SYNTAX

```
{
    declarations
    statements
}
```

FUNCTIONALITY

Allows several statements to be grouped together and treated as one statement, and allows variables inside block to be hidden from the outside block. Executed by sequentially processing declarations and executing statements.

See examples in Section 2.2 and throughout the book.

The continue **Statement**

SYNTAX

```
continue;
```

FUNCTIONALITY

Used in conjunction with the while loop, the for loop and the do-while loop. Causes control to pass to the end of the loop body to prepare and test for another iteration.

See example in Section 6.4.

The do-while **Statement**

SYNTAX

```
do
      statement
while ( expression );
```

FUNCTIONALITY

A test-at-the-bottom loop. The statement is repeatedly executed and the expression evaluated. Loop terminates when the expression evaluates to zero.

See example in Section 6.2.

The Expression Statement

SYNTAX

```
expression;
```

FUNCTIONALITY

Causes the expression to be evaluated.

See examples in Section 2.1.

The `for` Statement

SYNTAX

```
for ( expr1; expr2; expr3)
      statement
```

FUNCTIONALITY

An iterative statement. Upon entering, `expr1` is evaluated. For each iteration, `expr2` is first evaluated; if it evaluates to zero, the loop terminates; otherwise it continues. The statement is executed and then `expr3` is evaluated to complete one iteration.

See example in Section 2.7.

The `goto` Statement

SYNTAX

```
goto label;
```

FUNCTIONALITY

Causes execution to jump to the designated labeled statement in the program.

See example in Section 6.6.

The `if` and `if-else` Statements

SYNTAX

```
if (expression)
      statement
```

```
if (expression)
      statement1
else
      statement2
```

FUNCTIONALITY

In the first syntax, the expression is evaluated. If it is nonzero, the `statement` is executed; otherwise, no action is taken.

In the second syntax, the expression is evaluated. If it is nonzero, `statement1` is executed; otherwise, `statement2` is executed.

See examples in Section 2.3.

Labeled Statements

SYNTAX

```
Named (identifier) labels
      identifier : statement
```

Case labels

```
case const-expr : statement
```

where const-expr is a constant and one of the integer types

Default label

```
default : statement
```

FUNCTIONALITY

The statement executes as it would without the label. The named (identifier) label is used in conjunction with the `goto` statement. The case and default labels are used in conjunction with the `switch` statement. Notice that the expression in a case label must be a constant.

See examples in Sections 6.3, 6.4, and 6.6.

The Null Statement

SYNTAX

```
;
```

FUNCTIONALITY

The statement does nothing, but serves to syntactically complete other statements.

See example in Section 2.7.

The `return` Statement

SYNTAX

```
return;
```

or

```
return expression;
```

FUNCTIONALITY

Used in a function to cause execution to return to the calling environment at the point immediately after the function call. In the syntax where return is followed by an expression, the expression is evaluated and passed back to the calling environment as the return value of the function.

See examples in Sections 1.7 and 3.9.

The `switch` Statement

SYNTAX

```
switch (expression) statement
```

Typical use:

```
switch (expression) {
    case label1 : statement1
    case label2 : statement2
    ...
    case labeln : statementn
    default : statement            /* optional */
}
```

where the expression must be one of the integer types and the case labels must be constant integral types.

FUNCTIONALITY

In the typical use, the expression is evaluated and compared with the labels. If a match is found, execution resumes at the statement associated with that label. All statements following that label are executed unless a break statement is encountered. If no match is found, the statement associated with the default is executed. If there is no default, no execution is done.

See examples in Sections 6.3 and 6.4.

The `while` Statement

SYNTAX

```
while (expression)
      statement
```

FUNCTIONALITY

An iterative statement. Upon entering, the expression is evaluated. If it is nonzero, the statement is executed and the expression is evaluated again. The loop will terminate whenever the expression evaluates to zero.

See examples in Section 2.5. and throughout the book.

F

The ANSI C Library

The ANSI Standards for C have specified the functions that are to be included in a standard library. Many of these useful functions are listed here with information about the functionality, the parameters, the return value, and possibly an example or a reference to an example in the text where it was illustrated. The list is not complete.

Input and Output Functions

Declarations of the input/output functions and associated types appear in the header file stdio.h.

Many examples of these functions appear throughout the text. References will be made to the program and section in which some of the examples appear.

File Handling

The definition of a FILE appears in stdio.h, which must be included in programs using a file. Files are buffered by default; terminal input and output are line buffered by default.

`fopen( filename, mode )` makes a file available for use by the program.

Parameters	filename	a null-terminated string containing the name of the file to be opened.
	mode	a null-terminated string indicating the mode of opening. (See Section 10.2.)
Return value		a value of type FILE * by which the file can be referenced within the program.
Example		See fopen2.c (Section 10.2).
Related functions	freopen()	

fflush(fp)   with a file opened for output, causes the contents of the buffer to be written to the file.

Parameters	fp	the FILE * variable associated with the open file.
Return value		0 for success, EOF (-1) for error.

---

fclose(fp)   closes the file. Flushes the associated buffer and releases it

Parameters	fp	the FILE * variable indicating the file to be closed.
Return value		0 for success, EOF (-1) for error.
Example		See fopen2.c (Section 10.2).

---

setbuf(fp, buf)   uses buf for buffering on the file associated with fp, instead of the default buffer. If buf is NULL, buffering is turned off.

Parameters	fp	the FILE * variable associated with the file.
	buf	the address of the memory buffer to be used instead of the default buffering or a NULL if buffering is to be turned off.
Return value		None, return type is void.
Example		`setbuf( stdout, (char *)NULL );` `/* defeats buffering for stdout */`
Related function	setvbuf()	

---

fseek(fp, offset, start)   changes the current position in the file associated with fp.

Parameters	fp	the FILE * value associated with the open file.
	offset	a long value indicating the number of bytes the new position should be from the start position.
	start	an int indicating the start position: SEEK_SET (0) indicates the start position is at the beginning of the file, SEEK_CUR (1) indicates the current position in the file, and SEEK_END (2) indicates the end of the file.

Return value	0 for success, nonzero for error.	
Example	`fseek(fp, 0L, SEEK_SET)` seeks to the file beginning.	

See also fseek.c (Section 10.7).

`ftell( fp )` — gives the current position in the file associated with `fp` in bytes.

Parameters	fp	the `FILE *` value associated with the file.
Return value	a `long` value—the current byte offset from the beginning of the file or `-1` if an error occurs.	
Example	See fseek.c (Section 10.7).	

`feof( fp )` — indicates if the end of the file associated with `fp` has been reached.

Parameters	fp	the `FILE *` value associated with the open file.
Return value	nonzero if end-of-file has been reached, 0 if not.	
Example	See ungetc.c (Section 10.3).	

`ferror( fp )` — indicates if an error has occurred on `fp`.

Parameters	fp	the `FILE *` value associated with the open file.
Return value	nonzero if an error has occurred; 0 if not.	
Example	See perror.c (Section 11.2).	

`clearerr( fp )` — resets the error flag on the file associated with `fp`.

Parameters	fp	the `FILE *` value associated with the open file.
Return value	None. Function type is `void`.	
Example	See perror.c (Section 11.2).	

`ungetc( iochar, fp )` — pushes `iochar` back into the input stream for the input file associated with `fp`.

Parameters	iochar	an `int` value, the value to be pushed onto `fp`. Note `iochar` will be the next value read from the file.
	fp	a `FILE *` value associated with a file that has been opened for input.

Return value	`iochar`, or `EOF` for error.
Example	See ungetc.c (Section 10.3).

Input Functions

Terminal Input Functions

`getchar()` reads a single character from standard input (the keyboard). Usually implemented as a macro.

Parameters	none.
Return value	the value input (a value of type `int`) or `EOF` when end-of-file is reached.
Example	See inout2.c (Section 2.5).

`gets( inbuff )` inputs a string from standard input

Parameters	`inbuff` the address of a buffer that will hold the input.
Return value	a `char *` value, the address of `inbuff` or `NULL` in case of error or end-of-file.
Example	See counter.c (Section 5.3) and struct2.c (Section 7.3).

File Input Functions

NOTE: The following functions do file input. When a parameter `fp` is mentioned, it should refer to a file that has been opened for input with a call to `fopen()` or an equivalent function.

`getc( fp )` gets a single character from the file associated with `fp`. Usually implemented as a macro.

Parameters	`fp`	of type `FILE *`, indicates the file for input.
Return value	the value input (as type `int`), or `EOF` when end-of-file is reached.	
Example	See cp.c (Section 10.3).	

`fgetc( fp )`		gets a single character from the file associated with `fp`. A functional version of the macro `getc()`.
Parameters	`fp`	of type `FILE *`, indicates the file for input.
Return value		the value input as type `int`, or `EOF` when end-of-file is reached.

`fgets( inbuff, n, fp )`		accepts input of a string of maximum length `n-1` from one line of the file `fp`.
Parameters	`inbuff`	the address of the buffer that will hold the string;
	`n`	an `int` representing the maximum length of the string;
	`fp`	a `FILE *` representing the open file from which the input is to come.
Return value		a `char *` value (the address of `inbuff`) or `NULL` in case of error or end-of-file.
Example		See the discussion in Section 10.4 and programs nl.c (Section 10.4) and fwrite.c (Section 10.5).

`fread( buffer, size, num, fp )`		reads a block of data from `fp`.
Parameters	`buffer`	the address of a memory buffer big enough to hold the input.
	`size`	the size of the items being read, of type `size_t` (an `unsigned` integral type in ANSI C);
	`num`	the maximum number of items to be read, of type `size_t`;
	`fp`	the `FILE *` value associated with the input file.
Return value		the number of items read.
Example		See fread.c (Section 10.5) and calloc.c (Section 11.5).

Formatted Input Functions

The following functions will accept input according to a format specified in the parameter `control_string`. The `control_string` contains conversion specifications much like those for the `printf()` family of functions. Each conversion specification has the following form where the items in square brackets (`[]`) are optional.

```
% [*] [field width][width] conversion
```

where

`*`	indicates suppression of conversion and storage of this input item.
`field width`	an unsigned decimal integer.
`width`	one of the characters `'h'`, `'l'`, and `'L'`. An `'h'` indicates a conversion to `short`; an `'l'` to `long` or `double` depending on the conversion character, and `'L'` indicates a conversion to `long double`.
`conversion`	a single character indicating which conversion is to be done. The list of character meanings is below.
`d`	a decimal integer. Corresponding argument: the address of a memory location for an `int`.
`i`	an integer. Argument: address of an `int`.
`o`	an octal integer. Argument: address of an `int`.
`u`	unsigned integer. Argument: address of `unsigned`.
`x`	hexadecimal integer. Argument: address of `int`.
`c`	a character. Argument: address of a `char`.
`s`	a string delimited by whitespace. Argument: the address of a memory buffer.
`p`	a pointer value. Argument: a pointer to `void`.
`n`	No input is read. No conversion is made. Instead, the number of characters read by this point in the call is stored in the corresponding argument.
`%`	a single percent sign. No argument.
`e`	a floating point number. Argument: address of a `float`, `double`, or `long double`.
`f`	a floating point number. Argument: address of a `float`, `double`, or `long double`.
`g`	a floating point number. Argument: address of a `float`, `double`, or `long double`.

scanf(control_string, args, ...)

scans input for characters requested by conversion specifications in the control string. For each conversion specification in the control_string, attempts to convert the input value and store in the corresponding argument.

Parameters   control_string   the address of a null-terminated string that specifies the format as described earlier;

args   one additional argument appears for each conversion specification in the control string. Each argument should be the address of the memory location where the input is to be stored.

Return value   The number of conversions made for specifications in the control string or EOF for end-of-file or an error.

Example   See input1.c (Section 1.5) and retval.c (Section 10.6).

fscanf(fp, control_string, args, ...)

same as scanf() except that the input is to come from the file associated with fp.

Parameters   fp   of type FILE *. Associated with the open file from which the input is to come.

The other parameters are the same as for scanf().

Return value   The number of conversions made for specifications in the control string or EOF for end-of-file or an error.

Example   fscanf(fp, "%c", &charvar); reads a single character from fp and stores it in charvar.

sscanf(buffer, control_string, args, ...)

same as scanf() except that buffer is scanned for the values to convert instead of standard input.

Parameters   buffer   is a memory buffer which is to be scanned for items in the control_string.

The other parameters are the same as for scanf().

Return value   The number of conversions made for specifications in the control string, or EOF in case of end-of-file or error.

Example   See prntscan.c (Section 10.6).

Output Functions

Terminal Output Functions

`putchar( iochar )`   displays a single character on standard output (the terminal). Usually implemented as a macro.

Parameters	`iochar` the character to be displayed, as an `int` value.
Return value	the value output, or `EOF` when end-of-file is reached.
Example	See inout2.c (Section 2.5).

`puts( outbuff )`   displays a string on standard output and appends a newline character.

Parameters	`outbuff` the address of a buffer containing the data that will be displayed.
Return value	`EOF` in case of error, nonnegative otherwise.
Example	See strngio2.c (Section 5.3).

File Output Functions

NOTE: The following functions do file output. When a parameter `fp` is mentioned, it should refer to a file that has been opened for output with a call to `fopen()` or an equivalent function.

`putc( iochar, fp )`   displays a single character to the file associated with `fp`. Usually implemented as a macro.

Parameters	`iochar`	an `int` with the character to be output stored;
	`fp`	of type `FILE *`, indicates the file for output.
Return value		the value output as a value of type `int`, or `EOF` for error.
Example	See cp.c (Section 10.3).	

`fputc( iochar, fp )`   displays `iochar` to the file associated with `fp`. A functional version of the macro `putc()`.

Parameters	`iochar`	the value to be displayed, stored as an `int`;
	`fp`	of type `FILE *`, indicates the file for output.
Return value		the value output or `EOF` for error.

`fputs( outbuff, fp )`   writes a string on the file `fp`.

Parameters	`outbuff`	the address of the buffer that holds the string;
	`fp`	a `FILE *` representing the open file to which the output is to go.

Return value `EOF` for error; a nonnegative value otherwise.

Example See nl.c (Section 10.4).

`fwrite( buffer, size, num, fp )`
writes a block of data to `fp`.

Parameters	`buffer`	the address of memory buffer holding the data.
	`size`	the size of each item to be written, of type `size_t`;
	`num`	the number of items to be written, of type `size_t`; fp a `FILE *` value associated with the output file.

Return value The number of items written. This number will be less than `num` if an error has occurred.

Example See fwrite.c (Section 10.5).

Formatted Output Functions

The following functions will output characters according to a format specified in the parameter `control_string`. The `control_string` contains conversion specifications much like those for the `scanf()` family of functions. Each conversion specification has the following form; the items in square brackets (`[]`) are optional.

```
% [flag] [field width] [.precision] [size] conversion
```

flags:	(optional)	
–		left justify
0		pad with zeros instead of spaces
+		always print the sign (+ or –)
space		print either a space or a - (minus sign)
#		use a variant of the usual conversion (see the documentation with your compiler)
field width:	(optional)	
		a decimal integer constant specifying the minimal field width.

precision specification: (optional)
a period followed by a decimal integer specifying the number of digits to be printed in a conversion of a floating point value after the decimal point.

size: 'h' for a short or unsigned short argument, 'l' for a long or unsigned long argument, 'L' for long double.

conversion: a single character indicating which conversion to make. The list of character meanings is below.

d   signed decimal conversion (types int, char, short, or long)

i   signed decimal conversion

u   unsigned decimal conversion (unsigned types)

o   unsigned octal conversion (integer types)

x   unsigned hexadecimal conversion using 0123456789abcdef (integer types)

X   unsigned hexadecimal conversion using 0123456789ABCDEF (integer types)

c   the argument will be printed as a character whenever it is a character or integer type and its value is a valid character code

s   the argument to be printed is a string

f   for floating point (double) - print in decimal form.

e,E   for floating point (double) - print in exponential form.

g,G   for floating point (double) - print in whichever format (f or e,E) that requires the least amount of space

p   a pointer value (implementation dependent)

n   no output is done, no conversion is made; the number of characters output by this point in the call is stored in the corresponding argument, which must be of type int *

%   print a single percent sign

---

printf(control_string, args, ...)

displays the control string with conversion specifications replaced with requested conversions of the arguments.

Parameters   control_string
the address of a null-terminated string that specifies the format as described earlier;

args   one additional argument appears for each conversion specification in the control string. Each argument should be an expression representing the value to be converted and output.

Return value	The number of characters written or a negative value in case of error.
Example	Almost every program in the text.

fprintf(fp, control_string, args, ...)

same as `printf()` but writes to the file associated with `fp`.

Parameters	fp	of type `FILE *`, associated with the open file to which the output is to go.
		The other parameters are the same as for `printf()`.
Return value		Same as for `printf()`.
Example		See prntscan.c (Section 10.6).

sprintf(buffer, control_string, args, ...)

same as `printf()` except that characters are written into the array `buffer`.

Parameters	buffer	a memory buffer which is large enough to hold the string and all the conversions.
		The other parameters are the same as for `printf()`.
Return value		Same as for `printf()` - the number of characters written to the string.

Mathematics Floating Point Library Functions

Declarations of these functions and related types and constants are contained in the header file math.h.

Types	Unless otherwise noted, all of these functions return a value of type `double`. Any additional information about the return values is given with the function description.
Parameters	Unless otherwise noted, all parameters are of type `double`. Any additional restrictions are given with the function description.

Trigonometric Functions

`sin( x )`	the sine of the angle x
`cos( x )`	the cosine of the angle x
`tan( x )`	the tangent of the angle x

Arguments   The argument x is a `double` value that represents the angle in radians. Note: x cannot be a multiple of `PI/2` for `tan(x)`.

Examples
```
#define PI 3.14159

double x, y = PI/3;
x = sin( PI/2 );
x = tan( y );

double sec( double x )
{
        return ( 1/cos(x) );
}
```

See also math.c (Section 11.3).

Inverse Trigonometric Functions

`asin( x )`	the inverse sine (arcsine) of x. x must be between `-1` and `1`. The result is between `-PI/2` and `PI/2`.
`acos( x )`	the inverse cosine of x. Domain: `-1` to `1`. Result: between `0` and `PI`.
`atan( x )`	the arctangent of x. Result: between `-PI/2` and `PI/2`.
`atan2( x,y )`	the angle made by the positive x axis and the ray through the origin and the point (x,y). The result is between `-PI` and `PI`.

Examples
```
double x, y;
x = asin( (double) 1/3);
y = acos( 0.5 );
y = atan( 1 );
x = atan2( 2, -3 );
```

See also polar.c (Section 11.3).

Hyperbolic Functions

`sinh( x )`	hyperbolic sine of the angle x: $(e^x - e^x)/2$
`cosh( x )`	hyperbolic cosine of x: $(e^x + e^x)/2$
`tanh( x )`	hyperbolic tangent of x: `sinh( x )/cosh( x )`

Examples
```
double x, y;
x = cosh( 1 );
y = -1/sinh( x );    /* csch( x ) */
```

Exponential and Logarithmic Functions

`exp( x )`	exponential function (e^x) with base `e` (`2.718`).
`log( x )`	natural logarithm function with base `e`. x must be greater than `0`.
`log10( x )`	base `10` logarithms. x must be greater than `0`.

Examples
```
double x, y;
x = log( 2.718 );  /* approximately 1 */
y = exp(x);        /* approximately e */
```

Other Mathematical Functions

`pow( x, y )`	x^y. See math.c (Section 11.3) for restrictions on the parameters.
`sqrt( x )`	the square root of x. (x must be greater than `0`)
`ceil( x )`	the smallest integer greater than or equal to x (returned as a `double`)
`floor( x )`	the greatest integer less than or equal to x (returned as a `double`)
`fabs( x )`	the absolute value of x

Examples
```
double x, y;
y = ceil(4.72934);   /* 5 */
x = floor(4.72934);  /* 4 */
```

See also math.c, polar.c (Section 11.3).

String Library Functions

The string library provides functions that manipulate strings. In the following discussions, a string is considered to be a sequence of ASCII characters terminated with a null character, '\0'. A buffer refers to a memory buffer that has been allocated in the program. Both a string and a buffer are referenced in the string library functions by the address of the first cell. The declarations of the string library functions are contained in the standard header file string.h. The type size_t is also declared in string.h and represents one of the unsigned integer types.

---

strlen (string)   calculates the length of string.

Parameters	string	a null-terminated string.
Return value	the length of string not including the terminating '\0', of type size_t.	
Example	See strnglib.c (Section 5.4) and malloc.c (Section 11.5).	

---

strcpy (buffer, string)   copies string into buffer.

Parameters	buffer	is the address of a memory buffer in the program;
	string	a null-terminated string.
Return value	the address of buffer, a char *.	
Example	see strnglib.c (Section 5.4) and linklist.c (Section 11.6).	

---

strcat (buffer, string)   concatenates string onto the end of the current string in buffer.

Parameters	buffer	the address of a memory buffer in the program that contains a null-terminated string;
	string	a null-terminated string.
Return value	the address of buffer, a char *.	
Example	See strnglib.c (Section 5.4).	

---

strcmp (string1, string2)

compares the contents of string1 with that of string2.

Parameters	string1	
	string2	both null-terminated strings.

Return value		a value of type int: 0, if the strings are identical; positive if string2 would occur before string1 in the ordering given by the ASCII character set, and negative if string1 would occur before string2.
Example		See strnglib.c (Section 5.4) and ptrptr.c (Section 9.6).

strncpy(buffer, string, n)

copies n characters from string to buffer, pads with null characters if string doesn't have n characters. Doesn't copy a terminating null character unless one occurs within first n characters of string.

Parameters	buffer	a memory buffer allocated in the program;
	string	a null-terminated string;
	n	a value of type size_t indicating the number of characters to copy.
Return value		the address of buffer, a char * value.
Example		See struct2.c (Section 7.3).

strncat(buffer, string, n)

concatenates at most n characters from string to the end of the current string in buffer. The new string in buffer is terminated with a null character.

Parameters	buffer	a memory buffer allocated in the program that contains a null-terminated string;
	string	a null-terminated string;
	n	an int, the number of characters to concatenate.
Return value		the address of buffer, a char * value.
Example		strncat(buffer, "the time", 4); if buffer is at least 11 bytes long and contains the string "NOW IS" before the call to strncat(), then after the call it will contain the string "NOW ISthe ".

strncmp(string1, string2, n)

compares the first n characters of string1 to the first n characters of string2.

Parameters	string1	
	string2	both null-terminated strings;
	n	an int indicating the number of characters to compare.

Return value   Same return value as strcmp().

Examples   strncmp("Daisy", "Daffy", 2); returns a zero while strncmp("Daisy", "Daffy", 3) returns a positive value.

---

strchr(string, ch)   looks for the first occurrence of ch in string.

Parameters	string	a null-terminated string;
	ch	a character.

Return value   a pointer to the first occurrence of ch in string or NULL if ch does not appear in string. A char * value.

Example   See strchrex.c (Section 5.5).

---

strrchr(string, ch)   same as strchr(), but looks at the string in reverse order.

Parameters   Same parameters as strchr().

Return value   A pointer to the last occurrence of ch in string or NULL if ch is not in string. A char * value.

---

strspn(string1, string2)

count the number of characters at the beginning of string1 that are contained in string2.

Parameters	string1	
	string2	both null-terminated strings.

Return value   A value of type size_t giving the length of the longest substring at the beginning of string1 that is composed entirely of characters of string2.

Example   strspn("??? why", "?\t !") would return 4.

---

strcspn(string1, string2)

the "complement" of strspn(), the number of characters at the beginning of string1 that are not contained in string2.

Parameters	string1	
	string2	both null-terminated strings.

Return value	a value of type `size_t` indicating the length of the longest substring at the beginning of `string1` that contains no characters from `string2`.
Example	`strcspn( "abc456","0123456789" );` would return 3.

strstr(string1, string2)

find the first occurrence of `string2` as a substring of `string1`.

Parameters	`string1`	
	`string2`	both null-terminated strings.
Return value	a pointer to the first character of the first occurrence of `string2` in `string1` or `NULL` if `string2` does not occur in `string1`. A `char *` value.	
Example	`strstr( "Mississippi", "is" );` would return the address of the `'i'` immediately after the `'M'`.	

strtok(buffer, delimiters)

A "token" in `buffer` is defined to be a sequence of characters between any two occurrences of characters in `delimiters`. A call to `strtok()` places a null character at the end of the first "token" and returns the address of the first character of the "token". Subsequent calls to `strtok()` with a `NULL` as the first parameter will find and isolate each "token" in `buffer`.

Parameters	`buffer`	a null-terminated string.
	`delimiters`	a null-terminated string. The characters in the string mark the beginning and end of "tokens" in `buffer`.
Return value	The address of the next "token" in `buffer`.	
Example	`strtok( "123¦abcd! efg", " ¦!.?" );` will return the address of the `'1'`, and the `'¦'` will be replaced with a `'\0'`. A subsequent call `strtok( NULL, " ¦!.?" )` will return the address of the `'a'` with the `'!'` replaced with a `'\0'`.	

Memory Manipulation Functions

The functions that manipulate memory have much the same functionality as those manipulating strings. One difference is that these functions will not depend on a buffer containing a null-terminated string. The addresses mentioned in the parameter descriptions refer to memory buffers allocated within the program. The declarations of these functions are also in string.h.

`memcpy ( buff1, buff2, n )`

copies n bytes from `buff2` to `buff1`.

Parameters	buff1	
	buff2	both memory buffers allocated in the current program. They should not overlap.
	n	a value of type size_t indicating the number of bytes to copy.
Return value	the address of `buff1`.	
Example	with the declarations	

`char array1[5], array2[8];`
`memcpy(array1, array2, 5);` will copy 5 bytes from array2 to array1.

`memcmp ( buff1, buff2, n )`

compares the first n characters of `buff1` and `buff2`.

Parameters	buff1	
	buff2	both memory buffers allocated in the program;
	n	a value of type size_t that indicates the number of bytes to compare.
Return value	the same return value as `strcmp()`.	

`memchr ( buff1, ch, n )`   finds the first occurrence of the character ch in the first n bytes of `buff1`.

Parameters	buff1	a memory buffer in the program;
	ch	the character to be located;
	n	of type size_t, is the maximum number of characters to search.
Return value	the address of the first occurrence of ch in `buff1` or NULL if ch does not occur in `buff1`. A char * value.	

Example	`memchr( "fizz", 'z', 2 );` returns `NULL`.
	`memchr( "fizz", 'z', 3 );` returns the address of the first `'z'`.

`memset( buff1, ch, n )`   initializes the first n bytes of `buff1` to hold the character `ch`.

Parameters	`buff1`	a memory buffer in the program;
	`ch`	the character.
	`n`	a value of type `size_t` indicating the number of bytes to initialize.
Return value		the address of `buff1`, a `char *` value.
Example		With the declaration, `char array[10];`
		`memset(array, '\0', 10);` initializes the array to bytes of `'\0'`.

Character Testing

All the facilities for character testing are similar. Most of them are implemented as macros, and are defined in the standard header file ctype.h. The following information is valid for all of the functions listed here.

Parameters	`ch`	is of type `int`, and either represents a character or `EOF` for end-of-file.
Return value		A value of type `int`: nonzero if the parameter passes the test; 0 if not.
Example		See ctype.c (Section 11.4) for an example involving several of these macros.

`islower( ch )`	tests whether ch is a lowercase alphabetic character, `'a'` to `'z'`.
`isupper( ch )`	tests whether ch is an uppercase alphabetic character, `'A'` to `'Z'`.
`isalpha( ch )`	tests whether ch is an alphabetic character, either uppercase or lowercase.
`isalnum( ch )`	tests to see if ch is either an alphabetic character or a decimal digit.
`isdigit( ch )`	tests whether ch is a decimal digit.
`isxdigit( ch )`	tests whether ch is a hexadecimal digit.

`iscntrl( ch )`	tests whether `ch` is a control character (a character in the ASCII character set corresponding to one of the integers in the range 0 through 31 or 127).
`isprint( ch )`	tests whether `ch` is a printing character (a character in the ASCII character set corresponding to one of the integers in the range 32 to 126).
`isgraph( ch )`	tests whether `ch` is a graphical character (all printing characters except space , ' ', make up the graphical characters).
`ispunct( ch )`	tests whether `ch` is a punctuation character (a graphical character that is not an alphabetic character or a digit).
`isspace( ch )`	tests whether `ch` is a whitespace character (a space, a tab, a newline, a formfeed, a carriage return, or a vertical tab).

Utility Library Functions

A large number of functions in the standard library do tasks like converting from a string of ASCII digits to one of the integer types, allocating and deallocating memory, providing execution control of a program and so on. Some of them are discussed here. The declarations of the functions in this section are in the standard header file stdlib.h. The necessary types and constants, like `size_t` and RAND_MAX, are also declared in that header file.

Functions That Do Conversions

`atof( buffer )`		converts a string of digits with a possible decimal point in `buffer` to type `double`.
Parameters	`buffer`	a null-terminated string of digits possibly containing a decimal point.
Return value		a `double` value represented by the contents of `buffer`.
Example		See struct2.c (Section 7.3).

`atoi( buffer )`   converts a string of digits in `buffer` to the represented `int`.

Parameters	`buffer`	a null-terminated string of digits.
Return value		an `int` value represented by the contents of `buffer`.
Example		See struct1.c (Section 7.3) and unions.c (Section 7.6).

`atol( buffer )`   converts a string of digits in `buffer` to the corresponding `long` value.

Parameters	`buffer`	a null-terminated string of decimal digits.
Return value		the `long` value represented by the contents of `buffer`.

`strtod( buffer, remainderptr )`

converts the string of digits with a possible decimal point to type `double`, and puts the address of the first character that could not be converted in the contents of `remainderptr`.

Parameters   `buffer`   a null-terminated string of digits possibly with an embedded decimal point and extra nonnumeric characters at the end.

`remainderptr`
the address of a `char *` variable that will hold the address of the first nonconverted character in `buffer`.

Return value   a `double` value represented by the first part of the string in `buffer`.

Example   See polar.c and the discussion in Section 11.3.

Functions That Manage Memory Allocation

`calloc( num, size )`   allocates a block of memory large enough to hold `num` objects of size `size`.

Parameters	num	the number of items for which to allocate memory;
	size	the size of each item.

Both parameters have type `size_t`.

Return value   the address of the allocated memory block of `num * size` bytes or a `NULL` pointer if memory cannot be allocated. Note that the return type is `void *`. The value returned should be cast to a pointer to the appropriate type so that the pointer arithmetic will behave correctly.

Example   See calloc.c (Section 11.5) and linklist.c (Section 11.6).

`malloc( size )`   allocates a block of memory with `size` bytes.

Parameters   size   has type `size_t`, the number of bytes to be allocated.

Return value   the address of the allocated block of memory or a `NULL` pointer if a block cannot be allocated. Note that the return type is `void *`. The value returned should be cast to a pointer to the appropriate type so that the pointer arithmetic will behave correctly.

Example   See malloc.c (Section 11.5) and linklist.c (Section 11.6).

`free( ptr )`   deallocates the block of memory pointed to by `ptr`.

Parameters   `ptr` is the `void *` pointer value that was returned by a previous call to `calloc()` or `malloc()`. Note that `ptr` must be recast to type `void *`.

Return value   none, `free()` is declared to return type `void`.

Example   See malloc.c, calloc.c (Section 11.5) and linklist.c (Section 11.6).

Other Utility Functions

qsort(buffer, num, size, funct)

sorts the array `buffer` according to the comparisons done by the function `funct()`.

Parameters
buffer	an array of items to be sorted.
num	has type `size_t`, the number of elements in `buffer`.
size	the size of each element in bytes - has type `size_t`.
funct	the address of a function that performs a comparison between two elements of `buffer`. The two parameters to `funct()` are pointers to the objects being compared. The return value from `funct()` is of type `int`; it is negative if the first parameter is less than the second parameter, 0 if both parameters are identical, and positive if the second parameter is less than the first.

Return value   None - `qsort()` has type `void`. The array `buffer` will have been sorted.

Example

```
#include <stdio.h>
#include <stdlib.h>
int compar( const void *, const void * );

void main( void )
{   int to_sort[5] = { 4, 2, 6, 1, 8 };
    int i;

    qsort( ( void * )to_sort, 5, sizeof( int ), compar );

    for ( i = 0; i < 5; i ++ )
        printf("%d\n", to_sort[i] );
}

int compar( const void *x, const void *y )
{
    return( *( int * )x - *( int * )y );
}
```

`rand( void )`

a random number generator that returns a random number between `0` and `RAND_MAX`, an implementation-defined constant.

Parameters   none.

Return value   a nonnegative value of type `int`.

Example   See discussion of `srand()` below.

`srand( seed )`

seeds (initializes) the random number generator `rand()`. The random number generator would always return the same sequence of random numbers unless seeded by a call to `srand()` with a different value of `seed`.

Parameters   `seed`   can be any unsigned `int` value, but is usually a value associated with the current time or some other value that will change from one execution of a program to another.

Return value   none – `srand()` has type `void`.

Examples   `srand(( unsigned )time(( time_t * ) NULL ));` `rand();` Note that the seeding in the example is done with a call to the `time()` library function. The parameters have been cast to match the types in the function definitions.

`exit( status )`

causes orderly program termination by closing all files, and so on.

Parameters   `status`   a value of type `int` that indicates the reason for program termination. The value of `status` is defined by the programmer, but a `status` of zero will always indicate normal termination.

Return value   none. `exit()` is declared to have type `void`.

Example   See cp.c (Section 10.3).

Related Function `atexit()`

`abs( n )`

returns the absolute value of `n`.

Parameters   `n`   a value of type `int`.

Return value   a value of type `int`.

Example   `x = abs( y );` where both `x` and `y` were declared of type `int`.

Miscellaneous Library Functions

The following list of library functions do not fit into one category, but represent a selection of other facilities that are available in the ANSI library.

`perror( string )`   issues an error message beginning with `string` and concluded with an implementation-defined reason for the error. Program should include the line `#include <errno.h>`

Parameters	`string`	a null-terminated string containing the first part of the error message to be output.
Return value		none - `perror()` is declared to have type `void`.
Example		See perror.c (Section 11.2) and math.c (Section 11.3).

`clock()`   gives the processor time used by the calling program. Program should include the line `#include <time.h>`

Parameters	none.
Return value	the number of clock ticks used by the program up to this point or `-1` if this information is not available. A constant, `CLOCKS_PER_SEC`, is declared in time.h so that the expression `clock()/CLOCKS_PER_SEC` gives the time in seconds.
Example	See timex.c (Section 11.1).

`time( tp )`   returns a value indicating the current time. Include the line `#include <time.h>`

Parameters	`tp`	an address of variable of type `time_t` (defined in time.h). The current calendar time is returned in `*tp`, in addition to being the return value of the function. `time()` can also be called with a `NULL` pointer and `time()` will not duplicate its return value in the parameter.
Return value		a value of type `time_t` that represents the current time or `-1` if the time is not available.
Example		See timex.c (Section 11.1)
Related Functions		`ctime()`, `localtime()`. See Section 11.1.

G

The C Preprocessor

Traditionally, the preprocess phase is the first phase of compilation. In many implementations (a UNIX C compiler for example) the preprocess phase is a separate phase of compilation and the preprocessed source code can be inspected. Even in implementations where the preprocess phase is not separate from the compiler, a facility for executing just the preprocessor may exist.

The tasks done by the preprocessor include stripping comments and processing the preprocessor directives. The directives include facilities for defining macros, including other source code files (usually referred to as header files), and facilitating conditional compilation.

The syntax of the preprocessor directives is independent of the rest of the C language. Each directive must start with the character '#' and is expected to lie entirely on one source code line. (The appearance of the "escape" character '\' immediately before the end of the line will escape the usual meaning of the end of the line (to terminate the directive) and allow the directive to continue onto the next line.) Some compilers require that the '#' appear in the first column of each line, and some do not allow any whitespace to appear between the '#' and the name of the directive. Both of those restrictions have been relaxed in the ANSI C standards.

List of Preprocessor Directives

Defining Macros

Directive   #define

Examples

```
#define MAX     100
#define MIN( a,b )         ( a < b ? a : b )
```

Including Source Code Files

Directive   `#include`

Examples

```
#include <stdio.h>      for a standard header file.
#include "myheader.h"  for a header in the current directory.
```

Conditional Compilation Directives

`#if constant_expression`

In case `constant_expression` is not zero, the preprocessor includes the following lines of source code until the occurrence of `#else`, `#elif` or `#endif`. If `constant_expression` is zero, the lines are not included.

`#ifdef identifier`

If `identifier` has been defined either through a `#define` directive or through a compiler option, then the preprocessor includes the following lines of source code until the occurrence of either `#else`, `#elif`, or `#endif`. If the identifier has not been defined, the code is not included.

`#if defined identifier`

Equivalent to `#ifdef`.

`#ifndef identifier`

If `identifier` has not been defined, the following code (until the occurrence of `#else`, `#endif`, or `#elif`) will be included. If `identifier` has been defined, the code will not be included.

`#endif`

Signals the end of conditionally included source code lines.

`#else`

Must be paired with a preceding `#if`, `#ifdef`, or `#ifndef`. In case the requirement for the preceding `if` directive is not met, include the following code (until the occurrence of `#endif`). If the requirement of the preceding `if` directive is met, the code is not included.

#elif constant_expression

Must be used in conjunction with a preceding #if or another #elif directive. If the requirements for the preceding directives are not met, then constant_expression is tested. If its value is nonzero, then the following code (until the occurrence of #endif, #else, or #elif) is included. If the value of constant_expression is zero, the code is not included. Note that the #elif directive is relatively new and may not be supported on all compilers.

#undef identifier

Causes identifier to be undefined. It is not an error to use #undef with an identifier that has not previously been defined.

Examples   (Conditional Compilation. See Section 11.8)

```
1. #define  DEBUG
   #ifdef DEBUG
        printf("i is %d, string is %s.\n", i, string);
   #endif
```

```
2. #if  FLAG >> 3      /* FLAG shifted right 3 bits */
       /* code dependent on FLAG's value goes here   */
   #elif FLAG >> 2
       /* code dependent on FLAG's value goes here   */
   #elif FLAG >> 1
       /* code dependent on FLAG's value goes here   */
   #else
       /* code dependent on FLAG's value goes here   */
   #endif
```

ANSI C Additions to the C Preprocessor

#line, #error, #pragma, and #.

The directives #line, #error, #pragma, and # (the null directive) are not as commonly used and will not be taken up here.

Trigraph Sequences

Three-character sequences can now be used for certain characters that are found in the ASCII character set but not in other character sets, like the ISO 646-1983 Invariant Code Set.

Trigraph Sequence	Char	Trigraph Sequence	Char
??<	{	??(	[
??>	}	??)	]
??=	#	??-	~
??/	\	??!	¦
??'	^		

Operators with Macro Expansion

The operator # is used with a parameter in the macro definition. When it appears immediately before the parameter, it causes the parameter to be enclosed in double quotes.

Example

```
#define print(s)     printf(#s)
```

When called

```
print(error) expands to printf("error");
```

The operator ## causes concatenation of the parameters on either side of it. Any whitespace is discarded.

Example

```
#define concat(s1,s2)     s1 ## s2
```

When called

```
concat ("Humpty ,Dumpty") expands to "HumptyDumpty"
```

Several Predefined Macros

__DATE__	date of compilation as a string
__FILE__	name of the file as a string
__LINE__	current line number in the source file
__TIME__	time of compilation as a string
__STDC__	1 if the implementation is ANSI Standard C

These macros cannot be undefined with the #undef directive.

H

Linking C Object Code with Object Code from Other Languages

Many times it may be desirable to link object code from a C compiler with object code from another compiler. In some cases this can be done relatively easily while in other cases it may require additional or different software. Several requirements must be met by the software on the computer. For simplicity, let us assume that we will be linking code from just two different language compilers, C and some other language.

First there must be a common format for executable object code from the two compilers. That is, once a program has been compiled and linked, the executable code should be independent of the compiler that was used. For example, on a UNIX system, every compiler must produce a code that meets the a.out format. On an MS-DOS system, there are two executable code formats: the .com format and the .exe format. In the case of more than one format for the executable code, the compilers for the languages involved should both target the same executable file format.

Second, facilities should exist with the compilers for both languages to suppress the link phase of the compilation and leave the code in an object file. This is commonly available if the compiler supports separate compilation of source modules.

Third, there must exist a linker that will take the relocatable (unlinked) object code from both compilers and link them together into the executable code format. This usually implies that the relocatable object code from both compilers must be compatible. On a UNIX system, the link editor, `ld`, is just such a linker. On MS-DOS systems, a linker, `link.exe`, is supplied with the macro assembler (and in some cases the operating system). It links object code files that have the .OBJ format.

If all of the above requirements are met, then it is realistic to start researching the properties of the individual compilers to see if the source code from two different languages could possibly be linked together into one executable file. The remaining discussion centers on the passing of information to and from the functions in C and the subroutines in the other language.

Three issues that must be explored are the passing of parameters between different subprograms, the values returned by subprograms, and compatible data types in the two languages. The documentation for the compilers will probably have to be consulted often.

First it must be determined where each compiler stores the values returned by functions. Although it is not specified, many C compilers will place the return values from functions on the stack. Another common practice is to place return values in registers. If the two languages implement return values differently, it may be difficult to make them communicate.

A similar situation arises with parameters to subprograms. Some compilers may place the parameters on a stack while others may pass the values in registers or designate a different location and method of communication between functions. If the two compilers do not use the same method, communication between the different subprograms will be limited at best. If the two compilers are both produced by the same software company, the method of passing information between program parts is more likely to be compatible, and many of these issues will be resolved.

It must also be determined which data types in C are equivalent to the data types in the other language. For example, if the other language has an `integer` data type, is it the same as a `short`, an `int`, or a `long` in C? Similarly, if the other language has a `real` data type, is it equivalent to `float`, `double`, or `long double`? What about character types? In designing programs to link with C code, only compatible data types should be used. The compiler documentation should contain the answers to many of these questions.

If linking the code from the two different languages still looks feasible, then the specific properties of parameter passing in the languages themselves must be considered.

For example, in C, parameters are always passed by value to a C function. That means that a location is set aside for the execution environment for the function and a copy of the current value of the parameters is put into that environment. The function acts only on a copy of the variables and not on the actual parameters themselves. If it is desired that a C function change the value of a variable to be passed in as a parameter, then the address of (pointer to) the variable to be changed should be passed in as a parameter.

In contrast, parameters to FORTRAN subroutines and functions are always passed by reference. This means that the address of the parameter is passed into the subprogram and when a change is made to a parameter, the change is being made in the memory location whose address was passed in. The variables in the calling environment are changed when a FORTRAN subprogram changes one of its parameters.

If FORTRAN routines are to be linked with C routines, these differences must be taken into account. If a FORTRAN program calls a C function, the C function must be written with parameters that are pointers, since FORTRAN will be passing in an address. The code for the C program would need to dereference its parameters if it needs to change a value passed in by FORTRAN. Similarly, if a C program calls a FORTRAN function or subroutine, the C program must pass in the address of the parameters since the FORTRAN subprogram expects an address.

Another example can be seen with the language Pascal. Standard Pascal does not support separate compilation of source modules, but many implementations of Pascal do provide this feature. The concepts discussed can be applied to other languages. As with the FORTRAN/C pairing, it is necessary to check on the methods used by the different language compilers for passing parameters and returning values from functions. Second, equivalent data types should be identified. Finally, since Pascal is very strict about identifiers being declared before use, the Pascal compiler must provide a way to declare the C functions used. If all this is accomplished, it is feasible to talk about the specifics of passing parameters. Pascal accepts two types of parameters to its functions and procedures, var (or pass-by-reference parameters) and value (or pass-by-value parameters). For a var parameter, the address of the parameter is passed into the subprogram and any changes to the parameter are reflected in the calling environment. A copy is made of a value parameter and changes to a value parameter are not known in the calling environment. If a Pascal program calls a C function, it should declare a var parameter for any parameter to the C function that is either a pointer type or an array. It should declare a value parameter for any other parameter to the C function.

Another way of combining code from a different language with code from C that is easier to use is sometimes available with a C compiler. A C compiler may allow code from another language, notably FORTRAN or assembly, to be placed in-line in a C source code program. This is usually done by adding words like `fortran` and `asm` to the list of keywords in C. For example, when the keyword `asm` appears in the C code, a segment of assembly code can follow it. A similar situation exists with the keyword `fortran`. The implementation of the `asm` keyword would involve having the compiler bypass the `asm` section until the assembly phase. The implementation of the `fortran` keyword would be more complicated.

In summary, there are many details to consider in trying to link source code from two different languages. If all the software requirements are met by the system software and the compilers, then it is up to the programmer to ensure that the two modules communicate properly through their data types, parameter passing, and handling of return values. If the code is linked successfully on one system, it would only port to another system if all the requirements are met.

I

The ASCII
Collating Sequence

The ASCII Character Set

DEC	HEX	CHAR	DEC	HEX	CHAR	DEC	HEX	CHAR	DEC	HEX	CHAR
0	00	^@ NUL \0	32	20	SPC	64	40	@	96	60	`
1	01	^A SOH	33	21	!	65	41	A	97	61	a
2	02	^B STX	34	22	"	66	42	B	98	62	b
3	03	^C ETX	35	23	#	67	43	C	99	63	c
4	04	^D EOT	36	24	$	68	44	D	100	64	d
5	05	^E ENQ	37	25	%	69	45	E	101	65	e
6	06	^F ACK	38	26	&	70	46	F	102	66	f
7	07	^G BEL \a	39	27	'	71	47	G	103	67	g
8	08	^H BS \b	40	28	(	72	48	H	104	68	h
9	09	^I HT \t	41	29	)	73	49	I	105	69	i
10	0A	^J LF \n	42	2A	*	74	4A	J	106	6A	j
11	0B	^K VT \v	43	2B	+	75	4B	K	107	6B	k
12	0C	^L FF \f	44	2C	,	76	4C	L	108	6C	l
13	0D	^M CR \r	45	2D	-	77	4D	M	109	6D	m
14	0E	^N SO	46	2E	.	78	4E	N	110	6E	n
15	0F	^O SI	47	2F	/	79	4F	O	111	6F	o
16	10	^P DLE	48	30	0	80	50	P	112	70	p
17	11	^Q DC1	49	31	1	81	51	Q	113	71	q
18	12	^R DC2	50	32	2	82	52	R	114	72	r
19	13	^S DC3	51	33	3	83	53	S	115	73	s
20	14	^T DC4	52	34	4	84	54	T	116	74	t
21	15	^U NAK	53	35	5	85	55	U	117	75	u
22	16	^V SYN	54	36	6	86	56	V	118	76	v
23	17	^W ETB	55	37	7	87	57	W	119	77	w
24	18	^X CAN	56	38	8	88	58	X	120	78	x
25	19	^Y EM	57	39	9	89	59	Y	121	79	y
26	1A	^Z SUB	58	3A	:	90	5A	Z	122	7A	z
27	1B	^[ESC	59	3B	;	91	5B	[	123	7B	{
28	1C	^\ FS	60	3C	<	92	5C	\	124	7C	¦
29	1D	^] GS	61	3D	=	93	5D	]	125	7D	}
30	1E	^^ RS	62	3E	>	94	5E	^	126	7E	~
31	1F	^_ US	63	3F	?	95	5F	_	127	7F	DEL

Note: ^A means Control-A, etc.

J

Preview of C++

by William B. Jones, California State University, Dominguez Hills

Contents

This appendix is a brief introduction to the most important and most basic ways in which C++ differs from the C language. It is an abridgement, without exercises, of the author's book *QuickStart in C++*, Scott/Jones, Inc., 1995

At various times we will indicate especially important statements visually. We will note Rules

▌This is a Rule, an absolute requirement of the C++ language.

and Rules of Thumb

‖ This is a Rule of Thumb, which is not a requirement of C++
but which the author thinks you should follow nonetheless.

1. Getting Started with C++

1.1 A Simple Program

Turning an ANSI C program into a C++ program is easy. If you have included prototypes for all the functions you use (which you should do anyway), all you have to do is change the extension on the file name. C++ compilers generally require an extension such as .C, .cxx, or .cpp to indicate that the program is C++ code. We will use .cpp where appropriate. Header files still use the extension .h. Thus the ubiquitous C hello program

```
/* hello.c -- say hello to the world */

#include <stdio.h>

void main( void )
{
    printf("Hello, world!\n");
}
```

becomes the potentially equally ubiquitous C++ hello program:

```
// hello.cpp -- say hello to the world

    #include <stdio.h>

void main( void )
{
    printf("Hello, world!\n");
}
```

new comment

simply by changing the file name from hello.c to hello.cpp. We have also used a second form of **comment** allowed by C++. At any time, the appearance of '//' indicates that the rest of the line is a comment. For example,

```
    x = 5;      // this is a comment
```

(Some C compilers now also allow this notation.)

1.2 Stream I/O

Even in a simple program like hello.cpp, C++ can make our lives easier in various ways. C++ has a style of I/O, called **stream I/O**, which is much easier to use than printf in simple situations. It also avoids errors that are easy to make with printf. The following is a version of the hello program using these new ideas:

```
// hello2.cpp -- say hello to the world

#include <iostream.h>

void main( void )
{
    cout << "Hello, world!" << endl;
}
```

new comment

The actual output is performed by the statement

easy output:
cout

```
    cout << "Hello, world!" << endl;
```

This statement is interpreted as first sending the string "Hello, world!", then an end-of-line, to the output stream cout, which is the user's display screen. The statement can be read 'cout **gets** "Hello, world!", **then** endl.' It is equivalent to

end output lines
with endl

```
    cout << "Hello, world!";
    cout << endl;
```

and to

```
    cout << "Hello, world!\n";
```

Stream I/O can be intermixed with traditional C I/O (e.g., printf) as long as stream and traditional I/O generate separate lines of output.

For a more elaborate example, consider

```
// add1.cpp -- add two numbers

#include <iostream.h>

void main( void )
{
    cout << "The sum of " << 3 << " and " << 5 << " is " << 3 + 5
        << endl;
}
```

which produces the line of output

```
The sum of 3 and 5 is 8
```

You can think of the 'cout <<...' statement as marching across the page, specifying the output fields in order:

```
cout << "The sum of " << 3 << " and " << 5 << " is " << 8;
```

                    The sum of 3 and 5 is 8

One can also do input from the keyboard using the stream cin. The statement

```
cin >> a >> b >> c;
```

(read 'cin **gives** a **then** b **then** c') reads values for the variables a, b, and c from the keyboard. The values must be separated by blanks or ends of lines. Note that the traditional C version of this statement would be

```
scanf( "%d %d %d", &a, &b, &c );
```

If some of the ampersands (&) were missing, C would not detect this fact. When using cin in C++, ampersands are not required (or allowed).

The following is a variation of the adding program using input:

```
// add2.cpp -- add two numbers

#include <iostream.h>

void main( void )
{
    int a, b;

    cout << "Type in two integers ";
    cin >> a >> b;
    cout << "The sum of " << a << " and " << b << " is " << a + b
            << endl;
}
```

A sample run of add2 (user input in **boldface**) is

```
Type in two integers 23 44
The sum of 23 and 44 is 67
```

Unlike scanf, cin will also read octal and hexadecimal numbers when typed in the usual C format. Consider the following execution of add2:

```
Type in two numbers 023 0x44
The sum of 19 and 68 is 87
```

(The leading '0' in 023 indicates that the number is in octal, base 8, and the leading '0x' in 0x44 indicates that the number is in hex (hexadecimal, base 16).)

It is also possible to have cin interpret numbers as octal or hex numbers without requiring the user to type the leading '0' or '0x'. Each stream has a **current base** that is decimal (initially), octal, or hex. The base of a stream is changed by feeding it one of the string manipulators dec, oct, or hex, to change the base to decimal, octal, or hex, respectively. For instance,

```
// basein.cpp -- experiment with number bases and cin

#include <iostream.h>

void main( void )
{
    int a, b, c;

    cout << "Enter one number in octal, then two in hex: ";
    cin >> oct >> a >> hex >> b;
    cin >> c;
    cout << "The numbers are " << a << ", " << b << ", and " << c
            << endl;
}
```

can produce the run

```
Enter one number in octal, two in hex: 23 44 ab
The numbers are 19, 68, and 171
```

The use of two separate cin statements in the program above shows that the current base of cin is remembered from one call to the next.

The same technique can also be used to change the base in which numbers are output:

```
// baseout.cpp -- changing number bases in cout

#include <iostream.h>

void main( void )
{
    int a;

    cout << "Enter a number: ";
    cin >> a;
    cout << a << " = 0" << oct << a << " = 0x" << hex << a << endl;
}
```

A sample run is

```
Enter a number: 123
123 = 0173 = 0x7b
```

Use of stream I/O is especially nice when mixing numbers of different types and sizes. Using scanf and printf, you can get quite strange results if the type or size specified in the format string doesn't agree with that of the variable coming in or expression going out. When stream I/O is used in C++, all of this is taken care of for you automatically. For instance,

```cpp
// types.cpp -- different data types and sizes using stream I/O

#include <iostream.h>

void main( void )
{
    int i;
    long int l; // (possibly) longer than an integer
    char c;     // generally shorter than an int
    float f;    // number with a decimal point
    double d;   // number with dec. pt. and more digits

    cin >> i >> l >> c >> f >> d;
    cout << i << " " << l << " " << c << " " << f << " " << d << endl;
}
```

can produce the run

```
123  123456#  3.1415926535  3.1415926535
123 123456 # 3.141593 3.141593
```

Cin skips over white space (blanks, etc.) to arrive at the next input item. Thus the input line above could just as well have been typed

```
123          123456        #3.1415926535    3.1415926535
```

The extra digits of precision are saved in d. Cout in the default form used here just doesn't display them. As an example of the formatting decisions made by C++ stream I/O, consider the program

```cpp
// float.cpp -- examples of output of float numbers with cout

#include <iostream.h>

void main( void )
{
    cout << 123.0 << endl;
    cout << 0.00123 << endl;
    cout << 1.2300 << endl;
    cout << 123000000000000000.0 << endl;
```

```
    cout << 0.000000000000000123 << endl;
}
```

which produces the output

```
123
0.00123
1.23
1.23e+17
1.23e-16
```

It is possible to change this default behavior and control output to a greater degree than `printf` using functions in the include file `iomanip.h`. However, I don't advise it. Simple stream I/O is a pleasure to use, but the fancy stuff is poorly designed, irregular, and not fun at all. I think you are better off using `printf` or other C functions if you want to do anything fancier than we have done here.

RULE

> In C, the `char` data type only determines the size of memory allocated. In all other ways, a `char` is identical to a (signed or unsigned) `int`. In C++, a `char` stays a `char` until it is used in a non-trivial expression, which forces it to be an `int`.

Stream I/O demonstrates this difference. In C,

```
char c;
...
c = 'A' + 1;        // = 66
printf( "%d %c %d %c\n", 'A' + 1, 'A' + 1, c, c );
```

produces the output

```
66 B 66 B
```

In C++ though, the code

in C++, char is a real data type

```
char c;
...
c = 66;        // = 'A' + 1
cout << 'A' + 1 << " " << c << " " << c + 1 << endl;
```

produces the output

```
66 B 67
```

Of course in C++, we can use **type casting** to get any interpretation we want.

```
cout << (char) ('A' + 1) << " " << (int) c << " "
         << (char) (c + 1);
```

produces the output

```
B 66 C
```

Neither C nor C++ can tell the difference between a pointer to a character and a pointer to a character string — they are, in fact, the same. When cout is fed a (pointer to a) character string, it chooses to do the thing it is most likely being asked to do, namely, it displays the string. Thus the C++ code

cout interprets char * differently than other pointers

```
long  l = 0x41424344, // ASCII ABCD, left to right
     *lp = &l;
char *cp = (char *)lp;

cout << cp << " " << lp << endl;
```

produces the output

```
DCBA 0x8d710ffc
```

Thus a char * pointer always displays a character string and any other pointer type always displays its hex value. Some machines, depending on their internal architecture, might display the characters in the order 'ABCD'.

To get the actual location in memory pointed to by a char pointer, we would need to code something like

```
cout << (void *) cp << endl;
```

When we use cin to read into a character array (or a string pointed to by a char * pointer), cin behaves just as scanf does: it reads and stores characters up to the first blank, tab, or end of line. Thus the code

```
char s[100];
...
cin >> s;
```

cin separates words

given the input

nothing but words

would assign to s the character string "nothing".

One final word. Some C++s *buffer* stream output to the screen, that is, cout collects output until either an endl or a cin occurs. This is to improve performance. In rare circumstances where this is a problem, one can use the special cout stream manipulator **flush**, which forces everything collected so far to be

use flush to force output to screen

displayed on the screen. To demonstrate the occurrence of buffering and the use of flush, consider the following situation: Programs often want to give some visual indication on the screen that they are working. One method, which we show below, is to output a period from time to time. We use a large do-nothing loop to simulate a lengthy process.

```
// pause.cpp -- test to see if cout buffers output
//  if the first line of output has different timing
//  from the second, buffering is occurring

#include <iostream.h>

#define PAUSELEN 500000L   // suitable for 33Mhz 486 or VAX

void main( void )
{
    int i; long j;

    for ( i = 1; i <= 10; ++i ) { // line without flushing
        cout << '.';
        for ( j = 1; j <= PAUSELEN; ++j ) ; // wait
        }
    cout << endl;

    for ( i = 1; i <= 10; ++i ) { // same but with flushing
        cout << '.' << flush;
        for ( j = 1; j <= PAUSELEN; ++j ) ; //wait
        }
    cout << endl;
}
```

If the program waits a long time to give the first line of output, then gives all the dots in quick succession, while the second line has short pauses between each dot, then buffering is in use. If both lines come out with the same timing, buffering is not in use. According to the author's experiments, GNU and Visual C++ buffer cout and Borland C++ doesn't. It never hurts to add the flush manipulators, except perhaps for a slight speed penalty. Note that flush isn't needed in baseout.cpp, above.

Another solution to the buffering problem is to use the cerr standard stream, which works exactly like cout except that it is never buffered and normal redirection doesn't send it away from the user's screen.

cerr is used for error output

2. Reference Types

The reference type in C++ is a feature which in elementary applications adds greatly to the safety of C++ programs and in more advanced usage adds greatly to the power of the language. A **reference type** is a sort of constant, automatic pointer.

The following example will give something of the flavor of variables of reference type. Suppose that we declare

```
int a;
int &ra = a;   // ra permanently refers to a
```

Then use of a or ra within a program is interchangeable — they will always have the same value.

```
a = 14;      // also sets ra = 14
ra = -425;   // also sets a = -425
```

In this situation &ra, the address of ra, would be the same as &a. Compare this to a similar treatment using pointers:

reference and pointer types compared

```
int a;
int *pa = &a;  // pa points to a until it is changed
   ...
a = 14;        // also sets *pa = 14, if pa still points to a!!!
*pa = -425;  // also sets a = -425 (same caveat)
```

Note the difference between using pointers and reference types:

> A reference type refers to the same variable for its entire life, whereas a pointer type can refer to many different variables during its life;
> When a pointer is set (e.g. pa = &a) the address-of operator '&' must be used explicitly, whereas when a reference type is initialized '&' must *not* be used;
> When the value pointed to by a pointer is set or used, the '*' operator must be used, whereas with reference types, the '*' is not needed and must *not* be used.

most important use of reference types is for parameters

The examples above use 'ordinary variables', and I can see no legitimate use for reference types with such variables. On the other hand, reference types are extremely useful in function parameters and occasionally as a function return type. The following tables compare these three kinds of uses. For simplicity all the references will be to ints, but 'int' can be replaced by any C++ type. The 'ordinary variable' case will be shown shaded to remind you of its dubious utility.

Declaration of int Reference Type		
Ordinary Variable	Function Parameter	Function Return
int &x = lvalue;	type Fun(...int &x...)	int &x(...)

There are two ways in which a reference type is assigned a value. When it is originally *created*, it is assigned an lvalue of the same type (here int) to reference. (An **lvalue** is anything that can appear on the left side of an assignment statement.) Once a variable of reference type has been created, it (and hence the lvalue it refers to) can be assigned any value of the correct type (here int). In what follows we will assume we have declared

```
int a, b[10]; // standard declarations for use with tables below
```

Creating References with an int Reference Type		
Ordinary Variable	Function Parameter	Function Return

`int &x = a,`
`    &y = b[3];`
	`type Fun( int &x,`
	`            int  &y )`
	`{`
	`    ...`
	`}`
	`    ...Fun(    a,    b[3]`
	`) ...`
		`int &x( ... ) {`
		`    ...`
		`    return a;`
		`}`
		`int &y( ... ) {`
		`    ...`
		`    return b[3];`
		`}`

Function parameters are created and initialized when the function is called, and cease to exist when the function is returned from. A function return reference type is created and initialized when the return statement is executed and destroyed when evaluation of the function call is finished. (Thus, function return types have an extremely short existence.)

To set a to 14 and b[3] to –257 in each case, we would code

Assigning Values to a and b[3]		
Ordinary Variable	Function Parameter	Function Return

`int & x = a,`
`    & y = b[3];`
`...`
`x = 14;`
`y = -257;`
	`type Fun( int & x,`
	`            int & y )`
	`{`
	`    x = 14;`
	`    y = -257;`
	`}`
	`    ...Fun(    a,    b[3]`
	`) ...`
		`int & x( ... ) {`
		`    ...`
		`    return a;`
		`}`
		`int & y( ... ) {`
		`    ...`
		`    return b[3];`
		`}`
		
		`    ...`
		`x( ... ) = 14;`
		`y( ... ) = -257;`

Note the following *illegal* ways of creating reference type variables:

ILLEGAL Creation of Reference Types		
Ordinary Variable	Function Parameter	Function Return

`float r;`
`int & x = 14,`
`    & y = &14;`
`    & z = a + 1;`
`    & w = r;`
	`type Fun( int & x,`
	`              int & y )`
	`{`
	`  ...`
	`}`
	`  ...Fun(    14,    &14`
	`)...`
		`int & x( ... ) {`
		`  ...`
		`  return 14;`
		`}`
		`int & y( ... ) {`
		`  ...`
		`  return &14;`
		`}`

14, &14, and a + 1 are illegal because they aren't lvalues, i.e., they cannot be used on the left side of an assignment statement, and r is illegal because it isn't a variable of the correct type.

Let's give some useful examples involving reference parameters and function return types.

Example 2.1: Write a program Swap(x, y) which swaps the values of its two integer arguments. The following program fails, because C and C++ normally pass parameters *by value*; that is, the value of the parameter is passed *to* the function, but any changes to that value are *not* passed back to the caller.

```
// Incorrect version of Swap

void Swap( int x, int y)
{
   int temp = x;
   x = y;
   y = temp;    // exchanges x and y within Swap, but doesn't
                // affect a and b
}
   ...
   Swap( a, b );
```

Note that the function call Swap(14, 24) would be legal here, and we certainly wouldn't expect it to swap the values of two *constants*! The following program works,

```
// Traditional C version of Swap

void Swap( int *px, int *py)
{
   int temp = *px;
   *px = *py;
   *py = temp; // exchanges a and b as well as *px and *py
}
   ...
   Swap( &a, &b );
```

but the C++ version is simpler and much safer:

```
// Swap using reference parameters

void Swap( int &x, int &y)
{
   int temp = x;
   x = y;
   y = temp;    // exchanges a and b
}

   ...
   Swap( a, b );
```

The method of passing parameters using reference types is exactly equivalent to Pascal **var** parameters and Ada **inout** parameters. Though use of parameters with reference types is safer and easier than passing pointers and dereferencing them manually, in fact the same code is generated in either method.

To show that a procedure such as Swap can be useful, consider the following:

Example 2.2: Write a function SelectionSort(A, n) to sort an array A of n integers using the selection sort. The selection sort works as follows:

```
for ( i = 0; i < n - 1; ++i ) {        // sorting A[0..n-1]
   let smallj be the index of the smallest element
       among A[i], ..., A[n - 1];
   Swap( A[i], A[smallj] );
   }
```

The function works because at the beginning of each iteration of the loop, we are assuming that A[0], ..., A[i - 1] are the smallest items in the array and are already sorted. The work of the loop is to allow us to add 1 to i and maintain that condition. The code is

```
// selsort.cpp -- selection sort

int &Swap( int &a, int &b )
   ...

void SelectionSort(int A[], int n)
{
   int i, j, smallj;

   --n; // n is 1 more than the top subscript
   for ( i = 0; i < n; ++i ) {
      for ( smallj = i, j = i + 1; j <= n; ++j )
         if ( A[j] < A[smallj] ) smallj = j;
      Swap( A[i], A[smallj] );
      }
```

```
}

void main ...
```

Note that we can pass parameters like `A[i]` with variable subscripts to reference parameters. However, if i = 22, the reference is fixed to `A[22]` on entry to the function, and the parameter continues to refer to `A[22]` even if i is changed in the function. Thus

```
int    i = 1,
       A[2] = { -18, 45 };

void aFun( int &x )
{
    cout << x << " ";
    i = 0;    // changes A[i] BUT NOT x!
    cout << x << endl;
}
    ...
    aFun( A[i] )
```

produces the output

```
45 45
```

Also, C++ declarations can occur anywhere, not just at the beginning of a { } block. I think this is a poor idea in general, but one place where it might be justified is in the declaration of the index for a `for` loop. For instance, the `SelectionSort` code could be replaced by

declarations can go anywhere in blocks

```
void SelectionSort(int A[], int n)
{
    for ( int i = 0; i < n; ++i ) {
        for ( int smallj = i, j = i + 1; j <= n; ++j )
            if ( A[j] < A[smallj] ) smallj = j;
        Swap( A[i], A[smallj] );
    }
}
```

The first `for` statement declares i and the second declares `smallj` and j. Such variables, once declared, become available throughout the remainder of the block, not just in the `for` loop. Thus if the following two statements are in a single block, the second is erroneous:

```
for (int i = ...
    ...
for (int i = ...    // ILLEGAL multiple declaration of i
```

Note though that smallj is available only within the block that is the body of the for i loop.

Now let us turn to reference return types for functions. It is harder to make a convincing case for these now, so I will give an unconvincing one. Returning large objects by reference saves copying, and for 'file objects' such as cout, a reference return is essential since a copy isn't the same thing.

Example 2.3: We are going to construct a function Bigger(a, b) which returns a *reference* to the larger of its arguments. Thus not only will we be able to use the larger value, as in x = Bigger(a, b), we will also be able to *alter* the variable with the larger value *without knowing which one it is*! Thus ++Bigger(a, b) will add 1 to whichever variable is larger. (I told you the example wasn't particularly compelling.) The function itself is easy to write:

```
int & Bigger( int & x, int & y )
{
    if ( x > y ) return x;
    else return y;
}
```

(Note that we could also replace the body of the function with return (x > y) ? x : y;) Then if we code

```
int a = 14, b = 25, x;
    . . .
    x = Bigger( a, b );  // sets x = 25
    ++ Bigger( a, b );   // sets b = 26
```

Note that if we defined Bigger as follows

```
int & Bigger( int x, int y ) // Does not work properly!!
{ //    no &s:  ^       ^
    if ( x > y ) return x;
    else return y;
}
```

The reason that this version of Bigger doesn't work properly is that it returns a reference to one of the *local variables* x or y. By the time the outside world comes to use that fact, the function has been exited and the parameters, which are local to Bigger, no longer exist. x = Bigger(a, b) will probably work for the second version, but it isn't guaranteed to. ++Bigger(a, b) on the other hand changes something which no longer exists, rather than a or b. I haven't found a C++ that indicates that there is a problem here.

3. Extensions to Functions

In this section we will discuss three extremely useful C++ extensions of C related to functions. They are inline functions, default parameters, and overloaded functions. In particular, the ability to overload functions is one of the most powerful in the C++ language, and we will be occupied with it in one form or another for the rest of the book.

3.1 Inline Functions

dangers of #defines with parameters

Often it would be nice to encapsulate small pieces of code as functions. The problem is that passing parameters, calling a function, and returning from the call in a small function can take more space and time than the function code itself. In C, the `#define` statement is the only solution. For instance, the following code

```
#define MAX( x, y ) (x > y) ? x : y
```

causes the actual code `(a > b) ? a : b` to be substituted for `MAX( a, b )` wherever it occurs in the program, and there is no overhead from call, return, and parameter passing. One must be careful with such code, though. The code `MAX( a++, b++ )` or `MAX( a, b ) + 1` would probably have unintended results.[1] Another common problem is demonstrated by

```
#define PROD( x, y ) x * y      // poor #define
```

If the user entered `PROD( a+b, c+d )` the result would be `a + b*c + d` rather than `(a+b) * (c+d)` as was probably intended. C programmers must learn to enclose parameters in parentheses automatically:

```
#define PROD( x, y ) (x) * (y)  // better #define
```

inline functions are real functions that (usually) compile like #defines

C++ allows one to define ordinary functions (presumably small ones) with the 'storage type' **inline**. C++ then makes an effort to copy the code into each place where the function is called. This cuts down on execution time, at the expense of having multiple copies of the function in your program. The two functions above could be written

```
inline int MAX( int x, int y ) { return (x > y) ? x : y; }

inline int PROD( int x, int y ) { return x * y; }
```

---

[1] `MAX( a++, b++ )` would cause either a or b to be incremented twice (and the final value is implementation dependent, depending on when the incrementation takes place). Because '+' has higher precedence than '?:', `(a > b) ? a : b + 1` compiles as `(a > b) ? a : (b + 1)` rather than `((a > b) ? a : b) + 1`.

Note that when you declare a function `inline` you must give the function body on the spot. If you didn't, you'd be saying to the compiler, 'include the code for this procedure wherever it is called, but I'm not going to tell you what the code is.'

When functions are declared `inline`, you must declare parameter types and a function value type. This is both an advantage and a disadvantage. On the plus side, it makes for safer programming but on the minus side, our `#defined` versions of `MAX` and `PROD` work for any numeric type as parameters. (As we will see in section 3.3, it is possible to get the effect of multiple parameter types by overloading inline functions, but it's more work.)

Functions declared `inline` can also use local variables:

```
inline void SWAP( int &x, int &y )
{
    int temp = x;
    x = y;
    y = temp;
}
```

The specification of a function as `inline` is only a *suggestion* to the compiler. If the function is long it is unlikely to be compiled inline and if it is recursive, it can't be.

3.2 Default Parameters

C++ allows **default** values to be specified for function parameters. The default value is used for the parameter when no value is given for it in a function call.

For instance, we can write

```
void printMe( int x = 3 )     // x is given the value 3 if
                              // no parameter is specified
{ cout << x << endl; }
    . . .
    printMe( 45 );            // displays 45
    printMe( );              // displays the default value 3
```

Usually functions are first **declared** in a prototype and then **defined**, that is, their actual code given, later on. Parameter defaults should be declared only once, in the prototype. For example,

```
void printMe( int x = 3 );   // declaration (note ';')
                              // x has default value of 3
    . . .
    printMe( 45 );            // displays 45
    printMe( );              // displays the default value 3
    . . .
void printMe( int x )            // definition (no ';')
```

```
                                              //Default must not be respecified.
       { ...
```

In a function with multiple parameters, once one parameter has been given a default value all the parameters that follow must also be given default values. For example, if we have declared

```
       void aFun( int x, int y = 5, float z = 18.2 );
```

then the call aFun(1, 2) is equivalent to the call aFun(1, 2, 18.2) and the call aFun(1) is equivalent to the call aFun(1, 5, 18.2). The call aFun( ) would be illegal (x has no default value). Also, the declaration

```
       void bFun( int x, int y = 5, float z ); // ILLEGAL
```

would be illegal. (Calling such a function without a second parameter would require two consecutive commas, which was deemed error-prone.) Expressions may be used in default values:

```
       int x = 1;
       void cFun( int d = 3 * x + 1);

         x = 15;
         cFun( );    // equivalent to the call cFun(46)
```

A variable used in the default expression may have two definitions, one in force at the time the function is *declared* and another where it is *executed*. The variables in force at the time of the declaration of the default value are used to evaluate it, not those at the time the function is called. Thus in the following example, the declaration int x = 15 is used rather than int x = 2 in the call to dFun.

```
       int x = 15, y = 27;
       void dFun( int e = x + y );      // always uses x and y above

       void main( void )
       {
          int x = 2;

          y = 300;
          dFun( );   // equivalent to dFun( 315 )
```

The variables involved in default value expressions must all be global. Thus the following declaration is illegal:

```
       void eFun( int x, int y = x );  // ILLEGAL
```

3.3 Function Overloading

A function name with more than one declaration is said to be an **overloaded function**. Each declaration of the name must have a different number of parameters and/or different types of parameters so that C++ can determine from the function call which version of the function to apply. (The type the function returns cannot be used to distinguish names.) C++ determines which version of the function to use by picking the one that most closely matches the actual function invocation in type and number of parameters. Consider the following examples:

```
void aFun( int x )          { /* definition 1 */ }
void aFun( int x, int y ) { /* definition 2 */ }
void aFun( double x )       { /* definition 3 */ }

  aFun( 3 );        // calls definition 1
  aFun( 3.5 )     // calls definition 3
  aFun( 1, 2 )    // calls definition 2
```

It would have been an error to give y a default value in definition 2 because the call aFun(3) would not have been able to distinguish between definitions 1 and 2.

If there isn't an exact match, C++ has a very complicated scheme for determining how actual parameter types are cast to make the function choice. The complete set of rules, with examples, occupies twenty-two pages in Ellis and Stroustrup *The Annotated C++ Reference Manual*, §§ 13–13.2 (Addison-Wesley, 1990). A simple example of the surprises that can occur is

overloading can be hazardous to your (mental) health

```
void ofun( int x );
void ofun( float x );

    ...
    ofun( 3.5 );
```

C++ refuses to compile this program because numbers with decimal points in expressions (here, '3.5') are assumed to be of type double, and C++ can't decide whether to convert 3.5 to float or int! The program was rewritten with an additional ofun with double parameter, with each ofun defined as follows:

```
void ofun( myType x )
{
    cout << "ofun called with myType parameter" << endl;
}
```

With a main program of

```
void main( void )
{
    ofun( 3 );
    ofun( 3.5 );
    ofun( (float)3.5 );
}
```

I got the output

```
ofun called with int parameter
ofun called with double parameter
ofun called with float parameter
```

My advice is not to try to figure out complicated type casts when using overloaded functions. I think it extremely confusing and error prone. Instead,

RULE

> To avoid problems with overloaded functions, either
>   i)   Include one version of the function for all possible combinations of parameter types,
>   ii)   Explicitly cast all variables that don't match parameter types, or
>   iii)   Add debugging messages to each version of the function so you can see which version is being called.

Method i) can be implemented efficiently by making the 'unnecessary' declarations `inline` functions. For instance, in the original example above, we could have declared

```
inline void ofun( double x ) { ofun( (float)x ); }
```

The problem with both methods i) and ii) is that they require anticipating that there might be a problem, which may not be so easy. For method iii), we could for instance use the standard C technique on the "ofun called..." messages:

```
void ofun( type x )
{
#ifdef DEBUG
   cout << "ofun called with type parameter" << endl;
#endif
   ...
```

Overloaded functions can be used as a substitute for default parameters. For instance, the declaration of aFun in section 3.2

```
void aFun( int x, int y = 5, float z = -18.2 );
```

could be rewritten

```
void aFun( int x, int y, float z );
inline void aFun( int x, int y ) { aFun( x, y, -18.2 ); }
inline void aFun( int x )        { aFun( x, 5, -18.2 ); }
```

4. Memory Allocation and Release

C++ has a type-safe way of allocating and freeing memory using the operators new and delete (which are reserved words in C++). For any C++ data type *myType*,

> new *myType*   returns a pointer of type *myType* *
> pointing to an object of type *myType*
> new *myType*[n]   returns a pointer of type
> *myType* * pointing to the first object of *n* type *myType*
> objects

If we have declared

        myType *p, *pa;

then the C++ statements

use new instead of malloc

        p = new *myType*;
        pa = new *myType*[20];

are equivalent to the C statements

        p = (*myType* *)malloc(sizeof(*myType*));
        pa = (*myType* *)malloc(20 * sizeof(*myType*));

As usual, p and/or pa will be set to the null pointer if the allocation cannot be performed.

New is generally safer than malloc because malloc returns a void * pointer, which can point to anything and whose value can be stored in any pointer type. Thus no type checking is done. In addition, if *myType* is a *class* (to be defined in Section 5), new causes any special initialization for the class to be performed, whereas malloc doesn't. In case an *array* of class objects is allocated using new, as in new *myType*[20] above, *every item in the array is initialized* in this way.

There are no corresponding replacements for calloc and realloc, though the fact (mentioned above) that new automatically initializes classes can be used for more powerful purposes than calloc.

As one often wishes to allocate storage for structs, unions, and enums, a difference from C should be noted. In C, a struct, union, or enum data type name must be used in company with the defining keyword (struct, union, or enum). In C++, the appropriate keyword need not be mentioned. Thus consider declarations:

        struct s { ... };

```
union u { ... };
enum e { ... }

s x1; u y1; e z1;     // ILLEGAL in C, legal in C++
struct s x2; union u y2; enum e z2     // allowed in both C and C++
```

and expressions in C++

```
... new s ... // = new struct s, returns s*( = struct s*) type
... new u ... // = new union u, returns u*( = union u*) type
... new e ... // = new enum e, returns e*( = enum e*) type
```

Memory allocated with new should be freed with the delete operation. To free the memory allocated above, use

use delete
instead of free

```
delete p;          // for single objects allocated by new
delete [] pa;      // for arrays allocated by new
```

Delete should be used only on pointers set by the new operation. Thus code like

```
myType *p, *q, r;
    ...
p = new myType[100];
q = &r;
++ p;          // now points to (original p)[1]
    ...
delete p;   // likely to be disastrous
delete q;   // likely to be disastrous
```

probably won't work. Delete applied to the null pointer is guaranteed to work properly (i.e., to do nothing).

New and delete should always be used with classes (to be defined in Section 5) as they guarantee that special constructor and destructor functions are invoked. You should not use free with new or delete with malloc.

5. Classes

The most important addition of C++ to C is the notion of the *class*. Classes are a powerful tool for implementing Object-Oriented Programs and in giving concrete representations for abstract data types.

An **abstract data type** (ADT) is a description of the properties and operations of a class of objects without concern for implementation. For instance, the *stack* as an ADT is an ordered collection of items accessible at only one end (the *top*) via the abstract operations *push(x)* (add x to the top of the stack) and *pop()* (remove the item from the top of the stack and return its value). This description says nothing about how the stack ADT will be actually implemented — whether for instance as an array or as a linked list.

The traditional way to implement an ADT has been with a `struct` to contain the actual data values (in the case of the stack ADT, the `struct` contains the list of items on the stack and the 'top' indicator) and a collection of functions performing the operations.

In C++, an ADT is implemented as a **class**, which is much like a `struct` except that in addition to the *data* associated with the ADT, the class definition also contains the functions to perform all of the abstract operations on objects of the class.

As the class corresponds to a data *type*, it is used to declare actual *instances* of that type, which are called **class objects**. The functions of a class are held in common by all objects of that class, while each individual object has its own set of values for the data items. These data items can be protected so that only those functions in the class or 'blessed' by the class can operate on the class data. This mechanism can be used to ensure data integrity, i.e., that all data items in the class have values which are legal and coherent with the other values of the object. As an example, a 'date' class can guarantee that such dates as Feb. 29, 1967 cannot occur.

Classes and objects were first used in the discrete system simulation language Simula 67 developed at the Norwegian Computer Center. C++ classes are recognizably similar to Simula 67 classes. However C++ has added protection techniques and a lot of syntactic sugar (some of which we have already seen) which can make working with C++ classes more like working directly with the ADT than working with the nitty-gritty of the concrete implementation.

5.1 Some Basic Terminology

The general form of a **class declaration** is

```
class classname {
    declaration₁
    declaration₂
        ...
    declarationₙ
};    // Note the terminating ';'. It's easy to forget.
```

where the *declarations* can be any C-style data declaration, any function declaration *or complete definition*, and certain special function declarations. The data items of a class are called **data members** and the functions in the class are called **member functions**. Declarations of data and function members can be interspersed in any order.

In addition the class declaration can contain the labels `public:` and `private:` which give protection to members of the class to access from outside the class. Declarations following the **public** label are accessible to everyone, while

| Declarations following the **private** label can only be accessed by member functions in the class.

One can change back and forth between `public` and `private` at will.[2]

The specification of private data members is also an aid in **information hiding**, the attempt to make information available only to those parts of the program which need it. This is an attempt to localize program behavior so that changes in one part are less likely to have unsuspected effects on other parts — rather like watertight doors in ships which allow the effect of a leak to be localized.

In C++ terminology, a block of storage at program run-time representing a particular type of data is called an **object**. Thus if we declare

```
int a, *pi = new int;
```

then `pi` is a pointer object, and `a` and `*pi` are integer objects. If the data type is a class, *its* objects are called **class objects**. For instance, if the class `classname` is declared as above, the declaration

```
classname C, D, *pC;
```

declares `C` and `D` as class objects of `classname` and `pC` as a pointer to such a class object. (Notice that the keyword `class` is optional when declaring class objects.)

When a class object is created, C++ only needs to reserve memory for the *data* members of the class. A single copy of the function members is used in common by all objects of the class. When a member function of a particular object is called, C++ passes a hidden parameter represented by the keyword **this**, which is a pointer to the data member storage for the object.

inside member functions, 'this' points to the object that called the function

Reference to function and data members of a class object is reminiscent of the notation for `structs`. Suppose we have declared

```
class aClass {
    . . .
    int d;          // typical data member
    . . .
    void f( aClass o )      // a member function, which has an aClass
                            //   object as parameter
    . . .
};

aClass   o1, o2,      // aClass objects
            *po = o1      // pointer to an aClass object, initially, o1;
```

Then

---

[2] There is also an intermediate level of protection, `protected`.

> o1.d and po -> d refer to o1's data member d
> o1.f(o2)   and   po->f(o2)   evaluate o1's version of
>   f() with parameter o2
>   When we evaluate o1.f(o2), this = &o1 and o =
> o2
>   During this evaluation, inside the definition of f(),
> this -> d is equivalent to d (= o1.d)
> this -> f(...) is equivalent to f(...) (= o1.f(...)
>)

Because of the last two statements,

RULE

> The keyword 'this' is usually only used to refer to the class object as a whole.

5.2 A Substantial Example

In this section we will construct an implementation of the ADT *Date*. A Date will record the month, day, and year. Initially there will be three operations defined on dates — addition or subtraction of an integer number (days) to a date giving another date and subtraction of two dates giving an integer number (days). The intuitive meaning of these operations should be clear from the following examples:

"March 24, 1983" + 14 = "April 7, 1983"
"January 3, 1954" – 25 = "December 9, 1953"
"June 24, 1996" – "June 24, 1995" = 366

A class is generally *declared* in a file `classname.h` and the non-trivial member function *definitions* are given in a file `classname.cpp`. In the case of the Date class, we might have three files

```
// date.h--declarations for the Date class

class Date {
    declaration of data items and member functions for Date
};
```

```
// date.cpp--implementations of Date class operations

#include "date.h"
    member function definitions
```

```
// myprog.cpp--a user program which uses the Date class

#include "date.h"
   ...
Date birthday, anniversary, *pd; // Date is now a data type
   ...
   code to perform operations on dates
```

When we are developing classes for reuse, date.cpp would be compiled and perhaps kept in a library. In the link stage of constructing myprog, the compiled version of date.cpp would be combined with it.

As was mentioned in the last section, data and functions can be declared private to protect them. To simplify things though, we will start with everything public and add the protection later on.

There are a variety of ways we could represent a date, for instance as three integers representing month, day, and year or as the number of days since some fixed date. The first representation is more convenient when communicating with the real world and the second is more convenient when doing arithmetic with dates, so to avoid making a decision, we will use *both* representations simultaneously. For days before the fixed date, 'days since' will be negative, and if we wish to represent as many as 100 years, we may need a long int for it. Our first pass at the date.h file is

```
// date1.h--a first pass at the Date class

class Date {
   public:
      int month, day, year;
      long daysSince;      // Jan 1, BASEYEAR

      Date add( long n );
      Date sub( long n );
      long sub( Date d );
};
```

public data members are dangerous! We will take care of this later

The declarations of member functions above assume that the actual definitions will be given elsewhere.

> If the *definition* of a member function is given inside the class declaration, the function is assumed to be *inline*.

If we declare

```
Date d1, d2; long n;
```

Then we can write operations on Dates as follows

```
d2 = d1.add( 3 );    // d2 = "d1 + 3"
```

```
d1 = d2.sub( 14 );      // d1 = "d2 - 14"
n = d1.sub( d2 );    // n = "d1 - d2"
```

Notice that the 'sub' member function is overloaded.

The '.add()' and '.sub()' notation is not very appealing, but C++ comes to our rescue by allowing us to use the more expressive '+' and '−' notation as on the right. We do this by declaring **operator functions** which **overload the + and − operations**:

```
Date operator + ( int n );
```

```
. . .
d2 = d1 + 3;
```

'd1 + 3' is actually short for the notation d1.operator+(3). Most C++ operators can be overloaded this way.[3] However,

> At least one of the operands of an overloaded operator must be a class object.

The revised form of date.h is

```
// date2.h--use of overloaded operators

class Date {
   public:
      int month, day, year;
      long daysSince;      // Jan 1, BASEYEAR

      Date operator + ( long n );
      Date operator - ( long n );
      long operator - ( Date d );
};
```

We can easily implement two of our operator functions inline. The new version of date.h is

```
// date3.h--implement member functions inline.

class Date {
   public:
      int month, day, year;
      long daysSince;      // Jan 1, BASEYEAR

      Date operator + ( long n )
```

---

[3]Included are new, delete, () (function evaluation), [] (subscripting), and unary operators such as *, !, and &. Excluded are ., ?:, and sizeof.

```
Date operator - ( long n ) { return *this + ( - n ); }
long operator - ( Date d )
    { return daysSince - d.daysSince; }
};
```

Note (1) the use of this as a pointer to the date on the left side of the subtraction operation, so that it can be passed to the + operator; (2) the use of daysSince unqualified, representing its value for the Date invoking the function, i.e., the Date on the left side of the subtraction; and (3) the use of d.daysSince to refer to the daysSince data member in another Date.

The keyword inline is not necessary for the two operator -'s because as we said before: functions defined within a class declaration are assumed to be inline.

Thus far we have avoided the messy question of how the Date member variables are initialized. Clearly it is very important that 'month, day, year' represent the same date as daysSince! One of the most powerful consequences of defining member functions within classes is that

RULE #9

‖ Classes can (and should) guarantee that their class objects always contain valid data.

The first way in which C++ helps us maintain the integrity of a class is that whenever a class object is created, C++ automatically initializes it using a special member function the programmer defines called a **constructor function**. The general form of the constructor function declaration is *ClassName(initialization parameters)*.[4] By overloading the constructor function, we can create class objects in a variety of useful ways. For the Date class we will use three, which are declared as follows:

```
// Constructors:
    Date( int m, int d, int y );     // init month, day, year
    Date( long dS );                 // init daysSince
    Date( void );                    // init with today's date
```

The general form of the first Date constructor will be

```
...Date( int m, int d, int y )
{
    // verify that m, d, and y constitute a legal date
    ...
    month = m; day = d; year = y;
    // compute daysSince
```

---

[4]Actually the term *constructor* is a little misleading. When an object of a class is created, C++ *automatically* creates the storage for its data members. The constructor then fills the members with values and/or does anything else it wants.

```
}
```

The constructors are sufficiently complicated that they will be defined in the date.cpp file, to be discussed later.

Notice that

> Constructors don't have return types (even void) or return values.

This is perhaps because the main work of the constructor, allocating and returning storage for member data, is not explicitly stated.

Date(void) is called the **default constructor** as it can be called without arguments (or parentheses). Whenever a Date is declared with no parameters, this constructor is used.

RULE of 7

> Always define a default constructor.

If you don't, C++ will define a *default* default constructor, which does nothing useful. (A constructor all of whose parameters have default values will act as the default constructor as it can be called with no parameters.)

We can now make declarations of Dates as follows:

```
Date  independence( 7, 4, 1776 ),
      today,   // uses default constructor
      birthday( 11, 19, 52 ), tomorrow = today + 1;
```

or create 'anonymous' Dates with pointers pointing to them:

```
Date *pd = new Date( 9, 21, 43 ), *qd;
   ...
   qd = new Date;   // defaults to today
```

The notation

```
Date independence = Date( 7, 4, 1776 ), today = Date();
```

can also be used and is in every way equivalent to the first way we initialized the variables independence and today. This second method, though, can be used to initialize *arrays* of Dates, as in

```
Date Birthday[] = { Date( 5, 1, 45), ... };
```

Expressions like Date(6, 6, 1944) can also be used in expressions, and serve as the 'constant' values of the Date data type.

A constructor can also be used to program operator+:

```
class Date {
```

```
        . . .
    Date operator + ( long n )
      { return Date( daysSince + n ); }
        . . .
};
```

We could also have written the code

```
// alternative form of operator+
  { Date d( daysSince + n ); return d; }
```

but the second version is less efficient since in it, C++ creates one Date d and then copies it into the return value of the function. The first version doesn't have to do that copy.

The second method of maintaining the integrity of data members is to make them private, so that only member functions can manipulate them directly. In fact I would suggest the following:

RULE

|| All data members in a class should be private.

We give access to data members where appropriate using simple inline member functions that I call **accessers**. For example,

```
// sample accesser member function
int getMonth( void ) { return month; }
```

There is no loss of efficiency because the function is inline, and C++ generates the same code it would if you could access the data item directly.

We may also want to allow the user to set values of some data members, while of course maintaining the integrity of the object data. I call functions to do this **setters**. For instance, we might postulate a member function void setDate(int m, int d, int y) which could be used by a user of the Date class, as well as by the corresponding constructor function. Thus we can allow the user to change Dates without allowing him or her to set the month to 42.

Let's collect all our ideas so far.

```
// date.h--final (for now) version

class Date {
  private:
     int month, day, year;
     long daysSince;        // Jan 1, BASEYEAR
  public:
   // constructors
     Date( int m, int d, int y ) { setDate( m, d, y ); }
     Date( long dS ) { setDate( dS ); }
     Date( void ) { setDate( ); }    // defaults to today
```

```
   // accessers
     int getMonth( void )  { return month; }
     int getDay( void )    { return day; }
     int getYear( void )   { return year; }

   // setters
     void setDate( int m, int d, int y );
     void setDate( long dS );
     void setDate( void );

// member functions
   Date operator + ( long n )
      { return Date( daysSince + n ); }
   Date operator - ( long n ) { return *this + ( - n ); }
   long operator - ( Date & d )
      { return daysSince - d.daysSince; } // see Note below
};
```

Note that even though daysSince is now private, it can still be accessed for other class objects in the same class *within a member function of the class*.

Note also that setDate doesn't have to be declared before it is used! This is because

> Any function body in a class can use all data and function members, *even those declared after it.*

This is an appropriate point to discuss another useful principle for writing functions which have class objects as parameters and/or return values.

RULE of 9

> Class objects should *almost* always be passed to functions and returned as function values by *reference.*

For instance, Date objects would be passed and returned as Date &. This rule is certainly reasonable because class objects usually have a lot of storage devoted to data members, so it is more efficient to pass and return a pointer to the object. The functions operator+ and operator- above show one of the few situations when *returning by value is necessary*: We cannot return a reference in operator+ since the reference would be to Date(daysSince + n), which is a temporary object that disappears when the function containing it exits.

Passing objects by reference works even where perhaps it shouldn't. For instance, passing a 'constant' Date object of the form Date(7, 4, 1776) as a reference parameter to operator+ can be used in an expression like

```
long N = Date( 5, 14, 1994 ) - Date( 7, 4, 1776 );    // LEGAL!!
```

Finally, we will implement the remaining three member functions, the three setter functions in a .cpp file of the following form:

```
// date.cpp--implement member function of class Date

#include "date.h"

Date::setDate(int m, int d, int y)
{
    ...
}


Date::setDate( long dS )
{
    ...
}


Date::setDate( void ) // Today's date
{
    ...
}
```

The prefix `Date::` indicates that the function being defined is a member function of the `Date` class. ':::' is called the **scope operator**.

Returning today's date is the easiest. We will use the UNIX functions `time` and `localtime`. The latter returns, among other things, the current month, day, and year. This function is also available in many non-UNIX C's and C++'s. The code for `Date()` is

```
#include <time.h>
    ...
Date::Date( void )
{
    time_t t;
    struct tm *pt;

    time( &t );                 // get mysterious t
    pt = localtime( &t );       // interpret mysterious t
    setDate( pt -> tm_mon + 1, pt -> tm_mday, pt -> tm_year );
}
```

The remaining two functions are rather complex and somewhat similar, so I'll only do the one that converts 'month, day, year' to 'daysSince'. The other is on the disk that comes with this book. Now we must finally choose BASEYEAR. I chose 1970 because that's what UNIX uses, and maybe that might someday come in handy.

We will deal with the possibility of an illegal date by using the C **assert** facility. Its general form is

```
#include <assert.h>
    ...
    assert( condition );
```

If *condition* is false when the assert statement is executed, a message to that effect is displayed and execution terminated. Otherwise execution continues as before. To test and set a Date we will use the following:

```
#define BASEYEAR 1970⁵

static monthDays[] = { 0 /* dummy */,
        31, 28, 31, 30, 31, 30, 31, 31, 30, 31, 30, 31 };

static int leapYear( int year )
{  return (year % 4) == 0 &&
              (year % 100 != 0 || year % 400 == 0); }
```

To make the calculations a little simpler, we will cheat a little and temporarily alter the length of February. The assertions are then simple:

```
#include <assert.h>
    ...
  monthDays[2] += leapYear( y );          // temporarily

  assert( m >= 1 && m <= 12 );
  assert( 1 <= d && d <= monthDays[m] );
  if ( y < 100 ) y += 1900; // allows dates like Date( 2, 3, 94 )
```

We can start the conversion process by computing the number of days since Jan. 1 of the given year y:

```
  daysSince = d - 1;   // gets us to the first of month m
  while ( --m ) daysSince += monthDays[m];
      // daysSince = number of days since Jan 1, y
  monthDays[2] = 28;   // NOW restore February
```

To account for the years, we have two possibilities depending on whether y is before or after 1970. We take care of this as follows:

```
  while ( y >= BASEYEAR ) {
      daysSince += 365 + leapYear( --y );
      }
```

---

⁵C++ allows a more structured way to declare such constants, by putting the keyword const in front of any variable declaration, as in const int BASEYEAR = 1970. The main use of const is in declaring parameters to functions and thus protecting them from change by the function. The rules for const parameters are messy and complex and in my opinion, not worth the trouble. The book *Windows++* by Paul DiLascia (Addison-Wesley, 1992) develops 140 pages of sophisticated C++ code and uses const perhaps half a dozen times, all in trivial ways.

```
    while ( y < BASEYEAR ) {
        daysSince -= 365 + leapYear( y++ );
        }
```

The beginning of date.cpp is now

```
// date.cpp--the implementations

#include "date.h"
#include <time.h>
#include <assert.h>

#define BASEYEAR 1970

static monthDays[] = { 0 /* dummy */,
      31, 28, 31, 30, 31, 30, 31, 31, 30, 31, 30, 31 };

static int leapYear( int year )
{  return (year % 4) == 0 &&
              (year % 100 != 0 || year % 400 == 0); }

void Date::setDate( int m, int d, int y )
{
    monthDays[2] += leapYear(y);  // temporary expedient

    assert( m >= 1 && m <= 12 );
    assert( d >= 1 && d <= monthDays[m] );
    if ( y < 100 && y >= 0) y += 1900;

    month = m;  // do the easy stuff
    day = d;
    year = y;

    daysSince = d - 1;   // move to beginning of month m

    while ( --m )          // move to beginning of year y
        daysSince += monthDays[m];

    monthDays[2] = 28;   // put it back like it belongs

    // now move year to Jan 1, BASEYEAR; only one of the
    // following loops will actually be executed

    while ( y >= BASEYEAR ) {
        daysSince += 365 + leapYear( --y );
        }
    while ( y < BASEYEAR ) {
        daysSince -= 365 + leapYear( y++ );
        }
}
```

```
void setDate( long dS )
{
    ...
```

We used different names for the parameters to `setDate` (m, d, and y) than we did for the data members we were initializing (`month`, `day`, and `year`). For instance, we used m as a parameter to initialize the `month` data member. This is because i f we used

```
void Date::setDate( int month, ...
    ...
    month = month;          // ERROR
```

the two occurrences of `month` in the assignment statement would both refer to the *parameter* month, and the data member month wouldn't get initialized! You could get around this by writing

```
this -> month = month;
```

but this kind of thing is easy to forget, and suggests another

RULE ‖ Avoid using the same name for more than one variable.

Answers to Selected Learning Activities

Chapter 1

1. `Which#` has the illegal character `#`.
   `Who's_on_first` has the illegal character `'`.
   `struct` is a keyword
   `3meninatub` doesn't start with a letter or underscore
   The rest are legal identifiers.

2. The list of tokens follows. A token is listed once even though it may appear more than once in the program. The tokens are: each of the two comments at the beginning of the program, `main`, `(`, `)`, `{`, `sub_funct`, `;`, `}`, `/* ` **Notes 1 and 2** ` */`, `/* ` **Note 3** ` */`

5.
```
#include <stdio.h>
void main( void )
{
        printf( "\07" );
}
```

7.   either   or
          `"whew`   `"whewps`

          `"`   `"`

   depending on whether the backspace key erases the characters beneath.

9. `"` starts the control string; `\` escapes the meaning of the `n` to indicate a newline; the comma `,` separates parameters; the period `.` ends the sentence that is output.

11. 1 line of output

13.
```
#include <stdio.h>
void main( void )
{
    int first = 1,
        second = 2,
```

1

```
        third = 3,
        fourth = 4;

    printf( "First %d, second %d, third %d, fourth %d.\n",
                        first, second, third, fourth );
}
```

16. In general, `scanf()` stops converting the input to decimal when it encounters a character other than a decimal digit.

26. With the modified statement

```
    celsius = 5/9 * ( fahrenheit - 32 );
```

the quotient $5/9$ is calculated first. The quotient of this truncating integer division is 0 and therefore, the right hand side of the assignment statement will always have value 0.

28. 40

33. in ANSI C:

```
#include <stdio.h>
int cube( int );

void main( void )
{
    int intvar;

    printf( "Enter an integer: " );
    scanf( "%d", &intvar );
    printf( "Result: %d\n", cube( intvar ) + 3 * intvar );
}
int cube( int x )
{
    return ( x*x*x );
}
```

37. The only change that is necessary is

```
#define BASE 7
```

38. If we change BASE to 12 and each 10 in `todecimal()` to 16, the program will convert base 12 numbers (using a for 10 and b for 12) to decimal.

Chapter 2

4. a. The conditional statement is

```
if ( sum < 20 )
        printf( "The number is small.\n" );
```

  b. The control expression is

   (sum < 20)

10. 17

11. The number of lines of output will be 4 since the first, the second and the last `printf()` statement will always be executed plus exactly one line for the compound `if-else` statement.

12. d.

20. a. 7 b. 8

26. the digit '9'
  the tab key
  the character '@'
  error: '64' is not a character. If this program compiles, it will produce an infinite
     loop when executed.

30.
```
int i;
for ( i = 1; i < 513; i *= 2 )
     printf( "%d     ", i );
```

32.
```
int i, col;
for ( i = 1, col = 1; i <= 10; i++, col++ ) {
     printf( "\t%d", i );
     if ( col == 5 ) {
          col = 0;
          printf( "\n" );
     }
}
```

Chapter 3

2. a. 0001000000000000, 1111111111111111, 000110101011, 00101110
  b. 4096, 65535, 427, 46

4. a.

Decimal	Octal	Binary
0	0	000
1	1	001
2	2	010
3	3	011
4	4	100
5	5	101
6	6	110
7	7	111

  b. 001111011101 011110001 001100011001101
  c. 326, 431, 32

12. `char charvar = 'c';`

13. If an `int` occupies 16 bits, the maximum `unsigned` value will be 65535. If an `int` occupies 32 bits, the maximum unsigned value will be 4294967295.

22.
```c
#include <stdio.h>
void main( void )
{
    unsigned number, factor;
    int first = 1;

    printf( "This program will print the prime factors " );
    printf( "of an integer that is greater than 2.\n\n" );

    /* Prompt for and input the integer. */
    printf( "Enter an integer that is greater than 2 : " );
    scanf( "%u", &number );

    printf( "%d = ", number );
    for ( factor = 2; factor <= number; factor++ )
        /* if factor divides number evenly */
        if ( ! ( number % factor )) {
                /* output factor */
                if ( first ) {
                        printf( "%d" , factor );
                        first = 0;
                }
                else printf( " * %d", factor );

                /* take the factor out of number */
                number /= factor;

                /* decrement factor so that it can test
                 * for a repeated factor.
                 */
                factor--;
        }
    printf( "\n" );
}
```

24. a. `w1 <<= 3;`
    b. `w3 <<= 6;` will multiply w3 by 64 unless either (1) overflow occurs or (2) w3 is negative.

29. a. `01111100`
    b. `?11111??`   `0?????00`

34.
```
#include <stdio.h>
void main( void )
{
    float x1, y1, x2, y2;              /* The points */
    float slope, y_int;

    /*  Input the coordinates of the points */
    printf( "Enter the first point.\n" );
    printf( "x: " );
    scanf( "%f", &x1 );
    printf( "y: " );
    scanf( "%f", &y1 );
    printf( "Enter the second point.\n" );
    printf( "x: " );
    scanf( "%f", &x2 );
    printf( "y: " );
    scanf( "%f", &y2 );

    /*  Check for a horizontal line */
    if ( y1 == y2 )             /* slope is 0 */
        printf( "The equation is y = %5.2f\n", y1 );
    else if ( x1 != x2 ) {    /* not a vertical line */
        slope = ( y2 - y1 ) / ( x2 - x1 );
        y_int = y1 - slope*x1;
        printf( "The equation is y = %5.2fx + %5.2f\n",
                                    slope, y_int );
    }
    else                              /* vertical line */
        printf( "The equation is x = %5.2f\n", x1 );
}
```

38. `c1 + 3` is an int, `(us + f) * i` is a float, `(ul % c1) / i` is an unsigned long, `us + c1` is either int or unsigned, `d + f + ul` is a double, `u + l` is either type `long` or type `unsigned long`, `3 * us` is an int, and `c1 + c2` is an int.

Chapter 4

1. 1 line of output.

5. `&ptr_to_intvar` is the address of the location of the variable `ptr_to_intvar`.

9. The statement "The value of `(intptr + 1)` is `sizeof(int)` more than that of `int_ptr`." is the only true statement.

11. The following program has examples for type `double`.

```
#include <stdio.h>

void main( void )
{
   double dble, *dble_ptr1 = &dble, *dble_ptr2;

   printf( "%x %x\n", dble_ptr1, dble_ptr2 );

   dble_ptr2 = dble_ptr1 + 1;

   printf( "%x\n", dble_ptr2 );
   printf( "%x\n", dble_ptr1 - 1 );
   printf( "%x\n", dble_ptr2 + 2 );
   printf( "%x\n", ++dble_ptr2 );
   printf( "%x\n", dble_ptr2 - dble_ptr1 );
}
```

14. `*char_ptr is 'H'`
    `*char_ptr + 1 is 'I'`
    `*(char_ptr + 1) is 'e'`
    `(*char_ptr) + 1 is 'I'`
    `*char_ptr + 3 is 'K'`
    `*&char_ptr is 108`
    `&char_ptr is 100`
    `&char_ptr + 2 is 102`

16.
```
#include <stdio.h>
void main( void )
{
   int intgr,
       *ptr_int = &intgr;

   *ptr_int = 7;

   printf( "The value of intgr is %d.\n", intgr );
   printf( "ptr_int points to %d.\n", *ptr_int );
   *ptr_int += 5;

   printf( "The value of intgr is now %d.\n", intgr );
   printf( "ptr_int now points to %d.\n", *ptr_int );
}
```

17. The variables `input_ptr` and c have been declared as types `int  *` and `int` respectively because they are used to store the values returned by `getchar()` which returns an `int` value. Even though variables of type `char  *` and `char` may work correctly some of the time, they may also create error conditions and should not be used with `getchar()`.

19. Just the code changes are given here.

    CHANGES TO `main()`:
    ```
    void switchxz( int *, int * );   /* fill in declaration */

    switchxz ( int_pointer , &z );     /* fill in the call */
    ```
    CHANGES TO `switchxz()`:
    ```
    void switchxz( int *int1, int *int2 )
    {
        int temp;

        temp = *int1;
        *int1 = *int2;
        *int2 = temp;
    }
    ```

20. ```
    In p1, *i is 5, j is 28.
    Back in main, int1 is 3, int2 is 7, and int3 is 5.

    In p1, *i is 8, j is 20.
    Back in main, int1 is 3, int2 is 7, and int3 is 8.
    ```

26. ```
    double avg( void )
    {
        double sum = 0.0;
        int i;

        for ( i = 0; i < 10; i++ )
            sum += test_scores[i];

        return ( sum / 10 );
    }
    ```

31. ```
    int arr1[] = {0, 2, 4, 6, 8, 10, 12, 14, 16, 18, 20};
    int arr2[11] = {0, 2, 4, 6, 8, 10, 12, 14, 16, 18, 20};
    int arr3[11];
    int i;
    for ( i = 0; i < 11; i++ )
            arr3[i] = 2 * i;
    ```

33. a. `intarray[5];`

    b. 0

    c. ```
        int sum;
        sum = intarray[2] + intarray[4];
        ```

    d. The two declarations have the same effect. The second has more information for the reader of the program. The first form might be used when there are many initializers; the compiler is less likely to count incorrectly than a programmer.

38. a.
```
int input_inventory( int inventory[], int maxnum )
{
    int index;

    for ( index = 0; index < maxnum; index++ ) {
        scanf( "%d", &inventory[index] );
        if ( inventory[index] < 0 )
            break;
    }
    if ( index == maxnum )
        printf( "No room for more items.\n" );
    return ( index );
}
```

b.
```
void print_inventory( int *inventory, int numitems )
{
    int index;

    for ( index = 0; index < numitems; index++ ) {
        printf( "Item number %d:\t\t", index+1 );
        printf( "Number on hand  %5d\n",
                        *( inventory + index ));
    }
}
```

41. LINE ADDED TO BOTTOM OF `print_inventory()`:
```
printf( "The total number of items:  %d\n",
                    sum( inventory, numitems ));
```

FUNCTION `sum()`:
```
int sum( int inventory[], int num )
{
    int i, tempsum = 0;

    for ( i = 0; i < num; i++ )
            tempsum += inventory[i];
    return ( tempsum );
}
```

Chapter 5

4.
```
#include <stdio.h>

void main( void )
{
    char *str1, *str2;
```

```
str1 = "One two, buckle my shoe.\n";
printf( str1 );
str2 = "Three four, shut the door.\n";
printf( str2 );

*( str1 + 7 ) = ' ';
*( str1 + 8 ) = '\0';
printf( str1 );

*str2   =   't';
*( str2 + 10 ) = '!';
*( str2 + 11 ) = '\n';
*( str2 + 12 ) = '\0';
printf( str2 );
}
```

5. Yes, `inputptr` and `inputarray` both evaluate to the address of the first character in the array.

7. The variable `inputptr` could be eliminated. The variable `inputarray` is necessary since its declaration causes the necessary space to be allocated.

9. When the value NULL (0) is assigned to a pointer variable, we refer to a NULL pointer. A null character is the character `'\0'` or the first ASCII character. A null string is a string where the only character stored is a null character. For example, `" "` designates a null string. As with other strings, this is handled as the address of the first character in the string. The first character in a null string is the terminating null character.

10. No, to take full advantage of the value returned by `gets()`, both variables are necessary. The variable `inputarray` contains the space for the input characters. The variable `inputptr` will store the value returned by `gets()` which may be equal to either `inputarray` or NULL.

17. The type of the function `countem()` is type int. Since int is the default return type for functions, the word int is not necessary in the declaration, but it could help the reader.

19. Parts a. and b. are incorporated in the following program. No error checking on the input is done.

```
/* Include Files */
#include <stdio.h>
#include <string.h>

void main( void )
{
   int retval;
   char workstring[512];/
   char *string1 = "I know an old lady";
   char *string2 = "who swallowed a fly";
```

```
        printf( "Enter two strings: \n1> " );
        gets( string1 );
        printf( "2> " );
        gets( string2 );
        retval = strcmp( string1, string2 );
        if ( retval > 0 )
               printf( "string1 is > string2.\n" );
        else if ( retval < 0 )
               printf( "string1 is < string2.\n" );
        else   printf( "string1 = string2\n" );

        printf( "The length of string1 is %d.\n",
                               strlen( string1 ) );
        printf( "The length of string2 is %d.\n",
                               strlen( string2 ) );

        strcpy( workstring, string1 );
        if ( !strcmp( string1, workstring ) )
               printf( "Copy completed successfully!\n" );
        else
               printf( "Error found in copy.\n" );

        strcat( workstring, " " );
        strcat( workstring, string2 );
        printf( "The work string now contains:\n\t\"%s\"\n",
                               workstring );
        printf( "The length of the work string is now %d.\n",
                               strlen( workstring ) );
    }
23. #include <stdio.h>
    #include <string.h>

    void main( void )
    {
       char inarray[512];
       int  line_count = 0,
            char_count = 0;

       printf( "Enter your text now\n" );
       printf( "> " );
       while ( gets( inarray ) != NULL ) {
            line_count++;
            char_count += strlen( inarray ) + 1;
            printf( "> " );
       }
       printf( "%d lines, %d characters\n",
                               line_count, char_count );
    }
```

24. It reads standard input and writes to standard output. Therefore, it is a filter.

27.
```c
#include <stdio.h>
#include <string.h>

void main( void )
{
    char instring[512];
    char *currentpos, *lastpos;

    printf( "Enter a line of text.\n >" );
    gets( instring );
    lastpos = instring;

    while (( currentpos = strchr( lastpos, ' ' ))!= NULL ) {
            *currentpos++ = '\0';
            puts( lastpos );
            lastpos = currentpos;
            while ( *lastpos == ' ' )
                    lastpos++;
    }
    puts( lastpos );
}
```

Chapter 6

1. b. 34891   d. -4-3-2

6. Only the function showtabsinline() needed to be changed. The use of the continue statement is no longer necessary.

```c
void showtabsinline( void )
{
    int iochar;

    while (( iochar = getchar() ) != '\n' )
            if ( iochar == '\t' )
                    printf( "\\t" );
}
```

8. There are many ways to accomplish this. One is presented here. The only change to main() was to change the string in the third call to printf().

```c
printf( "\n\nThat was the second part of the line.\n" );
```

The function `readtosentinel()` could be changed as follows:

```
void readtosentinel( void )
{
    int iochar;

    while (( iochar = getchar() ) != EOLN )
            if ( iochar == SENTINEL )
                    break;
        if ( iochar != EOLN )
                while (( iochar = getchar() ) != EOLN )
                    putchar( iochar );
}
```

13. a. To get the program to compile it is necessary to change both declarations of `look_for_delimiter()` to declare the function as type `int` as well as make the changes suggested in the Learning Activity. The program should compile and execute in most C environments. Any change in execution will not be apparent to a person running the program.

   Generalization: The program sets up a location to hold the return value from a function; after execution the value in that location is returned and assigned. The error would only become apparent when the program needed to access the return value (the value assigned to `found` in this program).

   b. The program will compile and run. A runtime error may occur when the value in `found` is accessed since it has not been initialized properly. The contents of its memory location are unpredictable.

15. b.
```
#include <stdio.h>
int my_islower( int );

void main( void )
{
    int iochar;

    while (( iochar = getchar() ) != EOF )
        if ( my_islower( iochar ))
            printf( "lowercase " );
        else
            printf( "notlowercase " );
}

int my_islower( int io )
{
    if ( 'a' <= io && io <= 'z' )
        return 1;
    else
        return 0;
}
```

18. This change should cause compile-time errors since the labelled statement is not in the same function as the `goto`.

21. b. The value returned by `scanf()` gives the number of conversions made. The program will run correctly with the following changes:

Declare a variable to store the value returned by `scanf()`. For example:

```
int scanned;
```

Replace the last two lines in `main()` with the following lines:

```
scanned = scanf( "%d", &n );
if ( scanned )
    printf( "\n%d! is %d.\n", n, factorial( n ));
```

28. a. The 3 and the 5 are field width specifiers. The integer `index+1` will be right justified in a field of at least 3 spaces; `array[index]` will be right justified in a field of at least 5 spaces.

b. Two ways to exit the `while` loop: when `count = MAX_ARRAY` and when `get_int()` returns DONE. The second method of exit would probably be used more often. If the first is used very often, the constant `MAX_ARRAY` should be increased.

Chapter 7

3. a. tag `x` members `x1`, `x2`, `x3`
       tag `y` members `y1`, `y2`, `y3`, `y4`

   b. Storage is allocated by the lines
       ```
       } structy1, structy2;
       ```
       and
       ```
       struct x s1;
       ```

   c. i. illegal   ii. array of 5 ints   iii. int
       iv. struct x   v. char   iv. address of a char

4.  ```
    struct student {
            char    name[30];
            char    ssn[11];
            double  gpa;
            int     totalunits;
            int     majorcode[4];
    };
    ```

15. Only three things need to be changed: In the function `main()`,

   1. Declare the pointer:
       ```
       struct auto_part *partptr;
       ```
   2. Initialize the pointer:
       ```
       partptr = parts;
       ```
   3. Pass the pointer to `get_part()`:
       ```
       while  ( !get_part( partptr++ ) && ++i < MAXPARTS )
       ```
       ```

18. The function:

```
struct auto_part *low_inv( struct auto_part *pp, int numparts )
{
    int i = 0;
        while (( pp->cur_inv >= 5 ) && ( i++ < numparts ))
                pp++;
        if ( i < numparts )
                return ( pp );
        else
                return NULL;
}
```

Declaration of the function:

```
struct auto_part *low_inv( struct auto_part *, int );
```

Code to call the function and process the result:

```
partptr = low_inv( parts, i );
if ( partptr != NULL )
   printf( "Less than 5 in stock: part %s\n",
                                    partptr->id );
else
   printf( "Adequate inventory of all parts in stock.\n" );
```

20. One method would be to include the following seven lines at the beginning of the function:

```
char ssnout[12];
strncpy ( ssnout,emp.ssn,3 );
*( ssnout + 3 ) = '-';
strncpy( ssnout + 4, emp.ssn + 3,2 );
*( ssnout + 6 ) = '-';
strncpy( ssnout + 7, emp.ssn + 5, 5 );
printf( "SSN:    %12s\n", ssnout );
```

30.
```
#include <stdio.h>
#include <stdlib.h>

enum boolean { FALSE, TRUE };

void main( void )
{
    enum boolean prime, done;
    int num, divisor;
    char inarray[80];

    done = FALSE;
    while ( !done ) {
        printf( "Enter a positive integer to be tested: " );
        num = atoi( gets( inarray ));
```

```
             if ( num <= 0 )
                     printf( "That number wasn't positive.\n" );
             else {
                     prime = TRUE;
                     printf( "List of divisors: 1 " );

                     for ( divisor = 2; divisor < num; divisor++ )
                             if ( !( num % divisor )) {
                                     printf( " %d ", divisor );
                                     prime = FALSE;
                             }

                     if ( num != 1 )
                             printf( " %d\n", num );
                     else
                             prime = FALSE;

                     if ( prime )
                             printf( "%d is a prime number\n", num );
             }
             printf( "Another number (Y/N)? " );
             gets( inarray );
             if ( inarray[0] == 'N' || inarray[0] == 'n' )
                     done = TRUE;
        }
    }

31. #include <stdio.h>
    #include <stdlib.h>
    enum boolean { FALSE, TRUE };

    void main( void )
    {
        enum boolean prime;
        int num, divisor;
        char inarray[80];

        printf( "Enter a positive integer to be tested: " );
        num = atoi( gets( inarray ));

        if ( num <= 0 ) {
            printf( "Sorry, that number wasn't positive.\n" );
            exit( 1 );
        }

        prime = TRUE;
        if ( num ==1 )
            prime = FALSE;
```

```
        else {
            for ( divisor = 2; divisor < num; divisor++ )
                if ( !( num % divisor )) {
                        prime = FALSE;
                        break;
                }
        }

        if ( prime )
            printf( "%d is a prime number\n", num );
        else
            printf( "%d is not prime.\n", num );
    }
```

34. english   13
    russian   14
    c   5
    swedish   6

35. legal, illegal, illegal, illegal, illegal, legal

36. Declaration of a variable:

```
    int correct;
```

Modification of the error check on the input of the paytype:

```
    correct = 0;
    while ( !correct )
        if (( *instring == 'h' ) || ( *instring == 'H' )) {
            correct = 1;
            emptr->paytype = hourly;
        }
        else if (( *instring == 's' ) || ( *instring == 'S' )) {
            correct = 1;
            emptr->paytype = salaried;
        }
        else {
            printf( "Enter 'h' or 's': " );
            gets( instring );
        }
```

38. Yes, the parameter to reademp() must be a pointer since reademp() needs to change the contents of the variable referenced by the parameter.

44. The sizeof() operator applied to a union returns the number of bytes occupied by the widest of the union members.

48. They are the same thing. Both syntaxes reference the address of the intmem member of the union which is the same as the address of the union.

Chapter 8

7. d. On most systems, the automatic local variables and parameters will be in the same section of memory, and static and global variables will be located close to each other.

9. a. `main()` can reference global variables b and c, and the local variable a.

   b. `f1()` can access the global variables a, b, and d, and the local variable c.

16. When the function `push()` is called, it calls `isfull()` to determine if there is room on the stack. This protects the bounds of the array from being overwritten.

21. The program position.c would not understand any input with a non-standard use of the characters `'.'`, `'?'`, or `'!'`. For example, position.c would have a hard time with a program written in C.

27. b. `what` is a function that takes two parameters, a `char *` parameter, and a pointer to a function that takes a single parameter of type `char *` and returns an `int`. The function `what()` returns a pointer to a function that returns a `float`.

    x is a pointer to a `char`.

    y is a pointer to a function that returns an `int` and takes a single parameter of type `char *`

    z has type `char *`.

    w has type `int`.

Chapter 9

1. `int two_d[3][3];`

3. The solution below uses an array of strings (array of pointers to type `char`) to hold the labels for each line. Arrays of pointers to `char` are discussed later in this chapter. Another method of labelling each line would be equally effective.

```
void output_results( void )
{
    int i,j;
    char *label[2] = { "Buying Price: ",
                                    "Current Price: "};

    for ( i = 0; i < 2; i++ ) {
        printf( "%s", label[i] );
        for ( j = 0; j < 6; j++ )
            printf( "%8.2f", stock_prices[i][j] );
        printf( "\n" );
    }
}
```

5. For example, the reference `stock_prices[0][i]` would be rewritten as
```
*( *( stock_prices + 0 ) + i )
```
The `+ 0` can be omitted in this special case.

8. These changes entail
   1. A change in the declaration of the functions:
   ```
   void input_prices( float sp[][] );
   void process( float sp[][] );
   void output_results( float sp[][] );
   ```
   2. A change in the calls to the functions:
   ```
   input_prices( stock_prices );
   process( stock_prices );
   output_results( stock_prices );
   ```
   3. A change in the first line of the function definitions: (Note that if a different name had been chosen for the parameter to `input_prices()`, additional changes to the function code would have been necessary.)
   ```
   void input_prices( float stock_prices[][6] )
   void process( float sp[][6] )
   void output_results( float sp[][6] )
   ```

10. The first dimension can be omitted from the declaration of a three-dimensional array as long as the array is initialized with the correct number of initializers.

11. `printf( "%5.1f\t", *( *( *( three_d + i ) + j ) + k ));`

14. `&t[1][0]` is the address of the `'d'`
    `*( *t+2 )` is the `'c'`
    `**( t+1 )` is the `'d'`

18. and 20.

Solutions to both Learning Activities are in the program below.

```
#include <stdio.h>
#include <string.h>

void main( void )
{
   char instring[512];
   char *words[50], *current;
   int   j, i = 1;

   printf( "Enter text with words delimited by blanks:\n" );
   gets( instring );

   if ( instring[0] == '\0' )
       i = 0;
   else {
       words[0]=current=instring;

       while (( current = strchr( current, ' ' )) != NULL ) {
```

```
                    *current++ = '\0';
                    words[i++] = current;
            }
    }

    printf( "There were %d words in that line.\n", i );
    if ( i > 0 ) {
        printf( "They are :\n" );
        for ( j = 0; j < i; j++ )
            printf( "%s\n", words[j] );
    }
}
```

22. Replace the first `for` loop with the following code:

```
for ( --ptrptr; strcmp( *ptrptr, "" ); ptrptr++ )
;       /* position the pointer at the last word */

for ( ; ptrptr >= ptrarray; ptrptr-- )
        printf( "%s ", *ptrptr );
printf( "\n" );
```

23. Replace the second `for` loop with the following code:

```
for ( ptrptr = ptrarray; strcmp( *ptrptr, "" ); ptrptr++ )
        printf( "%c", *( *ptrptr + strlen( *ptrptr ) -1 ));
printf( "\n" );
```

24. c. `**ptrptr` is the character   `'G'`
    e. `*(ptrptr + 1)` is the string   `"Elliot's"`
    g. `*(*(ptrptr + 1) + 2)` is the character   `'l'`
    i. `*ptrptr+1` is the string   `"eorge"`
    k. `*(*ptrptr +2)` is the character   `'o'`

25. a. `float (what[3])();`   Illegal
    b. `float what[3]();`   Illegal
    c. what is a pointer to a function returning type `char`.
    d. what is a function returning a pointer to type `char`
    e. `double (*what())[3];`   Illegal
    f. `double *(what()[3]);`   Illegal
    g. what is an array of three pointers to pointers to type `int`.
    h. what is a function returning a pointer to a pointer to type `int`
    i. what is a pointer to a pointer to an array of three `int`s.
    j. what is an address of an array of three pointers to type `int`.

30. The changes consist of
    1. Including a header file:
       ```
       #include <ctype.h>
       ```
    2. Declaring some variables
       ```
       int i, j;
       ```
    3. Adding the following code
       ```
       for ( i = 1; i < argc; i++ )
            for ( j = 0; j < strlen( argv[i] ); j++ )
                if ( !isdigit( argv[i][j] )) {
                     printf( "Non-digit found\n" );
                     exit( 2 );
                }
       ```

Chapter 10

5. a.
   ```
   if (( fp = fopen( "info", "w" )) == NULL ) {
        printf( "Input file could not be opened\n" );
        exit( 1 );
   }
   ```
   b. After running the program a file named info is in the directory. It is empty.

   c. After running the program, the file info is empty. The contents were destroyed.

   d. When fopen() opens a file for writing, it creates it if it did not previously exist and truncates it if it did previously exist.

7. One other action might be to allow the user to enter a different file name.

9. The modes "a", "a+", and "w+" would allow the program to write to the file so that the program will work with these modes. Modes "a" and "a+" would cause the program to write at the end of the file which may not be desired. Modes "a+" and "w+" would also allow the program to read from the file; if the program is not going to read from the file, these modes might cause a point of confusion to a person reading the source code.

15. a. Changes:

    1. Declare the command line parameters:
       ```
       void main( int argc, char *argv[] )
       ```
    2. Add code to check on the correct number of command line parameters.
       ```
       if ( argc != 2 ) {
            printf( "Usage: ungetc filename\n" );
            exit( 1 );
       }
       ```

3. Change the code to open the file named on the command line.
```
if (( fp = fopen( argv[1], "r" )) == NULL ) {
    printf( "%s couldn't be opened\n", argv[1] );
    exit( 1 );
}
```

17. b. To allocate room for the terminating null character.

19. Changes:

1. Declare a FILE * variable for the output file.
```
FILE *fp, *fpout;
```

2. Add code to open the file when argc is 3 and substitute stdout when it is not 3.
```
if ( argc == 3 ) {
    if (( fpout = fopen( argv[2], "w" )) == NULL ) {
        printf( "Unable to open %s\n", argv[2] );
        exit( 1 );
    }
}
else
    fpout = stdout;
```

3. Change the output statements to access fpout instead of stdout.
```
while ( fgets( inarray, NUMCHARS, fp ) != NULL ) {
    fprintf( fpout, "%d\t", linecount++ );
    fputs( inarray, fpout );
}
```

22. `fwrite( array, sizeof( struct trans ), 5, fp );`

or

`fwrite( array, sizeof( array ), 1, fp );`

25.
```
read_trans( struct trans *trans_ptr, FILE *fp )
{
    return ( fread( trans_ptr, sizeof( *trans_ptr ), 1, fp ));
}
```

29. Yes, the only change necessary to the prntscan.c is in the final loop:
```
while ( fscanf( fp, "%s %s %f%*c", first, last, &gpa ) == 3 ) {
    fprintf( name_fp, "%s, %s\n", last, first );
    fprintf( gpa_fp, "%4.2f\n", gpa );
}
```

32. b. i. The space between hi and 7 terminates the string.

ii. The space is the character converted in the %c conversion specification. Since the 'r' cannot be part of a floating point number, the scanning stops at that point and scanret is 3. No values will be stored in floatvar.

iii. The space separates the character 'r' from the floating point number 4.5. Whitespace is skipped by scanf() when it looks for the floating point number.

34. The minimum value is 26. There are 18 characters specified in the control string plus at least 1 character for the string, 1 character for the decimal, 1 character for the input character, and 5 characters for the floating point number.

37. The only changes are to the function `browse()` and only deal with adjusting the user values.

   1. Change the error check on the number of records and adjust the number of bytes in the parameter to `fseek()`.

   ```
   if ( recnum > numrecs )
      printf( "Enter a number between 1 and %d\n",
                                           numrecs );
   else {
      fseek( fp, (long) (recnum-1) * sizeof( transact ), 0 );
      if (read_trans( &transact ,fp ))
            print_trans( &transact );
      else
            printf( "Transaction %d not found.\n",
                                       recnum );
   }
   ```

40. The change in values for `stdin` should reflect the progression through the input buffer. The value for `level` decreases, the position in the buffer increases, the contents of the buffer position reflects the next character to be read. The values for `stdout` may not appear to change because the output buffer is emptied after each output and may not be filled until after the conversions are made.

Chapter 11

3. For example, a program in California might include the following lines to output the time on the east coast since there is a 3 hour time difference between the two coasts. Note the conversion specifications `%02d` which will right justify the output in a field of two spaces and pad on the left with zeros. Also note the expression

   ```
   (tptr->tm_hour + 3 ) % 24
   ```

   which will calculate the correct time when the value of `tm_hour + 3` exceeds 24.

   ```
   tptr = localtime( &t1 );
   printf( "On the east coast it is %d:%02d:%02d.\n",
                           ( tptr->tm_hour + 3 ) % 24,
                           tptr->tm_min, tptr->tm_sec );
   ```

9. One method consists of
   1. A preprocessor definition:
      ```
      #define PI 3.14159
      ```
   2. Declaration of a new variable:
      ```
      int degrees;
      ```

3. The declaration of a new function `to_degrees()`:

```
int to_degrees ( double angle )
{
    return ( (int) (angle *360 / (2*PI) ));
}
```

4. In `main()`, a call to `to_degrees()` and a modification to the `printf()` call.

```
degrees = to_degrees( ppoint->angle );
printf( "Polar coordinates: " );
printf( "radius %5.2lf, angle %d degrees\n",
                        ppoint->radius, degrees );
```

11. The function `error()` might be modified as follows:

```
error( char *s )
{
    if ( errno ) {
            perror( s );
            return 1;
    }
    return 0;
}
```

Each call to `error()` might be made in a conditional statement. For example, the call

```
error( "sqrt" );
```

might be replaced with

```
if ( !error( "sqrt " ))
    printf( "sqrt( %4.2f ) is %5.2f\n",x, y );
```

13. When the experiment was run using the Borland Turbo C++ compiler, both the tab character and ^M were counted both as whitespace and control characters. So was ^L. The character ^J was not counted in any category.

14. It would be expected that the version with the `else` keywords would run faster since it would bypass several of the tests in the case of alphabetic input. Note that the test should be made with a file as input instead of the keyboard so that the user's response time would not affect the timing.

16. c. In convert.c, the variable num is initialized to zero and the conversion is accumulated in num. In la15.c, `scanf()` only stores a value in num after a conversion is made. Another difference is that convert.c will only read a single line from standard input while the `scanf()` call in la15.c will skip over newlines and other whitespace to find the start of the string of decimal digits.

19. b. The program modification follows:

```
#include <stdio.h>
#include <stdlib.h>
#include <string.h>

void main( void )
{
    char instring[512], *place, *neword, *word;

    printf( "Enter a line of text " );
    printf( "with words separated with blanks:\n" );
    gets( instring );
    place = instring;
    while (( neword = strtok( place, " \t.," )) != NULL ) {
            place = NULL;
            word = (char *) malloc( strlen( neword )+1 );
            strcpy( word, neword );
            printf( "I read that as \"%s\".\n", word );
            free(( void * ) word );
    }
}
```

21. When this experiment is run on Borland's Turbo C compiler, the error message "Unable to get the space" is output. Apparently, when `calloc()` is requested to allocate zero bytes, it returns a NULL pointer. This could be corrected by only calling `calloc()` when there is space to allocate. For example,

```
if ( nrecs > 0 ) {
        if (( t_array = ( struct trans * ) calloc( nrecs,
                    sizeof( struct trans ))) == NULL ) {
            printf( "Unable to get the space.\n" );
            exit( 1 );
        }
        .
        .
        .
```

23. The program linklist.c does not work properly as it is. It attempts to get another line of input and outputs garbage since the list is non-existent. It can be corrected by extending the compound statement that is associated with the line

```
    if ( gets( inputbuffer ) != NULL ) {
```

to encompass the rest of the code in `main()`.

27. One version that will work in simple cases is

```
    #define isdigit( a )  ( a > ='0' && a <= '9' ) ? 1 : 0
```

See the discussion in the **A Word of Warning** for cautions.

Index